Professional ASP.NET
Web Forms Techniques

By

Alex Homer

Wrox Press Ltd. ®

Professional ASP.NET
Web Forms Techniques

© 2002 Wrox Press

First Printed November 2002

wrox

Published by Wrox Press Ltd.,
Arden House, 1102 Warwick Road, Acocks Green,
Birmingham, B27 6BH
United Kingdom
Printed in the United States of America
ISBN 1-86100-786-8

Trademark Acknowledgments

Credits

Author
Alex Homer

Technical Reviewers
Damien Foggon
Shefali Kulkarni
Mark Horner
Craig McQueen
Paul Churchill
David Schultz

Managing Editor
Louay Fatoohi

Commissioning Editor
Daniel Kent

Technical Editor
Matthew Cumberlidge

Project Manager
Charlotte Smith

Production Coordinator
Neil Lote

Cover
Natalie O'Donnell

Indexer
Andrew Criddle

Proofreader
Susan Nettleton

About the Author

Alex Homer

Alex Homer is a computer geek and web developer with a passion for ASP.NET. Although he has to spend some time doing real work (a bit of consultancy and training, and the occasional conference session), most of his days are absorbed in playing with the latest Microsoft Web technology and then writing about it. Living in the picturesque wilderness of the Derbyshire Dales in England, he is well away from the demands of the real world – with only an Internet connection to maintain some distant representation of normality. But, hey, what else could you want from life? You can contact Alex through his own software company, Stonebroom Limited: alex@stonebroom.com.

WANTED
WEB DEVELOPER

Table of Contents

Table of Contents

Table of Contents

Table of Contents

Table of Contents

WANTED
WEB DEVELOPER

Introduction

ASP.NET makes it easy to create interactive and intuitive interfaces for web applications, and attractive and exciting web pages. The server-based postback architecture, combined with the comprehensive array of server controls that are provided as part of the .NET Framework, allow developers to quickly build browser-based interfaces for web sites and web applications – using much the same event-driven approach as in 'traditional' executable programs developed in languages like Visual Basic, Delphi, and C++.

This is a completely new and different way of working from previous versions of ASP, and the underlying principles and workings of server-based events, which occur in response to actions made by the user in the page, can prove to be difficult to grasp in their entirety. However, constructing ASP.NET pages, especially with some of the tools that are available or under development now, is very much easier and often less error-prone than in classic ASP.

Nevertheless, a completely server-based approach to user interaction does have its downsides. In high-latency scenarios, or over slow network connections, the need to hit the server every time that the page content needs to be modified can intrude on the working of an application, or reduce the perceived responsiveness of a web site.

Although the ASP.NET philosophy tends to engender a server-based mechanism, where postbacks to the server are used to generate and update the pages, some of the server controls (notably the Validation controls) also encompass client-side interactivity through JScript that is sent to the client for execution there. And there is no reason why a developer cannot add to this functionality for other controls by handling client-side events in the same way as has become the norm in most web sites and web applications today.

What Is This Book About?

So, based on the title and the preamble above, you can safely assume that this book is aiming to examine the possibilities for developing user interfaces that are driven by ASP.NET. We will discuss and explore a range of techniques and approaches predominantly for creating web sites and web pages that are:

- ❑ Intuitive and easy to use

- ❑ Attractive and full-featured

- ❑ Interactive where this is appropriate

- ❑ Based (loosely) on a real-world scenario

- ❑ Fulfill a predefined set of design requirements

- ❑ Are fun, memorable, and provide user satisfaction

The pages we build are, for the most part, elements of an overall application that – while being somewhat optimistic as regards consumer buying patterns – does form the basis for the kind of web site/application that is becoming one of the basic ingredients of the World Wide Web today. We'll be building a site that allows the user to choose, customize, and purchase a new car or truck from the world-famous **Wrox Car Company**.

To do so, we'll focus on the steps of requirements analysis and design (though not in extreme detail), followed by planning and mapping out the site. While this seems like the natural way to get started, it's often skimped or even omitted, allowing the site to develop in a haphazard and unpredictable way. While this is not always categorically wrong, it does make development and maintenance that much more difficult. Even the most simplistic 'starting plan' can reduce development and maintenance time, as well as avoiding many common frustrations that result from the 'no plan' approach.

Once the basic design is in place we'll look at the development of the various resources that make up the complete site. Of course, repetition is commonplace in a web site, and so to make the book as useful as possible we've taken some liberties to try and cover as many useful topics as possible. It means that we can look at a range of things such as:

- ❑ A central 'Home' page that makes navigation of the whole site easy

- ❑ Displaying data about the products available from the site from a backend database

- ❑ Interactive content that is driven by either (or both) server-side and client-side code

- ❑ Creating graphics on the fly, and other animations to liven up the site

- ❑ A 'login' feature that recognizes users and provides optional personalization

- ❑ An online order facility with order tracking and status reports via e-mail

- ❑ Some ASP.NET development tools that are available now, or are on the way

What we won't be doing is concentrating on the backend data processing tasks in any more detail than we need to in order to get the site running. In a sister publication, *ASP.NET Distributed Data Applications* (Wrox Press, ISBN 1-86100-492-3), we covered the whole reasoning behind, and implementation of *n*-tier architectures and componentized design. In that book, however, we steered clear of as much complexity in the client as possible, in order to concentrate on the data processing aspects.

On the grounds that we don't have 1,500 pages available here, this book does the reverse by concentrating on the user interface, and using fairly simple data access techniques. Of course, that doesn't mean we won't be doing it 'properly', it just means that you won't see detailed discussions of the workings of all of the .NET data access classes, or the long diatribes on catching and reporting concurrency errors.

All the ASP.NET code you see listed in the book, with the exception of simple abstract snippets that demonstrate a specific principle or just show the syntax, is available in both VB.NET and C#. The listings you see in the book are mostly written using VB.NET syntax, but avoiding any language-specific features wherever possible, so that it can easily be converted to other languages by any reasonably capable developer who prefers to work in a different language. Where there is an obvious difference between VB.NET and C# in the way that a specific feature is implemented, we show the C# version as well. Meanwhile, the client-side code is predominantly written in JavaScript/JScript.

You can download all the code for this book from http://www.wrox.com/. You can also run many of the examples online on our server. For details go to http://www.daveandal.com/books/7868/

> *If you worked with ASP 2.0 and/or 3.0, and read either of the previous Wrox "ASP Webmaster" books, you'll find that this book is somewhat similar to those in both the kinds of topics it covers, and the approach to these topics that it takes. But, of course, now we're talking about ASP.NET – and so the range of possibilities and the fundamental implementation are very different.*

Who Is This Book For?

As is becoming clear, ASP.NET and the accompanying .NET Framework class library are far more comprehensive – and complex – than anything we used in ASP 3.0 or earlier (or, in fact, in other environments like PHP and JSP). The result is that it's not possible for every ASP.NET book to cover an introduction or brief tutorial to ASP.NET as well as the more advanced content that forms the core of the book.

Mind you, this is a good thing from your point of view, as you don't want to pay for material that covers topics you are already familiar with. What it does mean is that you *do* need to be familiar with ASP.NET and, to some extent, the .NET Framework classes to be able to use this book successfully. We assume that you have already installed and are using ASP.NET to build pages, perhaps using a text editor or with Visual Studio .NET or another development tool.

We also assume that you have a reasonable grasp of using a database to drive a web site. We'll explain the data access code we use, how it works, and discuss alternatives where appropriate. But we won't be covering the basic techniques for setting up and administering your database.

What This Book Is Not

- ❏ It's not a dry reference book on any particular area of the technologies
- ❏ It's not an academic text that follows every thread or aspect of any one technology
- ❏ It's not about hardware performance or software configuration for ASP.NET
- ❏ It's not about SQL programming, server optimization, or data access theory
- ❏ It's not aimed at system or database administrators – it's aimed at developers

What This Book Is

❑ It is a practical approach aimed at achieving useful goals without drowning in complexity

❑ It is a guide to many of the useful and powerful interface-oriented features of ASP.NET

❑ It is an exploration of a process for designing and building an interactive web site

❑ It is a useful introduction to many peripheral techniques, such as drawing and e-mail

❑ It is a demonstration of how easy ASP.NET makes building great web sites

❑ It is, hopefully, informative, useful, and fun to read

What Do You Need To Use This Book?

Providing that your level of experience and knowledge meets the not-excessive requirements of the earlier sections, the only other things you need are:

❑ A development environment. At minimum your favorite text editor, or perhaps Visual Studio .NET, Microsoft ASP.NET Web Matrix, or any other suitable tool from a third party manufacturer.

❑ Internet Information Server and the .NET Framework installed and configured on a server that you can access. Alternatively, if you are using Matrix, you can take advantage of its built-in web server. We also recommend that you install the complete version of the .NET SDK that includes all the reference material, as it makes it easy to look up specific items when you aren't using Visual Studio .NET.

❑ A database such as Microsoft SQL Server or MSDE, although you can use any other SQL database system – or even a desktop database such as Microsoft Access – as long as there is a .NET Data Provider available so that it can be accessed via ASP.NET.

For development and experimentation you can run the database, IIS, .NET, and your chosen development environment on the same machine. This often makes debugging easier as well.

Conventions

We have used a number of different styles of text and layout in the book to help differentiate between the different kinds of information. Here are examples of the styles we use and an explanation of what they mean:

Code has several fonts. If it's a word that we're talking about in the text, for example, when discussing a `For...Next` loop, it's in `this font`. If it's a block of code that you can type in as a program and run, then it's also in a gray box:

```
Private Sub bthAdd_Click(ByVal sender As System.Object, _
                         ByVal e As System.EventArgs) Handles btnAdd.Click

  Dim n As Integer
  n = 27

  MessageBox.Show(n)

End Sub
```

Sometimes you'll see code in a mixture of styles, like this:

```
Private Sub bthAdd_Click(ByVal sender As System.Object, _
                     ByVal e As System.EventArgs) Handles btnAdd.Click
    Dim n As Integer
    n = 27

    n = n + 2

    MessageBox.Show(n)

End Sub
```

The code with a white background is code we've already looked at and that we don't wish to examine further. The line highlighted in gray is a new addition to the code since we last looked at it, or code that we want to highlight for some other reason.

Occasionally, there are commands, code lines or URLs that should be presented as a single line, but can't (because of the limited width of the page). In this case we indicate the overflow by using a ⏋ symbol, like this:

```
vbc /t:exe /out:logClient.exe logClient.vb ⏋
/r:System.dll,System.Runtime.Remoting.dll,../bin/logger.dll
```

Advice, hints, and background information come in an italicized, indented font like this.

> **Important pieces of information come in boxes like this.**

We demonstrate the syntactical usage of methods, properties (and so on) using the following format:

```
Regsvcs BookDistributor.dll [COM+AppName] [TypeLibrary.tbl]
```

Here, italicized parts indicate object references, variables, or parameter values to be inserted; the square braces indicate optional parameters.

Bulleted lists appear indented, with each new bullet marked as follows:

❑ **Important Words** are in a bold type font.

❑ Words that appear on the screen, or in menus like File or Window, are in a similar font to the one you would see on a Windows desktop.

❑ Keys that you press on the keyboard like *Ctrl* and *Enter* are in italics.

Customer Support and Feedback

We value feedback from our readers, and we want to know what you think about this book: what you liked, what you didn't like, and what you think we can do better next time. You can send us your comments, either by returning the reply card in the back of the book, or by e-mail to feedback@wrox.com. Please be sure to mention the book's ISBN and title in your message.

Source Code and Updates

All the source code used in this book is available for download at http://www.wrox.com. Once you've logged on to the web site, simply locate the title (either through our Search facility or by using one of the title lists). Then click on the Download Code link on the book's detail page and you can obtain all the source code.

The files that are available for download from our site have been archived using WinZip. When you have saved the attachments to a folder on your hard drive, you need to extract the files using a de-compression program such as WinZip or PKUnzip. When you extract the files, the code is usually extracted into chapter folders. When you start the extraction process, ensure that you've selected the Use folder names under the Extract to option list (or its equivalent).

The code can also be run online at the author's own web site, which you can find at the following address:

http://www.alanddave.com/books/7868

Errata

We have made every effort to make sure that there are no errors in the text or in the code. However, no one is perfect and mistakes do occur. If you find an error in this book, like a spelling mistake or a faulty piece of code, we would be very grateful to hear about it. By sending in errata, you may save another reader hours of frustration, and of course, you will be helping us provide even higher quality information. Simply e-mail the information to support@wrox.com; we'll check the information, and (if appropriate) we'll post a message to the errata pages, and use it in subsequent editions of the book.

To find errata on the web site, log on to http://www.wrox.com/, and simply locate the title through our Search facility or title list. Then, on the book details page, click on the Book Errata link. On this page you will be able to view all the errata that has been submitted and checked through by editorial. You will also be able to click the Submit Errata link to notify us of any errata that you may have found.

Technical Support

If you would like to make a direct query about a problem in the book, you need to e-mail support@wrox.com. A typical e-mail should include the following things:

❑ In the Subject field, tell us the **book name**, the **last four digits of the ISBN** (7868 for this book), and the **page number** of the problem.

❑ In the body of the message, tell us your **name**, **contact information**, and the **problem**.

We *won't* send you junk mail. We need these details to save your time and ours. When you send an e-mail message, it will go through the following chain of support:

1. **Customer Support** – Your message is delivered to one of our customer support staff – they're the first people to read it. They have files on most frequently asked questions and will answer anything general about the book or the web site immediately.

2. **Editorial** – Deeper queries are forwarded to the technical editor responsible for the book. They have experience with the programming language or particular product, and are able to answer detailed technical questions on the subject. Once an issue has been resolved, the editor can post the errata to the web site.

3. **The Authors** – Finally, in the unlikely event that the editor cannot answer your problem, he or she will forward the request to the author. We do try to protect the author from any distractions to their writing; however, we are quite happy to forward specific requests to them. All Wrox authors help with the support on their books. They will mail the customer and the editor with their response, and again all readers should benefit.

> Note that the Wrox support process can only offer support to issues that are directly pertinent to the content of our published title. Support for questions that fall outside the scope of normal book support is provided via the community lists of our http://p2p.wrox.com/ forum.

p2p.wrox.com

For author and peer discussion join the **P2P mailing lists**. Our unique system provides **programmer to programmer**™ contact on mailing lists, forums, and newsgroups, all *in addition* to our one-to-one e-mail support system. Be confident that your query is being examined by the many Wrox authors, and other industry experts, who are present on our mailing lists. At p2p.wrox.com you will find a number of different lists that will help you, not only while you read this book, but also as you develop your own applications.

To subscribe to a mailing list just follow these steps:

1. Go to http://p2p.wrox.com/ and choose the appropriate category from the left menu bar.

2. Click on the mailing list you wish to join.

3. Follow the instructions to subscribe and fill in your e-mail address and password.

4. Reply to the confirmation e-mail you receive.

5. Use the subscription manager to join more lists and set your mail preferences.

1

Getting Started

There's a saying that goes something like "You can't make an omelet without breaking some eggs". OK, so perhaps if you subscribe to the same school of culinary arts as this particular author (take it out of the freezer and put it in the microwave), then perhaps it's possible to avoid the physical experience of egg-breaking yourself. But someone has had to do it somewhere down the line – unless they've started breeding chickens that lay omelets directly, of course.

But what has all this to do with building a web site or web application? Well (as you probably guessed from the title and introduction) this book is about designing and building interfaces for your applications using ASP.NET as the driving force. In the culinary terms we started out with, this comes down to a simple question that you will keep coming back to at almost every stage of your ASP.NET application design process: "Can you build an ASP.NET web application without using server controls?"

The answer to any technical question posed to a programmer is almost invariably "it depends", but in general you can safely say that somewhere down the line most of your ASP.NET pages will contain at least a sprinkling of these clever little beasts. After all, they form the core around which many ASP.NET page design techniques are wrapped – rather like (to continue the culinary introduction) a tortilla. Although perhaps comparing server controls to the contents of a flour or corn pancake is stretching the allegory just a little too far.

So, following this customary off-topic wandering, what are we actually going to be looking at in this chapter? As the title suggests, the aim here is to think about how we can get started building an interactive web site or web application, based on ASP.NET, which provides an interesting and usable interface for our users. We'll look at:

❑ Why ASP.NET provides a great environment for building interactive pages and sites

❑ The fundamental ways that ASP.NET makes building dynamic pages easier

❑ The built-in features of ASP.NET that we can use in our pages and applications

❑   The impact and reasoning behind using client-side and server-side processing

❑   How we approach designing a site in order to get the most from ASP.NET

Towards the end of this chapter, we'll start with the basics of the design approach – pen and paper – and from there, by the end of the chapter, we should be in a position to start constructing some pages. However, first, we'll look at how ASP.NET provides new tools and enables new techniques that we can take advantage of to make building these pages much quicker and easier than ever before.

Why ASP.NET?

The fact that you are reading this book probably means that you are already a confirmed ASP.NET developer, and looking to see how you can get the most from the techniques you've learned from other books and publications. Alternatively, you may be thinking about trying ASP.NET to see if it is any better than your current development environment when it comes to building high-performance dynamic web sites and applications.

If you fall into the first category, then you should find the following sections useful in giving you some guidance about how you might plan your site to take full advantage of ASP.NET. If you fall into the second category, then you may find that you need to look at something more introductory to start with. However, the overall approach to the design of the site should still be useful in giving you more idea about what ASP.NET can do – and how easy it makes it to accomplish.

A Note on Terminology

In the not-so-distant past, it was easy to differentiate a web **site** from a web-based **application**. Web sites used mainly static HTML pages to display information, while web-based applications were ordinary applications that had often been converted from an executable running locally on your machine into something that you can execute across the Internet.

However, the continuing trend towards making **everything** web-enabled means that most new applications are designed and built with a remote interface that allows them to run over HTTP. And many web sites being constructed today are much more interactive than their predecessors – providing dynamic access to back-end systems both for exposing and collecting information.

So, if both web sites and web-based applications are really becoming just interfaces to some back-end data store, aren't they the same thing? Should we stop thinking about them as two different things, and approach both in the same way as far as design and implementation are concerned?

Certainly, there will still be some web sites that are not "interactive" (they just present information), but it's also fair to say that some web-based application interfaces only present information as well – in other words they are not really "interactive" either.

Is It a Bird? ... Is It a Plane? ... No, It's a Wapplisite!

So, we propose dropping the distinction. It's time that we moved away from thinking about the two as different things and treated them all the same. What's important is the level of interactivity that they expose. But what do we call them? In this book, you'll generally see us refer to just 'the site' or 'the application', and both should be taken to mean much the same thing.

One word that has been in circulation for a while is a combination of the words 'web' and 'application': **weblication**. However, this doesn't encompass the fact that we are also dealing with web sites. So, our new favorite word, and our pitch for everlasting fame (online glossary and dictionary webmasters please take note) is **wapplisite**. If you should happen to see this popping up in the remainder of the book, instead of the more cumbersome phrase "web application or web site" you'll now know exactly what we're referring to. And, as a bonus, you get value for money because there is more room for useful words on each page.

ASP.NET Fundamentals

Before we get started looking at how we might put together the recipe for a site, it's worth exploring in some detail why and how ASP.NET can provide the ingredients we need to make the task as easy and as productive as possible. The answers center around the fundamental change in the way that ASP.NET allows us to approach the whole concept of creating distributed applications that work across the Web using HTTP as the only transport mechanism.

Event-Driven Applications

Modern applications that are built to run on a 'window-based' interface to the operating system need to be **event-driven**, rather than **procedural**, in the way that they work (here we use the term 'window-based', with a lower-case 'w', to indicate that it applies to systems other than Microsoft Windows).

Procedural-based applications (generally with text rather than GUI interfaces) follow an execution path that is pre-defined, using menus that are effectively conditional statements that execute the code in a specific order, depending on user intervention that occurs only when the application prompts for input.

On the other hand, an event-driven application generally provides and displays several interface elements at a time (one or more windows, which can each contain more than one control or input element). The user can interact with the elements whenever, and in whatever order, they wish. As they do so, the elements raise events that are handled by the code in the application.

However, providing an event-driven environment has always been a difficult task in a web application. Web browsers were never designed to act as application interfaces. Their original purpose was to display (and allow editing of) information that is delivered in the form of structured HTML-encoded documents.

OK, so they have always offered a range of simple "form controls", such as the `<input>` and `<textarea>` elements, but it's only over the last few years that they have developed to include features such as client-side scripting, executable applets and ActiveX controls, and programmatic access to the content of a page that allows something other than a basic data-input form.

Programming Dynamic Pages on the Web

The traditional approach to building a web application is to provide a page containing the form controls that collect the user's input, and then have the user submit (or post) this page to a separate dynamic page that handles this user's input. There are plenty of existing technologies that can achieve this, for example scripting languages such as Perl, PHP, JSP and ASP. Another approach is to build executables that interact with the web server directly, using technologies like ISAPI (Internet Server Application Programming Interface) or the CGI (Common Gateway Interface).

Irrespective of the technology that is used, however, the basic technique is the same. The code in the dynamic page has to retrieve the values sent from the previous page, process them as required, and then, step-by-step, generate the output required to create the returned page that is sent to the client:

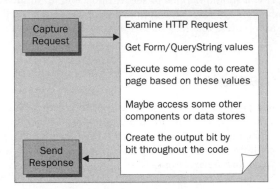

Yes, it works, but is it the best approach? The code in the page is executed in a procedural way, in that execution starts at the top of the page and continues until the page is complete. In other words, this model for handling the user's input means that we are simply responding to a single event (that of the page being submitted to the server), and we have to generate output as the execution proceeds. It can lead to a tangle of intermixed code, HTML and other content, making maintenance and debugging a nightmare, and often preventing the page from being extended or adapted without a huge redesign effort.

Event-Driven Programming on the Web

What we really want is a clean and easily extensible model that allows us to react to specific events as the user interacts with the interface we provide in their browser. As in traditional event-driven programming environments, we'd like to be able to create a form containing the controls and content, then react to events that are raised for the individual controls:

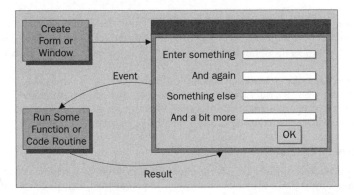

In this scenario, we only need to execute code in response to specific events, and generate output to update the areas of the page that need to be changed. Of course, to some extent, this isn't directly achievable using a web browser and a web server, because there is no persistent connection in the stateless environment that HTTP provides. The user still has to submit the page to our server for processing, whereupon it is processed in a procedural manner.

However, ASP.NET does provide an architecture that allows us to get close to our stated requirements. It is achieved through the **postback architecture** upon which ASP.NET is built, and the features that are implemented as part of this overall architecture. To get the most from ASP.NET it's important to be familiar with this architecture and we'll be looking at it in some detail.

But before then, we need to explore the underlying construction and processing of ASP.NET pages in relation to their script-based predecessors. In particular, it's important to realize just how different these underlying processes are, and how they provide the environment we're looking for to create applications that are truly event-driven.

The ASP.NET Page as a Compiled Class

In previous versions of ASP, and in other web server scripting environments such as JSP and PHP, code is executed as it occurs within the page, in the order that the page-parsing engine and the script interpreter encounter it. Anything that is not server-side script code is simply fed back to the client, via the web server, 'as is'. So, for an ASP 3.0 page, for example, the process might look something like the following diagram:

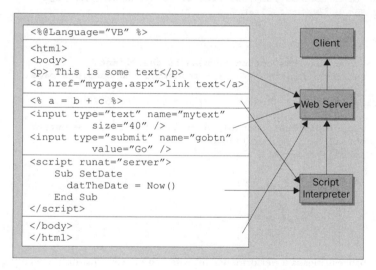

However, in ASP.NET, the process is completely different. The appropriate .NET Framework language compiler converts every page into a **class** file, using **MSIL** (Microsoft Intermediate Language) code. Content that is not server-side code is converted into a series of output.Write statements within the class, in much the same way as we might have used response.Write in ASP 3.0 (this is similar to the way that JSP pages are converted to servlets by most Java application servers). In extremely simplified form, what ASP.NET is actually executing looks something like the following (we've added the comments to indicate what's happening):

```
Public Class MyPage_aspx
  Inherits System.Web.UI.Page     '<-- the base class for the page
  ...

  'your own server-side code and event handlers go here
  Sub Page_Load()
    ...
  End Sub

  'routines to create the server-side controls declared in the page
  Private Sub BuildControlMyControl1
    ...
  End Sub
  Private Sub BuildControlMyControl2
    ...
  End Sub

  'routine to build the complete tree of controls for the page
  Private Sub BuildControlTree
    ...
  End Sub

  'routine to create the output to send to the client
  Private Sub Render_Control1     '<-- rendering the complete page
    ...
    output.Write("<html><body><h1>Welcome to my page</h1>")
    ...
    'tell each individual control to render itself to the output
    ChildControl.RenderControl(output)
    ChildControl.RenderControl(output)
    ...
    output.Write("</body></html>")
    ...
  End Sub

End Class
```

Obviously, this process means a performance hit when compared to simply executing the server-side code as in ASP 3.0, but ASP.NET also writes this code to a disk file within the folder \Winnt\Microsoft.NET\Framework\ *[version]* \Temporary ASP.NET Files\ using a randomly generated file name and with the .dll file extension. It becomes a .NET assembly that is then executed by the Framework the next time that this page is requested, without having to be parsed and compiled again.

You can view the contents of these compiled assemblies using the ildasm tool that is provided with the Framework, however, an easier way to confirm what is going on is to look at the code that the compiler has generated when a compilation error occurs in a page:

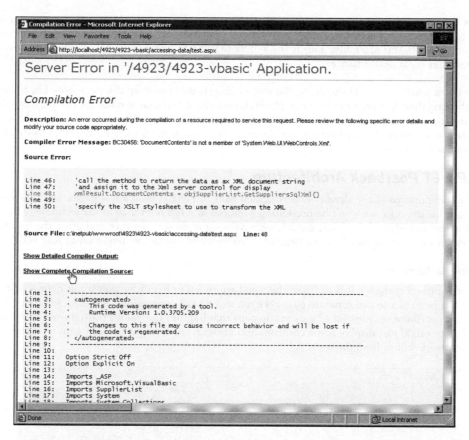

Within the code that will form the class file (once you sort out the compilation error) you'll see any server-side code that you placed in the page, plus the code that builds the complete tree of objects that will make up the final class. The point to take away from this is that everything you place within an ASP.NET page becomes an object, and not just some arbitrary text or HTML that will be sent to the client as it stands. The class exposes a Page object, and within that a host of other objects that represent every server control, every block of text and other content, and every other object that is referenced:

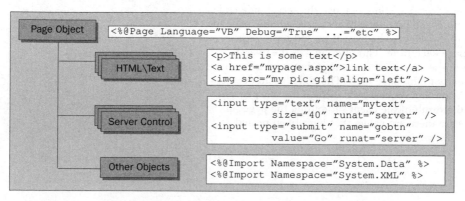

Why is this useful? We'll see more as we look at server controls shortly, but what it does mean is that now – to send this page to a client after it has been compiled – all ASP.NET has to do is execute the MSIL code within this assembly. This is something that the Framework is optimized to do very quickly, and so we get great performance.

All the extra work involved in building the tree of objects that make up the page only has to be done once, the first time it is requested by any client. Of course, if the source code for the page is edited, the compiled assembly file is automatically invalidated and removed, so the next request for the page will generate a new assembly. Furthermore, as the assemblies are written to disk, the MSIL code also survives a server reboot.

The ASP.NET Postback Architecture

As we assume that you have already experimented with ASP.NET, built a few pages, and understand the basic way that it works, we won't be presenting a tutorial or a full reference to the technology here. Having looked at the underlying processing model, what we want to do is make sure you grasp the fundamentals of the various features upon which we depend when we build interactive pages using ASP.NET.

Posting To the Same Page

As we mentioned earlier in this chapter, the usual approach to handling user input before ASP.NET arrived has been to use two separate pages. First a static page containing a <form> section, which has its action attribute set to point to a dynamic page that handles the values posted from that form. The second page might just display some confirmation message, or it might contain another <form> section to collect more values from the user.

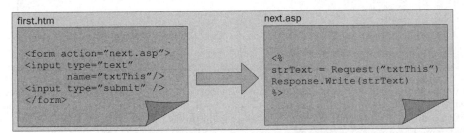

However, one technique that has grown in popularity is to create a single dynamic page that contains not only the <form> section, but also the server-side code that handles the input and generates a suitable page to return to the client. The form is posted back to this same page each time. This often makes the overall design of the site easier to manage, but it adds complexity to the page itself. The code has to decide if this is the first request by the client for this page, or if it is the result of the client submitting the page (in which case there are values that have been posted back to the server).

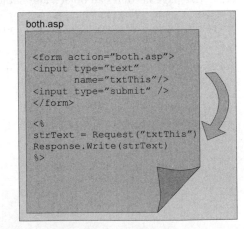

Server-Side ASP.NET Forms

In ASP.NET we have the concept of a **server-side form**, where the `<form>` element is itself a server control that contains the `runat="server"` attribute. In this case, we have no choice but to post back to the same page – ASP.NET prevents the `action` attribute from being set to a different page. In fact, all we need to declare is the `<form>` control element itself, and allow ASP.NET to fill in all the attributes that are required when it creates the control at runtime:

```
<form runat="server">
... form controls here ...
</form>
```

This is where the term '**postback architecture**' comes from, because we always post the values from a server-side ASP.NET `<form>` to the same page that contains the `<form>` declaration. If the page we are creating is called `both.aspx`, the simple definition above produces the following output and sends it to the client:

```
<form name="_ctl0" method="post" action="both.aspx" id="_ctl0">
... form controls here ...
</form>
```

Notice that as well as setting the `action` attribute to the current page, it also sets the `method` to 'post' so that the values will be available in the `Form` collection. In ASP 3.0 (and, of course, in HTML) the default for the `method`, if not specified, is the value 'get'. In this case the values are sent as part of the query string when the form is submitted, and they appear within the ASP `QueryString` collection.

What the postback architecture gives us is the ability to create a page containing HTML form controls, and have it displayed all the time so that the user can interact with it and submit the values they enter to the server – but all the time seeing the same page. It becomes more like the event-driven approach that we discussed earlier, and certainly resembles a normal window-based application more closely than the earlier technique of having a separate page that handles the submitted values.

However, we are still some way from being able to replicate the behavior of a normal executable application window. There are three obvious limitations:

❑ The form still has to be submitted to the server in full each time for processing

❑ The values of the controls will not normally be maintained when the postback occurs

❑ The user sees a page reload each time

ASP.NET attempts to answer these limitations for us in various ways. We'll look at these next.

Emulating Individual Control Events

Although we have a page that appears like an event-driven window-based application interface, we still have the limitation that we are only reacting to a single event – the page being submitted to the server. However, recall that our page is compiled into a class file that gets executed by the .NET Framework. This means that code in the page, and in the ASP.NET runtime processor, can provide an extra layer of capabilities on top of the simple `Request` and `Response` objects that we use in ASP 3.0 and earlier.

In effect, it can tell from the request (we'll see how later) if this is a postback, or if this is the first time that the page has been loaded. It can also tell which control on the page caused the page to be submitted, and even if the current value of any control has changed since the page was sent to the client. This means that ASP.NET can expose a whole range of different events, depending on what interaction took place client-side in the page.

For example, it can expose a `Click` event for the control that was clicked to cause the page to be submitted, or a `Change` event if the currently selected value in a list control is different from that selected when the page was sent to the client. All this is baked into the architecture, and we don't have to do anything to implement it ourselves. We just write event handlers to react to the individual events.

For example, the following code creates an ASP.NET server-side form containing four controls: a textbox, a drop-down list, a checkbox and a **Submit** button:

```
<form runat="server">

<asp:textbox id="MyText" text="OriginalValue"
              ontextchanged="MyChangeCode" runat="server" />

<asp:dropdownlist id="MyListBox"
                  onselectedindexchanged="MyChangeCode" runat="server">
  <asp:listitem text="Option 1" value="Value1" runat="server" />
  <asp:listitem text="Option 2" value="Value2" runat="server" />
  <asp:listitem text="Option 3" value="Value3" runat="server" />
</asp:dropdownlist>

<asp:checkbox id="MyCheckBox"
              oncheckedchanged="MyChangeCode" runat="server" />

<asp:button id="MySubmitButton" text="Submit"
            onclick="MyClickCode" runat="server" />  

</form>
```

We've attached an event handler to one of the events of each control, for example the `OnTextChanged` event for the textbox control, and the `OnClick` event of the **Submit** button. We can handle these events by inserting an event handler into the server-side code section of the page. In fact, we've included two event handlers – one for the change events from the textbox, list and checkbox controls, and a separate one for the click event from the button:

```
<script runat="server">

Sub MyChangeCode(objSender As Object, objArgs As EventArgs)
   divResult.InnerHtml += "Change event detected for control '" _
                          & objSender.ID & "'<br />"
End Sub

Sub MyClickCode(objSender As Object, objArgs As EventArgs)
   divResult.InnerHtml += "Click event detected for control '" _
                          & objSender.ID & "'<br />"
End Sub

</script>
```

Now, if we change the values in the three controls and submit the page by clicking the Submit button, the following is displayed:

Change event detected for control 'MyText'
Change event detected for control 'MyListBox'
Change event detected for control 'MyCheckBox'
Click event detected for control 'MySubmitButton'

Other events can be handled in a page; these are only a few examples. And, as well as client-initiated events like those we've just seen, there are also server-initiated events that we can handle. Examples are the Page_Load event, or events such as OnItemDataBound that occur for data-bound controls.

Server-Side and Client-Side Event Handling

What is important to grasp is that all the events we saw in the previous code listing are **handled server-side**, in our ASP.NET code, even though they represent actions that **occurred client-side** in the browser. Some occur immediately, because they cause a postback to occur (as is the case with the Click event for the Submit button). Others occur belatedly, such as the Change events for the other controls. This is because they can't be raised on the server until a postback occurs.

Of course, there's nothing to prevent the page containing the usual client-side event handlers as well, for example we can still write client-side code that is executed in response to a form being submitted or a button being clicked. That code can manipulate the controls on the page, or the page content via Dynamic HTML. But this is an entirely separate process from the handling of events on the server. Client-side code can't be used to handle ASP.NET-specific events.

This can be a confusing state of affairs until you start to get it straight in your head. There are three ways that events can occur and be handled:

❑   Events that are **initiated on the client** and **handled on the client**. These include, for example, the OnClick event for an HTML <input> element, the OnChange event for an HTML <select> list, and the OnSubmit event for an HTML <form> element.

❑   Events that are **initiated on the client** and **handled on the server**. These include, for example, the OnTextChanged event for an ASP.NET Textbox control and the OnCheckedChanged event for an ASP.NET Checkbox control.

❑   Events that are **initiated on the server** and **handled on the server**. These include, for example, the Page_Load event, or the OnItemDataBound event for a data-bound control.

Where things often get complicated is when we come to events like OnClick or OnChange. If we declare a textbox element using an <input> server-side control, and define a value for the OnChange attribute, what we are actually doing is specifying a client-side event handler for this element:

```
<input type="text" id="txtThis" onchange="MyChangeCode()" runat="server"/>
```

When this is rendered in the browser, the attribute is still present and the browser will expect to find a **client-side** event handler named MyChangeCode:

```
<input name="txtThis" id="txtThis" type="text" onchange="MyChangeCode()" />
```

19

If we want to specify a server-side event handler for this control, we have to use the `onserverchange` attribute:

```
<input type="text" id="txtThis" onserverchange="MyChangeCode" runat="server"/>
```

When this is rendered to the client, no event handler attribute is included:

```
<input name="txtThis2" id="txtThis2" type="text" />
```

However, when the page containing this element is posted back to the server, a 'change' event will be raised and ASP.NET will look for a **server-side** event handler named `MyChangeCode`.

Specifying Both Server-Side and Client-Side OnClick Event Handlers

The `OnServerXxxxxx` events are only defined for the HTML server-side controls (controls from the namespace `System.Web.UI.HtmlControls`). The ASP.NET Web Forms' controls (controls from the namespace `System.Web.UI.WebControls`) generally have specifically named events such as `OnTextChanged` and `OnCheckedChanged`, which can't be confused with the standard client-side events that are defined in HTML.

The ones that differ, and cause most confusion, are the ASP.NET Web Forms' `Button`, `ImageButton` and `LinkButton` controls. These do have an `OnClick` property, but the matching event is handled **server-side**, and **not** client-side. This is down to the way that the Web Forms' controls work internally. When they see an `OnClick` attribute in the control declaration, they use it to set up a connection for the event server-side, and they do not render the attribute to the client. So we can specify a handler in an ASP.NET page for one of these controls, using something like:

```
<asp:Button id="btnDoIt" Text="Do It" runat="server"
            OnClick="ServerClickCode" />
```

In this case, the event handler named `ServerClickCode` will be executed **on the server** when the page is posted back. This postback happens automatically anyway, when the button is clicked, because ASP.NET renders this control as an `<input type="submit" />` element in the page it creates.

One trick we can use with the `Button` control, if we want to run code on the client when the button is clicked but before the page is submitted, is to manually add a client-side attribute to the element that the ASP.NET control creates:

```
btnDoIt.Attributes.Add("onclick", "clientClickCode()")
```

What this does is add an `onclick` attribute to the `<input>` element itself, but without affecting the way that ASP.NET processes the event. When the button is clicked this time, the client-side code defined in the `onclick` attribute is executed. After that, the form is submitted to the server and ASP.NET will execute the server-side code in the event handler that is defined for the `OnClick` property of the control. So, effectively, we can arrange for an event to be raised on both the client and the server. Hopefully, the following code makes this clearer:

```
<%@Page Language="VB" %>
<html>
<head>
<script language="JavaScript">
<!--
// client-side script section
function clientClickCode() {
  alert("Event executed on client");
}
//-->
</script>
</head>
<body>
<form runat="server">
  <!-- declare Button control with server-side event property -->
  <asp:Button id="btnDoIt" Text="Do It" runat="server"
              OnClick="ServerClickCode" />
</form>
</body>
</html>

<script language="VB" runat="server">
' server-side script section
Sub Page_Load()
  ' add client-side "onclick" attribute to element when page loads
  btnDoIt.Attributes.Add("onclick", "clientClickCode()")
End Sub
Sub ServerClickCode(o as Object, e as EventArgs)
  Response.Write("Event executed on server")
End Sub
</script>
```

The same approach works with the other two controls we mentioned earlier, the ImageButton and LinkButton. The ImageButton control is rendered on the client as an <input type="image" /> element, and this automatically submits the form it's on when clicked. The process is exactly the same as with a Button control. The code that gets rendered on the client from an ImageButton, when we add our own onclick attribute to the element, looks like this:

```
<input type="image" name="btnTest" id="btnTest" src="myimage.gif"
       border="0" onclick="clientClickCode()"/>
```

However, the LinkButton control works in a different way, as we'll see in more detail in the next chapter. It relies on a client-side script function that is automatically added to the enclosing <form>, and which causes the form to be submitted when the link created by the control is clicked. It works by specifying a **JavaScript URL** (a function name preceded by the word javascript:) as the href attribute of an <a> element.

So our own onclick attribute can be added as well, and will execute our client-side event handler before the function defined in the href attribute. Again, this is the kind of result that is rendered in the browser from the control when we add our own onclick attribute to the element:

```
<a id="btnTest" onclick="clientClickCode()"
   href="javascript:__doPostBack('btnTest','')">test</a>
</form>
```

Of course, you can use the `Attributes` collection to access any attributes of an element that an ASP.NET control creates, and add any attribute you want to the output of the control. You'll see more examples later in the book as we build our sample web site.

So, after all this, you should be able to see how the ASP.NET approach to server-side programming in a web page is extremely innovative when compared to previous technologies, and also gives us the clean and extensible structure that we are looking for. We can handle individual events for controls, and benefit from the kind of event-driven programming technique that we were looking for. More to the point, this also reduces the code that we have to write, as well as making it much simpler to develop and maintain dynamic pages.

Control Values and ViewState

The second major issue with building dynamic pages, once we adopt the 'one-page' approach using postbacks to the same page, has always been how we maintain the values of the controls as the user submits data for processing. In ASP 3.0 and earlier (and in most other dynamic page generation technologies), the values that the user entered into the HTML controls on the page disappear each time the page is reloaded, unless we specifically write code to reinstate them.

The usual approach has been to simply insert the values from the `Request.Form` or `Request.QueryString` collection into the appropriate controls as we rebuild the page:

```
<input type="text" name="txtThis"
       value="<% = Request.Form("txtThis") %>" />
```

Of course, it gets more complicated with list controls and radio buttons, as we then have to figure out which one was selected and add a `selected="selected"` attribute to the appropriate `<option>` element, or a `checked="checked"` attribute to the appropriate `<input type="radio">` element.

ASP.NET does away with all this messing about for us. When a page is posted back to the server, ASP.NET automatically extracts the values of the controls from the request and populates these controls with the values that they contained when the page was submitted. This feature alone can save a great deal of coding when we are providing pages that behave like our proverbial window-based executable application.

This is because ASP.NET implements a new concept called **viewstate**. No doubt you've already seen the hidden-type `<input>` control that ASP.NET automatically adds to a server-side `<form>`:

```
<form name="_ctl" method="post" action="test.aspx" id="_ctl">
   <input type="hidden" name="__VIEWSTATE" value="dDwxNzI5M...qQThw" />
   ... other controls here ...
</form>
```

The viewstate contains an encoded representation of two aspects of the current page: the **control tree** that makes up the page (which means that it can prevent spoofing by only allowing the viewstate to be posted back to the same page as that in which it was created), and the **values of various controls** on the page. Viewstate can be enabled or disabled for a page, or individually for each control. By default, it is enabled and persisted for all the controls on a server-side <form>.

When the page is posted back to the server, it can extract from the viewstate the values that were in the controls when the page was last generated by ASP.NET, and compare these with the current values. This is how it can detect if the user has changed the value of a control – as in our earlier example of the OnTextChanged and OnCheckedChanged events. It's also how it detects if this is a postback, or if it is the first time that this client has loaded the page.

Viewstate is also used to store values that are required for more specific purposes. For example, when we use an ASP.NET DataGrid control and take advantage of the automatic paging feature it provides, viewstate is required to store details about which is the current page, and which page should be shown next.

Using Viewstate as a Storage Medium

Viewstate also has the advantage of being independent of things like ASP.NET Sessions, or other server-dependent techniques for storing user-specific data, because it is encoded within the page that they submit to the server each time. And while server controls automatically persist their values to the viewstate, and extract it when a postback occurs, we can also use this feature ourselves to pass values between pages. It makes a useful alternative to hidden-type <input> controls or the query string.

To add a value, which must be a String, to the viewstate for a page, we just use:

```
ViewState("keyname") = ValueToStore
```

We extract the value when the page is reloaded using:

```
ValueExtracted = CType(ViewState("keyname"), String)
```

In C#, the equivalent is:

```
ViewState["keyname"] = ValueToStore;
ValueExtracted = (String) ViewState["keyname"];
```

If there is no value in the viewstate for the key name we provide, we get nothing returned. As with the Request.QueryString and Request.Form collections, the returned value is an empty string in this case.

To store objects that are not of type String, and which cannot be automatically cast into a String, we must serialize them into a String first and then resurrect them after extracting them from the viewstate. So an Integer type can be stored directly, whereas a dataset cannot. However, we could serialize a DataSet object to a String containing an XML representation of the data, store in the viewstate, and then extract it afterwards and read it back into a DataSet.

Disabling Viewstate

Viewstate applies to many types of controls, not just the HTML form controls. For example if you set the text or content of a `<span>` or `<div>` element that contains the `runat="server"` attribute in your server-side code, this will be maintained across postbacks by default, using the viewstate. Likewise, the complete contents of a `DataGrid` control placed on a server-side `<form>` will be persisted.

However, there are often occasions where we don't actually need the viewstate to be persisted between postbacks. In these cases, the processing needed to generate it, decode it upon postback, and pass it twice across the network can be avoided by disabling it. For a complete page, including all the controls on it, we can add an instruction to the `Page` directive:

```
<%@Page Language="VB" EnableViewstate="False" %>
```

Some content is always stored in the hidden control named "__VIEWSTATE", even when viewstate is turned off for the page as a whole. This is the encoded representation of the control hierarchy, which is used to ensure that the page is correctly posted to the same one as it was generated by, in order to give some protection against a user spoofing the server by submitting a different page.

If viewstate is disabled in the `Page` directive, it cannot be 'turned back on' for individual controls. However, we can leave viewstate enabled for the page as a whole, and then selectively disable it for individual controls to limit the viewstate size:

```
<span id="status" enableviewstate="false" runat="server" />
```

For 'status' elements, perhaps an `<asp:Label>`, `<span>` or `<div>` that you use to display interactive messages or feedback, be sure to add the `enableviewstate="false"` attribute so that the existing values are removed when the page is regenerated on the server each time.

Preventing a Page Reload

The third issue we mentioned earlier about the way that ASP.NET attempts to provide a rich event-driven architecture over the Web is the problem of page reloads. No matter how clever our server-side processing is, the user still goes through the process of submitting the whole page, and then waiting for it to be reloaded.

One way to get round this is to use some component or browser feature on the client that can submit a request to the server and receive the response without actually reloading the visible page. Some developers implement this using a Java applet or even the XMLHTTP object that is part of the MSXML parser. However, it was always hard work, and usually limited to occasions where the server was only returning specific values. In other words, it was like calling a remote function or method on the server, receiving the result in the response, and using it to update some value in the page.

In ASP.NET, a new feature called **smart navigation** has been added. It only works at the moment in Internet Explorer 5 and above, as it uses the MSXML parser and Microsoft's own brand of Dynamic HTML to update the page being viewed in the client's browser.

Simply adding the `SmartNavigation` attribute to the `Page` directive automatically enables smart navigation:

```
<%@Page Language="VB" SmartNavigation="True" %>
```

This causes ASP.NET to add a hidden `<iframe>` element to the page, as well as accessing a special client-side script file stored within the `aspnet_client\system_web\` folder that is created within the default web site on your server when ASP.NET is installed:

```
<IFRAME ID=_hifSmartNav NAME=_hifSmartNav STYLE=display:none
        src="javascript:smartnav=1"></IFRAME>
```

Now the client immediately reaps the benefits. When they request a page, the client-side script code that implements smart navigation automatically requests the new page behind the scenes, without allowing the existing page to be submitted to the server. When it receives the response from the server, it figures out which parts of the page have changed, and updates just these parts by injecting the new content into the DHTML object model for the page.

Smart navigation doesn't always produce 'invisible' page reloads, a lot depends on how much of the page has changed. However, it certainly makes it appear a lot more like a 'real' window-based application (rather than a web page). It also has by-product advantages; such as the fact that it prevents long pages being scrolled back to the top each time the user hits a Submit button.

ASP.NET Server Controls

We've talked about ASP.NET server controls in the previous sections of this chapter, and no doubt you are already pretty familiar with them and how they are used. However, there are a few points worth mentioning here – in particular when you should actually consider using them and when an ordinary declarative HTML control will do the job.

Any controls or elements declared in your ASP.NET pages that are **not** marked with the `runat="server"` attribute are not server controls. The HTML that declares them becomes just part of the various string values that the `output.Write` statements in the compiled class file (which implements the page) send directly to the client.

However, server controls are implemented within an ASP.NET page as objects that become part of the control tree for that page. They are individually constructed by the compiler, and compiled into the page itself as a separate object. This obviously has an impact on the performance of the page, so you should really only use them when necessary. In general this is when:

❑ You need to access them in your server-side code, perhaps to set their property values, or react to events that they raise.

❑ You want to use controls from the `System.Web.UI.WebControls` namespace (controls that are prefixed with "asp:") that are not available as normal HTML controls. These controls must be defined with the `runat="server"` attribute. Examples are the `DataGrid`, `Calendar` and `AdRotator`.

You should **not** need to use a server control where:

❑ The element is only used to run some client-side script, such as opening a new browser window or interacting with the content of the page through Dynamic HTML.

❑ For a Submit button that only submits the <form>, and you don't need to interact with the button itself in your server-side code.

❑ For a hyperlink that opens another page, and you don't need to set the properties for the hyperlink on the server.

❑ Any other times when there is no requirement to access the properties, methods or events of the control.

Server-Side Data Binding

We mentioned that we often choose to use an ASP.NET server control when there is no equivalent HTML control. Of course, all the server controls actually emit HTML (and sometimes JavaScript) – because that's all the browser understands.

> *Some specialist controls can emit other types of output, for example the controls from the Microsoft Mobile Internet Toolkit (MMIT) can emit WML instead of HTML.*

What makes some of the ASP.NET Web Forms controls special is that they can automatically emit a series of HTML elements that make up more complex compound output, rather than just a single control. One simple example of this is the <asp:checkbox> control, which outputs a <span> element for the caption of the checkbox as well as the <input type="checkbox"> element itself.

Where the ASP.NET server controls really become useful is for building complex output such as lists. There is a range of list controls from the simpler Repeater and CheckBoxList to the more complex DataList and DataGrid. These can be bound to data sources on the server, and they automatically create a list of items based on the contents of the data source.

The techniques for formatting the output that several of these controls generate is also easy to grasp, yet at the same time extremely powerful. By using templates for each part of the list, it's easy to create attractive lists in an ASP.NET page with minimum effort.

Other Useful ASP.NET Features

As we work through building the example site for this book, we'll be taking advantage of as many of the useful features of ASP.NET as we can, and showing you how they make the whole process easier, faster and less error prone. Amongst these techniques are:

❑ Using the ASP.NET Session object to store user-specific values

❑ Using ASP.NET built-in caching features to improve performance and efficiency of the site

❑ Using the authentication and authorization features that ASP.NET provides for web pages

We'll very briefly touch on these next, before we move on to look at the design for our example site.

ASP.NET Sessions

Like ASP 3.0 and earlier, ASP.NET provides both an Application and a user-specific Session object that we can use to store values that we want to persist across postbacks. These are useful, though they do absorb resources on the server and may not be an ideal solution for a very heavy traffic site. One advance over ASP 3.0, however, is that sessions can now be maintained using **URL munging**, where the session identified is encoded into the URL itself rather than depending on the client supporting cookies.

The actual session content, the data, can also be stored in several ways. Rather than always storing it on the server that responds to the request (a problem in a web farm where requests may be passed to different servers each time), the data can be stored on one specific server using the new ASP.NET State Server service, or even in a SQL Server database table.

Sessions provide an alternative to viewstate for storing data that has to be passed between pages. This approach avoids the extra overhead in bandwidth use that comes from storing it within the page in a hidden-type <input> control. However, it does add extra loading to the server-side processing as the session is located and 'opened' with each request.

To avoid or reduce the overheads connected with using sessions in ASP.NET, we can disable session support for individual pages that don't need to access session data (in ASP 3.0 sessions could only be enabled or disabled at application level for all pages). We can also specify that session access is read-only for specific pages, which reduces the overhead somewhat by avoiding the extra stage of writing the data back to the session when page execution is complete.

ASP.NET Caching

ASP.NET provides a rich caching environment that we can take advantage of when building applications. As well as a global cache for each application, within which we can store values with pre-defined expiry conditions and triggers, we can take advantage of **output caching**. This is a great way to speed up delivery of pages that are always the same, or which do not vary much between each other (based on parameter values sent in the request).

When output caching is enabled for a page, the resulting HTML and content that ASP.NET generates by executing the page is cached automatically for a period defined by the OutputCache directive in the page. All subsequent requests for this page are met by ASP.NET simply sending back the output it created by executing the page that last time, up until the cached page expires.

Of course, this is only going to work if the content is not supposed to be different for each request, based on some value sent from the client in a <form> or in the query string. However, caching can be configured to take this into account, and a different copy of the page will be generated and cached when the values sent from the clients differ.

While some care is required when configuring output caching, to take into account the requirements for different clients and different request values, it's clear that it can be hugely beneficial in improving performance.

ASP.NET Authentication and Authorization

One area where web developers have always had to build quite complex custom code routines is when you need to protect some or all of a site by demanding that the user logs in by presenting some type of credentials. ASP.NET makes it much easier to implement this type of feature in any web site or application through a range of security features that are built in.

The most common for public web sites is **forms-based authentication**, which depends on a specially encoded cookie being delivered to the client, and then used to access secured pages. It is easy to implement using the objects that are part of the .NET Framework, and we demonstrate it in our example application in this book.

For intranet sites, another option that ASP.NET provides is integration with the built-in Windows authentication features, using the accounts and groups that are defined within Windows itself. Finally, there are also features that allow ASP.NET sites to take advantage of Microsoft's own Passport authentication service.

All of the topics we've been discussing are covered in depth in other Wrox publications that are devoted to ASP.NET itself, and so we haven't gone into any more detail here. For more information, check out: *Professional ASP.NET 1.0* (ISBN 1-861007-03-5) and *ASP.NET Namespace Reference with VB.NET* (ISBN 1-861007-45-0) or its C# equivalent (ISBN 1-861007-44-2).

Designing an Interactive Web Site

Having spent some considerable time looking at why we should choose ASP.NET as the foundation for our web sites, and seeing some of the extremely useful features it provides, we can move on now to look at the process we used to design the example site you'll see being developed throughout the remainder of this book. We start with a look at the overall aims of the site, the general approach to planning it, and the design we came up with for the basic structure.

The Overall Site Design

Designing a web site is a process that you can tackle in many different ways. However, more than probably most other kinds of application that you might build, the design process involves two completely different areas of expertise. A competent programmer can build the back-end interfaces, components and logic code, and probably put together a half-reasonable user interface as well. But, for a public web site, there needs to be input from one or more people who have at least a modicum of flair for graphical design and appearance.

We don't profess to be accomplished in this area, and for others in the same position it might prove beneficial to employ an outside agency or contractor who is expert in this field. However, even when you separate the graphical design from the physical development process, both the basic structural design of a site and its actual appearance should be based on something that meets the requirements of both the site owner and the visitors who will use it.

Requirements Analysis

As with any other software project, a good place to start is with **requirements analysis**. There are plenty of authoritative textbooks out there that describe the complete process for collecting the information required, and pulling it all together into a cohesive plan. And while this is no doubt extremely necessary for applications that have to manage the day-to-day running of your corporation, the process for a web site is harder to specify in absolute terms.

You might decide to ask visitors to an existing site what they feel is wrong with it, and what they would like to see. It's also a good idea to ask your own staff the same questions, plus any existing customers or users that you can track down directly. You might also decide to take a look at competitors' sites, or even just surf around looking at different kinds of web sites to see if their approach would suit your requirements.

But, even after all this, you may still end up with a mixed set of requirements. It's just too easy to end up with a list that contains things like "we want it to look like this but in red", or "we ought to have a page where you can read product reviews". All this is useful input, but it needs to be carefully separated out into the two areas we mentioned at the start: the structure and workings of the site versus the physical appearance and 'look and feel'.

The Basic Site Structure

So, having said all that, how do we get started once the opinions, preferences, bright ideas and other input have all been collated? My favorite approach involves the minimum of tools – a pen and lots of paper. Step one is then to get down on paper the overall structure for the site, showing the main pages we think will be required to give the features we want, and how they are related and linked to each other.

Next, we can add in other features if required, for example those miscellaneous requirements such as a page to display the terms and conditions of trading, or a contact page. What's important is to make sure that the pages we don't include in the first iteration are not "foundation" pages, in other words they are pages or features that we can add later without causing a complete redesign of the original structure.

Of course, you can never be sure that future requirements won't upset the whole applecart and prompt a major re-design. But it's usually possible from the requirements analysis to tell which features are the most important, and form the basis for the complete site. They're usually the ones at the top of everyone's list, and crop up most often in discussions about the site requirements.

The Wrox Car Company

OK, so it's time to take the plunge. The following is the completed list of the requirements we used to start designing and building the Wrox Car Company site:

Feature	Description	Notes on Description
Home Page	Display news about the company	
	Show special offers and new models	
	Display details of events that might interest visitors and customers	
	Provide a list of car models that links to more details pages about each one	
	Include links to Terms and Conditions, Contact page, and so on	

Table continued on following page

Feature	Description	Notes on Description
Page for Each Car Model	Show options, colors, and extras available for that model	
	Display vehicle image in chosen color	
	Allow visitors to customize the vehicle and see the cost of that customized version	
	Show the credit (hire-purchase) terms and calculate the payments required	
	Provide a link to reviews about that model	
	Provide a link to allow visitors to place an order for the car they choose	
Page to Compare Model Features	Allow visitors to choose different sets of features to compare	Economy, Performance, Standard Features, Running Costs, and so on
	Use graphical displays, pie charts, line graphs, and bar charts	
	Open from 'Home' page, and possibly from individual model pages (to be decided)	
Order Page	Collect data on the configuration already specified by the customer	
	Collect payment and delivery information	
	Process order and send email confirmation	Maybe print invoice as well?
Future Extensions	Allow visitors to configure site style and appearance	Personalization
	Provide a Search feature	Although everything should be easy to find anyway

This is probably a far simpler set of requirements than many 'real-world' sites during their design phase, but it is compact enough for us to have a chance of building it all without requiring a book six inches thick to describe it. It also includes all the major user interface implementation features that we want to be able to investigate in this book.

So, coming back to our pen and paper (and just to prove that we actually do follow our own advice) the following diagram shows the first working sketch we made for the **Wrox Car Company** site based on the requirements listed earlier:

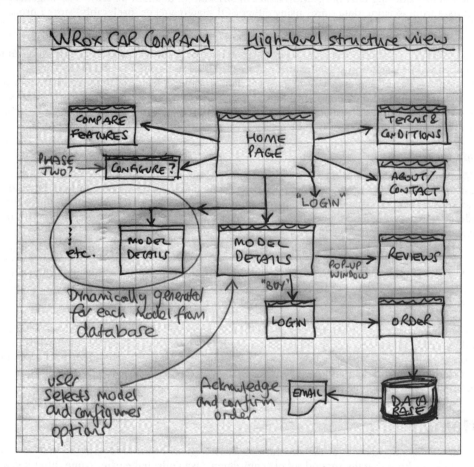

The design is a fairly common approach for any site that has multiple products to sell. The main functionality is in the dynamic page that will generate the details of each vehicle model, based on a key or ID value that we pass into the page appended to the query string in the usual way. The Home page will also be interesting to build in that it needs to obtain the data for the news, events and special offers from the back-end database that we'll be using to power all this.

The Data Source

Having just slipped into the narrative the topic of a database, this is also something that we need to consider before the design proceeds too far. In our **Wrox Car Company** example site, we have the luxury of being free from any existing constraints on the nature and source of the data that will drive our site. We're building the database as well as the site, so we can provide a set of data structures, tables, and columns that suit our requirements.

Of course, this isn't always the case. Often you have an existing database or other data source that you need to connect to and access. This book is about user interfaces, and not about data management, so we won't be considering data integration issues in any kind of detail here. However, in general you can extract data from existing data stores using either SQL statements or (preferably) stored procedures to get almost any combination of table and column values.

This might not be as efficient as a purpose-designed database, and you may consider using some kind of data replication or staged bulk data transfer process to fill a more suitable database from the 'production' data store that contains the original data. For more details of the ways that you can consolidate and convert data between different formats, take a look at the Wrox Press book *ASP.NET Distributed Data Applications* (ISBN 1-861004-92-3). This book is devoted to the 'data side' of building applications rather than the user interface side.

Client-Side Processing

One focus of the book we just mentioned is a detailed examination of how we can distribute the processing load in a data management application to the client, using client-side scripting and objects such as an XML parser instantiated on the client machine. This approach not only relieves the server of considerable processing load by minimizing postbacks, but also produces a more interactive interface in the browser and better-perceived performance by the client.

In our Wrox Car Company application, we're focusing on the use of the ASP.NET Web Forms' controls, and other server controls, so most of the interaction with the pages will produce a postback to the server. However, we will still consider including client-side processing where it provides appreciable improvements in either interactivity or perceived performance.

For example, we can get far better control over the location and appearance of pop-up windows if we open them using client-side script rather than an ordinary hyperlink. However, this means that clients that don't support client-side scripting (or where it is disabled) won't be able to open the window. We can get round this problem by implementing a client-side script check within the application, and changing the behavior of the pages to suit each client.

The Home Page

Now that we have an idea about the structure of the site, we can start to look at the individual pages in more detail. It's here that the second set of requirements we collected earlier come into play, as we can start to think about what the pages might look like as well as what they contain and how they might be implemented. The sketch we made of our Home page layout is shown next:

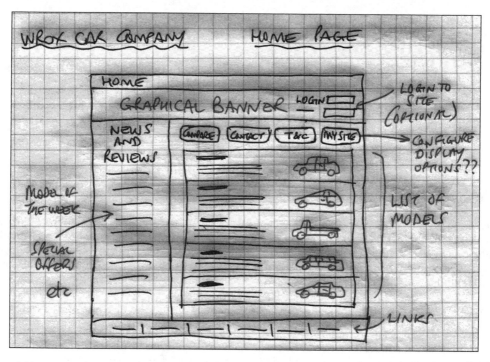

It would be nice if the graphical banner was animated in some way, and we'll perhaps be able to implement this using some client-side script where it is available. We will also omit the 'login' controls in the first iteration, though it's useful to have an idea about how they will be integrated into the site later on.

The list of text links at the bottom will appear on every page of the site, so we need to build some kind of reusable control for this. The most obvious approach, and one we'll implement, is to create it as a User Control that we can insert into any page.

The remainder of the page content is generated dynamically from our database, containing the news, events and special offers in the left-hand column and a list of car models in the right-hand column. Probably we'll use a different background color to separate them visually. Even though these lists are dynamically generated, the data doesn't change very often – perhaps daily at the most – so this page will be a good candidate for output caching to improve performance.

The Ingredients for the Home Page

So, the ingredients we'll need for this page are:

❑   Something eye-catching and graphical for a banner at the top.

❑   Some 'button' controls to open the other pages linked from the Home page. We should consider dynamically changing the page to use 'submit' buttons, rather than the Web Forms' Button control, if the client doesn't support client-side scripting (you'll see why in the next chapter).

- ❑ A list-type control for the news and events section, probably a `DataList` or `Repeater`. Items displayed here might contain links to open other pages containing detailed reviews or more information on any topic shown in the list.

- ❑ A control to display a list of car models, again probably a `DataList` or a `Repeater`. Each car image and model name will be a link to the detail page for that model.

- ❑ A server-side `<form>` and two textbox controls for the 'login' section, when we decide to implement this.

- ❑ A User Control for the reusable page footer, probably one that displays the current page link in a different color to aid navigation.

The Car Model Details Page

This page is at the heart of our application, and will be the one that visitors use the most. We want to provide a lot of information about each vehicle, and allow visitors to specify a lot of quite complex configuration options and 'add-on' extras (so that they spend more money!). We could implement several different pages for each model of vehicle, for example one for the colors, one for the engine details and one for the finance packages that are available.

The Color Options Section

However, we chose a more compact approach that we think makes it feel more like a one-stop operation. It also has extra benefits, in that users can easily see where they are and what options are available. We chose to incorporate a tabbed dialog appearance. This is the sketch we produced, showing what the page will look like when choosing the color of your new car:

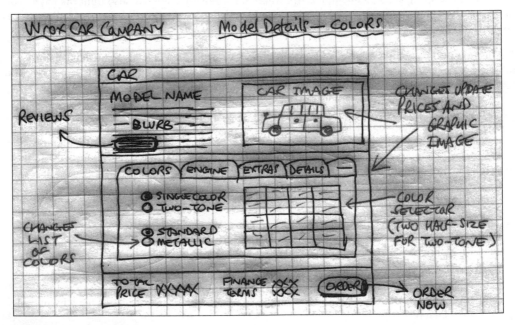

An image of the car and a brief description (marketing 'blurb') are shown in the top section, with a link to open a page where we'll display reviews about the car. In the central section is the tabbed 'dialog' page showing the different areas of customization and information that are available for each model. The visitor can choose the type of color scheme they are interested in here, and we'll respond by changing the color of the image in the top section to match so that they can see what their new car will look like.

The lower section contains the calculated cost for the vehicle with the currently selected options, and the finance terms for the vehicle. There's also the all-important button to allow them to place their order whenever they are ready.

Using a Frameset

We could implement this page using an HTML frameset. One immediate issue that many readers will raise, however, is that using frames is "old-fashioned", and they are no good on many kinds of simple web-browsing devices. They also make navigating the site more complicated, and prevent the Back button working properly in the browser. It's a formidable list of objections, but frames also have some distinct advantages.

We want to make the page as interactive as possible, but it is obviously going to be a big page (source-code wise), and will require quite a lot of processing on the server each time it's requested. By breaking it up into three frames, and only reloading the ones that actually need to be changed, we reduce the bandwidth usage and processing effort.

Frames also allow the user to carry on interacting with the page in one frame while the other frame is reloading. This is ideal for our lower frame, which can go off and recalculate the price while the user decides what other extras for their new car they can afford to lavish money on.

Other Approaches

In some respects, smart navigation could help to minimize the page reloads that the user would see if we do not use frames, but this still requires the complete page to be sent from the server to the client each time. While the user wouldn't see the page reloading, our server would still have to work just as hard, and the time taken for the page to be delivered over the network would not be reduced either. On top of this, smart navigation will only work in Internet Explorer 5.0 and above anyway.

Alternatively, we might decide to use <iframe> elements to build separate areas of the page that could be refreshed individually. This has the advantage over using a <frameset> in that it has less impact on navigation, but (despite being defined in the HTML 4.0 recommendations) the <iframe> element is relatively Internet Explorer-specific. Up until version 6.0, Opera and Navigator do not recognize it.

The Ingredients for the Color Options Section

So, the ingredients we'll need for this page can be divided into three sections: one for each section within the page. For the top section, we'll need:

❑ A panel of some kind to hold the description, perhaps within a table that fills the window, or in an ASP.NET `Panel` control.

❑ A button of some type, perhaps a clickable image, to show reviews for this model.

❑ An `Image` control to display the picture of the vehicle, and we'll color it as visitors select a color in the central section.

❑ Possibly another button to open the 'compare features' page, if we decide to implement a link from this page to it.

For the central section we'll need:

- A tabbed dialog or 'tabstrip' control to display the five 'option section' tabs.
- A few RadioButton controls to display the color style options.
- An ASP.NET List control, to create the table of vehicle colors dynamically as the color style is selected.

For the lower section, we'll need:

- Some Label controls to display the price and finance terms.
- A button of some type, perhaps a clickable image, to start the 'order' process.

The Engine Options Section

Each model is available with a choice of engines, and the second tabbed page in the central section will show these options. For each one, we'll display the technical specifications of the engine, and we'll update the price and finance details in the lower section when a visitor chooses an engine for their new car:

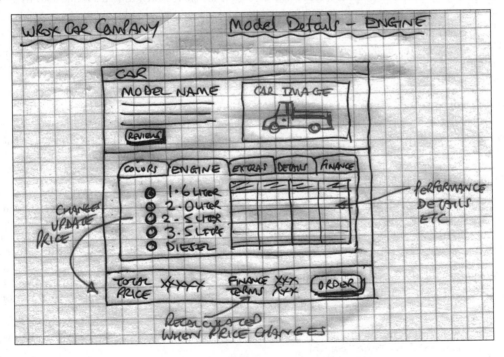

The Ingredients for the Engine Options Section

For this page, as well as the controls we specified for the top and bottom sections, and the tabstrip in the central section, we'll need:

- ❑ A `RadioButtonList` control to show the engine options, which will be different for each model.

- ❑ A list control of some type to show the engine specifications. It might be a `DataGrid` or a `DataList`, or we may even resort to using XSLT to build the display if the specifications are provided in XML format.

The Optional Extras Section

Probably the most complex of the central section pages will be the Optional Extras page. Each model will have a range of optional extras available for it, and the user will be able to choose the ones they want from the list in this window. Again, as they do so, the price and finance terms in the lower section will be updated to reflect their current selection:

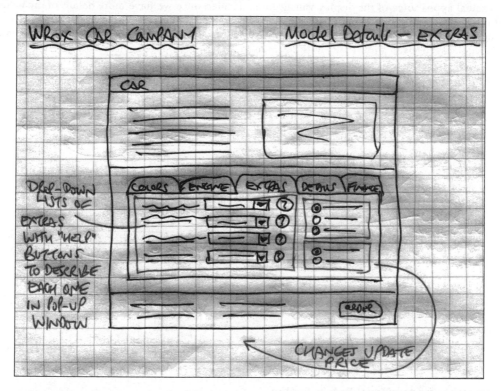

The Ingredients for the Optional Extras Section

For now, until we investigate the types of optional extra that are available, we'll assume that we can use drop-down lists and/or option buttons to select each one. So, the list of requirements looks like this at the moment:

□ A selection of `DropDownList` controls to display options where there are many different variations.

□ A selection of `RadioButtonList` controls for options where there are only a few variations.

□ Some clickable `Image` controls to display details and help for each optional extra category – probably in a pop-up window.

□ Possibly some `Validation` controls to check user input and make sure that the combination of options chosen is valid.

The Model Details Section

This page is designed to show details of a whole range of the features of a vehicle that are not configurable. At the moment we don't have a definitive list of what they will all be, but it's likely to be things like the overall dimensions of the vehicle, the weight and fuel tank capacity, the number of seats, and so on.

The actual appearance of the display will again be decided once we have more details of the actual data, but the ideal is probably to provide a list divided into sections like those listed in the previous paragraph. It would also be nice if we could display these in such a way that the visitor can expand and collapse the sections to show the details:

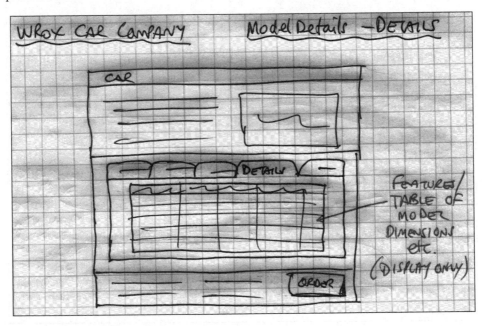

The Ingredients for the Model Details Section

To implement a collapsible list, we have a range of options. We might use any of the following:

□ A `TreeView` control of some type, or perhaps two side-by-side. A client-side version would provide a highly responsive interface here.

- A list control such as a `DataList` or `DataGrid`, with child list controls to show the individual values for each section.

- An ASP.NET `Xml` control that uses an XSLT stylesheet to transform the data into a collapsible list format that relies on client-side script.

- Alternatively, a simple list control such as a `Repeater` or `DataList` if we decide to avoid the expand/collapse feature.

The Finance Options Section

This section is relatively simple from the user interface point of view, but will involve some more complex server-side or client-side processing to calculate the values as the user selects the payment plan they require. For speed and interactivity, it would be nice to perform the calculation client-side and update the totals in the lower section without requiring a postback. However, as the previous sections will probably rely on a postback to obtain the values, this might not be possible.

Other opportunities are to use a Web Service to fetch the payment terms calculated on the server, but this is likely to be Internet Explorer-specific. It might prove in the long term to be better just to force a page reload and calculate the new terms on the server each time. Either way, the design we want for the page as a whole looks like the following:

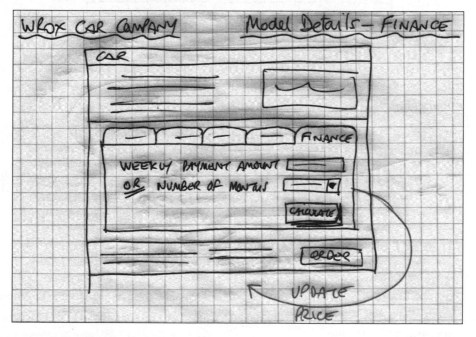

The Ingredients for the Finance Options Section

As far as controls go, our only requirements are:

- A `TextBox` to enter the monthly payment amount.

- One or more `Validation` controls to check that a valid value has been entered.

- ❏ A DropDownList to select the number of months for the finance package to run.

- ❏ A Button control (probably a Submit button) to calculate the new terms.

The Compare Features Page

We want to make sure that our customers purchase a vehicle that is right for them, and which meets all their needs. The best way to do this is to allow them to compare various features of our range of vehicles directly, within the same page. It also gives us a chance to explore how ASP.NET can create various charts and other graphical output directly using the Drawing classes that are included in the Framework class library.

The Compare Features page will consist of a list of models, a list of comparison types, and an area where a chart or other graphic that reflects the chosen model comparisons is displayed. We'll allow the user to compare as many models from the range as they wish:

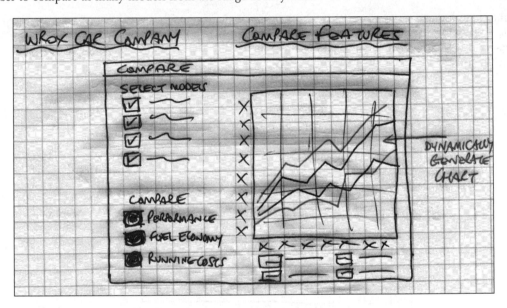

The Ingredients for the Compare Features Page

To implement this page, we're going to need:

- ❏ A CheckBoxList control where the user selects the models to be included in the comparison.

- ❏ A RadioButtonList control (or individual RadioButton controls) to select the type of comparison they require.

- ❏ An Image control to display the results of the comparison.

- ❏ Possibly a Button control to initiate the process, or it could be done directly when a comparison type is selected.

The Order Pages

One section of the site that we haven't paid much attention to so far is how we will actually place an order for a vehicle after our visitor has configured it and decided on the finance package that suits them best. The process of building up and placing the order is intertwined with the way that we'll store details of the vehicle as the user configures it.

The focus of this book (as we've already said several times) is on the user interface design and construction, and not on the back-end processing. However, our dynamic site requires a back-end database, and this will be used to store vehicle configurations and order data, as well as supplying data for the user interface. In later chapters, as we build the pages for our site, we'll see how we connect to and work with this database.

The actual design and appearance of the order pages themselves is going to follow a fairly predictable path, as they will just contain a series of textboxes, drop-down lists and buttons that collect the remaining data we need to place an order.

Along the way, we'll be providing the visitor with a username and password that identifies them, and so we'll also implement a 'login' dialog so that they can come back and buy more cars without having to fill in all the information again. This will be achieved using ASP.NET Forms-based security techniques, and we'll examine this, together with the various pages and code we use to create the login dialog and place the order, later in the book.

Other "Peripheral" Pages

The other pages we'll be implementing on our site are fairly simple, and probably not interactive. They include the Terms and Conditions, an 'about' and 'contact' page, and possible pages to display other news, events, reviews or features concerning the site or the products. At the moment, all of these are 'peripheral' pages, in that they will not form part of the foundation structure of the site. They are simply opened from links on other appropriate pages. So, as far as design goes, we can put off any final decisions until we get the main parts of the site working.

What we do know is that most will probably carry the same footer as we'll be using in the main site pages, and perhaps a header graphic that will also appear in most of the pages on the site. We'll be adding these pages to our example application, but we won't be spending any time discussing them in detail, as they are unlikely to add anything extra to our exploration of user interface design and implementation.

Is It All Actually Achievable?

One thing you can see as we go along is that we are still relatively relaxed about the exact techniques we'll use to build the pages. Rather than tying everything down too precisely yet, this kind of exploration of possibilities is useful in finding issues that might arise later on, while allowing the design to evolve (and hopefully improve) as it becomes clearer in your mind.

The one risk is that something you plan to do will prove to be impossible when you actually start writing code, and there is nothing to protect you from this except experience and a thorough knowledge of ASP.NET and the server controls it provides. Usually, nothing is actually **impossible**, though it may turn out to be difficult to achieve, or hit performance so badly that it has to be abandoned.

The point here is that we haven't spent a huge amount of effort on the actual design process for the individual pages yet, and so backtracking and adapting the design is an acceptable option. We still have the original design for the overall site layout and structure in place to fall back on, and from where we can explore other possible approaches to implementation.

All in all, however, we're fairly well satisfied with the design we now have, and we're ready to crank up a computer and start building some pages. The recipe is open at the appropriate page, the oven is hot, and it's time to get cooking.

Summary

In this first chapter, we started out by considering why ASP.NET provides a great environment for building interactive user interfaces for web applications and web sites (or wapplisites). At the heart of this is the event-driven programming model that the combination of server-side controls and the postback architecture provides. It makes it easier than ever before to build applications that look, feel and work more like the traditional executable applications that we were building before the Web was invented.

We also spent quite some time looking at the whole topic of the ASP.NET page-processing model, and the use of server controls. This was followed by a brief review of some of the other features that ASP.NET provides to make it easier to build high-performance applications.

Following this, we moved on to look at some of the basic principles involved in designing a web site that will take advantage of the features of ASP.NET. The first steps involved analyzing requirements for the site, and then planning the overall structure. All this is done without too much concern over the appearance of the site or the technical implementation, as it's more important to get the foundations right first.

Then we followed up by trying to plan the pages themselves, or at least the ones that form the core of the site. This is an iterative process, as you'll see, because it's difficult at this stage to combine the need for an attractive appearance and intuitive layout with the technical details of how the pages will actually be implemented. However, until you have a feel for the appearance and layout of the pages, it's even harder to try and envisage how they might be implemented – a kind of vicious circle that you often only escape from through trial and error.

We ended the chapter with some sketches and lists of ingredients for the main pages we'll be building, but these are still somewhat vague specifications. What's important is that we have somewhere to start the construction process, and a relatively well-defined path to follow. Through the remaining chapters of this book, you'll be able to see whether the original design was anywhere near to meeting the original requirements, or whether we end up redesigning some of the pages to suit the needs of the users, requirements imposed on us by the data store, or the limitations of ASP.NET itself.

In summary, this chapter covered:

❑ Why ASP.NET provides a great environment for building interactive pages and sites

❑ The fundamental ways that ASP.NET makes building dynamic pages easier

❑ The built-in features of ASP.NET that we can use in our pages and applications

❑ The impact and reasoning behind using client-side and server-side processing

❑ How we approach designing a site in order to get the most from ASP.NET

Before we do get started building pages, however, we'll use the next chapter to get a better understanding about how the output generated by the ASP.NET Web Forms server controls can vary depending on the client that hits our site.

2

Browser Compatibility with ASP.NET Server Controls

As you get used to using ASP.NET, it becomes very easy to throw together attractive and usable web sites and applications by just dropping a few server controls, such as the DataGrid, Hyperlink, or Label, onto your pages. To get the appearance you want, you only have to set a few common properties, and leave the rest to the wonders of the ASP.NET runtime framework. After all, Microsoft has sorted out the issues of generating the appropriate HTML output from their server controls, so you don't need to worry about it.

In fact, this isn't always the case, and you **should** worry about the output that you are sending to the clients that access your pages. OK, so it's only in a few circumstances that it does affect the visible appearance or the workings of the page, but it's extremely useful to be aware of just what's going on behind the scenes when you use these controls.

The topics we'll be covering in this chapter are:

❑   A simple test application for examining the output generated by server controls

❑   How Microsoft defines which are 'up-level' and which are 'down-level' clients

❑   How the style attribute and <font> elements are used in up-level and down-level clients

❑   Working with more complex controls like the DataList and DataGrid

❑   How the controls are affected by the lack of client-side scripting capabilities

❑   How the Panel control completely changes its output for the two types of client

❑   How output caching can affect browser compatibility

We start with a look at what we actually mean when we say that the ASP.NET Web Forms' server controls are 'intelligent'.

Built-In Intelligence

When I originally wrote about the ASP.NET Web Forms server controls for the Wrox book *Professional ASP.NET* (now updated as ISBN 1-861007-03-5), I repeated the information provided by Microsoft (during the Beta cycle) that these controls are intelligent. They change their output depending on the client type that is accessing the page – allegedly to provide a better user experience in modern browsers. However, it turned out that the only really visible evidence of this in the release version was in the validation controls, which provide client-side interactivity via Dynamic HTML in Internet Explorer 5 and above.

In fact, I was forced to apologize publicly in the errata for the first edition of the book when it turned out that the Calendar control did not use client-side script to rebuild the display each time on the client and avoid the extra post-backs required when you select a date or change the month. I still have the rash brought on by the sackcloth, but that's another story...

So, while there is little obvious evidence of the server controls being intelligent, there is stuff going on inside them that does affect the output they generate, depending on the type of client that hits the page. In the main (with a couple of interesting exceptions that we'll come to later), the differences are confined to the controls from the namespace System.Web.UI.WebControls (the controls prefixed "asp:"), and to the way that the visible appearance of the control is generated through the browser's rendering process.

As an example, the following screenshot shows a DataList control that sets the size for the text in the header, item, and alternating item rows to different sizes. You can see that in Navigator on the left, the sizes are not set correctly when the control is rendered in the page:

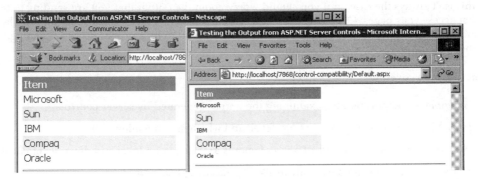

The code we used to create the control (omitting the section that generates the actual values) is shown next. You can see that we set the fonts for each row to specific pixel sizes. If we only test the page in Internet Explorer, we'll never know that it doesn't provide the effect we want in some other browsers:

```
<asp:datagrid id="dgrTest" runat="server"
              forecolor="#000000"
              backcolor="#ffffff"
              cellpadding="3"
              gridlines="none"
              width="50%"
              font-name="tahoma,arial,sans-serif"
```

```
                     font-size="14px">
   <headerstyle forecolor="#ffffff"
                     backcolor="#808080"
                     font-name="tahoma,arial,sans-serif"
                     font-size="12px"
                     font-bold="true"
                     wrap="false" />
   <itemstyle    font-name="tahoma,arial,sans-serif"
                     font-size="10px" />
   <alternatingitemstyle font-name="tahoma,arial,sans-serif"
                     font-size="16px"
                     backcolor="#ffff00" />
</asp:datagrid>
```

A Test Application

We'll come back to look at this example later on, and see why the appearance is different and how we can cure this. In the meantime, to demonstrate the controls and techniques we'll be using in this chapter, we built a simple test application that allows us to see the output created for different browsers, including those that we don't actually have installed. The code for this application is available to download from http://www.wrox.com/ along with all the samples for this book. You can run it on your own server, and modify it to experiment with other controls. Alternatively, you can just run it online directly from our server at http://www.daveandal.com/books/7868/.

The page you see shows a list of the test pages we've provided, options to select the browser type you want to pretend to be, and a button to fetch the page:

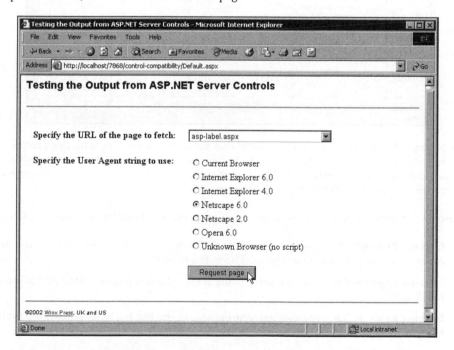

After you request the page, the content is shown below these controls in the same page. It includes the user agent string that was sent to the test page, the content of the page rendered (as it would be if opened directly), the source (HTML and text) that was created by the page and returned to the browser, and the actual source code of the original test page file on disk:

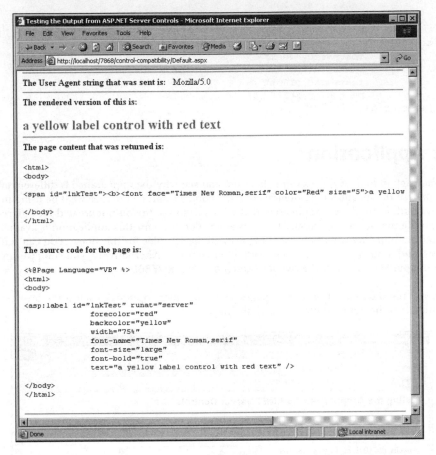

The list of pages that are available includes ones that demonstrate working with the `TextBox`, `Hyperlink`, `Calendar`, `Label`, `DataList`, `DataGrid`, `LinkButton`, `RequiredFieldValidator`, and `Panel` controls. In later sections, we'll use all these to see how the output they generate affects the appearance of the page in different types of browser.

The browsers that you can 'pretend to be' in our application when sending the request to the test page are:

❑ **Current Browser** – the user-agent string of the browser you're using to run the test application is passed to the test page you request. This is the default.

❑ **Internet Explorer 6.0** – the user agent string sent to the test page is: "Mozilla/4.0 (compatible; MSIE 6.0)"

❑ **Internet Explorer 4.0** – the user agent string sent to the test page is: "Mozilla/4.0 (compatible; MSIE 4.0)"

❑ **Netscape 6.0** – the user agent string sent to the test page is: "Mozilla/5.0" (note that it's not 6.0 as you might expect).

❑ **Netscape 2.0** – the user agent string sent to the test page is: "Mozilla/2.0"

❑ **Opera 6.0** – the user agent string sent to the test page is: "Opera/6.0"

❑ **Unknown Browser (no script)** – the user agent for this option is just this: "Unknown Browser (no script)". It allows you to test your pages with what ASP.NET specifies as the default for browsers or other clients that it does not recognize, such as web crawlers and spiders.

One interesting feature in Opera 6.0 is that you can tell it to pretend to be another browser. In the File / Quick Preferences menu, you can tell Opera to send a specific user-agent string to the server, and pretend to be Mozilla 3.0, 4.78 or 5.0, or Internet Explorer 5.0. In theory, Opera can support all the features of these browsers, and so you can see the different pages that are generated depending on the browser type.

Use a Selection of Browsers

One point to be aware of right from the start is that the control appearance you see is generated **by the actual browser you are using to run the test page**. In other words, if you open the application in Internet Explorer and view a page pretending to be Navigator, you'll see IE's version of rendering the output. Navigator may render the same output differently.

So, while you do get the convenience of seeing what the server controls generate as output, you still need to make sure that this actually does produce what you want in that particular browser. Of course, Microsoft has done a good job of tailoring the output for each client to give the closest result possible, but it's always worth a final check. We use Internet Explorer 6.0, Navigator 4.5, Opera 6.0 and Amaya 6.0 (the W3C reference browser) on the same machine with no problems. You can get the various browsers from the following sites on the Web:

❑ **Internet Explorer**: http://www.microsoft.com/windows/ie/default.asp

❑ **Netscape Navigator**: http://home.netscape.com/computing/download/index.html

❑ **Mozilla**: http://mozilla.org/

❑ **Opera**: http://www.opera.com/

❑ **Amaya**: http://www.w3.org/Amaya/

> **An extremely useful site that lists the available browsers is http://www.browserlist.browser.org/.**

Viewing the Test Pages

Starting with a simple example, the test page `asp-textbox.aspx` contains a formatted textbox. The `TextBox` control must be placed on a server-side `<form>`, and the code we use is simply:

```
<form runat="server">
<asp:textbox id="txtTest" runat="server"
```

```
        font-name="Arial,sans-serif"
        font-size="16px"
        font-bold="true"
        forecolor="red"
        backcolor="yellow"
        columns="30"
        width="75%"
        text="a yellow text box with red text" />
</form>
```

In Internet Explorer, using the **Current Browser** setting, this creates an `<input type="text">`
element that includes the `style` attribute to get the formatting we specified in our code:

```
<input name="txtTest" type="text" value="a yellow text box with red text"
      size="30" id="txtTest" style="color:Red;background-color:Yellow;
                                    font-family:Arial,sans-serif;
                                    font-size:16px;font-weight:bold;width:75%;"
/>
```

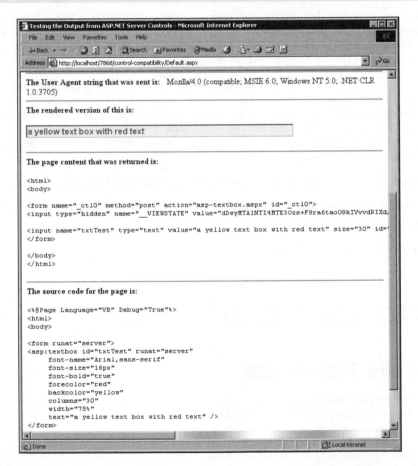

However, when we run the same page in Navigator or Opera (or specify a user-agent string other than Internet Explorer 4.0 or 6.0), we get different output from the control:

```
<input name="txtTest" type="text" value="a yellow text box with red text"
       size="30" id="txtTest" />
```

There is no `style` attribute, so the page contains a simple version of the `<input>` element that just specifies the `name`, `type`, `value`, `size`, and `id` attributes. The font used is the default, and the textbox is not 75% of the page width – and there's nothing we can do to change this behavior:

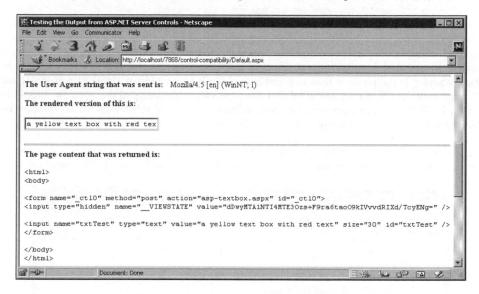

The Hyperlink Server Control

The next test page demonstrates a hyperlink `<a>` element, created by an ASP.NET `Hyperlink` server control. The code in our test page `asp-hyperlink.aspx` contains the following definition of a `Hyperlink` server control:

```
<asp:hyperlink id="lnkTest" runat="server"
               navigateurl="not-there.htm"
               forecolor="red"
               backcolor="yellow"
               font-name="Times New Roman,serif"
               font-size="large"
               font-bold="true"
               width="75%"
               text="a yellow hyperlink with red text" />
```

In Internet Explorer 5.0 and 6.0, as with the `TextBox` control, we get a `style` element that specifies the appearance and the width of the link:

```
<a id="lnkTest" href="/output-test/test-pages/not-there.htm"
   style="color:Red;background-color:Yellow;
          font-family:Times New Roman,serif;font-size:Large;
          font-weight:bold;width:75%;">a yellow hyperlink with red text</a>
```

However, in Navigator, Opera, and other browsers, the control generates a `<b>` and a `<font>` element within the hyperlink instead:

```
<a id="lnkTest" href="/output-test/test-pages/not-there.htm">
   <b><font face="Times New Roman,serif" color="Red" size="5">
   a yellow hyperlink with red text</font></b></a>
```

This makes sense, as the `<b>` and `<font>` elements have been around for a long time and are widely supported. Notice also that the `size` attribute of the `<font>` element is set, but this can only be a number (where 1 is the smallest font size and larger numbers give larger sizes). If you look back at the ASPX page code, you'll see we specified that the `font-size` property of our element should be `"large"`. In IE this was interpreted as a `font-size:Large` style selector, whereas in other browsers this becomes a `size="5"` attribute of the `<font>` element.

The rendered output generated by the `Hyperlink` control in these two cases is shown in the next screenshot – where you can see that only IE displays the proper width and background color:

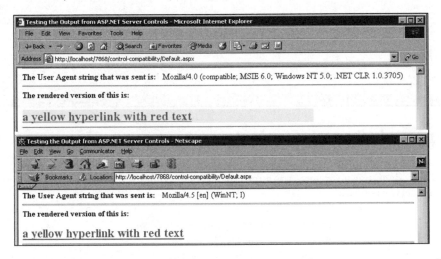

Note that, if we specify the `font-size` property as a specific pixel or point measurement (for example `"16px"` or `"12pt"`), it does not appear at all in the `<font>` element for non-IE browsers. In this case, the text of the hyperlink appears in the default font size for the page. The value for the `font-size` attribute has to be one of `"xx-small"`, `"x-small"`, `"small"`, `"smaller"`, `"medium"`, `"large"`, `"larger"`, `"x-large"` or `"xx-large"`.

> *You might be wondering about specifying one of these values for the `font-size` property in the `TextBox` example we looked at earlier, rather than the value `"16px"` we used in that test page. Don't bother – it makes no difference. In HTML, you can't place a `<font>` element inside an `<input type="text">` element, so the server control just ignores it.*

Viewing the same page in Opera 6.0 (again with the **Current Browser** setting for the User Agent string) provides almost identical output to Navigator. But remember that Opera always uses the default link color for the underline, though you can turn off the display of the underline in this particular browser if you wish:

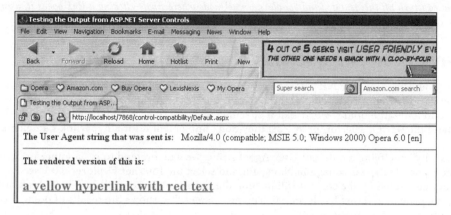

And what about Amaya? If you haven't tried this browser, you'll probably be surprised at the way it renders things that are familiar to Windows developers in a totally different way. The next screenshot shows the same `Hyperlink` test page in Amaya 6.0 for Windows NT/2000/XP, for which the same output as created for Navigator and Opera is generated. Notice that Amaya indents hyperlinks from the left margin automatically:

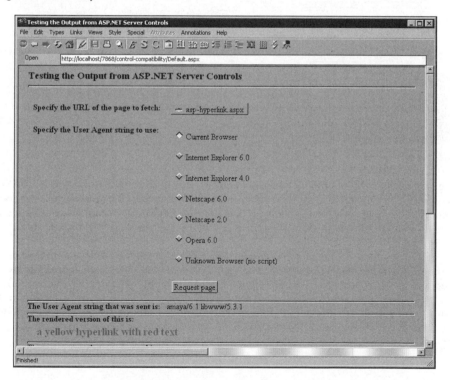

You might be interested to test all your pages against Amaya, as it is a good way to detect errors that other browsers have a neat habit of ignoring. Amaya also follows the original principles of the World Wide Web when it first came into being by allowing you to edit the page that is displayed. You can turn off this feature, and enable 'normal' mode where single-clicking a link opens it, using the commands in the Edit and Special menus.

But Navigator Understands the Style Attribute!

Of course, just because ASP.NET doesn't send a `style` attribute to other browsers doesn't mean that they don't know what it is. In fact, all three of our 'non-IE' browsers will happily display a yellow background and large bold red text that is specified in a `style` attribute. However, none of them understand the `width` selector, or at least they don't implement it for a hyperlink `<a>` element.

Of course, by specifying a different User Agent string, we can 'pretend to be' another browser. If we open the `hyperlink.aspx` page in Navigator and select the Internet Explorer 6.0 User Agent string, the output generated by the control will include the `style` attribute. ASP.NET will think that it's serving the page to Internet Explorer 6.0. The next screenshot shows the results of doing this in the other three of our test browsers:

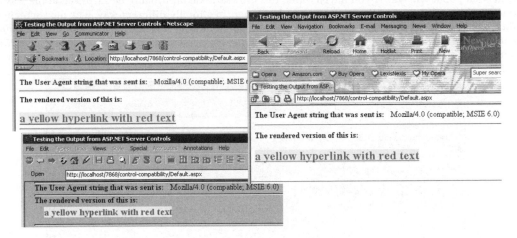

So, is the server control misbehaving? It really comes down to the fact that the ASP.NET Web Forms server controls only support two 'modes' for formatting (and, in fact, for other output generation). The client accessing the page is classed as being either Internet Explorer 4.0 and above (called an **Up-level** client), or it's 'one of the rest' (a **Down-level** client). We'll see more about all this later in this chapter.

The alternative would be to detect and generate specific output for lots of different types of browser, and for the different versions of each one. The problem is that they vary quite considerably in their published and actual support for different elements and attributes, even between versions of the same browser, making it very hard to satisfy them all. Of course, there's nothing to stop you from building your own server controls that inherit from the ones provided, and adding specific browser support yourself.

The Calendar Control

Before moving on to look at the next main option for controlling formatting, we'll take a quick look at the `Calendar` control. While the automatic use of client-side interactivity that was originally mooted for inclusion in the control never materialized, it does perform in two different modes for 'up-level' (Internet Explorer 4.0 and above) and 'down-level' (all other) clients. We used the following code to create a calendar using the ASP.NET `Calendar` control:

```
<asp:calendar id="calTest" runat="server"
              BackColor="#ffff80"
              BorderColor="#c0c0c0"
              BorderStyle="ridge"
              BorderWidth="5" />
```

The screenshots below show the result in the four browsers we're using. You can see that only Internet Explorer displays the "ridge" border. The others quite happily display the main part of the calendar, except for Amaya – which has problems with the background color:

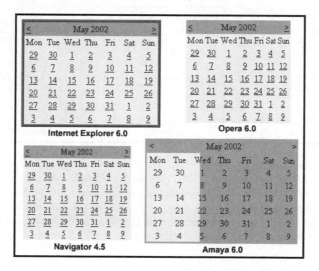

The actual output generated by the `Calendar` control for 'up-level' browsers contains a raft of style selectors within the `style` attribute of the HTML `<table>` and each table row and cell. You can see the `border-style:Ridge` selector that creates the raised border for the calendar:

```
<table id="calTest" cellspacing="0" cellpadding="2" bordercolor="Silver"
       border="0" style="background-color:#FFFF80;border-color:Silver;
                    border-width:5px;border-style:Ridge;
                    border-collapse:collapse;">
  <tr>
    <td colspan="7" style="background-color:Silver;">
    ...
    <td align="Center" style="width:14%;">
      <a href="javascript:__doPostBack('calTest','857')"
         style="color:Black">7</a></td>
```

Unlike the controls we've looked at so far, the `Calendar` control does not try to achieve a similar appearance for 'down-level' clients by using `<font>` elements. Instead, it still generates a series of style selectors for the `style` attribute, but with a reduced set for the main `<table>` element. The `border-style` selector is omitted, so the browser does not attempt to display the raised border in this case:

```
<table id="calTest" cellspacing="0" cellpadding="2" bordercolor="Silver"
        border="0" bgcolor="#FFFF80">
...
  <td align="Center" width="14%">
    <a href="javascript:__doPostBack('calTest','857')"
        style="color:Black">7</a></td>
```

What happens if we pretend to be Internet Explorer in the other three browsers? Navigator 4.5 fails to do any better, although later versions (Navigator 6.0 and Mozilla 1.0) do work fine. Opera gets very close, with just a problem in one place with the "ridge" border. However, Amaya doesn't handle the style attributes too well at all:

To check if it's the output from the control that is the problem in Amaya (which is very strict in its interpretation of HTML), we saved the HTML generated by the page as an `.htm` *file and loaded it into* **Mozquito** *– an XHTML validation tool that is available from http://www.mozquito.org/. It wasn't too happy with the attributes in the* `<form>` *for some reason, but otherwise reported that the structure of the document was correct according to the XHTML 1.0 strict recommendations from W3C. So we can't blame the server control in this case.*

Specifying Up-level or Down-Level Clients

We've spent enough time looking at the basic issues of `style` attributes and `<font>` elements for simple controls. However, before we go on to look at more complicated controls, we need to quickly investigate the situation with regard to specifying if a client is an 'up-level' or 'down-level' one.

The ASP.NET `Page` directive accepts an attribute named `ClientTarget`, which specifies if the Web Forms server controls on the page should perform the browser detection we've been seeing earlier on in this chapter. The default, if omitted, is 'Up-level', but it can be set to 'Down-level' to prevent the controls from creating different output that is specially tailored to 'up-level' clients:

```
<%@Page ClientTarget="Down-level" Language="..." %>
```

In fact, the values that you can use for this property of the Page *depend on the contents of the* web.config *file. The values* "Up-level" *and* "Down-level" *are the defaults, but you can add your own. For full details, look up "<clientTarget> element" in the .NET SDK Help file.*

You can investigate the effect of this using the two test pages in our sample application named asp-label.aspx and asp-label-down-level.aspx. They both define a Label control using the code:

```
<asp:label id="lblTest" runat="server"
           forecolor="red"
           backcolor="yellow"
           width="75%"
           font-name="Times New Roman,serif"
           font-size="large"
           font-bold="true"
           text="a yellow label control with red text" />
```

Without the ClientTarget attribute in the @Page directive (or if it is set to "Up-level"), the output is a <span> element 75% of the window width, with a yellow background and large bold red text:

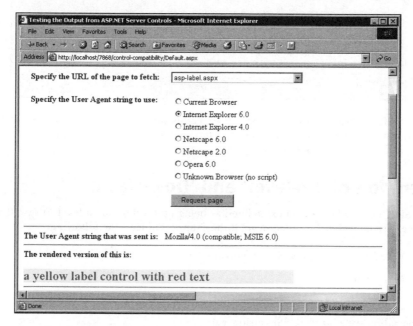

This is the output created by the page asp-label.aspx in Internet Explorer 6.0. It contains the style attribute that is usually delivered to 'up-level' clients. However, the page asp-label-down-level.aspx has the ClientTarget="Down-level" attribute added to the Page directive. In this case, the page always creates the 'down-level' output shown next:

```
<span id="lnkTest"><b><font face="Times New Roman,serif" color="Red" size="5">
a yellow label control with red text
</font></b></span>
```

There is no `style` attribute, and we're back to the `<b>` and `<font>` elements to create the appearance. So now the page looks the same in Internet Explorer 6.0 as it would in 'down-level' browsers:

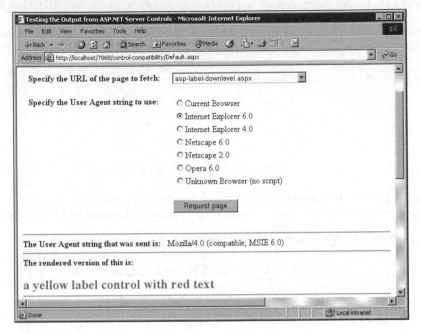

Thankfully, there are ways that we can get a more compatible appearance across lots of different client browsers, by using CSS styles directly instead of having the server control create them for us. We'll look at this topic in more detail in the next chapter.

The Definition of 'Up-level' and 'Down-level'

The .NET SDK defines how a client is defined as being up-level or down-level. It says that browsers and client devices are considered to be up-level if they support at least the following:

- ❑ ECMAScript (JScript, JavaScript) version 1.2
- ❑ HTML version 4.0
- ❑ The Microsoft Document Object Model (MSDOM)
- ❑ Cascading style sheets (CSS) version 1.0

Down-level browsers and client devices only need to support HTML version 3.2. More details can be found in the SDK at:

ms-help://MS.NETFrameworkSDK/cpguidenf/html/cptskDetectingBrowserTypesInWebForms.htm

We also discuss ways that you use code to detect if a specific client is up-level or down-level in the later section of this chapter that looks at *Output Caching*.

List Control Formatting and Templates

The Web Forms server controls include several that are predominantly used to create 'lists' or 'tables' of information. These include the `DataGrid`, `DataList`, and `Repeater` controls. They can be used with **templates** that specify the output to be generated by the control. In most cases an object such as a `DataSet`, `DataReader`, `Array`, `Hashtable`, or `Collection` provides the data through server-side data binding. Templates are predominantly used to specify which 'fields' or 'columns' in the data are to be shown. However, they can also be used to control the formatting and appearance of the data.

The `DataGrid` and `DataList` (by default) create output that is an HTML `<table>`, and the format of each row and cell can be specified separately using the syntax we already met for the simpler controls. For example, our test page named `asp-datalist.aspx` contains this definition of a `DataList` control:

```
<asp:datalist   id="dlTest" runat="server"
                forecolor="#000000"
                backcolor="#ffffff"
                cellpadding="3"
                gridlines="none"
                width="50%" >
  <itemstyle    font-name="tahoma,arial,sans-serif"
                font-size="12"
                backcolor="#ffffff" />
  <alternatingitemstyle font-name="tahoma,arial,sans-serif"
                font-size="2"
                backcolor="#ffff00" />

  <itemtemplate>
    <%# Container.DataItem %>
  </itemtemplate>

</asp:datalist>
```

The data source is a single-column array, and you can use the sample application to view the code that creates it and binds it to the control. In the code above, you can see that we've specified quite a few attributes that affect the control's output, including the appearance of the table itself and the font name and size for the item and alternating item rows.

So what does the output from this page look like in the various browsers? All can display the styles we specified without a problem (except that Amaya doesn't recognize the font name), and the table appears at the correct width of 50% of the page width. However, notice that the text in the alternating item rows in Internet Explorer is extremely small compared to the other browsers:

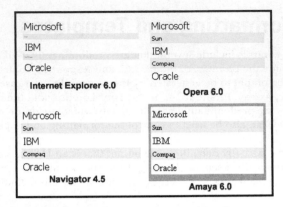

The Output from the DataList Control

Looking at the actual generated output from the control explains why this is the case. The next listing shows the output generated for Internet Explorer, and you can see that all the formatting is provided by style attributes – as we saw with the simpler controls earlier on. Notice also how the list controls convert the color we specified using hexadecimal values (for example "#ffff00") into the color names. However, the text size for the alternating item rows is set to 2pt:

```
<table id="dlTest" cellpadding="3" border="0"
        style="color:Black;background-color:White;width:50%;">
  <tr>
    <td style="background-color:White;font-family:tahoma,arial,sans-serif;
            font-size:12pt;">
      Microsoft
    </td>
  </tr><tr>
    <td style="background-color:Yellow;font-family:tahoma,arial,sans-serif;
            font-size:2pt;">
      Sun
    </td>
  </tr><tr>
    <td style="background-color:White;font-family:tahoma,arial,sans-serif;
            font-size:12pt;">
      IBM
    </td>
  </tr><tr>
    <td style="background-color:Yellow;font-family:tahoma,arial,sans-serif;
            font-size:2pt;">
      Compaq
    </td>
  </tr><tr>
    <td style="background-color:White;font-family:tahoma,arial,sans-serif;
            font-size:12pt;">
      Oracle
    </td>
  </tr>
</table>
```

The reason for this can be seen in the original code. We specified the font-size property for the item and alternating item rows as:

```
font-size="12"      'for item rows
font-size="2"       'for alternating item rows
```

These numbers were interpreted as 12pt and 2pt by the control. But when the target browser is a 'down-level' client, the situation is different. The next listing shows the output from the control when the browser is Navigator, and you can see that the font name, color and size are now specified with <font> elements instead of a style attribute on the opening <td> tag. The font sizes are also translated into the appropriate number of the size attribute for the <font> element – and as 1 is the lowest, this is used for the alternating item rows where Internet Explorer used 2pt:

```
<table id="dlTest" cellpadding="3" border="0" bgcolor="White" width="50%">
  <tr>
    <td bgcolor="White"><font face="tahoma,arial,sans-serif"
                             color="Black" size="3">
      Microsoft
    </font></td>
  </tr><tr>
    <td bgcolor="Yellow"><font face="tahoma,arial,sans-serif"
        color="Black" size="1">
      Sun
    </font></td>
  </tr><tr>
    <td bgcolor="White"><font face="tahoma,arial,sans-serif"
        color="Black" size="3">
      IBM
    </font></td>
  </tr><tr>
    <td bgcolor="Yellow"><font face="tahoma,arial,sans-serif"
        color="Black" size="1">
      Compaq
    </font></td>
  </tr><tr>
    <td bgcolor="White"><font face="tahoma,arial,sans-serif"
        color="Black" size="3">
      Oracle
    </font></td>
  </tr>
</table>
```

In fact, the control has managed the differences between the up-level and down-level clients very well. In the up-level version, the <table> element contains the style attribute:

```
style="color:Black;background-color:White;width:50%;"
```

On the other hand the down-level version uses attributes of the <table> element to achieve the same overall background color and width:

```
<table id="dlTest" cellpadding="3" border="0" bgcolor="White" width="50%">
```

The cells within each table row for the up-level client are formatted with the following `style` attribute on each `<td>` element. There is no need to specify the font color as this is done in the `style` attribute for the `<table>` element:

```
style="background-color:White;font-family:tahoma,arial,sans-serif;font-size:12pt;"
```

However, the down-level client receives a `<td>` element with a series of appropriate attributes plus a `<font>` element within the cell that also sets the font color:

```
<td bgcolor="White"><font face="tahoma,arial,sans-serif" color="Black" size="3">
```

Adding Templates to the DataList Control

One way of getting round the issue of the font size in a list control is to abandon (or override) the settings made by the `style` attribute for up-level clients with a `<font>` element within each cell, producing output that is the same as that created automatically for down-level clients. You do lose some control over the font size, in that you can then only set it to the numeric values that are supported by a `<font>` element. However, it does mean that you get the same overall appearance in all browsers.

The test page named `asp-datalist-format-item.aspx` demonstrates this, by adding specific formatting elements to the templates within the definition of the `DataList` control. Instead of an ordinary array as the data source, we also switched over to using a `Hashtable`. This allows us to store two values for each item (as the `Key` and `Value`). We also removed the `font-size` attributes from the declaration of the `<itemstyle>` and `<alternatingitemstyle>` as they will now be specified within the templates for these rows.

The next listing shows just the templates we use in our `DataList` control for this example:

```
<itemtemplate>
  <%# DataBinder.Eval(Container.DataItem, "Key", _
                      "<font size='1'>{0}</font>") %>
  <%# DataBinder.Eval(Container.DataItem, "Value", _
                      "<font size='1'>${0:f2}</font>") %>
</itemtemplate>

<alternatingitemtemplate>
  <%# DataBinder.Eval(Container.DataItem, "Key", _
                      "<font size='4'>{0}</font>") %>
  <%# DataBinder.Eval(Container.DataItem, "Value", _
                      "<font size='4'>${0:f2}</font>") %>
</alternatingitemtemplate>
```

The idea is simple enough, we want to insert a `<font>` element manually into each cell and specify the required font details. We do this by taking advantage of the `Eval` method of the `DataBinder` that is actually performing the binding of the data to the control. We specify the data item itself as `Container.DataItem`, the name of the column or field we want to bind to, and a string that defines the format of the output. Our string, `"<font size='1'>{0}</font>"`, will generate a `<font>` element with the actual value for the cell inserted where the `{0}` placeholder is within the format string.

Of course, this doesn't prevent us from carrying out other formatting of the value itself, for example in the second column we format the value as a fixed two decimal places number, and include the dollar currency symbol within the `<font>` element as well. The only downside is that using the `DataBinder.Eval` method is marginally less efficient in execution at runtime than just using `Container.DataItem` (as we did in the previous example page).

Now, when this row is generated by the control for an up-level client, the actual output is:

```
<td style="background-color:White;font-family:tahoma,arial,sans-serif;">
  <font size='1'>Microsoft</font>
  <font size='1'>$49.56</font>
</td>
```

For a down-level client, we get the usual switch from a `style` attribute to separate attributes of the `<td>` element, and the `<font>` element that wraps the entire content. However, inside this are the same set of elements and values that we get for the up-level client:

```
<td bgcolor="White">
  <font face="tahoma,arial,sans-serif" color="Black">
    <font size='1'>Oracle</font>
    <font size='1'>$41.10</font>
  </font>
</td>
```

The result is that all the browsers now provide the same appearance (with Amaya's exception of not recognizing the font name):

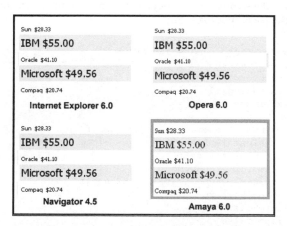

One point worth mentioning is that many experienced web page builders avoid any white-space between the `<font>` element and the enclosing `<td>` element in tables (or in fact in any container-type control such as a `<div>`, `<span>`, etc.). This is because any white-space characters here, be they spaces, tabs, carriage returns, etc., are formatted in the default page or parent container font. This can upset the layout, often in unpredictable ways. However, the ASP.NET server controls that create tables often do insert unwanted white-space (though not always). Sometimes you can prevent this by removing all the spaces and carriage returns from the content of your templates within source code of the page.

More Complexity – the DataGrid Control

Having seen one way that the `DataList` can be persuaded to generate a common appearance for the content in both up-level and down-level browsers, we'll look at a slightly more complex example. The `DataGrid` control works in a similar way to a `DataList`, but offers far more in the way of features. For example it can provide paging and sorting with only minimal extra development effort. However, the same issues arise with regard to formatting the output to suit all types of browser.

The following screenshot (repeated from the start of the chapter) shows the same page in two different browsers – Internet Explorer and Navigator (the result in Opera is the same as in Navigator). You can see that the formatting instructions we provide in the declaration of the `DataGrid` control do not provide the same output in Navigator as they do in Internet Explorer:

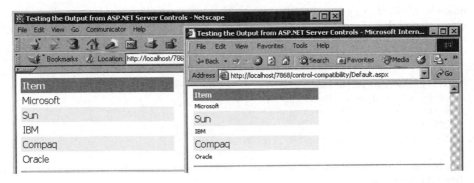

The reason for this is just the same as we encountered with the `DataList` component earlier on. Our control declaration in the page looks like this:

```
<asp:datagrid id="dgrTest" runat="server"
              forecolor="#000000"
              backcolor="#ffffff"
              cellpadding="3"
              gridlines="none"
              width="50%"
              font-name="tahoma,arial,sans-serif"
              font-size="14px">
  <headerstyle forecolor="#ffffff"
               backcolor="#808080"
               font-name="tahoma,arial,sans-serif"
               font-size="12px"
               font-bold="true"
               wrap="false" />
  <itemstyle font-name="tahoma,arial,sans-serif"
             font-size="10px" />
  <alternatingitemstyle font-name="tahoma,arial,sans-serif"
                        font-size="16px"
                        backcolor="#ffff00" />
</asp:datagrid>
```

You can see that we are formatting the content using fixed pixel values for the `font-size` attributes of the header, item and alternating item rows. The result in Internet Explorer contains the usual set of `style` attributes that set the visible appearance:

```
<table cellspacing="0" cellpadding="3" border="0" id="dgrTest"
      style="color:Black;background-color:White;
             font-family:tahoma,arial,sans-serif;font-size:14px;
             width:50%;border-collapse:collapse;">
  <tr nowrap="nowrap"
      style="color:White;background-color:Gray;
             font-family:tahoma,arial,sans-serif;font-size:12px;
             font-weight:bold;">
    <td>Item</td>
  </tr><tr style="font-family:tahoma,arial,sans-serif;font-size:10px;">
    <td>Microsoft</td>
  </tr><tr style="background-color:Yellow;
                  font-family:tahoma,arial,sans-serif;font-size:16px;">
    <td>Sun</td>
    ...
  </tr>
</table>
```

In Navigator and other down-level browsers, we get a mixture of attributes on the `<table>`, `<tr>`, and `<td>` elements, plus `<font>` elements within each cell:

```
<table cellspacing="0" cellpadding="3" border="0" id="dgrTest"
      bgcolor="White" width="50%">
  <tr nowrap="nowrap" bgcolor="Gray">
    <td><font face="tahoma,arial,sans-serif" color="White"><b>Item</b></font></td>
  </tr><tr>
    <td><font face="tahoma,arial,sans-serif" color="Black">Microsoft</font></td>
  </tr><tr bgcolor="Yellow">
    <td><font face="tahoma,arial,sans-serif" color="Black">Sun</font></td>
  ...
  </tr>
</table>
```

Specifying Column Information in a DataGrid Control

The `DataGrid` control doesn't need any information about the structure of its data source to be provided if that data source exposes the values as an array or a collection. It automatically creates a column for each 'field' within the items of the data source. In our previous example we are using a simple array of string values as the data source, and the header displays the word Item automatically.

However, we can exert more control over the output of the `DataGrid` by specifying what columns we actually want to display, and how we want them to appear. In the test page named `asp-datagrid-format-item.aspx` we add an `autogeneratecolumns="false"` attribute to the declaration of the `DataGrid` control itself, and then specify a `<columns>` element that defines the columns we want to display. In the next listing you can see these highlighted (we also removed the `font-size` attributes from the `<itemstyle>` and `<alternatingitemstyle>` elements):

```
<asp:datagrid id="dgrTest" runat="server"
              forecolor="#000000"
              backcolor="#ffffff"
              cellpadding="3"
              gridlines="none"
              width="50%"
              font-name="tahoma,arial,sans-serif"
              font-size="14px"
              autogeneratecolumns="false" >
  <headerstyle forecolor="#ffffff"
               backcolor="#808080"
               font-name="tahoma,arial,sans-serif"
               font-size="12px"
               font-bold="true"
               wrap="false" />
  <itemstyle font-name="tahoma,arial,sans-serif" />
  <alternatingitemstyle font-name="tahoma,arial,sans-serif"
                        backcolor="#ffff00" />
  <columns>
    <asp:boundcolumn headertext="Key" datafield="Key"
                     dataformatstring="<font size='4'>{0}</font>" />
    <asp:boundcolumn headertext="Value" datafield="Value"
                     dataformatstring="<font size='1'>${0:f2}</font>" />
  <columns>
</asp:datagrid>
```

In this example, we're using a Hashtable as the data source, which contains two values for each item – the key is a company name and the value is a number. Each <asp:boundcolumn> element specifies the column name to use in the header row (the headertext) and the 'field' from the data source item to display in that column (the datafield). To get the formatting we want, we use the dataformatstring attribute to enclose the value for that cell in a <font> element with a specified size.

Now the result in each row of the table is the same for each browser, with just the header text being different (and, of course, Amaya's inability to recognize the font name):

66

To get the same size for the header text, we could replace the `font-size="12px"` attribute in the `<headerstyle>` element with a value that works better across both up-level and down-level browsers. For example, using `font-size="10"` causes the `DataGrid` to create a `style` attribute in up-level browsers that contains `font-size:10pt`, while down-level browsers receive a `<font>` element that includes the attribute `size="2"`. If the user has the text size setting of their browser set to Medium (usually this is an option in the View menu), they will appear in the same size.

Formatting Within a TemplateColumn in a DataGrid Control

Often when working with the `DataGrid` control, the limitations of the `<asp:boundcolumn>` element prevent you from achieving exactly what you want. The usual solution in this case is to use an `<asp:templatecolumn>` element for one or more of the columns, and within this provide templates in exactly the same way as we do for a `DataList` (or `Repeater`) control.

The next listing, taken from the test page `asp-datagrid-template-format-item.aspx` shows this approach. Each column declaration is now an `<asp:templatecolumn>`, containing a `<headertemplate>` and an `<itemtemplate>` (we could provide an `<alternatingitemtemplate>` and `<footertemplate>` template as well if required). Inside each template we place the controls that will create the visible output – in this case `<font>` elements with the appropriate `size` attribute that enclose each call to the `DataBinder.Eval` method that generates the value for the cells:

```
<columns>

  <asp:templatecolumn>
    <headertemplate>
      <font size="2">Key</font>
    </headertemplate>
    <itemtemplate>
      <font size="4">
        <%# DataBinder.Eval(Container.DataItem, "Key") %>
      </font>
    </itemtemplate>
  </asp:templatecolumn>

  <asp:templatecolumn>
    <headertemplate>
      <font size="2">Value</font>
    </headertemplate>
    <itemtemplate>
      <font size="1">
        $<%# DataBinder.Eval(Container.DataItem, "Value", "{0:f2}") %>
      </font>
    </itemtemplate>
  </asp:templatecolumn>

</columns>
```

The result from this example page (`asp-datagrid-template-format-item.aspx`) is the same as that we saw in the previous example – though now with the same size font in the header rows due to our explicit definition in the `<headertemplate>` shown in the listing. You can view the complete source code and the actual HTML and other content that is created by viewing this test page in the application we provide as a sample.

What If There's No Client-Side Script Support?

As you'll no doubt be aware, several of the ASP.NET Web Forms server controls generate output that contains, and depends on, client-side JavaScript. As an example, the `LinkButton` control generates an `<a>` element that uses client-side JavaScript to submit the form containing it. The example page `asp-linkbutton.aspx` declares a `LinkButton` control, which must be placed on a server-side `<form>`. The code in our test page is shown next:

```
<form runat="server">
  <asp:linkButton id="lnkTest" runat="server"
                  forecolor="red"
                  backcolor="yellow"
                  width="50%"
                  font-name="Times New Roman,serif"
                  font-size="larger"
                  font-bold="true"
                  text="a yellow link button with red text" />
</form>
```

In Internet Explorer, as expected, we get a `style` attribute that defines the formatting of the `<a>` element The `href` attribute, shown below, calls a JavaScript function named `__dopostback` that ASP also inserts into the page:

```
href="javascript:__dopostback('lnkTest','')"
```

You can see the JavaScript function in the following screenshot:

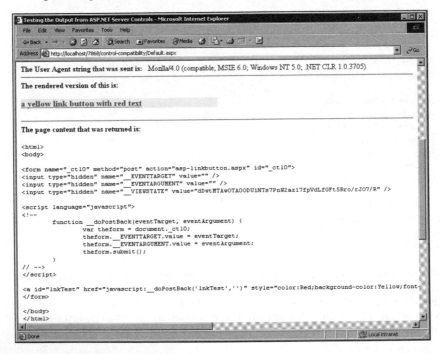

In down-level browsers, the only difference is that the formatting of the <a> element is set using <b> and <font> elements, as we discovered is the case with the controls we examined earlier. The href is the same as the output for up-level clients, as is the JavaScript code:

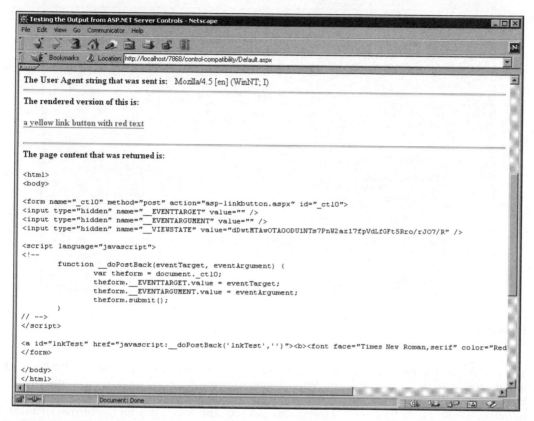

But what happens in clients that don't support JavaScript? OK, so most browsers do support JavaScript, but it's also possible that the user may have disabled script execution in their browser. In this case, clicking the link will have no effect. You might expect the control to recognize one or both of these situations, but it doesn't.

Example: a LinkButton in Amaya

For example, if you open the test page in a browser that doesn't support script, you'll see that the same output is generated and so the link does not function. The next screenshot shows what happens in Amaya (which does not support client-side scripting) – you can see the error message in the status bar at the bottom of the window:

Likewise, if you disable Active Scripting in the Tools | Internet Options | Security | Advanced dialog in Internet Explorer, the page generates the same client-side JavaScript code as before, but the link no longer works.

You can use the test page named `asp-linkbutton-uatype.aspx` to determine if ASP.NET thinks that the browser you are using does or does not support client-side scripting. The only difference between this page and the one we've just been using is that it queries two properties of the `Request.Browser` object to see if it thinks that `javascript` is available for the current client, and to get the 'alias' or short type description for the client.

```
JavaScript supported: <% = Request.Browser("javascript") %><br />
Reported type: <% = Request.Browser("type") %>
```

The results for Internet Explorer and Amaya are shown in the next compound screenshot:

ASP.NET populates the properties of the `Request.Browser` *object by matching a set of patterns in the* `<browserCaps>` *section of the* `machine.config` *and any applicable* `web.config` *files with the User Agent string sent by the browser. The* `machine.config` *file is in the folder:*

`C:\WINNT\Microsoft.NET\Framework\[version]\CONFIG\`

Updates to this section of the file can be obtained from cyScape, Inc. at http://www.cyscape.com/browsercaps/.

Solving the 'No Script' Problem

The problem of lack of client-side scripting support affects not only the `LinkButton`, but other controls as well. If you look back at the output generated by the `Calendar` control, you'll see that it uses the same technique as the `LinkButton` to cause a postback to the server when a date is selected. On top of that, several other controls (the `CheckBox`, `RadioButton`, `TextBox`, and some list controls) support a property called `AutoPostback`. This adds the same kind of JavaScript function and element attributes to the page as we've seen for the `LinkButton` control. None of these will work without client-side script support.

So, should Microsoft have made the controls more intelligent? It would certainly have made them more complex, and might also have prevented them from working properly in some browsers if the `<browserCaps>` file is not up to date. For example, newly released or beta versions of browsers may not be properly detected, and in this case functionality would be lost even when the client in question probably supports it.

So, you have a choice – you can avoid using the `LinkButton` and `Calendar`, and the `AutoPostback` feature of some of the other Web Forms controls – but this reduces the functionality of your application in all clients, when only a minority may not have client-side scripting available. Alternatively, you could just use it and hope for the best, perhaps including a message for clients that don't support scripting by using a `<noscript>` element:

```
<noscript>
  NOTE: this page requires a browser that supports JavaScript
</noscript>
```

When Scripting Is Supported but Disabled

But even this is no help if the client **supports** JavaScript but has it **disabled** in their browser options. In this case, you might resort to using a common trick with a redirection that detects if scripting is actually available **and enabled**:

```
<html>
<head>
<meta http-equiv="refresh" content="1;url=no-client-script.aspx %>" />
<title>Checking for Active Scripting Support</title>

<script language="JavaScript">
<!--
function jumpScripting() {
// jump to page using client-side JavaScript - if jump not executed
// then client does not have scripting available or it is disabled
```

```
window.location.href='client-script-ok.aspx';
}
//-->
</script>

</head>
<body onload="jumpScripting()">
Checking support for Active Scripting...
</body>

<noscript>
  Your browser does not support client-side script.
  <a href="no-client-script.aspx">Click here to continue</a>
</noscript>

</html>
```

The JavaScript code in this page will automatically load the page named `client-script-ok.aspx` if scripting is supported and enabled. If the code is not executed, the `<meta>` element will instead load the page `no-client-script.aspx` after one second. And if the browser does not support script at all, the `<a>` element will display a normal hyperlink to load the page `no-client-script.aspx`. You'll see this technique used in our example site in the next chapter.

The ASP.NET Validation Controls

Having discussed the shortcomings of client-side JavaScript detection in the previous sections, we need to mention the situation with regard to the ASP.NET **validation** controls. In fact, these are more intelligent than the other controls we've been discussing – though still not as intelligent as they could be.

If you've used the validation controls before, you'll know that – like most Web Forms controls – they generate different output for up-level and down-level clients. For up-level clients (basically Internet Explorer 4.0 and above), they take advantage of the ability to change the content of a page dynamically while it is displayed, using Dynamic HTML.

As you move the input focus from one visible UI control in the page (such as a text box) to another (by clicking or tabbing), any validation control attached to that visible control is activated. If the validation fails, the text content of the validation control is displayed in the page. You can see this if you open the test page named `asp-validator.aspx` in Internet Explorer 4.0 or above. The page contains a text box to which is attached a `RequiredFieldValidator` control:

If there is an invalid value in any control on the page (that has a validator attached), the form cannot be submitted. Instead, the `ValidationSummary` control we placed in the page displays a summary of the errors:

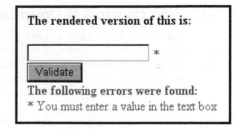

The rendered version of this is:

The relevant parts of the source code for this page are shown in the next listing. You can see the declaration of the `TextBox`, `RequiredFieldValidator`, `Button`, and the `ValidationSummary` controls:

```
<form runat="server">

<asp:textbox id="txtTest" text="delete this" runat="server" />

<asp:RequiredFieldValidator
        id="valRequired" runat="server"
        ErrorMessage="* You must enter a value in the text box"
        ControlToValidate="txtTest"
        Display="dynamic">
*
</asp:RequiredFieldValidator>

<br />

<asp:button text="Validate" runat="server" />

<asp:ValidationSummary
        id="valSummary" runat="server"
        HeaderText="<b>The following errors were found:</b>"
        ShowSummary="true"
        DisplayMode="List" />

</form>
```

Viewing the output that is generated from this page for an up-level client, it's possible to get an idea of how it works. We haven't listed it all here, but in essence there is a client-side `<script>` element that loads a JavaScript code file from the server's `aspnet_client` folder. There are also a couple of other client-side script sections that handle the events raised by the controls in the page to display the asterisk and the error message.

The `<input>` element that submits the page to the server calls a function within these script sections to validate the values in the controls on the page, and either submit the page to the server or cancel the submit event if any of the values are invalid:

```
<input type="submit" name="_ctl1" value="Validate"
        onclick="if (typeof(Page_ClientValidate) == 'function')
                Page_ClientValidate();" language="javascript" />
```

The Validation Controls in Down-Level Clients

The same page when loaded into a down-level browser does not, however, perform the same way. Instead, the page is always submitted to the server, and it's only there that the validation is carried out. If a control contains an invalid value, the returned page contains the asterisk and the error message. In appearance (other than the asterisks not appearing as you move from one control to another), the result is the same as for an up-level client - but requiring a postback to the server.

The page also contains the same <input> element as that generated for up-level clients. Of course, in this case the separate client-side script functions are not loaded from the server. This means that the code in the onclick attribute does not detect the function named Page_ClientValidate - the statement typeof(Page_ClientValidate) will return "null" - and the page is always submitted to the server for validation.

> *If you want to see all the code that is generated, run the test page* asp-validator.aspx *in different browsers, or select different User Agent string values. You can also open the* WebUIValidation.js *script file from the* \aspnet_client\system_web\[version]\ *subfolder in your default web site to see the functions that it provides for performing validation.*

So what happens in a browser that doesn't support scripting when we use the validation controls? The great thing is that it actually does still work in exactly the same way as with down-level clients that do support scripting. The code in the onclick event attribute of the <input> element does not execute, but the page is still submitted to the server for validation there. And the controls still work with an up-level client that has scripting disabled – though again only in the same way as they do with a down-level client.

The ASP.NET Panel Control

There is one ASP.NET Web Forms control that exhibits an interesting change of behavior when used with different clients. The Panel control is used to create a separate section within a page, representing the kind of effect that is obtained by controls of the same name in environments such as Visual Basic 6.0. By adding style attributes, we can generate a section of the page that looks like a 'panel' – useful for grouping related controls or other output together.

Our test page, named asp-panel.aspx, contains the following code to create a panel with a grooved border, some text content, plus a TextBox and Button control. In this case, to make it easier to concentrate on the working of the Panel control itself, we've used <b> and <font> elements within the content rather than confuse the matter by using the properties of the Panel control:

```
<body bgcolor="silver">
<center>
<form runat="server">
<asp:panel id="pnlTest" runat="server"
           forecolor="black"
           backcolor="silver"
           bordercolor="darkgray"
           borderwidth="5"
           borderstyle="groove"
           width="50%" >
  <font face="Arial,sans-serif" size="2">
    <b>A test panel</b><p />
```

```
      Enter some text:
      <asp:textbox id="txtTest" runat="server" text="some text" /><p />
      And click this button:
      <asp:button runat="server" text="click me" /><p />
   </font>
 </asp:panel>
 </form>
 </center>
 </body>
```

In Internet Explorer, it looks like this:

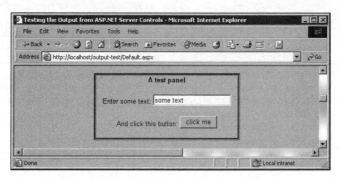

Looking at the code that the `Panel` control generates, you can see that the content of our panel is enclosed in a `<div>` element that defines the style for the foreground and background colors, and the grooved border. It also specifies, in response to the `width="50%"` attribute we included, that the `<div>` should be 50% of the page width:

```
<body bgcolor="silver">
<center>
<form name="_ctl0" method="post" action="asp-panel.aspx" id="_ctl0">
<input type="hidden" name="__VIEWSTATE"
       value="dDwtMTczMzcxMDE3Mjs7PjvcvBfJpdIovdPOMh4rCi0ehaBU" />

<div id="pnlTest" style="color:Black;background-color:Silver;
                        border-color:DarkGray;border-width:5px;
                        border-style:Groove;width:50%;">

  <font face="Arial,sans-serif" size="2">
    <b>A test panel</b><p />
    Enter some text:
    <input name="txtTest" type="text" value="some text"
          id="txtTest" /><p />
    And click this button:
    <input type="submit" name="_ctl1" value="click me" /><p />
  </font>

</div>
</form>
</center>
</body>
```

The Panel Control in Down-Level Clients

However, if we open the same page in Navigator and Opera, we get different results. The content is no longer centered within the panel, although the panel itself does appear as 50% of the width of the page. We also lose the space below the button in Navigator:

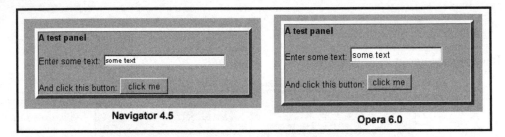

A more surprising feature of the output is visible if you look at the code that is generated by the `Panel` control in these cases. Instead of a `<div>` element, we get a single-row HTML `<table>` that contains one cell:

```
<body bgcolor="silver">

<center>
<form name="_ctl0" method="post" action="asp-panel.aspx" id="_ctl0">
<input type="hidden" name="__VIEWSTATE"
        value="dDwtMTczMzcxMDE3Mjs7PjvcvBfJpdIovdPOMh4rCi0ehaBU" />

<table id="pnlTest" cellpadding="0" cellspacing="0" bgcolor="Silver"
        border="5" width="50%">
<tr><td><font color="Black">

  <font face="Arial,sans-serif" size="2">
    <b>A test panel</b><p />
    Enter some text:
    <input name="txtTest" type="text"
            value="some text" id="txtTest" /><p />
    And click this button:
    <input type="submit" name="_ctl1"
            value="click me" /><p />
  </font>

</font></td></tr></table>
</form>
</center>

</body>
```

This is because the `<div>` element (defined in HTML 3.0) was a relatively late addition to many browsers, as well as behaving quite differently in different browsers. For example, some browsers do not support setting the width of a `<div>`, and some don't support background colors. It's also possible to specify a background image for a `Panel` server control, but as some browsers don't support background images for a `<div>`, they would not be able to display this image either.

Therefore, to maximize compatibility across as many browsers as possible, Microsoft designed the Panel control to generate a <table> for down-level clients. The HTML <table> will generally support setting the background color and/or a background image. Most browsers also allow us to specify the width of the table (or the columns within it) as well. So it will, in most cases, give a similar appearance to the <div> element used in up-level clients.

The reason that the <center> element in our page does not provide centered output in Navigator and Opera is because this 'property' is not inherited from the page itself by a table cell in HTML, whereas it is inherited by a <div> element. The same applies to any <font> settings that are active in the page or another container control that holds the Panel element.

What this does mean is that you will quite often get a difference in appearance between browsers when using a Panel control, and it's well worth keeping your eye open for this. However, there are a couple of useful attributes you can add to the Panel control declaration that affect the output of down-level clients as well as up-level ones. Add an align attribute to control the horizontal alignment of the content for down-level clients:

```
align="center"
```

This will force the Panel control to add this attribute to each <td> element in the resulting <table> for down-level clients, centering the content. Unfortunately, however, some of the other obvious and useful attributes don't work as expected. A prime example of this is:

```
wrap="false"
```

For up-level clients it adds the attribute nowrap="nowrap" to the <div> element, preventing the content from wrapping if the <div> is narrower than the content or the page width. For down-level clients, it adds the same attribute to the <table> element, but **not** to the <td> element. In most browsers, this does not prevent the content from wrapping if it is wider than the table or the page width.

Don't Get Caught Out by Output Caching

So far, we've concentrated on what differences there are in the output of the ASP.NET Web Forms server controls between up-level and down-level clients – and some of the ways we can make sure that we get the appearance we want in different browsers. However, there is one great feature of ASP.NET that can break all our hard work.

ASP.NET can automatically perform caching of the output that it generates by executing a page, and then sending this cached output to other clients that request the same page. This saves the page from being executed every time, and can considerably reduce server loading and resource usage. While we don't have the space to discuss the workings of output caching in full, we'll see an unfortunate side effect when we are supporting different types of client.

The page asp-panel-cache-all.aspx contains an OutputCache directive that instructs ASP.NET to cache the page for ten seconds. The rest of the page is just a simple declaration of a Panel control into which we write the date and time that the page was executed:

```
<%@Page Language="VB" Debug="True"%>
<%@OutputCache Duration="10" VaryByParam="none" %>
<html>
<body>

<asp:panel id="pnlTest" runat="server">
  Page executed: <% = Now() %>
</asp:panel>

</body>
</html>
```

If we open the page in Internet Explorer, then immediately afterwards in Navigator (or use the appropriate User Agent string options in the example page to load it first for Internet Explorer and then for Navigator), we get the following result:

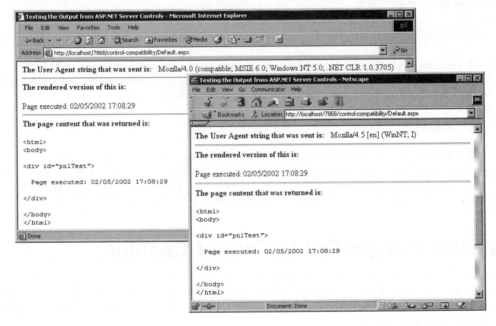

Notice that Navigator receives the up-level page designed for Internet Explorer this time, because this is what is cached by ASP.NET. If the output depended on features that are specific to Internet Explorer, Navigator might fail to display the content correctly.

Caching by Browser Version

To get round this, if you expect to receive hits from different clients, you may prefer to set up output caching so that it still sends the appropriate page to up-level and down-level clients. The easiest way to do this is to add the attribute VaryByCustom="browser" to the OutputCache directive:

```
<%@OutputCache Duration="10" VaryByParam="none" VaryByCustom="browser" %>
```

Now, as you can confirm by running the test page `asp-panel-cache-by-browser.aspx`, the cached page is only sent to the same browser as it was originally created for. Each browser creates a specific copy of the page, and all these different copies are cached.

In our test page the output is cached for ten seconds, and served from the cache every time during that period when you reload it in the **same browser** (or specify the same User Agent string setting). However, changing to a different browser (or changing the User Agent string setting) causes the page to be re-executed and a separate copy is cached. If you then go back to the first browser within ten seconds you'll see that the originally cached copy of the page is served again.

Of course, this means that you will cache lots of pages that are the same – every different version of every different browser will cause a copy of the page to be cached. In reality, there are only two different pages that need to be cached – one for up-level clients and one for down-level clients. We can achieve this by extending the custom caching approach we just used.

Caching by Client Target

We create a function within the `global.asax` file for our site that returns a string value. This value should be different only for situations where we want a separate copy of the page to be cached. If it returns the same value for more than one client request, the same page from the cache will be used for all these requests. So, if we can decide whether our client is up-level or down-level, and just return one of two values, we'll only get two copies of the page cached.

The function we used for our test page is shown next. Note the declaration has to be a `Public` function that overrides `GetVaryByCustomString`, and which takes the `HttpContext` and a `String` as the two parameters:

```
Public Overrides Function GetVaryByCustomString(context As HttpContext, _
                                    arg As String) As String
  If (arg = "clientlevel") Then
    Dim iEcmaVersion As Decimal = 0
    Dim iDomVersion As Decimal = 0
    Dim iMajorVersion As Integer = 0

    Try
      iEcmaVersion = Request.Browser("EcmaScriptVersion")
      iDomVersion = Request.Browser("MSDomVersion")
      iMajorVersion = Request.Browser("MajorVersion")
    Catch
      Return "downlevel"
    End Try

    If iEcmaVersion >= 1.2 _
    And iDomVersion >= 4 _
    And iMajorVersion >= 4 Then
      Return "uplevel"
    Else
      Return "downlevel"
    End If
  End If
End Function
```

In the function, we collect three values from the `Request.Browser` object for the current client: the ECMAScript version, the MSHTML DOM version, and the major version of the browser. Then we can do a test to see if it meets the criteria laid down earlier in this chapter of supporting at least ECMAScript version 1.2 and the MSHTML DOM (version 4.0 or above for Dynamic HTML support). To test for HTML 4.0 and CSS support is more difficult, as these are not available as properties of the `Request.Browser` object. Instead, we demand that the major version be at least 4.0.

This works because only Internet Explorer supports the MSHTML DOM version 4.0, and we know that Internet Explorer 4.0 and above support HTML 4.0 and CSS. An alternative would be to demand a major version of 4.0 and above if the browser type is "IE", or 5.0 and above for other browsers (as the main version 5 and 6 browsers from other companies do support HTML 4.0 and CSS):

```
...
If (Request.Browser("browser") = "IE" And iMajorVersion >= 4) _
Or (iMajorVersion >= 5) Then
  Return "uplevel"
Else
  Return "downlevel"
End If
...
```

Once this function is complete, we can specify it in the `VaryByCustom` attribute of the `OutputCache` directive in our pages:

```
<%@OutputCache Duration="10" VaryByParam="none"
            VaryByCustom="clientlevel" %>
```

Now the page is only cached for the appropriate client type. All requests from Internet Explorer get the same up-level cached page, while all requests from other clients get the same down-level cached page. We've provided a test page named `asp-cache-by-level.aspx` that you can use to experiment with, but you will have to copy the function `GetVaryByCustomString` into your `global.asax` file first. This override also prevents the previous example from working until you remove the function from `global.asax` again.

Summary

We've tried in this chapter to get to grips with the way that the ASP.NET Web Forms server controls generate different output depending on the type of client that is accessing the page. While in most cases you can leave it to the control to generate the output you want, understanding what it is doing and why is a useful addition to your web design and development skills.

In fact, there are occasions when knowing about all this stuff actually means that you can provide a better and more uniform output across different types of client browser. All that is really involved is two things: knowing when your property settings and other page content may affect the output that is generated, and how to get round this.

Usually, all you need to do to provide the best user experience possible is to add a few extra elements, or make minor modifications to the control's property settings, to satisfy the needs of all your down-level clients. In particular, when using the more complex server controls such as the DataList and DataGrid, a little extra care when declaring the controls, their properties and the templates they include can make all the difference.

We haven't looked at all the server controls that are included with ASP.NET, or covered all the ways that the output might affect every browser. Such a comprehensive study might sound useful, but in fact would be extremely repetitive because so many of the issues are the same across several controls. Instead, we looked at the areas where you do need to be aware of the issues, including:

❑ A simple test application for examining the output generated by server controls

❑ How Microsoft defines which are 'up-level' and which are 'down-level' clients

❑ How the style attribute and <font> elements are used for up-level and down-level clients

❑ Working with more complex control like the DataList and DataGrid

❑ How the controls are affected by the lack of client-side scripting capabilities

❑ How the Panel control completely changes its output for the two types of client

❑ How output caching can affect browser compatibility

Having looked at some of the important issues involved in using the ASP.NET Web Forms server controls, we move on in the next chapter to consider how we'll be putting the design for our site into practice. We'll still be doing groundwork to some extent, covering issues like checking the client's browser capabilities and designing our pages to provide the most compatible and accessible output possible.

3

Laying the Foundations

In the previous two chapters, we've been discussing recipes and ingredients for our web site. We've decided what we want to achieve, and examined some of the techniques that we will take advantage of within the pages. Of course, there are several other factors that we need to consider when building the site. Amongst these factors, two important points are achieving as wide-ranging browser compatibility as possible, and providing optimum accessibility for all types of user.

In this chapter, we'll get the groundwork done for the site by looking in some detail at the two issues we highlighted in the previous paragraph, and show you some interesting approaches that achieve both aims. We'll also discuss the technical requirements for our site, in terms of ASP.NET sessions and client-side scripting support. More importantly, we'll show you how we implement checks for these features, and ensure that our visitors can use the site to the fullest extent. By the end of this chapter, we should have all the remaining ingredients ready to build our 'Home' page.

So, in this chapter, we cover:

- ❑ The client-side technical requirements for our Wrox Car Company web site
- ❑ Some of the major issues we have to consider with browser compatibility
- ❑ How our example site checks for session and client-side scripting support
- ❑ Some important issues for making sites accessible to all visitors

Once we have seen where you can obtain the samples for this chapter and the book as a whole, we'll continue by looking at the technical requirements for our site.

Obtaining the Example Files

All the examples you see in this book can be obtained from our web site to run on your own server. The code is available in VB.NET and C#, and can be download from http://www.wrox.com/ (go to the page for this book, where you'll find a link to download the samples as a zip file). Alternatively, you can just run the examples online directly from our server at http://www.daveandal.com/books/7868/.

Installing the Wrox Car Company Site

After downloading the example files, you must configure them for your own server. The tasks required are:

❑ **Install the files into a subfolder of your web site**. Unzip the files using the Use folder names, Restore Folders or Restore Directories option of your zip file manager software to recreate the correct folder tree within the sample files. It doesn't matter what the subfolder is called, though we used the last four numbers of the ISBN for this book – 7868 – as you'll see in the screenshots.

❑ **Create virtual applications** for the wroxcars and cookieless-wroxcars folder. In Internet Services Manager (available from Start | Programs | Administrative Tools), expand the tree in the left-hand window to reveal the wroxcars folder, right-click on it, and select Properties. In the Application Settings section of the Directory page, click the button marked Create next to the Application name textbox, then click OK to close the Properties dialog. Then repeat this for the cookieless-wroxcars folder.

❑ **Install the database**. We've provided SQL scripts and instructions for creating the database in the folder named database of the samples. We've also provided a SQL Server 2000 compatible database backup that you can restore instead of running the SQL scripts. Be sure to create a new Logon named anon, with a blank password, before restoring the database from the backup file. If you use the SQL scripts, the new logon is created automatically.

Then navigate to the folder you just created, for example http://localhost/7868/, where a menu provides access to all the examples:

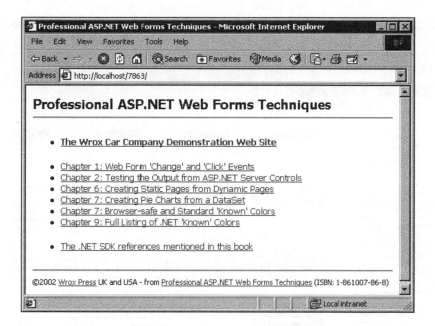

Wrox Cars' Client-Side Technical Requirements

We all know that software comes with a set of 'minimum requirements' – usually the platform, operating system, version, and other prerequisite software that must be available. In some cases, this specification is easy. For executable applications, it could be as simple as "requires Windows 2000 or Windows XP". If the user has purchased the product, it's reasonable to expect that they have read the label on the side of the box.

With a web site, things should be easier. As long as our site conforms to the specifications laid down for the World Wide Web (basically, it outputs HTML), it should work no matter what platform, operating system, version or web browser our visitor is using. After all, that's the whole principle of the Web.

Nevertheless, as we are all so aware these days, it's not that simple. Rarely will pages written to HTML 2.0 standards provide a site that is visually acceptable in today's competitive world. We need to take advantage of features in more recent browsers such as HTML 3.2 or HTML 4.01, client-side scripting, CSS stylesheets, cookie support, and more.

There are plenty of other web-based technologies that we can use as well, but the level of client-side support (and user acceptance) tends to taper off as we get to the more esoteric features. For example, we can only use graphics filters and the Remote Data Service in Internet Explorer 4 and above. And many users may have features such as Java applets and Flash graphics disabled in their browser, or blocked by a proxy server or firewall.

So, can we build attractive, interactive and accessible sites that do work in most browsers and other web-based clients while sticking within the limitations of the more widely accepted features of the Web? We believe that the answer is "yes", and we'll aim to prove it with the site we're building here. To give you an idea, the next screenshot shows the completed 'Home' page:

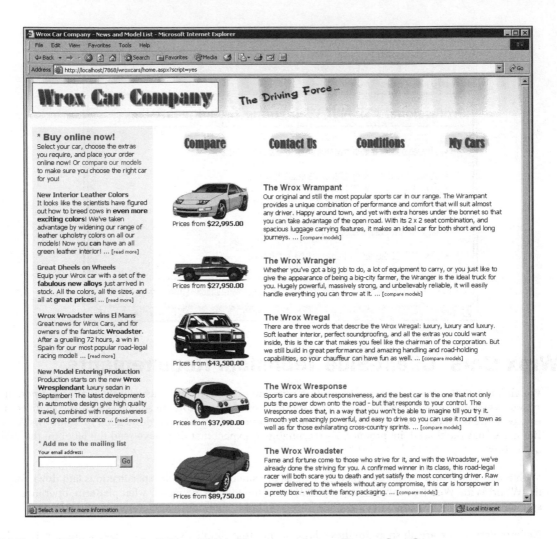

What 'Standards' Do We Support or Require?

The 'Home' page you see above, like the rest of the site, uses markup that is generally compatible with HTML 3.2. However, we do include other elements and attributes that are not part of HTML 3.2, but which do not affect the output in HTML 3.2 clients. You'll see many such examples throughout this chapter. The HTML recommendations insist that a client should ignore any elements and attributes that it doesn't recognize, so it's acceptable to include this 'extra' markup.

The 'animated banner' feature requires extra client-specific support, such as Cascading Style Sheets version 2.0 (CSS2) support, but the page will still work for CSS1 clients and clients that don't support CSS at all. We also use CSS stylesheets to implement the formatting of text and other content, but we include extra formatting elements so clients that do not recognize CSS at all will still produce an acceptable appearance.

Some features of the site depend on support for ASP.NET sessions, and we also include client-side code written in JavaScript 1.0 in some of the pages. We can't manage without session support in this application (this is a design decision we took when planning the site), but we have designed the pages to work without client-side script as far as possible. We'll look at all these issues when we build the individual pages, explain our design decisions, and see how we implement the features to support as many different types of client as possible.

ASP.NET Sessions

When building an interactive site that has to collect and store information provided by the user, as is the case with our example site, we have to find a way to save this data between page requests. We mentioned a few of the options that are available in Chapter 1, such as using `hidden`-type form controls, storing it in the viewstate of the page, or using ASP.NET sessions.

We chose the last of these, ASP.NET sessions, as being the most suitable for our site. Why? Well we are going to be collecting quite a lot of information from each user about the car they want to purchase, and so storing this in the page each time will be laborious and will increase the size of the page. It will also absorb extra bandwidth, as the complete set of values will be sent over the network twice with each page request/response made by the user.

Instead, it makes sense to store the values on the server between requests, and access these only when required. And the easiest way to store values that are specific to each user is by using the ASP.NET `Session` object.

ASP.NET is very good at managing sessions for us automatically, far better than previous versions of ASP where sessions could just occasionally 'get lost' between requests. ASP.NET is also more efficient, with session support adding less of an overhead to the processing and loading of the server. There is still some extra overhead required to manage sessions, however, but the saving in bandwidth and page size can make up for this. We also, of course, save the processing that our code would have to carry out to handle the values any other way.

Requirements for Session Support

For ASP.NET to be able to handle sessions properly, there are two things that must be considered:

❑ Does the client support cookies? If not we must use the cookie-less session features of ASP.NET to provide session support through 'URL munging'.

❑ Will the site run on a web farm, or in a multiple-server environment? If so, we have to ensure that the configuration of the site and servers properly supports sessions for each user.

We'll look at both of these issues next.

Cookies, Cookie-Less Sessions, and URL Munging

ASP.NET uses a 'session cookie' (a cookie that only remains on the client for 20 minutes or until the browser is closed down) to connect each client with their session information stored on the server. A unique session ID is stored in the cookie, and the `Expires` property of the cookie is updated each time a request is received so that it will expire 20 minutes after the last page request from that user (we'll see how you can configure the time out yourself later).

Session configuration in ASP.NET is through the `machine.config` file (stored in your `Winnt\Microsoft.NET\Framework\[version]\config\` folder), and `web.config` files placed in the web site root folder and sub-folders. The default within the `<system.web>` section of these files is:

```
<sessionState mode="InProc" cookieless="false" timeout="20" />
```

This configuration causes the session data to be stored in memory on the server that handles the request, in much the same way as in ASP 3.0 and earlier (`mode="InProc"`). It also defines the way that sessions will be identified – in the default case using a cookie because the `cookieless` attribute is set to `"false"`. The final attribute is, of course, the time-out for sessions, and it can be edited as required.

However, the behavior can be changed in various ways. For example, if the client does not support cookies (in which case the default configuration will not provide session support), we can change it to force ASP.NET to use **cookie-less sessions** through a process called **URL munging**. All that's required is to change the value of the `cookieless` attribute to `"true"`. Then the session ID is automatically inserted into the URL when the response is sent to the client, for example:

```
http://localhost/7868/cookieless-wroxcars/(s3vs5y55dsmkrqubtrvzvw55)/home.aspx
```

The session ID is also inserted into each hyperlink on the page automatically by the ASP.NET process:

```
<a href="cookieless-wroxcars/(s3vs5y55dsmkrqubtrvzvw55)/news.aspx">
  read this news article
</a>
```

The only issue is that this setting can only be used in `machine.config` (where it applies to the whole machine) or in a `web.config` file that is in the root directory of a web site or in a virtual application root directory. We'll see the ramifications of this when we look at our example application later on.

The Session ID and Session Timeout

The ID used by ASP.NET for each user's session can be obtained from the read-only `Session.SessionID` property. You might want to use this ID to store data or identify specific sessions in some custom code of your own. However, in general, you should not need to concern yourself with the actual ID, as ASP.NET manages all this for you automatically.

The session timeout can be changed in ASP.NET by editing the value for `timeout` in the `machine.config` or `web.config` files on your server. It can also be changed within your code by setting the `Session.Timeout` property to an integer value for the number of minutes that a session should remain available after the last request from a client. A common scenario is to set it to something like ten minutes to reduce the number of sessions that are stored on a busy server, but take care that you don't annoy your users.

For an application that handles sensitive data, such as the web interface to your bank account, short session time outs are usually acceptable (and are a good idea for security reasons to prevent users leaving a browser open after logging in). However, they might take more than ten minutes to read and absorb a complex page (or stop to answer the phone or make a cup of coffee). For more mundane tasks, they might be upset if this means that they have to start all over again.

Session Support Across Multiple Servers

The second issue we mentioned earlier is how ASP.NET manages sessions when there is more than one server responding to requests. This is common in a web farm or server cluster. If the session data is stored only on the machine that responds to the initial request, subsequent requests from this user must be routed to the same server every time. If not, the request will start a new session on the server it is directed to, and this new session won't contain the current session data.

Some web farm software, routers, and load-balancing algorithms allow for **affinity** to be enabled. In general, this works by detecting the client's IP address and using this to decide which server in a cluster or web farm will receive the request. In Windows Application Center and Windows 2000 Load Balancing, affinity divides requests amongst servers based on their Class 'C' IP address space.

> *Class 'C' address spaces use the first three of the four values in the 'dotted format' IP numbering system as the address mask. In other words, all clients that have the same values for these parts of their IP address fall into the same Class 'C' address space. As an example, the Class 'C' address space (namespace mask) for the IP address* 194.75.229.98 *is* 194.75.229.

Other techniques exist – including using a cookie that is sent to the client to indicate which server should respond to the next request that is received. However, all of these techniques mean that the effectiveness of load balancing for the cluster can be compromised, and that a server failure can disrupt existing sessions.

Instead, ASP.NET allows us to centralize the session data so that any server in a cluster or web farm can respond to the request, and then get the session data for that client from the central store. The two types of 'central store' we can use are the ASP.NET State Service or a SQL Server database. Both hit performance, being less efficient than the default `"InProc"` session data storage method, but the effects can be minimized (as we'll see later).

Using the ASP.NET State Service

The ASP.NET State Service uses one or more separate servers that are dedicated to storing session data, and these are assigned as the **session store**. The dedicated State Service runs on these servers, and all the other servers connect to it to obtain the session data each time. In `machine.config` or a `web.config` file, change the entry for the `<sessionState>` element within the `<system.web>` section. Set the mode to `"StateServer"` and add an attribute to specify the IP address of the server cluster that is running the ASP.NET State Service. For example

```
<sessionState mode="StateServer" cookieless="false" timeout="20"
              stateConnectionString="tcpip=194.75.229.123" />
```

The State Service is installed by default with ASP.NET, but not automatically started. It can be started from the command line by typing:

```
net start aspnet_state
```

However, you probably want to go into the Properties dialog for this service (go to Start | Programs | Administrative Tools | Services) and change the Startup type to Automatic. Cookie-less sessions can still be used when the ASP.NET State Service is holding the session data.

Using SQL Server for Session Support

Rather than using the ASP.NET State Service on a web farm or server cluster, we can use a SQL Server database to hold the session data in a table. This technique can also improve reliability for very busy sites, as two SQL Server machines can be clustered to give some redundant backup in case of failure.

A SQL script file named `InstallSqlState.sql` is provided with ASP.NET (stored in the `Winnt\Microsoft.NET\Framework\[version]\` folder) that you can execute to create the required database, table and procedures within your SQL Server. Then it's just a matter of setting the `mode` attribute in `machine.config` or a `web.config` file to `"SQLServer"`, and adding the `sqlConnectionString` attribute that specifies how to connect to the SQL Server database:

```
<sessionState mode="SQLServer" cookieless="false" timeout="20"
    sqlConnectionString="data source=194.75.229.123;user id=uid;password=pw" />
```

Cookie-less sessions can still be used when SQL Server is holding the session data.

Maximizing Performance When Using Sessions

No matter how they are implemented, sessions do hit the performance of ASP.NET. For `"InProc"` sessions this hit is reasonably low, and is generally acceptable in exchange for the advantage of automatic per-user state support that sessions provide. And, since ASP.NET uses an MTA thread pool to read and update session state (as opposed to an STA thread pool in classic ASP 3.0) when using the `"StateServer"` and `"SQLServer"` methods, it provides better system throughput than classic ASP. There is no thread affinity in the MTA thread pool, and hence no blocking and contention.

However, irrespective of how we actually implement the session storage, we can limit the loading they impose by only accessing the session data when required, and by accessing it in read-only mode when possible. By 'accessing the session data', we don't mean reading and writing it in code. What we mean is reducing the work ASP.NET has to do behind the scenes to manage the session data for us. Every request for an ASP.NET page raises a series of events on the server, and the appropriate modules that make up the ASP.NET runtime handle these events.

Two events that are executed by default for every page manage the values stored in a user's session. Near the start of the page execution cycle, before any of our own code in the page is executed, the session data is fetched from the state store (either `"InProc"`, `"StateServer"`, or `"SQLServer"`) ready for use in the page. Then, once the page has been rendered and sent to the client, the session data is written back to the state store again so that any changes are persisted ready for the next request.

If we have a page that does not use any of the session data, we should indicate this by adding the attribute `EnableSessionState="False"` to the page:

```
<%@Page Language="VB" EnableSessionState="False" %>
```

Then the two processes that load and save session state are not executed for this page (the default if we omit this attribute is for session data to be loaded and saved each time). We'll also get a compiler error if we try to access the user's session in code when sessions are not enabled for the page.

Alternatively, if we want to read session values but not **write** (update) them, we can use the value `"ReadOnly"` for the `EnableSessionState` attribute. This means that ASP.NET avoids the processing step required to write back (update) the stored session data:

```
<%@Page Language="VB" EnableSessionState="ReadOnly" %>
```

We use these attributes in the pages of our site where appropriate – you'll see them in the code listings later in this chapter, and throughout the remainder of the book.

Client-Side Scripting

Client-side script that runs within the browser can produce an interactive user experience that can never be matched by posting back to the server. For example, changing the value or selection in <form> controls as the user interacts with the page, or moving the input focus to a specific control. If the user's browser supports Dynamic HTML or CSS2, then there are even more opportunities to make the page interactive, by changing the content within the page dynamically without requiring a postback to the server. An example might be showing or hiding controls as the user makes selections in the page.

However, there are some browser clients that do not support client-side scripting, and there are also situations where support for it is not appropriate. An obvious example is a 'page reader' designed to allow blind or partially sighted people to hear the content of the page read to them. There are also many users who still prefer text-based browsers such as Lynx (http://lynx.browser.org/).

Security is a big issue with web browsers these days, and some users also disable client-side scripting in their browser to protect against malicious activity in the pages they view (although, in general, client-side scripting is perfectly safe). So, for all these situations, we should make sure that our pages work without client-side script support wherever possible. Reduced interactivity might be a direct result, but the pages should still **work** (i.e. not appear to be 'broken').

In our example site, we make only marginal use of client-side scripting in the 'Home' page. It's limited to the animated banner at the top of the page, and opening a new window for the 'Configure' page where the user can select the optional extras for their new car before placing an order. Where client-side script is disabled or unavailable, a static banner replaces the animated one, and the links to open the new window become 'normal' <a> elements. We do use client-side script a great deal in the vehicle configuration page, however it still works (albeit less intuitively) when client-side scripting is not available.

Users and User IDs in the Wrox Car Company Site

We want to allow our visitors to interact with the site by choosing a vehicle, and then configuring it by adding optional extras. Having done so, we will give them the opportunity to place an order for the vehicle, or save their selected configuration and come back to it again later. We'll also allow them to come back and view orders they have previously placed and cars that they bought in the past. All this will happen when they select the My Cars link in the 'Home' page.

While we won't be looking at these features until much later in the book, it's clear that we'll need to implement some kind of login system so that we can tell which cars and configurations belong to each particular visitor. So, we decided to automatically allocate *every* visitor a user ID as soon as they enter the site, and store it in their ASP.NET session. This user ID value is used to track the configuration options that the user makes when deciding to purchase a car, and allows them to save configurations and come back and edit them again.

However, we don't want to ask users to log in straight away, as this may put them off browsing the site and being tempted by our special offers. Instead, we store their user ID in a cookie with a long Expires value on their machine. If a visitor arrives and they don't already have a user ID cookie, we'll use a temporary randomly generated user ID instead and then store this in a cookie, as well as storing it in their current session. We could alternatively use a GUID, or the unique ASP.NET session ID, but our random generation is extremely unlikely to create the same temporary ID twice.

This means that the visitor doesn't have to provide any login details to enter the site or configure vehicles. We'll just use their user ID as a key in the database for any data we save for this user. Only when they come to place an order, or view existing orders or cars (using the My Cars link) will we prompt them to either register with us, or enter the password that matches their current user ID.

And, to make it more user friendly, we'll allow each visitor to select their own user ID when they register, and simply copy any data we stored against their temporary ID to their new registered ID (and update their user ID cookie). Then, when they visit the site in future, our code will use their own registered ID for access to their saved information.

Of course, if they destroy the cookie on their machine or use a different machine to access the site (or if their browser does not support cookies), they will always start off with a new temporary randomly generated user ID. However, they can use the My Cars link to access the login dialog and then log in using their registered user ID and password. This means that they are reconnected to the saved data again.

Checking for Sessions and Scripting Support

We've decided that we need to change the behavior of the site to handle clients that don't support cookies (by using cookie-less sessions) and clients that don't support client-side scripting (by changing the way that the page works). Of course, to be able to do this, we have to detect whether each client does provide cookie and scripting support.

The techniques have been described in other books, and we also mentioned the client-side scripting detection code we use in the previous chapter of this book. Our site has a default.aspx page that carries out two specific tasks:

❑ It stores a value in the user's session, which we can look for in the next ('Home') page to see if a session is available.

❑ It redirects the client to the 'Home' page, adding a name/value pair to the query string if client-side script is supported. Then, if we can find this name/value pair within the Request.QueryString collection in our 'Home' page, we know that client-side scripting is both available and enabled.

However, before we look at the code in detail, we also need to take into account how we will identify users that come back to the site to view their current orders, their own vehicle details, and any configurations that they may have saved during previous visits. As we saw earlier, we depend on a user ID that is saved in a cookie, or if none is available we need to create a new one for every visitor.

Client Capabilities and User ID Detection

The next schematic shows the overall process we implement to collect a user ID from each visitor as they enter the site (or create a new one), and at the same time detect if the client supports sessions and scripting:

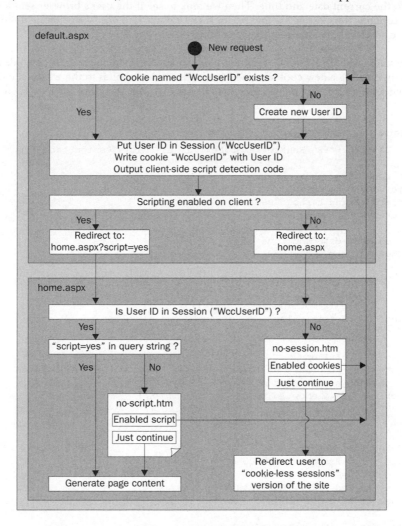

Most of the work is done in the two pages default.aspx and home.aspx, with the other two pages (no-script.htm and no-sessions.htm) only there to act as warnings that scripting or cookie support is not available, and to give the user a choice of what to do about it. We'll look at the code itself in detail next.

The Code in default.aspx

The next listing shows the server-side code `<script>` section for the page `default.aspx`. We declare a `String` variable to hold a user ID that we'll need within the site as a whole, and a `DateTime` variable that we set to the current date and time. Then we look to see if the user's browser sent a cookie with the request that contains the existing ID for this user. If we don't find one, we generate a new unique value using the date and a random number between 0 and 999.

Now that we know what the user ID is, either an existing one or one we've just created, we write it back to the client by creating a new cookie named `WccUserID` that applies to the whole site (`Path = "/"`), and which has a long `expires` value (five years from now). We also store the user ID in this user's session:

default.aspx

```
<%@Page Language="VB" EnableViewState="False" EnableSessionState="True"%>

<script runat="server">
Sub Page_Load()
  ' declare string to hold user ID
  Dim sUserID As String = ""

  ' get current date and time
  Dim dNow As DateTime = Now()

  ' get UserID from long-expiry cookie if possible
  Dim oCookie As HttpCookie = Request.Cookies("WccUserID")
  If Not oCookie Is Nothing Then
    sUserID = oCookie.Value
  End If

  If sUserID = "" Then
    ' no value, so create new UserID
    Dim oRandom As New Random()
    sUserID = "~" & dNow.ToString("yyMMddhhmmss") _
              & oRandom.Next(0, 999).ToString()
  End If

  ' update UserID cookie
  oCookie = New HttpCookie("WccUserID", sUserID)
  oCookie.Path = "/"
  oCookie.Expires = dNow.AddYears(5)
  Response.Cookies.Add(oCookie)

  ' store UserID in Session object
  Session("WccUserID") = sUserID

End Sub
</script>
...
```

The HTML and Content in default.aspx

The remainder of the default.aspx page contains the output that the user will see, and the client-side script detection code. As we indicated towards the end of the previous chapter, we can use a <meta> directive (element) to redirect the client to another page – in our case after one second to the page no-script.htm. However, default.aspx also contains a client-side script section that will be executed as the page loads, and which redirects the client to the page home.aspx, with the name/value pair "script=yes" appended to the URL if client-side scripting is available and enabled:

default.aspx

```
...
<!doctype html public "-//IETF//DTD HTML 2.0//EN">
<html>
<head>
<meta http-equiv="refresh" content="1;url=no-script.htm" />
<title>Checking for Client Scripting Support</title>

<script language="JavaScript">
<!--
function jumpScripting() {
// jump to page using client-side JavaScript - if jump not executed
// then client does not have scripting available or it is disabled
window.location.href='home.aspx?script=yes';
}
//-->
</script>
</head>
...
```

The <body> section of the page contains some text that is displayed as the next page is loading, plus a <noscript> section. Only clients that do not implement client-side scripting at all should display the contents of this section, and we included it in case the client does not implement the <meta http-equiv="refresh"> directive we placed in the <head> section of the page. Within the <noscript> element we provide some text information about our site, plus links to some locations from which script-enabled browsers can be obtained:

```
...
<body onload="jumpScripting()">
<font size="2" face="Tahoma,Arial,sans-serif">
Checking for script support in your browser... </font>
<noscript>
  <p><font size="2" face="Tahoma,Arial,sans-serif" color="#ff0000">
  <b>Please note:</b></font></p>
  <p><font size="2" face="Tahoma,Arial,sans-serif">Your browser does
  not support Active Scripting or client-side JavaScript, or it is
  disabled in your security settings. For best results, you should
  enable this before using the application. If not, you will be
  unable to take full advantage of the features of this site. Some
  will require extra requests to the server, or involve extra steps
  on your behalf.</p>
  <p><font size="2" face="Tahoma,Arial,sans-serif">
  Suitable browsers can be downloaded from:
```

```
  <ul>
   <li><font size="2" face="Tahoma,Arial,sans-serif">
    <a href="http://www.microsoft.com">http://www.microsoft.com</a></font>
   </li>
   <li><font size="2" face="Tahoma,Arial,sans-serif">
    <a href="http://www.netscape.com/">http://www.netscape.com</a></font>
   </li>
   <li><font size="2" face="Tahoma,Arial,sans-serif">
    <a href="http://www.opera.com/">http://www.opera.com</a></font>
   </li><p />
   <li><font size="2" face="Tahoma,Arial,sans-serif">
    However, in the meantime, you can still:</font>
   </li>
   <li><font size="2" face="Tahoma,Arial,sans-serif">
    <b><a href="home.aspx">Continue to Wrox Car Company</a></b></font>
   </li>
  </ul>
  </font>
</noscript>
</body>
</html>
```

Note that, as our site will generally work OK without client-side script, we also provide a link at the bottom of the page where the user can enter the site anyway. Here's what the page looks like in Amaya, which does not support client-side scripting at all and so displays the contents of the <noscript> section:

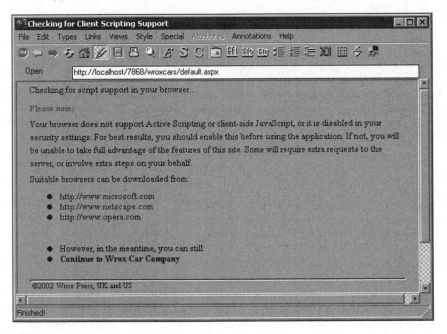

The no-script.htm Page

The `default.aspx` page we've just seen contains a `<meta>` directive that will be executed by the browser if it does not support scripting, but does react to a redirection directive:

```
<meta http-equiv="refresh" content="1;url=no-script.htm" />
```

Amaya does not process `<meta>` redirection directives, which is why we saw the `<noscript>` section in the previous screenshot. However, most other browsers do process this directive, and so are redirected to the page `no-script.htm`. This allows us to display a more informative message, and provide the user with a couple of options. Here's the complete listing of that page:

no-script.htm

```
<!doctype html public "-//IETF//DTD HTML 2.0//EN">
<html>
<head><title>Client-side Scripting Not Available</title></head>
<body>
<h3><font size="4" face="Tahoma,Arial,sans-serif">
Client-side Scripting Not Available</font></h3>
<font size="2" face="Tahoma,Arial,sans-serif" color="#ff0000">
<b>Please note:</b></font><br />
<font size="2" face="Tahoma,Arial,sans-serif">
Either you entered the site directly without starting from the
<a href="default.aspx">default page</a>, or your browser<br />
does not support Active Scripting or client-side JavaScript.
It might be disabled in the options<br /> page for security settings.
For best results, you should enable this before using the application.
<br /> If not, you will be unable to take full advantage of the features
of this site. Some features will<br />require extra requests to the
server, or involve extra steps on your behalf.</font><br />
<ul>
  <li><font size="2" face="Tahoma,Arial,sans-serif">I have
      <a href="default.aspx">enabled client-side scripting</a>
      and I want to use the application</font></li>
  <li><font size="2" face="Tahoma,Arial,sans-serif">I want to
      <a href="home.aspx">continue into the site</a> anyway</font></li>
</ul>
</body>
</html>
```

You can see that we provide a link to `default.aspx` for our visitor to use if they originally entered the site elsewhere (in which case they will not have a user ID in their session and so will be redirected back here by certain pages that require a user ID). We also provide a second link to `default.aspx` that they can use once they have enabled scripting in their browser.

The `default.aspx` page will then check for scripting support again, and (provided that it is now available) redirect them to the 'Home' page. The final link allows our visitor to go to the 'Home' page using a browser that does not support client-side scripting, or without enabling script support if that is the way they prefer to work:

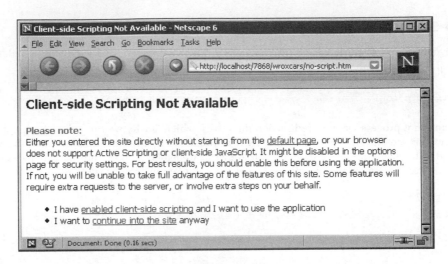

Enabling and Disabling Client-side Scripting

You can test the redirection feature in `default.aspx` page in most browsers that do support client-side scripting by turning it off. In Navigator 6, client-side script can be disabled in the Edit | Preferences | Advanced dialog:

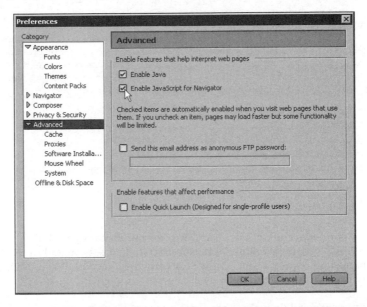

In Internet Explorer 5 and 6, client-side script can be disabled in the Tools | Internet Options | Security | Custom Level dialog. You can also elect to be prompted, and then choose whether to allow script to run or not as the page is displayed each time:

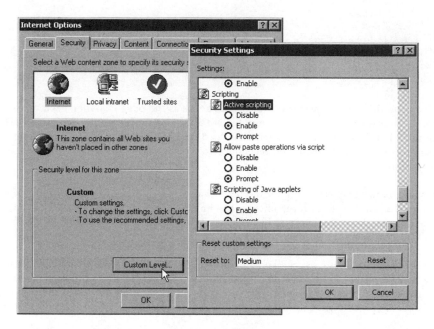

Interestingly, when you disable client-side script in Navigator 6 or Internet Explorer 6, the contents of the <noscript> element in default.aspx are displayed. So users will see this flash up when they first enter the site, but only for the one second until the <meta> directive loads the 'No Script' page.

The Detection Code in home.aspx

We'll be looking at the 'Home' page (home.aspx) in detail in the next chapter. However, to complete the session and scripting detection, we'll show you the code in home.aspx that carries out the remainder of the task now. The next listing shows this code:

home.aspx

```
Sub Page_Load()

  ' get UserID from Session put there by default.aspx
  ' if not there, browser does not support Sessions (cookies)
  ' or did not load default.aspx first
  If CType(Session("WccUserID"), String) = "" Then
    Response.Clear()
    Response.Redirect("no-sessions.htm")
    Response.End()
  End if

  ' get value of "script" from query string *or* Session to see
  ' if browser supports client-side scripting and it is enabled
  If Request.QueryString("script") = "yes" _
  Or CType(Session("WccCanScript"), Boolean) = True Then
    bCanScript = True
    Session("WccCanScript") = "True"    ' store in Session
  End If
```

```
      ...
      ...  {remainder of Page_Load event handler code is here}
      ...

   End Sub
```

You can see from this that we perform two sets of checks as the page is loaded each time. We collect the user ID from the session, where it was stored by `default.aspx`. If we can't find a user ID, it means either that the client has entered the site without loading `default.aspx` first, or that their browser does not support cookies. Our code redirects them to a page named `no-sessions.htm`, which we'll look at very soon.

Secondly, we look in the query string for the name/value pair `"script=yes"`, or in the session for the value `WccCanScript="True"`. If the client is just entering the site from `default.aspx`, the name/value pair will be in the query string. If they are coming back to the 'Home' page from another page, it will be stored in their session instead.

If either of these values does exist, we know that the client's browser supports client-side scripting, and so we set a page-level `Boolean` variable named `bCanScript` to `True`, and update the session value `WccCanScript`. Now, in any page of the site, we can extract the user's ID from their session, and check if their browser supports client-side scripting.

The no-sessions.htm Page

Providing that our client's browser supports cookies, and they are not disabled or blocked in their browser's security options, they will now be looking at our 'Home' page. However, if their browser does not support standard (cookie-based) sessions, the user will now be looking at the page `no-sessions.htm`.

The next listing shows `no-sessions.htm`. We provide our visitor with a similar explanation of the problem as in the `no-script.htm` page, together with a link to go to `default.aspx` if they entered the site elsewhere (so no user ID was created and stored in the session). We also provide a link that they can use to go back to `default.aspx` after enabling cookies in their browser:

no-sessions.htm

```html
<!doctype html public "-//IETF//DTD HTML 2.0//EN">
<html>
<head><title>Cookie Support Not Available</title></head>
<body>
<h3><font size="4" face="Tahoma,Arial,sans-serif">
Cookie Support Not Available</font></h3>
<font size="2" face="Tahoma,Arial,sans-serif" color="#ff0000">
<b>Please note:</b></font><br />
<font size="2" face="Tahoma,Arial,sans-serif">
Either you entered the site directly without starting from the
<a href="default.aspx">default page</a>, or your browser<br />
does not support cookies, or they have been disabled in your security
settings. You must<br />either enable cookies before using the
application, or use the alternative version that does<br />
not require cookie support.</font><br />
```

```
<ul>
  <li><font size="2" face="Tahoma,Arial,sans-serif">I have
    <a href="default.aspx">enabled cookie support</a>
    and I want to use the application</font></li>
  <li><font size="2" face="Tahoma,Arial,sans-serif">I will use the
    <a href="/7868/cookieless-wroxcars/default.aspx">alternative
    version</a> of the application</font></li>
</ul>
</body>
</html>
```

Cookie Based or Cookie-less Sessions?

What we use for the final link in the no-sessions.htm page depends on what we decide to do about clients that don't support cookies, and for whom we therefore cannot support cookie-based sessions in our site. We could simply turn them away, but that certainly isn't good business practice. A better alternative is to take advantage of the 'cookie-less sessions' feature we discussed earlier in this chapter. We could:

❑   Set up the site to always use cookie-less sessions for all clients. The downside with this is the ugly URL that they see in the browser, and the extra work that ASP.NET has to do to modify all the links and URLs for each page.

❑   Provide a mirror copy of the site that uses cookie-less sessions, to which we redirect visitors that do not support cookies.

As you can see from the final link in the previous listing, and in the next screenshot, we chose the second option for our site. As long as we are aware of a few minor issues when we code the pages (we'll look at these for our 'Home' page in the next chapter), the two copies of the site will be identical and so can be mirrored on the same server, on separate clustered servers, or even in different geographical locations:

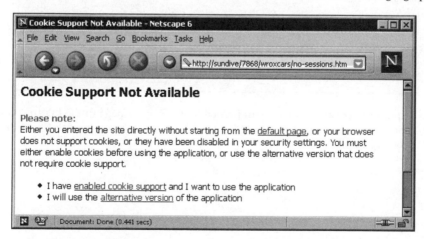

Of course, in the 'Home' page where we redirect the client to the no-sessions.htm page, we could just redirect them straight to the 'cookie-less' version of the application. However, recall that they might enter the site somewhere other than default.aspx, and so it makes sense to give them the option to use the default version of the site (as in our example).

Remember that you have to create a separate virtual application for the cookie-less version of the site if you want to run both cookie-based and cookie-less versions on the same server. The sample files contain the appropriate web.config *file for cookie-less session support in the folder* cookieless-wroxcars, *and you must configure this folder as a virtual application root as discussed at the start of this chapter.*

Enabling and Disabling Cookie Support

You can test our site, or your own session detection code, by disabling cookies in your browser. In Netscape 6, this is done in the Privacy & Security section of the Preferences dialog. You can disable cookies altogether, or have the browser prompt you before accepting one:

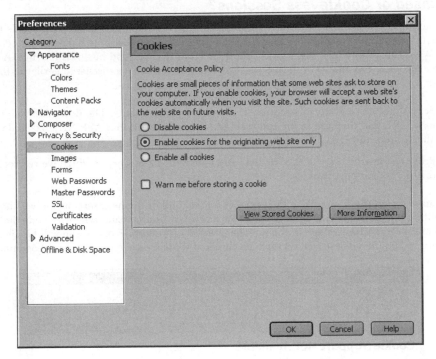

In Internet Explorer 6, cookie support is configured in the Privacy page of the Internet Options dialog. As well as 'general' settings such as High, Medium and Low, you can use the Advanced dialog to specify exactly how cookies should be handled:

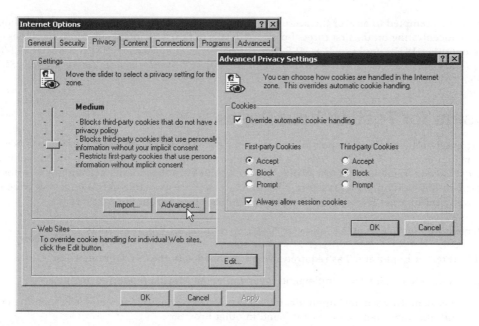

First-party cookies are those that come from the same domain as the page itself. Third-party cookies are those sent by other domains, perhaps when the browser loads an image from a different domain into this page. Turning off third-party cookies is the same as selecting the "Enable cookies for the originating Web site only" option in Netscape 6.

> *Notice that Internet Explorer also has an option to allow per-session cookies while blocking other (persistent) cookies. The difference between per-session cookies and persistent cookies is that the latter are stored on disk, while per-session cookies are automatically destroyed when you leave the web site.*

Cross-Browser Compatibility Issues

As time progresses, we should expect the issues of browser compatibility that used to make life so hard for web developers to become much less of a problem. All the major browser manufacturers have committed to follow the current and emerging recommendations from the World Wide Web consortium (the W3C at http://www.w3.org/). However, things are still made awkward by several factors:

❑ We should still attempt to support older and less well-known browsers where possible.

❑ Not all browsers interpret the recommendations in exactly the same way.

❑ A proportion of our visitors will have special needs, for example they may be blind or have difficulties using a standard keyboard and mouse. They are likely to be using a special browser, and we should endeavor to provide as much extra support as we can for these types of client.

❑ There are lots of different display mediums appearing, such as pocket PCs, mobile phones, WebTV, and many more. Some of these (in particular mobile devices) may require something other than HTML, or may support only a subset of HTML.

We haven't attempted to answer the last of these issues in this book, or in our example site, though we will be concentrating on the first three. For more details of how you might support other types of client, check out other Wrox books such as *ASP.NET Distributed Data Applications* (ISBN 1-86100-492-3), *Professional ASP.NET 1.0* (ISBN 1-86100-703-5), and *ASP.NET Mobile Controls Tutorial Guide* (ISBN 1-86100-522-9).

Browsers for Testing Your Pages

It's extremely difficult (if not impossible) to test your pages on all the different types of browser that you may encounter on the Web. Not only are there many different manufacturers and individual versions, but most have incremental updates available as well. And even this doesn't account for how they perform on different operating systems. Netscape browsers are available to run on a very wide range of platforms, and Internet Explorer has long been a popular browser on the Apple Mac.

We have tested our pages in the following browsers running on Windows 2000:

❑   Internet Explorer 6.0 as required by and installed with the .NET Framework.

❑   Netscape 6.2.2, which implements a version of the Mozilla rendering engine.

❑   Netscape Navigator/Communicator 4.5, which uses a highly non-standard rendering engine and includes many features not found in other browsers.

❑   Mozilla 1.0 Release Candidate 2, available from http://www.Mozilla.org/. Although only at version 1.0, it is fundamentally a 'version 6' browser that renders content with a version of the same rendering engine as Netscape 6.

❑   Opera version 6.02, available from http://www.opera.com/.

❑   Amaya 6.1, released in April 2002 by the W3C as a reference and test browser for HTML and CSS.

It's difficult to use earlier versions of many browsers, because you can't install them once a later version is in place. Internet Explorer is a good example of this, and in mid 2002 we were unable to find a machine that we could test pages with Internet Explorer 4. One possible solution is to make a test page available on the Web and get as many users as possible to access it and report problems. We regularly do this on our own web site (http://www.daveandal.com/) when building new sample applications.

Having said all this, it's good to see that some uniformity is beginning to appear. The four main players (Microsoft, Netscape, Opera and Mozilla) have 'version 6' browsers available which are remarkably compliant with HTML 4.01 and CSS2 recommendations, and pages generally work the same on these browsers.

Standing out from the crowd is Amaya. It does not support many 'modern' features, such as frames, client-side script, cookies and other features. However, it does provide a good guide to what your pages might look like in some of the more basic browsers and rendering engines.

Other User Agents

We also test our pages in two other user agents. Technically these are browsers, though they tend to be used mainly by people that have a disability, or who don't want to take advantage of the usual graphical appearance that (almost without exception these days) web sites provide. We use:

❑ Lynx version 2.8.3, which is a text-only browser available from http://lynx.browser.org/. The following screenshot shows the 'Home' page of our Wrox Car Company site in Lynx:

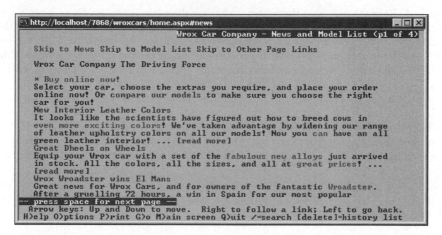

❑ IBM Home Page Reader (HPR) version 3.02, which is a special user agent that reads web pages aloud for people who suffer from impaired vision. A trial version can be obtained from http://www-3.ibm.com/able/hpr.html. It's a great way to see (or hear) how your web site actually appears to some visitors. You can see what our Wrox Car Company 'Home' page looks like in HPR 3.0 in the next screenshot, where the word currently being read out is highlighted:

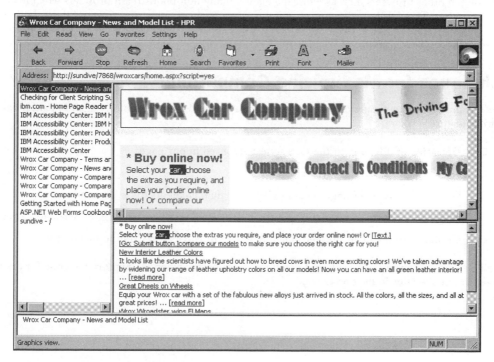

Solving Browser Compatibility Issues

Having talked about the browsers themselves, what are the main issues involved when we come to build pages and web applications? As we discussed earlier, almost all browsers in use today (with the exception of some special devices such as mobile or cellular phones) support HTML 3.2 – or a broad subset of it. So the usual types of formatting we use, including tables, <font> elements, direct formatting, and structure elements (such as <b>, <br>, <h1>, and so on) are going to work fine.

Almost every browser will recognize <span>, and most recognize <div>. And without exception 'active' elements such as <a>, <input>, <select>, and <textarea> will work fine. Frames are less universally compatible, and certainly Amaya and Lynx do not support them directly. However, they do provide support for navigating between frames; so if we do need to use them we can generally get away with it (we discussed our design decisions as regards frames towards the end of Chapter 1).

The other good news is that most recent browsers recognize a few extra attributes, which are technically not part of the HTML 3.2 standards. Examples are topmargin and leftmargin for a <body> element, and face for a <font> element.

> *You can view and download the full recommendations for HTML 3.2, and other versions of HTML, CSS, and other recommendations, from the W3C Web site at http://www.w3.org/.*

As we move towards the more esoteric presentation methods, however, support becomes less universal. ActiveX controls will only work in Internet Explorer (or with a special 'ActiveX wrapper' plugin installed in other browsers such as Netscape 6), and many non-mainstream browsers won't load Java applets either. Thankfully it's becoming commonplace for many new sites to avoid these, both for compatibility reasons and because most 'savvy' users consider them to be a security risk and so block them in their security settings.

Techniques for Maximizing Compatibility

For our purposes, the main areas where we do have issues to resolve in our site, and in sites that rely on similar feature sets, are:

- ❑ Declaring and linking to the CSS stylesheets used in our pages
- ❑ Specifying font styles, types and sizes
- ❑ Getting the layout of page sections and individual elements to be the same
- ❑ Making script-driven animations and other 'actions' work correctly in all scriptable clients
- ❑ Coping with the often-indeterminate behavior of Navigator/Communicator 4.x

We'll look at some solutions next, and you'll see more details when we explore the code for the various pages in our site later in the book.

Declaring and Linking to CSS Stylesheets

In general, the recommendation for using CSS is to **link** to the stylesheet rather than inserting the individual style definitions into the page within a `<style>` section. This not only makes it easier to change the styles later, and have all pages use the same style, but it also allows the browser to decide whether or not to download the stylesheet at all. On top of this, the browser can download the stylesheet once and cache it, thereby improving response times and reducing bandwidth usage.

For example, there would be no point in Lynx downloading a stylesheet, as it only displays text. If you insert the style information into the page, you are just making the page bigger for no reason, and with no benefit for some clients.

The recommended way to link to a stylesheet is with a `<link>` element placed within the `<head>` section of the page:

```
<link rel="stylesheet" title="Default" href="stylesheets/wccStd.css" />
```

You can also provide more than one stylesheet for a page. Add the `title` attribute to each one, and all those that carry the same value for this attribute are combined – effectively the individual style selectors are inherited from all these stylesheets. If you provide more than one stylesheet, but don't want them to be combined, use the `title` attribute to indicate the purpose of each one. The value `"Default"` for this attribute indicates the stylesheet that is used by default, and in some browsers the user can choose from the other linked stylesheets as well.

When using more than one stylesheet, change the `rel` attribute from `"stylesheet"` to `"alternate stylesheet"`, and be sure to use a different value for the `title` attribute for each `<link>` you include. As an example, we could have added links to six of the standard stylesheets that are available from W3C to our existing style sheet link in the 'Home' page of our example site:

```
<link rel="stylesheet" title="Default" href="stylesheets/wccStd.css" />
<link rel="alternate stylesheet" title="Modernist"
      href="http://www.w3.org/StyleSheets/Core/Modernist" />
<link rel="alternate stylesheet" title="Midnight"
      href="http://www.w3.org/StyleSheets/Core/Midnight" />
<link rel="alternate stylesheet" title="Ultramarine"
      href="http://www.w3.org/StyleSheets/Core/Ultramarine" />
<link rel="alternate stylesheet" title="Swiss"
      href="http://www.w3.org/StyleSheets/Core/Swiss" />
<link rel="alternate stylesheet" title="Chocolate"
      href="http://www.w3.org/StyleSheets/Core/Chocolate" />
<link rel="alternate stylesheet" title="Steely"
      href="http://www.w3.org/StyleSheets/Core/Steely" />
```

Then, in Netscape 6, we would be able to choose which stylesheet to apply to the page:

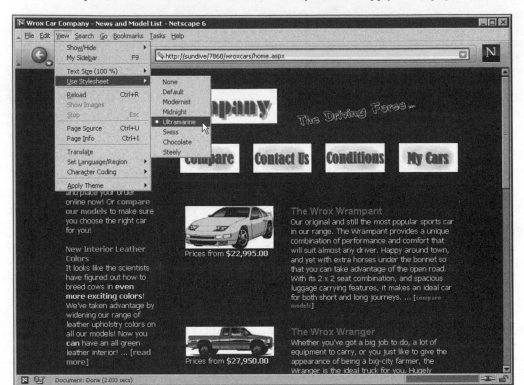

While the W3C stylesheets are mainly 'decorative', you might also decide to provide alternative stylesheets that use a simpler color range (or even just two colors), or which change the text size or layout, so that visitors who suffer poor vision can more easily use the pages.

Font Styles, Types, and Sizes

We saw in the previous chapter how the ASP.NET server controls vary their output depending on the type of client (up-level or down-level) that accesses the page where they are used. In general, there are two approaches to specifying the font style, type and size: we can use CSS stylesheets or the more universally acceptable `<font>` element.

CSS is the better solution, giving finer control over the appearance of text. We can specify the font family, color and size (to within very fine limits, such as by pixel, point, or em). We can also specify things like the padding and margin widths (top, bottom, left, and right), the alignment, the text decoration (underlined, strikeout, and so on), and whether elements should be visible, hidden, or not occur within the rendered output at all (`display:none`).

In CSS2, we can also add definitions for the positioning and layout, such as absolute positioning (specifying the top, left, width, and height), the z-order, and we can animate the images using script (many of these features also work as 'Dynamic HTML' in Internet Explorer 4 onwards).

However, CSS as a whole only works properly (with some minor exceptions) in Mozilla 1.0, Internet Explorer 4.x and above, Netscape 6.x and above and Opera 3.x and above. In earlier browser versions, it's difficult to rely on getting the appearance you actually want just by using CSS.

Probably the easiest way to get maximum compatibility is to combine `<font>` elements with CSS styles. For example, in our 'Home' page, we have the following section of HTML:

```
<font face="Arial,Helvetica,sans-serif" size="4" color="#b50055">
<span class="large-red-text"><b>* Buy online now!</b></span><br /></font>
<font face="Tahoma,Arial,Helvetica,sans-serif" size="2">
<span class="body-text">Select your car, choose the extras you require,
and place your order online now! Or </span><a class="std-link"
href="compare.aspx">compare our models</a><span class="body-text"> to make sure
you choose the right car for you!</span></font>
```

The innermost nested formatting instructions take precedence, so in our example the CSS styles are given preference over the `<font>` elements. However, if we had placed the `<font>` elements within the `<span>` elements instead, the `<font>` elements would take precedence.

Any aspects of the formatting that are not specified in the innermost instruction are inherited from the parent (enclosing) element in line with the inheritance rules of CSS. So, if our `body-text` style class did not define the font color, it would be inherited from the enclosing `<font>` element.

So, after all this, it's clear that we can get better overall control over the appearance of our pages in a wide range of browsers by using a combination of nested `<font>` elements and CSS styles. When our 'Home' page is viewed in our six test browsers, you can see that all of them produce acceptably similar output:

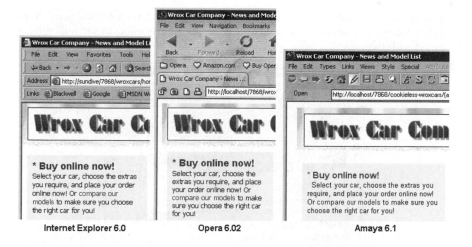

Internet Explorer 6.0   Opera 6.02   Amaya 6.1

| Mozilla 1.0 RC2 | Netscape 4.5 | Netscape 6.2.2 |

One problem is that font size can only be specified in fairly broad steps in a `<font>` element, as numbers from 1 to 7 (or as relative sizes against a `<basefont>` definition using +1, -2, and so on). So you may have to juggle the CSS `font-size` selectors to match this if you want to get exactly the same font size in all browsers.

Using Pre-Defined Font Sizes

Better still is to do as we have in our example site – use the pre-defined font sizes in the CSS stylesheet. These were discussed in the previous chapter, and the values available are `"xx-small"`, `"x-small"`, `"small"`, `"smaller"`, `"medium"`, `"large"`, `"larger"`, `"x-large"` and `"xx-large"`. The big advantage with these is that it allows visitors to change the size of the text displayed in the browser window using the features of their browser.

For example, in Internet Explorer, they can use the Text Size item on the View menu to enlarge the font size if they have problems reading small text. You can see the effect in the following screenshot if you compare it with the previous ones:

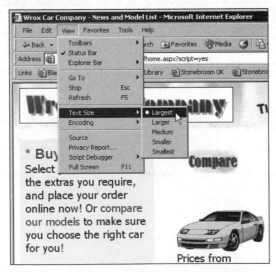

If we define the font sizes in our stylesheet using absolute values (such as "12px" or "10pt"), the user will not be able to resize the text when viewing the page.

Font Names and Colors

One point to remember, especially if you only test your pages on one operating system (for example, only on Windows 2000 as we have already owned up to doing!) is that font names are often O/S-specific. We prefer a sans-serif font in our pages, and so we specify our `font-family` as:

```
font-family:Tahoma,Arial,Helvetica,sans-serif;
```

The browser will use the first one it recognizes. If none of them are actual font names on the platform where the browser is running, it will use the 'generic' font names to give a font that has the same basic properties. The generic font names are "`serif`", "`sans-serif`", "`cursive`", "`fantasy`" and "`monospace`".

In a `<font>` element, we use the `face` attribute to specify the same series of fonts:

```
<font face="Tahoma,Arial,Helvetica,sans-serif" size="2" color="#cc3333">
```

It's also worth using numeric values for any colors you specify, rather than the color names. While most modern browsers do recognize a series of standard color names, you can be certain that all of them will be able to interpret the color from its hexadecimal equivalent (as seen in the `<font>` element listed above). You might also like to stay with using just the 216 'browser-safe' colors, rather than mixing your own.

A search of the Web for 'browser-safe colors' will bring up plenty of sites that list the safe colors and their hexadecimal equivalents (Google found 8,400 such sites!). A reference that we use most often is at the W3C: http://www.w3.org/MarkUp/Guide/Style.

ASP.NET Server Controls and the CssClass Property

You may recall from the previous chapter that the ASP.NET server controls are clever enough to change the output they generate based on the client type – either 'up-level' or 'down-level'. Our examples in that chapter used specific combinations of style elements to control the appearance of the output. Or, to put it another way, we specified values for the many different attributes of the controls that affect the appearance when rendered.

For example, in the demonstration of the ASP.NET `Label` control, we used this code to declare the control (we've used color names here so that you can more easily see how they relate to the output that the control generates):

```
<asp:label id="lblTest" runat="server"
          forecolor="red"
          backcolor="yellow"
          font-size="large"
          font-bold="true"
          bordercolor="black"
          borderwidth="3"
          text="a yellow label control with red text" />
```

For up-level clients (basically, Internet Explorer 4 and above), the control generates a `<style>` element that combines all the attribute values we specified:

```
<span id="lblTest" style="color:Red;background-color:Yellow;border-
color:Black;border-width:3px;border-style:solid;font-size:Large;font-
weight:bold;">a yellow label control with red text</span>
```

And the appearance is much as we would expect:

a yellow label control with red text

However, when we access the same page with a 'down-level' client, such as Netscape 6, we get totally different output generated (as we discussed in the previous chapter). Instead of a `style` attribute we only get a nested `<font>` element:

```
<span id="lblTest"><b><font color="Red" size="5">a yellow label control with red
text</font></b></span>
```

Obviously, this cannot provide the formatting information required to produce the yellow background and black border:

a yellow label control with red text

However, all the ASP.NET Web Forms controls that create visible output in the page expose a property named CssClass. We can set this to the name of the CSS class defined in a stylesheet (or in a `<style>` section within the page), and it will be added as the class attribute of the element(s) generated by the control.

So, we first create a stylesheet or a `<style>` definition within the page like this:

```
.body-text {
    font-size:large;  font-weight:bold;    color:red; background:yellow;
    border-width:3;   border-color:black; border-style:solid;
}
```

Then we define our server control like this:

```
<asp:label id="lblTest" runat="server"
           cssclass="body-text"
           text="a yellow label control with red text" />
```

Now, irrespective of the type of client that hits our page, the output of the control is just:

```
<span id="lblTest" class="body-text">a yellow label control with red text</span>
```

The only issue now is what happens if the client does not support CSS? The solution is easy – we declare our server control with specific properties for the appearance, *and* we set the CssClass property:

```
<asp:label id="lblTest" runat="server"
           forecolor="red"
           backcolor="yellow"
           font-size="large"
           font-bold="true"
           bordercolor="black"
           borderwidth="3"
           cssclass="body-text"
           text="a yellow label control with red text" />
```

Now, in an 'up-level' client, we get both a class attribute on the <span> element, and a full set of style selectors that mirror the individual attribute values we specified for the server control. Following the CSS rules for the inheritance of style values, the selectors in the style attribute override the selectors we defined for the CSS "body-text" style. But, because we used values for the server control attributes that replicate the styles defined for "body-text", the result is the same:

```
<span id="lblTest" class="body-text" style="color:Red;background-
color:Yellow;border-color:Black;border-width:3px;border-style:solid;font-
size:Large;font-weight:bold;">a yellow label control with red text</span>
```

However, in any other browser, we get a combination of the class attribute on the <span> element, and a nested <font> element:

```
<span id="lblTest" class="body-text"><b><font color="Red" size="5">a yellow label
control with red text</font></b></span>
```

This means the result in browsers that are classed as 'down-level', but which do support CSS, is much better. For example, this is the result in Netscape 6:

a yellow label control with red text

It will still give us at least large red text in clients that don't recognize CSS at all. But while this seems like the best of both worlds, there are a couple of points to bear in mind:

❑ As the <font> element is nested inside the <span> element, all of the formatting it specifies (which could at most be the face, color, and size) takes precedence over the selectors in the CSS style "body-text".

❑ Applying styles to individual elements 'hard-coded' into the page like this makes it much harder to maintain and update the page in the future than when using only a linked stylesheet to specify the formatting and styles.

Layout of Page Sections and Individual Elements

Most graphically-oriented sites try to achieve a pleasing display that is as near to the printed page as possible. However, the nature of the display in a web browser often gets in the way. Some issues we often come up against are:

❑   Specifying page widths, and coping with different screen resolution and text sizes

❑   Removing excess white space around full-width banners and other elements

We'll briefly consider these topics next.

Different Screen Resolutions and Text Sizes

Many sites attempt to achieve the 'same as the printed page' effect by using only a fixed-width area within the browser window. In general there is no excuse for this, and it is a constant source of annoyance for many users. They are forced to scroll the page to read content, while half of the browser window is empty.

Often the reason this approach is taken is to limit the length of the lines of text on the screen, because long lines are harder to read. This is why newspapers and magazines break the content into columns. But there is no reason why we can't use columns in our web pages as well. Our preferred approach is to create the complete page within a two- or three-column table, and use each column for different parts of the content.

The left-hand column is the natural area for a menu bar if you use one on your site, but it works equally well with other content – as you can see from the 'Home' page of our example Wrox Car Company site shown near the start of this chapter. The one disadvantage is that the user has to wait for all the content of the table to be received before their browser can render any of it.

It is possible, in browsers that support CSS2, to arrange for fixed width tables to be progressively rendered, by adding the style selector "table-layout:fixed" to the <table> element and specifying values for the width and height selectors for every <td> element in the first row. But if the content is all in two or three cells in one **row** of the table, progressive rendering will not make any difference.

We prefer to set the column widths using percentage values where possible, so that the columns are spaced evenly irrespective of the browser window width:

```
<table width="100%" border="0" cellspacing="10" cellpadding="10">
 <tr>
  <td width="25%" rowspan="2" bgcolor="#ffffaa" valign="top">
    ... left-hand column contents ...
  </td>
  <td width="75%">
    ... left-hand column contents ...
  </td>
 </tr>
</table>
```

However, if you have a menu bar in one column, you may prefer to set this column to a specific width. Just bear in mind the effects that setting fixed column sizes may have when the user resizes the text within the page. Test your pages with browser window widths from 640px up to 1280px (the common range of screen resolutions), and with different text sizes selected in the browser options or View menu.

Removing Excess White Space in Page Margins

We briefly mentioned in the previous chapter how unwanted white space can affect our page layout. There are a couple of areas worth bearing in mind: setting the page margins, and preventing excess characters creeping into formatted elements.

Quite a few browsers, such as Navigator 4 and Opera 6, do not recognize the leftmargin, rightmargin, and topmargin attributes for a <body> element. And Netscape 6 and Mozilla 6 do not recognize the rightmargin attribute. This is understandable, as these attributes are not part of the latest HTML recommendations. Instead, a good solution is to use CSS to define the style for the <body> element (as well as specifying zero for the leftmargin, rightmargin, and topmargin attributes):

```
body {
    font-family:Tahoma,Arial,Helvetica,sans-serif;
    font-size:x-small;
    padding-left:0;
    padding-right:0;
    padding-top:0;
}
```

This removes the white space from the left, top, and right of the page in Opera 6, though has no effect in Navigator 4. It also fails to remove the right-hand margin white space in Netscape 6 and Mozilla, but it's a simple technique that is certainly worth including in your pages if you aim to achieve full-width display.

Removing Excess White Space from Text in Block Elements

The other point to consider is how white space affects text that is placed in a containing element such as a table cell or <div>. For example, consider the following screenshot from a test page that contains a two-row table:

The Wrampant provides a unique combination of performance and comfort that will suit almost any driver. Happy around town, and yet with extra horses under the bonnet so that you can take advantage of the open road. With its 2 x 2 seat combination, and spacious luggage carrying features, it makes an ideal car for both short and long journeys.

Whether you've got a big job to do, a lot of equipment to carry, or you just like to give the appearance of being a big-city farmer, the Wranger is the ideal truck for you. Hugely powerful, massively strong, and unbelievably reliable, it will easily handle everything you throw at it.

You can see that the last line of text in the first table cell has extra white space above it. To understand why, we'll examine the source code that creates this table:

```
<table cellpadding="5">
<tr>
 <td><font size="2" face="Tahoma">
   The Wrampant provides a unique combination of performance and comfort
   that will suit almost any driver. Happy around town, and yet with extra
   horses under the bonnet so that you can take advantage of the open road.
```

```
    With its 2 x 2 seat combination, and spacious luggage carrying features,
    it makes an ideal car for both short and long journeys.</font>
   </td>
 </tr>
 <tr>
  <td><font size="2" face="Tahoma">
    Whether you've got a big job to do, a lot of equipment to carry, or
    you just like to give the appearance of being a big-city farmer, the
    Wranger is the ideal truck for you. Hugely powerful, massively strong,
    and unbelievably reliable, it will easily handle everything you
    throw at it.</font></td>
 </tr>
 </table>
```

Look at the closing </td> tags. In the first cell of the table, we allow unformatted white space to exist between the closing </font> tag and the </td> tag. The layout rules for browsers stipulate that any number of consecutive white space characters (carriage returns, spaces, tabs, and so on) should be replaced by a single space when rendering the page.

However, this space character is outside the formatted content we placed in the cell. So, as the overall physical size of the default font for the page is larger that the size 2 'Tahoma' font that we specified for the text in the table cell, the baseline of the last line of text moves down to accommodate this larger character.

The solution is shown in the second row of the table listed above – make sure that there are no extraneous characters between the closing tag of the formatting element and the closing tag of the block element that holds it. An equally valid way to code the page, if you don't like having the </td> tag at the far right of the content, is like this:

```
   ...
    and unbelievably reliable, it will easily handle everything you
    throw at it.
   </font></td>
 </tr>
 ...
```

Many web page editing tools, and several of the ASP.NET server controls, automatically format your source code and insert white space before a </td> tag, so check for this if you find layout problems like this occurring.

The visible effect of this extra white space is worse in Internet Explorer and older versions of Navigator. It also applies to other elements and types of content. For example, if you apply CSS styles using a <span> element, make sure there is no white space after the closing </span> tag and the closing tag for any containing element (such as a table cell, <div>, <li>, etc.).

Script-Driven Animations and Other 'Actions'

We've already decided that we want to include 'something different' in our 'Home' page in order to attract the viewer's attention, as well as demonstrating a few techniques that combine client-side and server-side code in ASP.NET. Our 'Home' page contains a banner at the top, which is animated in Internet Explorer 4.x and above, Netscape 4.x and above, and Mozilla 1.0.

We also planned to include the animation feature for Opera 6.0, which implements the CSS2 recommendations in the same way as Internet Explorer 6, Netscape 6 and Mozilla. However, at present (in version 6.02), Opera has problems with the absolute positioning of images through client-side script. Once this is cured, we'll be able to use the standard CSS2-based version of the banner in Opera as well. You can use the test page we provide with the samples (`dom2-test-banner.htm`* in the* `wroxcars` *folder) to test for support in your version of Opera.*

We only show the animation once in each session, the first time that the visitor opens the 'Home' page. After that, and in all the other pages (and in other browsers), we use a static representation of the banner instead.

We'll look at the implementation of the banner itself in Chapter 5. Here, we want to briefly look at the different categories of support for such animations in the different browsers. The following table shows the four categories into which almost all browsers fall:

Browser	Techniques for script-based animation
Internet Explorer 6.x Netscape 6.x Mozilla 1.0 Opera 6.x (in future revisions)	Support for CSS2 and JavaScript 1.0. Use standard HTML DOM2 methods to interact with the page content.
Internet Explorer 6.x Internet Explorer 5.x Internet Explorer 4.x	Support for Microsoft Dynamic HTML and JavaScript 1.0 (using the JScript interpreter). Use DHTML methods against the MSHTML rendering engine to interact with the page content.
Netscape Navigator 4.x	Support for Netscape-specific Dynamic HTML features such as Layers
Most other browsers	No support for dynamic interaction with the page content.

So, we can build client-side script powered animations into pages for all the most recent and common browsers, and therefore accommodate a high percentage of the total number of visitors. The problem is that we need to code the animation (and some of the other 'actions' that we might need to accomplish) in three different ways, to suit the first three categories.

In essence, we can write JavaScript code so that it detects certain features of the client as it runs, and have it modify its behavior automatically. In other situations, especially when using images or building complex scripts, it's often easier to code three different versions and then just send the appropriate one to the client.

We'll see some examples of detecting the client type in ASP.NET, and delivering appropriate content, in Chapter 5 when we look at our page banner in more detail. In the meantime, it's useful to explore the overall techniques for detecting the abilities of the browser in client-side code.

Client-Side Browser Feature Detection

The traditional way to identify a browser in client-side code is to query the properties of the navigator object that is exposed by the root window object. For example:

```
var sBrowserName = window.navigator.appName;
var sVersion = window.navigator.appVersion;
```

However, this requires some complex parsing and decision constructs to figure out which kind of features our client supports. An easier and generally more accepted approach is to check if the client implements various object model collections and/or methods.

Only Internet Explorer version 4.x and above implements the document.all collection for accessing the contents of a rendered page. And only Navigator 4.x implements the document.layers collection for accessing the <layer> elements contained in a page. Meanwhile, any browser that supports the DOM Level 2 and CSS2 will support the document.getElementById method.

So, we can use detection code like the following – note that, as Internet Explorer 5.x implements the getElementById method, we have to check for this when looking for CSS2 and DOM2 compliant browsers:

```
if (document.all) {
  //
  // code for Internet Explorer 4.x and above goes here
  //
}
if (document.layers) {
  //
  // code for Netscape Navigator 4.x only goes here
  //
}
if (document.getElementById && !document.all) {
  //
  // code for DOM2 and CSS2 compliant clients goes here
  //
}
```

Internet Explorer versions 4.x and 5.x implement a fairly compliant version of CSS, extended to include a great many features that are now part of CSS2. One annoying difference is that the technique for getting a reference to an element using its id property is different to that used in CSS2. In Internet Explorer 4.x and above, we can access the all collection that is exposed by the document object:

```
var oElementRef = document.all['my-element-id'];
```

In CSS2 and DOM Level 2-compliant clients, we have to call the document object's getElementById method instead:

```
var oElementRef = document.getElementById('my-element-id');
```

Coping with Navigator/Communicator 4.x.

Before we finish this section, we'll very quickly summarize some of the compatibility problems that arise when supporting Navigator 4.x clients – especially early versions up to 4.5. You'll see how we implement support in our example site in the coming chapters, but the main points to watch out for are:

❑   Navigator does not fully inherit <font> settings into things like lists (<ul> and <ol>) and table cells, leaving text in a default font and size inside these elements. It's wise to include extra nested <font> elements to ensure that the correct formatting is applied to these elements.

❑   If HTML controls are placed within the cells of a <table>, the <form> and </form> tags also have to be within the table, otherwise the controls may not be rendered. However the <form> tags can be placed between the corresponding <table> and <tr> tags if required, for example:

```
<table>
 <form runat="server">
  <tr>
   <td>
      ... table contents here ...
   </td>
  </tr>
 </form>
</table>
```

❑   A client-side <script> section cannot be placed within a <table>. In reality, this is a limitation only when using the ASP.NET RegisterClientScriptBlock method, which insists on placing the client-side <script> section immediately after the opening <form> tag – therefore conflicting with the limitation described previously (we discuss the RegisterClientScriptBlock method towards the end of Chapter 8).

❑   Textbox <input> elements and lists do not always display text in the same size as their surroundings, and it's often necessary to specifically format the text for these elements one size larger than the surrounding elements.

❑   Positioning text and other content at absolute positions requires a completely different approach, using <layer> elements, to that adopted in other browsers. Each <layer> contains its own document object, complete with a hierarchy of all the other objects normally found within the document object. So accessing elements within a <layer> requires more code than is required to access any element within the page directly, as is possible with DOM Level 2 and CSS2.

Making Sites Accessible to All Visitors

The final topic for this chapter – and one that is extremely important – is how we make our web pages accessible to visitors that suffer from various types of disability. For example, have you any idea how your pages might be used by a blind user, or how easy it might be for someone who cannot use a mouse to access them?

Providing optimum accessibility often means adding extra elements or attributes to our pages, or just using the existing ones in a more sensible way to make the page more intuitive for visitors. It makes us 'good players' in the field of the World Wide Web, and much of what's involved is generally just good practice anyway. However, there is an even more persuasive reason for considering how universally accessible our site actually is, as we'll see next.

Why Provide Universal Accessibility?

It's long been the case that companies and government departments have to provide facilities for disabled people to be able to use their facilities. This varies from installing wheelchair ramps at shop doorways, to making written contracts and forms available in Braille or large-print formats.

While the Web was just a communication network for scientists, and a playground for computer geeks, no one bothered about universal accessibility that much. However, now that it has become a major feature in almost everyone's life, a primary distribution channel for governmental and commercial information, and an access portal for a huge array of services, people are realizing that the laws and regulations governing accessibility in the physical world can also be applied to the Internet.

What this means is that we really do have a duty to comply with the recommendations, and there have already been several law suits in places like the US and Australia against sites that are unusable by blind or disadvantaged visitors. A United States government department called the Access Board (http://www.access-board.gov/) has published a document called the *Section 508 Standards for Electronic and Information Technology*, and it applies to both hardware and software (see http://www.access-board.gov/sec508/guide/ for more details). It lays down exactly how we should aim to provide universal access for all visitors to our web sites.

A great book that covers all the topics you'll see summarized here is Accessible Web Sites *from Glasshaus (ISBN: 1-90415-100-0).*

A Summary of Techniques for Accessibility

We strive to provide good accessibility for visitors in all the web sites we build, and the example Wrox Car Company site is no exception. In the following chapters, you'll see how we implement various accessibility features. However, we'll summarize them here as a reference point, and so that you have a feeling for what is involved.

Accessibility centers around making it as easy as possible for people to navigate to and within the pages we create, to read and understand the content, and to do so with the minimum of extra effort compared to the more usual techniques such as clicking with a mouse. Special user agents, browsers and other access software designed for use with different types of disabilities depends on some or all of the following guidelines to make pages more easily accessible.

Assisting Navigation

❑ Include a meaningful `<title>` element in every page so that software and users can tell immediately if the page covers what they are looking for. Remember that, if they are using an aural page reader, they don't want to have to wait while it reads the contents to find out that it is the wrong page.

❑ Provide 'skip to' links as the first items in every page, allowing users with text browsers or page readers to jump directly to the area of the page that interests them. We'll look in detail at how we can provide 'skip to' links in the 'Home' page we discuss in the next chapter.

❑ Try and make the structural layout of every page similar if this is appropriate for the content, for example put menus in the same place on each page.

❑ Avoid self-referring links, in other words links that load the same page again. If you use a common menu bar or footer section, you should arrange for it to exclude the current page amongst the links.

❑ Try and lay out the content of any tables you use so that they can be read from left to right, and still make sense. Use <th> elements for the heading row, or add a scope attribute to identify if the cell contains data that applies to the row (scope="row") or column (scope="col").

❑ For HTML <form> controls, always place the caption for a textbox or list to the left of the control. For a radio button or checkbox, place it to the right of the control. If the layout of a form is complex, use <label> elements to contain the caption, and in each one set the for attribute to the name or id (which should be the same) of the control it applies to.

❑ Avoid meaningless text in hyperlinks, such as 'click here'. Instead, indicate in the text of the link what the target actually is.

Identifying Elements

❑ Include a name and a title attribute in all <frame> elements, and a title attribute in all interactive elements, such as <a>, <input>, <select>, <textarea>, and so on.

❑ Include an alt attribute in every image element you use, with a brief but meaningful text description of the image. If the image does not contribute to the meaning of the page, for example, a spacer image, bullet or horizontal rule image, include alt="" (an empty string) so that access software knows that it can be ignored.

❑ Include an alt attribute in each <area> definition of a client-side image map, and try and avoid using server-side image maps – which access software cannot usually describe to the user in any kind of meaningful way.

❑ Where an image contributes a lot towards the meaning of a page, use the longdesc attribute to point to a text file or web page that contains a full description of the image.

General Recommendations

❑ Use the standard generic font sizes, such as "x-small" and "large" rather than fixed sizes, allowing visitors to enlarge the font in their browser if required.

❑ Provide alternative text content where possible, for example *inside* the declaration of an <object> element or <applet> element, but *outside* any contained elements such as <param>. This text will be available to the client if their software does not load the object or applet.

❑ Avoid generating important content through client-side scripting, where this content is not available if clients do not or cannot execute the script. Use a <noscript> section to provide alternative content if necessary.

❑ Try accessing your pages in Lynx, to see if they are usable in a text-only browser.

❑ Try accessing your site in one of the 'page reader' applications, such as the IBM Home Page Reader we saw earlier in this chapter. Close your eyes or turn off your screen and see if you can navigate through your own site!

Summary

This chapter has ranged far and wide over many varied topics, mainly in order to prepare for the task of building the first of the pages for our site. As you've seen, the task of building a site that conforms to current standards, works well in most browsers, and is accessible for disadvantaged visitors, is not like falling off a log. There are a lot of things to keep in mind, and a lot of different techniques available. And we still need to make it look attractive!

In this chapter we've attempted to round out the topics we started in the previous two chapters, such as figuring out what standards we will support (basically HTML 3.2 and CSS), deciding on the technical requirements we will impose on our visitor's browsers, and the way that we can detect if each browser is suitable. We also looked at how we can take advantage of features in more recent browsers to make our pages work even better.

The third topic we spent time investigating was that of general browser compatibility. With so many different makes, versions and operating systems out there, we can never be sure that we've covered everything. However, we have tried to show you how you can cover most bases, along with some useful techniques that work in most browsers.

We finished the chapter with a brief summary of accessibility issues, both how they are panning out legally and how we can be better 'Net citizens' by following the (generally common-sense) guidelines.

The topic areas we covered were:

❑ The client-side technical requirements for our Wrox Car Company web site

❑ Some of the major issues we have to consider with browser compatibility

❑ How our example site checks for sessions and client-side scripting support

❑ Some important issues for making sites accessible to all visitors

And at last, in the next chapter, we can start building some pages and see some results for all the work we've put in so far. We'll get started on the 'Home' page for our example Wrox Car Company web site, and you'll see many of the techniques from this and the previous chapters put to good use.

The Home Page

It's taken us a while to get this far, but at last we're in a position to start building the 'Home' page for our Wrox Car Company site. In this chapter we'll look at how it works, the coding techniques we used, and how ASP.NET server controls make the task so much easier than in ASP 3.0 and earlier. Building on much of the theory and design issues we covered in earlier chapters, we'll produce a page that satisfies all our original criteria, and which works well in each of the 'test' browsers we described in the previous chapter.

As you'll see, our 'Home' page can be easily divided into separate logical sections. We'll describe each of these sections in turn so that you can follow the design, and see how each section is implemented. The data access techniques we use in our page are relatively simple, so we'll also discuss this aspect as we look at each section of the page.

However, we don't have room to cover every section of the 'Home' page in detail in this chapter. We'll carry over to the next chapter the animated banner, page footer and mailing list sections of this page. Meanwhile, in this chapter, you'll see:

- ❏ The overall structure of the 'Home' page
- ❏ How we specify the styles and appearance of the page, and each page section
- ❏ How we provide additional accessibility and navigation features for specialist clients
- ❏ The section containing the links to other pages
- ❏ The 'News and Special Offers' section of the page
- ❏ The list of car models and descriptions
- ❏ How the page changes behavior for script-enabled and non-script-enabled clients

We start with a look at the overall page structure.

The Overall Page Structure

In Chapter 1 we showed you the first sketches of the design for our site. We decided that the 'Home' page would be divided into sections. The main sections we identified were:

- ❑ Some kind of animated page banner that will attract our visitors' attention when they first come to the site (possibly with a facility to log in, if we implement this later on).

- ❑ News about our company, the cars themselves, and any other special offers or features that we want to draw visitors' attention to.

- ❑ A list of links that make it clear to visitors what other features our site offers, such as comparing models, contact details, terms and conditions, and so on.

- ❑ A section showing the full range of vehicles, including a short description of each one and links to see more about that vehicle.

- ❑ A page footer containing a set of text links to other pages, plus our copyright notice and the e-mail address of the webmaster.

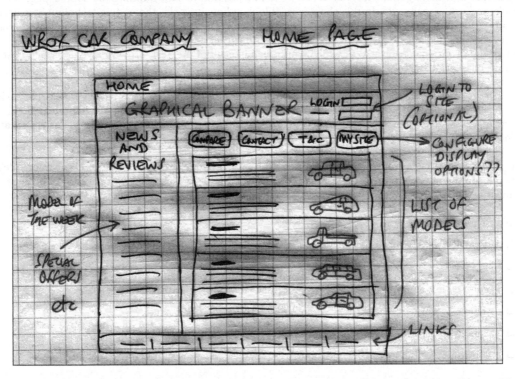

As we moved from initial design into a more in-depth study of the implementation details, we added one more feature – controls where visitors can add themselves to our mailing list. This is a common feature on many sites, and it is easy to implement using ASP.NET server controls. So, the design now translates into the high-level layout shown in the following schematic:

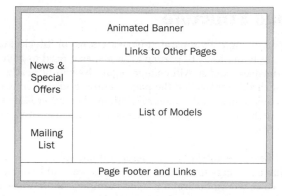

The next screenshot shows the finished page, so that you can see how well it compares to our original design (the page footer is off-screen at the bottom in this screenshot):

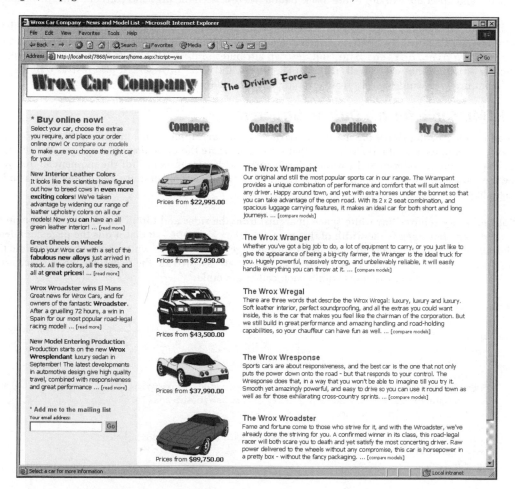

Creating the Page Structure

We could create this layout of logically separated page sections (or 'blocks') using CSS and absolute positioning, though this has limitations. In particular, it makes it hard to guarantee that the content (which is drawn from a database, and so will change regularly) will fit neatly into each section. The 'absolute position' approach also means that the page sections and content will probably not resize well to fit different browser window sizes and screen resolutions. The other issue with CSS to bear in mind is that support is, at best, 'patchy' in many older browsers, and can also confuse non-graphical user agents that do not recognize CSS at all.

Another approach could be to use an HTML frameset and individual frames to create the outline structure of the page. One advantage this would have is that we could enable scrolling on separate sections of the content, which would be useful if – for example – there were a lot more news items to show but we wanted to maintain the narrow left-hand 'column' appearance. Users could scroll each section (the news or the list of models) separately. However, multiple frames can make navigation more difficult, and upset the working of the 'Back' button (we discussed the pros and cons of frames in Chapter 1).

In the end, we decided to go with the time-honored approach of using an HTML table to break the page into separate sections. By specifying percentage values for the column widths, and some judicious use of the `cellpadding`, `cellspacing`, and `nowrap` attributes of the table and its individual cells, we can create a structure that works well in almost all current and older browsers. It also resizes well for different browser window sizes, from around 600px to 1200px wide.

The HTML Table for the Outline Structure

The following listing shows the main HTML outline for our 'Home' page, including the <head> and <body> elements, and the HTML table that we use to create the basic display structure. We've replaced the main 'content' sections and various other features with 'placeholders' for the moment so that you can see the page structure more clearly. We'll cover all of these sections in more detail later in this and the next chapter.

Notice that we remove any white space (margins) from the sides and top of the page in the opening <body> tag, then specify the width of the main <table> as "100%" so that it fills the page completely. This allows our page banner to completely fill the page width with no white space above it, while the `cellspacing` and `cellpadding` attributes of the <table> provide the necessary white space around and between the content sections within each cell of the table:

home.aspx

```
<!doctype html public "-//W3C//DTD HTML 3.2 Final//EN">
<html>
<head>
... links to stylesheet (and other stuff) go here ...
</head>
<body id="BodyTag" runat="server" leftmargin="0" topmargin="0"
      rightmargin="0" bgcolor="#ffffff" class="body-text">
... "Skip to" links go here ...
... animated banner is here ...
<table width="100%" border="0" cellspacing="10" cellpadding="10">
<form runat="server">
<tbody>
 <tr>
```

```
    <td width="25%" rowspan="2" bgcolor="#ffffaa" valign="top">
      ... News and Special Offers section ...
    </td>
    <td width="75%" wrap="nowrap">
      ... Links to Other Pages ...
    </td>
  </tr>
  <tr>
    <td valign="top">
      ... List of Models and Descriptions ...
    </td>
  </tr>
  </tbody>
  </form>
  </table>
  ... page footer goes here ...
  </body>
  </html>
```

The first cell uses `rowspan="2"` so that it spans the two sections for the page links and model list, as shown in the page layout schematic earlier on. We also specify that it should be 25% of the page width, and have a light yellow background to lift it out from the rest of the rest of the page content. The second column fills the remaining 75% of the page width. We also set the `nowrap` attribute so that the column will not shrink to too small a width – the entire page content is still visible without scrolling in 640 x 480 screen resolution.

The <form> Section

Notice also that we include a pair of `<form>` tags within the table, but outside the content, as discussed in the previous chapter. This form is used to submit the visitor's e-mail address, if they decide to join our mailing list. Because we're using the ASP.NET postback architecture, we only need to set the `runat="server"` attribute, and ASP.NET will provide the rest of the attributes required. As an example, the ASP.NET process automatically creates output like the following when a page containing a server-side `<form>` is executed:

```
<form name="_ctl0" method="post" action="home.aspx?script=yes" id="_ctl0">
<input type="hidden" name="__VIEWSTATE"
value="dDwtMjg0OTUwMzc4Ozs+u6uIRM6eSAupZaljlW1AdRVS2KY=" />
```

You can see the `method` and `action` have been set (the page is posted back to itself, and the query string `script=yes` is persisted as well). The `hidden-type` `<input>` element that holds the viewstate for the page is also included in the form. In our 'Home' page, we use the ASP.NET Validation controls to check that the user's input is valid (as you'll see when we look at the mailing list section of the page in the next chapter). In this case, the actual output that we get looks like this:

```
<form name="_ctl0" method="post" action="home.aspx?script=yes"
language="javascript" onsubmit="ValidatorOnSubmit();" id="_ctl0">
<input type="hidden" name="__VIEWSTATE"
value="dDwtMjg0OTUwMzc4Ozs+u6uIRM6eSAupZaljlW1AdRVS2KY=" />
```

You can see that the Validation controls change the attribute list for the <form> element by adding the language attribute and an onsubmit event handler declaration that these controls rely on to perform client-side validation.

The <body> Element as a Server Control

One point that might have prompted a question in your mind is why we have added the runat="server" attribute to the opening <body> tag. After all, there is no dedicated ASP.NET server control for a <body> element. The reason is that we want to be able to manipulate the <body> element in our server-side code as the page is being created.

This is because we want the client-side script within our animated banner to be executed once the page has finished loading, and we accomplish this by specifying the name of the function that provides the animation as the onload attribute. However, we only want to animate the banner once – the first time that the visitor accesses the 'Home' page. After that, they will see a static version of the banner instead, and so we won't need the onload attribute to be set.

ASP.NET includes many dedicated server controls, but these are mainly for the 'interactive' elements found in HTML. For example, there are specific server controls for textboxes, lists, hyperlinks and radio buttons. But we can specify that **any** element becomes a 'server control' simply by adding the runat="server" attribute to it, as we did with the <body> element in the listing above:

```
<body id="BodyTag" runat="server" ...>
```

The HtmlGenericControl Class

When ASP.NET finds an element that has the runat="server" attribute, but for which there is no specific server control in the class library, it uses the HtmlGenericControl class to implement this element. The HtmlGenericControl class is defined within the System.Web.UI.HtmlControls namespace. Compared to the more specialist server controls in the class library, HtmlGenericControl has quite a limited set of members (properties, methods, and events). These members apply to any control that is generated from this class – irrespective of the actual element type (tag name). The most useful of these members are:

Member	Description
Attributes property	Returns a collection of all the attribute name/value pairs for the opening tag of the control.
Controls property	Returns a ControlCollection object that references all the child controls defined for this control.
Disabled property	Sets or returns a Boolean value indicating if the control is disabled (has a disabled="disabled" attribute.
EnableViewState property	Sets or returns a Boolean value indicating if the control will persist its viewstate, and the view state of any child controls it contains, between requests.
ID property	Sets or returns the programmatic identifier of the control.

Member	Description
InnerHtml property	Sets or returns the entire content between the opening and closing tags of the control, as it will be rendered in the page.
InnerText property	Sets or returns just the text content between the opening and closing tags of the control, as it will be rendered in the page.
Page property	Returns a reference to the Page instance that contains this control.
Parent property	Returns a reference to the parent control for this control within the page's control hierarchy, if it has a parent.
Style property	Returns a collection of all the cascading stylesheet (CSS) properties (selectors) that are applied to this control when rendered.
TagName property	Sets or returns the tag name of the element that this control generates.
Visible property	Sets or returns a Boolean value that indicates if the control will be rendered when the page is generated.
FindControl method	Searches through all the child controls of this control to find a specific one using its ID value.

A full list of the members for the HtmlGenericControl *can be found in the .NET SDK at:*

ms-help://MS.NETFrameworkSDK/cpref/1
html/frlrfSystemWebUIHtmlControlsHtmlGenericControlClassTopic.htm

Effectively, what this means is that we can generate **any** kind of HTML element using the HtmlGenericControl class. For example, we can create a paragraph of text using this code:

```
<script runat="server">
Sub Page_Load()
  Dim MyPara As New HtmlGenericControl("p")
  MyPara.Attributes.Add("align", "center")
  MyPara.InnerHtml = "This is a new paragraph with TagName '" _
                  & MyPara.TagName & "'."
  Page.Controls.Add(MyPara)
End Sub
</script>
```

This creates a new HtmlGenericControl with the tag name "p", adds an align="center" attribute to it, sets the content to the value of the InnerHtml property, and then adds it to the Controls collection of the page so that it is displayed after any other controls. The HTML that this code creates is:

```
<p align="center">This is a new paragraph with TagName 'p'.</p>
```

Of course, in our 'Home' page, we aren't creating the <body> control from scratch (as we did in the previous listing). However, our 'Home' page code does demonstrate how we can get server-side access to any element in the page if required, simply by defining it as a server control (by adding the runat="server" attribute).

Setting the Styles for the Page

In the previous chapters, we've spent quite a lot of time discussing the ways that we can apply styles and text formatting to our Web Form pages and the output from ASP.NET server controls. In our Wrox Car Company site, we've already decided that we want to provide maximum support for all kinds of browser and user agent, and we do this with a combination of CSS styles and the traditional <font> element. You'll see <font> elements used in several places within the HTML declarations later in this chapter and in other chapters.

We also set the base font size for the page using a <basefont> element within the <head> section of the page:

```
<basefont size="2" />
```

While this is only useful for relative sizes within <font> elements, it's worth putting it onto every page where we might use <font> elements. It can save a lot of effort trying to fix wayward output later on if you decide to include a relative font size, for example <font size="-2"> or <font size="+1">.

Specifying the CSS Style Sheet

To specify the CSS styles, we include them in a separate style sheet and then link this to all the pages in our site using <link> elements. However, there is an issue that needs to be addressed first. We already know that we need to declare the sizes for the text in our pages using the generic 'size names', such as x-small and xx-large, rather than as specific pixel or point sizes (we discussed this in the previous chapter). Unfortunately, not all browsers can agree on the actual display size that these generic sizes represent.

Browsers based on the Netscape and Mozilla engines render these generic sizes 'one smaller' than most other browsers; for example they render small in the same size as Internet Explorer and Opera render medium. So, if we want to get the same text size in both kinds of browser, we need to provide a different stylesheet for each one!

We could go even further and fine-tune the stylesheets for each different type of browser, but this is generally unnecessary. Two will suffice – with the one for Netscape/Mozilla-based clients and any clients that ASP.NET does not recognize (through its browser-detection process) specifying a text size 'one size larger' than the stylesheet for other clients.

The Standard Style Sheet

For example, the following listing shows the stylesheet named wccStandard.css that we use in our Wrox Car Company site for browsers that are recognized by ASP.NET *other than* the Netscape/Mozilla-based ones. We have definitions for the basic page text (body-text) plus a version in a dark red color, definitions for large text in the default color (black) and dark red, and a definition for small text (such as that used above the 'mailing list' text box). There is also a fixed-point-size definition we only use for the tree view controls in the Model Details page, where we require an even smaller font (less than the small-text style):

wccStandard.css

```
.body-text {
  font-family:Tahoma,Arial,Helvetica,sans-serif;
  font-size:x-small;
  padding-left:0; padding-right:0; padding-top:0;
}

.body-red-text {
  font-family:Arial,Helvetica,sans-serif; font-size:x-small; color:#b50055
}

.large-text {
  font-family:Arial,Helvetica,sans-serif; font-size:small;
}

.large-red-text {
  font-family:Arial,Helvetica,sans-serif; font-size:medium; color:#b50055
}

.small-text {
  font-family:Tahoma,Arial,Helvetica,sans-serif; font-size:xx-small;
}

.fixed-small-text {
  font-family:Tahoma,Arial,Helvetica,sans-serif;
  font-size:8pt;
}
```

We also specify the style and colors for hyperlinks. We remove the underline when the link is not active, and prevent it changing to purple after being visited (these might be contentious issues from the navigation usability point of view, but they do preserve the appearance of the page better). We also include a definition that makes the link change to red and become underlined when the mouse hovers over it. These three definitions for 'standard-sized' text links are then repeated for large links (such as the model names in our 'Home' page) and small links (such as the 'read more' links in the 'News' section):

```
.std-link {
  font-family:Tahoma,Arial,Helvetica,sans-serif;
  font-size:x-small; text-decoration:none;
}

.std-link:visited {
  color:#0000ff;
}

.std-link:hover {
  color:#ff0000; text-decoration:underline;
}

.large-link {
  font-family:Arial,Helvetica,sans-serif;
  font-size:small; text-decoration:none;
}
```

```
.large-link:visited {
  color:#0000ff;
}

.large-link:hover {
  color:#ff0000;  text-decoration:underline;
}

.small-link {
  font-family:Tahoma,Arial,Helvetica,sans-serif;
  font-size:xx-small;  text-decoration:none;
}

.small-link:visited {
  color:#0000ff;
}

.small-link:hover {
  color:#ff0000;  text-decoration:underline;
}
```

The Netscape/Mozilla Stylesheet

To provide the two different sets of font sizes, we've chosen to provide a different linked stylesheet for Netscape/Mozilla-based clients and all other clients. We could have defined both 'sets' of styles in one stylesheet using different style names, but this would mean that we would have to dynamically change the `class` attribute for each element in the page depending on the browser type. By using two separate stylesheets, we just need to link the correct one to our page depending on the browser type.

So, our Netscape/Mozilla stylesheet (named `wccLarge.css`) is identical to the one we've just shown, except that each font-size selector is 'one larger'. For example, the `body-text` style is defined as:

wccLarge.css

```
.body-text {
  font-family:Tahoma,Arial,Helvetica,sans-serif;
  font-size:small;
  padding-left:0;  padding-right:0;  padding-top:0;
}
```

This means that we must detect the client type when the site is first accessed, and see which stylesheet we should send to the client. Once we've decided, we can specify the correct one in the `<link>` element within the `<head>` section of our page.

Detecting the Client Type

Within the server-side script section of our page, we declare a `String` variable named `sStyleSize` that will hold part of the name of the stylesheet for the current client, and set the default value to `"Standard"`:

home.aspx

```
<script runat="server">

' page-level variable to client browser type
Dim sStyleSize As String = "Standard"
```

In the `Page_Load` event handler for our 'Home' page, after the code we looked at in the previous chapter that checks for ASP.NET sessions and client-side scripting support, we include code that extracts the current browser 'type' (the manufacturer/browser name) and the major version number (such as 4 or 6):

```
Sub Page_Load()
  ...
  ... code to get UserID from Session (put there by default.aspx)
  ... and get value of "script" from query string *or* Session to see
  ... if browser supports client-side scripting and it is enabled
  ...
  ' get the browser type and version
  Dim sUAType As String = Request.Browser("Browser")
  Dim sUAVer As String = Request.Browser("MajorVersion")
```

As we saw in Chapter 2, the information to populate the `Request.Browser` collection comes from the user agent string that is exposed by the browser. Netscape and Mozilla browsers do not specifically include the manufacturer's name in their user agent string, and so they are both treated as being `Netscape` by the browser detection process, and exposed as such by the `Request.Browser("Browser")` property.

Notice that, if the browser type cannot be determined, we also use the larger size text styles as a precaution in case the client renders them too small to be easily read by the visitor. After figuring out which stylesheet to use, we store the string name (either `"Standard"` or `"Large"` in the user's ASP.NET session as well as in the page-level variable named `sStyleSize`:

```
  ' specify appropriate stylesheet for <link> element
  ' cannot server-side <link> control element as the
  ' presence of an ID attribute stops some browsers
  ' from loading the stylesheet! Netscape and Amaya
  ' require larger font sizes to be specified
  If sUAType = "Netscape" Or sUAType = "Unknown" Or sUAType = "" Then
    sStyleSize = "Large"
  End If
  Session("WccStyleSize") = sStyleSize    ' store in Session
  ...
  ... code to build rest of dynamic page content goes here
  ...
End Sub
```

Linking to the Correct Stylesheet

Now that we have the correct stylesheet name part, we can populate the `<link>` element in our page with the full style sheet `href` value. We want our page to contain one of the following two `<link>` elements, depending on the browser we are serving this page to:

```
<link rel="stylesheet" type="text/css" href="stylesheets/wccStandard.css" />
```

or:

```
<link rel="stylesheet" type="text/css" href="stylesheets/wccLarge.css" />
```

Having seen the earlier discussion about using an `HtmlGenericControl` for the `<body>` element of the page, so that we can dynamically add an `onload` attribute, it would also seem to be a good way to add the appropriate `href` attribute to the `<link>` element. In the page, we could declare the server control as:

```
<link id="lnkStyle" rel="stylesheet" type="text/css" runat="server" />
```

Then, in our `Page_Load` event handler we could add the appropriate `href` attribute:

```
lnkStyle.Attributes.Add("href", "stylesheets/wcc" & sStyleSize & ".css")
```

This is what we tried first, but unfortunately we came up against a problem in Netscape 4.x. Some minor versions seem to ignore the `<link>` element if it has an `id` attribute before the `href` attribute. But we need one to be able to access the control in our server-side code, and ASP.NET automatically places it before any dynamically added attributes.

While this effect was not 100% repeatable in tests, we decided to use the more traditional (ASP 3.0 style) technique for inserting the `href` attribute value instead. We simply place the variable inside an ASP 'render block' (a pair of `<%` and `%>` tags). OK, so it's not as elegant as the first suggestion, but it works fine and avoids any issues that may arise when an `id` attribute is included:

```
<link rel="stylesheet" type="text/css"
      href="stylesheets/wcc<% = sStyleSize %>.css" />
```

In other pages of the site that use the same stylesheets, we can simply extract the value for the stylesheet 'name part' from the user's session. We don't need to query the `Request.Browser` object properties again. For example, in the **Compare Features** page (`compare.aspx`), we use:

compare.aspx
```
' get style sheet size from Session
sStyleSize = CType(Session("WccStyleSize"), String)
```

Then we use the same `<link>` element definition as in our 'Home' page, which takes this value and selects the correct stylesheet.

Providing Accessibility Navigational Aids

It's very easy to forget how the majority of visitors to your site just click away with their mouse on anything that looks interesting, without really worrying too much about where these links are within the page. Stick some nice big graphic on the middle of the page, and visitors can click on it to see what it's all about.

But, if that visitor is not as physically able as the majority of visitors, they may well be using a non-graphical user agent or specialist client. Then, navigation goes from being a happy point and click affair to something that requires a lot more effort. For a simple example, look at our 'Home' page in the Lynx text-only browser:

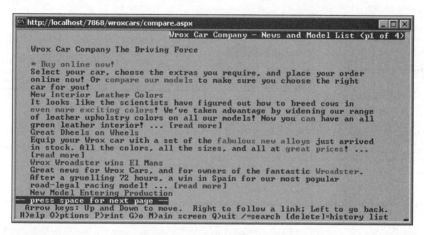

The content looks fine. The `alt` attribute we defined for the banner graphic shows up at the top of the page, so the user can tell what the site 'name' is. However, all that they see on this first section ("p1 of 4" because Lynx breaks each page down into sections based on the size of the DOS window) is the first few 'News' items. To see what vehicle models we offer, and the links to other pages on the site, they have to scroll through the sections looking for what they require. And that's assuming that they have been here before, remember the page and site layout, and know where to find what they're looking for!

For visitors with poor or no vision, and who rely on a page reader client, things are even worse. The page reader will announce the site name and slogan, using the `alt` attributes from our banner graphics, and then start to read the list of 'News' items – pausing on each 'read more' hyperlink as it goes. You can tell what the user will hear by looking at the central section in the next screenshot of the IBM Home Page Reader:

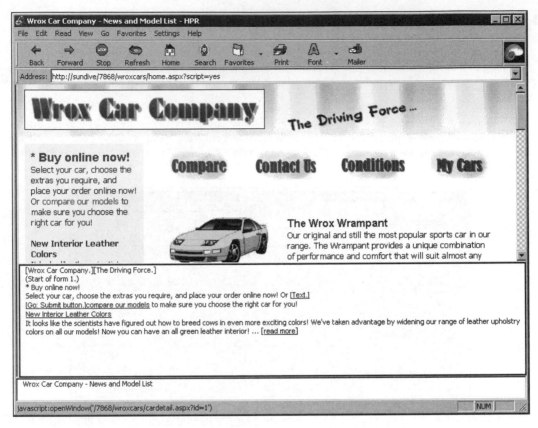

Obviously we need to do something to help visitors using these types of user agent find the content they are looking for on the page. The generally accepted way to do this is with 'Skip To' links.

Implementing 'Skip To' Links

It's clear from the previous section that we aren't making life easy for visitors who use these kinds of clients. Some sites are even worse than ours, for example they may have myriad links to other pages at the top of each page, or long 'menu bars' down the left-hand side of the page. How long will your visitor sit listening to these links being read out to them on every page, or spend scanning each page for useful content in a text-only browser? And maybe they might even decide to start a legal action based on Section 508 (see the end of the previous chapter) because your site is obviously not 'properly accessible'.

In fact, we removed some content from our 'Home' page when we took the preceding screenshots to demonstrate just how these often ignored issues affect some disadvantaged visitors. In our actual 'Home' page, and in every other page, we include 'skip to' links that appear as the first items in the page. They allow the visitor to go directly to specific parts of the page. In the next screenshot of the 'Home' page in Lynx (after we put them back into our page), you can see these links above the site name:

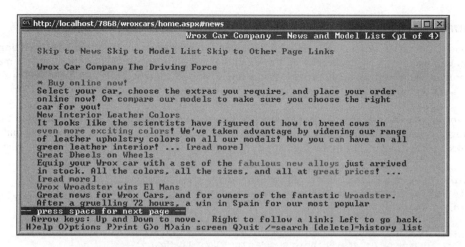

When the same page is opened in the IBM Home Page Reader, these links are read to the user first – as you can see in the central section of the next screenshot. In the case of visitors who suffer vision problems and depend on aural browsers like this one, 'skip to' links are probably one of the most useful navigational aids we can provide:

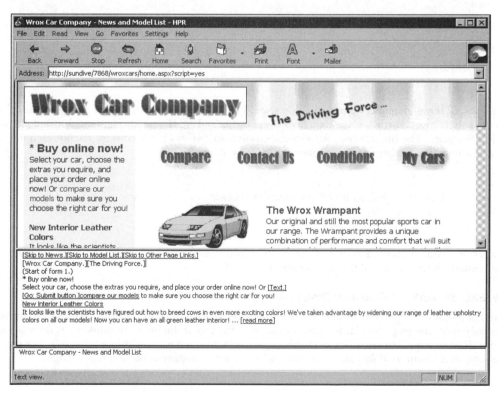

The Source Code for the 'Skip To' Links

Obviously, the set of 'skip to' links we include depends on the page content, and which sections we feel visitors will want to navigate directly to. For example, in a simple page that contains only a menu bar and content, we would probably provide just a single 'skip to content' link. You'll see this in some of the other pages on our site.

However, in our 'Home' page (as you've seen in the previous screenshots) we provide three links, allowing the visitor to skip directly to the 'News' section, the list of models, or the section that contains the links to other pages. The following listing shows the code we use to implement these links:

```
<div style="position:absolute;height:0px;"><font size="1" color=#ffffff>
<!-- skip links for aural page readers -->
<layer visibility="hidden">
<a href="#news" style="color:#ffffff;font-size:1px;text-decoration:none">
  <img width="1" height="1" hspace="0" vspace="0" src="images/_blnk.gif"
      border="0" style="height:0" alt="Skip to News" />
</a>
<a href="#models" style="color:#ffffff;font-size:1px;text-decoration:none">
  <img width="1" height="1" hspace="0" vspace="0" src="images/_blnk.gif"
      border="0" style="height:0" alt="Skip to Model List" />
</a>
<a href="#links" style="color:#ffffff;font-size:1px;text-decoration:none">
  <img width="1" height="1" hspace="0" vspace="0" src="images/_blnk.gif"
      border="0" style="height:0" alt="Skip to Other Page Links" />
</a>
</layer>
</font></div>
```

Amongst all these elements we include, you should be able to pick out the three `<a>` elements that have, as their `href` attributes, the names of three ordinary HTML anchor elements located elsewhere within the page. The first of these, for example, points to `"#news"`, which is an anchor element named news located in the table cell that contains the 'News' items:

```
...
<td width="25%" rowspan="2" bgcolor="#ffffaa" valign="top">
  <a name="news" />
  ... cell content goes here ...
```

The same technique is used to provide anchors named models and links in the relevant table cells that contain these sections of the page content.

Hiding 'Skip To' Links in Graphical Browsers

One issue that often puts site designers off implementing 'skip to' links (besides laziness, of course) is that they want the page content to appear flush with the top of the browser window, as does the banner in our 'Home' page. However, if the visible page content is contained within a table or other block element, these 'skip to' links can cause extra white space to appear at the top of the page.

The common approach to solving this problem is to use single pixel transparent GIF images within the hyperlink, as we have done in our code above, and even specify the width and height as zero rather than one pixel. However, this still forces white space to appear as a narrow band above any following block-level element(s). It's worse in some browsers than in others (for example Internet Explorer 6 shows more white space that Netscape 6).

You might be tempted to set the CSS style for the images to prevent them upsetting the display, for example using "visibility:hidden" or "display:none". However, doing this is an own-goal, because then the browser or page reader will ignore them. After all, you've told it that they aren't visible or that they aren't part of the page, so why would the browser display them?

Getting rid of the unwanted white space altogether, in all browsers, therefore involves a more cunning approach. We found that a combination of settings does the trick in all browsers we could find to test our page. You might decide to implement only a subset of these settings (after all, we have gone somewhat to extremes here), but if you do, make sure you test the page in all your target browsers:

- ❑ Remember to include the alt attribute on the <img> element, as this is the sole reason for using 'skip to' links in the first place!

- ❑ Make sure that the <img> element contains the minimum height and width sizes (preferably one pixel in case a browser decides that the image will be omitted with zero height and width).

- ❑ Set the horizontal and vertical spacing attributes (hspace and vspace) to zero for the <img> element, and include the attribute border="0" on the <img> element to hide the border.

- ❑ Include a style="height:0" attribute on the <img> element to reduce the height to zero in browsers that support CSS.

- ❑ For the <a> element, specify a style that reduces the text to a minimum size, set the color to that of the page or banner background, and remove the underline to help it disappear if none of the other settings hide it.

- ❑ Wrap this lot in a <layer> element with the visibility="hidden" attribute for Navigator 4, which doesn't properly recognize the CSS settings. It's unlikely that any text-based browser or aural page reader will use the Navigator 4 rendering engine.

- ❑ Then, to make sure that any following relatively-positioned elements are not misplaced, wrap all this in a <div> element that is absolutely positioned with zero height. Maybe even include a <font> element inside the <div> to enforce the text sizes specified for the <a> elements as an extra precaution.

Note that some browsers, notably Opera, still place white space above, and to the left and right of the banner. However, as we discovered in the previous chapter, this is because Opera does not allow the page margin to be reduced to zero.

Remember those 'title' and 'alt' Attributes

One other point worth reinforcing here is to remember the 'rules' about alt and title attributes that we discussed at the end of the previous chapter. They are vital for non-graphical user agents, and also make it easier for graphical browser users as well. For example, if you use icons to represent links or options, you can use the alt and title attributes to provide extra information (the meaning of the link as text).

In HTML 4, almost every element (including all visual elements) accepts the `title` attribute. Some elements will not actually display this in a graphical browser, though most do. More important, however, is that any suitably-equipped user agent will be able to read these `title` attribute values, and it might find ways to present this information to the user so that it makes their life much easier.

As an example, we include the `title` attribute in the `<td>` element that creates the table cell holding the links to other pages on our site:

```
<td width="75%" wrap="nowrap" title="Links to other pages">
```

Within this cell are the links themselves, made up of images and hyperlinks like this:

```
<a title="Compare Models" href="compare.aspx">
  <img src="images/btn_compare.gif" width="100" height="49"
       alt="Compare Models" border="0" /></a>
```

We've set the `alt` attribute of the image, and the `title` attribute of the hyperlink, to the same text values. The result is that when the mouse moves over the table cell it displays the title of the cell, but when over the link images it displays the `title` of the `<a>` element or the `alt` value of the `<img>` element:

This could well prove useful in a page reader user agent. It could indicate that the table cell it is currently 'reading' contains "Links to other pages", and then read the `title`/`alt` values for each link in turn. It doesn't require that much extra effort, and yet provides a far more accessible interface.

However, one point to watch out for is that child elements or other contained elements often inherit the `title` value. For example, if we set the `title` attribute of a table cell (as just demonstrated), but then use `<a>` elements as hyperlinks without setting their own `title` attributes, the value of the `title` attribute from the table cell will be displayed when the mouse pointer is over the hyperlink.

So, if the cell has the title 'Main news section', a text-only hyperlink within it saying 'New Leather Colors' will display the text 'Main news section' as the pop-up tool-tip for this link. To avoid this, we have to set the `title` attribute of the hyperlink – probably to something more suitable like 'Read more about this topic'.

The Links to Other Pages

Our 'Home' page contains prominent links to the other main sections of the site as four clickable images. We used images to maintain the 'look and feel' of the page, and they are implemented (as we saw in the previous section) simply as a combination of `<a>` and `<img>` elements:

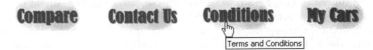

This whole section is a single cell within the main table that provides the structure for the page. However, to achieve the layout we want, these four images must be equally spaced within the table cell (between the 'News' section and the right-hand edge of the page). We get this effect by inserting them into a `<table>` within the existing table cell. The following listing shows the HTML source for this section (we'll discuss the validation summary control located in this section when we come to examine the way that the mailing list feature works):

```
...
<!-- cell in main page table -->
<td width="75%" wrap="nowrap">
  <table width="100%" border="0" cellpadding="0" cellspacing="0"
        title="Links to other pages">
    <tr>
      <td align="center">
        <a name="links" />
        <a title="Compare Models" href="compare.aspx">
          <img src="images/btn_compare.gif" width="100" height="49"
              alt="Compare Models" border="0" /></a>
      </td>
      <td align="center">
        <a title="Contact Us" href="contact.aspx">
          <img src="images/btn_contact.gif" width="100" height="49"
              alt="Contact Us" border="0" /></a>
      </td>
      <td align="center">
        <a title="Terms and Conditions" href="tandc.aspx">
          <img src="images/btn_tandc.gif" width="100" height="49"
              alt="Terms and Conditions" border="0" /></a>
      </td>
      <td align="center">
        <a title="My Cars" href="secure/mycars.aspx">
          <img src="images/btn_mycars.gif" width="100" height="49"
              alt="My Cars" border="0" /></a>
      </td>
    </tr>
    <tr>
      <td colspan="4" align="center">
        ... a validation summary control is declared here and this is ...
        ... discussed in next chapter in connection with mailing list ...
      </td>
    </tr>
  </table>
</td>
...
```

So there is nothing really exciting or unexpected here – it's just a conventional use of HTML elements. We set the `alt` attribute for each one as well as specifying the `width` and `height`. If the browser window is less than 640px wide, this table cell (with the nowrap attribute) will control how wide this cell is and how wide the cell below, which holds the list of models, is. So the browser can figure out these dimensions, plus the height of this cell, from the `width` and `height` attributes – without waiting to load the images.

Why not use ASP.NET server controls here? The reason is that we don't need to access the elements in our server-side code, so they don't have to be server controls (no `runat="server"` attribute). By using 'normal' HTML elements, we avoid the extra processing overhead that server controls would require.

The ASP.NET Hyperlink Control

However, if we did need to access the page link elements on the server, perhaps to change the image depending on whether a visitor has registered with us in the past, we would probably use ASP.NET `Hyperlink` controls here. A simple definition such as the following will cover our requirements for each of the clickable images:

```
<asp:Hyperlink id="lnkCompare" runat="server"
               NavigateUrl="compare.aspx"
               ImageUrl="images/btn_compare.gif"
               Tooltip="Compare Models"
               Text="Compare Models"
               Width="100"
               Height="49" />
```

In an "up-level" client (Internet Explorer 4 and above), the resulting HTML that this control generates is:

```
<a id="lnkCompare" title="Compare Models" href="compare.aspx"
style="height:49px;width:100px;"><img title="Compare Models" src="PlayButton.gif"
alt="Compare Models" border="0" /></a>
```

In a "down-level" client, the control generates similar visual output, setting the `title` and `alt` attributes of the `<a>` and `<img>` elements as required. However, there is one area where the control could have been a bit more intelligent. We specified the image width and height in the properties of the `Hyperlink` control, but these are ignored when output is generated for "down-level" clients.

The reason is that there is no `style` attribute generated in this case (behavior we'd expect after seeing the way that the controls work in different browsers in Chapter 2). However, we would probably also expect the control to go that extra distance and use the values we provide to set the `height` and `width` attributes of the `<img>` control. Unfortunately, it doesn't. And to make matters worse, we can't access the `<img>` element ourselves in code to add these attributes dynamically (because the HTML elements generated by the control are not themselves server controls).

Setting the 'title' and 'alt' Attributes

You can't actually tell by looking at the output generated by the `Hyperlink` control in the previous example, because we used the same values for the `Tooltip` and `Text` properties, but it is important to set both of these properties. The value we supply for the `Tooltip` property is used to set the `title` attribute for the `<a>` and `<img>` elements. However, the value we provide for the `Text` property is used in different ways depending on the type of link we're creating.

If we don't provide a value for the `ImageUrl` property, the control will generate a simple `<a>` element and use the value of the `Text` property as the text for the hyperlink. However, when we **do** provide a value for the `ImageUrl` property, the control generates the nested `<a>` and `<img>` elements we've seen earlier, and then uses the value of the `Text` property as the `alt` attribute of the `<img>` element. This is what most non-graphical and specialist user agents will use to 'describe' the image to the user.

The 'News and Special Offers' Section

The section that shows news, events, special offers, and so on sits at the left-hand side of our 'Home' page, with a light yellow background separating it from the remainder of the page content. The section heading ("Buy online now!") and the first paragraph of text are static – they are declared within the HTML source of the page. However, the remaining news items are generated dynamically from a database each time the page is accessed.

This book is not really aimed at teaching you about data access techniques, and so we're not going to be building complex *n*-tier data access components. Instead, we use code in our pages to directly access stored procedures within the database. In this book, we're more interested in how we display the data rather that how we manipulate it behind the scenes (for a discussion of *n*-tier data access techniques, see *ASP.NET Distributed Data Applications* from Wrox Press (ISBN 1-86100-492-3)).

Only a précis of each news item is shown in this section of the page, but the heading and the 'read more' hyperlinks can be used to view the complete item (we'll see an example of this in the next chapter).

> *** Buy online now!**
>
> Select your car, choose the extras you require, and place your order online now! Or compare our models to make sure you choose the right car for you!
>
> **New Interior Leather Colors**
> It looks like the scientists have figured out how to breed cows in **even more exciting colors**! We've taken advantage by widening our range of leather upholstry colors on all our models! Now you **can** have an all green leather interior! ... [read more]
>
> **Great Dheels on Wheels**
> Equip your Wrox car with a set of the **fabulous new alloys** just arrived in stock. All the colors, all

The Data Access Code for the 'News' List

The `WroxCars` database (which you can install from the downloadable samples) contains a table named `tblNews`, which itself contains four columns. The `NewsID` column is a numeric (`int`) column that forms the primary key, and it is also an `Identity` column (unique values for this column are generated automatically as rows are added to the table). The remaining three columns, `NewsTitle`, `NewsPrecis` and `NewsText`, are all of type `varchar` (the values are 'text' strings).

The GetNewsList Stored Procedure

The database also contains a stored procedure named `GetNewsList` that returns all the news items from the `tblNews` table:

Stored procedure: GetNewsList

```
SELECT NewsID, NewsTitle, NewsPrecis FROM tblNews ORDER BY NewsID DESC
```

This is a simple approach, and means that the page will show all the news items in the database table every time, in reverse order in which they were added. We would have to add and delete rows to change the items that are displayed. Instead, you may prefer to include extra columns in the table that define when each news item should be shown from (`DisplayFrom`), when it should no longer be displayed (`DisplayUntil`), and even the order that they should be displayed (`DisplayOrder`). For example:

```
SELECT NewsID, NewsTitle, NewsPrecis FROM tblNews
WHERE DATEDIFF(day, DisplayFrom, getdate()) >= 0
AND DATEDIFF(day, DisplayUntil, getdate()) < 0
ORDER BY DisplayOrder DESC
```

We're using Microsoft SQL Server as our database, and so we can use the classes and objects from the `System.Data.SqlClient` namespace to access this stored procedure (and any other data we need). To use these classes in our page, we must import the appropriate namespaces. Visual Studio .NET imports these into your projects automatically, but when using other editors you will probably have to add them yourself:

```
<%@Import Namespace="System.Data"%>
<%@Import Namespace="System.Data.SqlClient"%>
```

To use any other database, you will need to import the `OleDb` or `Odbc` namespaces instead:

```
<%@Import Namespace="System.Data"%>
<%@Import Namespace="System.Data.OleDb"%>
```

or:

```
<%@Import Namespace="System.Data"%>
<%@Import Namespace="System.Data.Odbc"%>
```

> *The classes that implement the namespace* `System.Data.Odbc` *are not part of the standard .NET installation in version 1.0, and must be downloaded and installed separately from the Microsoft Universal Data Access web site at http://www.microsoft.com/data/.*

The GetNewsListDR Function

We execute the `GetNewsList` stored procedure from within a function named `GetNewsListDR`, declared in our `home.aspx` 'Home' page. This function is shown in the next listing, and you can see that it uses standard ADO.NET data access techniques:

home.aspx

```
' function to get list of new items for Repeater control
Function GetNewsListDR() As SqlDataReader
  Try
    Dim sqlConnect As SqlConnection = New SqlConnection(sConnect)
    Dim sProcName As String = "GetNewsList"
    Dim sqlComm As SqlCommand = New SqlCommand(sProcName, sqlConnect)
    sqlComm.CommandType = CommandType.StoredProcedure
    sqlConnect.Open
```

```
      Return sqlComm.ExecuteReader(CommandBehavior.CloseConnection)
   Catch
      Return Nothing
   End Try
End Function
```

This code creates a new `SqlConnection` object using the connection string that we've previously placed in a page-level variable named `sConnect` (you'll see where this is done shortly). Then it defines the name of the stored procedure we want to call, and creates a new `SqlCommand` object using this name and the `SqlConnection` object. The `CommandType` for the `SqlCommand` object is set to `CommandType.StoredProcedure`. This makes access more efficient as ADO.NET then knows what the command itself represents – a stored procedure and not a table name or SQL statement.

To get the data from the database, we open the connection and call the `ExecuteReader` method of the `SqlCommand` object. This returns a `SqlDataReader` object which points to the results set generated by the stored procedure, ready for use in our page. We simply return this `SqlDataReader` as the result of our function.

The CommandBehavior Parameter for the ExecuteReader Method

Notice that we include the value `CloseConnection` for the `CommandBehavior` parameter in the call to the `ExecuteReader` method. This is extremely important, because the underlying connection to the database remains open after we return the `DataReader` from our function to the calling routine. It has to be open so that the data can be accessed. However, once we've finished with the `DataReader`, the connection will remain open until explicitly closed, wasting precious resources.

When we specify the value `CloseConnection` for the `CommandBehavior` parameter, the `DataReader` will automatically close its underlying connection to the database when the `DataReader` itself is destroyed (when it goes out of scope in our page, or when we destroy it explicitly by setting it to `Nothing` in VB.NET or `null` in C#).

Data Binding the Repeater Control

So, now that we've got a function that returns a `DataReader`, all we need to do is bind the `DataReader` it returns to the ASP.NET `Repeater` control in our page. It will then generate the output to fill our 'News' section (we'll look at the declaration of the `Repeater` control in the next section).

We have a page-level variable named `sConnect` declared within the server-side `<script>` section of the page (you saw this being used in the `GetNewsListDR` function earlier on):

home.aspx

```
<script runat="server">
' page-level variable to hold database connection string
Dim sConnect As String
```

In the `Page_Load` event handler, we set this variable to the value of the connection string for our `WroxCars` database. The connection string is stored in the `appSettings` section of the two `web.config` files we use for our site (in the `wroxcars` and `cookieless-wroxcars` folders):

web.config

```
<configuration>

  <appSettings>
    <add key="WroxCarsConnectString"
         value="server=localhost;database=WroxCars;uid=anon;pwd=;" />
  </appSettings>

</configuration>
```

So, to get the connection string from within any page, all we need to do is reference the AppSettings collection of the default ConfigurationSettings object that is exposed by the page:

home.aspx

```
Sub Page_Load()
  ...
  ... other code to get user ID, etc. goes here
  ...
  ' get database connection string from web.config
  sConnect = ConfigurationSettings.AppSettings("WroxCarsConnectString")
  ...
```

Then we can use the DataReader we get back from the GetNewsListDR method as the DataSource of our Repeater control, and call the DataBind method to display the data:

```
  ...
  ' set DataSource for "news" list and data-bind it
  repNews.DataSource = GetNewsListDR()
  repNews.DataBind()
  ...
  ... other non-relevant code here, omitted for clarity
  ...
End Sub
```

Choosing the Appropriate ASP.NET 'List' Control

As you can see from the earlier screenshot, the output we're looking for in our 'News' list is simply a series of separate paragraphs, each containing the précis of the new items in our database (taken from the NewsPrecis column of our tblNews table).

ASP.NET provides several types of list control that we can use to generate repeated content from a range of data sources. We use a range of list controls in the pages of our Wrox Car Company site. Choosing which control to use involves thinking about what you actually want the control to achieve. The following table showing all the list controls should help. While the first four are relatively obvious in the way that they are used, the last three often do need some extra consideration when selecting which is the most appropriate:

Control	Useful when you need to ...
CheckBoxList	... create a list of checkboxes, from which more than one can be selected.
RadioButtonList	... create a list of radio or option buttons, from which only one can be selected.
DropDownList	... create a drop-down selection list, from which only one item can be selected and you want to minimize the space used on the page.
ListBox	... create a list where more than one item is visible. Can be configured so that users can select only one item, or so that they can select more than one item.
Repeater	... repeat any type of content that you specifically define, without the control applying any of its own structuring or formatting to the content. Simpler, lighter and more efficient than the DataList or DataGrid, but with fewer features. Templates are used to define the format and layout of the content, and any line breaks, paragraph divisions, etc. must be specifically declared within these templates.
DataList	... lay out content in the cells of a table, or repeated across or down the page in columns. A powerful control, which is one-step up from the Repeater in complexity and in use of resources. By default it lays out the content generated for each item in the data source within one cell of an HTML <table>, though it can also be used like the Repeater (without generating a <table> – called "flow layout" mode). It also provides a header and footer than can be formatted separately, and it can lay content out vertically or horizontally in columns when in "table layout" mode.
DataGrid	... build an HTML table where each value is in a separate column, so that it looks like a grid. It provides the most control over content, and the most extra features. As well as headers and footers, the control can divide the list of items across multiple 'pages', provide automatic in-line editing features, easily link code to events raised by controls in each row, and even automatically generate the columns based on the data source contents. A wide range of formatting options allows attractive layouts to be constructed.

From the table above, it's pretty easy to see that the best choice for our 'News' list is a Repeater control. We can define all the content and formatting within the control's templates – as you'll see when we come to look at the code for our 'Home' page shortly.

The Static Section of the 'News' List

Before we look at the Repeater control in our page, however, the following listing shows the outline of the 'News' section and the static content it contains. You can see the anchor named news for our 'skip to' link. For the headings and text in the first paragraph of this section we use a combination of CSS styles (defined as the class attribute of the <span> elements) and <font> elements to format the content. Because the <span> elements are inside the <font> elements, the CSS styles take precedence in browsers that support CSS. For other browsers and clients, the <font> elements still provide a close approximation to the formatting we want:

```
...
<td width="25%" rowspan="2" bgcolor="#ffffaa" valign="top">
  <a name="news" />
  <font face="Arial,Helvetica,sans-serif" size="4" color="#b50055">
  <span class="large-red-text"><b>* Buy online now!</b></span><br />
  </font><font face="Tahoma,Arial,Helvetica,sans-serif" size="2">
  <span class="body-text">Select your car, choose the extras you
    require, and place your order online now! Or
  </span>
  <a class="std-link" href="compare.aspx">compare our models</a>
  <span class="body-text"> to make sure you choose the right
    car for you!</span><br /><br />
  ...
  ... Repeater control declaration goes here
  ...
  ... Controls for the mailing list section go here
  ...
</td>
...
```

We'll be looking at how the mailing list controls work (declared at the end of this section of code) in the next chapter. We'll move on and look at the 'News' `Repeater` control declaration next.

The ASP.NET Repeater Control for the 'News' List

A `Repeater` control provides no 'structure' of its own (it doesn't create an HTML table, or even separate the items with a `<br />` element). This means that we must specify how we want the items within the data source of the control to be displayed, using at least an `<ItemTemplate>` section.

> *The `Repeater` control supports five templates, for the header, footer, item, alternating item and separator. For a full reference to the Repeater control, see the .NET SDK page:*
>
> ms-help://MS.NETFrameworkSDK/cpref/html/frlrfSystemWebUIWebControlsRepeaterPropertiesTopic.htm

The ASP.NET `Repeater` control we use to display the list of 'News' items is shown in the next listing. The contents of the `<ItemTemplate>` section are automatically repeated for each item in the data source (once for each row in the rowset exposed by our `DataReader`). Within this template we use an ASP.NET `Hyperlink` control for the news item title (displaying the text as a hyperlink) followed by a normal HTML `<span>` element that contains the précis of the item. After this comes the [read more] hyperlink, which is created by another ASP.NET `Hyperlink` control, within a `<span>` element that specifies the format of the text and the square brackets:

```
<asp:Repeater id="repNews" runat="server">
  <ItemTemplate><font face="Tahoma,Arial,Helvetica,sans-serif" size="2">
    <b>
    <asp:Hyperlink runat="server" CssClass="std-link"
      Text='<%# Container.DataItem("NewsTitle") %>'
      NavigateUrl='<%# DataBinder.Eval(Container.DataItem, "NewsID", _
                                       "readnews.aspx?id={0}") %>' />
    </b><br />
    <span class="body-text"><%# Container.DataItem("NewsPrecis") %>
     ... </span>
```

```
        <font size="1"><span class="small-text">
          [<asp:Hyperlink runat="server" CssClass="small-link"
                        Text='read more'
          NavigateUrl='<%# DataBinder.Eval(Container.DataItem, "NewsID", _
                                    "readnews.aspx?id={0}") %>' />]
        </span></font><br /><br /></font>
      </ItemTemplate>
    </asp:Repeater>
```

Notice that the complete output for each of the rows (the content of the <ItemTemplate> section) is wrapped in a <font> element that defines the format and appearance of the text for clients that don't support CSS. However, within the <font> and </font> tags of this element each <span> element has its class attribute set so that browsers which do recognize CSS will use this to format and style the output.

The [read more] text is one size smaller than the rest of the text, achieved with a nested <font> element with the attribute size="1" (the font face is inherited from the enclosing <font> element), or by the CSS styles small-text and small-link that are applied as the class attributes of the enclosed <span> elements.

The <ItemTemplate> content ends with two <br /> elements. Remember that, as the Repeater control does not generate any layout information, we have to specify it all ourselves within the templates we define for the control. The two <br /> elements we use here are inserted into the HTML output after the rest of the content that is generated by the <ItemTemplate> for each row or item in the data source.

Data Binding Syntax in a List Control Template

To get the values from the data source rowset into the page, we use the special data binding syntax shown in the previous listing. There are two basic approaches for working with data that is exposed as a rowset, as is the case with our DataReader object: we can specify the data source column name directly, or we can use the Eval method of the DataBinder object to extract and optionally format the data.

The simplest approach is to specify the column name directly, using the syntax:

```
<%# Container.DataItem("column-name") %>
```

In our listing above, we use this statement directly (within the <span> element that specifies our text formatting and style) to provide the précis of the news item, specifying the column NewsPrecis:

```
<%# Container.DataItem("NewsPrecis") %>
```

We can also use this syntax within the declaration of an attribute for a control, for example we use it to set the Text property of the first Hyperlink control to the value of the NewsTitle column in our rowset:

```
<asp:Hyperlink runat="server" CssClass="std-link"
            Text='<%# Container.DataItem("NewsTitle") %>'
            ...
```

*Notice that we have to use double-quotes around the column name within the data-binding block
(the statement or code within the <%# and %> delimiters). So, when we use this to specify the value
of an attribute for the control, we must use single quotes around the complete block.*

However, if we want to format the values contained in the rowset when they are displayed, we can use
the `Eval` method of the `DataBinder` object that is exposed by the list control itself. This method takes
two or three parameters. The first is a reference to the data source item (`Container.DataItem` – the
same as we used directly in the previous example), and the second is the name of the column within this
row or item that we want to display:

```
<%# DataBinder.Eval(Container.DataItem, "column-name") %>
```

The optional third parameter is a 'format string' that defines how the output will appear. We can use
standard format strings as defined within .NET, with `{0}` being the placeholder for the value. For
example, to format a number as currency, we could use:

```
<%# DataBinder.Eval(Container.DataItem, "column-name", "{0:C}") %>
```

*See the .NET SDK topic:
ms-help://MS.NETFrameworkSDK/cpguidenf/html/cpconformattingtypes.htm
for more details about the format strings that can be used.*

Where the `Eval` method is really useful is when we need to build up a string value that contains the
value of a column. In our example, we want the URL of our hyperlink to be the page `readnews.aspx`,
with the `id` of the current item appended to the query string. For this, we can use the format string
`"readnews.aspx?id={0}"`. The `{0}` part will be replaced by the value of the column when the data
is bound:

```
<asp:Hyperlink runat="server" CssClass="std-link"
               Text='<%# Container.DataItem("NewsTitle") %>'
               NavigateUrl='<%# DataBinder.Eval(Container.DataItem, "NewsID", _
                                      "readnews.aspx?id={0}") %>' />
```

Exactly the same approach is taken to set the `NavigateUrl` property of the second hyperlink in the
`<ItemTemplate>`, which generates the [read more] link. The only difference here is that the text for
the link is the same for each item. Notice how we avoid extra white space around the hyperlink by
careful placing of the square brackets and closing `</font>` and `</span>` tags:

```
...
<font size="1"><span class="small-text">
[<asp:Hyperlink runat="server" CssClass="small-link"
      Text='read more'
      NavigateUrl='<%# DataBinder.Eval(Container.DataItem, "NewsID", _
                              "readnews.aspx?id={0}") %>' />]
</span></font><br /><br /></font>
```

*Remember that the content of the data-binding block is code that is executed when the binding takes
place. So if we break the block across more than one line in VB.NET, we have to include the line
continuation character, as shown above. In C#, this is not, of course, required.*

Also in C#, because there is no implicit type conversion, it's common practice to use the `Eval` *method for all data binding statements, and avoid the simpler syntax we used earlier in VB.NET. The* `Eval` *method is marginally less efficient than directly specifying the column name, but the advantage of the automatic output-formatting feature generally outweighs this.*

The List of Car Models

The main right-hand section of our 'Home' page contains a list of the different vehicles that are available from the Wrox Car Company. For each one, we provide a small graphic image and the model name, both of which are hyperlinks that visitors can follow to see the standard features, configure the vehicle to suit their requirements, and discover how much it costs to purchase.

Under the image is the basic price for the vehicle, and below the model name in the right-hand column is a short description of the vehicle followed by a hyperlink where visitors can compare various features of the different vehicles:

Prices from **$22,995.00**

The Wrox Wrampant

Our original and still the most popular sports car in our range. The Wrampant provides a unique combination of performance and comfort 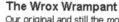almost any driver. Happy around town, and yet with extra horses under the bonnet so that you can take advantage of the open road. With its 2 x 2 seat combination, and spacious luggage carrying features, it makes an ideal car for both short and long journeys. ...
[compare models]

Prices from **$27,950.00**

The Wrox Wranger

Whether you've got a big job to do, a lot of equipment to carry, or you just like to give the appearance of being a big-city farmer, the Wranger is the ideal truck for you. Hugely powerful, massively strong, and unbelievably reliable, it will easily handle everything you can throw at it. ... [compare models]

Choosing the Appropriate List Control

As you can see from the screenshot, we wanted two distinct columns for this part of the page. The easiest way to achieve this is with a two-column table placed within the current cell of the main page structure table. If we had chosen a `Repeater` control, we would have to create this nested table ourselves, by placing the `<table>` and `</table>` around the complete control declaration, and then creating each two-column row within the `<ItemTemplate>` section of the control.

The next choice would be a `DataList` control, as this can create a complete HTML table containing a single row for each item in the data source. However, this would have made it awkward to get the two-column layout, as we would then have to use the `align` attribute of each image to force the text to wrap to the right of it, and it would be very difficult to get the price below the image while guaranteeing that the layout remained constant irrespective of the browser window width.

Of course, we could create a two-column table within each cell that the DataList control creates. This involves using the ASP.NET Table, TableRow, and TableCell server controls, and setting the ExtractTemplateRows property of the DataList to True as well. Without this, the DataList control ignores any table elements that are placed within its templates. And doing it this way, we'd have ended up with tables nested three deep – the main structure table for the page would have a table generated by the DataList control inside the current cell. This table would consist of a single-cell row for each item, with a nested table inside each of these cells!

Instead, to best meet our layout requirements, the obvious choice here is a DataGrid control. This will create a table containing a row for each item in the data source, and each row will have the number of cells that we specify when we declare the DataGrid control in our page. We'll see what this declaration looks like shortly.

Changing the Behavior for Script-Enabled Clients

One other aspect of this part of the page is that the way it works changes depending on whether the current user's browser supports client-side scripting or not. We decided that the hyperlinks in this section, which open the page where the user can configure the vehicle, should display that page in a separate browser window.

The reason is that this allows users to view and configure more than one vehicle at a time, and decide on the final configuration they require afterwards. There is some interesting debate amongst web designers and users as to whether pop-up windows like this are acceptable, but there are several quite legitimate reasons for using them – and we feel this is one. Besides, it gives us the opportunity to demonstrate some extra features of ASP.NET Web Forms and server controls.

> *The 'compare models' link opens its target page in the same window, and not in a new browser window like the other two hyperlinks for the image and the model name.*

So, if the current user's browser supports client-side scripting, we use hyperlinks that execute a client-side script function to open a new browser window at a specific position, and with specific window furniture (menus, toolbars, and so on) that we specify in this client-side code. However, if the user's browser does not support client-side scripting, we use a normal <a> element but with the target attribute set to "_blank" so that it opens within a new window. We'll look at how this is done at the end of this section of the chapter, after we've seen how we extract and display the data for this section of the page.

The Data Access Code for the 'Car Models' List

You won't be surprised to learn that the code to extract the data for the list of models is almost identical to that we used to extract the list of 'News' items in the previous section of this chapter. We have a stored procedure named GetModelList within our database, which accesses the tblCars table and extracts the required columns from each row. This stored procedure is executed from within a function named GetModelListDR, which returns a DataReader that we bind to the DataGrid control in our page.

The GetModelList Stored Procedure

In the `GetModelList` stored procedure, we extract the ID of each vehicle, the model name, and the short précis from the `tblCar` table. We also need the lowest price for this model (so that we can display "Prices from $xx,xxx.xx". We get this using a sub-query that selects the lowest value for this model from the `CarEnginePrice` column of the `tblCarEngines` table, joining this table to `tblCar` on the `CarID` column. Finally, we order the results alphabetically by model name:

Stored procedure: GetModelList

```
SELECT CarID, Model, Precis,
(SELECT MIN(CarEnginePrice) FROM tblCarEngines
        WHERE tblCarEngines.CarID = tblCar.CarID) As Price
FROM tblCar ORDER BY Model
```

You could, of course, extract the rows in any other order you wish, for example by price (or price descending), by ID, or by adding a column to the table that specifies the order in which you want them to be displayed.

The GetModelListDR Function

Our `GetModelListDR` function looks just like the `GetNewsListDR` function we described for the 'News' section of our page, and so we don't need to describe the workings again. The only difference is that it uses our `GetModelList` stored procedure this time:

home.aspx

```
' function to get details of car models for DataGrid control
Function GetModelListDR() As SqlDataReader
  Try
    Dim sqlConnect As SqlConnection = New SqlConnection(sConnect)
    Dim sProcName As String = "GetModelList"
    Dim sqlComm As SqlCommand = New SqlCommand(sProcName, sqlConnect)
    sqlComm.CommandType = CommandType.StoredProcedure
    sqlConnect.Open
    Return sqlComm.ExecuteReader(CommandBehavior.CloseConnection)
  Catch
    Return Nothing
  End Try
End Function
```

Data Binding the DataGrid Control

We saw the relevant parts of the `Page_Load` event handler when looking at the 'News' list earlier on. Code there declares and sets the value of the `sConnect` variable that holds the connection string. The only things we need to do otherwise are assign the `DataReader` that is returned from the `GetModelListDR` function to our `DataGrid` control, and then initiate the data binding process:

```
Sub Page_Load()
  ...
  ... other code to get user ID, etc. goes here
  ...
  ... get database connection string from web.config as seen earlier
  ...
```

```
' set DataSource for "car models" list and data-bind it
dgrModels.DataSource = GetModelListDR()
dgrModels.DataBind()

End Sub
```

The DataGrid Control for the 'Car Models' List

The declaration of the 'models list' section of our page is shown in the next listing. You can see the table cell that is part of the main page structure table, together with the anchor that our 'skip to' link at the top of the page points to. Below that, within the table cell, is the outline declaration of the DataGrid control that generates the list of models:

```
<tr>
  <td valign="top">
    <a name="models" />
    <asp:DataGrid id="dgrModels" runat="server" Width="100%"
                  Font-Name="Tahoma,Arial,Helvetica,sans-serif"
                  Font-Size="10"
                  BorderStyle="None"
                  GridLines="None"
                  CellSpacing="10"
                  CellPadding="10"
                  ShowHeader="False"
                  AutoGenerateColumns="False"
                  OnItemDataBound="SetNavigateUrl">
      <ItemStyle VerticalAlign="top" />
      <Columns>
        ... column declarations go here ...
      </Columns>
    </asp:DataGrid>
  </td>
</tr>
```

You can see that we've included values for quite a few attributes of this control. We've specified the font name (face) and size, turned off display of borders and grid lines (the individual cell borders), set the cell spacing and padding to "10", and told the control not to display a header row.

The next attribute, AutoGenerateColumns="False", tells the control that we don't want it to create the columns automatically. The default, if not specified, is "True", which means that the control will automatically generate a column in the resulting grid (an HTML table) for each column or field it finds in the rows of the data source. We want to exert fine control over the output, without having a separate column for each field in our rowset, and so we'll define the columns ourselves.

The OnItemDataBound attribute specifies the name of an event handler that will be executed once for each row in our data source, after the control has figured out what values are in the data row but before it creates the output for that row. We use this event handler to modify the URL of the hyperlinks in the resulting page, depending on whether the current user's browser supports client-side script. We'll see how this is done later on.

Specifying Styles and Templates

After the opening tag of the DataGrid control, we come to the elements that define the content and appearance of each section of the control's output. Any styling or other information we provide within the <ItemStyle> element is applied only to the rows in the resulting grid. There are equivalent elements to define the style and appearance of the alternating item rows, the header, the footer, the selected item row and the row currently being edited (if there is one). We'll see examples of these elements and templates in later examples from other pages in our site.

Notice that we mentioned a 'selected row' style. Both the DataList and DataGrid controls provide a SelectedIndex property. When the control generates its output, the row at the index specified in this property is rendered using the style values specified in the <SelectedItemStyle> element.

It's also possible to switch a row into 'edit' mode in a DataList or DataGrid control, by setting the EditItemIndex to a value greater than -1. In this case, the styles specified in the <EditItemStyle> element are used to render the output for the row at the specified index.

If we are using templates to create the output (as will always be the case with a DataList control), the contents of the <SelectedItemTemplate> are displayed instead of the <ItemTemplate> or <AlternatingItemTemplate> contents for the row at the SelectedIndex position. Likewise, the contents of the <EditItemTemplate> are displayed instead of the <ItemTemplate> or <AlternatingItemTemplate> contents for the row at the EditItemIndex position.

> For a full reference to the DataGrid control, see the .NET SDK page:
> ms-help://MS.NETFrameworkSDK/cpref/html/frlrfSystemWebUIWebControlsDataGridPropertiesTopic.htm

Specifying Column Information in a DataGrid Template

The final element shown in the previous listing is the <Columns> element, which contains the definitions of the columns we want the DataGrid control to display. This element and its content are only required because we have told the control that we don't want it to generate the columns automatically – we'll be doing that ourselves.

When specifying the column information for a DataGrid control, we can take advantage of several ready-built column types. This is the 'next step up' from having the control generate the columns automatically based on the structure of each data source item. It gives us more control over the appearance and formatting of the column and its values.

The column types we can use are:

- ❑ asp:BoundColumn – values are displayed as text in the output. If the EditItemIndex of the control is not -1, values from the row at that index position are displayed in text boxes.

- ❑ asp:HyperlinkColumn – values in this column are displayed as hyperlinks, and the target URL can be created dynamically from the value if required.

- ❑ asp:EditColumn – displays <u>Edit</u>, <u>Update</u> and <u>Cancel</u> command links in this column for each row, depending on the value of the EditItemIndex property of the control (which specifies the row that is currently being edited if there is one).

- ❑ asp:ButtonColumn – displays a button in this column for each row. The caption and action of the button can be specified to create custom behavior for the grid.

There is also one more type of column, and this is used when we want absolute control over the content and appearance of the column:

❑ asp:TemplateColumn – all the information to generate the column is provided by declaring templates. These work in the same way as the templates for a DataList or Repeater control, and we can define the content to be displayed for this column in each row, each alternating row, the selected row and the row currently being edited (if there is one).

We only want two columns for our DataGrid control – one for the graphic of the vehicle and price, and one for the name, description and link to compare models. However, we need to build the content for these columns using data from several columns (or fields) in our data source rows. So we have to resort to using an asp:TemplateColumn column type for both of these columns.

The Graphic Image and Price Column

The next listing shows the first column declaration, within the <Columns> element of our DataGrid control. We only need an <ItemTemplate> for this column, as all the rows have the same format (we aren't formatting alternate rows in a different style). Within the <ItemTemplate> we declare an ASP.NET Hyperlink control, followed by a <br /> element and a <span> where the price will be inserted:

```
<Columns>
  <asp:TemplateColumn>
    <ItemTemplate>
      <asp:Hyperlink id="lnkCarImage" runat="server" Target="_blank"
            ImageUrl='<%# DataBinder.Eval(Container.DataItem, _
                       "Model", "images/{0}150.gif") %>'
            ToolTip='<%# DataBinder.Eval(Container.DataItem, _
                       "Model", "The Wrox {0} in detail") %>'
            NavigateUrl='<%# DataBinder.Eval(Container.DataItem, _
                       "CarID", "cardetail-noscript.aspx?id={0}") %>' />
      <br />
      <span class="body-text">
        <%# DataBinder.Eval(Container.DataItem, "Price", _
                       "Prices from <b>${0:#,##0.00}</b>") %>
      </span></ItemTemplate>
  </asp:TemplateColumn>
```

We could, of course, provide an <AlternatingItemTemplate> as well if we wanted alternate rows to look different, and a <SeparatorTemplate> if we wanted to insert some HTML or other output between each row.

The Hyperlink control is used to display a clickable graphic image, as we suggested was possible when we looked at the 'links to other pages' section earlier in this chapter. The image is a picture of the vehicle, and we need to specify the path and name of the appropriate image as the ImageUrl attribute of the Hyperlink control.

This is achieved by using the DataBinder.Eval method, as we did with the Repeater control earlier on in this chapter, and specifying as the format string the value "images/{0}150.gif". This will resolve to a value such as "images/Wrampant150.gif" when data binding takes place, and so the correct image will be used in the page for this row. Likewise, we specify the ToolTip attribute in the same way, using a format string that will give a result such as "The Wrox Wrampant in detail".

The `NavigateUrl` attribute is set in the same way, but this time it's bound to the `CarID` column and not the `Model` (name) column, and so will resolve to a value such as `"cardetail-noscript.aspx?id=4"` after binding is complete. As we've also included the attribute `Target="_blank"` in the `Hyperlink` declaration, the page `cardetail-noscript.aspx` will be opened in a new browser window.

Following the `Hyperlink` control and the `<br />` element is a `<span>` element that uses the CSS style class named `body-text`, and which contains the value from the `Price` column of our data source. We use the format string `"Prices from <b>${0:#,##0.00}</b>"` within the `Databinder.Eval` method here to produce the formatted output you can see in the following screenshot – it's permissible to include HTML in the format string and have it rendered by the client. The screenshot also shows the value for the `ToolTip` attribute that we specified in the `Hyperlink` declaration:

The Wrox Wrampant

Our original and still the most popular sports car in our range. The Wrampant provides a unique combination of performance and comfort

The Wrox Wrampant in detail almost any driver. Happy around town, and yet with extra horses under the bonnet so that you can take advantage of the open road. With its 2 x 2 seat combination, and spacious luggage carrying features, it makes an ideal car for both short and long journeys. ...
[compare models]

Prices from **$22,995.00**

Viewing the output that is generated for this column in the browser, you can see the results of the format strings we specified for the various properties of the `Hyperlink` control and the price. Notice that (as we discovered in Chapter 2) Internet Explorer generates a `style` attribute in the opening tag of the `<table>` element that the control creates (and which will hold all the rows from the data source):

Result in Internet Explorer 6 (with client-side scripting disabled):

```
<table cellspacing="10" cellpadding="10" border="0" id="dgrModels" style="border-
style:None;font-family:Tahoma,Arial,Helvetica,sans-serif;font-
size:10pt;width:100%;">
 <tr valign="Top">
  <td>
   <a id="dgrModels__ctl2_lnkCarImage" Target="_blank"
     title="The Wrox Wrampant in detail"
     href="cardetail-noscript.aspx?id=1">
    <img title="The Wrox Wrampant in detail"
        src="images/Wrampant150.gif" border="0" /></a><br />
   <span class="body-text">Prices from <b>$22,995.00</b></span></td>
```

However, as all the text generated by the control is within `<span>` elements, which each have a `class` attribute that defines the CSS styles for that text, the overall text styles specified in the opening `<table>` tag are ignored in browsers that support CSS.

In "down-level" clients, the `DataGrid` control does not create the `style` attribute for the opening `<table>` tag. Instead, it wraps the entire content of each column inside a `<font>` element that uses the values we specified in the attributes to the `DataGrid` control (remember that `Font-Size="10"`, without any unit specifier such as `px` or `em`, is translated into `<font size="2">` by the control):

Result in Netscape 6 (with client-side scripting disabled):

```
<table cellspacing="10" cellpadding="10" border="0" id="dgrModels"
       width="100%">
  <tr valign="Top">
   <td><font face="Tahoma,Arial,Helvetica,sans-serif" size="2">
    <a id="dgrModels__ctl2_lnkCarImage" Target="_blank"
       title="The Wrox Wrampant in detail"
       href="cardetail-noscript.aspx?id=1">
     <img title="The Wrox Wrampant in detail"
          src="images/Wrampant150.gif" border="0" /></a><br />
    <span class="body-text">Prices from <b>$22,995.00</b></span></font></td>
```

Other than that, the output is the same. And the same `<span>` elements with the same `class` attribute values ensure that the appearance is correct in any client that supports CSS.

The Name and Description Column

The column that displays the model name, description and [compare models] link is very similar in declaration and workings to the previous column we've been looking at. The model name is generated by an ASP.NET `Hyperlink` control, but this time using text as the link and not a graphic image. This is followed by a `<br />` element, and the text description of the vehicle within a `<span>` element. After this comes another `Hyperlink` control, with the text "compare models" for every row:

```
<asp:TemplateColumn>
  <ItemTemplate>
    <b><font face="Arial,Helvetica,sans-serif" size="3">
    <asp:Hyperlink id="lnkCarName" runat="server"
        CssClass="large-link" Target="_blank"
        Text='<%# DataBinder.Eval(Container.DataItem, "Model", _
                          "The Wrox {0}") %>'
        NavigateUrl='<%# DataBinder.Eval(Container.DataItem, "CarID", _
                            "cardetail-noscript.aspx?id={0}") %>' />
    </b><br /></font>
    <span class="body-text"><%# Container.DataItem("Precis") %> ...
    </span><font size="1"><span class="small-text">
    [<asp:Hyperlink runat="server" CssClass="small-link"
      Text='compare models'
      NavigateUrl='<%# DataBinder.Eval(Container.DataItem, "Model", _
                              "compare.aspx?compare={0}") %>' />]
    </span></font></ItemTemplate>
  </asp:TemplateColumn>
</Columns>
```

Notice that we provide a `CssClass` attribute for the two hyperlinks, specifying the class names that we want placed in these elements (as the `class` attribute). However, to provide the correct appearance on non-CSS-enabled browsers, we also need to include the appropriate `<font>` elements. We wrap the model name in a `<font>` element with the size set to `"3"`, and the compare models link in a `<font>` element with the size set to `"1"`. In "down-level" clients, the `DataGrid` control itself will automatically wrap all this inside another `<font>` element (with the correct font face and with a font size of `"2"`). The result is shown in this screenshot:

The Wrox Wranger

Whether you've got a big job to do, a lot of equipment to carry, or you just like to give the appearance of being a big-city farmer, the Wranger is the ideal truck for you. Hugely powerful, massively strong, and unbelievably reliable, it will easily handle everything you can throw at it. ... [compare models]

Looking at the HTML output that the `DataGrid` control generates for this column, you can see the effects of the `CssClass` attributes we added to the `Hyperlink` controls, and the extra `<font>` elements. In Internet Explorer 6 (and other "up-level" browsers), the control generates the following output, including a `class` attribute on each `<a>` element:

Result in Internet Explorer 6 (with client-side scripting disabled):

```
  <td><b><font face="Arial,Helvetica,sans-serif" size="3">
  <a id="dgrModels__ct12_lnkCarName" class="large-link" Target="_blank"
     href="cardetail-noscript.aspx?id=3">The Wrox Wranger</a></b>
  <br /></font>
  <span class="body-text">Whether you've got a big job to do ...
  </span><font size="1"><span class="small-text">
    [<a class="small-link" href="compare.aspx?compare=Wranger">
    compare models</a>]
  </span></font></td>
<tr>
...
... row for next car here ...
```

In "down-level" clients, the control generates a slightly different output. Inside the table cell we get the `<font>` element generated from the `Font-Name` and `Font-Size` attributes we specified in the opening tag of the `DataGrid` control declaration. Inside this is the content we specified in our template, and it is the same as that for "up-level" clients that we've just seen:

Result in Netscape 6 (with client-side scripting disabled):

```
  <td><font face="Tahoma,Arial,Helvetica,sans-serif" size="2">
   <b><font face="Arial,Helvetica,sans-serif" size="3">
   <a id="dgrModels__ct12_lnkCarName" class="large-link" Target="_blank"
      href="cardetail-noscript.aspx?id=3">The Wrox Wranger</a></b><br /></font>
   <span class="body-text"> Whether you've got a big job to do ...
   </span><font size="1"><span class="small-text">
     [<a class="small-link" href="compare.aspx?compare=Wranger">
     compare models</a>]
   </span></font></font></td>
</tr>
...
... row for next car here ...
```

So, as before, the appearance of the output in clients that support CSS is guaranteed by the fact that every visible element has a `class` attribute that specifies the CSS style we want to apply to that element. Outside these `<a>` and `<span>` elements are nested `<font>` elements that will provide a very similar appearance in clients that do not support CSS.

Handling the ItemDataBound Event for a DataGrid

The results we showed you being generated by the `DataGrid` control in the previous sections are what you will see in a browser or client that does not support client-side scripting, or which has it disabled. You'll recall that we want to change the way that the hyperlinks in the models list work for clients that do support client-side scripting:

❑ Firstly, we want to open the new window using client-side script so that we can control the size, position and window furniture.

❑ We'd also like to be able to prevent multiple instances of the same model window being opened, and instead use an existing window if the user selects the same model again. And, in this case, we want to bring the existing window to the front so that it is visible.

❑ Most important of all, we have to load a **different page** into the pop-up window if our visitor's browser *does* support client-side scripting. By default (as you saw above) we load the page `cardetail-noscript.aspx`. However, if they have client-side scripting enabled, we want to load the page `cardetail.aspx` instead.

When we declared our `DataGrid` control earlier on, we included a value for the `OnItemDatabound` attribute:

```
<asp:DataGrid id="dgrModels" runat="server" Width="100%"
              ...
              ...
              OnItemDataBound="SetNavigateUrl">
```

This value is the name of an event handler that will be executed each time the control processes a row from the data source. The control passes two parameters to the event handler – a reference to itself (the 'sender'), and a `DataGridItemEventArgs` object. This object contains a wealth of information about the event that is occurring, including information about the type of row that is being bound, and a reference to the row in the data source that is providing the data from this output row.

The SetNavigateUrl Event Handler

The next listing shows the complete `SetNavigateUrl` event handler we've defined within our page. We first check the page-level variable `bCanScript`, as this will only be `True` if the current client supports client-side scripting (we set this in the `Page_Load` event handler when we test for script support, as you saw in the previous chapter).

We also need to check that the event is being raised for an 'item' row or an 'alternating item' row. It's only these rows that will contain the hyperlink controls whose properties we want to modify. The `DataGridItemEventArgs` object passed to our event handler exposes information about the row in the `DataGrid` control as the `Item` property, and the type of row is stored in the `ItemType` property of the `Item` object:

```
Sub SetNavigateUrl(sender As Object, args As DataGridItemEventArgs)
  If bCanScript And (args.Item.ItemType = ListItemType.Item _
  Or args.Item.ItemType = ListItemType.AlternatingItem) Then
```

```
        ' it's a data row that is being bound so create appropriate
        ' URLs for hyperlinks and remove Target attributes
        ' use separate function to ensure session ID is munged into URL
        ' in case the page is running in "cookieless sessions" mode
        Dim sCarID As String = args.Item.DataItem("CarID")
        Dim sHref As String = "javascript:openWindow('" _
                        & InsertSessionId(Request.Path) _
                        & "/cardetail.aspx?id=" & sCarID _
                        & "', '" & sCarID & "')"

        ' update href in controls to new value
        CType(args.Item.FindControl("lnkCarImage"), _
                                Hyperlink).NavigateUrl = sHref
        CType(args.Item.FindControl("lnkCarImage"), _
                                Hyperlink).Target = ""
        CType(args.Item.FindControl("lnkCarName"), _
                                Hyperlink).NavigateUrl = sHref
        CType(args.Item.FindControl("lnkCarName"), _
                                Hyperlink).Target = ""

    End If
End Sub
```

Once we've decided that we do need to process this row, inside the `If...End If` construct, we create a `String` containing the appropriate value to use as the `NavigateUrl` of the hyperlinks in this row. We want it to be something like:

```
javascript:openWindow('cardetail.aspx?id=1', '1')
```

When the user clicks on such a link, the browser will execute the client-side function named `openWindow`, passing it the URL of the page we want to display with the ID of the current vehicle appended as the query string, and the ID of the vehicle as a separate parameter as well.

After we've created the string for the URL, we access the two `Hyperlink` controls that are in the current row of the `DataGrid` by using the `FindControl` method of the current `Item` (the current row in the `DataGrid`) and by specifying the value of the `id` property for the control we want to find. We have to cast (convert) the returned object to the appropriate type (a `Hyperlink` object), and then we can set the `NavigateUrl` property to the new value:

```
CType(args.Item.FindControl("lnkCarImage"), _
                        Hyperlink).NavigateUrl = sHref
```

The two hyperlinks we declared in our `DataGrid` also contain `Target` attributes, set to open the new page in a new browser window (`Target="_blank"`). However, when we use a function to open the new window, we need to remove these attributes. We do this by setting the `Target` property of the `Hyperlink` controls to an empty string:

```
CType(args.Item.FindControl("lnkCarImage"), _
                        Hyperlink).Target = ""
```

If you view the result created by the `DataGrid` in a script-enabled browser, you can see the effect this event handler has. The `href` attributes of the two `<a>` elements now have the new values, and there are no `target` attributes:

```
<a id="dgrModels__ctl2_lnkCarImage"
   title="The Wrox Wrampant in detail"
   href="javascript:openWindow('cardetail.aspx?id=1', '1')">
<img title="The Wrox Wrampant in detail"
     src="images/Wrampant150.gif" border="0" /></a><br />
<span class="body-text">Prices from <b>$22,995.00</b></span></td><td>
<b><font face="Arial,Helvetica,sans-serif" size="3">
<a id="dgrModels__ctl2_lnkCarName" class="large-link"
   href="javascript:openWindow('cardetail.aspx?id=1', '1')">
  The Wrox Wrampant</a></b><br /></font>
```

Of course, we also need to include the client-side `openWindow` function in our page. This is declared within the `<head>` section of our `home.aspx` page (it is inserted into the page every time, irrespective of whether the client supports scripting or not). As there is no `runat="server"` attribute in the opening `<script>` tag, the script is simply sent to the client as it is:

```
<head>
...
<script language='JavaScript'>
<!--
function openWindow(sHref, sCarID) {
  // open cardetail.aspx page in new window and bring to front
  var newWin = window.open(sHref, 'WCCDetail' + sCarID,
    'scrollbars=yes,toolbar=no,location=no,resizable=yes,directories=no,'
   + 'status=no,menubar=no,width=635,height=550,top=5,left=5');
  newWin.focus();
}
//-->
</script>
</head>
```

Notice that we use the first parameter (`sHref`) to specify the page that will be loaded into this window. To prevent multiple instances of the same model being displayed in different windows, we use the second parameter (`sCarID`) to specify the name of the window that we'll open. If a window with this name is already open, the browser automatically loads the page into this existing window instead of opening a new one.

However, in this case, the window that it uses may not be visible – it may be hidden behind other windows. So, in the last line of the function, we bring it to the front and give it the 'input focus' by calling its `focus` method.

> *If we decided to allow users to open more than one instance of the window for each model, as they can when client-side scripting is not enabled, we would just change the window name parameter to the* `window.open` *method from* `'WCCDetail' + sCarID` *to* `'_blank'`.

You may have noticed in the `SetNavigateUrl` event handler, when we were creating the string for the new URL, that we called a function named `InsertSessionId`, and passed to it the virtual path to the current page:

```
Dim sCarID As String = args.Item.DataItem("CarID")
Dim sHref As String = "javascript:openWindow('" _
                    & InsertSessionId(Request.Path) _
                    & "/cardetail.aspx?id=" & sCarID _
                    & "', '" & sCarID & "')"
```

The reason is that our application is designed to work with both normal cookie-based sessions, and with cookie-less sessions. In the latter case, the URLs in the page must contain the session ID, 'munged' into the URL. In cookie-less sessions mode, ASP.NET automatically performs this 'munging' for all hyperlinks in the page, as we saw near the start of the previous chapter. However, when we are building URLs dynamically in code, as in the `SetNavigateUrl` event handler, we have to perform our own 'munging'.

While we could do this by querying the `SessionID` property of the user's `Session` object, and performing some fairly simple string manipulation, there is an easier way. The `Response` object exposes a method named `ApplyAppPathModifier`, which returns the path to the current page with the session ID 'munged' into it if the page is running in 'cookie-less session' mode. If not, it doesn't insert the session ID.

So, our `InsertSessionID` function can take the path passed to it as a parameter and call the `ApplyAppPathModifier` method. This returns the same virtual path, but with the session ID 'munged' into it when running in 'cookie-less sessions' mode. However, we want to return just the path, and not the complete modified path and file name. Remember that we pass to this function the virtual path to the current page, so we need to strip off the page name before returning just the path:

```
Function InsertSessionId(sPath As String) As String
  ' function to insert SessionID into path if running in cookieless
  ' session mode, and return just the path with no filename
  ' does not insert session ID if not in "cookieless" mode
  Dim sResult As String = Response.ApplyAppPathModifier(sPath)
  Return sResult.Substring(0, sResult.LastIndexOf("/"))
End Function
```

The code in the `SetNavigateUrl` event handler can then add the name of the target page to the result, and use it to build the final URL – as we saw earlier.

Summary

In this chapter we started to build our example site 'Home' page, keeping in mind all the issues we discussed in previous chapters. In particular, we've tried to make the page work properly, and give the same appearance, in as many client browser types as possible by using a combination of CSS styles and the more traditional `<font>` elements.

We also put in quite a lot of effort to make the page accessible to users who suffer a disability, such as limitations in movement or vision, that require them to use specialist user agents rather than graphical browsers. We included all the features, and followed all the guidelines we discussed near the end of the previous chapter to make navigation within our site as easy as possible for users of text browsers and 'page reader' clients.

Our 'Home' page is neatly divisible into several sections, and we looked at the way that the overall structure of the page and these sections is achieved. We also looked in depth at three of these sections: the links to other pages, the 'News' section, and the list of vehicle models available from the Wrox Car Company.

We also spent time discussing how the various list controls provided with ASP.NET can be used to make building pages easier, and we showed how we used a `Repeater` and a `DataGrid` control in the 'Home' page.

Finally, we discovered how we can modify our pages to take into account features available on the client to which we are serving the page. By handling events raised by the list controls, we can selectively change the output generated by the control. We used this technique to modify the way that hyperlinks work in our page when the user's browser supports client-side scripting.

In all, the topics we covered were:

- ❑   The overall structure of the 'Home' page
- ❑   How we specify the styles and appearance of the page, and each page section
- ❑   How we provide additional accessibility and navigational features for specialist clients
- ❑   The section containing the links to other pages
- ❑   The 'News and Special Offers' section of the page
- ❑   The list of car models and descriptions
- ❑   How the page changes behavior for script-enabled and non-script-enabled clients

In the next chapter, we'll complete our exploration of the 'Home' page by looking at the animated banner, the page footer, and the mailing list sections of the page.

5

Banners, Footers, and E-Mail

In the previous chapter, we saw the basic structure of the 'Home' page of our site, and examined the three main sections of the page: the links to other pages, the list of 'News' items, and the list of vehicle models available from the Wrox Car Company. However, there are three other features of the 'Home' page that we didn't have room to cover in the previous chapter.

We'll look at these in more detail in this chapter, including the animated page banner, the page footer, and the way that visitors can sign up for our mailing list. The first two of these topics introduce an extremely useful generic technique in ASP.NET – wrapping up reusable sections of code into **user controls**.

So, the topics for this chapter are:

❑   The animated banner we use in most of the pages

❑   The page footer we use in most of the pages

❑   How we add users to the mailing list in our 'Home' page

We'll start with a look at the topic of user controls, which we take advantage of for the animated banner and page footer in our example site.

About ASP.NET User Controls

When we work with ASP.NET, we tend to use its in-built elements (server controls, the .NET Framework classes, and so on) for building our own web sites and web applications without a second thought. After all, these elements provide the foundations of the whole ASP.NET postback architecture, and all the advantages that this brings.

However, the server controls provided with ASP.NET are sometimes not exactly what we want, especially when we have some esoteric purpose in mind. Neither are they directly customized to suit our own web sites – which is not surprising, as they have to be generic in nature.

One solution is to write and compile our own server controls. However, custom server control creation, while not difficult to do, is a little complex – and the topic as a whole is outside the remit of the book. You can find out more from other books, such as *Professional ASP.NET Server Controls – Building Custom Controls with C#* (Wrox Press, ISBN 1-86100-564-4).

In the meantime, there is an easier way to build custom controls that can behave in a similar way to server controls, and which provide most of the features that server controls do as well. We can build **user controls**.

Reusable Code and Content

User controls can be extremely useful when building a web site or web application. They provide several advantages over 'inline' code that occurs in every page:

❑ They are reusable – the same single source file that defines a control can be inserted dynamically at runtime into any number of pages, as long as they reside within the same ASP.NET application (they are all in the same virtual application root folder or subfolders of that root folder).

❑ They can contain anything that we can put into an ordinary ASP.NET page (.aspx), including HTML, text, other content, server-side script, client-side script, and so on.

❑ Their content becomes part of the hosting page, so we can refer to the controls, script functions, and other objects within the user control as properties of the control.

❑ They can expose custom properties as simple data types, or as objects (classes), allowing values to be passed into the user control dynamically each time it is instantiated in an ASP.NET page.

❑ Code within the user control can reference objects in the parent ASP.NET page that is hosting the user control, through the Parent property of the control.

❑ Output caching can be configured for just the control, separately from the ASP.NET page that hosts it. This allows the content of just the user control to be cached between requests in just the same way as we use output caching in an ASP.NET page, but with the content of the hosting page being regenerated on each request.

Of all these advantages, the primary one is usually the ability to write one 'page' (user control) and then use it in several other pages. If the control has to be fixed when a bug is found, or updated to suit new requirements, only that single file needs attention. Each page that uses it will pick up the new version the next time it is requested. And moving blocks of content and/or code out of an ASP.NET page and into a user control also makes the hosting page simpler and easier to manage and debug:

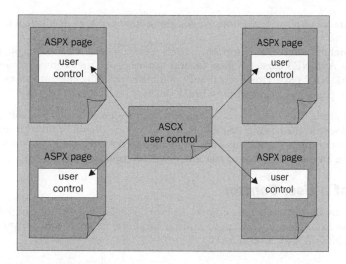

Building a User Control

Building user controls is trivially easy, in fact a common approach is to discover some content in a page that you need to reuse, and just lift it out and convert it into a user control. Of course, those of us with a more organized approach to site and page design will already be aware of which user controls will be needed when we design the site (and there are a few pigs passing overhead right now!).

The only things that define a user control as being different to an ASP.NET page are the directive at the start of the file and the file extension. Instead of a `Page` directive, we use a `Control` directive:

```
<%@Control Language="VB" %>
```

The file extension for a user control must be `.ascx`, although it can be placed in any folder within the virtual application where it is used. Unlike .NET assemblies (compiled `.dll` files), user controls *do not* have to reside in the `bin` folder.

We can use many of the same attributes within the `Control` directive of a user control as we do in an ASP.NET page, for example `EnableViewState="True|False"` and `Debug="True|False"`, and these override the settings for the parent page. And we can include other directives as well. For example, as mentioned earlier, we can include an `OutputCache` directive:

```
<%@OutputCache Duration="60" VaryByParam="*" %>
```

We can also import namespaces from the .NET class library, or for custom components and assemblies that we create ourselves:

```
<%@Import Namespace="System.Data.SqlClient" %>
<%@Import Namespace="MyAssembly.MyNewClass" %>
```

However, there are a couple of limitations on the things that can appear inside a user control:

❑ Do not include a server-side form (a <form runat="server"> control), as there can only be one in an ASP.NET page, whereas several instances of a user control could be inserted into a single ASP.NET page. However, if only one instance of the control will ever be used in any ASP.NET page, you might want to break this rule.

❑ Do not include the <html>, <head>, and <body> elements, as these will generally be provided within the hosting ASP.NET page. However, if your control is used – for example, to create the complete <head> or <body> section of the page – and only one instance will ever be used in any ASP.NET page, you might want to break this rule.

The Contents of a User Control

So, what do we actually put into a user control? As we discussed earlier, we can put almost anything into one. A simple example is if we want to insert a corporate image and hyperlink into every page of a site. We could define the user control as:

```
<%@Control Language="VB" %>
<center>
<a href="http://mysite.com/about.aspx" title="About Us">
  <img src="corp-hq.jpg" alt="About us" border="0" />
</a>
<hr />
<a href="http://mysite.com/about.aspx" title="About Us">
  Read about our company ...
</a>
</center>
```

Then, when the CEO decides to change the text in the hyperlink to "Read all about our wonderful corporation", we only have to edit this .ascx file. All the pages that use it will display the new content when next requested.

A completely different way of using user controls is where they simply act as a way to centralize non-visible parts of a page, or even just server-side code blocks. For example, if we have a function that performs some complicated calculation, and we want to use it in several pages, we can create it as a user control like this:

```
<%@Control Language="VB" %>
<script runat="server">
Function CalculateSomethingDifficult(iInput As Integer) As String
  ...
  ... code to calculate and return the result ...
  ...
End Function
</script>
```

Now we can use this function as a method of the control – just like we would use a method of any other server control. And, of course, we can mix all kinds of content in a user control. The examples you'll see later in this chapter, which come from our example Wrox Car Company site, contain several different types of content as well as server-side code.

Exposing Properties from a User Control

One useful aspect of user controls is that they can expose properties – again, much like any other server control. There are two ways that we can expose properties: as a `Public` variable or by creating `Get` and `Set` methods within the control.

If we just want to expose a simple value type, such as an `Integer` or `String`, we can declare it within the user control as a `Public` variable, and even give it a default value:

```
<%@Control Language="VB" %>
<script runat="server">
Public MyProperty As String = "Not specified"

Sub Page_Load()
  ...
  ... use the value of the variable MyProperty here
  ...
End Sub
</script>

<p>Or even insert it into the output like this: <% = MyProperty %></p>
```

If the hosting ASP.NET page does not set the value of the property when it instantiates the user control, the value will be the default we provided: `"Not specified"`.

Alternatively, we can expose properties of objects within the user control. For example, if we have a text box with the `id` value `"MyTextbox"`, we can set up access to its properties like this:

```
<%@Control Language="VB" %>
<script runat="server">
Public Property TheText() As String
  Get
    Return MyTextbox.Text
  End Get
  Set
    MyTextbox.Text = value
  End Set
End Property
</script>

<asp:Textbox id="MyTextbox" runat="server" />
```

One final aspect of user controls that helps to demonstrate how powerful they can be is that we can even use templates within a user control – to create a **templated user control**. We don't cover this topic here, or use templated user controls in our site, but you can read more about them in the .NET SDK here:

ms-help://MS.NETFrameworkSDK/cpguidenf/html/cpconcreatingtemplatedusercontrol.htm.

Using a User Control in an ASP.NET Page

Having seen how we build user controls, we need to look at how we insert them into our ASP.NET pages and then access them. User controls must first be registered in the ASP.NET pages that use them, with a `Register` directive. We specify the tag prefix and tag name that we'll use to identify the control, and the path to the `.ascx` file that implements the control:

```
<%@Register TagPrefix="wrox" TagName="mynewcontrol"
            Src="ascx/my-user-control.ascx"%>
```

Once it has been registered, we insert the control into the page as an XML element, using the tag prefix and tag name we just specified. We can also give it an ID, so that we can refer to it afterwards in our code if required. Note that we must include the `runat="server"` attribute so ASP.NET knows that it has to process this element, and insert the user control into the page at this point:

```
<wrox:mynewcontrol id="MyControl" runat="server" />
```

This is all that's required if the user control just contains HTML and static or dynamically generated content, and does not require any further interaction from us. The HTML and content will appear in the output at the point where we place the XML element you've just seen.

However, if the user control contains code that we want to access, for example a function that we want to use in our server-side code, we refer to it using the ID of the user control. So, to call the `CalculateSomethingDifficult` function we defined in an earlier example, we would use:

```
Dim sResult As String = MyControl.CalculateSomethingDifficult(42)
```

Setting Properties

If our user control exposes any properties, we can set these in the ASP.NET page that hosts the control. And it's done in exactly the same way as we would any other server control. For example, if the user control with the ID value `"MyControl"` exposes a `String` property named `MyProperty`, we can set the value when we insert the control into our page:

```
<wrox:mynewcontrol id="MyControl" runat="server"
               MyProperty="This value" />
```

If the user control also exposes an `Integer` property named `MyNumber` (or a property that is of any other simple value type), we still set it the same way, using attributes of the user control element:

```
<wrox:mynewcontrol id="MyControl" runat="server"
               MyProperty="This value" MyNumber="42" />
```

Furthermore, just as with the 'standard' server controls, we can set the properties dynamically in our server-side code. This time, however, we should make sure that the values are of the correct data type (while VB.NET will convert most data types implicitly, C# does not):

```
MyControl.MyProperty = "Another value"
MyControl.MyNumber = 42
```

The Animated Page Banner

So, after a detour to talk about user controls, we can now get back to our Wrox Car Company site, and the remainder of the 'Home' page that we started to look at in the previous chapter. We'll examine in detail how we implement the animated banner that appears at the top of the page when first opened in browsers such as Internet Explorer 4.0 and above, Netscape 4.0 and above, and Mozilla 1.0.

As you'll have guessed by now, the animated banner section of the page is a user control, and we insert it into each page as required. It exposes properties that we can set to manage the way it behaves. As output, the user control generates a mixture of HTML and client-side script – depending on the type of client that is accessing the page in which the control is hosted.

To be able to modify its output, our user control contains server-side script that is executed each time it is instantiated in an ASP.NET page. This selects the appropriate sections of output for insertion into the hosting page. As part of this process, the server-side code also accesses an element within the hosting page itself.

The following screenshots show what the banner looks like while the animation is running. The old car tows the Wrox Car Company logo onto the page, then trundles off to the right and disappears; after which the slogan appears:

Building the Animated Banner Control

To achieve the animation you see above, we have to use different techniques in different browsers. We looked at the scripted animation techniques available in different browsers in Chapter 3, and we can summarize this as:

❑ Internet Explorer 6.x, Netscape 6.x, Mozilla 1.0, and Opera 6.x (in future revisions, when a bug in the absolute positioning feature is fixed) all support CSS2 and JavaScript 1.0. We can use standard HTML DOM2 methods along with CSS2 absolute positioning techniques to interact with the page content.

❑ Internet Explorer 4.x and above support Microsoft's version of Dynamic HTML (DHTML), and can execute JavaScript 1.0 using the built-in JScript interpreter. We can use DHTML methods against the MSHTML rendering engine to interact with the page content.

❑ Netscape Navigator 4.x supports Netscape-specific Dynamic HTML features such as Layers, plus JavaScript 1.0. We use custom scripting techniques to interact with layers that contain fragments of the content.

To support all these browsers, we have to create content and client-side script that is specific to the three approaches for interacting with the page content. However, by covering all three approaches, we will be providing support for the vast majority of graphical clients that visit our site.

As we saw in Chapter 3, it's possible to write code that detects features of the browser it's running on, and executes the appropriate methods. However, this results in complicated code that is often hard to debug, and to update as new browsers arrive. And if we have to include other content (in our case images with the correct combination of attributes), it can be difficult to make it all work correctly in all the target browsers.

Instead, we chose to expose only browser-specific content and client-side script. Our user control will only generate one of the three 'sets' of output we defined above, depending on which client hits the page. We also want to ensure that the user only sees the animation once during each session, as it soon becomes boring if we show it on every page they open!

The Structure of the 'Page Banner' User Control

The page banner user control, `pagebanner.ascx`, is stored in a folder named `ascx` under the main `wroxcars` and `cookieless-wroxcars` folders of our site. There is a lot of code in it, but it can be logically divided into five sections.

The first is the server-side code that exposes the properties of the control and implements a `Page_Load` event handler, and the HTML table in which the background image (`bgmain.gif`) and the images for the animation will be placed. After that come three separate sections that define the HTML and client-side code we send to each of the three different categories of client listed above, followed by another section that we send to any other type of client.

The server-side code in the `Page_Load` event handler of our user control (which is executed when the page hosting the control is opened each time, just after that page's own `Page_Load` event handler) selects the appropriate one of these four sections, and displays in it the ASP.NET page that is hosting our user control. The following listing shows the contents of our user control in outline, with the code that implements the functionality removed for clarity:

pagebanner.ascx (in outline)

```
<%@Control Language="VB" EnableViewState="False" %>
<script runat="server">
```

```
'property declarations
Public UAType As String = "Unknown"
Public UAVer As String = "Unknown"
Public Animate As Boolean = False

Private sBannerType As String = "Base"

Sub Page_Load()
  ...
  ... code to select the appropriate section of output
  ...
End Sub

</script>

<!-- start of table that holds the banner output -->
<table id="tblBack"
       background="images/bgmain.gif" style="width:100%"
       width="100%" border="0" cellspacing="0" cellpadding="0">
<tbody>
<tr><td nowrap="nowrap">

<asp:Literal id="blockIE4" runat="server" Visible="False">
<!-- animated page banner for IE 4.x and 5.x only -->
  ...
  ... code and HTML to implement banner for IE 4.x and 5.x
  ...
</asp:Literal>

<asp:Literal id="blockStd" runat="server" Visible="False">
<!-- animated page banner for IE 6.x, Nav 6.x and above -->
  ...
  ... code and HTML for IE 6.x, Netscape 6.x and Opera 6.x (when fixed)
  ...
</asp:Literal>

<asp:Literal id="blockN4" runat="server" Visible="False">
<!-- animated page banner for N4.x only -->
  ...
  ... code and HTML to implement banner for Netscape 4.x
  ...
</asp:Literal>

<asp:Literal id="blockBase" runat="server" Visible="False">
<!-- page banner with no animation -->
  <img src="images/wccheader.gif" width="370"
       height="61" hspace="10" vspace="8" alt="Wrox Car Company" />
  <img src="images/force.gif" width="200"
       height="40" hspace="20" vspace="5" alt="The Driving Force" />
</asp:Literal>

<!-- end of page banner table -->
</td></tr>
</tbody>
</table>
```

177

You should be able to see from this listing that we use four <asp:Literal> controls to manage the output of the control. Each has a unique ID, and has its Visible property set to "False". So, unless we change this property to "True", the content of that Literal control will not be sent to the client. When we set the Visible property of a server control to "False", it does not create any output in the response sent to the client:

```
<asp:Literal id="blockIE4" runat="server" Visible="False">
   ... content here ...
</asp:Literal>
```

The ASP.NET Literal Control

The ASP.NET Literal control is a useful way to insert content into a page dynamically, or to remove it from a page programmatically. It's a relatively simple control, and the main advantage it provides is that it doesn't create any output of its own. Only the content of the control as defined for the Text property, or the HTML and other content declared between the opening and closing <asp:Literal> tags, is sent to the client.

The commonly used properties for the Literal control are shown in the table below:

Member	Description
Controls property	Returns a ControlCollection object that references all the child controls defined for this control.
EnableViewState property	Sets or returns a Boolean value indicating if the control will persist its viewstate, and the viewstate of any child controls it contains, between requests.
ID property	Sets or returns the programmatic identifier of the server control.
Page property	Returns a reference to the Page instance that contains this control.
Parent property	Returns a reference to the parent control for this control within the page's control hierarchy (if it has a parent).
Text property	Sets or returns the text and other content that the control will generate within the output if the Visible property is True.
Visible property	Sets or returns a Boolean value that indicates if the control will be rendered when the page is generated.
FindControl method	Searches through all the child controls of this control to find a specific one using its ID value.

A full list of the members for the LiteralControl can be found in the .NET SDK at: ms-help://MS.NETFrameworkSDK/cpref/html/ ᒋ frlrfSystemWebUIWebControlsLiteralMembersTopic.htm.

So, coming back to our user control, you can see that all we have to do is decide which section of the output we want to send to the client, and flip the Visible property to True for that section.

The Properties of our User Control

Our user control exposes three properties, shown in the listing you saw earlier and repeated here. They are used to specify the manufacturer or name of the current client's browser, the major version, and to indicate if we want an animated or a static banner to be displayed:

```
Public UAType As String = "Unknown"
Public UAVer As String = "Unknown"
Public Animate As Boolean = False
```

There is also a `Private` (member) variable named `sBannerType`:

```
Private sBannerType As String = "Base"
```

This variable is used to indicate which section of content we want to send to our client, and the value we place in it is the ID of the `Literal` control that we want to make visible. This is done with code in the `Page_Load` event handler, which we'll be looking at shortly. The default value, `Base`, indicates that we'll send the non-animated version (shown at the end of the previous listing, and repeated here):

```
<asp:Literal id="blockBase" runat="server" Visible="False">
<!-- page banner with no animation -->
  <img src="images/wccheader.gif" width="370"
      height="61" hspace="10" vspace="8" alt="Wrox Car Company" />
  <img src="images/force.gif" width="200"
      height="40" hspace="20" vspace="5" alt="The Driving Force" />
</asp:Literal>
```

In this case, in conjunction with the table start and end declarations that are always present in the output of our user control, the client will receive the following content:

```
<table id="tblBack"
      background="images/bgmain.gif" style="width:100%"
      width="100%" border="0" cellspacing="0" cellpadding="0">
<tbody>
<tr><td nowrap="nowrap">
  <img src="images/wccheader.gif" width="370"
      height="61" hspace="10" vspace="8" alt="Wrox Car Company" />
  <img src="images/force.gif" width="200"
      height="40" hspace="20" vspace="5" alt="The Driving Force" />
</td></tr>
</tbody>
</table>
```

So, if we simply insert our page banner user control into a page, and do not set any of its properties, we get this static banner sent to the client:

The Page_Load Event Handler

When our user control loads, as a visitor requests the ASP.NET page that hosts it, the server-side code in the control's Page_Load event handler is executed. In this code, we examine the values of the three properties that our control exposes, and set the page-level sBannerType variable to the appropriate value.

The first step is to see if we are going to generate an animated banner or not. If the Animate property is True, we first examine the values of the UAType and UAVer properties to see which client we are serving the current page to. For Internet Explorer 4.x or 5.x, we set our private sBannerType variable to "IE4", and for Internet Explorer 6.x and above (which support CSS2), we set it to "IE6"":

```
Sub Page_Load()

  ' if Animate property is True get client type
  If Animate Then

    ' see if the current client is Internet Explorer
    If UAType = "IE" Then
      If (UAVer = 4 Or UAVer = 5) Then
        sBannerType = "IE4"
      End If
      If UAVer >= 6 Then
        sBannerType = "IE6"
      End If
    End If
  End If
```

If the current browser is a Netscape product, or one that does not provide manufacturer details directly (such as Mozilla), we again check the major version number. If it's a version 4.x browser, we set our sBannerType variable to "N4", while if it's version 5.x or above (Netscape 6.x has the user agent version string Mozilla/5.0, so is detected as version 5), we set sBannerType to "N6":

```
    ' see if the current client is Navigator
    If UAType = "Netscape" Then
      If UAVer = 4  Then    ' version 4 only
        sBannerType = "N4"
      End If
      If UAVer >= 5  Then  ' version 5/6+
        sBannerType = "N6"
      End If
    End If
```

Finally, we check to see if it's Opera 6.x or above. While this browser has problems with absolute positioning at the time of writing, Opera are actively looking into the problem and should have a fix available soon. So, we detect it and set the sBannerType variable to "O6" in this case:

```
    ' see if the current client is Opera
    If (UAType = "Opera" And UAVer >= 6) Then
      sBannerType = "O6"
    End If
```

Selecting the Content Block to Send to the Client

Now that we have a definite fix on the current browser type, we can use a `Select Case` construct to choose the appropriate content block that we will make visible and send to the client. However, there is one more task that we have to perform if we want to use an animated banner.

We must add an `onload` attribute to the opening `<body>` tag in the page that hosts our user control. The value of this attribute must be the name of the client-side JavaScript function that we want to be executed when the page itself has finished loading on the client. In each page where the banner will be animated (in our case just the 'Home' page), we specify the `<body>` element as a server control:

```
<body id="BodyTag" runat="server" ... >
```

We discussed this near the start of Chapter 4, and explained that we would be adding an `onload` attribute to it from within our server control.

To add the `onload` attribute, we need to get a reference to the `<body>` element in the hosting page. We access the `Parent` property of our control, which returns a reference to the `Page` object for the ASP.NET page that is hosting the control. Then we use the `FindControl` method of the `Page` object to get a reference to the element with the ID `"BodyTag"`. We have to cast the returned value to the correct object type, an `HtmlGenericControl`:

```
Dim oBodyTag As HtmlGenericControl = Parent.FindControl("BodyTag")
```

Then it's simply a matter of adding the `onload` attribute. We use the `Add` method of the element's `Attributes` collection, specifying the attribute name and the value for that attribute. In our case, the value is `"startAnimation()"` – the name of the client-side script function that we'll place in the page, and which will provide the animation we want:

```
oBodyTag.Attributes.Add("onload", "startAnimation()")
```

So, in our `Select Case` statement, we can use the value we previously assigned to our variable `sBannerType` to decide which ASP.NET `Literal` control's content block should be visible for the current client, and add the `onload` attribute to the `<body>` tag as well if we are sending an animated banner:

```
' insert the appropriate block of code into the page
' currently Opera has a problem with positioning, but
' should be able to use blockStd section when fixed
' also add "onload" attribute to <body> tag in main page
Select Case sBannerType
  Case "IE4"
    Dim oBodyTag As HtmlGenericControl = Parent.FindControl("BodyTag")
    oBodyTag.Attributes.Add("onload", "startAnimation()")
    blockIE4.Visible = True
  Case "N6", "IE6"          ' plus Opera6 when fixed
    Dim oBodyTag As HtmlGenericControl = Parent.FindControl("BodyTag")
    oBodyTag.Attributes.Add("onload", "startAnimation()")
    blockStd.Visible = True
  Case "N4"
    Dim oBodyTag As HtmlGenericControl = Parent.FindControl("BodyTag")
```

```
        oBodyTag.Attributes.Add("onload", "startAnimation()")
        blockN4.Visible = True
    Case Else
        blockBase.Visible = True
  End Select
...
```

If the `Animate` property is `False`, we don't need to do anything other than make the `Literal` control that contains the `"Base"` banner content visible:

```
    ...
  Else

    ' no animation required, show base version
    blockBase.Visible = True

  End If

End Sub
```

Notice that the <body> element in any page where the banner will be animated must be declared as a server control with the id of "BodyTag" for this to work. In other pages, where we don't animate the banner, there is no need for the <body> element to be a server control.

The Animation Content for CSS-Enabled Clients

All that remains to look at in our banner is the content that we send to each of the three types of client we are serving an animated version to. For any browser that supports CSS2 and the HTML DOM Version 2, we can use the content in the 'standard' block – defined within the `Literal` control with an id value of `"blockStd"`. The next listing shows the first part of this content. It consists of five images, with a range of attributes applied to each one:

```
<asp:Literal id="blockStd" runat="server" Visible="False">

<!-- animated page banner for IE 6.x, Nav 6.x and above -->
<!-- NOTE: also Opera6+ when positioning error is fixed -->

  <img src="images/bgsizer.gif" width="1px" height="83px" alt="" />
  <img id="CarImg" src="images/animtow1.gif"
      width="134px" height="61px" alt=""
      style="visibility:hidden; position:absolute; display:block;
            left:0px; top:8px" />
  <img id="CarImg2" src="images/animtow2.gif"
      width="134px" height="61px" alt=""
      style="visibility:hidden; position:absolute; display:block;
            left:0px; top:8px" />
  <img id="HeadImg" src="images/wccheader.gif"
      width="370px" height="61px" alt="Wrox Car Company"
      style="visibility:hidden; position:absolute; display:block;
            left:0px; top:8px" />
  <img id="Force" src="images/force.gif"
```

```
         width="200px" height="40px" alt="The Driving Force"
     style="visibility:hidden; position:absolute; display:block;
             left:420px; top:15px" />
```

The first image, `bgsizer.gif`, is used simply to force the HTML table that contains the banner to be exactly 83 pixels high. It's a one-pixel-wide transparent GIF image, so does not show up in the browser. Notice that we also set the `alt` attribute to an empty string so that text-only browsers and page readers know that it should be ignored.

Next come the two 'old car' images, one with a towrope and one without. These are actually three-frame animated GIF files that we built using Microsoft GIF Animator. They are absolutely positioned eight pixels down from the top of the page, and to the far left of the page. The CSS styles also specify that both images will be hidden when the page loads.

> *For information about Microsoft GIF Animator, see:*
> *http://www.microsoft.com/FRONTPAGE/previous/imagecomposer/page5.htm*

After the 'old car' images comes the Wrox Car Company logo itself, and the image of the slogan "The Driving Force". The logo is positioned eight pixels down from the top of the page, and at the left-hand side, while the slogan image is located at its final position. However, like the 'old car' images, both are hidden when the page first loads.

Animating the Banner

Animation of the banner is implemented with client-side JavaScript code. The `onload` event of the page (defined in the `<body>` element, as we saw earlier) causes the function named `startAnimation` to be executed once the page has loaded into the user's browser. The next listing shows that function, complete with the rest of the client-side code.

We have a series of 'global' variables defined in the client-side `<script>` section. In the `startAnimation` function we place a "welcome" message in the browser's status bar, then set the global variables `objCar` and `objHead` as references to the two images we want to move across the screen first. We also set the initial positions of these images so that they will gradually appear at the left-hand side of the page:

```
<script language="JavaScript">
<!--
//--- Version for IE 6.0 and higher, Netscape 6.0 and ---
//--- higher, Mozilla 1.0 and higher, plus Opera 6.0. ---
//--- Uses W3CDOM Level2 + CSS methods and properties ---
// declare the global variables
var objTimer;       // reference to window.setInterval timer
var objCar;         // reference to old car image
var objHead;        // reference to Wrox Car Co banner image
var bLoaded;        // flag to show if images are finished loading
var bSwapped;       // flag to show we've swapped to the 2nd car image
var iWindowWidth;   // width of client window

function startAnimation() {
  window.status = 'Welcome to the Wrox Car Company';
  objCar = document.getElementById('CarImg');
  iCarLeft = - 150;
```

```
    objHead = document.getElementById('HeadImg');
    iHeadLeft = -520;
    bSwapped = false;  // using first car image
    // need width of page to detect car reaching right-hand side
    // table holding contents of page is sized to 100% of page width
    // use this except in Navigator and other browsers where we have to use
    // innerWidth property of the window instead:
    if (document.all)
      iWindowWidth = document.getElementById('tblBack').style.pixelWidth
    else
      iWindowWidth = window.innerWidth;
    // start the interval timer
    objTimer = window.setInterval('moveImages()', 10);
  }
```

As you can see towards the end of this code, we need to figure out the width of the browser window so that we can stop the animation when the car gets to the right-hand side. In most CSS2-enabled clients we tried, the window object exposes a property named innerWidth that returns the width in pixels. However, Internet Explorer doesn't do this, so we use the width of the table within which we're animating the images instead. Only Internet Explorer has a document.all collection (we discussed this in Chapter 3), and so we can detect IE by looking for this collection.

The final line of the code above starts an interval timer running, and specifies that the function named moveImages should be executed every 10 milliseconds (effectively, this means as fast as the client can process the interval events).

Moving the Images

The moveImages function, which is responsible for the complete animation sequence, is shown next. In Internet Explorer, we can take advantage of a specific feature it provides to make sure that all the images have finished loading before we start the animation – we check that the readyState property of the document object is "complete". This doesn't work in other clients, however, so again we check for the presence of a document.all collection here.

Next we can make our car and logo images visible, and see if the car has reached the right-hand side of the window. If it has, we stop the interval timer, hide the car image, change the status bar message, and display the 'slogan' image by making it visible:

```
function moveImages() {
  // wait until all images have loaded (IE only)
  if ((document.all) && document.readyState != 'complete') return;
  // make the images visible, they're off screen
  objCar.style.visibility = 'visible';
  objHead.style.visibility = 'visible';
  if (iCarLeft > iWindowWidth - 135) {
    // car has got to right-hand end
    window.clearInterval(objTimer);        // so stop timer
    objCar.style.visibility = 'hidden';    // and hide it
    window.status = 'Select a car for more information';
    // display the slogan image
    document.getElementById('Force').style.visibility = 'visible';
  }
  ...
```

The two global variables we declared earlier, `iCarLeft` and `iHeadLeft`, store the current position of the 'old car' and logo images, and we set them to positions off to the left of the page when we first started the animation. So now, if the car has not yet reached the right-hand side of the window, we need to move it right by one pixel. We also need to move the logo image right by one pixel if it has not yet reached its final position (ten pixels in from the left). All that's required is to increment the two global variables, and assign their new values to the `left` property of the images' `style` objects:

```
...
else {
  // move the images
  iCarLeft += 1;
  objCar.style.left = iCarLeft;
  if (iHeadLeft < 10) {
    iHeadLeft += 1;
    objHead.style.left = iHeadLeft;
  }
  else {
    if (! bSwapped) {
      // swap to the second car image (no towrope)
      objCar.src = document.getElementById('CarImg2').src;
      bSwapped = true;
    }
  }
}
//-->
</script>
</asp:Literal>
```

The other check we need to make, if the 'Wrox Car Company' logo image *has* reached its final position, is if we have already swapped the car images over so as to show the one *without* the towrope. The global variable bSwapped is initially set to `false` in the `startAnimation` function, but when the 'Wrox Car Company' logo image reaches it final position (ten pixels in from the left of the window) we set it to `true` and then change the `objCar` variable to reference the other car image. Then this image is displayed instead of the one with the towrope.

The Animation Content for Internet Explorer 4.x and Above

The client-side code we use to animate the image in Internet Explorer 4.x and 5.x is almost the same as we use in CSS2-enabled clients, and which we've just been examining. These two versions implement Microsoft Dynamic HTML, which is actually very close to the final CSS2 recommendations. Many of the properties, methods and techniques are the same, or extremely similar.

The reason that we provide a separate function for Internet Explorer 4.x and 5.x is that there is one fundamental difference between Microsoft DHTML and CSS2 – the way that we get a reference to an element within the page. In DHTML we query the `document.all` collection, while in CSS2 (as you've just seen) we use the `getElementById` method of the `document` object (we discussed our decision to use two different versions of the server-side script code, rather than detecting the client type within this code, earlier in this chapter).

So, here's the listing of the functions we use for Internet Explorer 4.x and 5.x. The HTML content (the images) is identical to the CSS2 version of the banner, so we haven't repeated it here. In the listing below, we've highlighted the lines that are different to the CSS2 version:

```
<script language="JavaScript">
<!--
//--- Version for Internet Explorer 4.x and 5.x only ---
//--- Uses IE-specific DHTML methods and properties  ---
// declare the global variables
var objTimer;      // reference to window.setInterval timer
var objCar;        // reference to old car image
var objHead;       // reference to Wrox Car Co banner image
var bLoaded;       // flag to show if images are finished loading
var bSwapped;      // flag to show we've swapped to the 2nd car image
var iWindowWidth;  // width of client window

function startAnimation() {
  window.status = 'Welcome to the Wrox Car Company';
  objCar = document.all['CarImg'];
  iCarLeft = - 150;
  objHead = document.all['HeadImg'];
  iHeadLeft = -520;
  bSwapped = false;  // using first car image
  // need width of page to detect car reaching right-hand side
  // table holding contents of page is sized to 100% of page width
  iWindowWidth = document.all['tblBack'].style.pixelWidth;
  // start the interval timer
  objTimer = window.setInterval('moveImages()', 10);
}
function moveImages() {
  // wait until all images have loaded (IE only)
  if ((document.all) && document.readyState != 'complete') return;
  // make the images visible, they're off screen
  objCar.style.visibility = 'visible';
  objHead.style.visibility = 'visible';
  if (iCarLeft > iWindowWidth - 135) {
    // car has got to right hand end
    window.clearInterval(objTimer);        // so stop timer
    objCar.style.visibility = 'hidden';   // and hide it
    window.status = 'Select a car for more information';
    // display the slogan image
    document.all['Force'].style.visibility = 'visible';
  }
  else {
    // move the images
    iCarLeft += 1;
    objCar.style.left = iCarLeft;
    if (iHeadLeft < 10) {
      iHeadLeft += 1;
      objHead.style.left = iHeadLeft;
    }
    else {
      if (! bSwapped) {
        // swap to the second car image (no towrope)
```

```
                    objCar.src = document.all['CarImg2'].src;
                bSwapped = true;
            }
        }
    }
}
//-->
</script>
```

The Animation Content for Netscape 4.x Only

In Netscape Navigator 4.x, the techniques we use to animate the banner are very similar to those we used in the two previous sections. However, we cannot reference images elements and manipulate them in the same way. The only way we can get the same type of effect is to place each image inside a separate <layer> element, and manipulate these instead. So, for a start, the HTML content we send to Navigator 4 has to be different:

```
<asp:Literal id="blockN4" runat="server" Visible="False">

<!-- animated page banner for N4.x only -->

  <img src="images/bgsizer.gif" width="1px" height="83px" alt="" />
  <layer id="HeadLayer" top="15px" left="-520px" visibility="hidden">
    <img src="images/wccheader.gif" width="370px" height="61px"
        alt="Wrox Car Company" />
  </layer>
  <layer id="CarLayer" top="15px" left="-150px" visibility="hidden">
    <img src="images/animtow1.gif" width="134px" height="61px" alt="" />
  </layer>
  <layer id="ForceLayer" top="25px" left="430px" visibility="hidden">
    <img src="images/force.gif" width="200px" height="40px"
        alt="The Driving Force" />
  </layer>
  <layer id="Car2Layer" top="15px" left="383px" visibility="hidden">
    <img src="images/animtow2.gif" alt="" />
  </layer>
```

We use the same bgsizer.gif image to force the table to be the correct height, but then each of the remaining images are placed within a separate <layer> element that is positioned on the page at the appropriate place, and hidden by setting the visibility attribute to "hidden" (note that we use attributes of the <layer> elements instead of selectors in a style attribute). We also have to use different values for the top property of each <layer> element, as the way that the layers are offset from the window is different to the way images are positioned in other browsers.

Moving the Layer Elements

In the code section, we again declare a series of 'global' variables, but this time we have four that we'll use to reference the <layer> elements (rather than the image elements, as we did in the previous sections for other browsers). We then collect references to the appropriate <layer> elements by accessing the layers collection of the document object:

```
<script language="JavaScript">
<!--
//--- Version for Netscape Navigator 4.x only ---
//--- Uses Netscape-specific layers & methods ---
// declare the global variables
var objTimer;          // reference to window.setInterval timer
var layHead;           // reference to Wrox Car Co banner image layer
var layCar;            // reference to old car (with towrope) image layer
var layCar2;           // reference to old car (no towrope) image layer
var layForce;          // reference to slogan layer
var bSwapped;          // flag to show we've swapped to the 2nd car image
var iWindowWidth;      // width of client window

function startAnimation() {
  window.status = 'Welcome to the Wrox Car Company';
  layHead = document.layers['HeadLayer'];
  layCar = document.layers['CarLayer'];
  layCar2 = document.layers['Car2Layer'];
  layForce = document.layers['ForceLayer'];
  bSwapped = false;  // using first car image
  iWindowWidth = window.innerWidth;
  // start the interval timer
  objTimer = window.setInterval('moveImages()', 10);
}
```

Having started the interval timer running, we react to each event it raises in the moveImages function as we did in the previous examples. While the overall process is much the same, we have slightly different values for the element positions in the various if...else constructs, and we also have to set the visibility attribute directly for the <layer> elements (in the previous sections, as you'll recall, we set the visibility property of the style object). The other major difference is that we position the images using the moveToAbsolute method, rather than by setting the style.left property:

```
function moveImages() {
  // make the images visible, they're off screen
  layCar.visibility = 'visible';
  layHead.visibility = 'visible';
  if (layCar.left > iWindowWidth - 50) {
    // car has got to right-hand end
    window.clearInterval(objTimer);           // so stop timer
    layCar.visibility = 'hidden';             // and hide it
    window.status = 'Select a car for more information';
    layForce.visibility = 'visible';          // show slogan
  }
  else {
    // move the images
    layCar.moveToAbsolute(layCar.left + 1, layCar.top);
    if (layHead.left < 20)
      layHead.moveToAbsolute(layHead.left + 1, layHead.top);
    else {
      if (! bSwapped) {
        // swap to the second car image (no towrope)
        layCar.visibility='hidden';
        layCar = layCar2;
```

```
            layCar.visibility='visible';
            bSwapped = true;
        }
      }
    }
  }
}
//-->
</script>
</asp:Literal>
```

Using the Animated Banner Control

Now that our banner control is complete, we can use it in our pages. In the 'Home' page, we want to animate the banner where possible, but only when the visitor first hits this page. For subsequent hits, and in all other pages, we want to show only the static version of the banner.

As we saw when building the banner control, it exposes three properties:

pagebanner.ascx

```
'property declarations
Public UAType As String = "Unknown"
Public UAVer As String = "Unknown"
Public Animate As Boolean = False
```

In our 'Home' page, we first register the banner control using the `Register` directive:

home.aspx

```
<%@Register TagPrefix="wcc" TagName="pagebanner"
            Src="ascx/pagebanner.ascx"%>
```

Then, after the 'skip to' links and before the start of the main page structure table, we insert our banner control into the page:

```
<wcc:pagebanner id="ctlBanner" runat="server" />
```

Setting the Banner Control Properties

The next step is to set the properties of the banner control each time our page loads. In the `Page_Load` event handler of our 'Home' page, `home.aspx`, we collect the browser type and major version into two variables (you saw this in the previous chapter, when we were deciding which stylesheet to send to our client).

Then we can check to see if the current browser supports client-side scripting, and has it enabled, by checking the `bCanScript` variable. If this is `False`, we can't animate the banner. However, if `bCanScript` is `True`, we can use the values for the browser type and major version to set the properties of our banner control:

```
    ...
    ' get the browser type and version
    Dim sUAType As String = Request.Browser("Browser")
```

```
      Dim sUAVer As String = Request.Browser("MajorVersion")
      ...
      ' set properties of "pagebanner" user control
      ' if client supports scripting and it is enabled
      If bCanScript Then
        ctlBanner.UAType = sUAType
        ctlBanner.UAVer = sUAVer

        ' check if user has seen animation in this session
        ' if not, show and set session value to indicate this
        If CType(Session("WccSeenAnimation"), Boolean) = False Then
          ctlBanner.Animate = True
          Session("WccSeenAnimation") = "True"
        End If

      End If
      ...
```

To decide whether to animate the banner, we check the user's ASP.NET session for a value named WccSeenAnimation. If this is False, we set the Animate property of our banner to True and set the session value to True as well. The next time this page is loaded during the current session, the banner control will not be animated and the user will see the static version.

When we use the banner control in other pages, where it will never be animated, we don't have to bother with setting its properties. The default values within the control will automatically provide a static banner. So, for these pages, we only need to register the banner control with a register directive, and insert it into the page. For example, in the 'Contact' page named contact.aspx, all we need is:

contact.aspx

```
<%@Register TagPrefix="wcc" TagName="pagebanner"
            Src="ascx/pagebanner.ascx"%>
...
...
<wcc:pagebanner id="ctlBanner" runat="server" />
```

The Page Footer Section

Every page in our site displays a 'standard' page footer section. This contains a set of text hyperlinks pointing to all the main pages on our site. This traditional type of page footer is the accepted way to provide alternate navigation features, plus the e-mail address of the site's webmaster for feedback purposes. Users generally expect to find something like this on web sites, and many go straight to it if they can't easily and quickly find any other links to pages that they want. And so, while we've tried very hard to make our site easy to navigate, we still provide these links:

Notice that we also provide the pop-up tool-tips for the links, using the `title` attributes of the `<a>` elements that implement these links. You'll see this shortly.

In ASP 3.0 and earlier, it was a common technique to build page footers like this as Server-Side Include (SSI) files. These are just text files containing the HTML and any other required content, and they are inserted into the page using a `#include` directive. Although this approach still works fine in ASP.NET, the preferred method is to use a control of some type. It could be a server control, compiled into a DLL and placed in the `bin` folder or into the Global Assembly Cache (GAC). However, equally valid, is the approach we've taken here of building it as a **user control**.

Dynamic Hyperlinks in the Footer

One reason for using a control for the page footer can be seen in the previous screenshot. Remember that the accessibility guidelines we discussed in Chapter 3 suggest that we should avoid self-referring links in our pages. There should not be any link in a page that refers to that page, as it can cause confusion for visitors who are using specialist clients or user agents.

This means that for the footer of our 'Home' page, we should *not* have a hyperlink to the 'Home' page, and you can see from the screenshot that this is the case in our page. We could, of course, omit this link – but leaving it in as text only (not a hyperlink) makes it obvious that this is the 'Home' page.

So, we want to build a footer control that we can use in any page on our site, but which shows the current page as text and not as a clickable hyperlink. Our page footer user control does just this, as we'll see next.

Building the Page Footer Control

Like the page banner, the page footer section is implemented as a user control that we can insert into any page within our site (within the same virtual application). We use fairly basic HTML within the control for maximum compatibility with all clients, centering the content in the page with a `<center>` element, and setting the font face and size using the `<font>` element.

However, notice that each of the `<a>` elements in the list of links to other pages is a server control. By adding the `runat="server"` attribute, we tell ASP.NET to use the `HtmlAnchor` class (from the namespace `System.Web.UI.HtmlControls`) to implement this control. We also provide an `id` for each one that reflects the text content of the hyperlink.

After these links comes the copyright statement, followed by an ASP.NET `Hyperlink` control that creates the link containing the e-mail address of the webmaster. Notice that we don't specify values for the `NavigateUrl` (the `href` attribute) or the `Text` (the clickable content). We set these values at runtime using code in the `Page_Load` event handler:

footerlinks.ascx

```
<%@Control Language="VB" EnableViewState="False"%>
...
... server-side script section here ...
...
<center>
<hr size="1" />
```

```
<font id="fHOME" runat="server" size="1" face="Arial,sans-serif">
<a id="aHOME" href="../home.aspx" runat="server"
   target="_top" title="Home Page">Home</a> |
<a id="aCOMPARE" href="../compare.aspx" runat="server"
   target="_top" title="Compare Models">Compare</a> |
<a id="aCONTACT" href="../contact.aspx" runat="server"
   target="_top" title="Contact Details">Contact</a> |
<a id="aTANDC" href="../tandc.aspx" runat="server"
   target="_top" title="Terms/Conditions">Terms &amp; Conditions</a> |
<a id="aMYCARS" href="../secure/mycars.aspx" runat="server"
   target="_top" title="My Cars">My Cars</a>
</font>
<hr size="1"/>
<font size="1" face="Arial,sans-serif">&copy;2002 <a href="http://www.wrox.com/"
title="Wrox Press">Wrox Press</a> UK and USA. Contact:
<asp:Hyperlink id="lnkWebmaster" runat="server" title="Support Email Address"
/></font>
</center>
```

We chose to use the HtmlAnchor controls for the text links here, rather than the ASP.NET Hyperlink, purely for efficiency reasons. As you'll see shortly, we need these to be server controls, but we don't need the extra complexity of the Hyperlink control. The HtmlAnchor is a simpler and lighter control, and so we might as well benefit from the reduced complexity.

We could have done the same with the link to the webmaster, but the approach we've taken shows both techniques together so that you can compare the way we set the properties.

The HtmlAnchor Control

The HtmlAnchor control inherits from the same base class (HtmlControl) as all the controls in the System.Web.UI.HtmlControls namespace, including the HtmlGenericControl we looked at in the previous chapter. However, because the HtmlAnchor control implements a specific HTML element (the <a> element), it has a few extra members that are specific to this type of element. In particular, it has four extra properties:

Member	Description
Href property	Sets or returns the URL that is used as the value of the href attribute when the element is rendered.
Name property	Sets or returns the text that is used as the value of the name attribute when the element is rendered.
Target property	Sets or returns the text that is used as the value of the target attribute when the element is rendered.
Title property	Sets or returns the text that is used as the value of the title attribute when the element is rendered.

A full list of the members for the HtmlAnchor can be found in the .NET SDK at:

ms-help://MS.NETFrameworkSDK/cpref/html/ ⌐
frlrfSystemWebUIHtmlControlsHtmlAnchorMembersTopic.htm

So, when we declare an `HtmlAnchor` control in our page (simply by adding the `runat="server"` attribute to an `<a>` element), we can set these properties to specify the matching attribute values we want the rendered element to have. This is what we did in the code for the 'Home' page you saw in the previous chapter, for example in the last link "My Cars" we specify the values for the `href`, `target` and `title`:

```
<a id="aMYCARS" href="../secure/mycars.aspx" runat="server"
    target="_top" title="My Cars">My Cars</a>
```

Including the `target="_top"` attribute means that we will always open the new page in the complete browser window, even if the current page is within a frameset.

The Code for the Page Footer Control

We know that our page footer control must have the ability to remove the hyperlink from one of the text links when it is inserted into a page. In fact, this is easy to do. We expose a property for our user control by defining a `Public String` variable named `CurrentPageLink`:

footerlinks.ascx

```
<script runat="server">
' control property set from ASPX page:
Public CurrentPageLink As String = ""
```

Then, in the `Page_Load` event handler for our control, we can find the control that implements this hyperlink, and remove the `href` attribute. This effectively renders the content of the control as text and not as a hyperlink. To remove an attribute from a control, we can access the `Attributes` collection using the attribute name:

```
MyAnchor.Attributes.Remove("href")
```

However, as the `href` attribute is exposed as the `Href` property of the control, it's easier to just set this property to an empty string. It gives us the same outcome – no `href` attribute:

```
MyAnchor.Href = ""
```

So, here's our `Page_Load` event handler so far. We convert the string supplied for the `CurrentPageLink` property of our control to uppercase, though this isn't strictly necessary as the `id` property is not case-sensitive, and prefix an "a" so that it will match the `id` value of the appropriate hyperlink. We also use a `Try...Catch` construct to prevent an error being raised if the value supplied in the `CurrentPageLink` property doesn't map to any of the hyperlinks:

footerlinks.ascx

```
Sub Page_Load()

  Try

    ' remove link for current page, leave as text
    Dim sCurrent As String = CurrentPageLink.ToUpper()
    CType(FindControl("a" & sCurrent), HtmlAnchor).Href = ""
```

```
        ' set the e-mail address of the webmaster
        ...

    Catch
    End Try

End Sub
```

Setting the Webmaster's E-Mail Address

Next we have to set the properties of the `Hyperlink` control that is used for sending e-mail to our webmaster. We store the e-mail address of our webmaster in the `<appSettings>` section of the `web.config` file, in the root folder of the samples (as we do with the connection string for our database – we discussed this technique in the previous chapter):

web.config

```
<appSettings>
  ...
  <!-- following is e-mail address used as "From" in e-mail messages -->
  <add key="WroxCarsWebmasterEmail" value="webmaster@your-own-site.com" />
  ...
<appSettings>
```

So all we have to do is extract this value from `web.config` and use it to create the values for our `Hyperlink` control's `NavigateUrl` and `Text` properties:

footerlinks.ascx

```
Sub Page_Load()

  Try

    ' remove link for current page, leave as text
    Dim sCurrent As String = CurrentPageLink.ToUpper()
    CType(FindControl("a" & sCurrent), HtmlAnchor).Href = ""

    ' set the e-mail address of the webmaster
    Dim sWebmasterEmail As String = _
            ConfigurationSettings.AppSettings("WroxCarsWebmasterEmail")
    lnkWebmaster.NavigateUrl = "mailto:" & sWebmasterEmail _
                            & "?subject=Wrox Cars Web Site"
    lnkWebmaster.Text = sWebmasterEmail

  Catch
  End Try

End Sub

</script>
```

Using the Page Footer Control

To use the footer control in our pages, all we need to do is register it and then insert it into the page at the point where we want the footer to appear (probably at the bottom of the page!). This is the `Register` directive:

```
<%@Register TagPrefix="wcc" TagName="footerlinks"
            Src="ascx/footerlinks.ascx"%>
```

When we insert the control into the page, we can specify the text of the link that we do *not* want to be displayed as a hyperlink. For example, in our 'Home' page we use:

```
<wcc:footerlinks runat="server" CurrentPageLink="Home" />
```

In a page that is not referenced in the links within the footer control we can just insert the control without specifying a value for the `CurrentPageLink` property. All the text links will be displayed as hyperlinks in this case.

Adding Users to the Mailing List

The final section of our 'Home' page that we have not looked at in detail is the area below the list of news items where visitors can submit their e-mail address to join our mailing list. We provide a text heading, a text box control with the caption "Your email address:", and a Go button to submit the value:

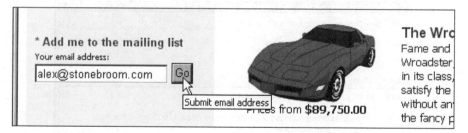

To try and avoid collecting invalid e-mail addresses, we validate the format of the e-mail address that the user enters. If the text box is empty, we display a message in the area below the four graphic links to other pages on our site telling them that they must enter an e-mail address. And if they enter a value that doesn't appear to be a valid e-mail address (it doesn't have the correct combination of 'dots' and the '@' character), we also display a warning:

Notice also that an asterisk appears next to the textbox caption when the value is missing or in an incorrect format (as shown in this screenshot, where we omitted the 'dot' before 'com'. OK, there is only one control on the page, so figuring out which one contains the invalid value doesn't require a diploma in computer science, but we'll show you later how we can achieve this effect very easily in our pages:

In an "up-level" client, where client-side validation is being performed, this asterisk appears when the content of the textbox is invalid and the user tabs to another control in the page, without requiring a postback to the server. The text error messages appear when the user attempts to submit the page by clicking the Go button – again without posting the page back to the server. However, this does not happen in "down-level" clients. The asterisk and the error message only appear after the page has been posted back to the server.

After a postback, and if the e-mail address they enter does appear to be valid, we add it to our database and display a "thank you" message:

We also send them an e-mail to confirm that they have been added to the mailing list:

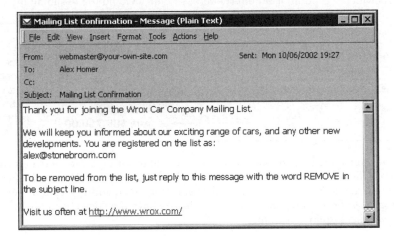

The Controls to Submit an E-Mail Address

To create the section of the page that contains the captions, e-mail address textbox, and Go button, we used a mixture of ASP.NET server controls and ordinary HTML elements. The next listing shows the source for this section of the page.

The heading "Add me to the mailing list" is declared within a <span> element that specifies the CSS class `body-red-text`, which defines the appearance we want for the text. However, for non-CSS browsers, we also wrap this in a <font> element that specifies the same font face, size, and color. Then the small text caption "Your email address: " is declared and formatted in the same way with a <span> and a <font> element.

Next come the two ASP.NET **validation controls** that we use to validate the e-mail address. We'll look at these in more detail shortly. They are followed by an ASP.NET `TextBox` control and `Button` control:

```
<font face="Arial,Helvetica,sans-serif" size="2" color="#b50055">
<span class="body-red-text">
<b>* Add me to the mailing list</b></span></font><br />
<font size="1"><span class="small-text">
Your email address:</span></font>

<asp:RequiredFieldValidator id="valRequired" runat="server"
    ControlToValidate="txtMailList"
    ErrorMessage="* You must enter a value in the email address textbox"
    Display="dynamic">
    *
</asp:RequiredFieldValidator>

<asp:RegularExpressionValidator id="valRegExpr" runat="server"
    ControlToValidate="txtMailList"
    ValidationExpression=".*@.*\..*"
    ErrorMessage="* You must provide a valid email address in the textbox"
    Display="dynamic">
    *
</asp:RegularExpressionValidator><br /></font>

<font face="Arial,Helvetica,sans-serif" size="3">
<asp:TextBox id="txtMailList" Columns="20" runat="server"
            title="Enter your email address" />
</font>
<font face="Tahoma,Arial,Helvetica,sans-serif" size="2">
<asp:Button id="btnMailList" OnClick="AddToMailingList" Text="Go"
            runat="server" title="Submit email address" /></font>
```

There are a few things we need to point out here. Notice how we wrap the `Textbox` control in a <font> element that specifies a sans-serif-style font face, and size `"3"`. Different browsers have different default fonts for the text controls on an HTML <form>, and different default widths for these controls. After some experimentation, we discovered that (at least in the various Windows-based browsers) this format creates a similar sized text box on all the clients we tested, and with similar sized text within the textbox.

However, for the Go button (which ASP.NET renders as a standard HTML `<input type="submit">` button, the best combination of font face and size to get the appearance we wanted appears to be that shown in the previous listing, a sans-serif font with size equal to `"2"`.

Notice also how we provide `title` attributes for the text box and Go button (you can see the effect of the `title` attribute on the Go button in the first screenshot of this section). An alternative would be to set the `ToolTip` attribute or property, which achieves the same thing (it also generates a `title` attribute when rendered to the client). This technique provides an extra hint to users of specialist browsers as to what the controls are for, and is especially useful on complex forms.

ASP.NET Form Controls and the <form> Element

The various ASP.NET controls that implement HTML `<form>` control elements (such as text boxes, checkboxes, lists, and so on) must be placed inside a server-side `<form>` section of the page – a `<form>` element with the `runat="server"` attribute. If not, the page will produce a compilation error when you try and open it.

This makes sense because, although Internet Explorer will display ordinary HTML form controls (elements that are not server controls) without placing them on a `<form>`, most other browsers will not. They just ignore the element declarations, and the controls do not appear in the page.

However, it does mean that we have to use a server-side form (with the `runat="server"` attribute) if we want to use server controls. Why would we need to use a `<form>` without the `runat="server"` attribute? Well, there are a couple of scenarios. We might want to submit the values to a different page rather than post them back to the same page. The ASP.NET postback architecture prevents this with a server-side `<form>`.

Secondly, we might want to have more than one `<form>` on a page, perhaps submitting values to different pages, or submitting different sets of values. Again, the ASP.NET postback architecture does not allow this. There can only be one server-side `<form>` on a page. OK, neither of these is a common technique in most of our pages – so the postback architecture can be used and we can benefit from the advantages it provides.

However, one other scenario to bear in mind is if you are using non-server control elements such as an `<input type="button">` or `<input type="text">`, and only interacting with them client-side (in other words, you are not submitting their values to the server). In this case you might prefer to put them on a `<form>` that does *not* contain a `runat="server"` attribute. But then you can't use server controls for these buttons or other control elements.

ASP.NET Validation Controls

We declared two ASP.NET validation controls in the previous listing, which will check the value that the user enters in the textbox on our page. Validation of submitted values is something that we know we should always do, but it never seems to be as easy as you would expect.

The common approach is to validate the values with client-side script, to avoid a postback to the server if the value is obviously invalid. However, how many of us then **repeat the validation on the server** to check that a user is not trying to spoof the code by creating a page of their own that submits invalid values.

The validation controls are the most intelligent of all the controls supplied with ASP.NET. They can perform validation on the client in "up-level" browsers using client-side script that is automatically added to the page when it is processed by ASP.NET. And they always validate the values sent from the client on the server as well.

In "down-level" clients there is no client-side validation (at least in ASP.NET version 1.0, though it may be added in future releases). Instead, the validation is performed only on the server, and we can check that it succeeded in our code. The validation controls also provide the facility to disable client-side validation in "up-level" clients, or to disable validation altogether if required. And there is also a 'validation summary' control that displays a list of all the validation errors found in the page. We use this to provide the error message you saw in the earlier screenshots.

A full list of the ASP.NET validation controls is:

Validation Control	Description
`<asp:RequiredFieldValidator>`	Checks that the validated control contains a value. It cannot be empty. Can be used in conjunction with other validators on a control to trap empty values.
`<asp:RangeValidator>`	Checks that the value in the validated control is within a specified text or numeric inclusive range. If the validated control is empty, no validation takes place.
`<asp:CompareValidator>`	Checks that the value in the validated control matches the value in another control or a specific value. The data type and comparison operation can be specified. If the validated control is empty, no validation takes place.
`<asp:RegularExpressionValidator>`	Checks that the value in the validated control matches a specified regular expression. If the validated control is empty, no validation takes place.
`<asp:CustomValidator>`	Performs user-defined validation on an input control using a specified function (client-side, server-side, or both). If the validated control is empty, no validation takes place.
`<asp:ValidationSummary>`	Displays a summary of all current validation errors.

The Validation Control Members

With the exception of the `ValidationSummary` control, all of the validation controls inherit from the base class named `BaseValidator`, which is part of the class library namespace `System.Web.UI.WebControls`. The most commonly used properties and methods of the `BaseValidator` base class are:

Member	Description
ControlToValidate property	Sets or returns the ID of the input control containing the value to be validated.
Display property	Sets or returns a value indicating how the validation control will display its content. Can be None (not displayed), Static (hidden when value is valid) or Dynamic (removed from page when value is valid).
EnableClientScript property	Sets or returns a Boolean value indicating whether client-side validation is enabled where the client supports this.
Enabled property	Sets or returns a Boolean value indicating if validation will be carried out.
ErrorMessage property	Sets or returns the text of the error message that is displayed by the ValidationSummary control when validation fails.
IsValid property	Returns a Boolean value indicating if the value in the associated input control passed the validation test.
Text property	Sets or returns the text and/or HTML content of the control.
Validate method	Performs validation on the associated input control and updates the IsValid property.

The validation controls also expose properties and methods (and in one case an event) that are specific to that control type:

Control	Properties	Events
RequiredFieldValidator	InitialValue	– *none* –
RangeValidator	MaximumValue, MinimumValue, Type	– *none* –
CompareValidator	ControlToCompare, Operator, Type, ValueToCompare	– *none* –
RegularExpressionValidator	ValidationExpression	– *none* –
CustomValidator	ClientValidationFunction	OnServerValidate
ValidationSummary	DisplayMode, HeaderText, ShowMessageBox, ShowSummary	– *none* –

Most of the property names are self-explanatory, and we don't have room to examine them all in depth here. However, we'll show you how we use the RequiredFieldValidator and RegularExpressionValidator controls in our 'Home' page next. We'll be looking at other ways we can use the validation controls later in the book when we see some pages from our Wrox Car Company site that use them.

A guide to the general techniques for using the validation controls can be found in the .NET SDK at:

ms-help://MS.NETFrameworkSDK/cpguidenf/html/ 7 cporiValidationWebServerControls.htm.

The reference section for each of the validation controls can be found within the System.Web.UI.WebControls namespace of the class library section at:

ms-help://MS.NETFrameworkSDK/cpref/html/frlrfSystemWebUIWebControls.htm.

The Validation Controls in the 'Home' Page

We've repeated the code we used to insert the two validation controls into our 'Home' page in the next listing. You can see from this how we use the ControlToValidate property to connect the validation control with the control we want it to validate (our Textbox control with the ID of txtMailList).

It's quite acceptable to connect more than one validation control to another control on the page, in fact it's often required. Remember that only the RequiredFieldValidator reports an invalid value if the control is empty. The others only validate the contents if the control is not empty, so we often use a combination of the RequiredFieldValidator to check that a value has been entered, along with another validator to check that value:

```
<asp:RequiredFieldValidator id="valRequired" runat="server"
    ControlToValidate="txtMailList"
    ErrorMessage="* You must enter a value in the email address textbox"
    Display="dynamic">
    *
</asp:RequiredFieldValidator>

<asp:RegularExpressionValidator id="valRegExpr" runat="server"
    ControlToValidate="txtMailList"
    ValidationExpression=".*@.*\..*"
    ErrorMessage="* You must provide a valid email address in the textbox"
    Display="dynamic">
    *
</asp:RegularExpressionValidator><br /></font>
```

We set the ErrorMessage property in both of the controls in our example above. This defines the text that is displayed by the ValidationSummary control we place elsewhere in our page – you can compare this text with the error message in the screenshot we showed earlier in this section of the chapter. In the case of the RegularExpressionValidator, we also have to provide the regular expression that we want the user's value to be compared to. Our example provides a rudimentary check for a valid e-mail address.

A guide to the syntax and general techniques for using regular expressions can be found in the .NET SDK at:

ms-help://MS.NETFrameworkSDK/cpguidenf/html/cpconcomregularexpressions.htm

Displaying the Validation Control Content

The `Display` property of the validation controls specifies how they will place the content of the control in the page, particularly when the value in the control they are validating is valid. The content of the validation control is (as you'd expect) the text and HTML placed between the opening and closing tags of the control. In our example above, we used just a single asterisk character.

When the value in the connected control is invalid, the validation control displays its content, by default in red (we can change the color, style, and size by setting various properties or attributes of the control, such as `ForeColor`, `Font-Size`, etc., just as we would any other Web Forms control). So, the position of the validation controls within the page defines where the content will be displayed. In our example, we place them after the caption for the textbox, but before the textbox and `<br />` element:

When the value in the connected control is valid, the content of the validation control is hidden. If the `Display` property of the validation control is set to `"Static"`, the space taken up by this content remains in the page – it is just hidden by setting the CSS `visibility` selector to `"hidden"`. This is useful when, for example, we place a validation control in a table cell, as it will not change the layout of the table when shown or hidden. However, if we set the `Display` property to `"Dynamic"`, the validation control actually removes the content from the page altogether by setting the CSS `display` selector to `"none"`, so the layout of the page may change.

The ValidationSummary Control in the 'Home' Page

To display the error messages from the validation controls when an invalid value is submitted, we use a `ValidationSummary` control. This is located in a table cell immediately below the four graphic links to other pages in our site, spanning the four columns of the table that holds these images:

```
...
<tr>
  <td colspan="4" align="center">
  <font face="Arial,Helvetica,sans-serif" size="3" color="#b50055">
  <asp:ValidationSummary Font-Name="Arial,Helvetica,sans-serif"
       id="valSummary" cssClass="large-red-text" runat="server"
       HeaderText="<b>You could not be added to the mailing list:</b>"
       ShowSummary="true" DisplayMode="List" />
  <asp:Label id="lblMessage" cssClass="large-red-text" runat="server" />
  </font></td>
</tr>
...
```

When we declare the control, we specify the formatting details in the same way as we have in other Web Forms controls, and in other parts of our page. We set the `CssClass` property to the name of the CSS class we want to use in CSS-enabled clients, and then specify the font details for other clients. We also wrap the complete content of the table cell in a `<font>` element for non-CSS-enabled clients.

Notice the three other attributes we set for the `ValidationSummary` control. The `HeaderText` attribute defines the text shown above the list of errors collected from the other validation controls in the page, and the `ShowSummary` attribute specifies if these error messages will be displayed or not (so we can just show the header text if required). The `DisplayMode` attribute defines how the list of errors is displayed. It can be `"List"` (the default, with line breaks between each one), `"BulletList"` (an HTML `<ul>` list), or `"SingleParagraph"` (with no line breaks).

Underneath the `ValidationSummary` control is an ASP.NET `Label` control with the ID `lblMessage`. We use this to display our own error messages, or a "thank you" message if we succeed in adding the user to our mailing list. You'll see how we set the values for this `Label` control when we look at the code to add addresses to the database shortly.

Online Server Controls Examples

A useful way to see all of the validation controls in action in one page is to run the example we created for the Wrox book *Professional ASP.NET* (ISBN 1-86100-703-5). To save downloading all the samples and installing them on your own machine (though you can if you wish), you can view them running on our server at http://www.daveandal.com/books/7035/. Select the Exploring Server Controls option, and open the Other Controls section of the menu to find the validation controls page:

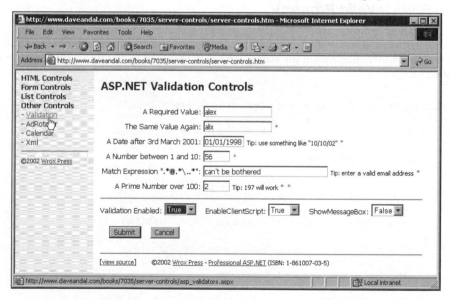

This page allows you to experiment with many of the ASP.NET server controls, and there are examples on this site that you can play with to see all the others (such as the list controls) in action as well.

203

The Code to Handle E-Mail Addresses

Having seen how we declare the validation controls in our page, we'll look at how we write the code that interacts with them. In fact, as you'll see, we don't have to do very much at all. The validation controls do all of the complicated work for us, and we are really just reduced to checking one property to see if the validation succeeded or not, then carrying out the actions required if validation did succeed.

So, the first section of code we need to look at in our 'Home' page is the `AddToMailingList` event handler. When we declared the Go button, we specified the value `AddToMailingList` as the `OnClick` attribute:

```
<asp:Button id="btnMailList" OnClick="AddToMailingList" Text="Go"
            runat="server" title="Submit email address" />
```

All ASP.NET Web Forms server controls (from the namespace `System.Web.UI.WebControls`) implement the `OnClick` event as a **server-side** event. As we discussed way back in Chapter 1, these controls do not provide the client-side `onclick` attribute. So, we can write a routine to handle this event on our server.

The first step is to see if the value submitted by the user is valid or not. While an "up-level" client will not allow them to submit an invalid value (unless client-side scripting is disabled), a "down-level" one will. OK, so it automatically generates the error messages, but we still have to make sure that we only execute our code when all the values in the page *are* valid. We do this by checking the `IsValid` property of the current (default) `Page` object.

Using the Page.IsValid Property

If all the validation controls agree that the values in their connected controls are valid, the `IsValid` property of our `Page` object will be `True`, and we execute some code that collects the e-mail address for the text box, trims any spaces from the start or end of it, and then passes it to a function named `UpdateMailingList`:

```
' subroutine executed when the user submits their e-mail
' address to add to the mailing list
Sub AddToMailingList(sender As Object, args As EventArgs)
  If Page.IsValid Then
    ' update database and display message
    Dim sMsg As String
    Dim sEmailAddr As String = txtMailList.Text.Trim()
    Select Case UpdateMailingList(sEmailAddr)
      Case 0
        sMsg = "You are already a member of our mailing list."
      Case 1
        sMsg = "Thank you for joining our mailing list."
        ' call routine to send e-mail confirmation
        SendEmailConfirmation(sEmailAddr)
      Case Else
        sMsg = "* Sorry, you could not be added to the " _
             & "mailing list.<br />Please " _
             & "<a href='contact.aspx' title='contact us'>contact us</a>" _
             & " for more information"
```

```
      End Select
      lblMessage.Text = "<p><b>" & sMsg & "</b></p>"
   End If
End Sub
```

Depending on the value returned by the UpdateMailingList function, we generate a suitable message as a String, and display it in the page by setting the Text property of the ASP.NET Label control named lblMessage that we placed underneath our ValidationSummary control. And if we do succeed in adding the user to our mailing list, we call another routine named SendEmailConfirmation that, as you can probably guess, sends the confirmation e-mail message we saw earlier on when we were experimenting with the page.

The UpdateMailingList Function

When a user submits their e-mail address to add to our mailing list, we must insert it into our database. The **WroxCars** database contains a table named tblMailingList, which contains two columns: a column named EmailAddr (the primary key and of type varchar) to hold the e-mail address, and a datetime column named DateAdded to indicate when the address was added. The value for this column is set to the current date automatically when a new row is added because we specify the function getdate() as the default value within the definition of the table.

The database also contains a stored procedure named AddMailingListAddress. It accepts a varchar (String) as the first (input) parameter named Email, and sets the output parameter named Result to an integer value that depends on the outcome of the procedure. If the e-mail address already exists in the table, the SELECT statement within the stored procedure (listed below) will set the internal ROWCOUNT variable to one (1). The following IF statement will then fail, and the INSERT statement will not be executed. However, executing an IF statement has the side effect of resetting ROWCOUNT to zero, so in the last line the Result variable will be set to zero and returned from the stored procedure.

If the e-mail address is not already in our database table, however, ROWCOUNT will be zero following execution of the SELECT statement, and so the stored procedure will execute the INSERT statement to add the e-mail address to the database. This will set ROWCOUNT to one (1), and the value of the Result variable will also be set to 1:

AddMailingListAddress (stored procedure)

```
CREATE PROCEDURE AddMailingListAddress
@Email varchar(255), @Result int OUTPUT
AS
SELECT EmailAddr FROM tblMailingList WHERE EmailAddr = @Email
IF @@ROWCOUNT = 0
    INSERT INTO tblMailingList (EmailAddr) VALUES (@Email)
SELECT @Result = @@ROWCOUNT
GO
```

Of course, because the e-mail address is the primary key of the table, we could just attempt an INSERT without bothering to check if it already exists. If it does the INSERT will fail. However, although this saves executing two distinct operations within the stored procedure (a SELECT and an INSERT), the more systematic approach we've used makes it easier to see what's going on, avoids an error being raised, and will work without a primary key definition if required.

Executing the AddMailingListAddress Stored Procedure

We execute the stored procedure AddMailingListAddress within a function in our 'Home' page named UpdateMailingList. The technique is similar to that we used in the previous chapter to execute the stored procedures to get a list of 'News' items and car models. However, now we have two parameters to contend with.

We can add parameters to a Command object in a range of ways – depending on what properties we need to set for these parameters. In our code we've chosen the simplest way to add parameters, by simply executing the Add method of the Parameters collection, and supplying the name of the parameter and the value. This method automatically figures out the data type of the value we provide, and creates a parameter of the correct type. All that remains is to tell it that the second parameter is an output parameter by setting the Direction property:

home.aspx

```
' function to add user's e-mail address to mailing list
Function UpdateMailingList(sEmailAddr As String) As Integer
  ' database connection string already in sConnect from Page_Load event
  Dim sqlConnect As SqlConnection = New SqlConnection(sConnect)
  Try
    Dim sProcName As String = "AddMailingListAddress"
    Dim sqlComm As SqlCommand = New SqlCommand(sProcName, sqlConnect)
    sqlComm.CommandType = CommandType.StoredProcedure
    sqlComm.Parameters.Add("@Email", sEmailAddr)
    sqlComm.Parameters.Add("@Result", -1)
    sqlComm.Parameters("@Result").Direction = ParameterDirection.Output
    sqlConnect.Open
    sqlComm.ExecuteNonQuery()
    Return sqlComm.Parameters("@Result").Value
  Catch
    Return -1
  Finally
    sqlConnect.Close
  End Try
End Function
```

The code then executes the stored procedure (using the ExecuteNonQuery method because we don't want to return a rowset), and returns the value of our parameter named Result to the calling routine. If there is an error of any kind (which we trap with a Try...Catch construct), we return the value –1 instead. Depending on the value we return from our UpdateMailingList function, the code we looked at earlier in the AddToMailingList event handler for the Go button on our 'Home' page will then create and display the appropriate message.

> *For a list of the six different overloads for the Parameters.Add method, see the .NET SDK topic: ms-help://MS.NETFrameworkSDK/cpref/html/⅂ frlrfsystemdatasqlclientsqlparametercollectionclassaddtopic.htm*

The SendMail User Control

Sending an e-mail message using the .NET Framework classes is easy, but there is one issue that we came across regularly while experimenting with these classes. If the code that uses these classes is not in a virtual application root folder (the root folder of an ASP.NET application), the process often proved to be unreliable.

While this isn't a problem in our 'Home' page, which *is* in the root of our **Wrox Car Company** application, we also want to be able to send e-mail messages from the **My Cars** page that you'll see described in Chapter 12. This page is in a sub-folder named secure, and so it will suffer from the problem we've just mentioned.

To get round this, we created another **user control** that we can use to instantiate and execute the Framework classes we need to send an e-mail message. Of course, we can't put this user control in the ascx sub-folder where all our other user controls reside – we have to put it into the root folder of the application.

The next listing shows the complete sendmail.ascx user control we created. To use the objects and classes that send SMTP mail from within ASP.NET, we must import the System.Web.Mail namespace into the page, as you can see in the second line of this listing. We describe how the rest of the code works in the following sections of this chapter:

sendmail.ascx

```
<%@Control Language="VB" EnableViewState="False"%>
<%@Import Namespace="System.Web.Mail"%>

<script runat="server">
' control properties set from ASPX page:
Public FromAddress As String = ""
Public ToAddress As String = ""
Public MessageSubject As String = ""
Public MessageBody As String = ""

' routine to send e-mail message
Function SendEmail() As Boolean
  Try
    Dim oMessage As MailMessage = New MailMessage
    oMessage.From = FromAddress
    oMessage.To = ToAddress
    oMessage.Subject = MessageSubject
    oMessage.Body = MessageBody
    oMessage.BodyFormat = MailFormat.Text
    ' specify SMTP server name if required, default is "localhost"
    ' EDIT THIS LINE: SmtpMail.SmtpServer = "my-mail-server"
    ' send mail - requires local mail server to be available
    SmtpMail.Send(oMessage)
    Return True
  Catch
    Return False
  End Try
End Function
</script>
```

Exposing the Properties and Methods of the Control

The first few lines of code within the `<script>` section of our `sendmail.ascx` user control define the four `Public String` properties that we will specify values for when we use this control. We expose the From and To addresses, the text for the subject line, and the text that will make up the body of the message.

The remainder of the code is a `Public Function` named `SendEmail` (exposed as a method of the user control) that sends the e-mail message. We take the values of the four properties and use them to set the properties of the .NET `MailMessage` object we're using to send the mail. We also specify that the format of the message (the `BodyFormat` property) is `Text` – though this is the default anyway. Finally, we call the `Send` method of the `SmtpMail` object.

Using the SmtpMail Class to Send the Message

If you've worked with the CDONTS objects in earlier versions of ASP, you'll find that using the `MailMessage` object in ASP.NET is a very similar technique. CDO (Collaborative Data Objects) is a COM-based technology for interacting with SMTP mail systems in Windows, and the classes in the .NET `System.Web.Mail` namespace simply wrap these objects and make them available as .NET classes.

> *Information about CDO for Windows 2000 can be found at:*
> *http://msdn.microsoft.com/library/en-us/cdo/html/_denali_cdo_for_nts_library.asp*

Once we've created our message, we have to find a way to deliver it. We use the local SMTP Service that is installed as part of Internet Information Services on Windows 2000 Server, Windows 2000 Advanced Server and Windows 2000 DataCenter Server (it is not available in Windows 2000 Professional). Alternatively, we can arrange for a separate 'smart host' to deliver the message instead.

Mail is sent using the `SmtpMail` object. The class that defines this object is static, and so we don't need to create a specific instance of it – we can just reference it directly. The `SmtpMail` object has one `Public` property, `SmtpServer`, which we use to specify the server that will be used to deliver the message. If we are using the local SMTP Service, we can omit this property, or set it to `"localhost"` (the default):

```
' specify mail server to be used to deliver message
SmtpMail.SmtpServer = "localhost"
```

The `SmtpMail` object also exposes a `Public` method named `Send`, which we use to pass the message to the SMTP Service or other mail server that will deliver it. In our 'Home' page, we use this code to send the message:

```
' send mail - requires mail server to be available
SmtpMail.Send(oMessage)
```

The SendEmailConfirmation Routine

So, in our 'Home' page, we can create a suitable e-mail message using our `sendmail.ascx` user control. At the top of this page we register this control, and then insert it right at the end of the page, just before the closing `</body>` tag. We give it an ID of `"ctlMail"`:

```
<%@Register TagPrefix="wcc" TagName="sendmail" Src="sendmail.ascx"%>
...
...
<!-- control containing the routine to send e-mail messages -->
<wcc:sendmail id="ctlMail" runat="server" />
```

Now, in the `SendEmailConfirmation` routine within our 'Home' page, we just have to build up a `String` holding the body of the message we want to send, and set the properties of our user control. Then we can call its `SendEmail` method to send the mail:

home.aspx

```
' routine to send e-mail confirmation of addition to mailing list
Sub SendEmailConfirmation(sEmailAddr)
   Dim sMessage As String
   sMessage = "Thank you for joining the Wrox Car Company Mailing List." _
           & vbCrlf & vbCrlf _
           & "We will keep you informed about our exciting range of " _
           & "cars, and any other new developments. You are registered " _
           & "on the list as: " & vbCrlf & sEmailAddr & vbCrlf & vbCrlf _
           & "To be removed from the list, just reply to this message " _
           & "with the word REMOVE in the subject line." _
           & vbCrlf & vbCrlf & "Visit us often at http://www.wrox.com/"

   ' use separate ASCX control to send the message
   ctlMail.FromAddress = _
           ConfigurationSettings.AppSettings("WroxCarsWebmasterEmail")
   ctlMail.ToAddress = sEmailAddr
   ctlMail.MessageSubject = "Mailing List Confirmation"
   ctlMail.MessageBody = sMessage
   ctlMail.SendEmail()
End Sub
```

Notice that we again use the value from `web.config` for the From address in our mail message, just as we did in the `footerlinks.ascx` user control we looked at earlier. It means that we only have to edit the value in the `<appSettings>` section of `web.config` to change the e-mail address in both the footer of every page in our site, and the 'From' address for all e-mail messages.

Configuration Issues for Sending Mail from ASP.NET

There are a few things to be aware of when you build ASP.NET pages that will send e-mail messages:

❑ The behavior of the `SmtpMail` object depends on the configuration of your mail server, and depends on the CDO objects installed with Windows 2000 for its functionality. Strange errors and other effects can occur if this is not available or properly configured.

❑ The page containing the code that sends the message should be in a virtual application folder, and not just in a sub-folder of the default web site. While we have not been able to discover the exact reasons for this, we found that the `SmtpMail.Send` method can cause a "550 Cannot Relay for Domain" message when the folder containing the page was not configured as a virtual application.

❑ ASP.NET must have permission to access the SMTP Service. For the local SMTP Service, you must give the ASPNET account (or whichever account you are running the ASP.NET process under if you changed it from the default) at least Read and Write access to the inetpub\mailroot\pickup folder. We generally give the ASPNET account Read, Write, and Modify permission for mailroot and all its sub-folders, so that ASP.NET can handle incoming mail as well.

❑ If you are delivering mail through a remote 'smart host' mail server, you may have to configure it to allow ASP.NET to send a message to it, and also allow the machine that generates the message to relay through the 'smart host'. The requirements depend on your network, mail server, and security configuration, and the type of mail server you are using.

❑ Make sure that you use a valid e-mail address for the From property of your messages. Some redirection servers and 'smart hosts' perform a reverse lookup, and may reject messages that do not have a valid 'from' address. The example page we provide in the samples for this book contains an invalid 'from' address, which you should change to suit your own system.

A full reference to the MailMessage and SmtpMail classes can be found in the .NET SDK at: ms-help://MS.NETFrameworkSDK/cpref/html/frlrfSystemWebMail.htm

Summary

In this chapter, we've completed our tour of the 'Home' page for our fictitious example Wrox Car Company web site. While it has taken two whole chapters to do so, we have covered a lot of ground in that time. In the previous chapter, we saw the design and implementation of the overall page structure, the way we apply styles and formatting, and how we extract content from our database and display it in the page.

In this chapter, we moved on to look at the concept of **user controls**, and how we built the two that provide the animated page banner and the intelligent page footer for our site. By exposing properties from these user controls, we can make them respond in various ways depending on the requirements of each page or specific situations. For example, our page banner provides different output depending on the type of client that we are serving the page to, and only creates the animated version when the user first visits the site.

We also looked at how we can send e-mail messages from our web site in this chapter. Exploring the controls we use to collect the information in our 'Home' page led to a fairly in-depth discussion of the ASP.NET validation controls, as well as looking at the way we use the objects from the System.Web.Mail namespace to create and send e-mail messages.

In all, we covered:

❑ The animated banner we use in most of the pages

❑ The page footer we use in most of the pages

❑ How we add users to the mailing list in our 'Home' page

In the next chapter, we'll leave our 'Home' page behind and see some of the other pages that we implement on our site.

WANTED
WEB DEVELOPER

6

The Ancillary Pages

Our site's 'Home' page is now complete, and we can move on to look at some of the other pages. As you will guess, most of the techniques we introduced in previous chapters are used in many, if not all, of the pages on our site. This includes the way we interact with the user's session, format the output for a wide range of client types, and provide accessibility features to assist users of specialist types of client.

You saw that the 'Home' page provides prominent links to four other pages, by way of the graphic buttons just below the banner at the top of the page. We'll be looking at three of these pages in this chapter, the 'Compare Models', 'Terms and Conditions' and 'Contact' pages. These pages include features that are standard across most of the 'ancillary' pages on our site, such as the links back to the 'Home' page and other pages, as well as having the same overall layout (we'll be looking at the 'My Cars' page in later chapters).

There are also two other pages that are opened from the 'Home' page, but not from the graphical button links. These are the page that displays a complete 'News' item (linked from the list of news précis in the left-hand column of the 'Home' page) and the 'Model Details' page (linked from the vehicle image and name in the right-hand section of the 'Home' page). We'll be looking at the first of these in this chapter, while we'll come back to the 'Model Details' page later in this book.

So, in this chapter, we'll examine:

- ❑ The general structure of the 'ancillary' pages, including layout and navigation
- ❑ The 'Terms and Conditions' and 'Contact' pages
- ❑ Deciding when to use static as opposed to dynamic content
- ❑ The page that displays the individual 'News' items
- ❑ The structure and workings of the 'Compare Models' page
- ❑ How we create the display of model comparisons as an HTML table

We start with a look at the overall page structure of our ancillary pages.

The Structure of the Ancillary Pages

In Chapter 3, while discussing the guidelines for providing good accessibility on our web pages for visitors who have restricted sight or movement, we pointed out that a great way to make a site easy to use was to have a common structure for the basic components or sections of every page. This makes it easier to find things like a menu bar, and to navigate between pages. And, as a bonus, it actually makes it easier for all our visitors to use the site – they don't have to hunt around for links and content that is placed in different positions on each page.

The Overall Layout

All of the ancillary pages on our site, with only a couple of minor exceptions, have a common layout for the page: a static banner, the link to the 'Home' page and other pages, the content section, and the page footer; as shown in the following diagram:

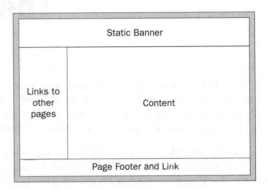

'Terms & Conditions' and 'Contact' Pages

As an example of the structure of the ancillary pages, the next screenshot shows the 'Contact' page – you can see all the sections shown in the diagram above within this page:

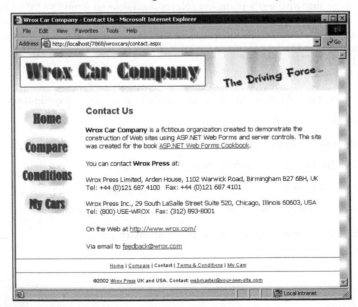

The HTML Table for the Ancillary Pages Structure

This overall layout is created with a standard HTML table, which includes three user controls that are common to all the ancillary pages. The page banner is the same user control named `pagebanner.ascx` that we used in the 'Home' page, but now it is not animated. The page footer is the same user control named `footerlinks.ascx` that we used in the 'Home' page, with the `CurrentPageLink` property set such that the current page is not a hyperlink.

The left-hand section containing the clickable image links is another user control – one that we haven't met so far. This control, named `mainlink.ascx`, is detailed later in this section of the chapter. Finally, the content of the page is displayed in the right-hand side of the page, within a single cell of our HTML table.

So, to get the overall page structure, we use the following abridged HTML declarations:

contact.aspx

```
<!doctype html public "-//W3C//DTD HTML 3.2 Final//EN">
<html>
<head>
<basefont size="2">
<link rel="stylesheet" type="text/css"
      href="stylesheets/wcc<% = sStyleSize %>.css" />
<title>Wrox Car Company - Contact Us</title>
</head>
<body leftmargin="0" rightmargin="0" topmargin="0"
      bgcolor="#ffffff" class="body-text">
<div style="position:absolute;height:0px;"><font size="1" color=#ffffff>

<!-- skip link for aural page readers -->
<layer visibility="hidden">
<a href="#content" style="color:#ffffff;font-size:1px;text-decoration:none"><img
width="1" height="1" hspace="0" vspace="0" src="images/_blnk.gif" border="0"
alt="Skip to Content" /></a>
</layer>

</font></div>

<wcc:pagebanner runat="server" /><br />

<table width="100%" border="0" cellspacing="0" cellpadding="10">
<tbody>
 <tr>
  <td valign="top" width="110px">
   <wcc:mainlink runat="server" CurrentPageLink="Contact" />
  </td>
  <td align="left">
   <a name="content" />
   <font face="Arial,Helvetica,sans-serif" size="4" color="#b50055">
   <p class="large-red-text"><b>Contact Us</b></p></font>
   <font face="Tahoma,Arial,Helvetica,sans-serif" size="2">
   <p class="body-text">
   <b>Wrox Car Company</b> is a fictitious organization created ...
     ... page content goes here ...
```

```
      </p>
     </font>
    </td>
   </tr>
 </tbody>
 </table>

 <wcc:footerlinks runat="server" CurrentPageLink="Contact" />

 </body>
 </html>
```

Looking through this, you should easily be able to pick out the important points:

❑   The page contains a section that declares the 'skip to' link for aural page readers and text-only user agents, linking to the main 'content' section of the page so that visitors can go straight to this section.

❑   The page banner user control is inserted into the page with the <wcc:pagebanner> element, as in the 'Home' page, but we don't need an id attribute as we are not going to be accessing the control in our server-side code.

❑   A two-column single-row HTML <table> contains the links to other pages, declared as the user control element <wcc:mainlink>, and the actual page content itself (our contact details) as text and HTML.

❑   Below the <table> is the user control that implements the 'footer' links. This is inserted into the page with the <wcc:footerlinks> element, just as we did in the 'Home' page, setting the CurrentPageLink property to the name of this page so that it is not included as a self-referencing hyperlink.

❑   The section containing the content uses both CSS styles and <font> elements to control the format and appearance of the text, as we've done in the 'Home' page of our site.

So, other than the content itself, which is simply inserted as text and HTML into the right-hand <table> cell, what haven't we seen before? There are a few lines of server-side code that we'll look at next. After that, the only thing that we need to examine in more detail is the <wcc:mainlink> user control – which we'll do in a short while.

The Code for the Ancillary Pages

There is very little code required in the 'Contact' and 'Terms and Conditions' pages. The only things we need to do are select the correct style sheet for the current browser type, and check that the user still has a current ASP.NET session available.

A page-level variable is declared to hold the part of the stylesheet name that we extract from the user's session (where it was stored by code in the 'Home' page). In the Page_Load event handler, we collect the value for this variable and then check to see if we actually did find it. If not, we know that either the user's session has expired, or that they entered our site at this page directly and not through the 'Home' page. In either case, we redirect them to the page default.aspx, where the client detection process will be performed to reestablish the session values we need:

contact.aspx

```
<script runat="server">
' -----------------------------------------------------------------

' page-level variable to style sheet size
Dim sStyleSize As String = "Standard"


' -----------------------------------------------------------------

Sub Page_Load()

  ' get style sheet size from Session
  sStyleSize = CType(Session("WccStyleSize"), String)

  ' if no value, session has expired or user entered
  ' site at page other than 'Home' page
  If sStyleSize = "" Then
    Response.Clear()
    Response.Redirect("default.aspx")
  End If

End Sub


' -----------------------------------------------------------------

</script>
```

The value for sStyleSize that we collect from the session is then used in the <link> element to select the correct stylesheet:

```
<link rel="stylesheet" type="text/css"
      href="stylesheets/wcc<% = sStyleSize %>.css" />
```

Redirection When No Session Is Available

We discussed our decision to demand session support for the **Wrox Car Company** site when we looked at the design of the site as a whole, and again when we discussed the client detection process. As the design we've chosen will not work correctly without an ASP.NET session, we have to check that one exists each time we load a page that uses any values stored in the session.

In the case of our 'Contact' and 'Terms and Conditions' pages, the only value we use is the stylesheet name, and so the page would work without a session. The <link> element would fail to find a matching stylesheet, and the <font> elements would provide the formatting we require.

However, other pages in our site will not work correctly without session support, and will have to redirect the visitor to the default.aspx page if a current session is not available. We felt that it makes sense for all the pages to exhibit the same behavior.

The other issue here is where we actually redirect the visitor to if session support is lost or a current session is not available. We chose to redirect them to the page default.aspx, which will then redirect them to the 'Home' page after reestablishing the user ID, stylesheet type and client-side script support values in their session.

Likewise, if the visitor has entered the site by loading one of the pages other than the 'Home' page (via `default.aspx`) first, they will be seamlessly redirected to the 'Home' page. This is not unusual behavior for a site that requires user interaction (try your own bank's online account management web site for an example).

As an alternative to redirecting them to `default.aspx`, we could redirect straight to `home.aspx`. Because there is no valid session available, the code in `home.aspx` will redirect them to the page `no-sessions.htm`. It displays details of why they are here, what might be the cause, and it provides a link to enter the site at the correct place – or to use the alternative cookie-less session version of the site instead:

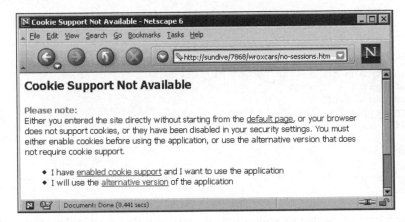

Of course, if we redirect to `default.aspx` and our visitor's browser does not support cookies, they'll see this page anyway. The code in the 'Home' pages causes this to happen, as we saw in Chapter 3. This is the reason that we decided to go with the 'seamless' option of redirecting to `default.aspx`, as it probably gives a better user experience, and less of an impression that the site has 'broken'.

The MainLink User Control

The graphical links in the left-hand side of our 'ancillary' pages are the same as we use near the top of the 'Home' page, with the addition of a link back to the 'Home' page itself. However, remember the accessibility guidelines that suggest we should never have a self-referring link in our pages (except when we need to post a `<form>` back to the server). So, we want to make sure that we only display links to other pages each time.

In the previous screenshot of the 'Contact' page, you can see that the links there do not include the 'Contact' clickable graphic button. However, the following screenshot of the 'Terms and Conditions' page does have this link – but not a 'Conditions' link:

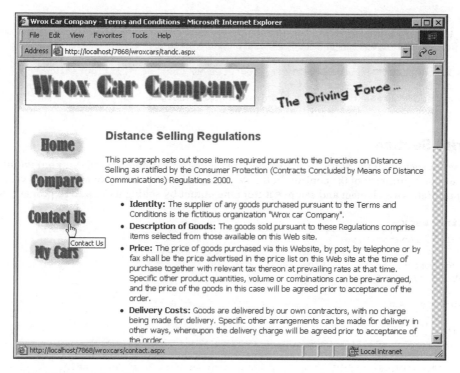

You can probably guess that the user control (`mainlink.ascx`) we use to implement these links works in much the same way as the `footerlinks.ascx` user control we examined in the previous chapter (which implements the text links and copyright notice at the bottom of every page).

The visible content of our `mainlink.ascx` control is shown in the next listing. You can see that we have five `<img>` elements, nested inside five `<a>` elements. Notice that the `<a>` elements are server controls (implemented by the `HtmlAnchor` control we examined in the previous chapter), and that the `id` for each one contains the page name. However, the `<img>` elements are not server controls and have no `id` attribute:

mainlink.ascx

```
<%@Control Language="VB" EnableViewState="False" debug="True"%>

<a id="aHOME" runat="server" Title="Back to List of Models"
   href="../home.aspx">
 <img src="images/btn_home.gif" width="100" height="49"
     hspace="3" vspace="2" alt="Home Page" border="0" /></a>
<a id="aCOMPARE" runat="server" Title="Compare Vehicle Models"
   href="../compare.aspx">
 <img src="images/btn_compare.gif" width="100" height="49"
     hspace="3" vspace="2" alt="Compare Models" border="0" /></a>
<a id="aCONTACT" runat="server" Title="Contact and Feedback Details"
   href="../contact.aspx">
 <img src="images/btn_contact.gif" width="100" height="49"
     hspace="3" vspace="2" alt="Contact Us" border="0" /></a>
```

```
<a id="aTANDC" runat="server" Title="Terms and Conditions of Trading"
   href="../tandc.aspx">
 <img src="images/btn_tandc.gif" width="100" height="49"
     hspace="3" vspace="2" alt="Terms and Conditions" border="0" /></a>
<a id="aMYCARS" runat="server" Title="View My Cars and Configurations"
   href="../secure/mycars.aspx">
 <img src="images/btn_mycars.gif" width="100" height="49"
     hspace="3" vspace="2" alt="My Cars" border="0" /></a>
```

The Script Section

In the script section of the user control, we declare a `Public` variable named `CurrentPageLink`, which acts as a property of the control. In the `Page_Load` event handler we can use this value to locate the appropriate <a> element and remove it from the output by setting its `Visible` property to `False`:

mainlink.ascx

```
<script runat="server">

' control property set from ASPX page:
Public CurrentPageLink As String = ""

Sub Page_Load()

  Try
    ' remove <a> from page - also removes child <img> element
    Dim sCurrent As String = CurrentPageLink.ToUpper()
    CType(FindControl("a" & sCurrent), HtmlAnchor).Visible = False
  Catch
  End Try

End Sub

</script>
```

When the page is executed, all the content of the page is built up into a 'control tree' – a hierarchical tree of objects that represent every part of the page. The <img> element becomes part of the content of the `HtmlAnchor` control that represents the <a> element (the <img> element is *not* a server control as it has no `runat="server"` attribute, and therefore cannot be a child control of the `HtmlAnchor` control). The result is that, when we remove the <a> element from the output, the <img> element disappears as well. So the page only contains the links that are not specified for the `CurrentPageLink` property.

Using the MainLink Control

We use the `mainlink.ascx` control in exactly the same way as we do the `footerlinks.ascx` control. We register it in the page, and then insert it where we want the links to appear. As we insert it into the page, we use an attribute to set the `CurrentPageLink` property of the control to the appropriate value that will hide the link for the current page:

tandc.aspx

```
<%@Register TagPrefix="wcc" TagName="mainlink" Src="ascx/mainlink.ascx" %>
...
```

```
<table width="100%" border="0" cellspacing="0" cellpadding="10">
<tbody>
 <tr>
   <td valign="top" width="110px">
     <wcc:mainlink runat="server" CurrentPageLink="TandC" />
   </td>
   <td align="left">
     <a name="content" />
     <p class="large-red-text"><b>Distance Selling Regulations</b></p>
     <p class="body-text">
       This paragraph sets out those items required pursuant to the ...
       ... page content goes here ...
     </p>
   </td>
 </tr>
</tbody>
</table>
```

For a more complete discussion of user controls, see the previous chapter of this book.

Choosing Static or Dynamic Content

In the 'Terms and Conditions' and 'Contact' pages, we use static text and HTML to create the content (as displayed in the right-hand section of the page). You can confirm this by viewing the ASPX source code for either of these pages. Using static text and HTML provides the best performance, as it is simply embedded into the compiled ASP.NET page and streamed to the client with the rest of the response.

However, this approach is really only acceptable when the content does not change over time, or when it changes only infrequently. Each change to the content means editing the page source directly. So it's worth looking at other ways that we could get this 'content' into the page.

Making Static Content Dynamic

In the 'Home' page, the content came from a database. We have tables containing lists of car models and news items that we want to display, and we did this using the various list controls that are provided with ASP.NET. And, of course, you'll see plenty more examples of this approach throughout the rest of the book.

The ASP.NET list controls provide not only an easy way to handle repeated values with only one relatively simple control declaration, but they also cope with the source data changing as regularly as is required. Each time the page is accessed, it collects the list of items from the database and builds the relevant section of the page dynamically.

So, if we only have one 'thing' to display, rather than a list of items, should we still do it dynamically? As you'd expect, the typical programmer's response of "*it depends...*" is again likely. So, what does it really depend on? Here are a few pointers:

❑   How easy is it to update the source code for the page and post it to the live server? If we are using a staging server and some kind of content publishing system, there should be no problem.

❑ How complicated is the content? If it involves a lot of complex HTML and other data, it might be easier to write it directly in the page as static content than try to load it into a database table for dynamic insertion into the page at runtime.

❑ How easy is it to update the database, if we decide to store the content in this way? Do we need to provide 'admin' pages that are used simply to update the database, and is the extra work involved for this worthwhile if the content changes only rarely?

❑ Are the servers under extreme loading, so that every extra bit of performance we can squeeze out of our pages is required to keep the site running well? While this seems like a good reason to use static content, investment in an extra server or two instead is probably quite justifiable – especially if we really do need to publish dynamic content.

❑ Are we using a multiple-server web farm that runs against a single central database? In this case, unless the web farm software includes features to replicate content between servers, pulling it from the central data store dynamically might be a good plan, and provide easier maintenance.

Dynamic Content Without a Database

Of course, even when the content is being loaded into the page dynamically, it doesn't always have to come from a database. It could be:

❑ **Stored as a text file**, which contains all the HTML and content required for that section of the page. We can read a text file from disk and stream it to the client as part of the response very easily using ASP.NET. We just call the WriteFile method of the Response object, passing in the physical path to the file we want to use:

```
Response.WriteFile("myfile.txt")
```

❑ **Declared within a User Control**, which is inserted into the page using a Register directive as we saw in the previous chapter. The content of the user control appears in the page wherever we place the element that we define for it:

```
<%@Register TagPrefix="wcc" TagName="pagecontent"
            Src="ascx/some-content.ascx" %>
...
  <wcc:pagecontent runat="server" />
```

❑ **Stored in an XML document**, and transformed into HTML and other content at runtime with an XSL or XSLT stylesheet. There is even an ASP.NET control (the Xml control) that we can use to do this (we'll look at this control in more detail in Chapter 10, where we use it in the pages of our site):

```
<asp:Xml id="ctlXml" runat="server"
         DocumentSource="content.xml"
         TransformSource="contentstyle.xslt" />
```

❑ It could even come from another source such as a **Web Service**, which returns the HTML and content as a text stream (String) that we insert into the page. However, this is probably not useful unless we absolutely must have the latest data, as it is likely to considerably reduce page performance. But it's another option if we really do need to go down this route.

Making Dynamic Content Static

There is also a converse situation, which we meet quite often in web sites that contain a lot of dynamic content, but which does not change very often. This is where the data comes from a dynamic source, and it doesn't make sense to use static content in the form of HTML and text placed directly in the source of the page. But, if the data only changes infrequently (maybe once a week, once a month or even once a year), it would be nice to have a way to convert it to static content.

The laborious way to do this is to view the delivered page source in the browser, copy it as text, and paste it into the static page. However, this is not a solution that is generally likely to find favor. Instead, we can do much the same thing using code. In fact, we take advantage of this technique in several of our existing sites, as do many developers of other well-known commercial sites.

Often referred to as 'bulk caching', 'pre-caching' or 'web caching' in ASP 3.0 days, the technique is not really *caching* at all – at least not in any sense that we understand it with ASP.NET. All we do is run some code that requests the page, captures the response, and writes it to disk as an HTML page with the .htm file extension. The client then loads the .htm pages instead of the dynamic ones.

Of course, all the links in the pages we generate must then point to the equivalent static .htm page, and not to the dynamic page that generates them. But, as long as the pages are written with this in mind, there's no problem.

Generating Static Pages with ASP.NET

The example that we used in Chapter 2 of this book to demonstrate how server controls react to different types of client uses techniques we can easily adapt to generate static pages with ASP.NET. Although we didn't discuss how that example page actually works in Chapter 2, it's not difficult to see what it does from the following listing that shows the relevant techniques:

```
<%@Page Language="VB" %>
<%@Import Namespace="System.IO" %>
<%@Import Namespace="System.Net" %>

<script runat="server">
Sub Page_Load()
  ' create a Web Request object with a specified virtual path
  Dim sVPath As String = "http://localhost/test/input-page.aspx"
  Dim oWRequ As WebRequest = WebRequest.Create(sVPath)

  ' send the request and collect the response in a Stream object
  Dim oWResp As WebResponse = oWRequ.GetResponse()
  Dim oStream As Stream = oWResp.GetResponseStream()

  ' create a StreamReader to read the stream
  Dim oReader As New StreamReader(oStream, Encoding.ASCII)

  ' create a StreamWriter and use it to write the stream to a disk file
  Dim oWriter As New StreamWriter(Server.MapPath("result.htm"))
  oWriter.Write(oReader.ReadToEnd())
```

```
    ' close all the objects
    oWriter.Close()
    oReader.Close()
    oWResp.Close()
End Sub
</script>
```

You'll find an example that uses very similar code to this in the static-pages sub-folder of the sample files for this book.

The WebRequest object fetches the page, and the entire content is written to disk as a file with the .htm file extension. This file can then be opened in a browser, and it is identical to the output of the dynamic page that it was created from. However, it avoids the necessity to re-execute the original page each time. Generation of the static page need only be done when the data that is used in the dynamic page changes.

However, there are a couple of unfortunate side effects with this technique. If the page relies on values posted from a <form> or provided in the query string to change its behavior or output, static disk file generation is not going to be of any use. The .htm page we generate cannot react dynamically to these values.

The other issue is that the page cannot react differently depending on the browser type that requests it. You'll recall that the ASP.NET Web Forms server controls change their output depending on whether the current request is from an "up-level" or a "down-level" client. By default, static .htm pages generated from a dynamic page using the code we showed above will contain content suited to "down-level" clients only.

We can set the value of the UserAgent property of the WebRequest object, and have this value sent to the server as the USER_AGENT HTTP header. However, this is a property of the specific object type HttpWebRequest (not the generic WebRequest class), so we have to convert (cast) the object to the correct type first:

```
Dim sUAString As String = "Mozilla/4.0 (compatible; MSIE 6.0;)"
CType(oWRequ, HttpWebRequest).UserAgent = sUAString
```

You could, if preferred, use the specific objects like HttpWebRequest and HttpWebResponse in our code instead of the generic WebRequest and WebResponse objects and avoid the type cast.

Now the dynamic page will think that the request came from Internet Explorer 6.0, and not our ASPX code that uses a WebRequest object, so the server controls in the page we request will create output suited to "up-level" clients instead.

Using ASP.NET Caching to Expose 'Static' Pages

While creating static disk files is a useful technique in some situations, don't forget that ASP.NET also provides *real* caching – built right into the .NET Framework. We discussed this at some length towards the end of Chapter 2, when we looked at the effect it has on the output from the ASP.NET server controls.

An `OutputCache` directive such as the following tells ASP.NET to store the HTML and other content it generates in the local cache for the period (in seconds) specified in the `Duration` attribute. The code below caches the page for 24 hours, and we can use larger values to cache it even longer if required:

```
<%@OutputCache Duration="86400" VaryByParam="none" %>
```

On top of this, we can tell ASP.NET to only cache the 'static' output for requests that have the same values within the HTTP headers. For example, as a 'catch-all' that ensures our server sends a different page in response to each request that has different parameters (different `<form>` and/or query string values), we can use:

```
<%@OutputCache Duration="86400" VaryByParam="*" %>
```

And to make sure that it sends the correct output from server controls to each type of browser ("up-level" or "down-level") we can use:

```
<%@OutputCache Duration="86400" VaryByParam="*" VaryByCustom="browser" %>
```

We even demonstrated in Chapter 2 how we can create custom `VaryBy` values so as to minimize the number of different versions of the page that are cached. Look back there for more details if you need to refresh your memory.

This discussion also leads us neatly on to the next page we want to look at – the page to read the complete content of a 'News' article. The content for this page is dynamic, being drawn from a database, so we need to consider how we get maximum performance and minimize loading on our server.

The 'Read News Item' Page

In the 'Home' page of our **Wrox Car Company** site, we provide a list of current news articles in the left-hand column. The title of each one is a hyperlink, as is the [read more] link at the end of the article précis. Clicking on one of these links opens the selected article in the main window so that the visitor can read it.

The links are created within the templates we defined for the `Repeater` control that generates the list of articles. We create a URL for each hyperlink that points to the page `readnews.aspx`, and append the ID of that article to the query string. You can see the complete URL and query string (in this case http://localhost/7868/wroxcars/readnews.aspx?id=4) in the status bar of the browser window in this screenshot:

The 'Read News Item' page (`readnews.aspx`) that opens from these hyperlinks follows the same outline structure as the 'Contact' and 'Terms and Conditions' pages we looked at earlier. It has the same page banner, a set of clickable image links to other pages, and the same footer section containing the text links and copyright information. The title and content of the selected article are displayed in the right-hand section of the page:

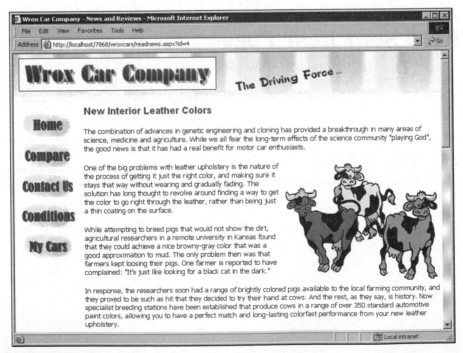

Before we look at the code that implements this page, we'll follow on from the discussion earlier about using static or dynamic content by quickly reviewing the options we have for inserting dynamic content into a page.

Inserting Dynamic Content into Pages

When we have decided that we have to include dynamic content, rather than using static HTML and text (as we did in the 'Contact' and 'Terms and Conditions' pages), we need to decide on the most appropriate technique for inserting that content into the page. We can still use the ASP 3.0 approach, but there are much better ways in ASP.NET. The following list attempts to explain the various options that are available.

- ❑ A traditional technique is to **write the content directly to the output** using a `Response.Write` statement at the point that we want the content to appear. This was a favorite approach in ASP 3.0, but is **not** recommended in ASP.NET. As the page is compiled into a class and then executed, `Response.Write` will probably not insert its output at the point you expect. It appears at the point where the statement is actually executed, and this is likely to be within an event handler, rather than during the procedural execution of the script in an ASP 3.0 page. For example, placing a `Response.Write` statement in the `Page_Load` event handler inserts the output before any other content – at the top of the page and before the opening `<html>` tag.

- ❑ We can still safely use the **ASP 3.0-style `<% =value %>` syntax** in the HTML section of the page, as we did with our stylesheet name in the `<link>` element. This is actually `Response.Write` in disguise, but it is executed as the content is generated and the output appears at that point in the page. The only issue here is that the value must be a page-level variable, and not a variable that is defined inside an event handler such as `Page_Load`. In general, it is not a preferred approach – though it is acceptable when required (as described in Chapter 4, we use it in our `<link>` element to avoid having to declare it as a server control).

- ❑ We can use **data binding with a list control**, such as a `Repeater`, `DataList`, or `DataGrid`, if the data is stored in a suitable data source object (such as a `DataReader`, a `DataSet`, a collection, an array, or a `HashTable`). Even though there is only one 'row' of data (containing, in our 'News' page example, the title and the article content) this is still a perfectly valid approach. We will only get one instance of the output that is declared in the list control's templates. If we want to place the values from this one 'row' into a table, using a `DataGrid` makes it easy as it will generate the HTML `<table>`, `<tr>`, and `<td>` elements automatically. However, it does mean extra processing overhead to instantiate the control and generate the output, which we can avoid using other techniques.

- ❑ We can use **simple single-value data binding**, either at `Page` level or to set an attribute or the content of any control on the page. The result of a function or expression, or the value of a property, can be inserted directly into the page using a data binding statement such as `<%# MyFunction() %>`. Just remember to call the `Page.DataBind()` method in the `Page_Load` event handler as well. This approach is faster and more efficient than using a list control, and it also allows the value to be inserted into an element that is *not* a server control. For example, we can use syntax such as:

```
<span><%# MyFunction(parameter1, parameter2, ...) %></span>
<input type="text" value="<%# MyProperty %>">
```

❑   We can **set the property of a server control in the page** (usually the `Text` property or the `InnerHtml` property) to the value we want to display. This is the preferred approach in ASP.NET when we have single values to display, especially where they are text rather than individual numeric values. It is the most efficient approach, and is what we do in our 'Read News' example page.

The HTML and Code for the 'Read News' Page

As you've seen, the 'Read News' page is fundamentally similar to the other ancillary pages in terms of structure, layout and appearance. The HTML code that creates these features of the page is therefore much the same as in the 'Terms and Conditions' and 'Contact' pages. The important differences are highlighted in the next abridged listing:

readnews.aspx

```
<table width="100%" border="0" cellspacing="0" cellpadding="10">
<tbody>
 <tr>
  <td valign="top" width="110px">
    <wcc:mainlink runat="server" />
  </td>
  <td align="left" class="body-text">
    <a name="content" />
    <font face="Arial,Helvetica,sans-serif" size="4" color="#b50055">
    <p id="pNewsTitle" class="large-red-text" runat="server" />
    </font>
    <font face="Tahoma,Arial,Helvetica,sans-serif" size="2">
    <p id="pNewsText" class="body-text" runat="server" />
    </font>
  </td>
 </tr>
</tbody>
</table>
```

As this page does not appear in the list of clickable graphic links generated by the user control `mainlink.ascx`, we don't have to set the `CurrentPageLink` property. We just insert the control and let it display all the links.

The other two highlighted lines show the controls where we will insert the dynamic content. We include two `<p>` elements in the page, specifying the CSS class that we want for them (they are also enclosed in the matching `<font>` elements as in the other ancillary pages). However, both of the `<p>` elements are server controls, because we've added the `runat="server"` attribute to them. This means that they will be implemented by ASP.NET as `HtmlGenericControl` objects, and so we can access their properties in our server-side code.

Getting the Content from the Data Store

But first, we need to get the dynamic content from the data source – in our case a SQL Server database. We've included a function in the page that calls a stored procedure named `GetNewsItem` within our database. This stored procedure returns the contents of all four columns in the row that has the ID value specified in the `@ItemID` parameter:

```
CREATE PROCEDURE GetNewsItem @ItemID int AS
SELECT * FROM tblNews
WHERE NewsID =  @ItemID
```

We could, of course, just return the two columns we are using in our page – we are not displaying the précis (from the column named NewsPrecis) in our page at the moment, and this would make it marginally more efficient. However, as the only thing we don't use is the précis, which is just a small text string, we decided to return all the columns here. This allows us to demonstrate a couple of ways that you can extract values from a DataReader, and also means that you can easily experiment and adapt the page to show the précis as well. Of course, if you know that a column will never be used in the page, you should not return it (especially if it is more than a few bytes).

The function GetNewsItemDR that calls this stored procedure is listed next. It works in the same way as the similar function we used in the 'Home' page to get a list of all the 'News' item précis, but this time we also have to provide a value for the @ItemID parameter:

```
' function to get selected news item from database
Function GetNewsItemDR(iItemID As Integer) As SqlDataReader
  Try
    Dim sConnect As String
    sConnect = ConfigurationSettings.AppSettings("WroxCarsConnectString")
    Dim sqlConnect As SqlConnection = New SqlConnection(sConnect)
    Dim sProcName As String = "GetNewsItem"
    Dim sqlComm As SqlCommand = New SqlCommand(sProcName, sqlConnect)
    sqlComm.CommandType = CommandType.StoredProcedure
    sqlComm.Parameters.Add("@ItemID", iItemID)
    sqlConnect.Open
    Return sqlComm.ExecuteReader(CommandBehavior.CloseConnection)
  Catch
    Return Nothing
  End Try
End Function
```

You can see that we specify the name of our stored procedure in the variable sProcName, create a Command object for this stored procedure, and set the CommandType. Then we create a new Parameter object using the Add method of the Parameters collection, setting the name to @ItemID and the value to that of the ID passed into this function as the iItemID parameter. The results of executing the stored procedure are then returned to the calling routine as a DataReader object.

Inserting the Content into the Page

The Page_Load event handler in our readnews.aspx page can use the GetNewsItemDR function to get a reference to a DataReader that will extract the values we need. It also has to collect the stylesheet type from the user's current ASP.NET session, or redirect them to the default.aspx page if there is no existing session. However, this code is the same as we used in the other ancillary pages. In the next listing, we've highlighted the code that calls the GetNewsItemDR function and inserts the data into the page:

```
Sub Page_Load()
  ' get style sheet size from Session
  sStyleSize = CType(Session("WccStyleSize"), String)
```

229

```
' if no value, session has expired or user entered
' site at page other than 'Home' page
If sStyleSize = "" Then
  Response.Clear()
  Response.Redirect("default.aspx")
End If

  ' get news item ID and display the contents
  Dim sNewsID As String = Request.QueryString("id")
  If sNewsID <> "" Then
    Dim dr As SqlDataReader = GetNewsItemDR(Integer.Parse(sNewsID))
    If dr Is Nothing Then
      pNewsText.InnerHtml = "Could not read from database"
    Else
      If dr.Read() Then
        pNewsTitle.InnerHtml = "<b>" & dr.GetString(1) & "</b>"
        pNewsText.InnerHtml = dr.GetString(3)
      End If
    End If
  End If

End Sub
```

The highlighted section of code first collects the value for the 'News' item ID, passed to this page in a name/value pair named id appended to the query string. If there is value here, we convert it to an Integer type using the shared Parse method, and pass it to the GetNewsItemDR function.

If there was no error, we'll get a DataReader back and we can call the Read method of this DataReader to access the first (and only) row of data. We then extract the values of the second and fourth columns (at index 1 and 3 because the columns are indexed from zero) to get the title and content of the 'News' item. These values are inserted into the two <p> elements by setting their InnerHtml properties. In the case of the article title, we also wrap the value in a pair of HTML <b> elements.

We'll look in more detail at the use of the DataReader.GetString method shortly.

Why Use <p> Elements?

To maximize the performance of the page, we used <p> elements rather than asp:Label controls, although these would work just as well. The HtmlGenericControl that implements the <p> elements is 'lighter' than the Label control, because it doesn't perform the client detection and other clever styling stuff that the Web Forms Label control does. So we get a marginal performance benefit.

Similar justification could be applied to using a <div> or <span> element in the same way, depending on whether we want output to be 'inline' or 'block' in HTML/CSS terms. The <p> element provides a blank line above and below its content, which is what we wanted here. If we use <div> elements, the content will appear on separate lines but without the blank line between each <div>. And if we use <span> elements, the content will be wrapped in the current line without any line breaks or blank lines.

In our example, each paragraph within the content is itself wrapped in <p> elements, so the kind of element we use in the page is not critical. However, if this was not the case, the choice of element will affect the layout of the page. Note that the HTML <p> element only generates a single line of white space before and after the content, irrespective of how many empty nested ones there may be in the page.

Alternatively, we could have used an `asp:Literal` control here, like we did in our page banner control in Chapter 5. However, this doesn't have a `class` or `CssClass` property, so we would not be able to specify the CSS style class we want for the content of the control. Another possibility would be to create a suitable control dynamically, and then insert it into the page. Again, there is an extra overhead here, but it is a useful technique to be aware of. We'll demonstrate it later in this chapter when we look at the 'Compare Models' page.

Before we move on, it's also worth mentioning how we access the contents of a `DataReader` when extracting values explicitly as we do in this page (as opposed to data binding, where they are 'implicitly' extracted by the data binding process).

Extracting Values from a DataReader

The `DataReader` provides a wide range of methods that can be used to return data from it, and we used only the simplest in our 'Read News' page. The values of a row in a `DataSet` table and in a `DataReader` are exposed as a collection of `Item` objects. We can access each `Item` by specifying the column name as a `String`, or the ordinal index as an `Integer` (with the first column being indexed as zero):

```
ItemValue = DataReader("column-name")
ItemValue = DataReader(column-index)
```

The value is returned in its native format, in other words as the data type that is defined for the column. So, if the column contains `String` values (column types `char` or `varchar` in SQL Server), both of the previous statements will return a `String`.

However, the `DataReader` also provides methods that return specific data types from a column (but the column can only be specified by its index within the collection of columns, and not by column name). This sounds really useful until you realize that they don't actually perform any type conversion. For example, if we use the `GetDateTime` method, and the column is not of type `datetime`, then an error may occur (VB.NET *might* be able to implicitly convert it to suit the variable type we assign the result to, but C# will not).

```
DateTimeValue = DataReader.GetDateTime(column-index)
```

It also means that we have to check if the column contains <NULL> first using the `IsDBNull` method. If it does contain <NULL>, we'll get an error when we try and extract the value. However, the specific methods are marginally more efficient, and you may prefer to use them when you can be sure of the data type and the presence of a value in every row.

In our code earlier on we used the `GetString` method, and specified the indices of the columns we want:

```
pNewsTitle.InnerHtml = "<b>" & dr.GetString(1) & "</b>"
pNewsText.InnerHtml = dr.GetString(3)
```

DataReader Methods that Return .NET Data Types

A summary of the methods that return specific data types from a `DataReader` is shown in the next table. These methods apply to both the `SqlDataReader` and `OleDbDataReader` objects (and to `OdbcDataReader` if you have installed the ODBC Data Provider for .NET).

231

Method	Description
Get*xxxxxx*	Returns a specific data type from a column of that type. The methods that are available are: GetBoolean, GetByte, GetChar, GetDateTime, GetDecimal, GetDouble, GetFloat, GetGuid, GetInt16, GetInt32, GetInt64, and GetString. The column required must be specified by index.
GetValue	Returns the value of the column specified by index, in its native format. Effectively the same as specifying the column index or column name only.
GetValues	Returns an array of Object types containing the column values in their native formats.
GetBytes	Reads a stream of bytes from within the specified column into a buffer (array), starting at the given buffer offset. You can also specify the start and end indices within the column to read only part of the content if required.
GetChars	Reads a stream of characters from within the specified column into a buffer (array), starting at the given buffer offset. You can also specify the start and end indices within the column to read only part of the content if required.

For a full description of all the members of the OleDbDataReader class, see the .NET SDK topic: ms-help://MS.NETFrameworkSDK/cpref/html/⏋ frlrfSystemDataOleDbOleDbDataReaderMembersTopic.htm

DataReader Methods that Return SQL Server Data Types

The SqlDataReader object also implements methods that are specific to SQL Server native data types, allowing us to extract data into variables that are declared as these data types (using the types specified within the System.Data.SqlTypes namespace). These methods only apply to the SqlDataReader class.

Method	Description
GetSql*xxxxxx*	Returns a specific SQL Server data type from a column of that type. The methods that are available are: GetSqlBinary, GetSqlBoolean, GetSqlByte, GetSqlDateTime, GetSqlDecimal, GetSqlDouble, GetSqlGuid, GetSqlInt16, GetSqlInt32, GetSqlInt64, GetSqlMoney, GetSqlSingle, and GetSqlString.
GetSqlValue	Returns the value of the specified column as a SqlDbType.Variant object.
GetSqlValues	Returns an array of Object types containing the column values in their native SqlType formats.

For a full description of all the members of the SqlDataReader class, see the .NET SDK topic: ms-help://MS.NETFrameworkSDK/cpref/html/⏋ frlrfSystemDataSqlClientSqlDataReaderMembersTopic.htm

DataReader Methods that Return Information About the Data

The `DataReader` also provides four methods that are useful for finding out more about the data. We can get the data type for a specific column, get the column name when we know the ordinal index within the row, or get the index when we know the column name. These methods apply to both the `SqlDataReader` object and the `OleDbDataReader` object (and to `OdbcDataReader` if you have installed the ODBC Data Provider for .NET).

Method	Description
GetDataTypeName	Returns a `String` containing the name of the data type for a column, as specified by its ordinal index within the row.
GetFieldType	Returns a `Type` object representing the data type of a column, as specified by its ordinal index within the row.
GetName	Returns a `String` containing the name of the column, as specified by its ordinal index within the row.
GetOrdinal	Returns an `Integer` that is the ordinal index of the column within the row, as specified by its column name.

The 'Compare Models' Page

When we were designing our site, we came up with the following rough sketch of the page where visitors can go to compare the performance and other features of all our vehicles. We decided that we'd provide a list of the models, some options on what type of comparison to carry out, and then show the results as a graphical chart of some type:

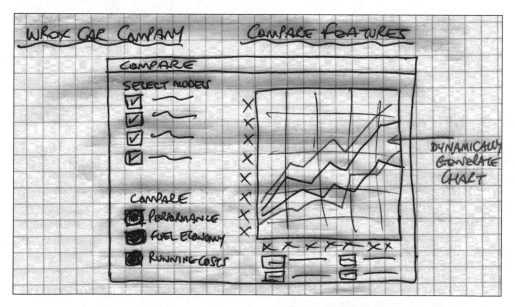

The next screenshot shows the finished page on our site, and it follows the original design quite well. The chart you see is a GIF image that is generated dynamically by ASP.NET from the information in our database, every time the page is accessed. We've added to the original design by including the standard set of links to other pages on our site, positioned as in all the other ancillary pages. And we also added one other feature (just above the chart): the option to show the results as a Table instead of a Chart:

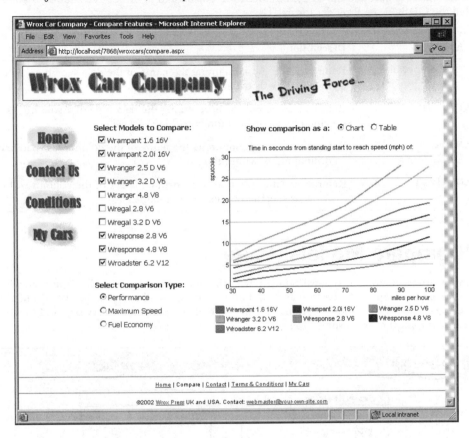

Accessibility Issues with Complex Images

The Section 508 Guidelines on Accessibility to Information Technology suggest that we should provide alternative content for any element on our web sites that does not contain plain text. This is because most specialist browsers and user agents can only make sense of text, and not of any other types of content. In our discussions of this topic at the end of Chapter 3, we talked about fulfilling this requirement by adding `alt` and `title` attributes that describe the purpose or content of these non-text elements.

The second issue that comes into play, particularly when we use charts and graphs, is the guideline that suggests no part of a site should rely solely on color for its meaning. Our visitors may suffer from varying levels of color blindness, applying to different colors as well, so this guideline makes a lot of sense. In all our pages up until now, we have only used color for aesthetic reasons anyway, as you'll see from the gray-scale screenshots in this book.

All of the precautions we've taken so far to comply with the guidelines are fine with things like text, hyperlinks and simple images, but what happens when we have something like a chart or graph – as in our 'Compare Models' page? It depends on colors to differentiate each line on the chart. And, for blind or partially sighted visitors, the chart is pretty much useless anyway. There's no way that any kind of user agent is going to be able to convert the information displayed in it to text or aural output.

Using a Long Description

The suggested technique for providing information that equates to the contents of a complex chart or graphic, where the alt attribute cannot reasonably contain this information, it to use the longdesc attribute and/or provide the same information in another format.

The longdesc attribute is part of the HTML 4.01 standard, and applies only to <img> elements. The W3C documentation for HTML 4.01 says that it is used to provide a 'long description' of the image to which it is attached, which supplements the text in the alt attribute. This 'long description' is the URL (or URI) of a page or text file that describes the content of the image in sufficient detail for the user to obtain as much information about the subject as is contained in the image. So, for a static image, it's possible to provide a long description quite easily.

However, it gets harder when we generate images or other non-text content dynamically. Of course, using ASP.NET, or any other dynamic page creation technique, we can easily generate a description as a text string. As an example, if the data comes from a data table, we can iterate through the table building up a string that contains all the column values. Then we just have to assign the URL of this dynamic page to the longdesc attribute. Or we could use the longdesc attribute to point to a dynamic page that uses the same source data, but which writes it into the page as text or as an HTML table.

Of course, there are other possibilities as well. For example, we might use the longdesc attribute to link to a streaming media source that contains an aural description or commentary. Or even link to a different site or resource that describes the object we feature in more appropriate ways.

Complex Images in Hyperlinks

One interesting issue arises when the image is used within a hyperlink, like this:

```
<a href="somewhere.aspx" title="go somewhere">
  <img src="image.gif" alt="go somewhere" longdesc="moredetails.aspx" />
</a>
```

A normal modern graphical browser may be aware of the longdesc attribute, but is unlikely to provide the user with any way to access it. However, specialist user agents should be able to do so (although few of them seem to at the moment), which means that we must find a way to present the link to the user so that they can make a choice – whether to load the page specified in the href attribute of the <a> element, or the page specified in the longdesc attribute of the <img> element.

Adding a 'Long Description' Attribute with ASP.NET

In ASP.NET, we can generate image elements in a range of ways, other than using a normal (non-server control) <img> element. For example we might use the HtmlImage or the Web Forms Image server controls, or the Web Forms Hyperlink server control with an image specified for the ImageUrl property (as we do to display the vehicle images in our 'Home' page). However, none of these controls expose a property that we can set to insert a longdesc attribute.

Instead, with an `HtmlImage` or a Web Forms `Image` control, we can add a `longdesc` attribute using the `Attributes` collection that all ASP.NET server controls expose. If we have a control named `MyImageControl`, and we have a `String` variable named `sDescription` containing the URL of our 'long description' page, we can add it as a `longdesc` attribute using:

```
MyImageControl.Attributes.Add("longdesc", sDescription)
```

However, as we discovered in Chapter 4, we can't add attributes to the `<img>` element that ASP.NET generates when we use a Web Forms `Hyperlink` control to display an image as a hyperlink. We can only add attributes to the enclosing `<a>` element, and in HTML this does not support the `longdesc` attribute. So, if you do need your complex graphics to be described by a 'long description', but also act as a hyperlink (OK, so it's probably not a common scenario), then you must avoid using the `ImageUrl` property of the `Hyperlink` control, and use separate `Hyperlink` and `Image` controls, or `<a>` and `<img>` elements, instead.

Using a 'D Link' Hyperlink

As most graphical browsers, and many other user agents, are not able to display or use the `longdesc` attribute value, other approaches are often used to provide alternative content formats for complex graphically presented information. The suggested technique, and the one most followed at the moment, is to use a 'D link'.

A 'D Link' is simply a hyperlink within the page containing the complex graphic or other non-text content that opens another page containing the text equivalent of this content. It is functionally equivalent to placing a URL in the `longdesc` attribute. The following screenshot shows how we might position a 'D Link' that provides this textual equivalent content – this is the generally accepted position for such a link:

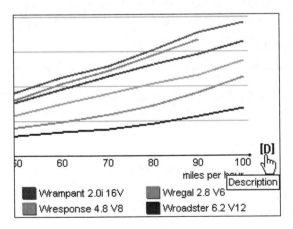

In fact, providing a 'D Link' is actually a great idea as it can benefit all of our visitors, not just those with restricted sight. As the hyperlink is visible in all browsers, any visitor can decide to view the text description if they prefer without requiring some specially-equipped user agent to be able to decode the `longdesc` attribute. Of course, this doesn't mean that we can forget `longdesc` altogether. It's easy enough to provide both, pointing them to the same URL.

Providing Alternative Content Formats

Having realized that we need to provide alternative content formats for complex images (usually a text description in the same page, or a separate page that contains the description), how do we do this in our 'Compare Models' page? We don't use a 'D Link' as such in the 'Compare Models' page of our **Wrox Car Company** site.

Instead, we've built alternative content format presentation into the page as an integral feature. In fact, you've already seen the answer in the two option buttons above the chart in earlier screenshots (and in the one here). Selecting Table causes a postback to the server and produces the following page:

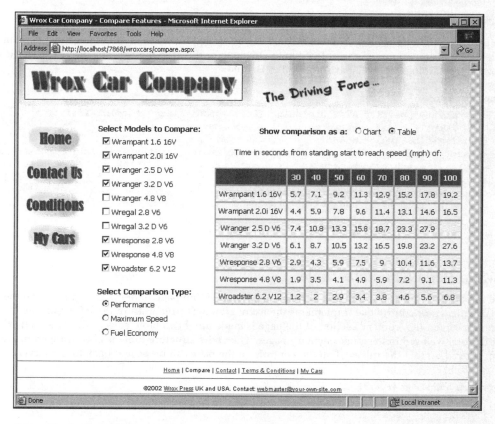

We could provide a [D] hyperlink next to the chart (when that mode is selected) that does the same as selecting the Table option button. However, the option buttons and the page itself use the ASP.NET `AutoPostBack` *feature. This means that the 'D Link' would have to run some code to resubmit the form, because the values stored within the form controls are required to be able to build the table of values. And if the client does not support client-side scripting (many text-only browsers and specialist user agents do not), the 'D Link' would have to be a* `submit` *button instead.*

Building the 'Compare Models' Page

The overall structure of the 'Compare Models' page, the way that we select the appropriate stylesheet, and the way that we redirect visitors to default.aspx if they have no current ASP.NET session are all very similar to the other ancillary pages. However, it's worth pointing out that we do need to provide an extra 'skip to' link in this page, because it contains more than one obvious 'content section' that visitors using text-based or aural page readers will want to be able to go straight to. Remember that each interaction with the controls on our page will cause a postback to the server, and so a visitor using one of these specialist user agents will 'start again' at the top of the page each time.

The 'Skip To' Links

We provide two "skip to" links, so that visitors can go straight to the area of the page that contains the "Select Models to Compare" controls (Skip to Options), or direct to the chart or the HTML table that contains the results of the comparison (Skip to Result):

compare.aspx

```
<div style="position:absolute;height:0px;"><font size="1" color=#ffffff>
<!-- skip link for aural page readers -->
<layer visibility="hidden">
<a href="#options" style="color:#ffffff;font-size:1px;text-decoration:none"><img
width="1" height="1" hspace="0" vspace="0" src="images/_blnk.gif" border="0"
alt="Skip to Options" /></a>
<a href="#result" style="color:#ffffff;font-size:1px;text-decoration:none"><img
width="1" height="1" hspace="0" vspace="0" src="images/_blnk.gif" border="0"
alt="Skip to Result" /></a>
</layer>
</font></div>
```

The Main Page Structure Table

The remainder of the page contains the usual page banner and page footer user controls, and the mainlink.ascx control that implements the list of graphical page links in the left-hand side of the page. However, the 'content' section of the page is made up of two table cells in this case, rather than just the one we used in the other ancillary pages. The entire structure table is also wrapped in a server-side <form> so that the values of all the controls on the page can be posted back to the server:

```
<form runat="server">
<table width="100%" border="0" cellspacing="0" cellpadding="10">
<tbody>
 <tr>
  <td valign="top" width="105px">
    <wcc:mainlink runat="server" CurrentPageLink="Compare" />
  </td>
  <td align="left" valign="top" nowrap="nowrap">
    <a name="options" />
    ...
    ... controls to select comparison options go here
    ...
  </td>
  <td align="center" valign="top">
```

```
      <a name="result" />
      ...
      ... chart or HTML table containing results goes here
      ...
    </td>
  </tr>
</tbody>
</table>
</form>
```

We'll look at the contents of the second and third cells (the ones with the 'skip to' anchors named options and result) next.

The Controls to Select the Comparison Type

The next listing shows the HTML declarations we include in the 'options' section of our page structure table. We have a couple of ordinary <span> elements that contain the headings for the two groups of controls, a CheckBoxList control to provide the selectable list of vehicle models, and a RadioButtonList that allows selection of one of the three types of comparison. Each element or server control has a class or CssClass attribute that specifies the CSS style to be applied, and the whole lot is enclosed in a <font> element to provide fallback for non-CSS browsers:

```
<font face="Tahoma,Arial,Helvetica,sans-serif" size="2">
<span class="body-text"><b>Select Models to Compare:</b></span>
<asp:CheckBoxList id="chkModels" CssClass="body-text"
                  Font-Size="10"
                  Font-Name="Tahoma,Arial,Helvetica,sans-serif"
                  AutoPostBack="True" runat="server" /><p />
<span class="body-text"><b>Select Comparison Type:</b></span><br />
<asp:RadioButtonList id="optCompareList" CssClass="body-text"
                     Font-Size="10"
                     Font-Name="Tahoma,Arial,Helvetica,sans-serif"
                     AutoPostBack="True" runat="server">
  <asp:ListItem Text="Performance" Selected="True" runat="server" />
  <asp:ListItem Text="Maximum Speed" runat="server" />
  <asp:ListItem Text="Fuel Economy" runat="server" />
</asp:RadioButtonList>
</font>
```

We specify details of the three option buttons we want in the RadioButtonList control directly using ListItem controls, and also indicate that we want the first one to be selected by default when the page is first loaded. However, we don't specify any content (ListItem controls) for the CheckBoxList. We'll be filling this 'list' using server-side data binding in the Page_Load event, as you'll see when we look at the code in this page later on.

Also notice that both the RadioButtonList and CheckBoxList controls include the AutoPostBack="True" attribute, so that the page will be submitted to the server each time the user changes the selections in either list – when they add or remove a vehicle from the list to compare, or when they change the comparison type.

The CheckBoxList Control Versus the RadioButtonList Control

The reasons for using these two controls will be obvious if you have any experience of building user interfaces in a web page. We want to allow the user to select as many models for the comparison as they wish, and the traditional way to present this choice is with a list of checkboxes. They can set (check) as many as they like.

However, we only want to generate a result for one of the three possible types of comparison. So we need to present a mutually exclusive set of options for this, and the traditional approach is with 'radio buttons' (sometimes called 'option buttons'). While it's possible to build pages that use the controls in a different way, it doesn't make sense to do so as it will tend to confuse our users. They recognize that they can select more than one checkbox in a list, but only one radio button from a group.

When we use the ASP.NET `RadioButtonList` and `CheckBoxList` controls, they actually enforce the standard and recognized approach. The output they produce in the rendered page limits us to using the controls in this way.

For example, the `RadioButtonList` control automatically sets the name attribute of each radio button element it generates to the same value – the value we provide for the `id` attribute of the control. This causes them to be mutually exclusive when rendered in the browser. On the other hand, the `CheckBoxList` control creates a different name attribute for each checkbox element that it generates, using the value of the `id` that we provide and adding on the index of the control within the list.

Select Models to Compare:
- ☑ Wrampant 1.6 16V
- ☑ Wrampant 2.0i 16V
- ☑ Wranger 2.5 D V6
- ☑ Wranger 3.2 D V6
- ☐ Wranger 4.8 V8
- ☐ Wregal 2.8 V6
- ☐ Wregal 3.2 D V6
- ☑ Wresponse 2.8 V6
- ☑ Wresponse 4.8 V8
- ☑ Wroadster 6.2 V12

Select Comparison Type:
- ⦿ Performance
- ○ Maximum Speed
- ○ Fuel Economy

Getting the Values of CheckBoxList and RadioButtonList Controls

The other great thing about these list controls is that we can easily access them in our server-side code to see which of the controls (radio buttons or checkboxes) were selected when the page was posted to the server. The constituent controls for the lists all have different `id` values within the rendered page (when viewed on the client), because this is a condition of the HTML standards. So, we could poke around in the `Request.Form` collection to see which ones are checked. But ASP.NET makes it much easier than that.

To get the index of the radio button that was selected when the page was posted to the server, we can simply query the `SelectedIndex` property of the `RadioButtonList` control. We can also get a reference to a `ListItem` object that represents the selected radio button from the `SelectedItem` property of the `RadioButtonList` control. The `ListItem` object exposes three useful properties:

❑ `Text` – returns the text caption of this item as a `String`

❑ `Value` – returns the value of this item (from the `value` attribute) as a `String`

❑ `Selected` – returns a `Boolean` value indicating if the item is checked (or selected)

So, to get the text caption of the selected radio button we can query the control like this:

```
sCaption = RadioButtonList.SelectedItem.Text
```

If you look up the `SelectedIndex` property for a `CheckBoxList` or `RadioButtonList` control in the .NET SDK, you'll find that it returns the index of the **first** selected item in a list control. With a `RadioButtonList`, there can only be one selected item, so there is no problem with using the `SelectedIndex` property like we did in the code example above.

However, a `CheckBoxList` control allows the user to make multiple selections, and in this case we will generally avoid the `SelectedIndex` property (unless we only want to get the index of the first one that is selected). Instead, we have to iterate through the `Items` collection that the `CheckBoxList` exposes and examine the `Selected` property of each `ListItem` control in this collection.

```
Dim lstItem As ListItem
Dim sMessage As String = ""
For Each lstItem In MyCheckBoxList.Items
  If lstItem.Selected Then
    sMessage &= lstItem.Text & " is selected.<br />"
  End If
Next
```

Of course, we can also iterate through the `Items` collection exposed by a `RadioButtonList` control if we wish, but this is only likely to be useful if we want to extract a list of the text captions for all the items. In fact you'll see this technique used when we look at the code in the 'Compare Models' page shortly.

The Controls to Display the Results of the Comparison

The third cell of our page's structure table contains the two radio buttons where the user can choose to view the results as a chart or as a table. In this case, to show how it can be done, we've provided the two buttons as separate controls rather than using a `RadioButtonList` control. We've also included the `AutoPostBack="True"` attribute, as we did with the other controls on this page:

```
<font face="Tahoma,Arial,Helvetica,sans-serif" size="2">
<span class="body-text"><b>Show comparison as a:</b> </span>
<asp:RadioButton id="optShowChart" CssClass="body-text"
            GroupName="ShowAs" AutoPostBack="True"
            Text="Chart" Checked="True" runat="server" /> 
<asp:RadioButton id="optShowTable" CssClass="body-text"
```

```
                      GroupName="ShowAs" AutoPostBack="True"
                      Text="Table" runat="server" /><p />
      ...
      </font>
```

The important point to note here is that we've set the `GroupName` attribute of both the `RadioButton` controls to the same value. This gives them the same `name` attribute when rendered in the browser, making them mutually exclusive.

> *Normally, the value we provide for the `id` attribute of a server control is also rendered as the name attribute, and `id` attributes have to be different for every control on the page or ASP.NET will report a compilation error. The `RadioButtonControl` is the only control where we can specifically set a different value for the `id` and `name` (GroupName) attributes.*

The Controls to Display the Graphical Chart

Following the two radio buttons is an ASP.NET `PlaceHolder` control. This control does not itself create any output in the page, but simply acts as a container into which we can place other server controls dynamically at runtime. We'll be using it to insert an `Image` control that displays our graphical chart when the user selects this option with the radio buttons shown in the previous section of the page:

```
...
<!-- placeholder to hold image of results -->
<asp:PlaceHolder id="ctlPlaceholder" runat="server" />
...
```

The Controls to Display an HTML Table of the Results

Next comes a `Label` control that we'll use to display a caption for the table of results when this mode is selected, followed by a `DataGrid` control to display these results:

```
...
<!-- label to display caption and/or error messages -->
<asp:Label id="lblTableCaption" EnableViewState="False" runat="server" />
<p />

<!-- Datagrid to display results as a table -->
<asp:DataGrid id="dgrResult" EnableViewState="False" runat="server"
            Font-Size="10" Font-Name="Tahoma,Arial,Helvetica,sans-serif"
            BorderStyle="None" BorderWidth="1px" BorderColor="#DEBA84"
            BackColor="#DEBA84" CellPadding="5" CellSpacing="1">
  <HeaderStyle Font-Bold="True" ForeColor="#ffffff"
            BackColor="#b50055" HorizontalAlign="center" />
  <ItemStyle BackColor="#FFF7E7" HorizontalAlign="center" />
  <AlternatingItemStyle backcolor="#FFFFC0" HorizontalAlign="center" />
</asp:DataGrid>
...
```

You can see that we've specified a number of formatting options in the `DataGrid` to give it an attractive appearance. It's often hard to figure out what values we need for all these attributes to give the required result, and we 'cheated' here by using a page designer tool to build the control declaration for us.

At the time of writing, Microsoft has just released a Technology Preview version of a new product called **ASP.NET Web Matrix**. This is a lightweight but extremely comprehensive and competent tool for building ASP.NET pages. It includes an Auto Format feature for the `DataGrid` and `DataList` controls that is just about identical to the one found in Visual Studio .NET. We used it to create a formatted `DataGrid`, then copied the resulting source code into our page and adjusted it to get the final appearance we wanted:

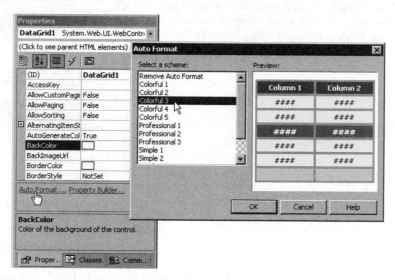

You can download Web Matrix from the ASP.NET community site at http://www.asp.net/. A useful introduction to Web Matrix is available from the same place, in the form of a free PDF document provided by Wrox Press.

The Invisible Submit Button

The final control we include in this section of the page is a `submit` button, implemented with an ASP.NET `Button` server control. We've specified `AutoPostBack` for all of the checkboxes and radio buttons in our page, so that users only have to make a selection in the various controls on the page and it is refreshed from the server automatically. So why do we need a `submit` button?

The reason is that we want our page to work without client-side scripting if possible – especially for text-based and aural page reader user agents that often do not provide this feature. In this case, we need a `submit` button to post the page back to the server:

```
...
<!-- button to submit form if no client-side scripting -->
<p class="body-text">
<asp:Button id="btnGo" CssClass="body-text"
            Text="Compare..." Visible="False" runat="server" /></p>
</font>
```

Of course, as the `Visible` attribute is set to `False`, the button will not actually be included in the page we send to the client. However, in our `Page_Load` event handler, we'll set the `Visible` property to `True` at runtime if we detect that the current browser or user agent does not support client-side scripting.

The Code To Make It All Work

Having looked at the declaration of the HTML, content, and server controls that make up the 'Compare Models' page, we can now move on and look at the server-side code that makes it all work. This page is opened from one of two links in the 'Home' page. The first possibility is that it is opened from the link in the left-hand 'News' section of that page. In this case, there is no query string appended to the URL, as you can see in the status bar of this screenshot:

However, the 'Compare Models' page can also be opened from the right-hand section of the 'Home' page where the list of models is displayed. Following the description of each of the five base models we offer is a [compare models] hyperlink. The data binding templates we use in the DataList control that creates this section of the page adds the ID of each model to the query string of the URL for these links. You can see it in the browser's status bar in the following screenshot:

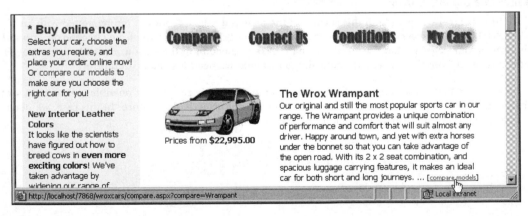

Summarizing the Requirements

So, when our 'Compare Models' page loads from one of these hyperlinks, we want to automatically set the appropriate checkboxes and generate the comparison results. However, when the page is opened from the link in the 'News' section, where there is no query string appended to the URL, we just want to display the page with no selections in the checkboxes and no results displayed. So, we can summarize the requirements for our code as follows.

When the page first loads (this is not a postback), we need to:

- ❑ Collect the name of the stylesheet for this client from the current ASP.NET session, or redirect the user to `default.aspx` if there is no value in the session (because it has expired or because they entered the site at this page instead of the 'Home' page).

- ❑ See if the client's browser supports scripting, and if not make the `submit` button visible.

- ❑ Generate a list of values to populate the `CheckBoxList` with the combination of car models and engine types.

- ❑ Look for an ID value in the query string. If there is one, select the appropriate checkboxes.

- ❑ Generate a chart (this is the default, rather than a table) showing the results of the comparison on 'Performance' (again, this is the default). But we only do this if one or more of the checkboxes are selected.

When the user changes any of the values in the checkboxes, or in either of the two radio button lists (and clicks **Compare** if client-side scripting is not available), a postback will occur. In this case, as the page loads, we need to:

- ❑ Collect the name of the stylesheet for this client from the current ASP.NET session, or redirect the user to `default.aspx` if there is no value in the session.

- ❑ See if the client's browser supports scripting, and if not make the `submit` button visible.

- ❑ See which type of display (**Chart** or **Table**) the user selected.

- ❑ Generate the chart or table showing the results of the currently selected comparison type, but again only if one or more of the checkboxes are selected.

The Page-Level Variables

We'll need to access several variables from within more than one function or routine in our page. Some of these variables will be passed as parameters to the other routines, or returned directly as the result of a function. However, for the most commonly used values, we can declare them as page-level variables that will automatically be available within any routine in the page. For the stylesheet name part, `sStyleSize`, this is actually a requirement anyway as we are inserting it into the page using the traditional ASP 3.0 technique with `<% = sStyleSize %>` as we've done in the other pages we've looked at previously:

```
<script runat="server">

' page-level variable to hold database connection string
Dim sConnect As String
```

```
' page-level variable to stylesheet size
Dim sStyleSize As String = ""

' page-level variable to hold client script ability
Dim bCanScript As Boolean

' page-level variable to hold text comparison description
Dim sCompareType As String = ""
```

The Page_Load Event Handler

Based on the requirements summary for our code that you saw earlier, the next listing of the Page_Load event should immediately make sense. We collect the database connection string from web.config, and from the current ASP.NET session we collect the name part of the stylesheet and the Boolean value that indicates if the current browser supports client-side scripting (remember that we detected this and set the value in the default.aspx and 'Home' pages when our visitor first entered the site).

If there is no ASP.NET session, we perform the redirection to default.aspx, and if there is no client-side scripting support available we make the submit button visible in the page:

```
Sub Page_Load()

  ' get database connection string from web.config
  sConnect = ConfigurationSettings.AppSettings("WroxCarsConnectString")

  ' get stylesheet size from Session
  sStyleSize = CType(Session("WccStyleSize"), String)

  ' if no value, session has expired or user entered
  ' site at page other than 'Home' page
  If sStyleSize = "" Then
    Response.Clear()
    Response.Redirect("default.aspx")
  End If

  ' see if client supports client-side scripting
  bCanScript = CType(Session("WccCanScript"), Boolean)

  ' if not make 'Compare' submit button visible
  ' because AutoPostBack will not work
  If Not bCanScript Then
    btnGo.Visible = True
  End If
...
```

The next screenshot shows the relevant section of the page when the client does not support client-side scripting. The page is still completely usable, except that visitors must click the **Compare** button after making their comparison selections:

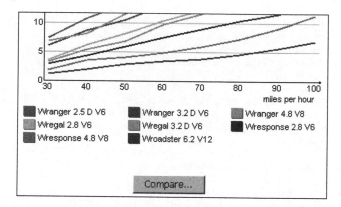

We could, of course, include this button in the page irrespective of the presence of client-side script support, but this is confusing for users. They might click the button after making a selection in one of the lists, and cause our page to be (partly) executed twice if client-side scripting is available. It also makes the whole thing a lot less intuitive and requires them to experiment to discover that they don't need to click the button (and, if not, why is it there?).

However, there is a flipside to consider. Would it be better to always show the **Compare** button and *not* use auto-postback? That way, users could make several changes in the lists of options without causing a postback and having to wait for the results of each individual selection. It really depends on how quickly we can get the results back to them. We chose the auto-postback scenario, but you might decide to use the other approach.

Checking for a Postback

The next step in our `Page_Load` event is to see if this is a postback, or if it's the first time the page has been loaded. In both cases we may have to generate the chart or table of results (depending on the current selections made in the checkboxes and radio buttons in the page), and we also have some extra work to do the first time the page is loaded.

We've written a couple of separate routines that, between them, carry out the bulk of the work of creating the page. A routine named `ShowComparison` is responsible for generating the results as a chart or table. It checks that at least one vehicle is selected, and takes into account the settings for the comparison type (performance, fuel consumption, or maximum speed) and the kind of result required (chart or table). We also have a separate function named `GetModelListDR`, which returns a `DataReader` containing the list of vehicle types and engine combinations to populate the list of checkboxes.

So, in line with our outline specification of the code requirements for the `Page_Load` event handler, we check the `IsPostBack` property to see if this request arises from the page being posted back. If it does, we simply call the `ShowComparison` routine to generate the results:

```
...
If Page.IsPostBack Then

   ' generate chart for selected items
   ShowComparison()

Else
```

```
' first time page has loaded, not a postback, so
' set DataSource for 'car models' list and databind it
chkModels.DataSource = GetModelListDR()
chkModels.DataTextField = "ViewName"
chkModels.DataBind()

' see if a model was specified in query string
' if so, need to generate chart or table this time
Dim sQuery As String = Request.QueryString("compare")
If sQuery <> "" Then

    ' select the appropriate checkboxes
    Dim lstItem As ListItem
    For Each lstItem In chkModels.Items
        If lstItem.Text.IndexOf(sQuery) = 0 Then
            lstItem.Selected = "True"
        End If
    Next

    ' generate chart of comparisons
    ShowComparison()

    End If

  End If

End Sub
```

If it is not a postback, the `Else` section of the code above is executed. In it we call our
`GetModelListDR` function to get a `DataReader` that will extract the list of vehicles, and assign this as
the `DataSource` property of our `CheckBoxList` control. We specify that the column named
`ViewName` should be used to provide the text captions for the checkboxes, and call the `DataBind`
method to display the results.

Managing and Using the ViewState

By default the ASP.NET postback architecture automatically maintains the values of all server controls
in a page between roundtrips to the server through the **viewstate** (we discussed this topic in Chapter 1),
unless we specifically 'turn it off' for a page or for individual controls within the page. This includes the
contents of list controls, such as our `CheckBoxList` control, and explains why we only need to
populate it when this is *not* a postback. When the page is posted back, ASP.NET automatically uses the
viewstate to populate the values of our `CheckBoxList` control.

However, it's worth bearing in mind how this useful automatic feature will affect the contents of our
page when we use server controls. A couple of particular issues here are the way that it affects the
`Label` and `DataGrid` controls we use in the right-hand section of our page. We use the `Label` control
to display captions or error messages each time the page loads, and we don't want it to remember any
previous values. So we added the `EnableViewState="False"` attribute to the control declaration to
prevent this.

Even more important is the DataGrid that we use to display the results as a table when the user selects this option. The entire contents of the table are created dynamically from the database every time, and there is absolutely no reason why we should want the table to be repopulated with the previous values following a postback. So, again, we've included the EnableViewState="False" attribute in the declaration of this control.

Just to give you an idea what effect this has, with the EnableViewState="False" attribute added to the DataGrid control, the viewstate that is included within the page (in the hidden-type input control that ASP.NET automatically generates within the <form> section) is around 850 characters when all ten vehicles are selected. Without the EnableViewState="False" attribute (remember that the default is "True" if it is omitted), the viewstate grows to over 6,500 characters.

Generating all this extra unnecessary data for every page interaction puts more load on our server, and it also gets sent over the wire twice with every postback – once when the user interacts with the page and submits it, and again when we deliver the new page to them.

Setting the CheckBoxList Control

We haven't quite finished with our Page_Load event handler yet. When this is not a postback, we need to collect any value that might be in the query string and set the appropriate matching checkboxes. As we saw earlier, the query string can contain a name/value pair such as compare=Wregal if the user clicked one of the [compare models] links in the right-hand side of the 'Home' page.

In this case, we need to iterate through the Items collection of the CheckBoxList control, and see if the caption (the Text property of the ListItem) starts with the model name contained in the query string. If it does, we can set (check) that checkbox by setting the Selected property of the corresponding ListItem to True. The relevant code is repeated here so that you can see what is happening:

```
' see if a model was specified in query string
' if so, need to generate chart or table this time
Dim sQuery As String = Request.QueryString("compare")
If sQuery <> "" Then

  ' select the appropriate checkboxes
  Dim lstItem As ListItem
  For Each lstItem In chkModels.Items
    If lstItem.Text.IndexOf(sQuery) = 0 Then
      lstItem.Selected = "True"
    End If
  Next

  ' generate chart of comparisons
  ShowComparison()

End If
```

If there is a value in the query string, after setting the appropriate checkboxes, we call our ShowComparison function to generate the results for the selected model in all available engine sizes.

If you are used to VBScript in ASP 3.0 and earlier, you may be wondering why we compare the result of the IndexOf method to zero (rather than one) when we want to find out if the match is at the beginning of the string. This is because the .NET language-agnostic IndexOf method treats strings as being zero-based rather than one-based.

Getting the Car and Engine Data

Earlier, we mentioned the two routines we use in the Page_Load event handler. The ShowComparison routine is discussed in detail later in this chapter. Next, however, we need to see how the other of these two routines works – namely the GetModelListDR function.

Our database contains several tables that provide information to drive the whole of the Wrox Car Company web site. Of particular interest here are the three tables that contain the bulk of the information about the vehicles themselves. The table named tblCar contains the details that are specific to each vehicle model, such as the model name, number of doors, and so on. Meanwhile, the table named tblEngine contains details that are specific to each of the engines we offer, such as the engine name (for example, "6.8 V12"), the cubic capacity, and the fuel type:

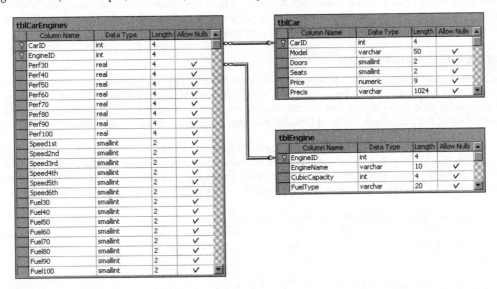

The third table shown in the screenshot above, tblCarEngines, links the other two tables. Although we only have five base vehicle models in our range, most are available with more than one engine option. For example, the Wregal sedan is available with the 2.8 liter V6 gas/petrol engine or the 3.2 liter V6 diesel engine. The tblCarEngines table contains a row for each of the available vehicle/engine combinations, using the key values of the vehicle (CarID) and the engine (EngineID).

Notice also that the tblCarEngines table contains other information. Some details about a vehicle depend on both the model and the engine, and not on just one of these factors. Examples shown in the screenshot above are the performance, maximum speed and fuel consumption. It's these values that we'll be using in the charts and tables that compare the features of each vehicle.

The GetModelEngineCombinedList Stored Procedure

To populate the CheckBoxList that contains the list of all available cars with an entry for each engine option for every car, we need a rowset that has a row for every possible valid combination of car and engine. However, we only need a single-column, containing the text for the captions of our checkboxes – as shown in the screenshot below.

This caption is made up of the car model name and the engine name, which are in the two tables `tblCar` and `tblEngine`. So, our stored procedure has to `JOIN` these two tables in turn with the `tblCarEngines` table, using the appropriate key columns (`CarID` and `EngineID`) in each table.

Select Models to Compare:

☑ Wrampant 1.6 16V
☑ Wrampant 2.0i 16V
☑ Wranger 2.5 D V6
☑ Wranger 3.2 D V6
☐ Wranger 4.8 V8
☐ Wregal 2.8 V6
☐ Wregal 3.2 D V6
☑ Wresponse 2.8 V6
☑ Wresponse 4.8 V8
☑ Wroadster 6.2 V12

Having done so, it extracts and returns a single column named `ViewName`, containing text string values that are made up by concatenating the values of the `Model` column from the `tblCar` table, a space character, and the `EngineName` column from the `tblEngines` table. The rows are then sorted by model name and engine name:

```
CREATE PROCEDURE GetModelEngineCombinedList AS
SELECT ViewName = tblCar.Model + ' ' + tblEngine.EngineName
FROM (tblCar JOIN tblCarEngines ON tblCar.CarID = tblCarEngines.CarID)
    JOIN tblEngine ON tblEngine.EngineID = tblCarEngines.EngineID
ORDER BY tblCar.Model, tblEngine.EngineName
```

Populating the CheckboxList of Models and Engine Types

The stored procedure we've just looked at is used in the `GetModelListDR` function that provides the `DataSource` property of our `CheckBoxList` control. We call it in exactly the same way as we did the stored procedures we used in our 'Home' page. The page-level variable named `sConnect` contains our connection string, and we use it when we create the `Connection` object. From this we can create a `Command` object that references our stored procedure, and call its `ExecuteReader` method to return a `DataReader`:

```
' function to create list of models for CheckBoxList captions
Function GetModelListDR() As SqlDataReader
  Try
    Dim sqlConnect As SqlConnection = New SqlConnection(sConnect)
    Dim sProcName As String = "GetModelEngineCombinedList"
    Dim sqlComm As SqlCommand = New SqlCommand(sProcName, sqlConnect)
    sqlComm.CommandType = CommandType.StoredProcedure
    sqlConnect.Open
    Return sqlComm.ExecuteReader(CommandBehavior.CloseConnection)
  Catch
    lblTableCaption.Text = "Sorry, the database cannot be accessed."
    Return Nothing
  End Try
End Function
```

If there is an error, we display a simple text message in the `Label` control above the 'results' chart or table.

Generating the Comparison Results

Our 'Compare Models' page now contains all the controls that the user can interact with, and we've populated the checkboxes showing the list of available model and engine combinations. The only feature of the page that we still need to look at is how we generate the table or graphical chart that displays the results of the selected comparison.

The ShowComparison Routine

The code in the Page_Load event handler we showed earlier calls a routine named ShowComparison when the page loads, and this does all the work of creating the chart or table of results. The first step is to see if any checkboxes are selected, and we can easily do this by examining the SelectedIndex property of the CheckBoxList control. You'll recall that this returns the index of the first selected item in the list.

We aren't concerned about *which* checkboxes are selected at the moment; we only want to know if there are any selected. If none are selected, the SelectedIndex property returns –1, and in this case we can just exit from our routine:

```
' routine to show the comparison image or table
Sub ShowComparison()

  ' see if any checkboxes are selected
  ' if not just exit from routine
  If chkModels.SelectedIndex = -1 Then Exit Sub
  ...
```

However, if there are any selected we continue by collecting the type of comparison that the user specified in the three radio buttons (**Performance**, **Fuel Consumption**, or **Maximum Speed**). These three options are exposed by the RadioButtonList control named optCompareList, and we can get a String value that describes the comparison type by querying the Text property of the currently selected radio button. This returns the caption for that button, which we can use in the caption displayed above the results table, and in the alt attribute of the chart:

```
  ...
  ' get text comparison description
  sCompareType = optCompareList.SelectedItem.Text
  ...
```

Next, we check to see which type of comparison we're performing. The two radio buttons above our chart or table are individual controls, rather than a RadioButtonList control, and have the values optShowChart and optShowTable for their id properties. So we can see if the **Chart** option was selected by examining the Checked property of this radio button directly:

```
  ...
  'see if we are generating a chart or a table
  If optShowChart.Checked Then
  ...
```

Creating the ASP.NET Image Element for the Chart

If the user is expecting us to generate a chart, we execute the code shown in the next listing. It creates a new ASP.NET Image element, and sets the ImageURL (which generates the src attribute) to the value returned by another function in our page named GetImageURL. We'll look at this function towards the end of this chapter, but for now just accept that it will provide a suitable value for the src property of the <img> element we're creating.

Next, our code sets the AlternateText property (which generates the alt attribute) to a string that includes the comparison type we previously collected in the variable named sCompareType. Then it creates a string suitable for the longdesc attribute, and adds it to the Image element using the Add method of the Attributes collection, as we showed earlier in this chapter:

```
...
' insert new Image element for chart into page
' could pass values in session but using the
' query string is probably more efficient
Dim ctlImage As New Image()
ctlImage.ImageUrl = GetImageURL()
ctlImage.AlternateText = " Chart showing comparison of " & sCompareType
Dim sLongDesc As String
sLongDesc = "Use the option buttons located just before this " _
        & "chart to display the data as a text-based table."
ctlImage.Attributes.Add("longdesc", sLongDesc)
ctlPlaceholder.Controls.Add(ctlImage)
...
```

The final line in the code above then inserts this new Image element into the page as a child of the ASP.NET PlaceHolder control that we declared within the page. When the page is rendered, the PlaceHolder itself produces no output, but the Image element is rendered just like it would be if we had declared it directly within the HTML section of the page.

For example, if we select just the **Wranger 2.5 D V6** model, the content that is rendered to the client looks like this (the Image control adds the border="0" attribute automatically by default):

```
<!-- placeholder to hold image of results -->
<img longdesc="Use the option buttons located just before this chart to display
the data as a text-based table."
    src="compare-chart.aspx?ctype=0&amp;list=Wranger+2.5+D+V6"
    alt="Chart showing comparison of Performance" border="0" />
```

Meanwhile, the DataGrid control that we also declared in the page will only produce output when it is databound, and so it will not appear when the **Chart** option is selected.

Creating the HTML Table of Results

However, if the user has selected the **Table** option rather than **Chart**, the Else section of our ShowComparison function is executed instead. In it we call a function named GetCompareDR, and assign the DataReader it returns to the DataSource property of the DataGrid in the right-hand side of the page, then call the DataBind method:

```
...
Else  'generate a table of the results

  ' Set DataSource and bind DataReader to DataGrid
  dgrResult.DataSource = GetCompareDR()
  dgrResult.DataBind()

End If

End Sub
```

This is all we have to do to show the comparison data as a table, and you can see that the result is well worth the small amount of effort involved:

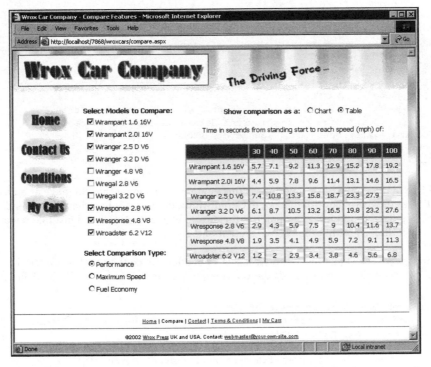

But, of course, the interesting part comes in how we actually access the database to get the values for our `DataGrid` control's `DataSource` property.

SQL Statement or Stored Procedure?

In all of our pages so far, we've used a stored procedure within the database to extract the rows we use in our various databound controls. However, there are cases where it makes sense to execute a SQL statement directly, rather than writing a stored procedure. For example, if we want to extract different sets of columns, pass in a varying number of parameters each time, carry out complex manipulation of the values, or perform some non-standard type of formatting of the data, a suitable stored procedure can soon become impossibly unwieldy. On top of this, the database may not be able to pre-compile and optimize the procedure, reducing the benefits that stored procedures can provide.

In our case, the WHERE clause that we need to specify the rows we want from our tblCarEngines table will contain anything between one and ten pairs of values (because the user can select any number of vehicles for a comparison at one time). So we would need a stored procedure to accept ten pairs of parameters – the car model name and engine name for each selected vehicle – and then test which of these should be used in the WHERE clause. It makes much more sense to build the WHERE clause dynamically within our ASP.NET code, and use it as part of the SQL statement that we'll execute to get the results we want.

Generating the Required SQL Statement

We created a function named GetSqlStatement that returns the complete SQL statement that we'll need to extract the required rows from our database. After declaring a couple of variables for use within the function, we examine the SelectedIndex property of the RadioButtonList control that contains the three comparison options (Performance, Fuel Consumption, or Maximum Speed). Depending on the current selection in this list, we generate a suitable 'first section' of the SQL statement. And, as a by-product within the Select Case statement, we create the matching caption that we'll place in the Label control above the table of results, and then display it by assigning it to that control's Text property:

```
' function to create SQL statement to extract comparison values
Function GetSqlStatement() As String

  Dim sResult, sCaption As String

  ' see which comparison type is selected
  ' and create SELECT part of SQL statement
  Select Case optCompareList.SelectedIndex

    Case 0    ' compare Performance
      sCaption = "Time in seconds from standing start to reach speed of:"
      sResult = "SELECT [ ] = Model + ' ' + EngineName, " _
              & "[30] = Perf30, [40] = Perf40, [50] = Perf50, " _
              & "[60] = Perf60, [70] = Perf70, [80] = Perf80, " _
              & "[90] = Perf90, [100] = Perf100 " _
              & "FROM (tblCar JOIN tblCarEngines ON " _
              & "tblCar.CarID = tblCarEngines.CarID) " _
              & "JOIN tblEngine ON " _
              & "tblEngine.EngineID = tblCarEngines.EngineID WHERE "

    Case 1    ' compare Maximum Speed
      sCaption = "Maximum speed (mph) in each gear:"
      sResult = "SELECT [ ] = Model + ' ' + EngineName, " _
              & "[1st] = Speed1st, [2nd] = Speed2nd, [3rd] = Speed3rd, " _
              & "[4th] = Speed4th, [5th] = Speed5th, [6th] = Speed6th " _
              & "FROM (tblCar JOIN tblCarEngines ON " _
              & "tblCar.CarID = tblCarEngines.CarID) " _
              & "JOIN tblEngine ON " _
              & "tblEngine.EngineID = tblCarEngines.EngineID WHERE "

    Case 2    ' compare Fuel Consumption
      sCaption = "Fuel consumption (mpg) at a steady speed (mph) of:"
      sResult = "SELECT [ ] = Model + ' ' + EngineName, " _
              & "[30] = Fuel30, [40] = Fuel40, [50] = Fuel50, " _
```

```
                  & "[60] = Fuel60, [70] = Fuel70, [80] = Fuel80, " _
                  & "[90] = Fuel90, [100] = Fuel100 " _
                  & "FROM (tblCar JOIN tblCarEngines ON " _
                  & "tblCar.CarID = tblCarEngines.CarID) " _
                  & "JOIN tblEngine ON " _
                  & "tblEngine.EngineID = tblCarEngines.EngineID WHERE "

      End Select

      ' set caption for table
      lblTableCaption.Text = sCaption
      ...
```

You can see that we perform the same JOIN on the three tables as we did when getting the list of models for the checkboxes earlier on. This is because we'll need to access the model name and engine name in our WHERE clause, as you'll see shortly. Also notice that we rename the columns ('alias' them in SQL Server terms), so that the names are suitable for use directly in our DataGrid control when displaying the results as a table.

The reason for this is that we haven't declared any templates for the DataGrid that will control the way the data is presented (you can confirm this by looking back at the HTML section of the page shown earlier in this chapter). Our DataGrid will be used to display three different sets of data, depending on the selected comparison type, and so we can't specify the column headings up-front in the HTML declaration. It's easier to extract the data rows with appropriate column names than to add suitable templates to the DataGrid dynamically afterwards (though it is possible to do it this way if you prefer).

Notice that, to specify a column name that starts with a non-alphabetic character, we must enclose it in square brackets. We also wanted to leave the column heading above the vehicle name empty, so we used the HTML non-breaking space character   for this column name – a useful trick when displaying data in a web page.

Specifying the WHERE Clause

The final section of the GetSqlStatement routine is used to create the WHERE clause for our SQL statement. However, this is not quite as simple as it might at first appear. Our CheckBoxList control does not have any facility to store values for each item in the list, other than as the Text property of each ListItem control within the list. There is no way to set the value attribute of the individual checkboxes that are generated by a CheckBoxList.

So, the only thing we can extract from each ListItem control is the value of the Text property, which is a combination of the model name and the engine name. We have to specify both of these in the WHERE clause, and match them to the values in the Model and EngineName columns of the tblCar and tblEngines tables. This is why we have to perform the three-way JOIN you saw earlier in our SQL statement.

This next listing shows the code we use to create the WHERE clause. We iterate through the Items collection of the CheckBoxList control, and test each one to see if it is selected. If it is, we extract the model name and the engine name from the Text property of that ListItem, and add a section to the WHERE clause for that particular vehicle:

```
...
' create WHERE clause section for each selected checkbox
Dim lstItem As ListItem
Dim sText, sModel, sEngine As String
For Each lstItem In chkModels.Items
  If lstItem.Selected Then
    sText = lstItem.Text
    sModel = sText.Substring(0, sText.IndexOf(" "))
    sEngine = sText.Substring(sText.IndexOf(" ") + 1)
    sResult &= "(Model = '" & sModel & "' AND EngineName = '" _
            & sEngine & "') OR "
  End If
Next
...
```

This does, of course, depend on the data content – it will fail if the model name contains a space. If you suspect that this is a possibility, and to provide more bulletproof code, you might instead prefer to use a specific delimiter character to separate the parts of the caption. Other techniques include building an array of the values, so that you can look them up in this array using the index of the button.

For each vehicle that is selected, this creates a matching section of the WHERE clause, for example:

```
"(Model = 'Wregal' AND EngineName = '2.8 V6') OR "
```

Then, after we've examined all the ListItem controls, we strip off the extra OR, and add an ORDER BY clause that sorts the rows by model name and then by engine name:

```
...
' remove final "OR" from string
sResult = sResult.SubString(0, sResult.Length - 4)

' add ORDER BY clause and return result
Return sResult & " ORDER BY Model, EngineName"

End Function
```

Getting a DataReader of Results for the DataGrid

All that remains now is to execute the SQL statement we just created to get the required rowset. This is done in the GetCompareDR function that you saw being used earlier to set the DataSource property of our DataGrid. It is very similar to the other functions we've used to get a DataReader, but this time we specify the SQL statement when we create the Command object rather than a stored procedure name, and we tell the Command that it's a SQL statement by setting the CommandType property to the value Text:

```
' function to get DataReader of values for comparison table
Function GetCompareDR() As SqlDataReader

  Try
    Dim sqlConnect As SqlConnection = New SqlConnection(sConnect)
```

```
      ' get SELECT statement to extract the data
      Dim sSQL As String = GetSqlStatement()

      Dim sqlComm As SqlCommand = New SqlCommand(sSQL, sqlConnect)
      sqlComm.CommandType = CommandType.Text   ' SQL statement
      sqlConnect.Open
      Return sqlComm.ExecuteReader(CommandBehavior.CloseConnection)
   Catch
      lblTableCaption.Text = "Sorry, the database cannot be accessed."
      Return Nothing
   End Try

 End Function
```

In fact, the default value for the CommandType, *if we don't specify otherwise, is*
CommandType.Text. *However, we prefer to specify it explicitly, as this makes it obvious what's*
going on to anyone using our code.

Creating the Chart Image URL and Query String

The one piece of code in our 'Compare Models' page that we haven't looked at yet is the GetImageURL
function. You'll recall that we use this function to set the ImageUrl property of the Image control (the
src attribute of the <img> element) that we insert into the page when we are displaying the data as a
chart rather than as a table.

Our graph chart is created as a GIF image by a separate ASP.NET page. This means that we must pass
all the values required to create the appropriate chart into that page. We'll discuss the reasons for using
a separate page, what other options are available, and some other ways that we can pass values between
pages in the next chapter when we look at how we create the chart.

In the meantime, here's the code we use for the GetImageURL function. It works much like the code we
used to create the SQL statement's WHERE clause earlier on, but this time the values are assembled into a
format that is better suited to use in a query string:

```
 ' function to generate URL and query string for image
 Function GetImageURL() As String

   Dim sQuery As String = ""

   ' create a string for each selected checkbox
   Dim lstItem As ListItem
   Dim sText, sModel, sEngine As String
   For Each lstItem In chkModels.Items
     If lstItem.Selected Then
       sText = lstItem.Text
       sModel = sText.Substring(0, sText.IndexOf(" "))
       sEngine = sText.Substring(sText.IndexOf(" ") + 1)
       sQuery &= sModel & " " & sEngine & "*"
     End If
   Next
```

```
' remove final "|" from string
sQuery = sQuery.SubString(0, sQuery.Length - 1)

' use string of models to build complete URL
Return "compare-chart.aspx?ctype=" _
      & optCompareList.SelectedIndex.ToString _
      & "&list=" & Server.UrlEncode(sQuery)

End Function
```

At the end of the function, we build up the complete URL by appending the query string we've created to the name of the page that creates the chart (`compare-chart.aspx`) plus a name/value pair that specifies the selection type (using the `SelectedIndex` value we extracted earlier from the `RadioButtonList`). As an example of the result, when the user selects the first two of the Wranger models we sell, the value that is returned from our function looks like this:

```
compare-chart.aspx?ctype=0&amp;list=Wranger+2.5+D+V6*Wranger+3.2+D+V6
```

In the next chapter, we'll be looking at the way we create the charts you see in the 'Compare Models' page as you select various types of comparison, as well as looking at how we can create other types of chart. However, to finish off this chapter, we'll very briefly see how the page works in a couple of specialist user agents that cannot handle graphics – and which benefit from the ability to display the data as an HTML table.

Testing for Accessibility

The 'Compare Models' page we've created looks fine in all the graphical browsers that we usually use to test our pages. However, we really do need to test it in the other specialist and non-graphical user agents we are aiming to support as well. So in the final section of this chapter, we'll show you how it works in the Lynx text-only browser and in the IBM Home Page Reader.

Using a Text-Only Browser

In the screenshot below, we've opened the 'Compare Models' page in Lynx from the [compare models] link in the 'Home' page for the Wrox Wrampant. You can see the two 'skip to' links we placed at the top of our page, with the Skip to Result link highlighted. The checkboxes for each vehicle, and the first two of the comparison-type radio buttons, can also be seen here:

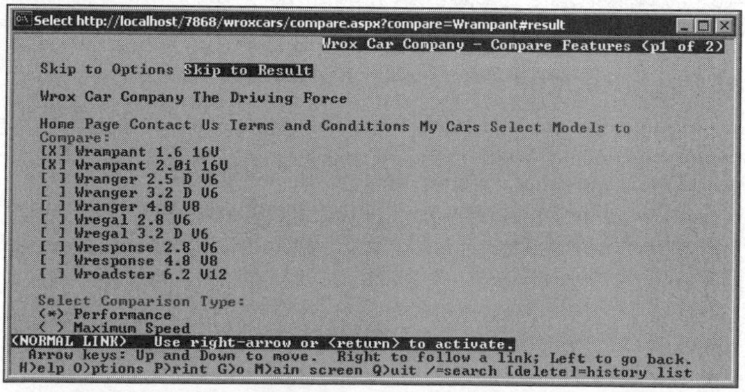

Following the Skip to Result link takes us to the radio buttons where we can select the way that the comparison results should be displayed. By default the display is a chart, and you can see that the only thing visible in our text-only client is the `alt` text we added to the `<img>` control that displays the chart:

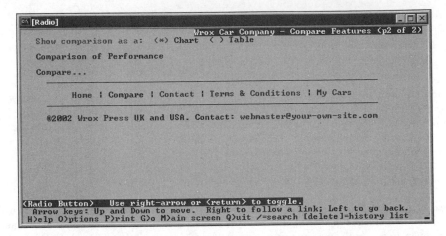

However, selecting the Table option displays the results as an HTML table, and you can see that Lynx can expose the contents in a useful and readable form – our page works fine and achieves our original aims:

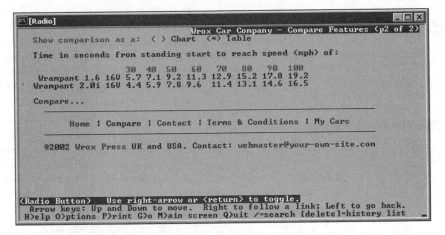

Using an Aural Page Reader

The next test for our page is in the IBM Home Page Reader, which you met in earlier chapters when we discussed the various types of specialist client that we should endeavor to support. This time we've hidden the graphical view and other windows, so only the text that is read to the user is visible. You can clearly see (in the section of the output that we've highlighted) the radio buttons to select a chart or table view of the results, followed by the `alt` text of our (default view) chart:

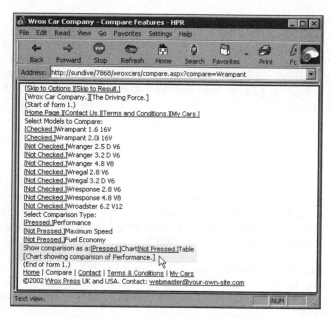

However, selecting the Table option returns the values as an HTML table, and they are read to the user row by row:

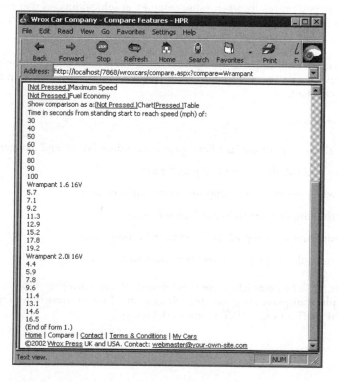

One interesting addition to our page might be to extend the checks we do on the user's client or browser type, when they first hit our site, to see if they are using a text-only client or a page reader. This isn't a trivial task, as the BrowserCapabilities routines provided by ASP.NET do not, by default, have the data available for this. However, if we could detect these types of client (perhaps by examining the user agent string available via the "USER_AGENT" value within the Request.ServerVariables collection), we could adapt our page code so that the Table option is the default for these types of client instead of the Chart option.

Summary

This is a relatively long chapter compared to most of the others in this book, and we used it to cover a lot of ground. Although the overall topics were few – looking at the ancillary pages of our site, the general page structure, and the way we display the information content – they did bring to light many areas where we felt that we should expand on the reasoning behind our design choices as well as showing you the implementation details and the results.

For example, we looked in some detail at the choices we made between static and dynamic content, and how we can implement this in various ways. We also focused in more detail than before on how we can insert content into a page at runtime, and discussed the ways that we can use a DataReader to extract content from a database.

In several places throughout the chapter, we also incorporated some pointers about maximizing accessibility in our pages, especially when using complex graphical images that contain information. This information is not generally available to users of non-graphical clients, and we looked at the ways we can present it in other formats as well as a graphic or chart.

We finished the chapter by testing our 'Compare Models' page in a couple of non-graphical clients to prove that the techniques we have chosen do work, including making the content available as a table instead of a graphical chart.

The topics we covered were:

- ❑ The general structure of the 'ancillary' pages, including layout and navigation
- ❑ The 'Terms and Conditions' and 'Contact' pages
- ❑ Deciding when to use static as opposed to dynamic content
- ❑ The page that displays the individual 'News' items
- ❑ The structure and workings of the "Compare Models" page
- ❑ How we create the display of model comparisons as an HTML table

In the next chapter, we'll be completing the construction of our 'Compare Models' page by seeing how the charts and graphs it displays are generated, along with a look at some other types of chart that we can create with ASP.NET and the .NET Framework classes.

7

Creating Graphs and Charts

In the previous chapter, we built the 'Compare Models' page for our Wrox Car Company site. This page allows visitors to compare the vehicles we sell in terms of their performance, fuel consumption, and maximum speed. The results of these comparisons can be displayed as a graph chart or an HTML table. We've already shown you how the table of results is created, but we didn't discuss how we create the chart that this page displays.

So, in this chapter, we'll continue where we left off, and look at how we can use the drawing classes that are part of the .NET Framework to create the charts you see in the 'Compare Models' page. This page only uses two basic types of chart: a line chart and a bar chart. However, before we look at these two specific examples, we'll explore a simpler type of chart. Probably the easiest type of chart to create is a pie chart, and we'll show you a generic example of this.

So, the topics for this chapter are:

- ❑ Looking at the various ways that we can generate graphics and images dynamically
- ❑ Exploring the ways that we can use these images in our pages
- ❑ The .NET Framework classes that allow us to generate these graphics and images
- ❑ How we create a simple pie chart as a generic function
- ❑ How we created the line charts for the Wrox Car Company site
- ❑ How we created the bar chart for the Wrox Car Company site

We start with a look at the whole concept of using dynamically generated images.

Dynamically Generated Graphics and Images

One of the long-standing issues with designing attractive web pages to display information is how to present information that is predominantly graphical in nature in such as way as it can be viewed by users of all kinds of browser, running on all kinds of operating systems.

Some of the available techniques for displaying static and dynamically generated graphics in a web browser are:

❑ Using a **Java Applet, a plug-in, or an ActiveX control** that runs on the client's machine and generates the output. The big issues here are compatibility with the operating system and browser, and concerns over security. Allowing code that is downloaded from the Web to run on your machine, even when sand-boxed (in the case of Java Applets) is something many people prefer to avoid.

❑ Using some built-in feature, add-in, or component that is pre-installed with the browser, such as the Internet Explorer **Structural Graphics Control** introduced with IE4. The problem with this technique is that it is not cross-browser compatible.

❑ Using a standard graphics rendering language, such as **Virtual Modelling Language** (VML, as implemented in Internet Explorer 5.0) or the **W3C Scalable Vector Graphics** (SVG) recommendations. Again, the issue with these techniques is lack of general browser support.

❑ Animation techniques that use a language and technology such as **Macromedia Flash**. This is a powerful and useful way to present moving and interactive images. Though it has traditionally been used more for dramatic effect than actual information presentation, and is frowned on for this reason by many users, it can be used to create extremely useful presentations as well as static output. It can also be scripted so that the content is generated dynamically – for more details see the Macromedia site at http://www.macromedia.com/.

❑ Converting the output to a static presentation using something like the **Adobe Portable Document Format** (PDF). Like Flash and many of the other techniques listed above, this requires client-side installation of a plug-in that can handle the PDF file. However, users often accept it more readily than other techniques. PDF documents can be generated dynamically on the server in a range of ways, for example using components provided by companies like ActivePDF (http://www.activepdf.com/).

While all of these are perfectly acceptable techniques within the limitations that they incur, many developers still prefer to provide normal GIF or JPEG images that are inserted into the page using a standard <img> element. This approach is almost guaranteed to work in all graphical browsers. And, increasingly, there is support in browsers for a relatively new image format, called **Portable Network Graphics** (PNG). This format avoids the issues that arise from the GIF format being a commercially patented technology. However, for maximum compatibility with old browsers, the GIF format is still the order of the day.

So, if we are going to use a GIF (or other format) image to present information that changes over time, we need to generate this image dynamically. There is a wide range of components available for ASP and ASP.NET that can do this. For some examples, check out:

❑ The ASP101 graphics components list at:
http://asp101.aspin.com/home/components/graphics

❑　HotScripts image manipulation tools at:
http://www.hotscripts.com/ASP/Scripts_and_Components/Image_Manipulation/

❑　And, of course, the component gallery on the Microsoft ASP.NET community site at:
http://www.asp.net/ControlGallery/default.aspx

Of course, being geeks and avid .NET developers, we chose to build our own graphics routines that use the .NET Framework classes. Before we see how, we'll look briefly at performance and caching issues with dynamic images, see why we chose to use dynamically generated GIF images, and find out how we can get them into our pages.

Performance and Caching

As well as choosing the technique for creating graphics and images based on our own technology and language preferences, plus the support available in the various client types we want to service, it's worth considering the affect that this choice has on performance and server loading.

Generating an image or graphic dynamically, especially a complex one, obviously takes more effort than just referencing a disk file that contains the image. The techniques we examine in this chapter generate the image as a stream of data using code running on the server, so we do cause a performance hit each time we generate the graphic. How much of a hit obviously depends on the complexity of the image, the efficiency of the algorithms in the code that creates it, and the raw speed of the language in which the code is written.

In other words, if we write the code in raw C or machine code, we're going to get better performance than using something like Visual Basic 6. However, in our new and exciting '.NET world', we can enjoy all the benefits of the Framework classes and runtime engine by using a managed language such as C# or VB.NET instead. OK, so the code won't be as fast as raw C, but it is still extremely efficient – as well as being a great deal easier to write.

Generating Graphics on the Client

To some extent we can minimize the performance hit by sending just the **instructions** for creating the image to the client, rather than the **complete data** for the image. In the case of 'line graphics', especially relatively simple ones such as charts or line drawings, this can reduce server loading and bandwidth usage, as the instructions are generally smaller than the amount of data contained in the rendered image. This is, for example, the way that VML, Macromedia Flash, and the Microsoft Structured Graphics control work. The downside is that we compromise compatibility, and often accessibility as well, as none of the available techniques work on all kinds of client.

ASP.NET Caching for Images and Graphics

When we use disk image files, referenced in the `src` attribute of an `<img>` element, the browser will usually cache the image file and reuse this where possible, rather than downloading the image every time. It just checks that the image is still 'current' by comparing the 'expires' date of the image in its cache with that on the server.

However, when we generate images dynamically, we lose this automatic support. It is possible to configure IIS to set the 'expires' date and time for files so that even dynamic pages are cached. We can do the same by setting the `Response.Expires` property in our page code in both ASP and ASP.NET. Unfortunately, this usually breaks the page when different values appear in the `Request.QueryString` or `Request.Form` collections, as it doesn't allow the code to be re-executed to take account of these values.

At this point you are probably jumping up and down and shouting "What about ASP.NET Output Caching?". A good point, but there is a problem here as well. Yes, ASP.NET can automatically re-execute the page if the values in the `Request.QueryString` or `Request.Form` collections differ. However, when it sends back a page from the Output Cache, it appears to always set the 'content type' (the MIME type of the response) to `"text/html"` – assuming that the cached output is being used to generate an HTML page in the browser.

While this is a reasonable assumption in most cases, it causes a problem when the ASP.NET code is generating a dynamic image that should have a different content type (`"image/gif"` or `"image/jpeg"` for example). Modern browsers will still display the image, but we can't always rely on this in other clients. It can also cause unpredictable behavior – for example, in Internet Explorer, when the user right-clicks to save the image as a file, it is saved as a `.bmp` file instead of a `.gif` or `.jpg` file. For these reasons, we chose to avoid using caching with our example pages.

Writing Images to Disk Files

If you find that the server loading caused by repeated execution of the code that creates the image is excessive, you may care to experiment with caching in your applications. Or, often an even better solution, write the images to disk files at specific intervals, or only when the source data changes, and use the appropriate file extension (`.gif`, `.jpg`, or whatever).

Using this approach, IIS will set the correct content type automatically, depending on the file extension. Plus, the browser will cache the image as well, so we get the best of both worlds. In the section *A Note About Saving a Bitmap* later in this chapter, we show how easy it is to create a disk file containing an image or graphic using the .NET Framework classes.

Using Dynamic Images in Web Pages

If we choose to present our graphical output as GIF or JPEG images, we can insert them into a page easily with an ordinary `<img>` element. Of course, as we discovered in the previous chapter, we still need to consider how we can provide the equivalent information for clients using a browser that is not capable of displaying images, or visually impaired visitors to whom images are of no use anyway.

In these cases, we must be sure to include an `alt` attribute to indicate the content of the image, plus a `longdesc` attribute and/or a 'D Link' to provide the same information as is contained in the image. However, all this is easy enough to implement, as we saw in our 'Compare Models' page in the previous chapter.

Alternative Elements for Inserting Images

Other ways that we can insert images in a range of formats into a web page are:

❑ Using an `<embed>` element. This was originally championed by Netscape in their Navigator browsers, and allows the insertion of documents in a wide range of formats. It depends on the appropriate plug-in being installed and available on the client's machine, though most popular plug-ins can be downloaded on demand if not already installed:

```
<embed src="myimage.gif" type="image/gif" height="100" width="150">
   The alternate text goes here for browsers
   that do not support embedded documents.
</embed>
```

❑ Using an `<object>` element. This is part of the recommendations for HTML 4.01, and was originally introduced by Microsoft in their Internet Explorer 3.0 browser. Most commercial browsers now support it, though the actual implementation and workings vary widely. It can be used to insert all kinds of document, including an image:

```
<object data="myimage.gif" type="image/gif" height="100" width="150">
   The alternate text goes here for browsers
   that do not support the <object> element.
</object>
```

In Internet Explorer 3.0 and above, using the `<object>` element, the image is inserted into a frame of the specified size, with scrollbars that allow the visitor to move the image around and view all of it if it is larger than the specified size. This might be useful in some situations, but will not work in many other browsers. The same effect can also be obtained in CSS2-enabled browsers using the CSS `overflow` and `clip` style selectors.

Using Multiple Static Image Files

When we want to display an image that may change depending on the selections made by the visitor, or in response to some outside factor (for example, a sun or cloud on a site that contains weather forecasts) a common technique is to have a series of images available and use code to choose the appropriate one.

So, for example, we could have a series of images of our cars on the **Wrox Car Company** site, each in a different color. When the user selects a color, we just change the `src` of the `<img>` element dynamically in our code to display the correct image. We can do this on the server in ASP.NET simply by assigning the value to the `ImageUrl` property of a Web Forms `Image` control, or to the `src` property of an `HtmlImage` control.

We can also do this client-side for most recent browsers. We access the `<img>` element and simply assign the URL of the image file we want to display to the `src` attribute – effectively this is what we did in the animated page banner we looked at in Chapter 5. As a simple example, in a browser that supports DOM2 and CSS2 techniques, we can use something like this:

```
document.getElementById('CarImg').src = 'newimage.gif';
```

You'll also see another trick in Chapter 8, where we use a GIF image containing sections that are marked as transparent. In this case, we can change the appearance of the image by simply changing the background color of the surface on which it's displayed.

However, none of these techniques use images that are created dynamically – they are all just different ways of using multiple *static* images. It is an easy way to achieve the result we want, but becomes more and more cumbersome as the number of images required grows.

What we'll be looking at in this chapter is actually generating the image itself dynamically. Before we do, however, there is one other minor topic we should consider. How do we pass values into the page or object that creates the image?

Passing Values to an Image Generation Page

If we are creating an image where the content of that image depends on some values that we specify at runtime, we need to be able to pass these values into the page or component that is creating the image. In ASP 3.0, when we use a custom or commercial component to create an image, we usually do so by instantiating the component within a page and then setting the appropriate properties.

But even here, the page that creates the image is separate from the page in which it is displayed. The client requests this page after the page containing the <img> element has finished loading, and the data returned by the second page is loaded into the <img> element and displayed. So we still need to be able to pass values from the first page into this second page (the one that creates the image) to indicate what we want our image to contain:

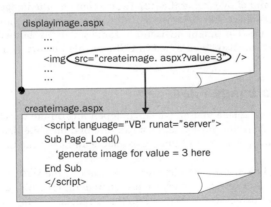

In the example above, and in our 'Compare Models' page in the previous chapter, we chose to pass the values using the query string. However, there are other options. You might be tempted to try passing them as the values in a <form> that is posted to the chart generation page. However, the target page is linked via the src attribute of an <img> element, and so this will not work. The only way we could do this would be to use the Server.Execute method to execute the page within the execution cycle of the current page.

Another option would be to store the values in the user's ASP.NET session, and then retrieve them in the target page. This is quite acceptable if you ensure that the client you are serving the pages to can support ASP.NET sessions (as we do in our **Wrox Car Company** site). The downside is that it can make it harder to see what's happening when experimenting, testing, and debugging the page because the values must be retrieved from a valid session each time.

However, the query string is generally the simplest option, and it means that that the target page (which creates the image) can include the `EnableSessionState="False"` directive to minimize server loading. The actual URL we use is not visible in the browser, except when viewing the source of the page, and hence will not confuse visitors even if it's a complex set of values.

The only real issue here is keeping the total length (the full path of the page plus the query string) below the maximum that the browser and server can accept. The usual working value for this is 1024 characters, so you should not run into problems unless you have an inordinately large number of parameters to pass to the image generation page.

The .NET Framework Drawing Classes

As the topic of this chapter is generating images with the .NET Framework classes, it's high time we actually started to investigate these classes. The root namespace is `System.Drawing`, and there are several other ancillary namespaces that include classes designed for more specific tasks or advanced image manipulation. The following table summarizes all the relevant namespaces:

Namespace	Description
`System.Drawing`	Provides access to the basic graphics functions used in GDI+, including bitmaps, brushes, pens, colors, points, and rectangles. Within this namespace is the `Graphics` class, which exposes most of the basic methods for drawing onto a bitmap.
`System.Drawing.2D`	Provides extra classes and enumerations for two-dimensional vector graphics use, including the classes required for generating gradient fills.
`System.Drawing.Imaging`	Provides advanced features for interacting with bitmaps and images, creating color palettes, specifying image formats, and managing the encoding of images.
`System.Drawing.Text`	Provides advanced font handling and management classes, allowing interaction with collections of installed fonts.
`System.Drawing.Printing`	Provides the classes required to manage printing of graphics, including access to all the necessary printer functions and settings.
`System.Drawing.Design`	Provides the classes required for developing designtime extensions to the UI, for example when creating custom classes and controls for use in Visual Studio .NET.

The System.Drawing Namespace

When creating reasonably simple GIF or JPEG images such as we use in our **Wrox Car Company** site, we mainly use just the classes from the `System.Drawing` namespace. The next table summarizes the most commonly used classes, indicating what we use them for:

Class	Description
Bitmap	The drawing surface on which the graphics tools will be used, and which stores the graphic image. Exposes methods to save the bitmap in a range of formats, and to interact with the bitmap on a pixel-by-pixel basis.
Graphics	This is the main tool for drawing on a bitmap. It provides methods to draw straight and curved lines; plus outlined or filled circles, ellipses, pie 'slices', rectangles, polygons, and so on. It also exposes a series of methods to transform, rotate, and scale sections of a bitmap.
Pen	Used to draw lines and curves. The width and color can be specified.
Brush	Used to fill shapes and draw text. This is a base class – the concrete classes that inherit from it are SolidBrush, TextureBrush, and LinearGradientBrush, allowing a range of fill styles to be used.
Color	Defines a color for a brush or pen, and provides methods to define the color in a range of different ways.
Rectangle	Defines a rectangular region within the bitmap, where the top, left, width, and height are specified as Integer values.
RectangleF	A Rectangle structure that use floating-point (Single) values for the dimensions and co-ordinates instead of Integer values.
Font	Specifies the font style, size, and weight to be used when drawing text onto a bitmap.
StringFormat	Specifies the alignment and other features of the text that is drawn onto a bitmap, including tabs, digit substitution and hot-key indicators.

A full reference to the System.Drawing namespace is provided in the .NET SDK at: ms-help://MS.NETFrameworkSDK/cpref/html/frlrfSystemDrawing.htm

It's All Very Simple

All this looks complicated, but in fact the principle is very simple. We just use a Pen or Brush object to draw our image elements onto a Bitmap object. You can think of the Graphics object as being the 'hand' that does the drawing, by creating the lines, fills, text, and other elements:

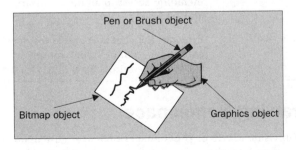

In more technical terms, the process is:

- Create a `Bitmap` – this represents the drawing surface
- Create a `Graphics` object based on the bitmap – this represents the 'hand' that manipulates the drawing tools
- Create a `Pen` – this is used to draw lines.
- Create a `Brush` – this is used to fill shapes and draw text strings
- Call the methods of the `Graphics` object to create the required content using the `Pen` and `Brush` objects
- Call the `Save` method of the `Bitmap` object to output the finished image
- Dispose of the objects

The next listing shows the outline code required in an ASP.NET page to generate a GIF image. Notice that we set the correct `ContentType` for the response, so that the client knows that it is a GIF image. While Internet Explorer will automatically display the result as an image without this, some other browsers will not:

```
' set content-type of response so client knows it is a GIF image
Response.ContentType="image/gif"

' create a new bitmap
Dim oBitMap As New Bitmap(iWidth, iHeight)

' create new graphics object to draw on bitmap
Dim oGraphics As Graphics = Graphics.FromImage(oBitMap)

'create a solid brush for writing text and filling shapes
Dim oBrush As New SolidBrush(Color.Yellow)

'create a red pen for drawing lines
Dim oPen As New Pen(Color.Red, 1)

...
...
'code here to draw the individual elements onto the bitmap
...
...

' write bitmap to response
oBitmap.Save(Response.OutputStream, ImageFormat.Gif)

' dispose of objects
oPen.Dispose()
oBrush.Dispose()
oGraphics.Dispose()
oBitmap.Dispose()
```

If it's as easy as this, we should have no problem generating our charts. In the remainder of this chapter, we'll show you a generic example for creating a pie chart, and then examine the page we use in our Wrox Car Company site to generate the model comparison charts.

Creating a Simple Pie Chart

Probably the easiest kind of chart to generate dynamically is a pie chart. The Graphics object exposes methods that generate an outlined or a filled 'pie slice', so all we need to do is call these methods for each row in our data to generate a complete pie chart. However, we also need to add the 'key box' for each slice in the chart, indicating what that slice represents.

The finished chart is shown in the next screenshot. We are charting the popularity of each vehicle model from the Wrox Car Company site. We've chosen to make the chart as attractive as possible by adding shadows to the various elements of the chart. This makes the code a little more complicated, but is well worth the extra effort. Without it, the chart looks quite flat and amateurish:

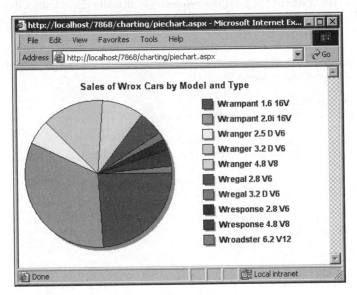

You'll find this example in the charting *sub-folder of the samples provided for this book. You can obtain the sample files from:*
http://www.wrox.com/Books/Book_Details.asp?isbn=1861007868 or you can run them online at: http://www.daveandal.com/books/7868/.

Providing the Data Source

In most cases, the data to build a chart like this will come from a database or perhaps an XML document, though it could, of course, be an array or a collection of some type. All we need are two items of information for each of the rows or objects that we want to include in the chart: the text string that describes the data item and the value itself.

The most likely data source will be a database of some kind, as in the example charts we use in our Wrox Car Company site. What's important is that the data must be available in a way that allows us to access the 'rows' or 'items' more than once. We will need to iterate through the data at least twice, and so we can't use the forward-only `DataReader` as the data source directly.

Instead, the best choice for accessing a database when creating charts is to use a `DataSet`. We can then pass the table from the `DataSet` that contains the information (as a `DataTable` object) to our charting routine. We can even extract a specific set of rows as a `DataRowCollection` and pass this to the routine. Furthermore, if the data is stored in an XML file rather than in a database, we can easily load it into a `DataSet` using the `ReadXml` method of the `DataSet` object.

Another approach is to make the data available as an `Array` or a `Collection` object. Of these, the `Array` is perhaps the most obvious, and we can easily create an array in code with the values we need if the source of the data is not a relational data store such as a SQL database. Plus, if the data is only available as a `DataReader` object, we can use the `GetValues` or `GetSqlValues` methods of the `DataReader` to return an `Array` containing the values. We discussed these methods briefly in the previous chapter.

Finally, if the data is created programmatically, we might create a custom class that holds the two values we need for each slice of the pie chart, and then use a collection based on this custom class as the data source for our charting routine.

In our pie chart example page, we're using a `DataSet` as the data source. However, to keep this demonstration of using the `System.Drawing` classes as simple as possible, we aren't fetching this data from a database. Instead, we just create the rows individually within our code. You'll see how next.

Creating the DataSet for the Pie Chart Example

Our example page charts the proportion of sales for each vehicle model. So we need a table in our `DataSet` that contains the vehicle name and the number of that vehicle sold. Note that this figure is *not* a percentage of the total number sold. It's extremely unlikely that any database would store percentages of the total for any specific quantity, because it would need to be recalculated for all the rows every time one quantity changed. Or, in terms of our example, we would have to recalculate the value for every row whenever we sold a vehicle.

The following listing shows the code we use to create our `DataSet` and table, returning it as the result of a function named `GetDataSet`. We create the empty `DataSet` object, add a new `DataTable` to it, and define two columns in this table. Then we can add rows to the table by specifying the values for these two columns (to avoid unnecessary repetition, we haven't shown the code for every row here):

piechart.aspx

```
' function to create a DataSet containing a few values
Function GetDataSet() As DataSet

  ' create a new DataSet object and a new table
  Dim dsResult As New DataSet()
  Dim tblData As New DataTable("Data")
  dsResult.Tables.Add(tblData)

  ' define two columns (fields) within the table
  tblData.Columns.Add("Caption", System.Type.GetType("System.String"))
  tblData.Columns.Add("Value", System.Type.GetType("System.Double"))
```

```
'declare a variable to hold a DataRow object
'fill in the values and add to table then repeat
Dim oRow As DataRow = tblData.NewRow()
oRow("Caption") = "Wrampant 1.6 16V"
oRow("Value") = 277
tblData.Rows.Add(oRow)

oRow = tblData.NewRow()
oRow("Caption") = "Wrampant 2.0i 16V"
oRow("Value") = 381
tblData.Rows.Add(oRow)

...
... repeat for other eight rows
...

Return dsResult    ' return DataSet

End Function
```

The Pie Chart Example Page

We've attempted to provide a routine that is reasonably generic in our pie chart example. However, to make all the possible features of the chart configurable through parameters to a method would mean a large number of parameters would be required. We chose just to expose four parameters to our 'generic' routine: the DataSet, the bitmap width and height, and the text for the caption at the top of the chart. So we can call our routine using something like:

```
DrawPieChart(dsMyDataSet, 420, 250, "A Test Pie Chart")
```

To make the chart more configurable, we could expose things like the offset of the shadows for the elements, the size and color of the text, the alignment of the 'key' boxes and text, the spacing between the chart and the 'key' boxes, and so on. However, this may not be the best approach in most practical situations.

In most cases, the variables we've just mentioned are not that important – they are not a vital part of the result we're hoping to achieve. Using some sensible hard-coded values for these variables within our routine is fine. It also marginally improves the efficiency of the code, reducing the variable references and subsequent calculations that would be required to position each element.

Of course, when you come to build your own charts and graphs, you might decide to make more features configurable via parameters, depending on your own requirements. However, as you'll see towards the end of the chapter, we actually reduced the level of configurability in the line charts that are a part of the Wrox Car Company site.

Adding the Import Directives

Before we do any drawing in our ASP.NET page, we should import the namespaces that we require. We only need the System.Drawing namespace for most of the tasks, however there are a couple of classes in the System.Drawing.Imaging namespace that we also take advantage of. And, because we're using a DataSet in our code, we also need the System.Data namespace:

```
<%@Page Language="VB" %>
<%@Import Namespace="System.Drawing" %>
<%@Import Namespace="System.Drawing.Imaging" %>
<%@Import Namespace="System.Data" %>
```

Instead of importing a namespace, we can refer to the classes within it directly by specifying the full class path within the .NET Framework's namespace hierarchy. In fact, we do this in a later example where we make use of the LineCap enumeration to add an arrowhead to the end of our axes. LineCap is part of the System.Drawing.Drawing2D namespace, but rather than importing the whole namespace we specify the full namespace and class name when we use it:

```
oPen.EndCap = System.Drawing.Drawing2D.LineCap.ArrowAnchor
```

This makes our code more wordy, and we use this approach only when we will refer to an item once or twice in a page. Any more than that and it probably makes more sense to import the namespace into the page. Importing a namespace does not make the page any 'heavier' or any less efficient, as the compiler only includes references to the classes actually used in the page, and not the complete namespace. You can use either approach in your code – we are simply demonstrating both here.

The Page_Load Event Handler

The next part of the code in our pie chart example page is the Page_Load event handler. All we do here is set the ContentType of the response, specify the caption for our chart, and call the DrawPieChart routine to create the chart. We pass to it the DataSet returned from the GetDataSet method we looked at earlier, and the width and height for the chart:

```
Sub Page_Load()

   ' set content-type of response so client knows it is a GIF image
   Response.ContentType="image/gif"

   ' specify the caption text for the chart
   Dim sCaption As String = "Sales of Wrox Cars by Model and Type"

   ' call routine to draw the pie chart - specify width and height
   ' for image that is created and the caption for top of image
   DrawPieChart(GetDataSet(), 420, 250, sCaption)

End Sub
```

The DrawPieChart routine creates the bitmap and draws the chart on it, and then saves the result to the response (as we saw in our outline of the process earlier on). Despite the fact that the browser accessed an ASP.NET (.aspx) page, it will think that the response is a normal GIF image (which, of course, it is) and will display it as an image. Of course, there is no HTML or other content in the page, as we must only send to the client the data that is generated by the Bitmap object.

Drawing Text on a Bitmap

Within our `DrawPieChart` routine, we'll need to write text strings onto the bitmap. In fact this is often the most complex part of creating a chart. The `Graphics` object exposes a method called `DrawString`, which takes as parameters:

- ❑ The text to write as a `String`.

- ❑ A `Font` object that defines the font to be used.

- ❑ A `Brush` object that defines the color and fill for the text. This is usually a `SolidBrush` object, though a `TextureBrush` or `LinearGradientBrush` can be used instead.

- ❑ A `Point` or `RectangleF` object that indicates the position of the text, or the X and Y coordinates of the starting position for the text.

- ❑ A `StringFormat` object that defines the alignment and various other attributes (such as digit substitution, trimming, and the hotkey character) for the text.

If we provide a starting point for the text, using a `Point` object or the X and Y coordinates, we lose some control over the actual alignment. We find that it's generally easier to use a `RectangleF` to define the area where the text should appear, and then control its position within this rectangle using the alignment properties of the `StringFormat` object we pass as the last parameter:

```
oGraphics.DrawString(sText, oFont, oBrush, oRect, oFormat)
```

Alternatively, you may prefer to calculate the start position for the text and use one of the other overloads of the `DrawString` method:

```
oGraphics.DrawString(sText, oFont, oBrush, iTop, iLeft, oFormat)
```

Or, if we create a `Point` object that defines the X and Y position:

```
oGraphics.DrawString(sText, oFont, oBrush, oPoint, oFormat)
```

Note that the `StringFormat` parameter is optional (in the sense that there are overloads of the `DrawString` method that do not accept this parameter), so we could just use:

```
oGraphics.DrawString(sText, oFont, oBrush, oPoint)
```

> *A full reference to the `DrawString` method is provided in the .NET SDK at: ms-help://MS.NETFrameworkSDK/cpref/html/ frlrfsystemdrawinggraphicsclassdrawstringtopic.htm*

A Custom Routine to Draw Text Strings

It's clear from the above that we have to do quite a lot of work to draw a text string on our bitmap, creating the various objects we need and then calling the `DrawString` method. For this reason, we built a generic routine that we can use to draw text strings. As well as accepting a reference to the current `Graphics` object that we're using to create the bitmap content, it allows us to specify the other variables such as the text itself, the rectangle in which it is drawn (using four integer values), the font style and size, the color, and the alignment:

```
' routine to draw text string in rectangle on bitmap
Sub DrawText(oGraphics As Graphics, iTop As Integer, _
            iLeft As Integer, iWidth As Integer, _
            iHeight As Integer, sText As String, _
            Optional eFontStyle As FontStyle = FontStyle.Regular, _
            Optional iFontSize As Integer = 8, _
            Optional sColor As String = "Black", _
            Optional eAlign As StringAlignment = StringAlignment.Near, _
            Optional eFlag As StringFormatFlags = Nothing)
    ...
```

Many of the parameters are optional, and are set to the basic commonly-used values, so we often only need to specify the first six parameters. Notice the last parameter named `StringFormatFlags`. This is used to set the `Flags` property of the `StringFormat` object we use to control the layout of the text within our rectangle. Amongst the extra controls it allows us to apply to the layout of the text are whether it should wrap within the rectangle, and whether any excess content should be clipped at the boundaries.

The value for this property of the `StringFormat` object is an integer made up by ANDing values from the `StringFormatFlags` enumeration. We really only included this so that we could take advantage of another value it exposes – `DirectionVertical`. We'll need this to place the text string vertically next to the Y-axis when we create line charts.

Within the `DrawText` routine, we first create a `RectangleF` object using the top, left, width, and height parameter values, and then create a new `Font` object using the font name, size, and style parameter values:

```
    ...
    ' create the rectangle to hold the text
    Dim oRect As New RectangleF(iTop, iLeft, iWidth, iHeight)

    ' create a Font object for the text style
    Dim oFont As New Font("Arial", iFontSize, eFontStyle)
    ...
```

> *There are actually 13 different constructors for a `Font` object, taking a range of different parameters. You'll find a full list in the .NET SDK at:*
> *ms-help://MS.NETFrameworkSDK/cpref/html/frlrfSystemDrawingFontClassctorTopic.htm*

Formatting and Drawing the Text

Next, we create a new `StringFormat` object, and specify the alignment we need. We only expose the horizontal alignment in the parameters to our custom `DrawText` routine, allowing text to be left aligned, right aligned, or centered within the rectangle. It's also possible to vertically align the text within the rectangle, but we always use `StringAlignment.Center` here. We can vary the vertical position of the text when we call our custom routine by changing the height of the rectangle.

```
    ...
    'create the format object to define the format and style
    Dim oFormat As New StringFormat(eFlag)
    oFormat.Alignment = eAlign      ' horizontal alignment
    ' always center vertically within rectangle area
    oFormat.LineAlignment = StringAlignment.Center
    ...
```

One interesting point is that the values we must use to horizontally align text are not quite what you may expect. For left-to-right (Western-style) text, we use `StringAlignment.Near` to align the text at the left of the enclosing rectangle, and `StringAlignment.Far` to align it to the right. For text that is written from right-to-left (which we specify by setting the `Flags` property of the `StringAlignment` object to `StringFormatFlags.DirectionRightToLeft`), the behavior is reversed. And the `LineAlignment` property, which controls vertical alignment, uses the same enumeration values; with `Near` being at the top of the rectangle, and `Far` being at the bottom of the rectangle.

Finally, we can create a `SolidBrush` object of the appropriate color, and then draw the text onto the bitmap:

```
    ...
    ' create a brush object and draw the text
    Dim oBrush As New SolidBrush(Color.FromName(sColor))
    oGraphics.DrawString(sText, oFont, oBrush, oRect, oFormat)

End Sub
```

Using our Custom DrawText Routine

To use our `DrawText` function, we must specify at least the first six parameters – the `Graphics` object reference, the rectangle boundaries, and the text string to draw. The other parameters can be omitted to use their default values. So, to draw a caption centered at the top of the chart, we can use:

```
DrawText(oGraphics, 0, 0, oBitMap.Width, 20, "My New Pie Chart")
```

If we want to control the font style, size, color, and alignment, we just add these parameters when we call the function:

```
DrawText(oGraphics, 0, 0, oBitMap.Width, 20, "My New Pie Chart", _
        FontStyle.Bold, 10, "Red", StringAlignment.Center)
```

To draw text vertically, as you'll see in the line charts we create later in this chapter, we specify the value `StringFormatFlags.DirectionVertical` for the final parameter. We can omit any intermediate parameters that we don't want to set specific values for, and the default values are used:

```
DrawText(0, 20, 12, 230, "seconds", , , , , _
        StringFormatFlags.DirectionVertical)
```

Creating and Using Colors in Images

We're going to need a range of colors for our chart. Probably the best way to do this is to create an `Array` of the colors we want to use, so that we can extract different ones as we iterate through the rows in our data source. In our example page, we create an `Array` of `Color` objects (rather than text color names as `String` variables).

Following is the code for the `GetColorArray` function in our example page. We only need ten colors, because our example will only have ten rows in the data source (one for each vehicle model in our `DataSet` table). However, you must make sure that there are sufficient colors for the maximum number of data rows or items you expect your own charting routines to handle – this routine will provide different colors for up to twenty data rows:

```
Function GetColorArray() As Color()

    ' declare an Array for 20 colors
    Dim aColors(19) As Color

    ' fill the array of colors for chart items
    ' use browser-safe colors (multiples of #33)
    aColors(0) = Color.FromArgb(204, 0, 0)       'red
    aColors(1) = Color.FromArgb(255, 153, 0)     'orange
    aColors(2) = Color.FromArgb(255, 255, 0)     'yellow
    aColors(3) = Color.FromArgb(0 ,255, 0)       'green
    aColors(4) = Color.FromArgb(0, 255, 255)     'cyan
    aColors(5) = Color.FromArgb(51, 102, 255)    'blue
    aColors(6) = Color.FromArgb(255, 0, 255)     'magenta
    aColors(7) = Color.FromArgb(102, 0, 102)     'purple
    aColors(8) = Color.FromArgb(153, 0, 0)       'dark red
    aColors(9) = Color.FromArgb(153, 153, 0)     'khaki
    aColors(10) = Color.FromArgb(0, 102, 0)      'dark green
    aColors(11) = Color.FromArgb(51, 51, 102)    'dark blue
    aColors(12) = Color.FromArgb(102, 51, 0)     'brown
    aColors(13) = Color.FromArgb(204, 204, 204)  'light gray
    aColors(14) = Color.FromArgb(0, 0, 0)        'black
    aColors(15) = Color.FromArgb(102, 204, 255)  'sky
    aColors(16) = Color.FromArgb(255, 204, 255)  'pink
    aColors(17) = Color.FromArgb(255, 255, 204)  'chiffon
    aColors(18) = Color.FromArgb(255, 204, 204)  'flesh
    aColors(19) = Color.FromArgb(153, 255, 204)  'pale green

    Return aColors

End Function
```

Color Modes and Color Palettes

Notice that we do *not* use the standard .NET color names here. There is an issue with using the standard colors when creating GIF images in .NET, and in fact whenever we use colors in a web page. It's easy to assume that every client we serve pages to has their system display set up in 'true color' mode – or so that it can display a minimum of 32,000 colors ('high color' mode).

In these modes, almost any color we use will be displayed without being dithered. They will appear as solid colors in the browser. However, some people still work in 256-color mode, and in this case the colors will be dithered – which can make the output look quite ugly.

And while it's very easy to forget about the problems of 256-color display with modern browsers, we come down to earth with a bump when we use .NET to generate GIF images. The standard method of encoding the bitmap we create when saving it as a GIF uses only the standard 'browser-safe' range of 216 standard colors. Any other colors are dithered, producing a non-solid appearance in all browsers (irrespective of the system display settings) that is often unacceptable. This enlarged view of the output when we use a different color (in this case "Khaki") shows the result:

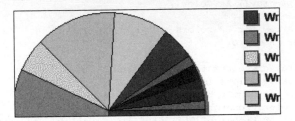

One way round this is to define the palette that the bitmap uses, by creating a new `ColorPalette` object and adding the colors we want to it. It's not trivial, but certainly an option. However, it doesn't solve the client-side issue. Just because we've generated the image with a specific color doesn't mean that the browser will be able to display it without dithering. If the user's system is configured in 256-color mode, it might not be able to display the color anyway – or it might be dithered when another window that uses a different palette is brought to the foreground, causing annoying color shifts as they work with the pages in the site.

Another option is to use a different encoding for the bitmap when we save it. Options include PNG and JPEG. As we mentioned earlier, support for PNG format is less universal in older browsers, so a JPEG is probably a better choice. However, the default high compression ratio that the standard encoding uses for JPEG output produces a rather 'muddy' and ill-defined output – even tinting the white background a light sepia color:

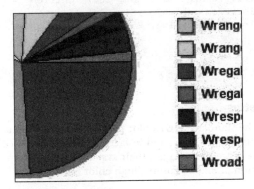

Again, there is a code-intensive solution where we reference an instance of the appropriate `Encoder` class, and change the properties to suit our image's requirements. However, after much experimentation, we found that the best solution to give maximum compatibility with all clients is to stick to using GIF images with the 216 browser-safe colors. For images that are 'pictures' rather than bitmaps (for example, an idyllic country scene taken with a digital camera, rather than a chart like that we're using here) JPEG is a better option, and you'll need to interact with the encoder to get the optimum results.

The Browser-Safe and Standard Colors

We've discussed the requirement to use only the **216 browser-safe colors** in our pages and images. But what are these colors? The simple answer is that they use values for their Red, Green, and Blue (RGB) components that are all multiples of the hexadecimal value #33 (51 in decimal). This allows an even spread of colors, as #33 is an integer divisor of the maximum value #FF (255 in decimal).

There are several sites on the Web that provide lists of these colors (we mentioned the W3C site in Chapter 3), however we've included a page that does this (and more) with the samples for this book. After all, it's not hard to calculate what they are!

The colors that are classed as 'browser-safe' are things like #003366 or #cc9966. What's really unfortunate is that only eight of these possible combinations of RGB values exactly match the standard 'known' colors defined by name in .NET. This is why we define the colors using RGB values in our example page. The only colors that do match exactly are:

.NET Name	Black	Blue	Lime	Cyan	Red	Magenta	Yellow	White
RGB Value	#000000	#0000ff	#00ff00	#00ffff	#ff0000	#ff00ff	#ffff00	#ffffff

The example page we've provided builds up a series of HTML tables that show the 216 colors as they appear in your browser, the decimal and hexadecimal values of each of the three components of the color (the RGB values), and the equivalent .NET color name if one exists. You can access this page (color-list.aspx in the charting sub-folder of the samples) from the opening menu of the sample files:

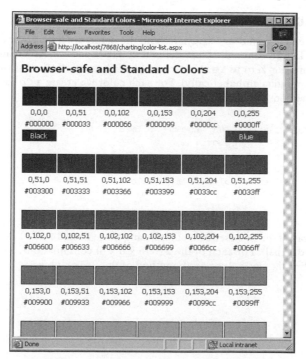

How the 'Browser-Safe Colors' Page Works

The Browser-Safe Colors page you've just seen appears to be quite simple. Each of the three components of the color that make up the RGB definition can have one of six values (#00, #33, #66, #99, #cc, or #ff). So all we need are 36 (6 x 6) tables that each display the six possible values for one of the components. However, rather than create 36 tables manually, it makes sense to allow ASP.NET to generate them dynamically for us.

So, in the HTML section of our page we just include the page title and some styling information for the text, followed by an ASP.NET PlaceHolder control where we'll insert out dynamically generated table:

```
<!-- placeholder to hold table of results -->
<asp:PlaceHolder id="ctlPlaceholder" runat="server" />
```

Then, in the Page_Load event handler, we create the table and add it to the Controls collection of the PlaceHolder control (we used this technique in the previous chapter to insert an Image control into a page dynamically):

color-list.aspx
```
Sub Page_Load()
  ...
  ... code to create an ASP.NET Table control named oTable here
  ...
  ctlPlaceholder.Controls.Add(oTable)

End Sub
```

Creating the Arrays of Colors

Before we start, we need to create two arrays to hold the colors we'll be displaying and examining in our code. There are 168 'known' (named) colors defined in .NET, and we can create an array of these by iterating through them from zero to YellowGreen (the last KnownColor, as they are stored in the Color structure enumeration alphabetically). For each color we create a Color object using the static FromKnownColor method:

```
' array to hold list of 168 'known' colors
Dim aKnownCols(167) As Color
Dim eValue As KnownColor
For eValue = 0 To KnownColor.YellowGreen
  aKnownCols(eValue) = Color.FromKnownColor(eValue)
Next
...
```

We can create an array of the browser-safe colors using three nested For...Next loops, with the 'step' value set to #33 (51 decimal). For each of the 216 (6 x 6 x 6) combinations, we create the equivalent Color object by calling the static FromArgb method of the Color object:

```
...
' array to hold list of 216 browser-safe colors
Dim aSafeCols(215) As Color
Dim rValue, gValue, bValue As Integer
Dim iPointer As Integer = 0
For rValue = 0 To 255 Step 51
  For gValue = 0 To 255 Step 51
    For bValue = 0 To 255 Step 51
      aSafeCols(iPointer) = Color.FromArgb(rValue, gValue, bValue)
      iPointer += 1
    Next
  Next
Next
...
```

Creating the Rows for Each Table

Now we declare the variables we'll need within our code. To display a cell with the correct background color, we'll be setting the BackColor property of that Cell object. As there is no other content in the cell, we use a string of large font non-breaking spaces (sColorCell) to ensure that the cell is large enough to show the color.

Then we can create five new TableRow objects that we'll add to the table once we've finished 'filling them in'. We also specify the horizontal alignment for the three rows that will contain text:

```
...
' declare variables, we'll create 5 rows simultaneously
Dim oRow1, oRow2, oRow3, oRow4, oRow5 As TableRow
Dim oCell As TableCell
Dim oColor, oKnown As Color
Dim sDecimalVals, sHexVals, sKnown As String

' to create empty cell with colored background
Dim sColorCell As String
sColorCell = "<font size=5>       </font>"

' create empty Table object and five Row objects
Dim oTable As New Table
oRow1 = New TableRow()
oRow2 = New TableRow()
oRow3 = New TableRow()
oRow4 = New TableRow()
oRow5 = New TableRow()

' set horizontal alignment for three rows
oRow2.HorizontalAlign = HorizontalAlign.Center
oRow3.HorizontalAlign = HorizontalAlign.Center
oRow4.HorizontalAlign = HorizontalAlign.Center
...
```

One of the great things about creating tables dynamically with the Web Forms controls is that we can generate multiple table rows at the same time, as we're doing in this example (the fifth row is empty, and is just there to add vertical white-space between each set of color rows). After all the rows are complete, we just add them to the Table object in the correct order. Where we display different types of output for each color in different rows of the table, it means that we can iterate through the array of colors once only, creating all the rows in one pass, rather than having to iterate through the array once for each row as we would if we were generating output directly to the response (like we do in ASP 3.0).

0,0,255
#0000ff
Blue

We can do much the same using the HtmlTable, HtmlTableRow, and HtmlTableCell controls from the System.Web.UI.HtmlControls namespace. However, we chose to use the Web Forms equivalents (Table, TableRow, and TableCell) from the System.Web.UI.WebControls namespace here, as they provide easier control of the format and layout.

Creating the Cells for Each Table Row

Now we can iterate through the safe colors in our aSafeCols array. We build up a String for the values in decimal and in hexadecimal (the format string "x2" indicates that the value should be formatted as two hexadecimal characters, using lower-case letters for values above 9):

```
...
' iterate through array of safe colors
For Each oColor In aSafeCols

  ' create the strings showing decimal and hex RGB values
  sDecimalVals = oColor.R.ToString() & "," & oColor.G.ToString() _
              & "," & oColor.B.ToString()
  sHexVals = "#" & oColor.R.ToString("x2") & oColor.G.ToString("x2") _
          & oColor.B.ToString("x2")
...
```

Next we can check to see if the current color is the same as any of the standard .NET 'known' colors. We iterate through the aKnownCols array, checking if the RGB value of each color is identical to the RGB value of our current browser-safe color. If it is, we set the String value sKnown to the .NET known color name. If not, it remains empty:

```
...
' see if this color is same as any standard color by iterating
' through 'known' colors array and comparing ARGB values.
' not breaking at first match avoids returning 'system' colors
' such as "DialogText" and "WindowTitleBarText" which come first
sKnown = ""
For Each oKnown In aKnownCols
  If oKnown.ToArgb = oColor.ToArgb Then
    sKnown = oKnown.Name
  End If
Next
...
```

Displaying the Color and Color Details

Time to start generating the cells for our rows, and we do this by creating a new `TableCell` object, and adding a `LiteralControl` to its `Controls` collection. The parameter to the `LiteralControl` is the text string we want to display in that cell. For the first cell, this is the `String` we declared earlier in the page, which contains a series of large non-breaking space characters. Then we can display the actual color by setting the background color of the cell to this color. We also give the cell a black one-pixel-wide solid border (by specifying the value 1 for the `Pixel` method of the static `Unit` object), before adding it to the first of our five rows:

```
...
' create a new cell, and add LiteralControl containing value
oCell = New TableCell()
oCell.Controls.Add(New LiteralControl(sColorCell))

'set properties for this cell, and add to row 1
oCell.BorderColor = Color.Black
oCell.BorderStyle = BorderStyle.Solid
oCell.BorderWidth = Unit.Pixel(1)
oCell.BackColor = oColor
oRow1.Cells.Add(oCell)
...
```

Next come the two cells that contain the RGB values in decimal and hexadecimal. Each is placed in a `LiteralControl` within a new `TableCell` object, and these two cells are added to the second and third of our `TableRow` objects:

```
...
' repeat for cells containing decimal and hex RGB values
oCell = New TableCell()
oCell.Controls.Add(New LiteralControl(sDecimalVals))
oRow2.Cells.Add(oCell)
oCell = New TableCell()
oCell.Controls.Add(New LiteralControl(sHexVals))
oRow3.Cells.Add(oCell)
...
```

Next we create the cell for the fourth of our rows. If the current color is one of those that matches the 'known' .NET colors, the string sKnown will not be empty, and so we can insert the color name into this cell. We then create a new `Color` object with this name, and use it to change the background color of this cell – adding a black border as we did earlier. We also change the foreground color of this cell to white if this color has values less than 124 (decimal) for its Red and Green components, so that the text will show up.

If the current color is not a 'known' color, we just leave the cell empty. It will generate only the `<td></td>` tags in this case, preserving the layout of the table when rendered in the browser. In either case, we complete this section of code by adding the cell to the fourth of our new `TableRow` objects, and then create an empty cell and add it to the fifth `TableRow` object:

```
...
' create cell for matching 'known' color if there is one
oCell = New TableCell()
If sKnown <> "" Then
  oCell.Controls.Add(New LiteralControl(sKnown))

  ' create color object using 'known' color name
  oKnown = Color.FromName(sKnown)
  oCell.BackColor = oKnown
  oCell.BorderColor = Color.Black
  oCell.BorderStyle = BorderStyle.Solid
  oCell.BorderWidth = Unit.Pixel(1)

  ' see if we need to use white text on this background
  ' color when displaying color name in cell
  If oKnown.R < 124 And oKnown.G < 124 Then
    oCell.ForeColor = Color.White
  End If

End If

' add 'known color' cell to row 4
oRow4.Cells.Add(oCell)

' create cell in row 5 to provide space between color rows
oCell = New TableCell()
oCell.Controls.Add(New LiteralControl(" "))
oRow5.Cells.Add(oCell)
...
```

Starting a New Row

We want to start a new row each time the Blue component of our color values reaches 255 – as it will with every sixth color, because we set the Blue component of the colors in our array in the innermost of the three nested loops when we filled the array. When it does reach 255, we add the five rows we've been creating to the table, then create five more new ones and set the horizontal alignment as we did before. Then we can go back and process the next color in our array.

After we've processed all the colors, and our table is complete, we insert it into the PlaceHolder control we defined in the HTML section of the page. When ASP.NET renders the page to the client, our newly filled Table control will generate a normal HTML table:

```
...
' if Blue element of color has reached 255 start a new row
' add five existing rows to table, create new ones and set
' horizontal alignment for the three of them holding text

If oColor.B = 255 Then
  oTable.Rows.Add(oRow1)
  oTable.Rows.Add(oRow2)
  oTable.Rows.Add(oRow3)
  oTable.Rows.Add(oRow4)
  oTable.Rows.Add(oRow5)
```

```
        oRow1 = New TableRow()
        oRow2 = New TableRow()
        oRow3 = New TableRow()
        oRow4 = New TableRow()
        oRow5 = New TableRow()
        oRow2.HorizontalAlign = HorizontalAlign.Center
        oRow3.HorizontalAlign = HorizontalAlign.Center
        oRow4.HorizontalAlign = HorizontalAlign.Center
      End If

    Next

    ' table complete, so insert into page within PlaceHolder control
    ctlPlaceholder.Controls.Add(oTable)

  End Sub
```

So, having taken a detour to look at browser-safe colors, color palettes, and image formats, and seen how we can create HTML tables dynamically with ASP.NET, we'll come back to our pie chart example.

Our Generic Pie Chart Routine

Our 'generic' DrawPieChart routine takes as parameters a DataSet containing our source data, the width and height of the chart to create, and the caption to place at the top of the GIF image that it generates. Earlier on, in our Page_Load event handler, we called the DrawPieChart routine using:

```
    DrawPieChart(GetDataSet(), 420, 250, sCaption)
```

In this section of the chapter, we'll see how the DrawPieChart routine works. We start by creating a BitMap object, a Graphics object, a new black Pen object and a new white SolidBrush object – exactly as we demonstrated earlier in this chapter in the outline description of the process of drawing using the .NET Framework classes.

The default for a new BitMap object is for all the pixels to be set to zero, giving a completely black bitmap. So the first thing we do after creating the various objects we'll need is draw a filled rectangle the same size as the bitmap with our new white SolidBrush object (in the last line of the following listing) so that we have a white background to work on:

piechart.aspx

```
  Sub DrawPieChart(dsData As DataSet, iWidth As Integer, _
                   iHeight As Integer, sCaption As String)

    ' create a new bitmap
    Dim oBitMap As New Bitmap(iWidth, iHeight)

    ' create new graphics object to draw on bitmap
    Dim oGraphics As Graphics = Graphics.FromImage(oBitMap)

    ' create a black pen for drawing lines and draw border
    Dim oPen As New Pen(Color.Black, 1)
```

```
          ' create a solid brush for the background and fill it
          Dim oBrush As New SolidBrush(Color.White)
          oGraphics.FillRectangle(oBrush, 0, 0, oBitMap.Width, _
                                 oBitMap.Height)
          ...
```

Next we can add the chart caption, centered at the top of the bitmap and allowing 20 pixels for the height of the rectangle in which the text is placed. We use a bold 10px font:

```
          ...
          ' draw caption centered at top of bitmap using routine in this page
          DrawText(oGraphics, 0, 0, oBitMap.Width, 20, sCaption, _
                   FontStyle.Bold, 10, , StringAlignment.Center)
          ...
```

Calculating the Position of the Main Chart Elements

Now we create some variables we'll need, and calculate the position of the various elements of our chart based on the size of the bitmap we're creating. We get an array of colors using the routine you saw earlier, and then specify the vertical spacing for the top of the 'pie' itself, allowing room for the chart caption. Then we calculate the diameter of the 'pie', allowing room for the caption above it and the shadow below it:

```
          ...
          ' fill the array of colors using routine later in page
          Dim aColors() As Color = GetColorArray()

          ' vertical space for chart caption
          Dim iCaptionHeight As Integer = 30

          ' variable to hold size of space above pie chart if it is
          ' smaller than available height of bitmap.
          ' Used to center it vertically with 'key' boxes and text
          Dim iPieTopOffset As Integer = iCaptionHeight

          ' calculate dimensions of pie chart, allowing space
          ' for 'key' text as 0.4 of width on right of chart
          ' and for shadow - which is 5 pixels below chart
          Dim iPieDiameter As Integer = oBitMap.Height _
                                      - iCaptionHeight - 6
          ...
```

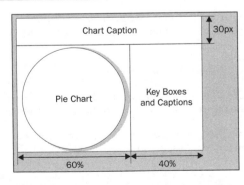

However, as the 'pie' is circular, we need to make sure that we have enough room for it plus the 'key' boxes and individual value captions (located to the right of the 'pie'). We decided that the 'pie' should only take up 60% of the horizontal width of the bitmap, so we check for this and adjust the diameter of the 'pie' if required (and adjust the vertical offset as well in this case, to keep it vertically aligned with the 'key' boxes alongside it):

```
...
If iPieDiameter > (oBitMap.Width * 0.6) Then
   iPieDiameter = oBitMap.Width * 0.6
   iPieTopOffset = ((oBitMap.Height - iPieDiameter) \ 2) _
                  + iCaptionHeight
End If
...
```

Creating Rectangles and Drawing Shadows

Now we're ready to start drawing some shapes. We create two rectangles – one for the 'pie', and one offset by 5 pixels vertically and horizontally for the shadow. Then we can change the color of our SolidBrush to dark gray and fill the shadow using the FillEllipse method of the graphics object. This method sizes the ellipse to fit inside the rectangle we pass as the second parameter and, as the width and height are the same, we get a circle:

```
...
' create rectangles for chart and shadow background
Dim oRectPie As New Rectangle(0, iPieTopOffset, _
                              iPieDiameter, iPieDiameter)
Dim oRectShadow As New Rectangle(5, iPieTopOffset + 5, _
                                 iPieDiameter, iPieDiameter)

' create color for shadows to objects
Dim cShadow As Color = Color.FromArgb(153, 153, 153)

' set brush color and draw circle for shadow
oBrush.Color = cShadow
oGraphics.FillEllipse(oBrush, oRectShadow)
...
```

There are also overloads of the FillEllipse method that accept four Integer or four Single values, instead of a rectangle object. And there is a DrawEllipse method that draws an outlined ellipse or circle using a Pen object instead of a brush object, with the size specified in the same way as for the FillEllipse method.

Next, we get a reference to a DataRowCollection that references all the rows in the single table of our source DataSet. Then we calculate the left position of the 'key' boxes, which will be 45 pixels from the right-hand side of the 'pie'. The vertical spacing between these boxes is the height of the bitmap minus the caption height, minus 15 pixels to allow a little extra space and room for the shadows, divided by the number of intervals between them (we use integer division here as we want an integer result). This value is the number of source data rows minus one:

```
...
' get reference to collection of data rows
Dim colRows As DataRowCollection
colRows = dsData.Tables(0).Rows

' calculate left position of 'value key' boxes
Dim iKeyBoxLeft As Integer = iPieDiameter + 45

' calculate vertical spacing for 'value key' boxes
Dim iKeyBoxSpace As Integer _
    = (oBitMap.Height - iCaptionHeight - 15) \ (colRows.Count - 1)
...
```

Declaring More Variables and Totaling the Rows

We'll need to store several values as we iterate through the rows in our data source, so we declare the variables for these values next. Notice that we use floating-point values for several of these variables. If the fSliceStart and fSliceDegrees values are forced to Integer values, the slices may not be exactly the right 'width', and not fully fill the pie chart (you'll see where these variables are used very soon). The other variables will hold values from our data rows, and so (depending on the values we're charting) these might not be Integer values:

```
...
' declare variables we'll need
Dim oRow As DataRow              ' reference to data row
Dim iRowIndex As Integer = 0     ' index for current row
Dim fSliceStart As Single = 0    ' start degrees of slice
Dim fSliceDegrees As Single      ' number of degrees for slice
Dim iKeyBoxTop As Integer        ' vertical offset of 'key' box
Dim fTotalValue As Double = 0    ' total of all values in table

' variables to hold values extracted from rows
Dim sSliceCaption As String
Dim fSliceValue As Double
...
```

We also need to find the total value of all the rows, so that we can work out what ratio of the total each 'slice' of our pie chart represents. We iterate through the rows summing the values from the second column (which contains the value), using a Try...Catch construct just in case there is a NULL value in any row:

```
...
' calculate total of all values in data table
' iterate through the rows in the table
For Each oRow In colRows
  Try
    fTotalValue += oRow(1)
  Catch
  End Try
Next
...
```

Drawing the Pie Slices

At last we're ready to start drawing the 'slices' of our pie chart, and for this we need to iterate through the rows again. For each row, we calculate the top position of the 'key' box using the spacing value we calculated earlier, and the row index that we set to zero when we originally declared this variable. Then we can set the color of our Brush, and draw a filled rectangle that creates the shadow for the 'key' box. We hard-coded the size (15 pixels wide by 14 pixels high):

```
...
' now ready to draw the pie chart itself
' iterate through the rows in the table again
For Each oRow In colRows

    ' calculate vertical position of 'key' box
    iKeyBoxTop = iCaptionHeight + (iKeyBoxSpace * iRowIndex)

    ' draw shadow for 'key' box
    oBrush.Color = cShadow
    oGraphics.FillRectangle(oBrush, iKeyBoxLeft + 3, iKeyBoxTop + 3, 15, 14)
    ...
```

The next step is to collect the values from the current data row, again using a Try...Catch construct as a precaution against NULL values in the row:

```
    ...
    ' get values from data row
    Try
        sCaption = oRow(0)
        fSliceValue = oRow(1)
    Catch
        sCaption = "Error"
        fSliceValue = 0
    End Try
    ...
```

The DrawPie and FillPie Methods

To draw a pie slice we use the DrawPie and FillPie methods of the Graphics object. Both of these can take a Rectangle object as their second parameter, the start position for the slice in degrees for the third parameter, and the number of degrees that the slice should take up as the fourth parameter.

So now we have to establish the number of degrees that this pie 'slice' will take up. We calculate the ratio of the total value for this 'slice', and then multiply by 360 to get a value in degrees. Then we can select the color for this 'slice' from our array of Color objects (using our row index variable) into our Brush, and draw our 'slice'. We first call the FillPie method with the Brush to create the colored 'slice', followed by a call to the DrawPie method. This uses our black Pen to draw an outline on top of the 'slice', giving a nice clean edge between the individually colored 'slices':

```
    ...
    ' convert to number of degrees for this value
    fSliceDegrees = (fSliceValue / fTotalValue) * 360
```

```
' set brush color from array of colors
oBrush.Color = aColors(iRowIndex)

' draw filled pie slice and then outline in black
oGraphics.FillPie(oBrush, oRectPie, fSliceStart, fSliceDegrees)
oGraphics.DrawPie(oPen, oRectPie, fSliceStart, fSliceDegrees)
...
```

There are also overloads of the `DrawPie` *and* `FillPie` *methods that accept parameters defining the top, left, width, and height instead of using a* `Rectangle` *object.*

Adding the Key and Caption

Now we can add the 'key' box for this 'slice', using the same color as we did to fill the 'slice', and then outline the box with our black pen. We've already calculated the position. We draw the text for this value to the right of the 'key' box using our own `DrawText` routine, placing it 7 pixels from the right of the box (22 pixels minus the width of the box). The width of the rectangle into which the text is drawn is calculated by subtracting the left position of the box and the 22-pixel offset from the width of the bitmap. The height of the text rectangle is the same as the box, so the text is centered vertically against the box:

```
...
' draw filled 'key' rectangle and then outline in black
oGraphics.FillRectangle(oBrush, iKeyBoxLeft, iKeyBoxTop, 15, 14)
oGraphics.DrawRectangle(oPen, iKeyBoxLeft, iKeyBoxTop, 15, 14)

' draw caption text next to 'key' box
DrawText(oGraphics, iKeyBoxLeft + 22, iKeyBoxTop, _
        oBitMap.Width - iKeyBoxLeft + 22, 14, sCaption, _
        FontStyle.Bold, 9)
...
```

We're only writing the text caption here, but you may like to add more information. For example, you might add the actual value of this 'slice' as a number to the text string. And, as you already know the total values for all the 'slices' of the pie, you can easily add the percentage as a number as well. We do this on one of our own web sites when displaying the relative number of visitors from each country that visit our site (by measuring and analyzing the language setting of their browser):

Completing the Loop

Before we start the next 'slice', we need to do a couple of things. The start position (in degrees) of the first 'slice' is zero, so this 'slice' is drawn starting at 3 o'clock and going clockwise. However, the next 'slice' must start at the end of the previous one, so we add the number of degrees for the current 'slice' to the starting position. We also increment our row index variable so that the 'key' box positions and colors for the next 'slice' are set correctly. Then we can go round and process the next row:

```
...
    ' save start position for next slice and increment row index
    fSliceStart += fSliceDegrees
    iRowIndex += 1

Next
...
```

Once we've processed all the rows, all that remains is to save the bitmap to the response so that it is sent to the browser, and destroy the objects we've used. In ASP.NET the objects are disposed of when page execution ends, but it is always good practice to do this explicitly:

```
...
    ' write bitmap to response
    oBitmap.Save(Response.OutputStream, ImageFormat.Gif)

    ' dispose of objects
    oPen.Dispose()
    oBrush.Dispose()
    oGraphics.Dispose()
    oBitmap.Dispose()

End Sub
```

A Note About Saving a Bitmap

Notice that we saved the bitmap in the code above directly to the current ASP.NET Response object. The output of the Bitmap object's Save method is a Stream, and so we can save the image data to any kind of object that accepts a Stream (in our case we used Response.OutputStream).

However, the other obvious requirement is to be able to save the bitmap as an image file to the server's disk. The Save method has an overload that saves the data as a disk file, and all we need to do is specify the full physical path and file name:

```
oBitmap.Save("c:\temp\piechart.gif", ImageFormat.Gif)
```

This might be useful if you want to create the images for your site only at specific intervals, perhaps to save on server loading if the values you are charting do not change very often.

The Vehicle Comparison Charts

Having seen how we create a pie chart, we can now move on and see how the comparison charts we use in our **Wrox Car Company** site are generated. The techniques are much the same as we used in our pie chart example, in particular the way that we create `BitMap` and `Graphics` objects, draw on the `BitMap`, and output the results to the browser. Where the pages really differ are in the set of drawing commands we use, and the way we calculate the values required to position each element of these charts.

The code in our 'Compare Models' page creates a complete URL for the chart image, including the name of the page that creates the image (`compare-chart.aspx`) and a query string that defines the comparison type and the list of models to include in the chart. For example, if the user selects the **Performance** comparison option for the two **Wregal** models, the URL used to load our chart image will be:

```
compare-chart.aspx?ctype=0&list=Wregal+2.8+V6*Wregal+3.2+D+V6
```

The `ctype` value is the index of the selected comparison radio button, so zero is performance, one is maximum speed, and two is fuel economy. The `list` value is just a list of the selected model names (taken from the checkbox captions), delimited with an asterisk character. The `URLEncode` method we used when creating the query string replaces any spaces with a 'plus' sign.

Getting the Values and Data for the Chart

Before we can even think about generating a chart, we must extract the appropriate data from our `WroxCars` database. In the `Page_Load` event handler we collect the value of `ctype` from the query string, and check that it is a valid value. If not we call a separate routine named `DrawErrorMessage`, which uses a very similar `DrawText` routine to that we used in our pie chart example to output the error message in bold red text (as the current `Graphics` object is held in a page-level variable in this example, we don't need to pass it to our `DrawText` routine).

However, if we do get a valid value, we collect the value for `list` from the query string. Providing that this is not empty, we call a routine named `DrawChart` located elsewhere in this page:

compare-chart.aspx

```
' extract from Page_Load() event handler
...
' get comparison type from query string
sCompareIndex = Request.QueryString("ctype")
If sCompareIndex >= "0" And sCompareIndex <= "2" Then

  ' get model list from query string
  sModelList = Request.QueryString("list")
  If sModelList <> "" Then
    DrawChart()
  Else   ' no vehicle list in query string
    DrawErrorMessage("No vehicles specified")
  End If

Else   ' no comparison type in query string
  DrawErrorMessage("Comparison type incorrect or not specified")
End If
...
```

Creating the SQL Statement

We need to create suitable SQL statements that will extract the values for each of the three types of chart. You'll recall that we had to do the same in the 'Compare Models' page to get the data for our table view of the comparison results. The only real difference between the first part of this routine and the one we used in the 'Compare Models' page is that we assign slightly different names to some of the columns:

```
Function GetSqlStatement() As String

  Dim sResult As String

  ' see which comparison type is selected
  ' and create SELECT part of SQL statement
  Select Case sCompareIndex

    Case 0      ' compare Performance
      sCaption = "Time in seconds from standing start to reach speed of:"
      sResult = "SELECT Caption = Model + ' ' + EngineName, " _
              & "[30] = Perf30, [40] = Perf40, [50] = Perf50, " _
              & "[60] = Perf60, [70] = Perf70, [80] = Perf80, " _
              & "[90] = Perf90, [100] = Perf100 " _
              & "FROM (tblCar JOIN tblCarEngines " _
              & "ON tblCar.CarID = tblCarEngines.CarID) " _
              & "JOIN tblEngine " _
              & "ON tblEngine.EngineID = tblCarEngines.EngineID WHERE "

    Case 1      ' compare Maximum Speed
      sCaption = "Maximum speed (mph) in each gear:"
      sResult = "SELECT Caption = Model + ' ' + EngineName, " _
              & "[1st gear] = Speed1st, [2nd gear] = Speed2nd, " _
              & "[3rd gear] = Speed3rd, [4th gear] = Speed4th, " _
              & "[5th gear] = Speed5th, [6th gear] = Speed6th " _
              & "FROM (tblCar JOIN tblCarEngines " _
              & "ON tblCar.CarID = tblCarEngines.CarID) " _
              & "JOIN tblEngine " _
              & "ON tblEngine.EngineID = tblCarEngines.EngineID WHERE "

    Case 2      ' compare Fuel Consumption
      sCaption = "Fuel consumption (mpg) at a steady speed (mph) of:"
      sResult = "SELECT Caption = Model + ' ' + EngineName, " _
              & "[30] = Fuel30, [40] = Fuel40, [50] = Fuel50, " _
              & "[60] = Fuel60, [70] = Fuel70, [80] = Fuel80, " _
              & "[90] = Fuel90, [100] = Fuel100 " _
              & "FROM (tblCar JOIN tblCarEngines " _
              & "ON tblCar.CarID = tblCarEngines.CarID) " _
              & "JOIN tblEngine " _
              & "ON tblEngine.EngineID = tblCarEngines.EngineID WHERE "

  End Select
  ...
```

However, now we need to create the WHERE clause for the SQL statement that we've been generating. The list of vehicles to include in the chart was extracted from the query string earlier in our code, and assigned to the String variable named sModelList. Each vehicle name is delimited with an asterisk character, and so we can convert this String into a String Array using the Split method. Then we can iterate through the array extracting the individual vehicle names and building up the WHERE clause:

```
   ...
   ' create WHERE clause section for each value in query string
   ' split list into an array, then extract each value
   Dim aList() As String = sModelList.Split("*")
   Dim sItem, sModel, sEngine As String
   For Each sItem In aList
     sModel = sItem.Substring(0, sItem.IndexOf(" "))
     sEngine = sItem.Substring(sItem.IndexOf(" ") + 1)
     sResult &= "(Model = '" & sModel & "' AND EngineName = '" _
                & sEngine & "') OR "
   Next

   ' remove final "OR" from string
   sResult = sResult.SubString(0, sResult.Length - 4)

   ' add ORDER BY clause and return result
   Return sResult & " ORDER BY Model, EngineName"

End Function
```

As an example, this is the SQL statement that is generated when we specify the 'performance' option and compare four of our vehicles:

```
SELECT Caption = Model + ' ' + EngineName, [30] = Perf30, [40] = Perf40, [50] =
Perf50, [60] = Perf60, [70] = Perf70, [80] = Perf80, [90] = Perf90, [100] =
Perf100 FROM (tblCar JOIN tblCarEngines ON tblCar.CarID = tblCarEngines.CarID)
JOIN tblEngine ON tblEngine.EngineID = tblCarEngines.EngineID WHERE (Model =
'Wrampant' AND EngineName = '1.6 16V') OR (Model = 'Wrampant' AND EngineName =
'2.0i 16V') OR (Model = 'Wranger' AND EngineName = '4.8 V8') OR (Model = 'Wregal'
AND EngineName = '3.2 D V6') ORDER BY Model, EngineName
```

We also have a GetCompareDS function in the compare-chart.aspx page that is similar to the GetCompareDR function we saw in the 'Compare Models' page. It uses the GetSqlStatement function listed above to get the appropriate SQL statement, and returns a DataSet containing the results.

Drawing the Appropriate Chart

The DrawChart routine that is executed from the Page_Load event handler simply calls the GetCompareDS function, and extracts the single table named Compare from the resulting DataSet. Then, providing there were some rows found, it calls a routine just like the one we used in our pie chart example to get an array of colors for the chart:

```
' routine to draw chart on bitmap
Sub DrawChart()
```

```
' get DataSet containing rows to chart
Dim dsResult As DataSet = GetCompareDS()

' get reference to table in DataSet
Dim tblResult As DataTable = dsResult.Tables("Compare")

' exit from routine if there was an error
If tblResult Is Nothing Then Exit Sub

' exit if there were no rows found
If tblResult.Rows.Count = 0 Then
  DrawErrorMessage("No matching vehicles found")
  Exit Sub
End If

' fill the array of colors for each item
FillColorArray()
...
```

Next we decide which chart we are going to create. We've written two routines, named `DrawLineChart` and `DrawBarChart`. We use the first of these for the 'performance' and 'fuel economy' line charts, and the other for the 'maximum speed' bar chart.

The `DrawLineChart` routine expects six parameters that define the low and high values for the Y-axis, the interval between each value on this axis, the caption for this axis, the caption for the X-axis, and the `DataTable` that contains the values to be used when generating the chart.

The `DrawBarChart` routine expects only three parameters. These define the interval between each value on the X-axis, the caption for the X-axis, and the `DataTable` that contains the values to be used when generating the chart.

The caption for the chart is held in a page-level variable named `sCaption`, and this is drawn onto the bitmap after we've executed the appropriate one of our two chart-generation routines to create the main section of the chart:

```
...
' decide which type of chart to draw and
' pass in suitable parameter values
Select Case sCompareIndex

  Case 0     ' compare Performance
    DrawLineChart(0, 30, 5, "seconds", "miles per hour", tblResult)

  Case 1     ' compare Maximum Speed
    DrawBarChart(10, "miles per hour", tblResult)

  Case 2     ' compare Fuel Consumption
    DrawLineChart(0, 55, 5, "miles per gallon", "miles per hour", _
                  tblResult)

End Select
```

299

```
    ' draw text caption onto chart
    DrawText(35, 0, 365, 12, sCaption)

End Sub
```

So, all that remains now is to see how the `DrawLineChart` and `DrawBarChart` routines work. They take advantage of many of the techniques we used to create our pie chart earlier in this chapter. We'll look at the line chart first, and then at the bar chart later on.

Drawing the Line Chart

The `DrawLineChart` routine in our page is used to draw both the 'performance' and the 'fuel economy' line charts. These are very similar, the only differences (apart from the actual plotted values) being the set of 'tick' values on the Y-axis and the caption of the Y-axis. The screenshot below shows an example of the 'performance' chart with all ten vehicles included in the comparison. You can see that the parameter values we used when we called this routine give Y-axis values that go from 0 to 30 seconds, spaced every 5 seconds:

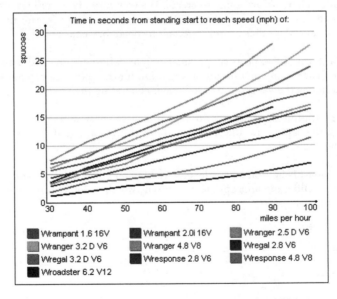

The same routine, when creating the 'fuel economy' chart, generates a Y-axis using the different values that we provide for these parameters. We get values from 0 to 55 miles per gallon, spaced every 5 miles per gallon:

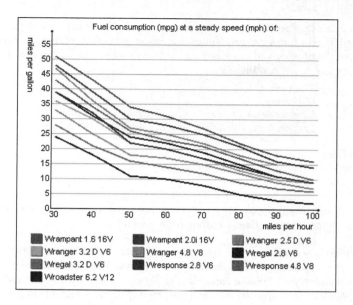

Declaring the Variables We'll Need

We start the `DrawLineChart` routine by declaring the variables we'll need. We have `Integer` variables to hold the position of the text caption and the 'key' boxes for each vehicle (which appear below the X-axis of the chart). There are also `Integer` variables to hold the start and end positions of each 'value line' segment we'll be drawing onto the chart. These are followed by a `String` to hold the description (caption) for each value, and a floating-point variable to hold the actual value. The last two variables will be used to reference the rows and columns in our source data table:

```
Sub DrawLineChart(iYMinVal As Integer, iYMaxVal As Integer, _
                  iYInterval As Integer, sYAxisText As String, _
                  sXAxisText As String, oXData As DataTable)

    ' variables required within routine
    Dim iLoop, iTextPos, iKeyXTop, iKeyXLeft As Integer
    Dim iLineXStart, iLineYStart, iLineXEnd, iLineYEnd As Integer
    Dim sValue As String
    Dim fValue As Single
    Dim oRow As DataRow
    Dim oCol As DataColumn
    ...
```

Creating Arrow Caps for the Axes

Each axis has an arrowhead at the 'high value' end. We can create these quite easily by assigning the value `LineCap.ArrowAnchor` to the `EndCap` property of the `Pen` object we use to draw the line (we can also add various line caps to the start of the line as well, by specifying the `StartCap` property of the `Pen` object). The `LineCap` enumeration is part of the `System.Drawing.Drawing2D` namespace, and as we haven't imported this into our page we have to specify the namespace when we reference the enumeration.

Once we've set the `EndCap` property of our `Pen`, we can call the `Graphics` object's `DrawLine` method to draw the X- and Y-axes for our chart. Notice that (as we discussed earlier) we've hard-coded the position and size of the elements of our chart, as we always want it to be the specific size we define – we won't be using it as a 'generic' routine:

```
...
'create arrow-head end point for pen and draw axes
oPen.EndCap = System.Drawing.Drawing2D.LineCap.ArrowAnchor
oGraphics.DrawLine(oPen, 35, 250, 399, 250)    ' X Axis
oGraphics.DrawLine(oPen, 35, 250, 35, 10)      ' Y Axis
oPen.EndCap = Nothing
...
```

After drawing the lines, we set the `EndCap` property of our `Pen` to `Nothing` (`null` in C#) so that the arrowhead will not appear on the lines we draw from now on.

Like the other methods in the `System.Drawing` namespace that we've used, the `DrawLine` method has several overloads. We used the one that accepts four `Integer` values here, and we'll use the one that accepts four `Single` values later in our code. There are also overloads that accept two `Point` objects (which define the start and end points of the line) rather than four individual coordinates.

Drawing the Y-Axis Values

Now we can calculate the position of each 'tick' value for the Y-axis and draw them onto our chart. We calculate the number of 'tick' values there will be, taking into account the start, end, and interval values specified in the parameters to this routine. From this, we can calculate the spacing in pixels between each 'tick' value (the chart is 230 pixels high), and the value that this represents in the units used within our data row:

```
...
' now add text and caption to Y (vertical) axis
' calculate spacing in pixels and value of each increment
Dim iYValCount As Integer = ((iYMaxVal - iYMinVal) / iYInterval) + 1
Dim iYSpacePX As Integer = 230 \ (iYValCount - 1)
Dim fYSpaceValue As Single = (iYMaxVal - iYMinVal) / (iYValCount - 1)
...
```

Then it's just a matter of iterating through the number of values we just calculated, working out the vertical position of each value on the axis, and drawing the text to show this value. The bottom of the Y-axis is 255 pixels down the bitmap, and by subtracting the index within the loop for this value, multiplied by the value per 'tick' on the axis, we get the vertical position. Notice that we draw the text aligned to the right (`StringAlignment.Far`). While we have this position in our variable, we draw a light gray horizontal line across the chart as well:

```
...
' for each value on Y axis
For iLoop = 0 To iYValCount - 1

    ' calculate value to display
    sValue = (iYMinVal + (iLoop * fYSpaceValue)).ToString()
```

```
    ' calculate vertical position and write text
    iTextPos = 244 - (iLoop * iYSpacePX)
    DrawText(11, iTextPos, 25, 12, sValue, , , , StringAlignment.Far)

    ' draw light gray horizontal line if not on X axis
    If iLoop > 0 Then
      oPen.Color = Color.FromArgb(204, 204, 204)  'light gray
      oGraphics.DrawLine(oPen, 36, iTextPos + 6, 395, iTextPos + 6)
    End If

  Next

  ' write Y axis caption vertically aligned left (top)
  DrawText(0, 20, 12, 230, sYAxisText, , , , StringAlignment.Near, _
          StringFormatFlags.DirectionVertical)
  ...
```

At the end of the loop, once we've drawn the 'tick' values for the Y-axis, we add the text description for this axis using the value passed into this routine as a parameter. The combination of the values `StringAlignment.Near` and `StringFormatFlags.DirectionVertical` causes the text to be drawn vertically, starting at the top of the rectangle we define with the first four parameters.

Drawing the X-Axis Values

The next step is to draw the 'tick' values onto the X-axis. This is a bit easier, because we have the values themselves in the rows of our data source table as the names of the columns (excluding the first, which contains the text description of the values in each row). So we can find out how many there are by querying the `Count` property of the table's `Columns` collection and subtracting one. From this we can calculate the pixel spacing per 'tick' value, by dividing the number of values into the size of the X-axis (355 pixels).

Then we iterate through the `Columns` collection of our table starting at the second column (at index 1), and extract the column name. The horizontal position is calculated using the index of the loop and the spacing between each 'tick' value, and we draw the column name at this point just below the X-axis. We specify the value `StringAlignment.Center` when we call the `DrawText` routine, so the text will be horizontally centered on the point we've just calculated:

```
  ...
  ' now ready to start X (horizontal) axis text and captions
  ' calculate spacing in pixels of values on X axis
  ' use DataColumns collection, but not first column (car name)
  Dim iXValCount As Integer = oXData.Columns.Count - 1
  Dim iXSpacePX As Integer = 355 \ (iXValCount - 1)

  ' for each value on X axis
  For iLoop = 0 To iXValCount - 1

    ' get column name to display
    sValue = oXData.Columns(iLoop + 1).ColumnName

    ' calculate horizontal position and write text
    iTextPos = 15 + (iLoop * iXSpacePX)
    DrawText(iTextPos, 252, 50, 12, sValue, , , , StringAlignment.Center)
```

```
Next

' write X axis caption aligned right
DrawText(40, 264, 355, 15, sXAxisText, , , , _
        StringAlignment.Far)
...
```

As before, once we've finished drawing the 'tick' values, we add the caption for this axis just below these values. Because we use the value `StringAlignment.Far` in this call to the `DrawText` routine, the text is right aligned under the axis.

Drawing the Value Lines

Now we can draw the 'value' lines onto the chart. We set our `Pen` width to two pixels, and calculate the multiplier for the Y-axis. We'll use this to convert each value in our data rows into the number of pixels above the X-axis for that point. We also declare an index variable that we'll use in the loop, just as we did in the pie chart example earlier on:

```
...
' now ready to draw lines of values for each row in data table
' set line width in pen to 2 and set start color
oPen.Width = 2

' calculate multiplier for Y values per pixel
Dim fYMultiplier = iYSpacePX / fYSpaceValue

' set the index of the current data row
' used to set colors and 'key' positions
Dim iRowIndex As Integer = 0
...
```

So, now we can start to iterate through the rows in our table, and for each one we set the color of the `Pen` using our array of colors, so that the line for each vehicle in drawn in a different color. Then we set the start position of the first line segment for this row at the left-hand end of the X-axis, and calculate the Y value for this point by multiplying the row value minus the start value of the Y-axis by the multiplier we calculated earlier, giving the number of pixels above the X-axis. To position this point on the chart, we also need to subtract the value we've just calculated from 250 (the vertical position of the X-axis):

```
...
' iterate through data rows
For Each oRow In oXData.Rows

    ' set pen color from array of colors
    oPen.Color = aColors(iRowIndex + 1)

    ' set starting values for line points for each row
    iLineXStart = 40
    iLineYStart = 250 - ((oRow(1) - iYMinVal) * fYMultiplier)

    ...
```

Now we know where the line for this row will start, and we can iterate through the rest of the columns in this row. In other words, we start here at the third column, indexed 2, because this contains the end point for the first line segment – we've already located the starting point for the first line segment.

For each column we access, we calculate the horizontal position of the current line segment end point and then extract the row value and calculate the vertical position. In both cases we use the same formula as we did in the previous section of code. However, here we use a `Try...Catch` construct when we extract the value, because we know that some vehicles will not have values in some columns (for example, two of our vehicles are not capable of reaching 100 mph, so the line for these must stop at the previous 'tick' value on the X-axis).

Once we've got the position of the end of the line segment, we can draw it onto the chart using the `DrawLine` method of our `Graphics` object:

```
...
' iterate through the columns in the row, omitting the
' first one which contains the vehicle name
For iLoop = 1 To iXValCount - 1

   'set the end X position of the line
   iLineXEnd = 40 + (iLoop * iXSpacePX)

   Try    ' in case database value is <NULL>

      ' get value from column in this row
      fValue = oRow(iLoop + 1)

      'calculate end Y position of line from value
      iLineYEnd = 250 - ((fValue - iYMinVal) * fYMultiplier)

      ' draw the line on the chart
      oGraphics.DrawLine(oPen, iLineXStart, iLineYStart, _
                      iLineXEnd, iLineYEnd)

   Catch
   End Try
   ...
```

The one other task within this loop, before we go round to draw the next line segment for this vehicle, is to save the end point co-ordinates of the current line segment. This will be the start point for the next line segment for this vehicle.

```
   ...
   ' save current position for start of next line segment
   iLineXStart = iLineXEnd
   iLineYStart = iLineYEnd

Next
...
```

Drawing the 'Key' Boxes and Descriptions

Once we've drawn all the line segments for this vehicle, and before we move to the next row in our table, we must add the 'key' box and text to the bottom of our chart. There is room for three of these 'key' boxes and text across the width of the chart, and we've allowed room for four vertically, so that we can get up to twelve values in this area of the chart (in our example site, we only have ten):

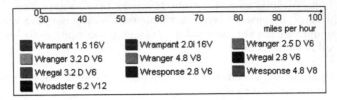

The position of these 'key' boxes is hard-coded into the routine, with the top left position of the first one being at X=9, Y=284. The space between them is 136 pixels horizontally and 17 pixels vertically, so we can calculate the position of the current one like this:

```
...
' now add the 'key' box and vehicle name
' calculate left and top positions for current row
iKeyXTop = 284 + ((iRowIndex \ 3) * 17)
iKeyXLeft = 9 + ((iRowIndex Mod 3) * 136)
...
```

By using integer division by three against the loop index for the vertical position, we know that it will only move the 'key' box down to the next row for every third one. Likewise, by using Mod 3 when we calculate the horizontal position, we know that it will return to zero for every third value of the loop index.

Now that we know the position of the 'key' box for the current row we can draw it onto our bitmap. We set the color of our page-level Brush to light gray and draw the shadow rectangle offset by one pixel horizontally and vertically, then set it to the current color for the value in this row and draw the colored box on top of this shadow.

To finish we draw the text we collected from the first column of this row (the vehicle description) next to the 'key' box, and then increment our row index variable, before going back to process the next row (the next vehicle) in our source data table:

```
' set brush color and draw shadow for box
oBrush.Color = Color.FromArgb(102, 102, 102)
oGraphics.FillRectangle(oBrush, iKeyXLeft + 1, iKeyXTop + 1, 15, 13)

' set brush color and draw box and text
oBrush.Color = aColors(iRowIndex + 1)
oGraphics.FillRectangle(oBrush, iKeyXLeft, iKeyXTop, 15, 13)
DrawText(iKeyXLeft + 18, iKeyXTop, 115, 14, oRow(0).ToString(), _
        , , , StringAlignment.Near)

'increment row index ready for next row
iRowIndex += 1
```

```
      Next

   End Sub
```

That's it for the line chart, and – as you've seen – we can use this routine for both the 'performance' and 'fuel economy' charts in our **Wrox Car Company** site.

Drawing the Bar Chart

The one type of chart that we haven't examined yet is the bar chart. We use this type of chart in our 'Compare Models' page to show the maximum speed in each gear for the vehicles we sell. We chose to use a horizontal bar chart, as the text descriptions for each vehicle fit better against the Y-axis, while the short 'miles per hour' values fit better on the X-axis. However, the technique for creating this type of chart is much the same for a vertical bar chart, and you should have no problem converting the code if you prefer that type of chart.

The next screenshot shows the 'maximum speed' comparison chart when all the vehicles we sell are selected. We achieve a semi-3D effect by drawing a shadow under each bar, as well as under the 'key' boxes like we did in the previous line chart example. Notice that not all vehicles have the same number of gears:

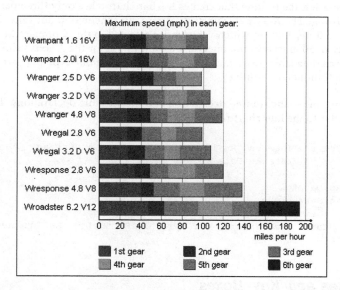

Unlike the line charts (where the maximum values of the axes stayed the same irrespective of which vehicles were selected, here we want to change the maximum value of the X-axis depending on the maximum speed of the selected vehicles. For example, when we select only some of the slower vehicles, the maximum value on the X-axis drops from 200 mph to 120 mph (or less if we only select the smallest engine version of the **Wrox Wranger**).

We also have to adjust the width and position of the bars as the number of selected vehicles changes, otherwise the bars will only fill the top part of the chart and this looks extremely 'odd'. The next screenshot shows both this change in bar width and the change in the maximum X-axis value:

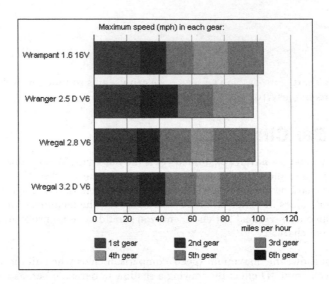

The Routine Parameters and Variable Declarations

As we mentioned earlier, the routine that creates the bar chart takes only three parameters. You can see them in the next listing. The X-axis always starts at zero, and the maximum value is calculated from the rows in our table, so it depends on which vehicles are selected in the 'Compare Models' page. This means that we only need to pass in the interval we want to use for the X-axis values, the caption for the chart, and the source data table (in fact, as we're only generating one type of chart here, we could have hard-coded the caption into the routine).

The following listing shows the routine declaration and the variable declarations. The list of variables we use is very similar to the line chart routine we've just seen:

```
Sub DrawBarChart(iYInterval As Integer, sXAxisText As String, _
              oXData As DataTable)

    Dim oRow As DataRow
    Dim oCol As DataColumn
    Dim iLoop, iTextPos, iKeyXTop, iKeyXLeft As Integer
    Dim iRectXStart, iRectYStart, iRectWidth, iRectHeight As Integer
    Dim sText As String
    ...
```

Drawing the Axes and 'Key' Boxes

The next step is to draw the axes, using an arrowhead LineCap as before for the X-axis:

```
    ...
    'create arrow-head end point for pen and draw axes lines
    oPen.EndCap = System.Drawing.Drawing2D.LineCap.ArrowAnchor
    oGraphics.DrawLine(oPen, 120, 261, 399, 261)    ' X Axis
    oPen.EndCap = Nothing
    oGraphics.DrawLine(oPen, 120, 17, 120, 261)     ' Y Axis
    ...
```

It is possible to vary the size and style of the arrowhead if you are not satisfied with the defaults, but this involves creating a custom `LineCap` object and setting its properties before assigning it to the `CustomEndCap` or `CustomStartCap` property of the `Pen` object. See the .NET SDK topic:

ms-help://MS.NETFrameworkSDK/cpref/html/ ⏎
frlrfsystemdrawingdrawing2dcustomlinecapclasstopic.htm

for more details about creating custom `LineCap` objects.

As we know that there can be a maximum of only six gears, we can draw the six 'key' boxes first; using the first six colors in our array of `Color` objects. The text descriptions for each one are the names of the columns in our source data table, omitting the first column as this contains the vehicle description that we'll display next to the Y-axis.

For each of the six 'key' boxes, we extract the column name into a `String` variable, and then calculate the top and left position using the same technique as in the line chart routine to get two rows of three 'key' boxes. After this we can set the `Brush` color to light gray and draw the shadow rectangle, then set the color to the appropriate one for this loop index and draw the colored rectangle. We finish off within the loop by drawing the text description (the column name) next to this 'key' box:

```
...
' draw the "key" boxes for each of the 6 possible
' values (gears) using column names from DataTable
For iLoop = 0 To 5

  ' get column name to display
  sText = oXData.Columns(iLoop + 1).ColumnName

  ' calculate position
  iKeyXTop = 295 + ((iLoop \ 3) * 17)
  iKeyXLeft = 120 + ((iLoop Mod 3) * 110)

  ' set brush color and draw shadow for box
  oBrush.Color = Color.FromArgb(102, 102, 102)
  oGraphics.FillRectangle(oBrush, iKeyXLeft + 1, iKeyXTop + 1, 15, 13)

  ' set brush color and draw box and text
  oBrush.Color = aColors(iLoop + 1)
  oGraphics.FillRectangle(oBrush, iKeyXLeft, iKeyXTop, 15, 13)
  DrawText(iKeyXLeft + 18, iKeyXTop, 115, 14, sText, _
           , , , StringAlignment.Near)

Next
...
```

Calculating the X-Axis Values

The X-axis for our bar chart is harder to build than in the previous line chart example, because we don't have the pre-defined maximum value available as a parameter. We have to calculate it from the values in the data rows. So we start by iterating through all the columns in all the rows to get the maximum value from any column in any row:

```
...
' next, find maximum value from all rows
Dim iValue, iRowsMax, iMaxValue As Integer
For Each oRow In oXData.Rows
  For iLoop = 1 To oXData.Columns.Count - 1
    Try
      iValue = oRow(iLoop)
      If iValue > iRowsMax Then
        iRowsMax = iValue
      End If
    Catch
    End Try
  Next
Next
...
```

Now we round up this maximum value to the next whole interval (the interval is specified as a parameter to this routine) by adding on the interval value, using integer division by the interval value, then multiplying by the interval again. From this value we can work out the number of values that will appear on the axis, and the spacing for these values in pixels (the X-axis is 270 pixels long):

```
...
' round up to next iYInterval
iMaxValue = ((iRowsMax + iYInterval) \ iYInterval) * iYInterval

' calculate number of values and pixel spacing
Dim iXValCount As Integer = (iMaxValue \ iYInterval) + 1
Dim iXSpacePX As Integer = 270 \ (iXValCount - 1)
...
```

The only problem now is that, if the maximum value is high and the 'tick' value spacing specified in the parameter to this routine is low, there may be more 'tick' values than will fit on the axis without overlapping – or looking 'odd' by being too close together. We decided that the minimum spacing between 'tick' values should be 25 pixels, and so we check if this is the case with the results we've calculated so far:

```
...
' see if the captions will overlap
While iXSpacePX < 25

  ' double the interval size
  iYInterval = iYInterval * 2

  ' recalculate values based on this interval size
  iMaxValue = ((iRowsMax + iYInterval) \ iYInterval) * iYInterval
  iXValCount = (iMaxValue \ iYInterval) + 1
  iXSpacePX = 270 \ (iXValCount - 1)

End While
...
```

If there are too many values, we double the interval that was provided as a parameter to the routine, and then recalculate the maximum value (to take into account the new interval value), the number of values, and the pixel spacing. It's most likely that we'll only have to do this once, but by enclosing it all in a While...End While construct, we know that the interval will always be doubled enough times to give the spacing we want.

Drawing the X-Axis Values

Finally, now that we have all the preliminary values we need, we can iterate through the number of 'tick' values and draw them just below the X-axis. The technique is much the same as we used in the line chart example earlier on, so we aren't detailing all the steps again here. The value 96 you see hard-coded here is the horizontal position of the pixel just to the right of the Y-axis, where the 'tick' values for the X-axis start and go along horizontally. Meanwhile, 263 is the vertical offset of the X-axis from the top of the bitmap:

```
...
' for each value on X axis
For iLoop = 0 To iXValCount - 1

   ' get value to display along axis
   iValue = iYInterval * iLoop

   ' calculate horizontal position and write text
   iTextPos = iLoop * iXSpacePX
   DrawText(96 + iTextPos, 263, 50, 12, iValue.ToString(), _
          , , , StringAlignment.Center)

   ' draw light gray vertical line if not on Y axis
   If iLoop > 0 Then
      oPen.Color = Color.FromArgb(204, 204, 204)  'light gray
      oGraphics.DrawLine(oPen, 120 + iTextPos, 17, 120 + iTextPos, 260)
   End If

Next

' write X axis caption aligned right
DrawText(40, 274, 355, 15, sXAxisText, , , , _
       StringAlignment.Far)
...
```

Within the loop, you can see that we draw a vertical line on the chart at each 'tick' value, rather like we did in the line chart. There they were horizontal lines, but vertical lines suit our horizontal bar chart better. Once we've drawn all the 'tick' values, the last line of the code above adds the text description (caption) for the X-axis just below them.

Drawing the Y-Axis Values

Before we can start drawing the Y-axis values or the bars themselves, we have to do some more calculations. First, we need the multiplier that determines the way we translate the values in the data rows to pixel values, and this can be obtained by dividing the width of the chart (270 pixels) by the maximum value on the X-axis.

Then, having declared our row index variable, we calculate the number of pixels that each horizontal bar of our chart can take up on the Y-axis (`iYSpacePX`) by dividing the chart height (240 pixels) by the number of rows in our data source:

```
...
' calculate multiplier for X values per pixel
Dim fXMultiplier = 270 / iMaxValue

' create index for row to set vertical position
Dim iRowCount As Integer = 0

' calculate vertical space for each row on Y axis
Dim iYSpacePX As Integer = 240 / oXData.Rows.Count
...
```

We now know how much vertical space each bar can use (it depends, of course, on the number of bars – which equates to the number of vehicles selected). However, we want to leave some space between them so that the light gray vertical 'tick lines' will be visible. So, we make each of the bars three-quarters (75%) of the available space (`iYBarHeight`), and center them vertically within the available space by offsetting them by 12.5% (`iYBarAbove`):

```
...
' make each bar 3/4 of available space to provide
' gap between each one so scale rules are visible
Dim iYBarHeight As Integer = iYSpacePX * 0.75
Dim iYBarAbove As Integer = iYSpacePX * 0.125
...
```

Drawing the Bars onto the Chart

At last we can start to draw the bars onto the chart. We iterate through the rows in our source data table, calculating the vertical position of the bar by multiplying the vertical space available by the row index and adding 18 pixels to allow for the caption at the top of the chart. Then we can draw the text description of the vehicle at this vertical offset, right aligning it against the Y-axis. The description comes from the first column of our data row:

```
...
' iterate through data rows
For Each oRow In oXData.Rows

   ' calculate vertical position for row values
   iRectYStart = 18 + (iRowCount * iYSpacePX)

   ' draw the vehicle name (caption) left of Y axis
   DrawText(0, iRectYStart, 118, iYBarHeight + iYBarAbove, _
         oRow(0).ToString(), , , , StringAlignment.Far)
   ...
```

We want to draw a shadow for the bar to give a 3D effect. However, we also need to think about how we'll create each different colored rectangular segment of the bar (each color indicating the maximum speed in a particular gear). We could start with first gear, and then draw subsequent rectangles starting from where the previous one ended – rather like we did when drawing the line segments in the previous example.

However, it is easier to draw each bar starting from the Y-axis, horizontally across the chart to its full actual value. This means that we don't have to keep track of the end of each bar, or subtract the previous data row value from the next one to get the correct size for the bar. As long as we draw the bars for the highest values first, and work backwards to the lowest value, each one will overlay correctly so that we get the result we want:

We also need to draw the shadow for the bar before we draw any of the segments. However, we only want to draw this for the largest segment (though you might like to try it with each segment for an even more exciting 3D effect). So we declare a `Boolean` variable that will indicate if we've already drawn the shadow. Remember that some vehicles will not have values for the fifth or sixth gear columns in the data row, so we can't just draw the shadow for the first column we process:

```
...
' flag so that shadow is only drawn once
Dim bDrawShadow As Boolean = True
...
```

Now we can iterate through the columns in the current data row, starting from the last one (`Columns.Count - 1`) and stepping backwards to the second column (at index 1 – remember that the first column is the text description of the vehicle). We collect the value of this column, within a `Try...Catch` construct because there may not be a value for this gear for this vehicle, and apply the value multiplier to get the length of the bar in pixels.

Before we draw the bar, we check if we've drawn the shadow yet, and if not we do so now using the current bar length value. We offset it by one pixel vertically and horizontally, and clear the shadow flag so that it won't be drawn again. After that, we can set the appropriate color for our `Brush` and draw the colored bar segment:

```
...
' iterate through the columns of this row
For iLoop = (oXData.Columns.Count - 1) To 1 Step -1
  Try
     iValue = oRow(iLoop)
     iRectWidth = iValue * fXMultiplier

     If bDrawShadow Then

        ' if this is the first value box for this row
        ' then set brush color and draw shadow for bar
        oBrush.Color = Color.FromArgb(102, 102, 102)
        oGraphics.FillRectangle(oBrush, 121, iRectYStart + iYBarAbove, _
                           iRectWidth + 1, iYBarHeight + 1)
        bDrawShadow = False     ' clear flag

     End If
```

```
              ' set brush color and draw value bar
              oBrush.Color = aColors(iLoop)
              oGraphics.FillRectangle(oBrush, 121, iRectYStart + iYBarAbove, _
                                      iRectWidth, iYBarHeight)

          Catch
          End Try

      Next
      ...
```

Having processed each column in this data row, we can now increment our row index variable, and go round to process the row for the next vehicle:

```
      ...
      iRowCount += 1

    Next

  End Sub
```

And that's it. The result is the attractive bar chart you saw earlier. It might seem like a long-winded and complicated process, but remember that it's just a matter of calling a few simple methods of the `Graphics` object to draw lines, ellipses and circles, rectangles, and text.

The hard part is calculating the positions of each element of the chart. One technique we used was to create a static view of the chart by drawing the elements manually in a paint program of some type – we used PaintShop Pro (from http://www.jasc.com/) but Windows Paint will do just as well. Once you've roughed out the chart, you can quite easily measure the positions and offsets of the various parts of the chart in pixels.

Summary

In this chapter, we showed you how we built the attractive and interactive charts that we use in the 'Compare Models' page of our fictitious **Wrox Car Company** site. However, we started off the chapter with a more general discussion of when and how you might consider using images or graphics that present information, rather than just being there for decorative effect. We also considered some of the options available for creating dynamic images, such as our performance comparison charts.

We followed this with a look at the easiest type of chart to create – the pie chart. Using some hard-coded values, we generated an attractive pie chart with 'key' boxes describing each value. And, in the middle of this, we wandered off to look at how we can build tables dynamically using the ASP.NET `Table`, `TableRow`, and `TableCell` server controls. While it might seem a little out of place here, we used this technique to discuss and demonstrate the browser-safe colors that you will probably want to stick to when generating GIF images with the .NET Framework `System.Drawing` classes.

The final sections of the chapter were devoted to the **Wrox Car Company** comparison charts. We built and discussed a line chart and a bar chart, both of which can accept a varying number of data rows as the source for the chart. The bar chart also scales the axes automatically to cope with varying maximum values within the data.

In summary, we:

- Looked at the various ways that we can generate graphics and images dynamically
- Explored the ways that we can use these images in our pages
- Described the .NET Framework classes that allow us to generate these graphics and images
- Showed how we create a simple pie chart as a generic function
- Showed how we created the line charts for the Wrox Car Company site
- Showed how we created the bar chart for the Wrox Car Company site

In the next chapter, we start to look at another of the interactive and dynamic pages on our Wrox Car Company site. We'll see how we build the page that allows users to configure a vehicle online.

8

Interactive Web Forms

So far, the pages we've created for our **Wrox Car Company** example site have been marginally interactive, in that they allow visitors to view performance details of our vehicles, select items such as News articles, and join our mailing list. However, when it comes to building pages that collect information, particularly multiple items such as the configuration of a vehicle, we need to provide much more in the way of interactivity.

As you'll see in this chapter, ASP.NET makes creating these kinds of pages much easier than it was in previous versions of ASP. The built-in features such as maintenance of viewstate, and the postback architecture, remove the need for a lot of code that we would have had to write in, say, ASP 3.0.

Our aim in this chapter is to build a page that allows visitors to configure any of our vehicles to their exact requirements, and then save this configuration as a quote so that they can place an order for that vehicle either immediately or at some point in the future. At the same time, we'll make the page as attractive and interesting as possible, tempting them to explore the various vehicles that we offer.

Of course, we should start by looking at the overall requirements, and coming up with a design for the page that provides all the features we want. So, before we start building the actual page that is part of the application, we'll explore some of the concepts and design decisions to help you understand how you can apply the same techniques to your own sites.

The aims of this chapter are to look at:

❑ How well our final page meets the original design requirements

❑ The **Model Details** page in outline, to understand how it is created

❑ The structure of the **Model Details** page, to understand how it works

We start with an overview of the requirements, and see how well we have met these requirements. This will also help to familiarize you with the way that the page works, making it easier to follow the detailed descriptions of the techniques we use that come later on in this and the next chapter.

Meeting the Design Requirements

In Chapter 1, we showed you the basic design for the Wrox Car Company site, and the rough sketches we created. The final site construction is based on these sketches and requirements, and follows them quite closely. Some of the original ideas have evolved into something more practical as construction was under way, but in general we have produced a close representation of both the appearance and the process that we originally planned. And, no, we didn't cheat and draw the sketches after the site was finished!

The Original Design

Our original design for the site includes a page where the user can go to see more details about each model, and configure it to suit their own personal requirements. As they do so, the page displays the total price for that configuration – including any monthly finance terms that they select. At the same time, a picture of the vehicle changes to reflect their color choice.

Selecting a Color for the Vehicle

The first of the original sketches we drew is shown again next, describing the section of the page where users specify the color they want:

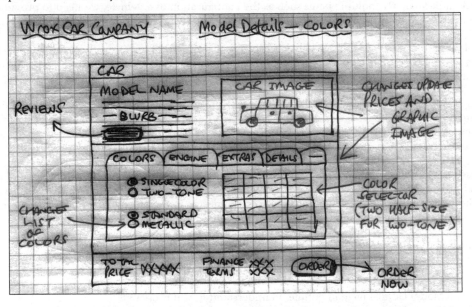

Some of the features of this page have been omitted in the final site. As far as implementation is concerned, a 'Reviews' section would probably have mirrored the operation of the 'News' feature that is available from the 'Home' page, and therefore would have demonstrated nothing new unless we extended it to accept user reviews and act as a list server.

The option of a two-tone 'paint job' has also been dropped; mainly because it again would add nothing extra to the techniques we are attempting to demonstrate. We've also moved the display of the price to the upper section of the page. However, all the other original design features are in place and working, as you can see in the next screenshot taken from the final application:

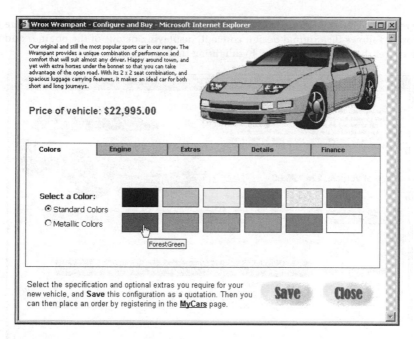

Selecting the Engine for the Vehicle

The second part of the 'Model Details' page allows the user to select the engine they prefer. All the vehicles can be provided with a choice of at least two different engines, and some with more than this. Our original sketch is shown below:

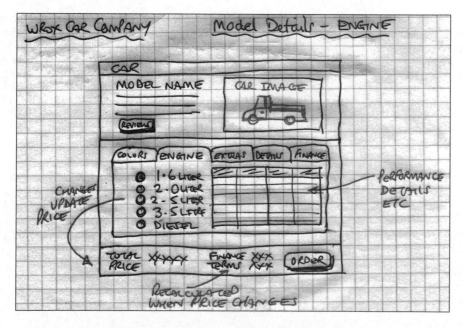

The next screenshot shows the section of the final application where the choice of engine is made. Again, it closely follows the original design concept, displaying details of the engines and indicating those of the currently selected engine by highlighting that row in the table:

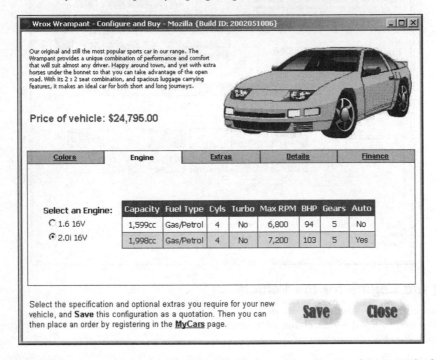

Comparing this screenshot with the previous one, you can see the effect on the price of selecting the larger engine. As with computers, you have to pay to get the extra performance! You may also notice that this screenshot shows the page displayed in Mozilla 1.0, whereas the previous one showed Internet Explorer 6. The appearance of the common content is just about identical. This was an early design decision in that we would attempt to provide the best support we could for all kinds of client browser.

Selecting the Optional Extras for the Vehicle

The third section of the page allows visitors to select from a range of optional extras. This is the original sketch:

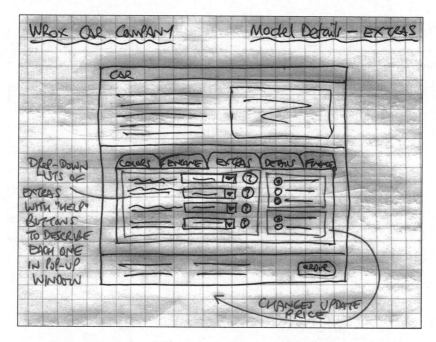

While we originally envisaged using a mixture of drop-down lists and option buttons, we ended up implementing a somewhat simpler interface. Each vehicle in our range can be equipped with a selection of optional extras, depending on the model. The page on the example site lists these options, and allows a visitor to select which they require. As they select each one, the price is updated to reflect the new total:

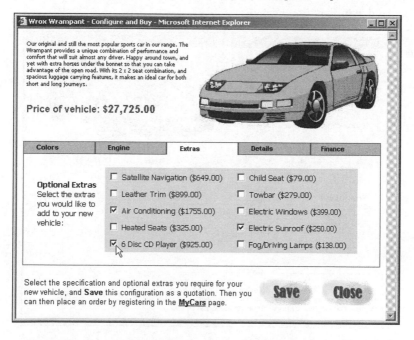

Viewing the Standard Features of the Vehicle

The fourth section of the 'Model Details' page allows visitors to examine the list of standard features for each vehicle. There is no requirement for interactivity in this section, as it is used simply to display information:

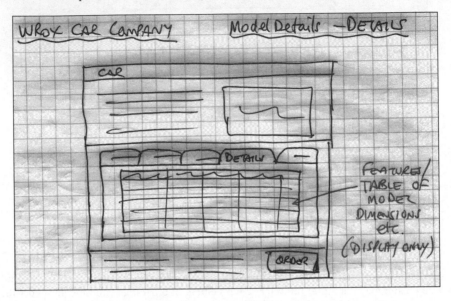

However, as you can see in the next screenshot of the finished page, we provide the information as a pair of collapsible 'tree view' lists. Each contains a subset of the standard features for this model, and the lists can be expanded to show these details:

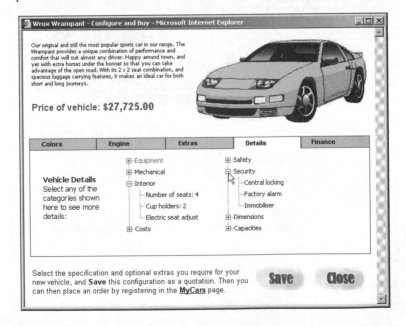

Selecting a Finance Package for the Vehicle

The final section of this page allows visitors to select a monthly payment finance package that suits them. The original design envisaged two options – specifying the number of months or allowing the page to calculate the number of months given the desired monthly payment:

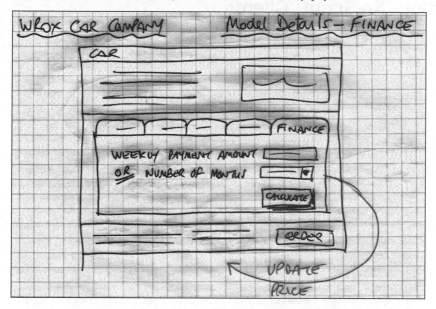

Again, we have implemented this feature almost exactly as per our design sketch. The next screenshot shows this page, after the user has selected the number of months required and clicked the Calculate button:

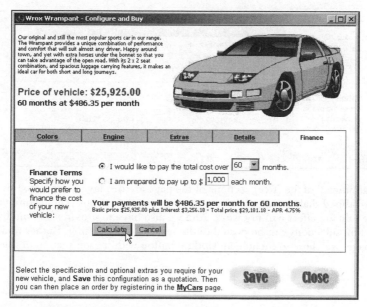

Notice that this screenshot shows the page in Opera 6.02, rather than Internet Explorer. Other than some very minor page layout details, the result is the same as we get in Internet Explorer, Netscape 6, and Mozilla.

Supporting 'No-Script' Clients

One other point of the original design is that we wanted to provide full support for non-script-enabled and non-graphical clients, as well as for traditional web browsers. The next screenshot shows what this page looks like when using a browser that does not support client-side script (or, in this case, has it disabled):

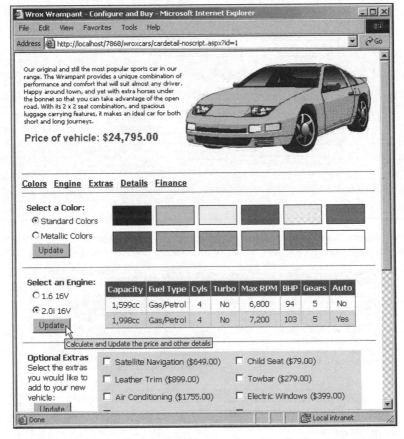

You can see that now all of the (five) sections of the page are displayed, separated by horizontal rules, rather than as a 'tabbed dialog' page. Without client-side script support, the techniques that we use to create the tabbed dialog effect will not work. And we also have to provide 'submit' buttons so that the user's configuration selections can be posted to the server for processing. Rather than just one at the bottom of the page, we chose to include an Update button within each section of the page to make it more intuitive.

Supporting 'Text-Only' Clients

As well as non script-enabled clients, we also want to support (as far as possible) text-only and other non-graphical clients. The next screenshot shows part of the same page displayed in Lynx – a text-only browser that we demonstrated in earlier chapters. Although the hyperlinks do not show up well when printed in black and white, you should be able to see from the screenshot that we can select the color, the engine, and (not shown in this screenshot) optional extras for a vehicle, as well as selecting the desired finance package:

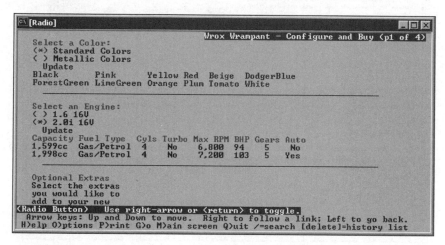

There are a couple of issues with Lynx, mainly caused by the fact that we are attempting to display this page in a separate window from the 'Home' page and the other pages on our site. Lynx opens all pages in the same 'window', and not in a new instance of the browser. We'll come back to this topic shortly, when we examine how our page works with non-script-enabled clients.

Supporting 'Page-Reader' Clients

As with the other pages in our site, we've tried to provide as good a level of support for visitors who use specialist user agents, such as an aural browser like the IBM Home Page Reader. The next screenshot shows the part of the page where the user selects the color for the vehicle. We've reduced the size of the top graphical section of the display so that you can see the text that is extracted from the page and read to the user:

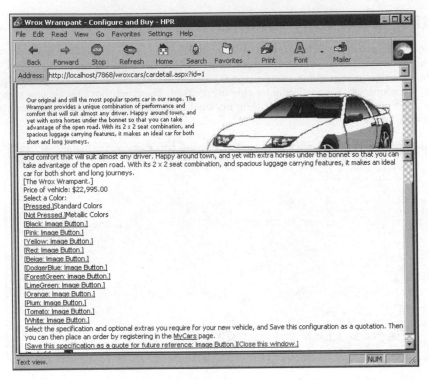

From our own experiments, with the screen turned off, we found that we could still specify all of the options and use all of the other controls on this page.

Saving Quotations and Closing the Window

Once the visitor has finished configuring their chosen model, we allow them to save the configuration to our server as a quotation – without having to log on. Afterwards they can register with our site, or log in if they have previously registered, view this quotation, and place an order based on it. This can be done immediately or at a later date, because we save all their quotes for when they come back to the site another time. You can see the instructions and the Save button in the next screenshot:

> Select the specification and optional extras you require for your new vehicle, and **Save** this configuration as a quotation. Then you can then place an order by registering in the **MyCars** page.
>
> **Save** **Close**

For client-script-enabled clients, the MyCars link can be used to go directly to the page that displays this user's quotes and previous orders. This page is displayed in the main window, and not in the current 'Model Details' window, but the link automatically closes the current window at the same time. This gives a reasonably seamless feel to the interface, rather like a traditional Windows executable application would. The Close link automatically closes the 'Model Details' window, but does not change the page that is displayed in the main window.

When client-side scripting is not available, the way that the 'Model Details' window is displayed and behaves in this respect is different. We can't use client-side code to open the window in the first place, or to control the size and position (as we saw in Chapter 4 when we looked at the code in the 'Home' page that opens this window).

The lack of client-side script support also means that we can't provide a Close link, or automatically change the page that is displayed in the main window when the Save link is clicked. In this case, we still display the Save link, but no Close link, and the instructions are slightly different. The user has to manually close this window in the traditional way using the buttons on the title bar:

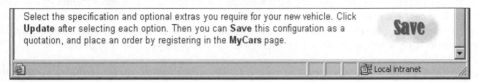

The Navigation Issue in Lynx

The one issue that our site does not address for navigation from the 'Model Details' page back to the other pages in the site is when we view the site using a text-only client such as Lynx. Many of these types of client display all the pages they load in the same window (in fact Opera can be configured to do the same). So in these cases, we should provide a link that simply navigates to the 'Home' page (or some other page, as required) and opens it in the same window.

But we don't want to do this if the 'Model Details' page is displayed in the new (pop-up) window that is part of our design. We could add some clever client-side script that detects whether this is a pop-up window or the only window, and then provide a suitable link. But without client-side script support (such as in Lynx), we can't implement this either.

However, the user can simply navigate back to the 'Home' page by entering the URL of the site into their browser, and then go to the 'My Cars' page from there to view a quote they have just received. As long as their browser supports cookies, or they have already registered and have a login ID and password, they will be connected to their new and existing quotations and orders. OK, so it's not a great site design feature, but it is the only option we can offer in this case.

The 'Model Details' Page in Outline

Having seen the page in action, and discussed some of the technical issues that arise from trying to mirror the original design specifications, we'll move on and look at the page in more detail. In this section we'll overview the operation of the page, and see how we use the query string, the postback architecture of ASP.NET, and ASP.NET Sessions to preserve data and pass it between requests to give optimum performance across all the different types of client we support.

Opening the 'Model Details' Page

You'll recall from our discussion of the 'Home' page that the links there to open the 'Model Details' page change depending on whether the current client supports client-side scripting or not. If they do support scripting, the page `cardetail.aspx` (in the same folder as the 'Home' page) is opened into a new (pop-up) window using client-side script. This allows the window size and position to be controlled – we place it to the top left and make it around 630 pixels wide and 550 pixels high.

This means that it will fit nicely onto the screen in 800 x 600 resolution and above (the usual minimum these days for most graphical script-supporting clients). On a 640 x 480 resolution screen it will be too long, but the full width of the title bar, and the buttons at the top right of this, will be visible. So the user can resize the window to suit. Scroll bars will be displayed automatically if required.

> *See Chapter 4 for more information and a code listing showing how the 'Home' page opens the 'Model Details' window.*

The 'Home' page also makes sure that, when client-side scripting is supported, there is only one instance of the 'Model Details' window open for each vehicle model (clicking the same model in the 'Home' page again just brings the existing 'Model Details' window for that vehicle to the front). Of course, you may choose to allow multiple windows for the same vehicle to exist, simply by changing the code. However, it does demonstrate a technique that you might want to adopt in your own applications.

If the current browser does *not* support scripting, however, we can do no more than just open the page in a new window (we can't control the window size or specify what 'window furniture' it will contain either). So there could be multiple windows for the same model in this case, but it makes no difference either way to how our code works in the 'Model Details' page. The other point is that we have a different page to implement the 'Model Details' for non script-enabled clients, named (not surprisingly) `cardetail-noscript.aspx`.

The only other feature of the way that we load the 'Model Details' page is that we include a query string in the URL when we open the page, which specifies the ID of the selected vehicle. So, in the 'Model Details' pages, we can detect which vehicle we need to fetch data for, and then display it within the page. You'll see how we use this when we look at the code for these pages in the next chapter.

Using the Postback Architecture

Continuing our overview, let's see how we actually manage the data about our selected vehicle, and how we interact with the user as they configure this vehicle. The advantages that the ASP.NET postback architecture brings (as we discussed in many places in earlier chapters) mean that we can just about leave the page to look after maintaining the user's selections all by itself.

We've enabled viewstate for the 'Model Details' pages (in the @Page directive), so all the values that the user enters, the content of the labels and text boxes, the current selection in the lists and option buttons, and the general 'state' of the page, will all be persisted between requests without us having to write any code at all.

Compare this to what would be required in (for example) ASP 3.0, JSP, or Perl, where we would have to save the values from around 20 different types of HTML 'form' controls in the user's session or in a database with each request, and then extract them all and use these to populate the controls correctly for the response. Simply adding an extra control to the page in these other environments can produce a lot of extra work, while in ASP.NET it's all handled automatically!

A Schematic of the Whole Process

The next schematic shows in overview the process of managing the data in the 'Model Details' page. When the page is first opened, we use some stored procedures to interrogate our database and build a `DataSet` that contains all the information required for this page. This process is quite resource-intensive, and so we cache the `DataSet` in the user's session afterwards. This means that we don't need to go back to the database and recreate it with each postback:

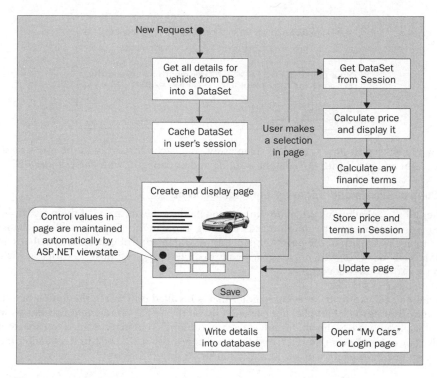

Recall that we are insisting that our client supports sessions. We do this either through the use of cookies or by redirecting the client to a copy of our application that uses the ASP.NET cookie-less session feature.

Calculating the Price and Finance Terms

As the user interacts with the controls on the page, it is posted back to our server each time (with a couple of exceptions if the client is Internet Explorer 5.5 or above, as we'll see later). With each postback, depending on which control caused the postback, we can calculate the price for the vehicle and update the display to reflect this.

However, we only display the finance terms (the number and amount of each monthly payment) when they specifically click the Calculate button in that part of the page. Each time the price of the vehicle is recalculated, we clear the previous finance terms. We could, of course, recalculate these as well each time the price changes, but there is an issue in that the price might exceed the limits we've defined for the maximum number of payments if the user has specified their maximum monthly payment amount. By forcing them to go back and recalculate it, we also have the option to comply with possible legal requirements by displaying the interest rate and amount each time.

Storing the Price and Finance Terms

After we have calculated the total price for the vehicle, and possibly the finance terms as well, we need to cache these somewhere where we can get at them again when the user decides to save the current configuration as a quotation. We could always extract them from the label controls where they are displayed, but this gets clunky because we are building up a string containing several values in the case of the finance terms, as shown in this screenshot:

> ○ I would like to pay the total cost over [36 ▼] months.
>
> ○ I am prepared to pay up to $ [1,000] each month.
>
> **Your payments will be $686.63 per month for 36 months.**
> Basic price $22,995.00 plus Interest $1,723.71 - Total price $24,718.71 - APR 4.75%
>
> [Calculate]   [Cancel]

Instead, we've chosen to store the values in an array, and cache this array in the user's session. We can easily extract it and work with the content (reading and updating it) with each request.

Detecting Control Events and Updating the Page Content

Then, after all the calculations are done, we can update the relevant parts of the page. In some cases, this may involve setting other values, such as selecting a row in the 'Engines' table or changing the color of the car image at the top of the page – it depends on which control caused the postback. Again, this is where ASP.NET makes our life easy, as each control on the page can raise its own specific event on the server as we process the request.

So, for example, we can write an event handler that is invoked only when the option buttons for the type of color (Standard or Metallic) are clicked. OK, so the Page_Load event is called as well with every postback, but we use this to our advantage by running code that we need to execute in every page load in the Page_Load event handler, and then any control-specific code in the handler for that control's own postback event (such as OnClick or OnCheckedChanged).

Later, you'll see all the event handlers we use, along with the remainder of the code and content in this page. However, there is one other feature of ASP.NET that we also find extremely useful in interactive pages, and which we take advantage of in our 'Model Details' page. This is the auto-postback feature.

Using Auto-Postback to Drive the Page

Most web users are familiar with the auto-postback effect in a web page, where simply making a selection in a list or checking a checkbox causes the page to be submitted to the server. In ASP.NET, this process can be implemented just by adding the AutoPostback="True" attribute to any of the interactive controls such as a checkbox, an option button, a drop-down list, or in fact any other type of list such as a CheckBoxList control or a RadioButtonList control. We discussed this technique in detail in earlier chapters.

Of course, we have a problem with auto-postback when there is no client-side scripting support, but we've already described how we use multiple 'submit' buttons on the cardetails-noscript.aspx page to get round this. We'll also look at this topic in a little more depth later in this chapter.

What Happened to the Frames?

In our original design, you may recall that we considered using HTML frames within the 'Model Details' page to allow the price and finance terms to be calculate in the background. Many sites use this technique, including well-known ones such as Dell Computers. An 'options' page (which can be a dynamic .asp or a static .htm page) contains a series of controls on an HTML <form>.

The `target` attribute of this `<form>` specifies a separate frame within the same browser window, and so any page generated in response to this form being submitted is displayed in the other frame. The current page that contains the `<form>` continues to be displayed. This means that, as the user makes selections and clicks a 'submit' button (or client-side script in the page submits the form automatically as they select from the lists of options), the other frame can be repeatedly reloaded to show the current price.

Why haven't we adopted this useful-sounding technique here? The answer is that ASP.NET effectively prevents us from taking this approach unless we are prepared to abandon the comforting and extremely supportive environment of the postback architecture. For the automatic maintenance of viewstate to work, we have to use a server-side `<form runat="server">`. This means that we must post each page back to itself every time, as the server-side `<form>` demands this and prevents us from specifying a different value for the `action` attribute. We can't submit the `<form>` to a different page.

OK, so we can still set the `target` attribute so that the page loads into a different frame, then post back to the same page and use some clever detection code (probably via a value placed into a `hidden`-type control on the form) that causes just the price to be displayed in the second frame.

However, having said all that, we've already seen that most of the actions that the user takes when interacting with the page require a postback to our server to update the page. And any actions that don't require a postback do not affect the price anyway, so there is no advantage to using a separate frame. This is why we ultimately chose to use just a single page in the 'Model Details' window.

Implementing a 'Tabbed Dialog'

Our design calls for a 'tabbed dialog' appearance in the 'Model Details' page, and you can see from the earlier screenshots that we have accomplished this for all the modern graphical script-enabled browsers such as Internet Explorer, Mozilla, Opera, and (not shown so far) Netscape. To achieve this we used two of the special controls that are part of the **Internet Explorer Web Controls** Pack. This pack contains several extremely useful controls that are designed for use in both ASP.NET, and client-side in Internet Explorer 5.5 and above.

About the IE Web Controls

The Internet Explorer team at Microsoft has been providing special tools and components for use client-side with IE for some time. Many of the controls were installed automatically with previous versions of Internet Explorer, such as the Structural Graphics control for drawing vector graphics in the page, a range of Data Source Controls for interacting with Remote Data Services and XML files to display data in the page, and several multi-media controls such as graphics filters and the Time control.

However, the IE Web Controls represent a breakthrough in that they are designed to interface directly with ASP.NET and produce compatible output on all kinds of browser – not just Internet Explorer. They include a set of components (Hyper-Text Components or HTCs) that are downloaded to the client as well as a set of server control classes that are installed into the .NET Framework on the server.

The IE Web Controls pack includes:

❑ The **MultiPage** control, which allows us to create several separate sections of a page and have just one of these sections displayed at a time.

❑ The **TabStrip** control, which provides the 'tab' effect you see in the previous screenshots to represent a tabbed dialog in a web page.

❑ The **TreeView** control, which can display an expandable and collapsible list of values or links.

❑ The **Toolbar** control, which can be used to create a Windows-style toolbar within a web page.

We use the first three of these controls in our application, and you'll see more about these when we look at the code in more detail later on in this and the next chapter. They do make it extremely easy to add these kinds of features to a page, and in Internet Explorer 5.5 and above provide superb client-side interactivity that can reduce the number of postbacks to our server. The bonus is that they are backwards compatible as well, so while the performance (and in some cases the appearance) is downgraded in clients other than IE 5.5+, they still function as expected.

You can obtain the IE Web Controls from the MSDN Web site at

http://msdn.microsoft.com/downloads/samples/internet/ ⅂ asp_dot_net_servercontrols/webcontrols/Default.asp

or individually from the ASP.NET site at http://www.asp.net/. Be sure to select the option(s) that install both the ASP.NET Server controls and the DHTML client-side Behavior components.

Fallback Support for Older Browsers

In Internet Explorer 5.5 and above, the **TabStrip** control uses an HTC that is loaded from the server and instantiated client-side within the page. This HTC integrates directly and automatically with the **MultiPage** control, which is another HTC that is loaded from the server and instantiated client-side. You can switch from one 'tab' or 'page' to another without any postback to the server being required, because the details of all the tabs and their content are stored within the client-side page.

Of course, none of this is going to work in other browsers. However, in this case, the controls detect that a different client is in use and automatically provide 'standard' HTML output (as an HTML `table`) that displays just the current 'tab' and its content. When the user clicks on a different tab heading, a postback to the server causes the contents of the 'tab' they selected to be displayed instead. As you saw in earlier screenshots, this works fine in browsers such as Mozilla and Opera 6.

However, one other point to watch out for is that the **TabStrip** uses Cascading Style Sheets (CSS 1.0) to control the positioning, font style, display of borders, and shading. The next screenshot shows the 'Model Details' page displayed in Netscape Navigator 4.5, and you can see that its lack of full CSS support means that the appearance is less than optimal. However, as long as we choose the background colors for the tabs carefully, the output is still reasonably close to our design requirements. And, other than using images to create the appearance of the 'tabs', there isn't much else we could do to get a 'tabbed dialog' effect anyway:

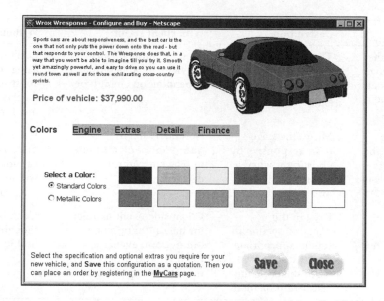

Coping Without Client-Side Scripting Support

You saw in our earlier discussions and screenshots that we implement two different pages for the Model Details – one that requires client-side scripting to be available and one that does not. We discussed some of the reasons why we chose this approach, and what the differences in the pages are. For completeness, we can summarize the differences here, as they relate to many of the topics we've been discussing so far.

The following table shows the differences between the two 'Model Details' pages, how this affects our original design requirements, and how we work around the limitations that the lack of client-side scripting imposes:

Task	Description	With client script	Without client script
Opening the 'Model Details' window.	We can open the 'Model Details' window at a specific position and size, and re-use the appropriate window.	Code demonstrated in Chapter 4 uses the client-side `window.open` and `focus` methods.	Set `target` attribute of hyperlink to `'_blank'` to open page in a new window.
Closing the 'Model Details' window.	There are several occasions where we change the page that is displayed in the main window in response to events in the 'Model Details' window, such as when a quotation is saved.	Change the value of `location.href` for the main window (`window.opener`) to display the required page, then call the client-side `window.close` method of this window.	Can't be done without using named frames in each window. Not implemented in our application, user has to manually close the 'Model Details' window and navigate in the main window.

Table continued on following page

Task	Description	With client script	Without client script
Displaying the 'tabbed dialog' and individual 'tabs' and their content.	The **TabStrip** control requires client-side script support in all cases.	Control automatically provides suitable output depending on client type.	Can't be done when using the **TabStrip** control, so we display them all in one long page.
Automatic postback as the user interacts with controls in the page.	Makes the page more responsive by updating it when a control is clicked or a value changed.	Add the ASP.NET `AutoPostback` attribute to relevant control declarations.	Use multiple 'submit' buttons (with the caption Update) within the page.
Setting option buttons in response to text entry or list selection.	Used in the 'Finance' section to set the appropriate option button when selecting the calculation method.	Client-side event handler for the `OnChange` and `OnKeyDown` events sets the `checked` property of the relevant option button.	Can't be done, though page is still usable without this.

We'll look at the `cardetail-noscript.aspx` page in Chapter 10, once we've seen how the version that requires client-side script works. You'll see that the bulk of the page content and code is identical, and there are only a few changes we have to make to cope with the lack of client-script support. Of course, this is because we originally designed the page to be implementable without client-side script. We'll look at this issue next.

Client-Side Versus Server-Side Page Updates

Modern browsers have great support for building dynamic pages that don't require regular postbacks to the server. Since the days of Internet Explorer 4 (and, to some extent Navigator 4), we've been able to use Dynamic HTML in conjunction with client-side script to change the appearance and content of a page while loaded into the browser. With the advent of the 'version 6' browsers, CSS 2.0 provides the same kinds of features. So, in our 'Model Details' page, why haven't we implemented more of this kind of approach to reduce server postbacks and provide a smoother and more responsive user experience? The reasons for this are four-fold:

❏ It's extremely hard to create dynamic pages that depend on client-side features, and yet which will work in different types of browser. We saw this when we were building the animated page banner back in Chapter 5.

❏ We can't provide support for older browsers and non-graphical clients and page readers, which either don't support Dynamic HTML or the very nature of its use makes it irrelevant (for example, in a 'page reader').

❏ The processes we need to carry out in calculating the price and finance terms are complex, and not easy to accomplish in client-side script alone. We would also have to remote all the data and algorithms required to perform the calculation to the client each time.

❏ We are using many of the ASP.NET server controls to reduce development time and effort, and to provide the appearance and functionality we want. With a few minor exceptions, these depend on a postback to the server to work properly.

All this doesn't mean that you should always avoid client-side processing. In some cases it can provide a real benefit. There are many techniques that are available for remoting data to a client, and processing it there. We are not going to cover them here, but you'll find a wealth of useful techniques and ideas in our sister publication *ASP.NET Distributed Data Applications* (Wrox Press, ISBN 1-86100-492-3).

An Example – Changing the Color of the Car

As an example of the decision process we went through, one of the features of our 'Model Details' page is that it changes the color of the car displayed at the top right of the page as you select a color from the list in the first page of the 'tabbed dialog'. Rather than have multiple images in all the possible colors, we 'cheat' by using a single GIF image where the bodywork of the vehicle is transparent. The image is displayed in the cell of an HTML `table`, and so we just have to change the background color of the cell to display the car in a different color. The screenshot here shows the results in Netscape 6.0:

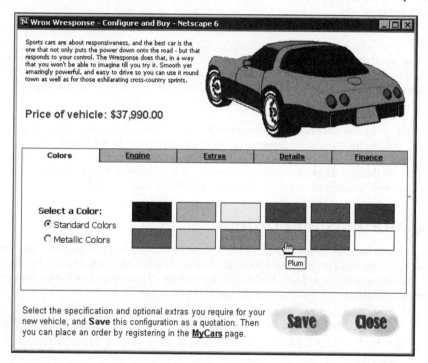

Almost all graphical web browsers, including some very old ones, allow us to specify the background color of a cell using the `bgcolor` attribute, so our technique is reasonably universal for all graphical clients. However, some browsers (notably Internet Explorer 4 and above, Netscape 4 and above, and the 'version 6' browsers) allow us to change the value of the `bgcolor` property of a table cell while the page is displayed in the browser, and they render this color immediately.

This means that we could execute some client-side code in response to the user selecting a color, and avoid a postback to the server. It would work in most of the common browsers in use today, and give a more responsive interface because the user would see the result immediately. However, there are a few reasons why we chose not to go down this route:

❑ It won't work if the browser does not support client-side scripting, so we'd have to code two different processes – one client-side and one server-side, or a combination of the two. This isn't too difficult, but it makes maintenance harder in the long run.

❑ The syntax for accessing elements in a page varies in different types of client, for example Netscape 4 and IE 4 are different to each other, and both are different to the CSS 2.0 techniques supported by 'version 6' browsers. So we'd need multiple versions of the client-side script code.

❑ We would still have to do some client detection if we wanted to support old browsers that do not allow the bgcolor attribute to be set, and force a postback to the server.

❑ We may need to change the price of the vehicle. The metallic colors add a premium to the cost of the vehicle, and so we would have to provide client-side code to handle price re-calculation as well.

The Conclusion

While you can see that we have tended towards using server-side processing and postbacks in our application, this doesn't mean that you should always go down this route. Client-side script support is extremely useful in many circumstances, as you can see from our earlier comparisons of the two versions of the 'Model Details' page that we implement.

So don't be put off by our decision here to stay with mainly server-side processing. Remember that we still use client-side script for several features of the page; much of it is implemented automatically by the ASP.NET server controls and the IE Web Controls. Furthermore, many of the basic client-side script-driven techniques that we do implement in our page, such as automatic postback of a <form> and setting the checked property of options buttons, use JavaScript code that is fully cross-browser compatible.

Saving Quotations and Orders

As well as allowing the user to see details of the vehicles we offer, and the price for their chosen configuration, our 'Model Details' page has to be able to save that user's quotation for later use (and, hopefully, conversion into an order!). We do this by writing all the details of the current configuration (all the selections made in the 'Model Details' page) into our database.

You'll recall that we establish a unique User ID for all visitors to our site, and store this in their ASP.NET session. Each page checks that a session exists and takes action to re-establish one if there isn't one present when that page loads (by redirecting the user to default.aspx where the User ID is created again). We saw the code to do all this when we looked at our client-detection routines and the 'Home' page, back in Chapters 3 and 4.

So, knowing that our user will have a unique User ID stored in their session, all we have to do is include this ID in the quote we store in the database. When the user comes back to our site, we can connect them with any existing quotations they have received. In fact, we also store the orders they place in the same table, with just a single 'flag' value indicating if it is a quotation or an order. This means that we can display a user's quotations and/or orders whenever we wish.

The 'flag' value also allows us to 'expire' quotations if we wish. We could delete any quotation rows automatically if they were more than, say, 14 days old, by executing a suitable SQL statement or stored procedure either when we display the 'My Cars' page or (even better) by running a separate executable application or service at specific intervals such as once a day.

We'll see the process of writing the configuration to the database as a quotation in this and the next chapter, as we examine the 'Model Details' page. Then, in later chapters, we'll look at the way that we authenticate users and allow them to log in and view their existing quotations and orders.

The Structure of the Model Details Page

So, having spent half a chapter in general overview, you should now have a good understanding of what the 'Model Details' page does – at least in outline. In the remainder of this chapter and throughout the next one, we'll examine the code we use to create the page, and the ASP.NET processing that makes it all work. We'll look at the version for script-enabled clients first, and then show you the way that we change the page to work with non-script-enabled clients towards the end of Chapter 10.

The overall layout of the page source is similar to that we use in most of the other pages on our site. We start with the @Page directive, which specifies that we want viewstate to be available and implemented in this page, and that we want to be able to read and write data in the user's ASP.NET session.

This is followed by the Import directives for the namespaces we'll need in the page. We include the System.Data and System.Data.SqlClient namespaces so that we can access our SQL Server database, and we need the System.Drawing namespace so that we can work with the colors defined for each car model. You'll see how and why later on:

cardetail.aspx

```
<%@ Page Language="VB" EnableViewState="True" EnableSessionState="True" %>
<%@ Import Namespace="System.Data"%>
<%@ Import Namespace="System.Data.SqlClient"%>
<%@ Import Namespace="System.Drawing" %>
...
```

Importing and Registering the IE Web Controls

We also have to import and register the namespace that implements the IE Web Controls we use in this page. This is not a default ASP.NET namespace, and so we have to include the Register directive to specify details of the assembly, and the 'tag' prefix we'll be using when we declare the controls in our page. Note that the Assembly attribute value must all be on one line, and not broken over two lines as we've had to do here in our code listing:

```
...
<%@ Import Namespace="Microsoft.Web.UI.WebControls" %>
<%@ Register TagPrefix="ie" Namespace="Microsoft.Web.UI.WebControls"
    Assembly="Microsoft.Web.UI.WebControls, Version=1.0.2.226,↴
    Culture=neutral, PublicKeyToken=31bf3856ad364e35" %>
<!-- note that preceding Assembly attribute must be all on one line -->
...
```

The values you see in the Register *directive are provided in the documentation for the controls, and will probably vary in later versions of these controls.*

After this comes the ASP.NET script section where our code to implement the page interactivity is located. We'll be looking at this code in detail in the next chapter:

```
...
<script runat="server">
...
... ASP.NET server-side code goes here ...
...
...
</script>
```

The HTML Section of the Page

The visible content of the page comes next. We have the same selection of elements at the beginning of the page as in most other pages, though we don't use the animated page banner in this page. However, we do include a 'skip to' link for text-only and page-reader clients, which points to an anchor element located in the main section of the page.

Notice that we also use the same technique as in other pages to insert the correct stylesheet name into the <link> element, and we have an empty server-side <title> element that we'll fill with the vehicle name in our ASP.NET code as the page loads:

```
<!doctype html public "-//W3C//DTD HTML 3.2 Final//EN">
<html>
<head>
<basefont size="2" face="Tahoma,Arial,Helvetica,sans-serif">
<link rel="stylesheet" type="text/css"
      href="stylesheets/wcc<% = sStyleSize %>.css" />
<title id="elmTitle" runat="server" />
</head>
<body bgcolor="#ffffff" class="body-text">

<div style="position:absolute;height:0px;"><font size="1" color=#ffffff">

<!-- skip link for aural page readers -->
<layer visibility="hidden">
<a href="#content" style="color:#ffffff;font-size:1px;text-decoration:none"><img
width="1" height="1" hspace="0" vspace="0" src="images/_blnk.gif" border="0"
alt="Skip to Content" /></a>
</layer></font></div>
```

```
<form runat="server">
...
... dynamic page content goes here...
...
</form>

</body>
</html>
```

The remainder of the page is a single server-side `<form>` section, within which all the rest of our dynamic and static content is located. This content is in five sections:

- ❑ The model description, price, and image
- ❑ The `TabStrip` control
- ❑ The `MultiPage` control
- ❑ A `Label` for displaying information and error messages
- ❑ The instructions for saving quotes, and the **Save** and **Cancel** buttons

We'll look at each of these sections in turn.

The Model Description, Price, and Image

The top section of our page contains nothing unexpected, simply an HTML table that displays the model description (précis) and the image. We use an `asp:Label` for the description, and we extract the text from our database and insert it into this `Label` during the `Page_Load` event. The image of the car is placed into a cell in the right-hand column that spans two rows, using an `asp:Image` control. We set the `ImageUrl` property of this control during the `Page_Load` event to load the appropriate image depending on which vehicle was selected in the 'Home' page:

```
<!-- model description and image -->
<table border="0" cellspacing="5" cellpadding="0">
<tr>
<td valign="top"><font face="Arial,Helvetica,sans-serif" size="1">
  <asp:Label class="fixed-small-text" id="lblPrecis" runat="server" />
  </font></td>
<td rowspan="2" id="tclColor" bgcolor="white" nowrap="true" runat="server">
  <asp:Image id="imgCar" runat="server" /></td>
</tr><tr>
<td><font face="Arial,Helvetica,sans-serif" size="3" color="#b50055"><b>
  Price of vehicle:
  $<asp:Label id="lblPrice" CssClass="large-red-text" runat="server" /></b>
  </font><font face="Arial,Helvetica,sans-serif" size="2"><br />
  <b><asp:Label id="lblTerms" CssClass="body-text"
              Text=" " runat="server" /></b>
  </font></td>
</tr>
</table><p />
<a name="content" />
...
```

Notice that we set the background color of the cell containing the car image to `"white"`. You'll see why in more detail in the next couple of chapters, when we come to examine how we calculate the price of the vehicle and save a quotation for it. Basically, we need to be able to extract the color name from the `BgColor` property of this cell in our server-side code (this is why it is also defined with the `runat="server"` attribute, so that it is implemented as a server control).

The lower cell in the left-hand part of the table shown in the listing above contains two `asp:Label` controls where we'll display the current price of the vehicle, and any finance terms that the user has specified. Notice that we use the same technique as in other pages you've seen previously to control the font, size, and color – we specify the CSS class name in the `Label` control, then wrap it in `<font>` tags for clients that don't understand CSS. After the end of the table is the 'skip to link' anchor that allows users to go straight to the page content.

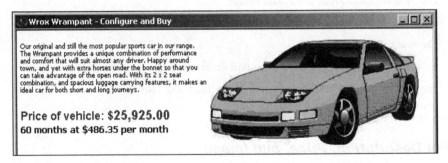

The 'Tabbed Dialog' Section

The main interactive section of our page is implemented as a 'tabbed dialog' in script-enabled browsers, and for this we've used the `TabStrip` and `MultiPage` controls from the IE Web Controls pack that we discussed earlier in this chapter.

To control the position of the 'tabbed dialog' on the page, we enclose it all inside a two-row single-column HTML table. The first row of the table contains the `TabStrip` control that implements the individual outlined 'tab' labels, and the second row contains the `MultiPage` control that manages the display of the appropriate set of controls depending on which 'tab' is selected:

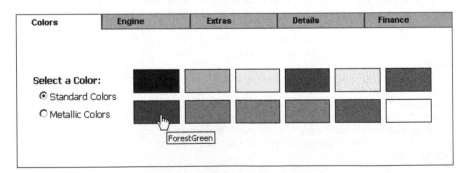

The TabStrip Control

The next listing shows the declaration of the `TabStrip` control within the first row of our table:

```
...
<!-- tab strip control -->
<table border="0" width="100%" cellpadding="0" cellspacing="0">
 <tr>
  <td>

   <ie:TabStrip id="tsCarDetail" runat="server"
       style="width:100%"
       TargetID="mpCarDetail"
       TabDefaultStyle="background-color:#cccccc; border-width:1px;
                        border-style:solid; border-color:#666666;
                        font-weight:bold; text-align:center;
                        font-family:Arial,Helvetica,sans-serif;
                        font-size:11px; height:21; width:79;"
       TabHoverStyle="color:#ff0000; text-decoration:underline;
                      background-color:#cccccc;"
       TabSelectedStyle="background-color:#ffffff; border-bottom:none"
       SepDefaultStyle="background-color:#ffffff; border-top:none;
                        border-left:none; border-right:none">
   <ie:Tab Text="Colors" />
   <ie:Tab Text="Engine" />
   <ie:Tab Text="Extras" />
   <ie:Tab Text="Details" />
   <ie:Tab Text="Finance" />
   </ie:TabStrip>

  </td>
 </tr><tr>
 ...
```

To insert the `TabStrip` control into the page we simply declare it just like we would any other ASP.NET server control – except that we use the 'tag' prefix `ie` we registered for the IE Web Controls earlier in our page. Then we can set the attribute values to specify the appearance we want for the control. We're using only a small selection of the available attributes in our example, taking advantage of many of the sensible defaults that the control implements.

The values we've used create a horizontal 'tab' strip (the default type) that fills the width of the enclosing table cell (`style="width:"100%"`). The 'tabs' can alternatively be aligned vertically if required. The appearance of each 'tab' is controlled by the various *xxxx*`Style` properties, such as `TabDefaultStyle`, `TabHoverStyle`, and `TabSelectedStyle`. The style properties specified for the `TabDefaultStyle` attribute are inherited by the style attributes for the other parts of the control (hover, selected, separator, and so on) so we don't have to repeat these.

Then, within the `TabStrip` element itself, we specify the 'tabs' that we want to appear using individual `Tab` elements, and the `Text` that we want to appear on each of these 'tabs'. The screenshots earlier and below show the result for the values we've used in our declaration of the `TabStrip` control:

| Colors | Engine | Extras | Details | Finance |

341

Using Images with a TabStrip Control

An alternative approach is to use images to create the visible appearance for the 'tabs' and the separators between them, and these are specified using a separate set of attributes; `DefaultImageUrl`, `SepDefaultImageUrl`, `SepHoverImageUrl`, and so on. Then we can declare a different image to be used on each 'tab', for example:

```
<ie:TabStrip id="tabWithImages" runat="server"
             SepDefaultImageUrl="center-default.gif"
             SepSelectedImageUrl="selected-centre.gif">

  <ie:TabSeparator DefaultImageUrl="left-tab-edge.gif"
                   SelectedImageUrl="selected-left-tab-edge.gif" />

  <ie:Tab DefaultImageUrl="tab1-image.gif"
          SelectedImageUrl="tab1-selected-image.gif" />

  <ie:TabSeparator/>

  <ie:Tab DefaultImageUrl="tab2-image.gif"
          SelectedImageUrl="tab2-selected-image.gif" />

  <ie:TabSeparator/>

  <ie:Tab DefaultImageUrl="tab3-image.gif"
          SelectedImageUrl="tab3-selected-image.gif" />

  <ie:TabSeparator DefaultImageUrl="right-tab-edge.gif"
                   SelectedImageUrl="selected-right-tab-edge.gif" />
</ie:TabStrip>
```

We haven't room here for a complete reference to the `TabStrip` or `MultiPage` controls, but you can access the documentation for them from the link that is added to your **Start** menu when you install the controls.

The IE Web Controls can be instantiated both from within ASP.NET, as we're doing, and directly within a page on the client just as you can instantiate any other HTC. Therefore there are two sets of references to the controls – the ASP.NET references for the server-side .NET assembly 'wrapper', and the client-side HTC references for the controls themselves. Both are available online at MSDN. Go to: http://msdn.microsoft.com/library/default.asp?url=/workshop/ ⅂ webcontrols/webcontrols_entry.asp

The MultiPage Control

The second row of the table that we 'opened' in the previous code listing contains the `MultiPage` control. This control will manage all the content that we want to display on all the 'tabs' of our 'tabbed dialog', with each page being declared within a separate `PageView` element. All these `PageView` elements are enclosed within the `MultiPage` element itself.

The next listing shows our declaration of the `MultiPage` control, with the HTML content of each 'tab' omitted to make it easier to see how the control itself is declared within the page. We'll come back and look at the content of each 'tab' later on:

```
...
<!-- multipage control -->
<td nowrap="nowrap">
  <ie:MultiPage id="mpCarDetail" runat="server"
                style="border-width:1px; border-style:solid;
                       border-color:#666666; border-top:none">

    <ie:PageView id="mpColors">
      <!-- controls for 'Colors' tab go here -->
    </ie:PageView>

    <ie:PageView id="mpEngine">
      <!-- controls for 'Engine' tab go here -->
    </ie:PageView>

    <ie:PageView id="mpExtras">
      <!-- controls for 'Extras' tab go here -->
    </ie:PageView>

    <ie:PageView id="mpDetails">
      <!-- controls for 'Details' tab go here -->
    </ie:PageView>

    <ie:PageView id="mpFinance">
      <!-- controls for 'Finance' tab go here -->
    </ie:PageView>

  </ie:MultiPage></td>

</tr>
</table>
...
```

Notice how the `style` attribute we use with this control adds a border round three sides of the control, but omits it from the top. This is what produces the 'tabbed dialog' appearance in the page. However, bear in mind that the `TabStrip` and `MultiPage` controls are inserted into rows of a table, and so it's vital to prevent white space appearing between them thus ruining the border effect. For this reason, in our opening `<table>` tag, we set the `cellpadding` and `cellspacing` attributes to zero:

```
<table border="0" width="100%" cellpadding="0" cellspacing="0">
```

Linking the TabStrip and MultiPage Controls

Our declarations above insert the two controls, the `TabStrip` and `MultiPage`, into our page and we get the appearance we want automatically. However, how do we switch between the 'tabs' and show the appropriate content in the `MultiPage` control when the user clicks on one of the 'tabs'? One way is to react to the `SelectedIndexChange` event that the `TabStrip` control raises when a 'tab' is clicked. We can do this on the server or on the client.

Note that the event name does not follow the normal pattern for other ASP.NET controls – it does not end with "d" like, for example, the `OnCheckChanged` event.

By handling the SelectedIndexChange event for the TabStrip control, we can determine which 'tab' was clicked by examining the SelectedIndex property of this control. Then we can tell the MultiPage control to display the content of the appropriate 'tab' or 'page' section by setting its SelectedIndex property to the required index value.

However, when we use a TabStrip and MultiPage control together, as in our example, we don't have to do even this minor amount of work to integrate the two controls. If you look back at the listing of the TabStrip declaration, you'll see that we specified the ID of our MultiPage control in the TargetID attribute of the TabStrip control:

```
TargetID="mpCarDetail"
```

This means that the two controls will automatically be linked together. As long as there are the same number of 'tabs' (Tab elements) defined for the TabStrip as there are 'pages' (PageView elements) for the MultiPage control, it will all work seamlessly without our help. Clicking the first 'tab' will display the first 'page' content, clicking the second 'tab' will display the second 'page' content, and so on.

So, all we have to do now is specify the content for each page. Though it might seem to be a rather strange order for doing things, we're going to postpone looking at the content of each 'tab' for now, however, and move on to look at the remainder of the HTML in this page. We'll come back and look at each 'tab' in more detail at the start of the next chapter, and examine the ASP.NET code that is used to implement the operation of the controls in each tab. This will save you from having to keep referring back to a listing here as we discuss the code; and, anyway, we have a lot more to cover before we're ready to start looking at this code.

What Output Do the TabStrip and MultiPage Controls Create?

The easiest way to understand what the TabStrip and MultiPage controls actually do is to look at the output they create in the browser. You can do this in most browsers by right clicking on the page and selecting View Source, or by using the Source option from the View menu.

In Internet Explorer 5.5 and above, the ASP.NET server controls that implement the TabStrip and MultiPage create XML elements within the page. These XML elements contain the data (content) that the client-side HTC controls will use to generate the visible appearance for the page. The section of the output created by the TabStrip control is shown in the next listing:

Output from the TabStrip control in Internet Explorer 5.5 and above

```
<?XML:NAMESPACE PREFIX="TSNS" /><?IMPORT NAMESPACE="TSNS"
IMPLEMENTATION="/webctrl_client/1_0/tabstrip.htc" />
<TSNS:TabStrip id="tsCarDetail" selectedIndex="0" targetID="mpCarDetail"
tabDefaultStyle="background-color:#cccccc;border-width:1px;border-
style:solid;border-color:#666666;font-weight:bold;text-align:center;font-
family:Arial,Helvetica,sans-serif;font-size:11px;height:21;width:79;"
tabHoverStyle="color:#ff0000;text-decoration:underline;background-color:#cccccc;"
tabSelectedStyle="background-color:#ffffff;border-bottom:none;"
sepDefaultStyle="background-color:#ffffff;border-top:none;border-left:none;border-
right:none;"
onSelectedIndexChange="JScript:document._ctl0.__tsCarDetail_State__.value=event.ind
ex"
onwcready="JScript:try{document._ctl0.__tsCarDetail_State__.value=selectedIndex}cat
ch(e){}" style="width:100%">
```

```
    <TSNS:Tab>Colors</TSNS:Tab>
    <TSNS:Tab>Engine</TSNS:Tab>
    <TSNS:Tab>Extras</TSNS:Tab>
    <TSNS:Tab>Details</TSNS:Tab>
    <TSNS:Tab>Finance</TSNS:Tab>
  </TSNS:TabStrip>
```

You can see that the `<?IMPORT ...?>` element in the first line of the code above references the HTC file `tabstrip.htc`, which is located in the `webctrl_client` folder of our web site. Installing the IE Web Controls automatically creates this folder for each web site on the machine, and installs the HTC files into it. From there, they are downloaded to the client and instantiated within the page to process the XML content you see in the listing above. If we subsequently create a new web site on our server, we have to copy this folder to it if we want to use the IE Web Controls in this new site.

The `MultiPage` control behaves much the same way. The next listing shows an abridged version of the output it creates, and again you can see the reference to the HTC file – in this case `multipage.htc`. Notice that all of the 'tab' or 'page' sections are sent to the client within the XML output. This allows it to display any of the pages, and switch between them, without requiring a postback to the server each time:

Output from the MultiPage control in Internet Explorer 5.5 and above

```
<?XML:NAMESPACE PREFIX="MPNS" /><?IMPORT NAMESPACE="MPNS"
IMPLEMENTATION="/webctrl_client/1_0/multipage.htc" />
<MPNS:MultiPage id="mpCarDetail" selectedIndex="0"
onSelectedIndexChange="JScript:document._ctl0.__mpCarDetail_State__.value=event.sel
ectedIndex" style="border-width:1px; border-style:solid; border-color:#666666;
border-top:none">
  <MPNS:PageView id="mpColors">
    <!-- section for "Colors" tab -->
    ... HTML elements as defined in ASP.NET page appear here ...
  </MPNS:PageView>
  <MPNS:PageView id="mpEngine">
    <!-- section for "Engine" tab -->
    ... HTML elements as defined in ASP.NET page appear here ...
  </MPNS:PageView>
  ... other page sections here ...
</MPNS:MultiPage>
```

The TabStrip and MultiPage Controls in 'Down-Level' Clients

In all other browsers and clients, where the HTC model is not supported (including IE 5.0, where HTC support is not robust enough for these controls), the `TabStrip` and `MultiPage` server controls generate standard HTML output. The output generated by the `TabStrip`, when the first 'tab' is selected, looks like this (for clarity, we're only showing the output for the first two 'tabs' here):

Output from the TabStrip control in all other browsers and clients

```
<table cellspacing="0" cellpadding="0" border="0" id="tsCarDetail"
style="width:100%">
<tr>
<td nowrap height="21" width="79" bgcolor="#ffffff" style="color:#000000;border-
width:1px;border-style:solid;border-color:#666666;font-weight:bold;text-
align:center;font-family:Arial,Helvetica,sans-serif;font-
size:11px;height:21;width:79;background-color:#ffffff;border-bottom:none;"><font
face="Arial,Helvetica,sans-serif" color="#000000"><b>Colors</b></font></td>
```

```
<td nowrap bgcolor="#cccccc" height="21" width="79"
style="color:#000000;background-color:#cccccc;border-width:1px;border-
style:solid;border-color:#666666;font-weight:bold;text-align:center;font-
family:Arial,Helvetica,sans-serif;font-size:11px;height:21;width:79;"><font
face="Arial,Helvetica,sans-serif" color="#000000"><b><a
href="javascript:document._ctl0.__tsCarDetail_State__.value='1';__doPostBack('tsCar
Detail','1')"><font color="#000000">Engine</font></a></b></font></td>
... other "tab" definitions go here ...
</tr>
</table>
```

You can see that the result is an HTML table, with the `style` of each cell set so that the appropriate borders are visible. However, the background color of the 'tabs' is set using the `bgcolor` attribute of that cell, which is why Navigator 4 can display the 'tabs' in different background colors even though it does not process the CSS styles (look back at the screenshot of Navigator 4 in the earlier section *About the IE Web Controls* to see what we mean).

The `MultiPage` control also generates standard HTML output in browsers and clients other than IE 5.5 and above. Only the content for one 'tab' or 'page' is visible because that's all that the control creates output for:

Output from the MultiPage control in all other browsers and clients

```
<table id="mpCarDetail" width="100%" style="border-width:1px; border-style:solid;
border-color:#666666; border-top:none">
  <tr>
    <td id="mpColors" valign="top">
      <!-- section for "Colors" tab -->
      ... HTML elements as defined in ASP.NET page appear here ...
    </td>
  </tr>
</table>
```

You can see that these clients must use a postback to the server to display a different page. So the result, compared to Internet Explorer 5.5 and above, is a reduction in responsiveness due to the repeated postbacks. On a slow connection this difference is quite noticeable, but there is no other way to reliably achieve the required result with all other client types.

The postback is caused by the **JavaScript URL** defined as the value of the `href` attribute for each of the links on the 'tabs' in the output of the `TabStrip` control, for example:

```
<a
href="javascript:document._ctl0.__tsCarDetail_State__.value='1';__doPostBack('tsCar
Detail','1')"><font color="#000000">Engine</font></a>
```

This code uses the same client-side script function (named `__doPostBack`) as the ASP.NET `AutoPostback` feature that we've discussed in previous chapters, which submits the form to the server. This is why, even when running in 'down-level' mode with clients other than Internet Explorer 5.5 and above, the controls still require client-side script support to be available.

The Information and Error Messages Label

After our 'tabbed dialog' comes a `Label` control where we can display error message or information to the user as they interact with our page. Hopefully, they will only see 'information' messages, and the most likely one is the confirmation that we successfully saved their chosen vehicle configuration as a quote.

The code for the `Label` is simple enough, specifying the font details and CSS class we want to apply to it. Notice that we also disable viewstate for the `Label`, so that any messages are not persisted across postbacks:

```
...
<!-- label to display information and error messages -->
<font face="Arial,helvetica,sans-serif" size="3" color="#b50055"><b>
<asp:Label id="lblMessage" EnableViewState="False" class="large-red-text"
           runat="server" /></b></font>
...
```

The next screenshot shows the `Label` after the user has saved a quotation. Notice that the **Save** button has disappeared now, and only the **Close** button is visible. We'll look at the code that creates these buttons next:

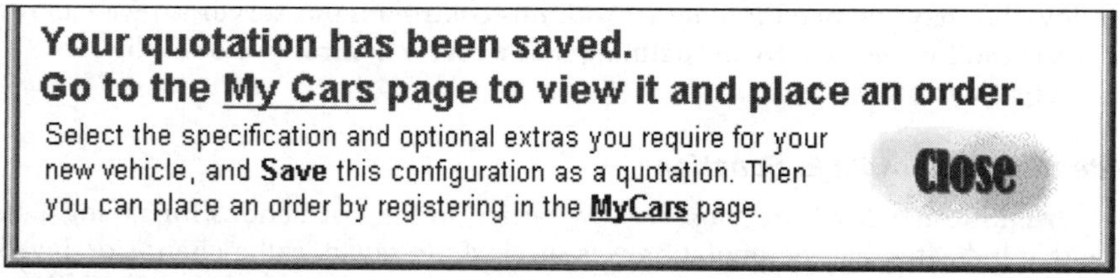

The Instructions, Save, and Close Buttons

The final section of the page contains the instructions for saving a quote, and the **Save** and **Close** buttons – as you've seen in several earlier screenshots. The instructions are simply static text defined within an HTML table cell, except that it contains a hyperlink that will execute a JavaScript function named `mainWindowPage` when clicked. This is the same `href` value as we use in the 'information' text (shown in the previous screenshot) when a quote is saved. We'll come back and look at this function shortly:

```
...
<!-- 'save quote' and 'window close' buttons -->
<table border="0" width="100%">
 <tr>
  <td><font face="Arial,helvetica,sans-serif" size="2">
    Select the specification and optional extras you require for your new
    vehicle, and <b>Save</b> this configuration as a quotation. Then you
    can place an order by registering in the
    <a href="javascript:mainWindowPage('secure/mycars.aspx', true)">
      <font color="#000000"><b>MyCars</b></font></a>
    page.</font></td>
  ...
```

After the instructions comes the cell that contains the Save and Close buttons. The Save button is not visible by default (the `Visible` attribute is set to `"False"`). The button is, of course, an image, and we are using an `<input type="image">` control to display it. This means that it will be implemented by ASP.NET as an `HtmlInputImage` control (as we used in the 'Home' page), and so we have to define the name of the function in our ASP.NET code that will run server-side when the button is clicked as the `OnServerClick` attribute:

```
   ...
   <td align="right" nowrap="nowrap">
     <input id="btnSave" type="image" src="images/btn_save.gif"
            Visible="False" runat="server" width="100" height="49"
            border="0" OnServerClick="SaveCarDetails"
            alt="Save specification as a quote for future reference" />
   <a href="javascript:window.close()">
      <img src="images/btn_close.gif" border="0"
           width="100" height="49" alt="Close this window" /></a></td>
  </tr>
 </table>
```

The last part of the code above implements the Close button. In this case we simply place the image inside an ordinary client-side HTML `<a>` element, with the `href` set to a JavaScript URL that closes the current window. We have no need to interact with this control on our server, so we can reduce the processing overhead for the page by *not* defining it as a server control (we omit the `runat="server"` attribute).

The Client-Side mainWindowPage Function

The two hyperlinks to the 'My Cars' page we saw earlier, in the instructions for saving a quote and in the message that indicates that the quotation was successfully saved, call a client-side JavaScript function named `mainWindowPage`. They pass two values to this function as parameters: the URL of the page that should be displayed in the main windows of our site, and a `Boolean` value to indicate if the 'Model Details' window should be closed (`true`) or left open (`false`):

```
     javascript:mainWindowPage('secure/mycars.aspx', true)
```

The function itself is shown in the next listing, and you can see that it is simple enough. Our 'Model Details' page was opened from a link in the main window (on the 'Home' page), and the browser automatically maintains a reference to this window as the `opener` property of the current ('Model Details' page) window object:

```
   function mainWindowPage(sHref, bClose) {
     window.opener.location.href = sHref;
     if (bClose) window.close();
   }
```

So, now we can change the page that is displayed in the main window by setting the `href` property of that window's `location` object to the URL we want to display. Then, if the value of the second parameter to our `mainWindowPage` function is `true`, we call the `close` method of the current window.

Using the ASP.NET RegisterClientScriptBlock Method

However, if you look at the HTML section of the 'Model Details' page, you'll find that this function is not declared there. This is because we insert it into the page using a method of the ASP.NET `Page` object called `RegisterClientScriptBlock`. This method is a useful way to insert client-side script code into the output that is sent to the client. The ASP.NET code we use to generate the 'Model Details' page contains, within the `Page_Load` event handler, the following code:

In the `Page_Load` event handler

```
' create the client-side script block for the control events in the page
Dim sScript as String = "<script language='JavaScript'>" & vbCrlf _
  & "<!--" & vbCrlf _
  & "function setOptionButtons(sName) {" & vbCrlf _
  & "  document.forms[0].elements[sName].checked = true;" & vbCrlf _
  & "}" & vbCrlf _
  & "function nodeExpanded(oSender) {" & vbCrlf _
  & "  var clickedNode = oSender.clickedNodeIndex;" & vbCrlf _
  & "  var colNodes = oSender.getChildren();" & vbCrlf _
  & "  for (var i = 0; i < colNodes.length; i++) {" & vbCrlf _
  & "    if (colNodes[i].getNodeIndex() != clickedNode)" & vbCrlf _
  & "      colNodes[i].setAttribute('expanded', false);" & vbCrlf _
  & "  }" & vbCrlf _
  & "}" & vbCrlf _
  & "function mainWindowPage(sHref, bClose) {" & vbCrlf _
  & "  window.opener.location.href = sHref;" & vbCrlf _
  & "  if (bClose) window.close();" & vbCrlf _
  & "}" & vbCrlf _
  & "//-->" & vbCrlf _
  & "<" & "/" & "script>"

' register it so that it is inserted into the page
If(Not IsClientScriptBlockRegistered("JSBlock")) Then
  RegisterClientScriptBlock("JSBlock", sScript)
End If
```

This code creates a `String` named sScript that contains the client-side script we want to include in the page, and then passes it to the `RegisterClientScriptBlock` method. This method automatically inserts a complete new client-side `<script>` section into the output, just after the opening tag of the server-side `<form>` section that must also exist in the page. At the same time, it registers this script section with the `Page` object using the name that we specify in the first parameter to the `RegisterClientScriptBlock` method – in our case `JSBlock`.

> *Obviously the code shown above creates more than just the* `mainWindowPage` *function that we looked at earlier. The other two functions,* `setOptionsButtons` *and* `nodeExpanded` *are used in other parts of the 'Model Details' page, and you'll see how in the next chapter.*

OK, so far this does nothing more than what we could achieve by simply placing the JavaScript (or VBScript) directly into the HTML section of the page (traditionally we would put it in the <head> section). So in general, when we only want to insert a single specific script section into a page, we would do so by coding it directly into the page. However, the `RegisterClientScriptBlock` method comes into its own when we create user controls or custom server controls, where multiple instances of that control might be inserted into the final ASP.NET page. In this case, we can prevent more than one instance of the client-side code section being inserted into the page, which would cause a client-side script error and prevent the page from working properly.

The `RegisterClientScriptBlock` method uses the name (or 'key') we allocate to the script section to identify it. So we can prevent it being inserted into the page more than once by using the `IsClientScriptBlockRegistered` method and specifying this 'key', as shown in the code above. Now only the first instance of a control will actually insert the client-side code, no matter how many instances of the control exist on the page.

Other ASP.NET Register Methods

The `Page` object also exposes some other similar methods that might be useful when building user controls and custom server controls. The following is a brief summary, and you can find out more about all of them from the `System.Web.UI.Page` section of the .NET SDK:

Method	Description
`RegisterClientScriptBlock`	Registers with the specified name ('key') a client-side script section that will be inserted into the page, directly **after** the **opening** <form> tag.
`IsClientScriptBlockRegistered`	Returns `True` if a client-side script section registered with the specified name ('key') has already been inserted into the page.
`RegisterStartupScript`	Registers with the specified name ('key') a client-side script section that will be inserted into the page, directly **before** the **closing** <form> tag.
`IsStartupScriptRegistered`	Returns `True` if a startup script section registered with the specified name ('key') has already been inserted into the page.
`RegisterOnSubmitStatement`	Registers with the specified name ('key') a client-side code statement (or series of statements) that will be added to the opening <form> tag as an attribute. The name of the attribute must be specified, for example `'submit'`.
`RegisterHiddenField`	Registers with the specified name ('key') an <input type="hidden"> control that will be inserted into the page. The name of the field and its value must be specified.

For more details about these and the other methods and properties of the `Page` *object, see the SDK documentation:*
ms-help://MS.NETFrameworkSDK/cpref/html/frlrfSystemWebUIPageMembersTopic.htm

Summary

In this chapter, we've begun our tour of the 'Model Details' page from our Wrox Car Company web site. This is by far the most complex part of the site, allowing visitors to view detailed information about each vehicle, and configure it by selecting the color, engine type, optional extras, and finance package that best suits them. At the same time, we display the current all-inclusive price, and a breakdown of the finance rates, total interest, and monthly payments required.

So the page has to provide a great deal of interactivity, as well as being intuitive and attractive. We feel that we've met the original design brief, and produced a page that works well, is relatively efficient in operation, and is easy to use.

So far, we've only really scratched the surface, however, looking in detail at just the simple parts of the page (the image and description at the top, and the instructions, information and Save/Close buttons section at the bottom). However, we have also sorted out how we'll provide the 'tabbed dialog' appearance, using two of the controls from the IE Web Controls pack.

In all, the aims of this chapter were to look at:

❑ How well our final page meets the original design requirements

❑ The 'Model Details' page in outline, to understand how it is created

❑ The structure of the 'Model Details' page, to understand how it works

In the next chapter we move on to look first at the data that drives our page, and then at the code and content we use to implement each of the five 'pages' that are displayed in turn within our 'tabbed dialog'. And, of course, we still have to figure out what we need to do differently to make the page work with browsers that do not support client-side script.

The Interactive Model Details

The previous chapter introduced you to the most complex of the pages in our example Wrox Car Company web site, where visitors can view details of any of the vehicles in our range, select the color, engine type, optional extras, and finance package that they require, and then save this configuration as a quotation. Now that you have a good understanding of what the page does, and you have seen an overview of the structure of the page, we can move on and look at how it actually works.

Our aim in this chapter is to look first at the data that drives the page, and then at the code we use to present this data to visitors who view the page with a script-enabled browser. We'll also look at the event handlers we use to make the page react to visitor interaction. However, we don't have room to cover all of the code in our 'Model Details' page in this chapter, so we'll save the tasks of calculating the price and the finance terms for the vehicle, and saving a quotation, until the next chapter.

In this chapter, the topics we'll be looking at are:

❑   The data that drives the 'Model Details' page

❑   How we extract this data for use in the page

❑   How we present the data to visitors in five distinct sections of the page

❑   How we react to events that occur for the controls in these sections

We start with a look at the parts of our database that are involved in this process, and the way that we extract this data for use in our page.

The Data for the 'Model Details' Page

Before we look at the ASP.NET code in our 'Model Details' page, we need to look in more detail at the database that drives our site. It contains all the data about our vehicles; plus the colors, engines, and optional extras that are available for each one. So, before we can really understand the code that presents and manipulates this data, we need to see how the data is stored, and how we extract it in a suitable format for use in our Model Details page.

The Vehicle Details Database Tables

We've looked at some of the tables in our database in previous chapters, as we've created procedures and functions that extract the data and display it. However, to help tie it all together, the next diagram shows all the tables that are related to storing information about each vehicle, each quotation or order that we store for these vehicles, and the users who generated these quotations and orders. It also shows the relationships between the tables:

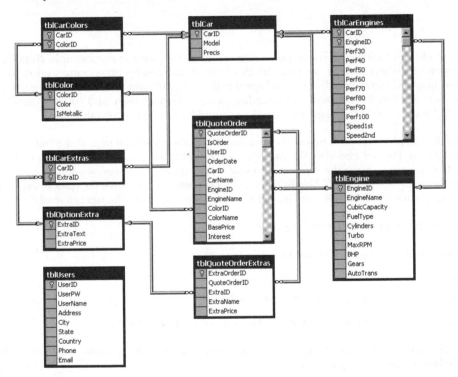

Note that not all of the 25 columns in the `tblCarEngines` *table are visible in this diagram. As well as those you see there are 4 more* `Speedxxx` *columns, 8* `Fuelxxx` *columns, and a final column named* `CarEnginePrice` *that contains the price for each available car/engine combination. Likewise, three columns are not visible for the* `tblQuoteOrder` *table. These are* `TotalPrice`, `PaymentMonths`, *and* `PaymentAmount`.

While it looks a little complicated, the structure we've chosen is the only really sensible way to approach the issue of allowing each vehicle to have a choice of engines, colors, and extras. The intermediate tables (tblCarColors, tblCarEngines, and tblCarExtras) simply link each vehicle with the color, engine, or optional extras that are available for that vehicle. In database terms, they resolve the many-to-many relationships that arise in situations like this – for example each car is available in more than one color, while each color is available for more than one car.

Each quotation or order consists of a single row in the tblQuoteOrder table, plus zero or more linked rows in the tblQuoteOrderExtras table that indicate the optional extras the customer selected. Notice the IsOrder column in the tblQuoteOrder table, which is used to indicate if this is an order or a quotation.

The other point worth mentioning is that the tblUsers table is not related through a foreign key constraint to any other table. Quotations might be stored against an anonymous User ID if our visitor has not previously registered or logged into the site. These IDs will not exist in the tblUsers table, preventing us from linking the tblUsers and tblQuoteOrder tables.

> *We'll be looking in detail at the design and operation of the user 'login' features in our site in Chapter 11.*

But in the Real World...

Our database is fine for our example application, but of course it doesn't provide the features you would probably need in a real-world site. Our site doesn't actually process orders, or collect payment information (mainly because we don't have any real cars to sell), but where this kind of backend processing is required it will probably involve a lot more in the way of data collection and storage.

However, the aim of this book is to demonstrate interface design and construction in ASP.NET, not backend data processing, so we make no apologies for stopping where we have with our example site. It's for the same reason that we do not use a separate data layer or middle tier in our application – we just access the stored procedures that expose the data directly from our ASP.NET pages.

The Stored Procedures for the 'Model Details' Page

The 'Model Details' page requires access to almost all of the data in the tables shown earlier, with the exception of the tblUsers table that stores details of each visitor as they register with our site. This table is used only during the registration process, and in the 'My Cars' page that we'll be looking at in Chapter 12.

We could extract this data directly from the database every time the page is opened, but we decided that for our requirements it makes more sense (as we discussed in the previous chapter) to extract it once, and then store it in the user's ASP.NET session. The best way to do this is to use a DataSet object, and take advantage of the ability it provides to store multiple tables within a single DataSet.

Extracting the Vehicle Details

We need a table that contains the basic details about each car/engine combination for the model that the user has chosen. For example, if the user selected the 'Wrox Wregal' by clicking on it in the 'Home' page, there are three car/engine combinations that are available for this model and our first stored procedure will need to extract these three rows from the database.

To do this we have to join the `tblCar` and `tblEngine` tables. However, as this is a many-to-many relationship, we must perform two joins. The `tblCar` table is joined to the `tblCarEngines` table, which is in turn joined to the `tblEngine` table. This also gives us access to the `CarEnginePrice` column in the `tblCarEngines` table, which we'll need in our page:

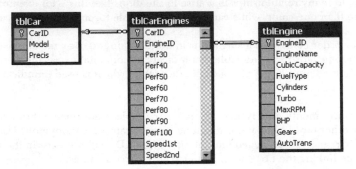

The stored procedure we use is shown next. It accepts a single parameter that is the ID of the vehicle we're displaying details for. Notice that we use a `CASE` statement within the SQL to return the text strings 'Yes' or 'No' for the columns that are effectively Boolean values (SQL Server `bit` columns). This makes it look a lot nicer when we display the results using data binding in our page:

```
CREATE PROCEDURE GetAllCarDetails @CarID int AS
SELECT tblCar.CarID, Model, Precis, tblEngine.EngineID, EngineName,
   CubicCapacity, FuelType, Cylinders, MaxRPM, BHP, Gears, CarEnginePrice,
   Turbo = CASE Turbo WHEN 1 THEN 'Yes' ELSE 'No' END,
   AutoTrans = CASE AutoTrans WHEN 1 THEN 'Yes' ELSE 'No' END
FROM (tblCar JOIN tblCarEngines ON tblCar.CarID = tblCarEngines.CarID)
   JOIN tblEngine ON tblEngine.EngineID = tblCarEngines.EngineID
WHERE tblCar.CarID = @CarID
```

From this stored procedure we get the details of the car model (the ID, model name, and précis), the engine details (ID, name, and technical data), and the price for that car/engine combination.

Extracting the List of Available Colors

We need to collect a list of colors that are available for the selected model. We can do this by joining the `tblCar` table to the `tblColor` table, using the intermediate table `tblCarColors`. Again we use a single parameter (the Car ID) to select the appropriate vehicle. We return the color ID and name, plus the `bit` column value that indicates if this is a metallic color or not:

```
CREATE PROCEDURE GetAllCarColors @CarID int AS
SELECT tblCarColors.ColorID, tblColor.Color, tblColor.IsMetallic
FROM (tblCar JOIN tblCarColors ON tblCar.CarID = tblCarColors.CarID)
   JOIN tblColor ON tblCarColors.ColorID = tblColor.ColorID
WHERE tblCar.CarID = @CarID
```

Extracting the List of Available Extras

We also need a list of the optional extras that are available for the selected vehicle in order to build the 'Extras' section of our page. Not all of the optional extras are available with all vehicles. Again, we have to join three tables – in this case `tblCar`, `tblOptionExtra`, and the intermediate `tblCarExtras` table. We provide the Car ID value as the single parameter to the stored procedure, and return the ID, name, and price of the available optional extras, plus a text string that is a combination of the name and price to display as the caption of each checkbox:

```
CREATE PROCEDURE GetAllCarExtras @CarID int AS
SELECT tblOptionExtra.ExtraID, tblOptionExtra.ExtraText,
       tblOptionExtra.ExtraPrice,
       DisplayText = ' ' + RTRIM(tblOptionExtra.ExtraText) + ' ($'
       + CONVERT(varchar(10), tblOptionExtra.ExtraPrice) + ')   '
FROM (tblCar JOIN tblCarExtras ON tblCar.CarID = tblCarExtras.CarID)
   JOIN tblOptionExtra ON tblCarExtras.ExtraID = tblOptionExtra.ExtraID
WHERE tblCar.CarID = @CarID
```

This gives us all the information we require about the vehicle itself, but there is one other set of values that we also need. These values are used to calculate the monthly payments when the user specifies the finance package they want.

The Finance PMT Values Table

One table that is not shown in the earlier schematics, but which relates to the data we use in the 'Model Details' page, is the list of values that we use to calculate the monthly payment amount required over a specified term to cover the cost of the selected vehicle plus the interest that is added during that term. This is referred to as a PMT (payment over a fixed term at a fixed interest rate) calculation.

You can find formulae for performing this calculation on the Web, though we usually take advantage of the PMT function in programs like Excel to perform this kind of calculation when working with Office-style documents. Within the .NET Framework, the `Pmt` function is implemented as part of the Visual Basic .NET namespace, and so we can use this instead. Interestingly, however, there is no equivalent in C#.

We chose to take an approach that uses the VB.NET `Pmt` function, and demonstrates a few other techniques that you might find useful as well. In particular, we'll use the `global.asax` file to execute some code when our application starts, and fill a database table named `tblFinancePMTData` with a list of values from which we can calculate the payment terms for any vehicle as our application runs.

Using global.asax to Handle Application-Level Events

Like 'classic' ASP, ASP.NET allows us to execute code in response to several 'application-level' events, outside the pages that make up the parts of the site that the user sees. The file `global.asax` works in almost exactly the same way as `global.asa` does in ASP 3.0 and earlier. In it we define event handlers that are executed in response to the events raised within the application as it starts, runs, or ends.

The events we can handle include these five most often used ones:

❑ `Application_Start` occurs when the application first starts up, such as when the site is first accessed, or when the `web.config` file in the root folder of the application is edited. For legacy support, `Application_OnStart` is included as an alternative for this event.

- ❑ Application_End occurs when the application stops, for example when the last active session expires or when the web.config file is edited and before a new instance of the application starts. For legacy support, Application_OnEnd is included as an alternative for this event.

- ❑ Session_Start occurs when a user who does not have an ASP.NET session already active requests any ASP.NET page within the application. For legacy support, Session_OnStart is included as an alternative for this event.

- ❑ Session_End occurs when a session expires, either after the timeout specified in machine.config or web.config, or when the Session.Abandon method is called. For legacy support, Session_OnEnd is included as an alternative for this event.

- ❑ Application_Error occurs when an ASP.NET compilation or runtime error is detected within the application. Details of the error can be obtained by using the Server.GetLastError method.

Remember that the global.asax file **must** be placed in the root folder of an ASP.NET application, and it will not be executed if this is not the case.

ASP.NET can spawn new instances of an application when errors occur in the default instance, and in response to changes in memory availability or (depending on the settings in the machine.config file) after a specified number of hours or number of hits. The Application_Start and Application_End events are raised whenever this occurs. If possible, ASP.NET will maintain a separate instance of the 'old version' of the application until all active sessions have expired, redirecting existing users to this instance so that their session values are preserved.

Running Code on Application Startup

From the previous section, it is obvious that we can handle the Application_Start event and use it to pre-fill our tblFinancePMTData table with the list of values we need to calculate the finance payments. We store the current finance interest rate for our site in the <appSettings> section of our web.config file, just as we do with the database connection string. When we edit web.config, the application is automatically restarted, and so the new rate will be used to refill the tblFinancePMTData table with the correct values each time.

web.config

```
<configuration>
  <appSettings>
    ...
    <!-- change following to adjust finance interest rates -->
    <add key="WroxCarsInterestRate" value="4.75" />
    ...
  </appSettings>
  ...
</configuration>
```

So, in our global.asax file, we start by importing the namespaces we'll need to access the database. We also import a couple of extra namespaces, which we'll use to write status messages to the event log and a text log file when we update the database:

global.asax

```
<%@Application Language="VB" %>
<%@Import Namespace="System.Data" %>
<%@Import Namespace="System.Data.SqlClient" %>
<%@Import Namespace="System.Diagnostics" %>
<%@Import Namespace="System.IO" %>
...
```

Then we declare a couple of application-level variables that we'll use within our event handlers – the name of the event log we'll write to and the path and name of the log file we'll be updating:

```
...
<script runat="server">
Dim sLogName As String = "WroxCarCompany"
Dim sLogFile As String = "C:\Temp\WroxCarCoLog.txt"
...
```

The Application_Start Event Handler

Next comes the event handler for the Application_Start event. After declaring some local variables we'll need in this event handler, we extract the current interest rate and the database connection string from web.config:

```
...
Sub Application_Start(Sender As Object, E As EventArgs)
   ' code that runs on application startup
   ' update database table containing calculated PMT values
   ' for calculating vehicle finance payments

   Dim sInterestRate, sStoredProc, sConnect, sMessage As String
   Dim fInterestRate, fPMTResult As Double
   Dim fPaymentPer1000 As Decimal
   Dim iMonth As Integer

   ' get values from web.config file
   sInterestRate = ConfigurationSettings.AppSettings("WroxCarsInterestRate")
   sConnect = ConfigurationSettings.AppSettings("WroxCarsConnectString")
   ...
```

Now we can update our database. We have a stored procedure in the database named UpdatePmtFinanceData that accepts a number of months and a decimal payment value. The payment value is the amount required to pay off a loan of $1000.00 plus interest at the current rate, over the specified number of months. So, for example, if the number of months is 36, the value is the monthly payment required to pay off a $1000.00 loan plus the interest over 36 months. We can use this payment amount to calculate the payment required for any vehicle later on by simply multiplying the payment by the car price divided by 1000.

The next listing shows the UpdatePmtFinanceData stored procedure. If the table is empty it inserts the row, or updates an existing row if there is already one present:

```
CREATE PROCEDURE UpdatePmtFinanceData @Months int, @Payment decimal(9,2)
AS
UPDATE tblFinancePMTData SET Payment = @Payment WHERE Months = @Months
IF @@ROWCOUNT = 0
  INSERT INTO tblFinancePMTData (Months,Payment) VALUES (@Months,@Payment)
```

Calculating the Payment Amounts

Returning to our event handler, all we have to do to fill the table is execute this stored procedure once for every monthly period over which we want to allow users to extend their loan. In our case, the range is from 6 to 120 months in six-monthly intervals. The techniques we use to execute the procedure are exactly the same as we've used in all our other pages. After establishing our connection to the database, we use a For...Next construct with a Step value of 6, and then call the VB.NET Pmt function with the appropriate values to get the result. We round it to two decimal places, then set the parameters for our stored procedure and execute it:

```
...
' declare stored proc name and data access objects
sStoredProc = "UpdatePmtFinanceData"
Dim sqlConn As New SqlConnection(sConnect)
Dim sqlComm As New SqlCommand(sStoredProc, sqlConn)
sqlComm.CommandType = CommandType.StoredProcedure

Try

   ' parse interest rate into a Double
   fInterestRate = Double.Parse(sInterestRate)

   ' open database connection
   sqlConn.Open()

   ' calculate payment rate per $1000 at six-month intervals
   For iMonth = 6 To 120 Step 6

     fPMTResult = - Pmt(fInterestRate / 1200, iMonth, 1000, 0)
     fPaymentPer1000 = Decimal.Round(CType(fPMTResult, Decimal), 2)

     ' set parameters and call stored proc to update database table row
     sqlComm.Parameters.Clear()
     sqlComm.Parameters.Add("@Months", iMonth)
     sqlComm.Parameters.Add("@Payment", fPaymentPer1000)
     sqlComm.ExecuteNonQuery()

   Next
...
```

The VB.NET PMT Function

The VB.NET Pmt function expects us to provide up to five parameters:

```
Pmt(interest-rate, #periods, present-value, [future-value], [due-date])
```

❑ *interest-rate* is a `Double` that specifies the interest rate per period. In our case this is per month, so we divide the value (for example 4.75) by 1200 to get a percentage value per month (for example, 0.00396).

❑ *#periods* is a `Double` that specifies the number of payments that are required or the number of periods over which the loan will run.

❑ *present-value* is a `Double` that specifies the present value (or lump sum) that must be paid, excluding interest. Effectively it is the value of the goods to the seller when the sale takes place.

❑ *future-value* (optional) is a `Double` that specifies the value or balance left after all the payments have been made. To completely pay off the loan, the value of this parameter must be zero, and this is the default that is assumed if you omit this optional parameter.

❑ *due-date* (optional) is a `Microsoft.VisualBasic.DueDate` object that specifies when payments are due, and can be `DueDate.EndOfPeriod` if payments are due at the end of the payment period, or `DueDate.BegOfPeriod` if payments are due at the beginning of the period. It is an optional argument, and `DueDate.EndOfPeriod` is assumed if omitted.

The return value of the function is a `Double` that specifies the amount for each payment. In accountancy terms this is a debit against the loan, and so is returned as a negative number. This is why we reverse the sign before we insert it into the database table.

> *A full reference to the Pmt function can be found in the .NET SDK at: ms-help://MS.NETFrameworkSDK/vblr7net/html/vafctPmt.htm*

Writing Status Messages to the Event Log and a Text Log File

After we have inserted all values into our `tblFinancePMTData` table, we write a status message to both the event log and a text log file so that the administrator can check that the process is working properly. We use the same two routines within our `global.asax` page for this as we did in the `Application_Start` event handler earlier on. Because we wrapped the database update code in a `Try...Catch` construct, we can output the appropriate message:

```
...
' write a 'succeeded' message to error log
sMessage = 'Updated FinancePMTData values in database'
WriteEventLogMessage(sLogName, sMessage, EventLogEntryType.Information)
WriteErrorFileMessage(sLogFile, sMessage)

Catch

' write a 'failed' message to error log
sMessage = "Unable to update FinancePMTData values in database"
WriteEventLogMessage(sLogName, sMessage, EventLogEntryType.Error)
WriteErrorFileMessage(sLogFile, sMessage)

Finally
sqlConn.Close()     ' close the database connection
End Try

End Sub
```

The WriteEventLogMessage Routine

The `WriteEventLogMessage` routine we've included in this page is shown in the next listing. One issue is that the ASP.NET account, under which our pages run by default, does not have permission to create a new Event Log, and so the code will always fail. However, you could, if you want to use the Event Log to record application events and errors, run this page once under the context of an administrative-level account to create the Event Log, or write a simple executable application that does the same and run it from the command line under the context of an administrative-level account. Once the new Event Log has been created, ASP.NET should be able to write events to it:

```
Sub WriteEventLogMessage(sLogName As String, sMessage As String, _
                    eType As EventLogEntryType)

  Try
    ' write a string message to the system's Event Log
    ' create the event log if it does not already exist
    ' however the ASP.NET account must have relevant
    ' permissions for this to work - it does not by default
    If (Not EventLog.SourceExists(sLogName)) Then
      EventLog.CreateEventSource(sLogName, sLogName)
    End if

    ' write event to log
    Dim oLog as New EventLog
    oLog.Source = sLogName
    oLog.WriteEntry(sMessage, eType)
  Catch
  End Try

End Sub
```

A full reference to the `EventLog` *class can be found in the .NET SDK at:*
ms-help://MS.NETFrameworkSDK/cpref/html/frlrfsystemdiagnosticseventlogclasstopic.htm

The WriteErrorFileMessage Routine

More generally useful is the ability to write messages to a text log file as our application runs. The `WriteErrorFileMessage` routine shown next does just that, taking the file path and the text of the message as parameters. We use a `StreamWriter` to append the text to the log file. The second parameter to the `StreamWriter` constructor determines if new text will be appended to the file (`True`), or if it will replace the existing file content (`False`). Then we call the `WriteLine` method, passing it the current date and time (using the `Now` function) and the text of the message we want to write to the file:

```
Sub WriteErrorFileMessage(sFilePath As String, sMessage As String)

  ' write a string to the text log file sFilePath
  ' creates the file if it does not already exist
  Dim oWriter As StreamWriter

  Try
    oWriter = New StreamWriter(sFilePath, True)
    oWriter.WriteLine(Now().ToString & " - " & sMessage)
  Catch
```

```
    Finally
      oWriter.Close()     ' remember to close it afterwards
    End Try

  End Sub
```

Just make sure on your server that the folder you specify for the log file (in our case `C:\Temp\`) does already exist, and that the ASP.NET account has permission to write to it.

> *A full reference to the `StreamWriter` class can be found in the .NET SDK at: ms-help://MS.NETFrameworkSDK/cpref/html/frlrfSystemIOStreamWriterMembersTopic.htm*

Running Code when an Application Error Occurs

One other feature of the `global.asax` file that we use in our application is the ability to handle the `Application_Error` event. We use this event to execute the `WriteEventLogMessage` and `WriteErrorFileMessage` routines that you've just seen, and thereby provide a log of application errors (compilation and run-time errors that occur in any of the pages in our application).

All that's involved is to extract the error details, create a suitable `String` value, and then pass it to the two methods that will record the error. We can call the `Server.GetLastError` method to get a reference to a standard `Exception` object that represents the error, and use the `ToString` method to get the complete error details as a `String`.

```
Sub Application_Error(Sender As Object, E As EventArgs)
  ' code that runs when an unhandled error occurs

  Dim sMessage As String = Server.GetLastError().ToString()
  WriteEventLogMessage(sLogName, sMessage, EventLogEntryType.Error)
  WriteErrorFileMessage(sLogFile, sMessage)

End Sub
```

The GetFinancePMTRates Stored Procedure

After that diversion to look at `global.asax`, we can now get round to looking at the last of the stored procedures we need for our 'Model Details' page. We want to extract all the payment data from the `tblFinancePMTData` table in our database, so that we can load it into the `DataSet` we're using to power our 'Model Details' page.

The stored procedure itself is as simple as you would expect. It just selects and returns all the rows from the `tblFinancePMTData` table:

```
CREATE PROCEDURE GetFinancePMTRates AS
SELECT Months, Payment FROM tblFinancePMTData ORDER BY Months
```

Fetching and Storing the Data for the Page

Now that we have all the stored procedures we need in place, we can look at the code that builds the `DataSet` we'll be using to drive the 'Model Details' page. The function `GetCarDetailsDS` takes the ID of the vehicle we're displaying details of, and returns a `DataSet` object. The next listing shows the first part of this function:

cardetail.aspx

```
Function GetCarDetailsDS(sCarID As String) As DataSet

  ' to hold DataSet for the results
  Dim dsCarDetail As DataSet = Nothing

  ' to hold Session key for DataSet
  Dim sSessionKey As String = "WroxCar" & sCarID & "Details"
  ...
```

We've already decided that we'll store the DataSet in the user's ASP.NET session after extracting it for the first time, so we need to create a suitable session key value. We may be storing more than one DataSet if the user is viewing the details of several cars, so the session key must include the Car ID. In the code above, you can see how we create this session key. The resulting key for the vehicle with ID value 3, for example, will be "WroxCar3Details".

Accessing the Database and Filling the DataSet

Once we know the session key, we can try and extract the DataSet from the session. If this is the first time the user has accessed the 'Model Details' page for this model, the DataSet will not be in the user's session. At this point in our GetCarDetailsDS function the variable dsCarDetail will still be Nothing (null in C#), and so the next line of code tests for this:

```
...
'try and get DataSet from user's Session
dsCarDetail = CType(Session(sSessionKey), DataSet)

If dsCarDetail Is Nothing Then     'not in Session - get from database
  ...
```

If our dsCarDetail variable is Nothing, we know that we'll have to go off to the database and fill the DataSet. We first declare the names of the four stored procedures that we described earlier in this chapter, then collect the database connection string from the web.config file. We also create the Connection and Command objects we'll need, and specify the CommandType as we've done in many previous examples:

```
...
' to hold stored procedure names
Dim sCarProcName As String = "GetAllCarDetails"
Dim sColorProcName As String = "GetAllCarColors"
Dim sExtrasProcName As String = "GetAllCarExtras"
Dim sFinancePMTProcName As String = "GetFinancePMTRates"

Dim sConnect As String = _
        ConfigurationSettings.AppSettings("WroxCarsConnectString")
Dim sqlConn As New SqlConnection(sConnect)
Dim sqlComm As New SqlCommand(sCarProcName, sqlConn)
sqlComm.CommandType = CommandType.StoredProcedure
...
```

Now we can create a new empty `DataSet`, and specify the single parameter of the `Command` using the Car ID value that is passed to our `GetCarDetailsDS` function. Then it's just a matter of opening the database connection and executing the `Fill` method four times, changing the value of the `CommandText` (the stored procedure name) each time.

However, before we execute the final call to the `Fill` method, we have to remove the parameter from the `Command` object, as the `GetFinancePMTRates` stored procedure does not accept any parameters. We can do this by calling the `Clear` method of the `Command` object's `Parameters` collection:

```
...
Try

    ' create a new empty DataSet for the results
    dsCarDetail = New DataSet()

    ' and fill it from the database
    sqlComm.Parameters.Add("@CarID", sCarID)
    Dim daCarDetail As New SqlDataAdapter(sqlComm)
    sqlConn.Open()
    daCarDetail.Fill(dsCarDetail, "CarDetails")
    sqlComm.CommandText = sColorProcName
    daCarDetail.Fill(dsCarDetail, "CarColors")
    sqlComm.CommandText = sExtrasProcName
    daCarDetail.Fill(dsCarDetail, "CarExtras")
    sqlComm.CommandText = sFinancePMTProcName
    sqlComm.Parameters.Clear()
    daCarDetail.Fill(dsCarDetail, "FinancePMTRates")
    ...
```

This gives us a `DataSet` containing four tables:

❑ `CarDetails` contains a row for each car/engine combination for this vehicle model

❑ `CarColors` contains a row for each color that is available for this vehicle model

❑ `CarExtras` contains a row for each optional extra that is available for this model

❑ `FinancePMTRates` contains the rows required to calculate the finance payments

Saving the DataSet in the Session

Now we have our `DataSet` ready for use, and we can save it in the user's ASP.NET session ready for the next (postback) request. The remainder of the code is the `Catch` and `Finally` sections of the `Try...Catch` construct we're using to trap any database access errors, followed by the statement that returns the `DataSet` (or `Nothing` if there was an error). Notice that we have to call the `Close` method of the `Connection` after we have finished with it. We opened the connection explicitly earlier on, and so the `Fill` method will not close it when it completes each time:

```
...
    'save DataSet in Session for next postback
    Session(sSessionKey) = dsCarDetail
```

```
     Catch
        Return Nothing
     Finally
        sqlConn.Close()
     End Try

   End If

   Return dsCarDetail

End Function
```

If the connection is closed when `Fill` is called, it is opened automatically (implicitly) by the `Fill` method and then closed again immediately afterwards. This is a considerable waste of processing resources when we are filling more than one table, and to get the best performance we open the connection first (before the first call to the `Fill` method) and then close it again after the last call to the `Fill` method.

Of course, as the data within the `DataSet` is the same for each user, and only depends on the `CarID` value (the selected model), we could store it in the `Application` object rather than in the user's `Session`. This would mean that the `DataSet` for each model would remain in the `Application` until it was restarted, whereas the ones in each user's `Session` disappear automatically when the session ends. If you have data that does not depend on the actual user, then you might like to consider testing if this alternative approach will reduce server loading and improve performance in your own application.

The Code in the 'Model Details' Page

Before we look at the main interactive 'tabbed dialog' sections of the 'Model Details' page, we should examine the code in the `Page_Load` event handler to see how the page behaves, and what it does, when first loaded and during each postback.

We have a few page-level variables declared within the page, outside any event handlers. These variables hold values such as the stylesheet size (as used in all our other pages), the ID of the selected vehicle, a reference to the `DataSet` holding the data to populate our page, and a variable to hold the ID of the current visitor (used when we come to save a quotation for them).

There is also an array of string values that we'll use to hold the calculated price and finance terms in the user's ASP.NET session, and a `String` to hold the session key that we'll use when storing this array in the user's session:

cardetail.aspx

```
' page-level variable to stylesheet size
Dim sStyleSize As String = "Standard"

' page-level variable to hold current car ID
Dim sCarID As String

' page-level variable to hold DataSet of values from database
Dim oCarsDS As DataSet
```

```
' page-level variable to hold User ID
Dim sUserID As String

' page-level array to hold current car price and finance terms
' (0) = Basic Price including extras and color option
' (1) = Annual interest rate applicable to purchase
' (2) = Interest amount included in Total Price
' (3) = Total Price including interest for finance plan (if selected)
' (4) = Number of months for finance plan (if selected)
' (5) = Monthly payment amount for finance plan (if selected)
Dim aCurrentPrice(5) As String

' page-level variable to hold Session key for prices array
Dim sPricesSessionKey As String
```

The Page_Load Event Handler

In the Page_Load event itself, we start by generating the client-side event handlers that we'll be using in our page. We discussed the use of the RegisterClientScriptBlock method and the client-side mainWindowPage function at the end of the previous chapter, and we'll look at where the other two client-side functions (setOptionButtons and nodeExpanded) are used later in this chapter:

```
Sub Page_Load()

  ' create the client-side script block for the control events in the page
  Dim sScript as String = "<script language='JavaScript'>" & vbCrlf _
    & "<!--" & vbCrlf _
    & "function setOptionButtons(sName) {" & vbCrlf _
    & "  document.forms[0].elements[sName].checked = true;" & vbCrlf _
    & "}" & vbCrlf _
    & "function nodeExpanded(oSender) {" & vbCrlf _
    & "  var clickedNode = oSender.clickedNodeIndex;" & vbCrlf _
    & "  var colNodes = oSender.getChildren();" & vbCrlf _
    & "  for (var i = 0; i < colNodes.length; i++) {" & vbCrlf _
    & "    if (colNodes[i].getNodeIndex() != clickedNode)" & vbCrlf _
    & "      colNodes[i].setAttribute('expanded', false);" & vbCrlf _
    & "  }" & vbCrlf _
    & "}" & vbCrlf _
    & "function mainWindowPage(sHref, bClose) {" & vbCrlf _
    & "  window.opener.location.href = sHref;" & vbCrlf _
    & "  if (bClose) window.close();" & vbCrlf _
    & "}" & vbCrlf _
    & "//-->" & vbCrlf _
    & "<" & "/" & "script>"

  ' register it so that it is inserted into the page
  If(Not IsClientScriptBlockRegistered("JSBlock")) Then
    RegisterClientScriptBlock("JSBlock", sScript)
  End If
  ...
```

Checking for an Active Session

Next, as in our other pages, we need to confirm that a session is currently active for this user. We extract the value for the stylesheet size from the session and check that we actually did get something. If not, we have to redirect the user to `default.aspx` to restart the session and re-establish the user ID and stylesheet size.

However, as the 'Model Details' page is running in a pop-up window that is opened from the 'Home' page in the main window, we need to do a little extra work compared to the action we take in the other pages. We have to change the URL of the main window to load the `default.aspx` page, and then close the 'Model Details' window.

Of course, if you remember what you read towards the end of the previous chapter (when we were discussing the links to the 'My Cars' page) you'll realize how we achieve this. We just output some client-side script that changes the `location.href` property for the main window (the `opener` property of the current window) to `default.aspx`, and call the `close` method of the current window. As this client-side script is not inside a function, but 'inline' in the page, it is executed automatically as soon as the client's browser receives it:

```
...
' get stylesheet size from Session
sStyleSize = CType(Session("WccStyleSize"), String)

' if no value, session has expired or user entered
' site at page other than 'Home' page
If sStyleSize = "" Then

    ' write client-side code that reloads 'Home' page and closes
    ' window to browser, plus message for non-script clients
    Dim sReload As String = "<html><body>" & vbCrlf _
        & "<script language='JavaScript'>" & vbCrlf _
        & "<!--" & vbCrlf _
        & "window.opener.location.href = 'default.aspx';" & vbCrlf _
        & "window.close();" & vbCrlf _
        & "//-->" & vbCrlf _
        & "<" & "/" & "script>" & vbCrlf _
        & "<center><b>Your session has expired.</b><p />" _
        & "<b>Please close this window and reload the Home page</b>" _
        & "</center></body></html>"

    ' then prevent rest of page from being processed
    Response.Write(sReload)
    Response.Flush()
    Response.End()
    Exit Sub

End If
...
```

Notice at the end of this code, after sending the script to the client, we prevent our server-side code from executing any further and flush the contents of the ASP.NET output buffer to the client.

Collecting the DataSet

Providing that there is an active session, the next step is to collect the DataSet containing the data we need to build our page. We also collect the current user ID from the session (as we now know that there is an active session), and store it away in our page-level variable for later use. Then we need to find out which model was selected, and we can extract this value from the query string – it is placed there by the links in the 'Home' page that open this page:

```
...
' get UserID from Session
sUserID = CType(Session("WccUserID"), String)

' get car ID from query string
sCarID = Request.QueryString("id")
If sCarID > "" Then
  ...
```

Providing that we do have a Car ID, we can now call the GetCarDetailsDS function we examined earlier to get our DataSet. If it is not available, we display a message and exit:

```
  ...
  ' get DataSet from function elsewhere in this page
  ' we'll also need it almost every time a postback occurs
  oCarsDS = GetCarDetailsDS(sCarID)
  If oCarsDS Is Nothing Then
    lblMessage.Text = "Sorry, the database cannot be accessed."
    btnSave.Visible = False
    Exit Sub
  End If
  ...
```

Collecting the Price and Finance Terms

You saw in the page-level declarations that we have an array to hold the price of the current configuration of the vehicle, plus the details of the currently selected finance package. We store this array in the user's session in between postbacks (this is easier than trying to extract the values from the controls on the page each time).

As with the DataSet containing the details of the vehicle, we have to build a session key that denotes the ID of the vehicle, so that we can store an array for each model if the user is configuring more than one at a time. However, this is only valid for the script-enabled version of the page, because our 'Home' page prevents visitors from opening more than one pop-up 'Model Details' window for the same model of vehicle.

In the version of the page for non-script-enabled clients, we'll have to handle the case where a visitor could be configuring more than one instance of the same vehicle, in which case using only the Car ID to differentiate the session-level variables is not a safe or valid approach – it would cause all instances of the page to use the same array values.

And, if we later decided to allow users to configure more than one instance of the same vehicle in our script-enabled version (by changing the code in the 'Home' page that opens the 'Model Details' window), we would face the same problem, so we might as well provide robust code in both versions of the page to make maintenance easier and avoid any possibility of an error in the future.

To achieve this we create a unique (random) session key to use for each array. However, the next question is where do we store this key so that we can get at it each time the page is loaded? We obviously can't keep it in the user's session, because that would defeat the whole object of the process. We could add it to the query string, but that means we would have to create it in the 'Home' page rather than here.

Saving Values in the ViewState of the Page

One great way to persist page-specific values across a postback is to use the **viewstate** of the page. Storing `String` values in the viewstate is easy. It works just like storing them in an ASP.NET session. We insert a value into the viewstate using:

```
ViewState("key-name") = value
```

And we extract it using:

```
value = CType(ViewState("key-name"), String)
```

Storing other data types (such as numbers) requires us to convert them to their `String` representation, but this is easy enough to do using the `ToString` method when we store them, and the `Parse` method when we extract them.

Viewstate is useful at times like this because the values are stored within the page, and not on the server, so it's a great approach for **page-instance-specific** values. When values are *not* specific to the page instance, and we can guarantee session support (as in our application), storing them in the session is often a better approach because it saves them being round-tripped to the client and back again.

In the case of our prices array we could, of course, just store the values themselves as individual values in the viewstate. However, remember that this adds to the page size, and so large or complex data structures (such as the `DataSet` that contains all the vehicle details), or values that can't easily be converted into a `String`, are not good candidates for storing in the viewstate. The technique we demonstrate here of using the session to store the data and the viewstate just to store the session key is probably more efficient.

So, returning to our `Page_Load` event handler, we check if this is a postback or if it's the first time that the page has been loaded. If it is a postback, we collect the key for our price and finance terms array from the viewstate and use it to access and collect our array:

```
...
If Page.IsPostback Then

  ' get key for Prices array from the page ViewState
  sPricesSessionKey = CType(ViewState("PriceArrayKey"), String)

  ' get array of current prices and finance terms from Session
  aCurrentPrice = CType(Session(sPricesSessionKey), String())
...
```

If this is the first time that the page has been loaded, there are different tasks to complete. First we must create the key for our prices array, and store it in the viewstate of the page. We generate a random number and use it in conjunction with the Car ID, so an example key might be something like `"WCCPricesKey3-814"`.

Then we can populate the controls on the page by calling two routines that are defined elsewhere: `ShowCarDetails` and `CalculateCarPrice`. You'll recall that we only need to populate the controls on the page the first time it loads, as the current values selected by our visitor will be maintained by the viewstate when a postback occurs:

```
...
Else

    ' create random key for storing price/finance terms array in
    ' user's session for this instance of the page, just in case
    ' they are configuring multiple instances of the same vehicle
    Dim oRand As New Random()
    sPricesSessionKey = "WCCPricesKey" & sCarID & "-" _
                    & oRand.Next(0, 999).ToString()

    ' store this key in the ViewState of the page
    ViewState("PriceArrayKey") = sPricesSessionKey

    ' display details of this vehicle
    ShowCarDetails(sCarID)

    ' calculate and display price for default configuration
    CalculateCarPrice()

    End If

  End If

End Sub
```

We'll be looking at the `ShowCarDetails` and `CalculateCarPrice` routines in detail in the next chapter.

The 'Model Details' 'Tab' Pages in Detail

At last we have everything in place to start examining the code for the five 'tabbed dialog' page sections of our 'Model Details' page. We've seen an outline view of the page in the previous chapter, and the HTML declarations that implement the parts of the page outside our 'tabbed dialog'. And now we've also seen how the data we require is accessed, and stored in a `DataSet` ready for use. So let's get on and look at the remaining code. We start with the section that displays the colors available for the current vehicle.

The Color Selection Section

The first of our five 'tabs' contains a list of all the colors that are available for the current vehicle. There are two ranges of colors, standard and metallic, and the option buttons on the left allow the visitor to choose which color range they want to select from. A pop-up tool-tip shows the color name when the mouse pointer hovers over a color:

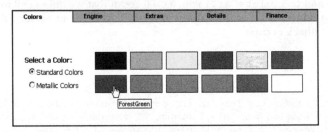

You'll recall that each of our 'tabbed dialog' sections is enclosed in a `PageView` element that is part of the IE Web Controls `MultiPage` control declaration. Inside the `PageView` we declare a three-column single-row HTML table to hold the dialog content.

The left-hand cell contains a small transparent image that we resize to force the 'tab' to be the correct vertical height (you'll see this used in all the 'tab' sections). The next cell contains the two option buttons, which are created with a `RadioButtonList` control containing an explicit declaration of the two buttons as `ListItem` controls:

```
<ie:PageView id="mpColors">
<!-- section for "Colors" tab -->
<table border="0" cellpadding="6">
  <tr>
    <td><img src="images/_blnk.gif" border="0"
            width="1" height="170" alt="" /></td>
    <td><font face="Tahoma,Arial,Helvetica,sans-serif" size="2">
      <span style="body-text"><b>Select a Color:</b></span><br />
      <asp:RadioButtonList id="optColorType"
                           OnSelectedIndexChanged="SelectColorType"
                           Font-Name="Tahoma,Arial,Helvetica,sans-serif"
                           Font-Size="10"
                           AutoPostBack="True"
                           CssClass="body-text" runat="server">
        <asp:ListItem Text="Standard Colors" Value="optColStandard"
                      Selected="True" />
        <asp:ListItem Text="Metallic Colors" Value="optColMetallic" />
      </asp:RadioButtonList></font>
    </td>
    ...
```

By default, we set (select) the **Standard Colors** option when the page first loads, but the actual selection after a postback will depend on the last setting chosen by the user, as stored in the viewstate for the page. You can also see that we set `AutoPostBack` to `True` for the `RadioButtonList` control so that a click will automatically post the page back to our server. And we specify a server-side event handler named `SelectColorType` for the `OnSelectedIndexChanged` attribute, so it will be executed when an option button is clicked. We'll be looking at all this code later on.

Displaying the Color Blocks

The main issue in this section of the page is how to display blocks of color in such a way that the user can click on one to select it. We could create the same outward appearance using an HTML table, setting the background color of each cell to the appropriate color. However, this gives us no easy way to react to a click event, because only Internet Explorer 4.0 and above, and the CSS2-enabled 'version 6' browsers, will recognize this event for a table cell.

Instead we chose to use standard `<input type="image">` controls, with the image being a GIF file of the appropriate color. Originally, when we experimented with stretching a single-pixel sized image to the required display size using the `width` and `height` attributes, we found that browser support for this was extremely variable. In particular, Opera failed to resize the image.

However, Opera is in fact behaving correctly, because HTML 4 does not define `width` and `height` attributes for an `<input>` element. A click on an `<input type="image">` control submits the `<form>` on which the control is declared to the server for processing, including the x and y co-ordinates of the mouse pointer within the image. So, if you think about it, how would rescaling an image affect these if you were allowed to do so? Should the coordinates be the actual position in pixels on the scaled image, or the equivalent position on the original-sized image?

So, the images we display are sized to the required final dimensions for the page, and stored in the `/images/colors/` folder of our site. There is one for each color listed in the `tblColor` table. While having to deliver all these images to the client might seem to be a waste of bandwidth, there is really no other cross-browser compatible solution. In any case, each image file is only 122 bytes (we used a bitmap editor to reduce the number of colors in the image to a minimum), and they will be cached on the client after the first access to the page.

The following listing shows the remainder of the **Colors** 'tab'. You can see that we use a `DataList` control with the `RepeatLayout`, `RepeatDirection`, and `RepeatColumns` attributes set so that we get a six-column wide table with the color blocks laid out horizontally:

```
...
<td><font face="Tahoma,Arial,Helvetica,sans-serif" size="2">
  <asp:DataList id="dlsColors" runat="server" CellSpacing="5"
                RepeatLayout="Table" RepeatDirection="Horizontal"
                RepeatColumns="6">
    <ItemTemplate>
      <input type="image" id="imgColor" runat="server"
          OnServerClick="SelectColor"
          Src='<%# DataBinder.Eval(Container.DataItem, "Color",
                                   "images/colors/{0}.gif") %>'
          Alt='<%# Container.DataItem("Color") %>'
          Width="60" Height="30" Border="1"
          Title='<%# Container.DataItem("Color") %>'
          Style="border-width:1px;border-style:solid;
                 border-color:Black;" />
    </ItemTemplate>
  </asp:DataList></font>
</td>
</tr>
</table>
</ie:PageView>
```

The `ItemTemplate` for our `DataList` generates the `<input type="image">` element for each color using data binding, and these elements have a range of attributes set so that the correct image is displayed, and a pop-up tool-tip is created for all different types of clients. Because we include the attribute `Border="1"`, we'll get an outline (albeit a blue 'hyperlink' one) in browsers that do not support CSS. However, for those that do, the `Style` attribute we've also included overrides this to add a one-pixel wide black border around each image (useful when the image is white!).

Where Do the Colors Come From?

In case you haven't noticed yet, we should admit that we cheated a little in selecting the colors that are available for our vehicles. We used the .NET Framework standard colors, allowing our code to automatically generate the appropriate color for the large car image at the top of this page. You'll see this code later on.

To assist in generating the images for our color blocks, and to view the available .NET Framework colors, we used a modified version of the 'color listing' page that we introduced in Chapter 7. That page, `color-list.aspx` in the `charting` sub-folder of the samples, was designed to show the browser-safe colors. However, in our application we've abandoned that approach for the car colors – most car buyers are not interested in whether their new vehicle is a browser-safe color, but more in whether it looks nice.

The page `dotnet-color-list.aspx` is also in the `charting` sub-folder of the samples, and it displays all of the .NET standard colors with their names and RGB values (in hex and decimal). The first few colors are the standard 'Windows furniture' colors such as `Desktop`, `ActiveCaption`, and `WindowText`. After that come the 140 other standard colors. The code is much the same as we used in the `color-list.aspx` page, so we aren't listing or describing it again here.

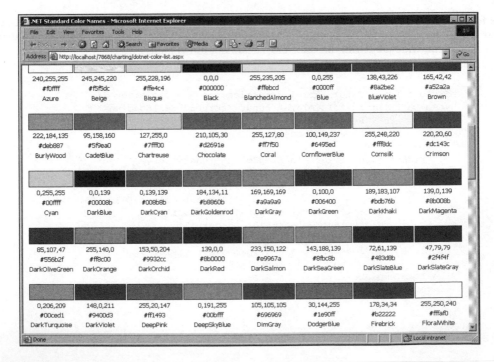

Populating the Page Heading and Colors Section

The `ShowCarDetails` routine that is called from the `Page_Load` event handler is responsible for populating the five 'tabbed dialog' sections. However, it also fills in a couple of items at the top of the 'Model Details' page. We've listed the first part of the routine next, and we'll be working through it section by section as we look at each of the 'tabs' in our page.

The routine starts off by getting references to each of the tables (`DataTable` objects) within the `DataSet` that holds all the data for this page. Then it gets a reference to the first row in the `CarDetails` table. This table contains a row for each car/engine combination for this model, but the model name and précis are the same in all the rows because they all refer to the currently selected model.

So, using the values in this row, we can fill in the précis and get the model name. From the model name we can figure out which image to load, and add the appropriate `alt` attribute to it. We also set the text of the `<title>` element (the element with the `id` value `elmTitle`) so that the title bar of our pop-up window shows the model name:

ShowCarDetails subroutine

```
' routine to show selected car details
Sub ShowCarDetails(sCarID As String)

  ' get references to the tables in the DataSet
  Dim oDTCar As DataTable = oCarsDS.Tables("CarDetails")
  Dim oDTColor As DataTable = oCarsDS.Tables("CarColors")
  Dim oDTExtras As DataTable = oCarsDS.Tables("CarExtras")
  Dim oDTFinance As DataTable = oCarsDS.Tables("FinancePMTRates")

  ' fill in precis and image of car
  Dim oDR As DataRow = oDTCar.Rows(0)
  lblPrecis.Text = oDR("Precis").ToString()
  Dim sCarName As String = oDR("Model").ToString()
  imgCar.ImageUrl = "images/" & sCarName & "300.gif"
  imgCar.AlternateText = "The Wrox " & sCarName
  elmTitle.InnerText = "Wrox " & sCarName & " - Configure and Buy"
  ...
```

Displaying the Appropriate Set of Colors

Now we can get a reference to a `DataView` object for the `CarColors` table in our `DataSet`. This table contains all the available colors, both standard and metallic ranges, and so we need to decide which ones should be displayed. We can find the current selection by examining the value of the `RadioButtonList` control named `optColorType` (the **Standard Colors** and **Metallic Colors** option buttons).

By good fortune rather than forward planning, the `SelectedIndex` property of the `RadioButtonList` control returns the same value as we use in our table to denote the color range (zero for standard colors and one for metallic colors). We can apply a filter to the rows in the `DataView`, so that only the appropriate colors are included, by using this value when we set the `RowFilter` property. Then we bind the filtered `DataView` to the `DataList` control named `dlsColors` that displays the color blocks. After the `DataList` output has been generated we remove the row filter to allow any other code that needs to access all of the data to do so:

```
...
' fill the DataList of colors depending on setting of
' the Standard/Metallic radio buttons
Dim oDTView As DataView = oDTColor.DefaultView
oDTView.RowFilter = "IsMetallic = " & optColorType.SelectedIndex
dlsColors.DataSource = oDTView
dlsColors.DataBind()
oDTView.RowFilter = ""
...
```

It's good practice to remove a `RowFilter` after use, as it can cause hard-to-find bugs in your code if you later reuse the `DataView` (or the underlying table) without remembering to remove the filter first.

Reacting to Events in the Colors Section

The code we've just seen will populate the `DataList` control named `dlsColors` with the standard colors when the page is first loaded. However, our page must handle both a click event arising from a visitor selecting a different color, and a change event that arises when they click on the option buttons to switch from standard colors to metallic colors or vice-versa.

The attributes we declared on the `RadioButtonList` control that implements the two option buttons specify that a postback will occur when an option is selected, and that the event handler named `SelectColorType` will be executed when this happens. All the `SelectColorType` event handler has to do is change the list of colors that are displayed in the `DataList` control. Effectively it's a copy of the code we just looked at:

```
' routine to show range of colors when Standard/Metallic is selected
Sub SelectColorType(oSender As Object, oArgs As EventArgs)

  ' get reference to table in the DataSet
  Dim oDTColor As DataTable = oCarsDS.Tables("CarColors")

  ' fill the DataList of colors depending on setting of
  ' the Standard/Metallic radio buttons
  Dim oDTView As DataView = oDTColor.DefaultView
  oDTView.RowFilter = "IsMetallic = " & optColorType.SelectedIndex
  dlsColors.DataSource = oDTView
  dlsColors.DataBind()
  oDTView.RowFilter = ""

End Sub
```

Meanwhile, the attributes we declared on the `DataList` itself specify that a postback will occur when a color block is clicked (each one is an `<input type="image">` element), and that the event handler named `SelectColor` will be executed when this happens. In this case, we just have to accomplish two things. We need to update the color of the car image at the top of the page, and we do this by simply changing the background color of the table cell that contains it.

As we mentioned in the previous chapter, each car image we use in this page is a GIF image where the bodywork of the vehicle is transparent. So the background color shows through, and it looks like the color of the vehicle has changed. In reality, however, you would probably want to display a more tempting (and better quality) image of the vehicle. You could just as easily change the `src` of the element containing the car image to load a different full-color image instead.

The only other step required for the `SelectColor` event handler is to recalculate the price. There is a price premium for the metallic colors, and so the current price might be incorrect if the user has switched from a standard to a metallic color, or vice versa. To recalculate the price we just have to execute the same `CalculateCarPrice` routine as we did when we first loaded the page (and which we'll be discussing in the next chapter):

```
' routine to select the color chosen by the user and update car image
Sub SelectColor(oSender As Object, oArgs As ImageClickEventArgs)
   tclColor.BgColor = oSender.Alt
   CalculateCarPrice()
End Sub
```

The Engine Selection Section

The second 'tab' in our page displays the list of available engines. The option buttons at the left of the 'tab' allow our visitors to select an engine from the list, and the table on the right indicates which one is selected by highlighting it. Notice the text strings in the **Turbo** and **Auto** columns that we created within the stored procedure we looked at earlier:

The HTML for this part of the page also uses an HTML three-column single-row table (as do all the 'tabs'). Again the left-hand cell contains the image that sets the height of the 'tab', and the next cell contains a `RadioButtonList` control – much like the **Colors** section we just looked at. However, this time the data to generate the list comes from our database, and is set dynamically when the page loads. So the `RadioButtonList` control contains no `ListItem` elements:

```
<ie:PageView id="mpEngine">
<!-- section for "Engine" tab -->
<table border="0" cellpadding="6">
  <tr>
    <td><img src="images/_blnk.gif" width="1" height="170" alt="" /></td>
    <td><font face="Tahoma,Arial,Helvetica,sans-serif" size="2">
      <span style="body-text"><b>Select an Engine:</b></span><br />
      <asp:RadioButtonList id="optEngine"
                    OnSelectedIndexChanged="SelectEngine"
```

```
                             Font-Name="Tahoma,Arial,Helvetica,sans-serif"
                             Font-Size="10" AutoPostBack="True"
                             CssClass="body-text" runat="server"/>
        </font>
      </td>
      ...
```

Again we use `AutoPostBack` to automatically submit the page to our server in response to a click on the option buttons. This will execute a server-side event handler named `SelectEngine`, which looks after highlighting the appropriate row in the table next to the option buttons and recalculating the vehicle price.

The Engine Details (DataGrid) Table

The right-hand table of engine details is also generated with server-side databinding, and to get the format, layout, and appearance we want, we use a `DataGrid` control this time. It is better suited to a purely columnar layout than other list controls. However, rather than allowing it to generate the columns automatically, we have specified these ourselves using `BoundColumn` controls. We want to change the column headings from those used in the database tables to something more appropriate (though we could have done this in our stored procedure, of course). We also specify the display format of the data in two of the columns:

```
    ...
  <td><font face="Tahoma,Arial,Helvetica,sans-serif" size="2">
    <asp:DataGrid id="dgrEngine" runat="server"
                AutoGenerateColumns="False" CellPadding="4"
                Font-Size="10" Font-Name="Tahoma,Arial,Helvetica,sans-serif"
                HeaderStyle-HorizontalAlign="center"
                HeaderStyle-BackColor="#b50055"
                HeaderStyle-ForeColor="#ffffff"
                HeaderStyle-Font-Bold="True"
                ItemStyle-HorizontalAlign="center"
                SelectedItemStyle-BackColor="#ffffcc">
      <Columns>
        <asp:BoundColumn HeaderText="Capacity" DataField="CubicCapacity"
                    DataFormatString="{0:#,###0cc}" />
        <asp:BoundColumn HeaderText="Fuel Type" DataField="FuelType" />
        <asp:BoundColumn HeaderText="Cyls" DataField="Cylinders" />
        <asp:BoundColumn HeaderText="Turbo" DataField="Turbo" />
        <asp:BoundColumn HeaderText="Max RPM" DataField="MaxRPM"
                    DataFormatString="{0:#,###0}" />
        <asp:BoundColumn HeaderText="BHP" DataField="BHP" />
        <asp:BoundColumn HeaderText="Gears" DataField="Gears" />
        <asp:BoundColumn HeaderText="Auto" DataField="AutoTrans" />
      </Columns>
    </asp:DataGrid></font>
  </td>
 </tr>
</table>
</ie:PageView>
```

Populating the Engine Section

The `ShowCarDetails` routine we execute when the page first loads continues by populating the controls for the 'Engine' section of our page. Using the reference to the `CarDetails` table that we obtained at the start of this routine, we can bind the data directly to the `RadioButtonList` control named `optEngine` that implements the list of option buttons for the engine types.

We want to display the engine name and use the ID of the engine as the value of each option button. We achieve this by specifying the appropriate column names from the `DataSet` table as the `DataValueField` and `DataTextField` property values:

`ShowCarDetails` subroutine (continued)

```
    ...
    ' fill RadioButtonList with available engines
    optEngine.DataSource = oDTCar
    optEngine.DataValueField = "EngineID"
    optEngine.DataTextField = "EngineName"
    optEngine.DataBind()
    ...
```

We also need to populate the table that displays the technical details of each engine. The `CarDetails` table in our `DataSet` contains all the information on each engine, so we can use this table again. We just have to bind it to the `DataGrid` control named `dgrEngine`.

There are also two more tasks. We want to be able to call the `CalculateCarPrice` routine when the page first loads, before the user has made any selections, so that they can see the price of the basic model. So we must set the option buttons to specify one of the engines, and we chose to select the first one – which should be the smallest and the least expensive. We also select the corresponding row in the `DataGrid` table by setting its `SelectedIndex` property to zero as well:

```
    ...
    ' fill the DataGrid with the details of each engine
    dgrEngine.DataSource = oDTCar
    dgrEngine.DataBind()

    ' and select the first engine in these two lists
    optEngine.SelectedIndex = 0
    dgrEngine.SelectedIndex = 0
    ...
```

Reacting to Events in the Engine Section

The only event that the 'Engine' section of our page can raise is the selection of a different engine. The `AutoPostBack` attribute will cause a postback to occur when this happens, and the `OnSelectedIndexChanged` attribute will cause our event handler named `SelectEngine` to be executed. All this does is set the `SelectedIndex` property of the `DataGrid` to the same value as the `SelectedIndex` of the `RadioButtonList` so that the correct row is highlighted, and then calls the routine to recalculate the price of the vehicle:

```
' routine to select row in DataGrid when an engine is selected
Sub SelectEngine(oSender As Object, oArgs As EventArgs)
  dgrEngine.SelectedIndex = optEngine.SelectedIndex
  CalculateCarPrice()
End Sub
```

The 'Optional Extras' Selection Section

The third 'tab' is the 'Extras' page, which shows the optional extras that are available for this vehicle. We've implemented it as a series of checkboxes, and the user can select as many as they wish from the list:

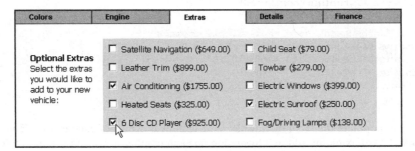

The HTML content of this 'tab' is relatively simple. There is some declarative text in the left-hand section, and a CheckBoxList control in the right-hand section. The captions for each checkbox are created through server-side databinding. As you'll recall, we carried out some text manipulation within the SQL of our stored procedure (described earlier in this chapter) to build these captions.

As in the previous two 'tabs', we set AutoPostBack for the CheckBoxList, and specify that the server-side event handler named SelectExtras will be executed when a postback occurs. And, as in the Colors 'tab', we use the RepeatLayout, RepeatDirection and RepeatColumns attributes to get a two-column table – though this time we lay out the controls in that table vertically rather than horizontally:

```
<ie:PageView id="mpExtras">
<!-- section for "Extras" tab -->
<table border="0" cellpadding="6">
  <tr>
    <td><img src="images/_blnk.gif" width="1" height="170" alt="" /></td>
    <td valign="top">
      <font face="Tahoma,Arial,Helvetica,sans-serif" size="2">
      <p> </p><span style="body-text"><b>Optional Extras</b><br />
      Select the extras<br />you would like to<br />add to your new<br />
      vehicle:</span></font>
    </td>
    <td nowrap="nowrap">
      <font face="Tahoma,Arial,Helvetica,sans-serif" size="2">
      <asp:CheckBoxList id="chkExtras"
                    OnSelectedIndexChanged="SelectExtras"
                    RepeatLayout="Table"
                    RepeatColumns="2" RepeatDirection="Vertical"
                    Font-Name="Tahoma,Arial,Helvetica,sans-serif"
                    Font-Size="10" CellPadding="3" BackColor="#ffffcc"
```

```
                              AutoPostBack="True" CssClass="body-text" runat="server">
        </asp:CheckBoxList></font>
      </td>
    </tr>
  </table>
  </ie:PageView>
```

Populating the 'Extras' Section

As our `ShowCarDetails` routine runs when the page first loads, the next part is responsible for populating our list of optional extras. We use the reference to the `CarExtras` table in our `DataSet` that we obtained at the start of this routine to bind that table to the `CheckBoxList` control named `chkExtras`. We use the value of the column that we created within our stored procedure (`DisplayText`) as the caption, so that each checkbox displays the 'extra's' name and price, followed by a couple of ` ` non-breaking space characters to separate the two columns:

ShowCarDetails subroutine (continued)

```
    ...
    ' fill the CheckBoxList with list of available extras
    chkExtras.DataSource = oDTExtras
    chkExtras.DataTextField = "DisplayText"
    chkExtras.DataValueField = "ExtraID"
    chkExtras.DataBind()
    ...
```

You can see in the code above that we attempt to bind the ID of each of the optional extras to the `value` property of each checkbox. However, as we discovered in the 'Compare Models' page in Chapter 7, this doesn't actually do anything. When we use a `CheckBoxList` control, the `value` attributes are never set. This is because their 'value' can't sensibly be accessed following a postback, due to the way that these controls work within the browser. You'll see how we have to work around this when we look at the routine to calculate the car price in the next chapter.

Reacting to Events in the 'Extras' Section

When our visitors check or un-check any of the boxes in our `CheckBoxList` control, the `AutoPostBack` and `OnSelectedIndexChanged` attribute values we specified cause a postback to occur, and the routine named `SelectExtras` is executed on the server. All we need to do here is recalculate the car price to take into account the change in the optional extras specified by our visitor:

```
    ' routine to update price as optional extras are selected
    Sub SelectExtras(oSender As Object, oArgs As EventArgs)
      CalculateCarPrice()
    End Sub
```

The 'Standard Features' (Details) Section

The fourth 'tab' does not provide any features for selecting options for the vehicle, but is still interactive. It contains two expandable 'tree view' lists that display categorized information about the vehicle. We wanted to prevent the user from changing the layout of our page by expanding these tree views beyond the current size of the 'tab' section, and thereby increasing its height, so we have used some code that automatically collapses any other open 'node' when you open a different one:

381

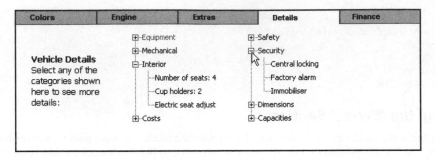

The HTML declaration for this page shows the two 'tree view' controls. These are implemented using two instances of the `TreeView` control from the IE Web Controls pack that we discussed in the previous chapter.

The IE Web Controls TreeView Control

This is the third of the four controls from the IE Web Controls pack that we use in our applications. It saves an inordinate amount of development time when building applications because, like the `TabStrip` and `MultiPage` controls we discussed in the previous chapter, the `TreeView` control automatically adapts its behavior to suit the client browser in use. All we have to do is declare the control and specify the source of the data that will be displayed within it.

The `TreeView` control expects the source data to be declared as a series of `<treenode>` elements within the source code, or supplied as an XML document or disk file. In Internet Explorer 5.5 and above, the XML or declarative data is sent to the client, along with an XML element that instantiates the `treeview.htc` behavior component on the client. In other browsers, the server-side `TreeView` control generates an HTML table containing images, text, and hyperlinks that provide the same visual appearance.

The Declarative Source Format for a TreeView Control

To declaratively define the nodes for a `TreeView` control, we use syntax such as the following:

```
<ie:treeview runat="server">
  <ie:treenode text="First top-level node">
    <ie:treenode text="First child node" />
    <ie:treenode text="Second child node" />
  </ie:treenode>
  <ie:treenode text="Second top-level node">
    <ie:treenode text="First child node" />
    <ie:treenode text="Second child node" />
  </ie:treenode>
</ie:treeview>
```

The nodes can be nested to any depth, though we have only shown two levels in the example above. The `text` attribute obviously defines the text that will appear for each item in the tree. To react to a user clicking on any node, all we have to do is handle the events that this raises (on the server or on the client).

DataBinding an XML Data Source File to a TreeView Control

When the `TreeView` control is instantiated within an ASP.NET page we can use server-side data binding to an XML document to build the visible output for the client, rather than having to declare it inline as in the previous example. The next listing shows the XML document format that is required (remember that XML is case-sensitive for element and attribute names!). This is one of the XML files we use as the source for our 'Details' page in the **Wrox Car Company** site:

```xml
<?xml version="1.0"?>
<TREENODES>
  <TreeNode Text="Equipment">
    <TreeNode Text="Power Steering" />
    <TreeNode Text="Cruise control" />
    <TreeNode Text="Tinted windows" />
  </TreeNode>
  <TreeNode Text="Mechanical">
    <TreeNode Text="Front wheel drive" />
    <TreeNode Text="Anti-lock brakes" />
  </TreeNode>
  <TreeNode Text="Interior">
    <TreeNode Text="Number of seats: 4" />
    <TreeNode Text="Cup holders: 2" />
    <TreeNode Text="Electric seat adjust" />
  </TreeNode>
  <TreeNode Text="Costs">
    <TreeNode Text="Insurance rate: 9" />
    <TreeNode Text="Cost per mile: $ 0.89" />
    <TreeNode Text="Service 12,000 miles" />
  </TreeNode>
</TREENODES>
```

To perform the server-side databinding, we just have to assign the URL of this document to the `TreeNodeSrc` property of the `TreeView` control and call the `DataBind` method:

```
tvwDetails.TreeNodeSrc = "xmldata/tvdata.xml"
tvwDetails.DataBind()
```

Alternatively, we can assign a `String` that contains valid XML, rather than a `String` that specifies the URL of an XML file on disk or at another location, to the `TreeNodeSrc` property. Another approach is to use XSLT to transform an existing XML document into the correct valid format for the `TreeView` control. The `TreeNodeSrc` property is set to the URL of, or a `String` containing, the XML document as before; and the `TreeNodeXsltSrc` property is set to the URL of, or a `String` containing, an appropriate XSLT stylesheet.

Reacting to TreeView Events

When the user clicks on a text item in the treeview, the `OnSelectedIndexChange` event fires. We can get the index of the node that was clicked by examining the `NewNode` property of the `TreeViewSelectEventArgs` object that is passed to our event handler, and the index of the node that was previously selected from the `OldNode` property.

```
Sub MyTreeView_Select(oSender As Object, oArgs As TreeViewSelectEventArgs)
   intOldNodeIndex = oArgs.OldNode
   intNewNodeIndex = oArgs.NewNode
   ... etc ...
End Sub
```

There are also `OnExpand`, `OnCollapse`, and `OnCheck` events, which are raised when the user expands a closed node, collapses an open node, or clicks on the checkbox for a node (the nodes of a treeview can be displayed as checkboxes). These events all expose a `TreeViewClickEventArgs` object to their event handler:

```
Sub MyTreeView_Event(oSender As Object, oArgs As TreeViewClickEventArgs)
   intNodeIndex = oArgs. Node
   ... etc ...
End Sub
```

To select a node in the treeview, all we have to do is set the `SelectedNodeIndex` property of the `TreeView` control.

> *A full reference to the `TreeView` control, and the other controls in the IE Web Controls pack, can be found using the link that they add to your* **Start** *menu when installed, or directly from:*
> *http://msdn.microsoft.com/library/default.asp?url=/workshop/ ̄*
> *webcontrols/webcontrols_entry.asp*

The HTML for the 'Details' Section

We are using two `TreeView` controls to create the appearance and data content for the 'Details' section of our page. In the next listing of the HTML section of the page source, you can see these two controls. As we use server-side databinding to populate them, there is no declarative content here.

Notice how we specify the style for each node. As we are simply displaying text (rather than using the nodes as hyperlinks), we don't want them to change color when the mouse hovers over them or when they are selected, so we set the `HoverStyle` and `SelectedStyle` style selectors to the same values as the default for all other nodes:

```
<ie:PageView id="mpDetails">
<!-- section for "Details" tab -->
<table border="0" cellpadding="6">
  <tr>
    <td><img src="images/_blnk.gif" width="1" height="170" alt="" /></td>
    <td valign="top">
      <font face="Tahoma,Arial,Helvetica,sans-serif" size="2">
      <p> </p><span style="body-text"><b>Vehicle Details</b><br />
      Select any of the<br />categories shown<br />here to see more<br />
      details:</span></font>
    </td>
    <td>   </td>
    <td valign="top">
      <font face="Tahoma,Arial,Helvetica,sans-serif" size="2">
      <span style="body-text">
      <ie:TreeView id="tvwDetailsLeft" runat="server"
```

```
            OnExpand="NodeExpanded"
            DefaultStyle="font-family:Tahoma,Arial,Helvetica,
                          sans-serif;font-size:11px;"
            HoverStyle="color:#000000;background:#ffffff;"
            SelectedStyle="color:#000000;background:#ffffff;" />
    </span></font></td>
  <td>   </td>
  <td valign="top">
    <font face="Tahoma,Arial,Helvetica,sans-serif" size="2">
    <span style="body-text">
    <ie:TreeView id="tvwDetailsRight" runat="server"
            OnExpand="NodeExpanded"
            DefaultStyle="font-family:Tahoma,Arial,Helvetica,
            sans-serif;font-size:11px;"
            HoverStyle="color:#000000;background:#ffffff;"
            SelectedStyle="color:#000000;background:#ffffff;" />
    </span></font></td>
  </tr>
</table>
</ie:PageView>
```

Another point to note is that we **do not** include the AutoPostBack attribute for the TreeView controls, but we have included the OnExpand attribute. In the code listing coming shortly, you'll see that we set the SelectExpands property of the controls to True, but only if the current browser **is not** Internet Explorer 5.5 and above. This seemingly random pattern of settings actually provides exactly the behavior we want. We'll see why next.

The Behavior of the TreeView Controls in the 'Model Details' Page

If you've experimented with the example site, you'll have seen that the treeview controls behave in such a way that, in browsers *other than* Internet Explorer 5.5 and above, you can open a top-level node by clicking either on the 'box' next to that node or on the text of the node itself. The nodes are not hyperlinks, so there can be no confusion about whether this action will navigate to another page or just open the node to display its child nodes. However, in Internet Explorer 5.5 and above you have to click the 'box' next to the node – clicking the node text has no effect in this case.

Secondly, you can only open one of the top-level nodes at a time. Opening a top-level node automatically closes any other top-level node that may be open in that control. We do this to prevent the height of the 'tabbed dialog' section changing – as it would do if more than one top-level node was open at the same time.

To achieve the 'automatic opening' of a top-level node, we just have to set the SelectExpands attribute or property of the TreeView control to True. The control looks after generating all the appropriate code automatically. To achieve the 'automatic collapse' of other top-level nodes, we have to react to the OnExpand event and use some code to collapse all the other top-level nodes.

Unfortunately, this combination of settings causes errors in Internet Explorer 5.5 and above, where the output is being created by the treeview.htc control on the client. We discovered that we could work around the problem by only allowing a click on a node to expand that node (SelectExpands) for browsers other than IE 5.5 and above. This is why the behavior is different for the different browsers.

In fact it turns out not to be a major problem because, in IE 5.5 and above, the text nodes are not underlined, so they do not look like hyperlinks. In other browsers that do underline the text nodes, such as Navigator 4 and 6, Mozilla and Opera, clicking the text node does cause it to expand.

Finally, to prevent Internet Explorer from submitting the page when a node is clicked, we have to omit the `AutoPostBack` attribute (as you saw in the code above). We don't want to handle this event, so there is no reason to post back in this case. Of course, for other browsers, we do need a click on a node to cause a postback – because this is the only way that the appearance of the 'tree' can be updated. But this happens automatically for these types of browser anyway (each node is a hyperlink that submits the page), even when `AutoPostBack` is `False`.

So, in summary, we need to:

❑ Handle the `OnExpand` event for all browsers to collapse any other open top-level nodes. In IE 5.5 and above we do this client-side using some JavaScript code that interacts with the client-side `treeview.htc` component. For all other browsers, we handle the event server-side and interact with the ASP.NET `TreeView` control. So we add the attribute `OnExpand="NodeExpanded"` to the declaration of the control, as you saw in the code above. However, in IE 5.5 and above, we modify this value later in our run-time code so that it raises the event client-side.

❑ Set the `SelectExpands` property of the `TreeView` controls to `True`, but only for browsers other than Internet Explorer 5.5 and above.

You'll see how we achieve all this, and the server-side and client-side event handlers we use, later in this section of the chapter.

Populating the 'Details' Section

So, let's see how we populate the `TreeView` controls in our example. We are using static XML disk files to fill the controls, but there is no reason why the data could not be extracted dynamically from a database instead. We could load it into a `DataSet` and export it as XML, or load it directly from the database into an `XmlDataDocument` and extract it that way.

We have ten XML files located in the `xmldata` subfolder of our application, two for each of the car models we offer. One file contains the **Equipment**, **Mechanical**, **Interior**, and **Costs** top-level headings and child nodes for the left-hand `TreeView` control, and the other contains the **Safety**, **Security**, **Dimensions**, and **Capacities** top-level headings and child nodes for the right-hand `TreeView` control.

You saw an example of these files earlier in this section of the chapter. The names of these XML files indicate which control they are aimed at, and the model that they apply to. For example, the file for the left-hand control for the vehicle with ID value 4 is named `tvdata-left-4.xml`.

Before we can bind the XML data to our `TreeView` controls, however, we have to sort out the issue of assigning the correct attributes to them. The first stage in this part of the `ShowCarDetails` routine is to figure out if we are talking to IE 5.5 and above. We can do this by looking at the property values exposed by the `Request.Browser` object:

ShowCarDetails subroutine (continued)

```
...
If (Request.Browser.Browser = "IE") _
And (Request.Browser.Version >= "5.5") Then
  ...
```

At this point we know that we are dealing with IE 5.5 or above, and so we can add the client-side event handler attributes to the `TreeView` controls. Setting the `OnExpand` property (directly in code, or through the `OnExpand` attribute as we've done in our page) specifies how the ASP.NET server-side `TreeView` control behaves when the `OnExpand` event occurs.

However, we can add an `onexpand` attribute to the client-side element that is created by the `TreeView` control, without affecting the server-side behavior, by referencing the `Attributes` collection of the control directly. We set the attribute value so that the `TreeView` control will execute a client-side event handler named `nodeExpanded`, and pass to it a reference to the client-side `TreeView` component:

```
...
' set up client-side event handlers for the onexpand event by
' adding attributes directly to tree-view control outputs
tvwDetailsLeft.Attributes.Add("onexpand", "nodeExpanded(this)")
tvwDetailsRight.Attributes.Add("onexpand", "nodeExpanded(this)")
...
```

However, if the current browser is not IE 5.5 and above, we set the `SelectExpands` property (as we discussed earlier):

```
...
Else  ' not IE 5.5 or above

  ' specify that we want the entries to auto-expand when clicked
  ' (setting these caused some versions of IE to misbehave)
  tvwDetailsLeft.SelectExpands = True
  tvwDetailsRight.SelectExpands = True

End If
...
```

The final steps required are to assign the appropriate XML files to the two controls, depending on which vehicle model we are displaying, and then call the `DataBind` method for each control. Notice that we do all this inside a `Try...Catch` construct so that we can trap an error if the XML file does not exist or cannot be loaded:

```
...
' specify XML source files for two Details treeview controls
' and call DataBind - works just like ASP.NET list controls
Try
  tvwDetailsLeft.TreeNodeSrc = "xmldata/tvdata-left-" & sCarID & ".xml"
  tvwDetailsLeft.DataBind()
  tvwDetailsRight.TreeNodeSrc = "xmldata/tvdata-right-" & sCarID & ".xml"
  tvwDetailsRight.DataBind()
Catch
```

387

```
        lblMessage.Text = "Error loading XML source for tree-view controls."
    End Try
...
```

Reacting to Events in the 'Details' Section

The only remaining task is to handle the events that are raised when the user expands a top-level node in either list. Both `TreeView` controls call the same event handler, but this may be the client-side version or the server-side version – depending on which browser is hosting the page. For browsers other than IE 5.5 and above, this server-side event will be executed by ASP.NET:

```
Sub NodeExpanded(oSender As Object, oArgs As TreeViewClickEventArgs)

    ' iterate through all the top-level child nodes of the control
    Dim oTopNode As TreeNode
    For Each oTopNode In oSender.Nodes

        ' if it is not the node that was just expanded, collapse it
        If Not oTopNode Is oSender.GetNodeFromIndex(oArgs.Node) Then
            oTopNode.Expanded = False
        End If

    Next

End Sub
```

As this event handler is used by both the `TreeView` controls, we need to be able to detect which one the event relates to. This is easy to do, as the first parameter to the event handler (`oSender`) is a reference to the control that raised the event. In the code you can see that we simply iterate through all the top-level nodes of the `TreeView` control, as exposed through the `Nodes` collection of the control.

For each node, we check if this is the one that was clicked. The only really non-familiar aspect of programming the `TreeView` control is that the `TreeViewClickEventArgs.Node` property returns the index of the node, and not (as you may expect) a reference to a `Node` object. This is probably because the control is running client-side, and references cannot be passed back to the server.

However, a reference to any `Node` object can be obtained using the `GetNodeFromIndex` method of the `TreeView` control. So we can compare each top-level `Node` object in the `TreeView.Nodes` collection with the `Node` object that caused the event to occur, and set the `Expanded` property to `False`, for all the nodes that did not cause this event, to collapse them.

The Client-Side nodeExpanded Event Handler

The previous server-side event handler takes care of collapsing the nodes in browsers other than IE 5.5 and above. However, in IE 5.5 and above we have specified that an `OnExpand` event should execute our client-side event handler named `nodeExpanded`. The client-side attribute that is added to the `TreeView` controls is:

```
onexpand="nodeExpanded(this)"
```

You'll recall from the end of the previous chapter, and earlier in this chapter, that we use the `RegisterClientScriptBlock` method to insert three client-side functions into our page. The `nodeExpanded` event handler is one of these functions:

```
function nodeExpanded(oSender) {
  var clickedNode = oSender.clickedNodeIndex;
  var colNodes = oSender.getChildren();
  for (var i = 0; i < colNodes.length; i++)
    if (colNodes[i].getNodeIndex() != clickedNode)
      colNodes[i].setAttribute('expanded', false);
  }
}
```

We are now working client-side directly with the `treeview.htc` control so, as you can see, the methods and properties that are available are different. However, it should be clear from this code that we are doing just the same thing as we did in our server-side event handler.

After collecting the index within the collection of top-level nodes of the node that was clicked, we can get a collection of these top-level nodes using the `getChildren` method of the `TreeView` control itself. Then we iterate through this collection setting the `expanded` attribute of each node except the current one to `false`.

Remember that the data to populate the `TreeView` controls on the client, in IE 5.5 and above, is sent to the client as an XML document. As you may have noticed, if you are familiar with coding against the XML DOM, the techniques we use client-side to interact with the control are effectively the same as those we would use to interact directly with the equivalent XML document.

The Finance Package Selection Section

The final 'tab' on our 'Model Details' page allows the visitor to select a finance package, and see the payment terms for the vehicle they are currently configuring:

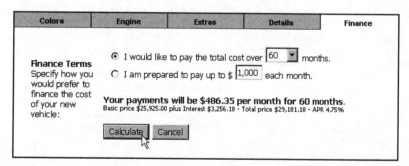

The HTML that creates this 'tab' section is shown in the next listing. There seems to be a lot of it, but most is layout and formatting information. The important parts are the two `RadioButton` controls for selecting the payment type, the `DropDownList` and `TextBox` to specify either the number of months or the maximum monthly payment, and the two `Button` controls to Calculate or Cancel the finance package:

```
<ie:PageView id="mpFinance">
<!-- section for "Finance" tab -->
<table border="0" cellpadding="6">
  <tr>
    <td><img src="images/_blnk.gif" width="1" height="170" alt="" /></td>
    <td valign="top">
      <font face="Tahoma,Arial,Helvetica,sans-serif" size="2">
      <p> </p><span style="body-text"><b>Finance Terms </b><br />
      Specify how you<br />would prefer to<br />finance the cost<br />
      of your new<br />vehicle:</span></font>
    </td>
    <td><font face="Tahoma,Arial,Helvetica,sans-serif" size="2">
      <span style="body-text">  
      <asp:RadioButton id="optByMonths" GroupName="optFinanceMethod"
          Checked="True" Text="" CssClass="body-text" runat="server"
          ToolTip="Select payment over a specified number of months" />
      I would like to pay the total cost over
      <asp:DropDownList id="lstFinanceMonths" CssClass="body-text"
          OnChange="setOptionButtons('optByMonths')" runat="server" />
      months.<br />  
      <asp:RadioButton id="optByAmount" GroupName="optFinanceMethod"
          Text="" CssClass="body-text" runat="server"
          ToolTip="Select payment of a specified monthly amount" />
      I am prepared to pay up to $
      <asp:TextBox id="txtMonthPayment" Text="1,000" Columns="4"
          MaxLength="7" CssClass="body-text" runat="server"
          OnKeyDown="setOptionButtons('optByAmount')"
          ToolTip="Enter the monthly payment amount" />
      each month.<p />
      <asp:Label id="lblFinanceResult" CssClass="body-text"
          runat="server" />
      <br /></span></font>
      <font face="Tahoma,Arial,Helvetica,sans-serif" size="1">
      <asp:Label id="lblFinanceInfo" CssClass="small-text" runat="server"
          Text="Select payment options you prefer and click Calculate" />
      <p /></font>
      <font face="Tahoma,Arial,Helvetica,sans-serif" size="2">
      <span style="body-text">
      <asp:Button id="btnCalculate" Text="Calculate"
          OnClick="ShowFinanceTerms" CssClass="body-text"
          ToolTip="Calculate the options selected above" runat="server" />
      <asp:Button id="btnCancel" Text="Cancel" Enabled="False"
          OnClick="ClearFinanceTerms" CssClass="body-text"
          ToolTip="Cancel existing finance package" runat="server" />
      </span></font>
    </td>
  </tr>
</table>
</ie:PageView>
```

Enabling and Disabling Buttons and Other Controls

You can see that the final control on this page, the Cancel button named btnCancel, is disabled by default when the page first loads. This is because there is no finance package specified, and it makes it obvious to the user that this is the case. We'll enable it once the user specifies the finance terms they want, so that they can change their mind later if required.

When you take advantage of this technique in your pages, just bear in mind that many older browsers do not recognize the disabled attribute (which is how ASP.NET disables buttons and other HTML controls). So you should never rely on a control being disabled. For example, your code should always be able to cope with a button being clicked, and the subsequent server-side event handler being executed, even when you have disabled that button.

Populating the 'Finance' Section

As our ShowCarDetails routine runs when the 'Model Details' page first loads, all we have to do is populate the drop-down list of months. This is done using server-side databinding, as with most of the other list controls on the page. We already have a reference oDTFinance to the DataTable in our DataSet that contains the PMT payment information we need to populate the control. We specify that the list should display the number of months, and use the payment information as the value of each item in the list:

ShowCarDetails subroutine (continued)

```
    . . .
    ' fill the DropDownList with months for 'Finance' page
    lstFinanceMonths.DataSource = oDTFinance
    lstFinanceMonths.DataTextField = "Months"
    lstFinanceMonths.DataValueField = "Payment"
    lstFinanceMonths.DataBind()

    ' select the "36 months" entry as the default
    lstFinanceMonths.SelectedIndex = 5

  End Sub
```

The only other task, at the end of the code above, is to select the entry for 36 months, which we feel to be the most appropriate default value, in the list. This entry is the sixth one (at index 5) and we select it by setting the SelectedIndex property of the DropDownList control.

Reacting to Events in the Finance Section

You may have noticed in the HTML listing for this section of the page that none of the controls carry the AutoPostBack attribute, as we only want to post the page for processing when one of the buttons is clicked. These buttons are rendered as <input type="submit"> controls, and so they will always initiate a postback when clicked.

The events we specify for these controls are defined in the OnClick attributes. The Click events will be raised server-side because these are ASP.NET Button controls:

```
<asp:Button id="btnCalculate" Text="Calculate"
            OnClick="ShowFinanceTerms" CssClass="body-text"
            ToolTip="Calculate the options selected above" runat="server" />
<asp:Button id="btnCancel" Text="Cancel" Enabled="False"
            OnClick="ClearFinanceTerms" CssClass="body-text"
            ToolTip="Cancel existing finance package" runat="server" />
```

We'll be looking at the ShowFinanceTerms and ClearFinanceTerms event handlers in the next chapter, when we see how we calculate the price of a vehicle and the finance terms for it.

Reacting to Client-Side Events in the 'Finance' Section

Although we don't want a postback to occur for any of the controls in this section of the page, other than the **Calculate** and **Cancel** buttons, we do want to execute some *client-side* code when two events occur. To provide a more intuitive and usable interface, we want the option buttons that select the finance package type to automatically reflect the user's actions when they interact with the drop-down list or the text box on the page.

In other words, selecting a number of months in the drop-down list should automatically select the first option, whereas typing into the text box should automatically select the second option. We achieve this by using some simple client-side code in the page. The DropDownList control named lstFinanceMonths has this attribute added to it in the declaration we saw earlier:

```
OnChange="setOptionButtons('optByMonths')
```

And the TextBox named txtMonthPayment has this attribute:

```
OnKeyDown="setOptionButtons('optByAmount')
```

So selecting a different value in the drop-down list, or typing in the text box, will execute the client-side setOptionButtons function. This is the third of the functions you saw being inserted into the page earlier on with the RegisterClientScriptBlock method:

```
function setOptionButtons(sName) {
  document.forms[0].elements[sName].checked = true;
}
```

All this function does is take the name of the control that is passed to it as a parameter, and set the checked property of that control. So the appropriate option button will be selected depending on whether the event is raised by the drop-down list or the text box.

Summary

With our look at the five 'tabbed dialog' sections, and the several distractions we've encountered and side streets we've traveled on the way, we have completed almost all of our investigations into the design, construction, and interactivity of the 'Model Details' page.

In the previous chapter we looked at the page in outline and discussed how easy it is to build this kind of page when we take advantage of the ASP.NET features like viewstate support and the postback architecture. In this chapter, we've looked at the data we use to drive the page, the way we extract it, and the way we use it to populate the controls on the page. We also looked in detail at most of the event handling code – both server-side and client side – that makes the page interactive.

Along the way we've examined the design of the database tables, the stored procedures that extract the data, and the function that builds this data into a DataSet that is cached in the user's session. We also diverted to look at using the global.asax file to run code when an application starts or when an error occurs.

Then, while exploring the five 'tabs' on our page where most of the interactivity is centered, we discussed the TreeView control from the IE Web Control pack, and saw how we can often react to events both server-side and client-side depending on the browser type and capabilities.

In all, the topics we covered were:

❑ The data that drives the 'Model Details' page

❑ How we extract this data for use in the page

❑ How we present the data to visitors in five distinct sections of the page

❑ How we react to events that occur for the controls in these sections

In the next chapter, we'll finally be able to complete our look at the 'Model Details' page by seeing how we calculate prices and finance terms, and how we save quotations for use later.

10

Car Prices and Quotations

The previous chapter looked in detail at the data we use to drive the 'Model Details' page, and the code we use to populate the controls on the page. We also saw how the viewstate automatically preserves the 'state' or settings of all the controls, so that we only need to populate the controls once and then write simple handlers to react to events that are raised as our visitors interact with the page.

The aim of this chapter is to complete our study of the 'Model Details' page. We'll look at how we calculate the price of the vehicle, the finance terms, and then how we save all this information as a quotation. We also need to see how the page designed for non-script-enabled client browsers works, and how different it is to the one we've been building for script-enabled clients.

So, the topics we'll be looking at are:

❑   How we calculate the price of a vehicle as the user configures it

❑   How we calculate the finance terms for a vehicle

❑   How we save the configuration as a quotation

❑   How the non-script-enabled version of the page works

We start with a look at how we calculate the current cost of a vehicle, including all the extras, as the user configures it.

Calculating the Price of the Vehicle

In the two previous chapters, you've seen how the 'Model Details' page in our Wrox Car Company sample web site allows visitors to configure the vehicles by selecting the color, engine type and optional extras they require. As they do so, the current 'all inclusive' price is displayed in the page. And if they specify a finance package, the payment terms and other details are displayed:

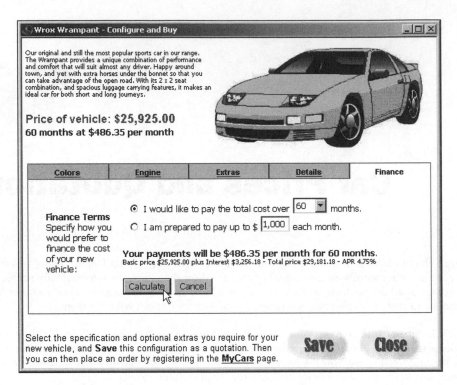

In this first section of the chapter, we'll look at how we calculate and display the price of the vehicle in its current configuration, and then later on we'll look at the code that calculates and displays the finance terms.

All the work of calculating the price of the vehicle takes place in one routine in our page, named `CalculateCarPrice`. As you saw in the previous chapter, it is executed as soon as the page is loaded to show the price of the standard (default) configuration. It is also executed by any event handlers that affect the price as the user makes their selections in the page, such as specifying a color from a different range (standard or metallic), choosing an engine, or adding optional extras.

The CalculateCarPrice Routine

The `CalculateCarPrice` routine is listed next, broken down into the stages that we discuss separately to make it easier to follow. We start by declaring a single variable to hold the running total as we perform our calculations:

cardetail.aspx

```
Sub CalculateCarPrice()
' routine to update price displayed in window when any options are changed

   Dim fPrice As Decimal = 0
   ...
```

Clearing Any Existing Finance Terms

Before we start calculating the price, we remove any existing finance terms from our stored array. We do this because the new price is most likely to be different from the existing price after our calculation is complete, and so any existing finance terms will be incorrect. In previous chapters, we discussed whether we should just recalculate the finance terms as well, but the issue we came across is that the new price may be greater than is valid for the user's currently selected finance package. If they have specified a maximum monthly payment, it might not be enough to cover the combined purchase price and interest within the maximum period we allow for loan repayments (120 months).

We have a separate routine that we can use to clear any existing finance terms (you'll see this in detail later in this chapter), and we can just call this directly. However, the routine is actually an event handler – it is executed in response to the user clicking the **Cancel** button in the 'Finance' section of the page. So we must provide the two parameters for the 'sender' and 'event arguments' that all ASP.NET event handlers expect to receive. As the `ClearFinanceTerms` event handler doesn't actually use the parameters, we can safely specify `Nothing` for these (or `null` if we were writing the code in C#):

```
...
' clear any existing finance terms from array and page
ClearFinanceTerms(Nothing, Nothing)

' hide Save button for quotations
btnSave.Visible = False
...
```

We also hide the **Save** button at the bottom of the page, which is implemented as an `<input type="image">` control, while we perform the calculation. If there is no error, we can show it again before we return from this routine. However, it does mean that, if an error should occur and we exit from this routine prematurely (in other words, we can't create a valid quotation) the **Save** button will not be available.

Notice that we choose to hide this button rather than attempt to 'disable' it. As we discussed in the previous chapter, not all browsers can disable controls – so you may decide it is better to hide them (remove them from the page) instead.

Getting the Price for the Current Car/Engine Combination

Now we are ready to start calculating the price of our vehicle. Within a `Try...Catch` construct, which will catch any data access error, we create a filter string that will select the appropriate row from the `CarDetails` table in our `DataSet`. We have to specify the car ID and the engine ID values, as the table contains a row for each car/engine combination available for this model.

Then we get a reference to the `CarDetails` table, which (as we saw in the previous chapter) is generated from joining the `tblCar`, `tblCarEngines`, and `tblEngine` tables. We apply the filter using the `Select` method, which returns an array of `DataRow` objects, and then extract the price from the `CarEnginePrice` column of the first `DataRow` in the array. This row is, of course, the single matching row within the table:

```
...
Try
```

```
' create suitable filter to get appropriate row from tblCarEngines
Dim sFilter As String = "CarID = " & sCarID & " AND EngineID = " _
                        & optEngine.SelectedItem.Value

' get reference to table in DataSet and select matching row
Dim oDTCar As DataTable = oCarsDS.Tables("CarDetails")
Dim aRows As DataRow() =  oDTCar.Select(sFilter, "")

' extract price for this car/engine combination
fPrice = aRows(0)("CarEnginePrice")
...
```

DataTable.Select Versus DataView.RowFilter

As an aside, it's worth pointing out the two different ways that the code in our 'Model Details' page has 'filtered' rows in a table to select a subset. In the previous chapter, when we were populating the controls in the ShowCarDetails routine, we had cases to deal with where we had to select a subset of the rows in a table before binding the data to a list control.

An example is when displaying the available color for a vehicle, where we have to filter the data depending on whether we are displaying colors from the standard or the metallic range. In that example, we created a DataView based on the table, and then filtered the rows that are available by setting the RowFilter property:

```
Dim oDTView As DataView = oDTColor.DefaultView
oDTView.RowFilter = "IsMetallic = " & optColorType.SelectedIndex
dlsColors.DataSource = oDTView
dlsColors.DataBind()
oDTView.RowFilter = ""
```

We remarked that we needed to remove the filter afterwards so other routines that accessed the table would be able to see all the rows. This is because a DataView is just what the name implies – an alternative view of (or series of references to) the data in the original table. Effectively, the row filter is applied to the table as well.

However, in this chapter we've used a different approach to get a subset of rows from a table, without creating a DataView at all. The Select method of the DataTable object returns an array of references to the rows in the table that match a given criteria, but without applying any kind of filter to the table. It also allows us to sort the rows that are returned into a different order. For example:

```
Dim oDTCar As DataTable = oCarsDS.Tables("CarDetails")
Dim sFilter As String = "CarID = " & sCarID
Dim sSort As String = "CarEnginePrice DESC"
Dim aRows As DataRow() =  oDTCar.Select(sFilter, sSort)
```

The Select method approach is handy when we want to select several sets of rows at a time, or when we only want to access the data using code. However, we can't bind the ASP.NET list controls to an array of DataRows (such as is returned from the Select method), so the use of a DataView and a RowFilter is the appropriate technique when using server-side databinding.

Adding the Extra Cost for a Metallic Color

Next, we must check to see if the user has selected a metallic color, as there is a price premium for these colors. The actual premium value is stored within the `<appSettings>` section of the `web.config` file, located in the root folder of the application (or, in our case, the root folder where you installed the samples):

web.config

```
<configuration>
  <appSettings>
    ...
    <!-- change following to adjust premium price for metallic paint -->
    <add key="WroxCarsMetallicPaint" value="375.00" />
    ...
  </appSettings>
</configuration>
```

The `web.config` file (introduced with ASP.NET) is a great way to store values that you need to access within an application. It's easy to edit them at a later date, and this action automatically causes ASP.NET to restart the application. All the pages will then use the new value. As you saw in previous chapters, we use this technique to store our database connection string, as well as several other 'global' values that are required in our application.

Back in the code of the 'Model Details' page, we first have to find out which color the user has selected before we can tell if it is a metallic color or not. You saw in the previous chapter that the selected color is used to set the `BgColor` property of the table cell that displays the image of the car, in the top right of the page. In the HTML declaration of this cell we include the attribute `bgcolor="White"` (all our cars are available in white) as the default.

The table cell is defined as a server control (it has an ID of `tclColor` and includes the `runat="server"` attribute), so the background color setting is automatically maintained across postbacks by ASP.NET through the viewstate. So we can extract the color name directly in our server-side code by accessing this element's `BgColor` property. We use it to create a filter that will select this row from the `CarColors` table in our `DataSet`, and then call the `Select` method to return only this matching row:

cardetail.aspx

```
...
' create suitable filter to get appropriate row from tblColors
' using color name set in background of car image cell
sFilter = "Color = '" & tclColor.BgColor & "'"

' get reference to table in DataSet and select matching row
Dim oDTColors As DataTable = oCarsDS.Tables("CarColors")
aRows = oDTColors.Select(sFilter, "")
...
```

The `CarColors` table is created by a stored procedure (which we examined in the previous chapter) that joins the `tblCar`, `tblCarColors`, and `tblColor` tables. As well as including the color ID and price, the stored procedure also extracts the SQL Server `bit` column named `IsMetallic` from the `tblColor` table. So we can check the value of this column in the selected row to see if this is a metallic color. A SQL Server `bit` column value is treated as being `True` (value 1) or `False` (value 0), so we can use the following code to perform our test:

```
...
' if it is a metallic color, add on the premium for this
If aRows(0)("IsMetallic") Then
  Try
    fPrice += Decimal.Parse(ConfigurationSettings.AppSettings _
                                  ("WroxCarsMetallicPaint"))
  Catch
    lblMessage.Text = "Error in metallic paint premium in web.config"
    lblPrice.Text = "* Error *"
    Exit Sub
  End Try
End If
...
```

If the column does contain 1 (True) we extract the price premium from the web.config file and parse it into a Decimal, then add it to the variable named fPrice that contains the running total for this vehicle. We do all this inside a Try...Catch construct to trap any error that might arise if the web.config entry is missing or not in the correct format. If there is an error, we display the message in our 'message' Label control at the bottom of the page, display the text *Error* in the price Label control at the top of the page, and exit from the routine.

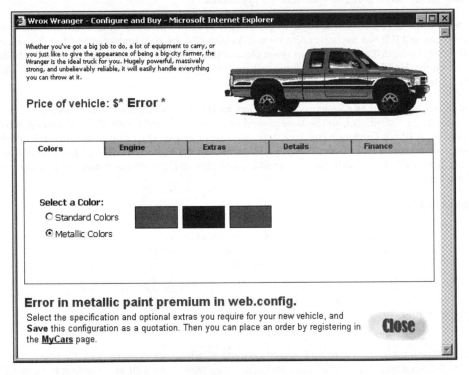

Of course, in a real-world application, you'll probably want to use a less developer-centric error message for these kinds of errors!

Adding the Cost of Optional Extras

If the user has selected any optional extras for the vehicle, we need to add these onto the price. Our `DataSet` contains a table named `CarExtras` that is created by the stored procedure we examined in the previous chapter, and this table is used to populate the list of optional extras. The stored procedure joins the `tblCar`, `tblCarExtras`, and `tblOptionExtra` tables, exposing the ID, name, and price of all the optional extras that are available for the current vehicle.

You'll recall that this stored procedure also generates a column named `DisplayText`, which contains a combination of the name and price for these optional extras. We use this column to populate the captions for the checkboxes where the user selects the options they require:

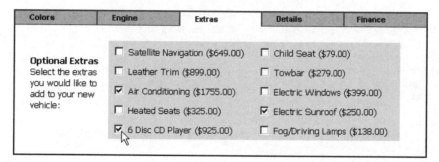

So the next step is to see which of these checkboxes were 'ticked'. The checkboxes are created by an ASP.NET `CheckBoxList` control, which means that we can use a `For...Each` construct to iterate through the `Items` collection and test each one to see if the `Selected` property is `True`:

```
    ...
    ' get reference to tblOptionExtra in DataSet
    Dim oDTExtras As DataTable = oCarsDS.Tables("CarExtras")

    ' iterate through the list of Extras to see which are selected
    Dim oItem As ListItem
    For Each oItem In chkExtras.Items
      If oItem.Selected Then
        ...
```

If the `Selected` property of a checkbox is `True`, we need to get the price for this optional extra from the `CarExtras` table in our `DataSet`, and add it to our running total variable `fPrice`. The only problem here is that, although we set the `DataValueField` property of the `CheckBoxList` control to the column that contains the ID of the optional extras when we populated the control, there is no `value` property available for the individual checkboxes (in other words for the `ListItem` controls that make up the list).

Instead, to create a suitable filter for our table, we either have to parse the name of the optional extra out of the caption text (the `DisplayText` column value) and use this to filter on the `ExtraText` column, or use the entire caption text to filter on the `DisplayText` column. This second alternative seems to be the most obvious approach, and is the one we've taken.

So, we create the filter we need and get a reference to the row that matches this filter. The price is extracted from the `ExtraPrice` column in the matching row, and added to the running total. Then we can go round and see if any other checkboxes are selected:

```
      . . .
              ' although we specified the ExtraID column as the DataValueField property
              ' of the CheckBoxList control, it does not render any value attributes.
              ' So instead we have to look up the selected items in the original DataSet
              ' using the DisplayText value from the caption of each button and then
              ' extract the Price column value - alternatively we could parse it out of
              ' the Text property (the caption) of the selected item

              ' create suitable filter to get appropriate row from tblOptionExtra
              sFilter = "DisplayText = '" & oItem.Text & "'"
              aRows = oDTExtras.Select(sFilter, "")
              fPrice += aRows(0)("ExtraPrice")


          End If
        Next

      Catch
        lblMessage.Text = "Sorry, the database cannot be accessed."
        lblPrice.Text = "* Error *"
        Exit Sub
      End Try
      . . .
```

At the end of the code above, you can see the `Catch` section of our `Try...Catch` construct. We just display suitable messages in the price `Label` control at the top of the page and in the 'message' `Label` control at the bottom of the page.

Storing the Total Price in the Prices Array

The final task in our `CalculateCarPrice` routine is to store the price we've just calculated in the array of prices and finance terms that we cache in the user's session. This means that, when the user places an order, we don't have to recalculate it again – we can just use the values that were calculated the last time that the user changed any of their configuration selections.

The array we use can contain up to six values. This is the page-level declaration of the array in the code of our page:

```
' page-level array to hold current car price and finance terms
' (0) = Basic Price including extras and color option
' (1) = Annual interest rate applicable to purchase
' (2) = Interest amount included in Total Price
' (3) = Total Price including interest for finance plan (if selected)
' (4) = Number of months for finance plan (if selected)
' (5) = Monthly payment amount for finance plan (if selected)
Dim aCurrentPrice(5) As String
```

Our `Page_Load` event handler extracts this array from the user's session into the `aCurrentPrice` variable each time the page is posted back to our server, so we can set or update the current price in the array by converting it to a `String` using the `ToString` method. As we do so, we format it so that it can be displayed directly in the 'My Cars' page you'll see in Chapter 12:

```
...
' store total price including extras in array
aCurrentPrice(0) = fPrice.ToString("#,##0.00")
...
```

We also need to store this array back in the user's session ready for the next postback. The session key is already stored in another page-level variable, named `sPricesSessionKey`. Then the last two tasks to complete the routine are to display the price we just calculated in the `Label` control at the top of the page, and show the **Save** button so that the user can save this configuration as a quotation if they wish:

```
...
' update Session with new array values
Session(sPricesSessionKey) = aCurrentPrice

' display price in page
lblPrice.Text = fPrice.ToString("#,##0.00")

' show Save button
btnSave.Visible = True

End Sub
```

Calculating the Finance Terms

The 'Finance' 'tab' on our 'Model Details' page allows users to specify how they want to pay for their vehicle. There are two options – they can specify the number of months over which they want to spread the cost of the vehicle, by selecting a value between 6 and 120 from the drop-down list, or they can type in the maximum monthly payment that they want to make:

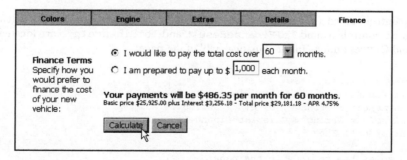

Clicking **Calculate** then works out the total interest, the monthly payment required, and the total price. This is displayed, together with the interest rate that was used in the calculation, within the 'Finance' 'tab'. It is also displayed (not shown here) just below the price of the vehicle near the top of the page. You can see this in the screenshot at the start of this chapter.

Clicking the Cancel button simply removes the selected finance package and clears the Label controls that display the payment terms. The Calculate button is disabled (in browsers that support this feature) when there is no finance package currently selected.

Calculating the finance terms involves three routines:

❑   The ShowFinanceTerms routine is responsible for displaying the results of the calculation, and manipulating the buttons on the page.

❑   The CalculateFinanceTerms function does the actual mathematical part of the task. It is called from the ShowFinanceTerms routine.

❑   The GetNumberPayments function, given a maximum monthly payment value, returns the number of months over which that payment will be required. It is called from the CalculateFinanceTerms function.

We'll look at each of these routines next, in the order they are listed above.

The ShowFinanceTerms Routine

The first step in calculating the payment terms for the selected finance package is to clear any existing values from the last calculation, using the ClearFinanceTerms routine in the same way as we did when calculating the price of the vehicle earlier in this chapter:

```
Sub ShowFinanceTerms(oSender As Object, oArgs As EventArgs)
' routine to display finance terms for "Calculate" button

   ' clear any existing finance terms from array and page
   ClearFinanceTerms(Nothing, Nothing)
   ...
```

Then we can call the separate CalculateFinanceTerms function in our page to calculate the payment terms. This function fills in the values in our prices array, and returns an empty String as the result if everything succeeds without any errors. If this is the case, we can build up three text strings from the values in this array and display them in our page.

The Label control named lblTerms is located just below the car price, near the top left of the page. The two Label controls named lblFinanceResult and lblFinanceInfo are located just above the Calculate and Cancel buttons in the 'Finance' 'tab' of the page:

```
   ...
   ' call function to calculate finance terms values
   ' returns error message, or empty string if all OK
   Dim sError As String = CalculateFinanceTerms()
   If sError = "" Then

      ' display the results in the page
      lblTerms.Text = aCurrentPrice(4) & " months  at $" _
         & aCurrentPrice(5) & " per month"
      lblFinanceResult.Text = "<b>Your payments will be $" _
         & aCurrentPrice(5).ToString() & " per month for " _
```

```
              & aCurrentPrice(4).ToString() & " months</b>."
    lblFinanceInfo.Text = "Basic price $" & aCurrentPrice(0) _
        & " plus Interest $" & aCurrentPrice(2) & " - Total price $" _
        & aCurrentPrice(3) & " - APR " & aCurrentPrice(1) & "%"
    ...
```

We also enable the Cancel button so that the user can remove this finance package selection if they wish, and we make sure that the Save button is visible:

```
    ...
    ' enable the button to cancel these terms
    btnCancel.Enabled = True

    ' show Save button
    btnSave.Visible = True
    ...
```

*If the previous calculation of the car price (as opposed to this calculation of the finance terms) had failed, the CalculateFinanceTerms function will also fail when it tries to parse and use the value for the vehicle price that is stored in the array (it will return the string '*Error*' in this case), and so the Save button will not be visible.*

Handling an Error in the Calculation

If the CalculateFinanceTerms function encounters an error, the String value it returns (which we stored in the variable named sError at the start of this ShowFinanceTerms routine) will be the error message. So, in this case, our code simply removes any existing values for the finance terms from the Label controls on the page and hides the Save button. Notice that we place a non-breaking space into the Label at the top of the page, which prevents any shift in the layout of the table that contains the vehicle price and the finance terms:

```
    ...
  Else

    ' display the error details in the page
    lblTerms.Text = " "
    lblFinanceResult.Text = "<b>" & sError & "</b>"
    lblFinanceInfo.Text = ""

    ' hide Save button
    btnSave.Visible = False

  End If

End Sub
```

The CalculateFinanceTerms Function

Having seen how the ShowFinanceTerms routine listed above handles the display of the finance terms, we'll look now at the CalculateFinanceTerms function that actually does the real work of calculating the payments required for the selected finance package.

We start by declaring a few variables that we'll need, and then collect the interest rate from web.config. We saw how it is stored there when we looked at filling the tblFinancePMTData table in the previous chapter. If the interest rate cannot be extracted and parsed into a Decimal, we simply exit from the function and return an appropriate error message:

```
Function CalculateFinanceTerms() As String
' function to calculate payment terms from current user selections

   Dim fInterestRate As Single
   Dim fBasePrice, fTotalInterest, fMonthlyPayment As Decimal
   Dim fTotalPrice, fPaymentPer1000 As Decimal
   Dim iMonths As Integer

   ' get interest rate from web.config file
   Try
      fInterestRate = _
      Decimal.Parse(ConfigurationSettings.AppSettings("WroxCarsInterestRate"))
   Catch
      Return "Interest Rate Error in web.config file"
   End Try
   ...
```

Now we can get the total price for the vehicle configuration the user specified from the first row of the prices array, where we stored it when we calculated and displayed this price. Again, any error attempting to retrieve it and parse it into a Decimal results in an error message being returned to the ShowFinanceTerms routine:

```
   ...
   ' get basic price including extras from prices array
   Try
      fBasePrice = Decimal.Parse(aCurrentPrice(0))
   Catch
      Return "Basic Price Error in Session Array"
   End Try
   ...
```

Processing the 'Maximum Monthly Payment' Finance Package

The next step is to see which type of finance package we are calculating. If the option button named optByAmount is checked, we are calculating the terms where the user has specified the maximum amount they wish to pay per month. So the first step in this case is to collect the value they entered into the text box control named txtMonthPayment. We attempt to parse it into a Decimal, and any error is reported back to the ShowFinanceTerms routine:

```
   ...
   ' see which payment option is selected
   If optByAmount.Checked Then    ' paying a specified amount each month

      Try

         ' get monthly payment from text box as a Decimal number
         fMonthlyPayment = Decimal.Parse(txtMonthPayment.Text)
```

```
Catch
  Return "The value for the monthly payment is not a valid number."
End Try
...
```

Provided that the value the user entered is a valid number we can now call another function named `GetNumberPayments`, located elsewhere in this page, to get the number of months required to pay off the specified total at the current interest rate. The first parameter is the price of the vehicle, and the second is a variable that we declared at the top of this function. The `GetNumberPayments` function updates this value (we pass it ByRef, as you'll see when we come to look at this function), and it also updates all the finance terms in the prices array:

```
...
' calculate the number of payments required and other values
' parameter fMonthlyPayment is ByRef and will be updated within
' the function to show actual payment required
iMonths = GetNumberPayments(fBasePrice, fMonthlyPayment)
...
```

The return value of the `GetNumberPayments` function is the number of months required, or zero if an error occurs during the calculation. So we can check if there was a problem by examining this returned value, and display a suitable message. We actually check that the result is not more than 120 as well, because we want to limit the number of payment months to this maximum value:

```
...
' see if the resulting term is acceptable
If (iMonths = 0) Or (iMonths > 120) Then
  Return "The monthly payment specified is not sufficient " _
       & "to repay the loan."
End If
...
```

In fact, in our example, the `GetNumberPayments` function cannot return any value greater than 120 because the `tblFinancePMTData` table does not contain any rows with 'number of months' values above this. It will always return zero if the maximum payment specified is less than the minimum value in the table rows. However, if the table did contain more rows, this check would be required.

Processing the 'Number of Months' Finance Package

We've seen how we calculate the number of months for a loan given a minimum monthly payment (although we still have to look at the `GetNumberPayments` function that the previous section of our code uses). If the option button named `optByAmount` is *not* checked, however, we have to perform the opposite calculation. We need to work out how much the monthly payments will be given the number of months over which the loan should extend.

In this case, the first step is to get the number of months selected by the user, and the equivalent payment amount per $1000, from the drop-down list named `lstFinanceMonths`. We get the number of months (as displayed by the list) by parsing the `Text` property of the `ListItem` object that is returned as the `SelectedItem` of the list control. The 'payment per $1000' figure comes from the `Value` property of the same `ListItem` object. This is because, when we populated the list, we declared the `DataTextField` and `DataValueField` properties as the `Months` and `Payment` columns of the `tblFinancePMTData` table.

As you've seen before, we use a `Try...Catch` construct to trap any number parsing errors, though the fact that we extract the values from a pre-populated drop-down list suggests that they will only ever contain valid numbers, and this might be seen as overkill:

```
...
Else  ' paying over a specified number of months

   Try

      ' get values from drop-down list
      iMonths = Int32.Parse(lstFinanceMonths.SelectedItem.Text)
      fPaymentPer1000 = Decimal.Parse(lstFinanceMonths.SelectedItem.Value)

      ' calculate payment for this vehicle price
      fMonthlyPayment = fPaymentPer1000 * fBasePrice / 1000

   Catch
      Return "The value for the number of months is not a valid number."
   End Try

End If
...
```

In the code above, you can see how easily we can use the 'payment per $1000' figure and the price of the vehicle to calculate the actual monthly payment amount for this vehicle. However, if there is an error, we just exit from this function and return a suitable error message.

Calculating the Interest and Filling the Prices Array

Now that we know the monthly payment required, whichever finance package is selected, we can calculate the other values that make up the complete finance package. The total price is just the number of payments multiplied by the number of months, and the interest part of the loan is the total price minus the actual price of the vehicle including any extras that were specified:

```
...
' calculate total price
fTotalPrice = fMonthlyPayment * iMonths
fTotalInterest = fTotalPrice - fBasePrice
...
```

The final steps are to update the prices array with the values we've just calculated, and the interest rate we extracted from `web.config` earlier in this routine. Then we save the array back into the user's ASP.NET session, and return an empty `String` to indicate that the process succeeded:

```
...
' fill in the finance terms section of the array of values
aCurrentPrice(1) = fInterestRate.ToString()
aCurrentPrice(2) = fTotalInterest.ToString("#,##0.00")
aCurrentPrice(3) = fTotalPrice.ToString("#,##0.00")
aCurrentPrice(4) = iMonths.ToString()
aCurrentPrice(5) = fMonthlyPayment.ToString("#,##0.00")
```

```
    ' update Session with new array values
    Session(sPricesSessionKey) = aCurrentPrice

    Return ""   ' empty string indicates all worked OK

End Function
```

The GetNumberPayments Function

The third and final routine that is used when calculating the finance terms is the `GetNumberPayments` function. This function accepts the price of the vehicle as the first parameter, and a `Decimal` variable as the second parameter. This parameter is declared as `ByRef` (by reference), so the function will receive a reference to the actual variable as declared in the calling routine rather than a copy of the value. This means that it can access and change the original value, and the calling routine will see this updated value:

```
Function GetNumberPayments(fBasePrice As Decimal, _
                          ByRef fMonthlyPayment As Decimal) As Integer
   ' get number of payments required given desired monthly payment
   ' by searching through PMT values in DataSet table
   ' Note that fMonthlyPayment parameter is ByRef and the value will
   ' be updated within function to actual payment required
   ...
```

We start the process of finding the number of months required by declaring a variable that will hold the 'payment per $1000' that is equivalent to the values in the `tblFinancePMTData` table column named `Payment`. Remember that the values in this column are what would be required to pay off a loan of $1000.00, and so we have to convert these values into 'real' payments that take into account the value of the car.

We get the value for `fPaymentPer1000` by multiplying the maximum monthly payment that the user specified by 1000, and then dividing that by the value of the vehicle they want to buy. Doing it this way means that we don't have to convert every value we extract from the `tblFinancePMTData` table into a 'real' payment – we just compare it to our `fPaymentPer1000` variable instead:

```
   ...
   Dim fPaymentPer1000 As Decimal

   ' calculate the maximum payment per 1000 acceptable to client
   fPaymentPer1000 = fMonthlyPayment * 1000 / fBasePrice
   ...
```

Finding the Matching Table Row

To find the nearest payment that is less than the maximum specified by the user, we could iterate through the `ListItem` controls in the drop-down list. After all, it contains all the values from the `tblFinancePMTData` table. However, it's faster and more efficient to search in the copy of this table (named `FinancePMTRates`) that we've already got cached in our `DataSet`. We can use a filter to select the rows, and then read the values directly.

So, the next step in our function is to create this filter, specifying that the value of the Payment column payment should be less than or equal to the value of our fPaymentPer1000 variable. We also specify that the results should be sorted in descending order by payment value, which means that the first row in the array of rows returned after applying the filter will be the highest value that is less than the maximum specified by the user:

```
...
' create suitable filter and sort criteria to get array of rows
' where first contains highest acceptable payment per 1000
Dim sFilter As String = "Payment <= " & fPaymentPer1000
Dim sSort As String = "Payment DESC"
...
```

We now apply this filter to the FinancePMTRates table in our DataSet and get back the array of matching rows. The required 'payment per $1000' is the value of the Payment column in the first row, and we just have to convert it into a 'real' payment for the vehicle by multiplying by the cost of the vehicle and dividing by 1000:

```
...
Try

    ' get reference to table in DataSet and select matching rows
    Dim oDTFinance As DataTable = oCarsDS.Tables("FinancePMTRates")
    Dim aRows As DataRow() = oDTFinance.Select(sFilter, sSort)

    ' calculate payment for this vehicle price using actual
    ' payment required from second column of data row
    fMonthlyPayment = aRows(0)("Payment") * fBasePrice / 1000
    ...
```

Now that we know what the actual payment will be, we can extract the number of monthly payments that will be required to fully cover the loan from the same row. We return this value as the result of the function, but remember that we've also set the value of the fMonthlyPayment parameter of this function (in the code above), so this will be available to the calling routine as well:

```
    ...
    ' extract number of months from first column of row
    Return aRows(0)("Months")

Catch

    ' return zero if cannot calculate the result
    ' will occur if payment is too low (no data rows selected)
    Return 0

End Try

End Function
```

At the end of the code above, you can see that we catch any error and return zero as the result of the function. This is most likely to be because no row was found with a low enough payment to match the one specified by the user. In other words, the payment they specified is not enough to cover the loan over the maximum term for which we have rows in the `FinancePMTRates` table.

The ClearFinanceTerms Routine

The previous sections of this chapter have covered all the code that we use to calculate the finance terms for our 'Model Details' page. There is just one other routine connected with the 'Finance' 'tab' on our page – the `ClearFinanceTerms` event handler. This routine is executed when the **Cancel** button in the 'Finance' 'tab' is clicked, and it just has to remove any existing finance terms.

This is easy enough to do. We just clear all the rows in the prices array except the first one (at index zero), as it contains the last calculated price for the vehicle. Then we can save the array in the user's session, clear the `Labels` on the page that show the finance terms, and disable the **Cancel** button. Notice that we use the `Label` above the **Calculate** and **Cancel** buttons to display brief instructions – it prevents the page from looking too 'empty':

```
' routine to clear any current finance terms for 'Cancel' button
Sub ClearFinanceTerms(oSender As Object, oArgs As EventArgs)

    ' clear the finance terms section of the array of values
    aCurrentPrice(1) = ""
    aCurrentPrice(2) = ""
    aCurrentPrice(3) = ""
    aCurrentPrice(4) = ""
    aCurrentPrice(5) = ""

    ' update Session with new array values
    Session(sPricesSessionKey) = aCurrentPrice

    ' clear any current finance terms text from page
    lblTerms.Text = " "
    lblFinanceResult.Text = "Select the payment options you prefer " _
                    & "and click <b>Calculate</b>."
    lblFinanceInfo.Text = ""

    ' disable the 'Cancel' button
    btnCancel.Enabled = False

End Sub
```

Remember that we suggested you write all your event handlers in such a way that they can still safely be executed if a button or other control that is supposed to be disabled causes a postback. Our `ClearFinanceTerms` *routine meets this criterion.*

Saving the Configuration as a Quotation

And so we come to the final section of code in the 'Model Details' page. As you will see when you experiment with this page, our visitors can save their current configuration of any vehicle, including the selected color, engine type, optional extras, and finance terms as a quotation. These details are stored in a pair of tables in our database, and can be viewed in the 'My Cars' page that we'll be looking at in Chapter 12. Any of these quotations can be converted into an order at any time, in the same page.

So, we'll now look at how we save the configuration to the database as a quotation. We start with a reminder of the database tables that are involved in the process.

The Saved Quotes and Orders Tables

Our database contains two tables that we use to store a quotation or an order for any of our vehicles. The parent table, tblQuoteOrder, contains all the relevant details of the vehicle itself. This includes the ID and name of the model, the engine and the color selected by the user, plus the price and any finance terms that were specified.

The related child table named tblQuoteOrderExtras contains details of any optional extras that were added to the vehicle. As there could be zero or more of these, we use a child table that has a one-to-many relationship with the parent table:

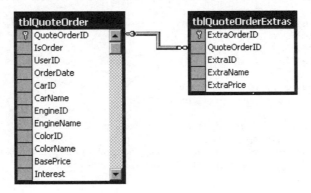

The relationship between the parent and child rows is through the primary key of the tblQuoteOrder table, the column named QuoteOrderID, and the matching foreign key column in the tblQuoteOrderExtras table. The UserID column in the tblQuoteOrder table identifies which user saved this quotation.

You'll notice that the tables are not fully normalized, in that there is 'redundant' information stored in them. For example, we store the names of the vehicle, engine, color, and optional extras, as well as their ID values. In theory we can always look up the names in the other tables of our database given the ID values, for example we can find the vehicle name from the tblCar table given the car ID.

However, we chose the less normalized approach for a couple of reasons:

❑ If the rows or column values in the original tables change, for example a car is no longer available and is removed, or the name is changed, we would not be able to find a match. OK, so good database management suggests that we should never remove rows like this, and instead flag them as 'unavailable' or 'not current' to allow the joins to still work, but our approach makes sure that we have the original value available at any point in the future.

❑ It makes it a lot easier and is more efficient when displaying the data, as you'll see in the 'My Cars' page we look at in a later chapter. We don't have to create multiple table joins to get the names of the car, engine, color, or optional extras.

Updating the Data within a Transaction

The design of the two tables we've just looked at means that, to save a quotation, all we have to do is add the appropriate rows to these tables. We add one row per quotation to the tblQuoteOrder table, and zero or more related rows to the tblQuoteOrderExtras table depending on which (if any) optional extras are specified by the user.

As we may have to update two tables to achieve the desired result (and there may be more than one update to the tblQuoteOrderExtras table if the user specifies more than one optional extra), we should consider using a **transaction** to make sure that the process either completes or fails as a single operation. In other words, either all the updates succeed, or they all fail.

If only some of the updates succeed, we leave the tables in an undefined state where the content is invalid. For example, if we insert a row in the parent table, but one or more updates to the child table fail, we have not saved the quotation accurately.

Using a transaction means that we can either commit all the updates in one go, once we are certain that they all succeeded, or roll them all back if any one stage of the process fails so that we leave the tables in the original state.

There are three basic types of transaction that we can use:

❑ **Database Server Transactions** are usually stored procedures that themselves contain the transaction statements. We pass in as parameters all the data required to perform all the updates on all the tables, and the stored procedure manages the entire process. It contains statements that execute the BEGIN TRANSACTION command before the updates are applied, and then either COMMIT TRANSACTION or ROLLBACK TRANSACTION after the updates have been applied – depending on whether they were all successful or not.

❑ **Distributed Transactions** are usually managed by external software or services (such as the Windows Transaction Service) that manages transactions across different databases, which can be located on separate servers. These servers may even be geographically remote from each other.

❑ **Connection-based Transactions** are managed by the data access software that applies the updates, rather than by the database or a separate service. This is the type of transaction we're using in our example. ADO.NET provides great support for these types of transactions.

The big advantage with using connection-based transactions is that we don't have to pass in all the values for all the updates in one go. In our example, we don't know beforehand how many 'optional extra' rows we'll need to insert into the tblQuoteOrderExtras table, and so it would be hard to write a stored procedure that accepted the appropriate number of values.

By using a connection-based transaction, we can execute different stored procedures, and execute them as many times as required, within the transaction. Then, once we know the outcome of all the updates, we can decide whether to commit all of them, or roll them all back. And as soon as one update fails, we can abandon the process and roll back all the previous updates.

Saving a Quotation

To see how our 'Model Details' page saves a quotation, we'll look at the SaveCarDetails routine next. This is called when the user clicks the **Save** button in the page, and it does all the work of saving the quotation to the database and displaying status messages to the user.

The plan is to first collect all the information required for the parent tblQuoteOrder table, and then insert this row. However, the QuoteOrderID primary key column in this table is of type IDENTITY (sometimes called an AutoNumber column), and so the value will be created automatically by the database when a new row is inserted. We can't specify a value for this column.

However, we need to insert the value that the database generates for the QuoteOrderID column into each row we add to the tblQuoteOrderExtras child table. This is required to create the relationship between the new quotation and any child 'optional extra' rows for that quotation.

So, the stored procedure we use to insert the parent row in the tblQuoteOrder table must return the value of the QuoteOrderID column. After checking that the new row was successfully inserted, we can use this value in the rows we add to the tblQuoteOrderExtras child table.

The only other point is that there are two other columns in the tblQuoteOrder table that we do not insert values for. Within the database table definition, the IsOrder column has a default value of zero specified. When we insert a new quotation, this default value indicates that this row is a quotation and not an order. The column named OrderDate also has a default value, in this case created by the function GETDATE(). So the new row will automatically have the current date and time inserted into the OrderDate column – we don't have to set it ourselves.

The Stored Procedures for the SaveCarDetails Routine

To add a new row to the tblQuoteOrder table, we use the stored procedure named InsertNewQuote. This is shown next, and you can see that it expects us to provide as parameters values for all twelve columns for which default values are not specified:

```
CREATE PROCEDURE InsertNewQuote
@UserID varchar(20), @CarID int, @CarName varchar(50),
@EngineID int, @EngineName varchar(10), @ColorID int,
@ColorName varchar(50), @BasePrice money, @Interest money,
@TotalPrice money, @PaymentMonths money, @PaymentAmount money,
@QuoteOrderID int OUTPUT
AS
INSERT INTO tblQuoteOrder(UserID, CarID, CarName, EngineID,
    EngineName, ColorID, ColorName, BasePrice, Interest,
    TotalPrice, PaymentMonths, PaymentAmount)
VALUES (@UserID, @CarID, @CarName, @EngineID,
    @EngineName, @ColorID, @ColorName, @BasePrice, @Interest,
    @TotalPrice, @PaymentMonths, @PaymentAmount)
SELECT @QuoteOrderID = @@IDENTITY
```

Notice also that the stored procedure declares an OUTPUT parameter named @QuoteOrderID. The last line of the procedure selects the value of the IDENTITY column named QuoteOrderID for the most recently inserted row in the current (connection) session. This is the value we need to create the links between this new row and any rows we insert into the tblQuoteOrderExtras child table.

The process of inserting optional extra rows into the tblQuoteOrderExtras table is much simpler. The primary key in this table is also an IDENTITY column (named ExtraOrderID), and so we don't need to insert a value for this column. Therefore the InsertNewQuoteExtraLine stored procedure takes only four parameters, and inserts a new row using these values. The first parameter is the QuoteOrderID value we returned from the previous stored procedure:

```
CREATE PROCEDURE InsertNewQuoteExtraLine
@QuoteOrderID int, @ExtraID int, @ExtraName varchar(50), @ExtraPrice money
AS
INSERT INTO tblQuoteOrderExtras(QuoteOrderID, ExtraID,
   ExtraName, ExtraPrice)
VALUES (@QuoteOrderID, @ExtraID, @ExtraName, @ExtraPrice)
```

The SaveCarDetails Routine

The SaveCarDetails routine starts by collecting the values we need to insert a row into the parent table. To make it easier to see what's going on, we save all the values in local variables before we attempt to call our stored procedures. Many of the values we need are stored in page-level variables, or in the prices array we save in the user's session, and so much of the process is just converting these to the correct data type. For example, the CarID column in the database is of type int (a 32-bit Integer value), whereas our sCarID variable contains a String:

```
Sub SaveCarDetails(oSender As Object, oArgs As ImageClickEventArgs)
' routine to save current configuration of vehicle in database

   ' collect the values we'll need for the tblQuoteOrder table
   Dim sAnonUserID As String = CType(Session("WccUserID"), String)
   Dim iCarID As Integer = Int32.Parse(sCarID)
   ...
```

We have a reference to the DataSet containing the tables we used to populate the controls on the page in the ShowCarDetails routine available in our page-level variable named oCarsDS, so we can also get some of the values we need from this. For example, the name of the current vehicle comes from the first row of the CarDetails table in this DataSet:

```
   ...
   Dim sCarName As String = oCarsDS.Tables("CarDetails").Rows(0)("Model")
   ...
```

Fetching the Price and Finance Values

The price and payment information we need for our stored procedure parameters can be extracted from the `aCurrentPrice` array in the user's session, where we store this data as they configure a vehicle. The 'base price' is the total price of the vehicle including the user's choice of color, engine and optional extras. We get this from the first row of the array, where it was saved by the `CalculateCarPrice` routine we looked at earlier. We also assign this value to the `dTotalPrice` variable, which will be used to set the `@TotalPrice` parameter to our stored procedure. If there is no finance package selected, the total price is the same as the base price:

```
...
Dim dBasePrice As Decimal = Decimal.Parse(aCurrentPrice(0))
Dim dTotalPrice As Decimal = dBasePrice
...
```

Now we can check to see if the user specified a finance package. We look at the third row in our prices array (at index 2) for a value. This is where the total amount of interest will be stored if the user has selected either of the two finance packages. If this value is not empty (remember that it's a `String` array), we can extract the values from the array for the total interest amount, the total price including the interest, the number of monthly payments required, and the monthly payment amount:

```
...
Dim dInterest, dPaymentAmount As Decimal
Dim iPaymentMonths As Integer
If aCurrentPrice(2) <> "" Then
   dInterest = Decimal.Parse(aCurrentPrice(2))
   dTotalPrice = Decimal.Parse(aCurrentPrice(3))
   iPaymentMonths = Int32.Parse(aCurrentPrice(4))
   dPaymentAmount = Decimal.Parse(aCurrentPrice(5))
End If
...
```

The row at index 1 of the array contains the interest rate at the time of the calculation, and we don't store this with our quotations. We don't need it because we already have all the calculated results we need. However, if required, an extra column could be added to the table and this value stored as well.

Fetching the Engine and Color Details

The next step is to collect the engine details. The ASP.NET viewstate automatically maintains the values of all the controls in the page as the user interacts with them, and all we need to do to get the values for the engine ID and name is query the `RadioButtonList` that specifies the engine type. The `SelectedItem` property of that control returns a reference to the currently selected `ListItem` object in the list, and we can extract the values of the `Text` and `Value` properties from this:

```
...
Dim iEngineID As Integer = optEngine.SelectedItem.Value
Dim sEngineName As String = optEngine.SelectedItem.Text
...
```

Getting the color details is just a little more difficult. We get the color name from the `BgColor` property of the table cell that holds the image of the vehicle, and use this to create a filter that we can use in the `Select` method against the `CarColors` table. The color ID is then extracted from the single row that is returned:

```
...
' extract color from DataSet as in CalculateCarPrice routine
Dim sColorName As String = tclColor.BgColor
Dim sFilter As String = "Color = '" & sColorName & "'"
Dim aRows As DataRow() = oCarsDS.Tables("CarColors").Select(sFilter, "")
Dim iColorID As Integer = aRows(0)("ColorID")
...
```

Preparing to Execute the Stored Procedures

Now we have all the values we need to insert the new quotation row, we specify the names of the stored procedures we'll be using and create the `Connection` and `Command` objects we'll need to execute these stored procedures. This is just like we've done in many earlier pages and routines:

```
...
' specify the stored procedure names
Dim sSaveQuote As String = "InsertNewQuote"
Dim sSaveExtraLine As String = "InsertNewQuoteExtraLine"

' create connection and command objects
Dim sConnect As String = _
            ConfigurationSettings.AppSettings("WroxCarsConnectString")
Dim sqlConn As New SqlConnection(sConnect)
Dim sqlComm As New SqlCommand(sSaveQuote, sqlConn)
sqlComm.CommandType = CommandType.StoredProcedure
...
```

Starting a Transaction

Before we go any further, we have to set up the transaction that will make sure we get a valid result across the two tables after inserting the new quotation and any related optional extra rows. We declare a variable to hold a `SqlTransaction` object (there are `OleDb` and `Odbc` versions of this object available as well if you are not using SQL Server). Then we start a `Try...Catch` construct:

```
...
' declare a variable to hold a Transaction object
Dim oTransaction As SqlTransaction

Try
    ...
```

We can only start a new transaction against an open connection, so we open our database connection next and then call the `BeginTransaction` method to start the transaction. A reference to the transaction is returned, which we save in our `oTransaction` variable:

```
...
' open connection and start a transaction
sqlConn.Open()
oTransaction = sqlConn.BeginTransaction()
...
```

Although we now have a transaction available for the connection, it will not be used by default. We have to specify which Command objects will use it, by assigning it to their Transaction property. This approach allows us to have more than one transaction in place for a connection if required (we can also nest transactions). So we can assign each Command to the appropriate transaction. However, in our code we only need one transaction, and we assign this to our Command object next:

```
...
' attach transaction to Command object
sqlComm.Transaction = oTransaction
...
```

Adding the InsertNewQuote Stored Procedure Parameters

Now we can add the parameters we need for our first stored procedure to the Command object's Parameters collection, using the values we collected earlier in this routine. Notice how we specify that @QuoteOrderID is an OUTPUT parameter:

```
...
' add parameters to Command
sqlComm.Parameters.Add("@UserID", sAnonUserID)
sqlComm.Parameters.Add("@CarID", iCarID)
sqlComm.Parameters.Add("@CarName", sCarName)
sqlComm.Parameters.Add("@EngineID", iEngineID)
sqlComm.Parameters.Add("@EngineName", sEngineName)
sqlComm.Parameters.Add("@ColorID", iColorID)
sqlComm.Parameters.Add("@ColorName", sColorName)
sqlComm.Parameters.Add("@BasePrice", dBasePrice)
sqlComm.Parameters.Add("@Interest", dInterest)
sqlComm.Parameters.Add("@TotalPrice", dTotalPrice)
sqlComm.Parameters.Add("@PaymentMonths", iPaymentMonths)
sqlComm.Parameters.Add("@PaymentAmount", dPaymentAmount)
sqlComm.Parameters.Add("@QuoteOrderID", 0)
sqlComm.Parameters("@QuoteOrderID").Direction _
                                = ParameterDirection.Output
...
```

Executing the InsertNewQuote Stored Procedure

We can now execute the InsertNewQuote stored procedure to add the new quotation row to our tblQuoteOrder table. The ExecuteNonQuery method will return 1 if the insert succeeds, and if not we create a new Exception object and Throw it. This causes execution to pass to the Catch part of our Try...Catch construct, with the string we provide when we create the Exception as the error message:

```
...
' execute the stored procedure
If sqlComm.ExecuteNonQuery() <> 1 Then
  ' throw an Exception to display error message
  Throw New Exception("* Could not insert new Quote into database.")
End If
...
```

However, if the stored procedure did succeed in adding the new row, the OUTPUT parameter named @QuoteOrderID will contain the row key value from the QuoteOrderID column of the row we just inserted. We save this in a variable named iQuoteID:

```
...
' get value of new quote ID from parameters
Dim iQuoteID As Integer = sqlComm.Parameters("@QuoteOrderID").Value
...
```

Adding the InsertNewQuoteExtraLine Stored Procedure Parameters

Now we're ready to add the rows to the tblQuoteOrderExtras child table, using the stored procedure named InsertNewQuoteExtraLine. We change the CommandText property of our command to this stored procedure name, clear the Parameters collection of the existing parameters we used for the InsertNewQuote stored procedure, and add the four parameters we have to provide to the InsertNewQuoteExtraLine stored procedure.

The first parameter is the value of the primary key column named QuoteOrderID in the parent tblQuoteOrder table for the new quotation row we just inserted. However, we set the other three parameters to 'dummy' values here. The reason is that we want to be able to just change the values of the parameters as we iterate through the list of optional extras for this quotation, rather than adding and removing them each time:

```
...
' change stored procedure name for updating Extras table
sqlComm.CommandText = sSaveExtraLine

' clear parameters collection and add parameters for Extras table
sqlComm.Parameters.Clear()
sqlComm.Parameters.Add("@QuoteOrderID", iQuoteID)
sqlComm.Parameters.Add("@ExtraID", 0)
sqlComm.Parameters.Add("@ExtraName", "")
sqlComm.Parameters.Add("@ExtraPrice", 0)

' get reference to tblOptionExtra in DataSet
Dim oDTExtras As DataTable = oCarsDS.Tables("CarExtras")
...
```

The final line of the code above gets a reference to the 'optional extras' table named CarExtras in our cached DataSet, as we'll need this to get information about each optional extra when we insert the rows into the tblQuoteOrderExtras table.

Iterating Through the Selected Optional Extras

Now we can see which optional extras the user specified for their vehicle. We iterate through the collection of `ListItem` objects for the `CheckBoxList` control named `chkExtras` that implements the list of optional extras in our page. For any of these that are selected, we must execute the `InsertNewQuoteExtraLine` stored procedure to add a row to the `tblQuoteOrderExtras` table.

So, inside the `For Each...Next` construct we create a filter that will select the matching row from the `CarExtras` table in our `DataSet`. Then, using the `Select` method with this filter string, we can extract the values for this optional extra from the row and use them to set the values of the parameters for our stored procedure:

```
...
' iterate through the Extras selected in the page and
' see if each one is selected in turn
Dim oItem As ListItem
For Each oItem In chkExtras.Items
  If oItem.Selected Then

    ' get a reference to the matching row in the DataSet
    sFilter = "DisplayText = '" & oItem.Text & "'"
    aRows = oDTExtras.Select(sFilter, "")

    ' set value of last three parameters
    sqlComm.Parameters("@ExtraID").Value = aRows(0)("ExtraID")
    sqlComm.Parameters("@ExtraName").Value = aRows(0)("ExtraText")
    sqlComm.Parameters("@ExtraPrice").Value = aRows(0)("ExtraPrice")
    ...
```

Next, we execute the stored procedure, and check the return value just as we did when we were inserting the new quotation row. If there is an error, the return value will not be 1, and we create an `Exception` and `Throw` it to abort the process:

```
    ...
    ' execute the stored procedure
    If sqlComm.ExecuteNonQuery() <> 1 Then
      ' throw an Exception to display error message
      Throw New Exception("* Could not insert new Optional " _
                    & "Extra row into database.")
    End If

  End If
Next
...
```

Committing or Rolling Back the Transaction

If all the updates completed without an error, we can commit them by calling the `Commit` method of the `Transaction` object we attached to our connection. However, an `Exception` will already have been raised if any of them failed. In this case, we call the `Rollback` method of the `Transaction` object to undo all the database updates, and display the error message from the `Exception`:

```
...
' no errors, so commit all the updates
oTransaction.Commit()

Catch objError As Exception

'error encountered so roll back all the updates
oTransaction.Rollback()

'display error details
lblMessage.Text = "* Error while inserting Quote. " _
                    & objError.Message
Exit Sub  ' and stop execution

Finally

sqlConn.Close()

End Try
...
```

And, of course, we have to close the database connection after we've finished. We do this in the `Finally` section of our `Try...Catch` construct – as you can see in the code listed above. And, in case you are concerned that the connection doesn't get closed when an error occurs, you'll be pleased to know that the code in the `Finally` block runs even when we exit from the routine using the `Exit Sub` statement.

Displaying the Result

Now we can display a message to the user indicating that the quotation was saved, and how they can view it. Notice that the message we display contains a JavaScript URL that calls the client-side `mainWindowPage` function. As you saw in Chapter 8, this function can be used to close the 'Model Details' window and show a specific page in the main window of our site – in this case the 'My Cars' page:

```
...
' display "OK" message and link to "My Cars" page
Dim sQUOT As String = Chr(34)
lblMessage.Text = "Your quotation has been saved.<br />" _
                  & "Go to the <a href=" & sQUOT _
                  & "javascript:mainWindowPage('secure/mycars.aspx', true)" _
                  & sQUOT & "><font color=" & sQUOT & "#b50055" & sQUOT _
                  & ">My Cars</font></a> page to view it and place an order."

' hide the Save button
btnSave.Visible = False

End Sub
```

The final step (in the code above) is to hide the **Save** button, helping to indicate that the quotation was saved and preventing our user from saving the same quotation twice. Of course, if they change the configuration, the price will be re-calculated and the **Save** button will reappear. So they can save multiple quotations for the same vehicle if required.

Your quotation has been saved.
Go to the My Cars page to view it and place an order.

Select the specification and optional extras you require for your new vehicle, and
Save this configuration as a quotation. Then you can place an order by registering in
the **MyCars** page.

Close

And with this, we've completed our study of the script-enabled version of the 'Model Details' page. The only remaining task in this chapter is to look at how we provide a version of this page that works in browsers and other user-agents that do not support client-side scripting.

The No-Script Version of the Page

As we've discussed at various points throughout the previous two chapters, the `cardetail.aspx` page relies on client-side script support for several of its functions:

❑ The `TabStrip` control can't be used without client-side script support, as this is required for the postback hyperlinks to operate.

❑ While the `MultiPage` control will still work (in that it will generate the appropriate output for the section of the page below the 'tabs'), the automatic interaction with the `TabStrip` control does not operate. So we have no obvious way to specify which section of output to create. The user would have to force a reload of the whole page using a submit button each time they wanted to view a different section.

❑ We can't depend on `AutoPostBack` to work for any controls, so the page will not be submitted automatically when the user makes a selection in a `RadioButtonList` or `CheckBoxList` control in the **Colors**, **Engine**, and **Extras** sections of the page.

❑ The `TreeView` control in the 'Details' section of the page will not work, as it also requires client-side script support for the postback hyperlinks to operate.

❑ The client-side `setOptionButtons` function we use to select the appropriate option button in the 'Finance' page when the user selects from the drop-down list containing the number of months, or types their maximum monthly payment amount in the text box, will not work.

❑ We can't use code to change the page that is displayed in the main window of the site (the client-side `mainWindowPage` function), so we can't automatically redirect users to `default.aspx` if their session has expired, or to the 'My Cars' page after saving a quotation.

❑ The **Close** button will not work, as it uses script to execute the client-side `window.close` method.

However, all the other features of the page do work, including selecting a color and a finance package, as these use submit buttons (the color blocks, you'll recall, are `<input type="image">` controls, which effectively are submit buttons).

Avoiding the TabStrip and MultiPage Controls

The list of things that do not work without client-side script seems formidable, but in fact it's not hard to solve all of these problems, or at least 'make do' and still provide a usable interactive page. We can't do much about the `TreeView` and `MultiPage` controls, and so (as you saw in Chapter 8), we decided to show all of the interactive sections of the page in one go. The following screenshot shows the top section of the `cardetail-noscript.aspx` page, and the one after it shows the bottom half of the same page:

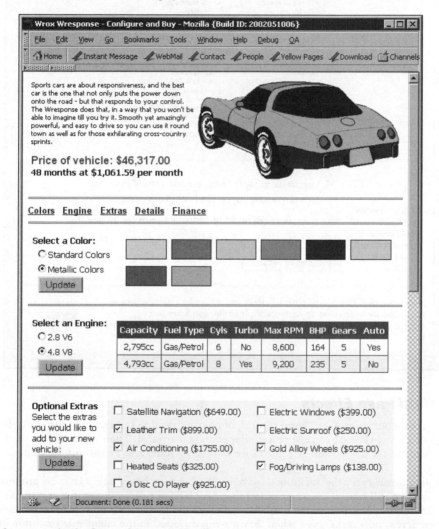

In this case, we're displaying the page in Mozilla, and we simply used the Edit | Preferences dialog to turn off client-side JavaScript before opening our site. We also tested the page in a completely non-script browser (Amaya from W3C at http://www.w3.org). Despite a few layout problems and the different appearance for the controls, it provides a very similar output to the screenshots shown here.

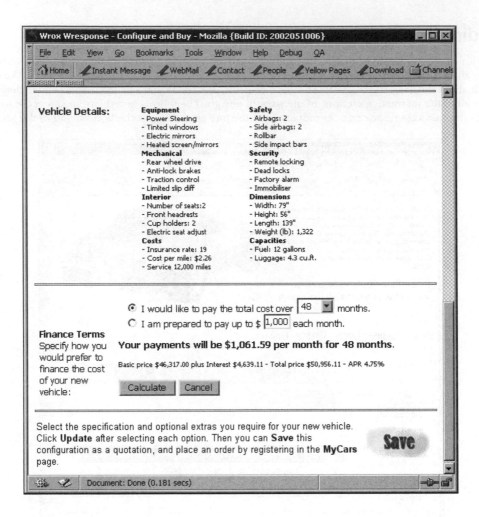

Custom Multi-Page Effects

We could create our own `MultiPage` control, of course, possible by wrapping the controls for each 'tab' page in an `asp:Panel` control or a similar container control. Then we would set the `Visible` property to `True` for the section of controls we want to include, and `False` for the others.

Even when controls carry the attribute `Visible="False"` (or have their `Visible` property set to `False`), they are still part of the `Page` object that ASP.NET is processing on the server. It's just that they are not rendered as part of the output to the client. So the viewstate for hidden controls is still maintained across postbacks, even when they are not included in the client-side rendition of the page.

Another approach would be to build an HTML table (perhaps using `asp:Table` elements like we did on our `color-list.aspx` page), putting each set of controls into a separate row. Then we could show and hide the appropriate rows by setting their `Visible` property in our server-side code.

Our Solution – Use Hyperlinks and Horizontal Rules

In our example no-script page, as you've seen, we abandon the concept of a 'tabbed dialog' effect and display all of the configuration sections in the page every time. We replaced the `TabStrip` control with a series of hyperlinks that target anchor elements within the page. So clicking the <u>Colors</u> link simply scrolls the page to the 'Colors' section, clicking the <u>Engine</u> link scrolls the page to the 'Engines' section, and so on:

`cardetail-noscript.aspx`

```
<hr size="1" />
<a href="#Colors"><font face="Arial,Helvetica,sans-serif"
   size="2" color="#000000"><b>Colors</b></font></a>  
<a href="#Engine"><font face="Arial,Helvetica,sans-serif"
   size="2" color="#000000"><b>Engine</b></font></a>  
<a href="#Extras"><font face="Arial,Helvetica,sans-serif"
   size="2" color="#000000"><b>Extras</b></font></a>  
<a href="#Details"><font face="Arial,Helvetica,sans-serif"
   size="2" color="#000000"><b>Details</b></font></a>  
<a href="#Finance"><font face="Arial,Helvetica,sans-serif"
   size="2" color="#000000"><b>Finance</b></font></a>
<hr size="1" />
...
```

Then, to separate each section, we placed horizontal rules in the page where previously the `PageView` elements ended and the next `PageView` element started. You can also see the anchors for the 'page section' hyperlinks here:

```
...
<!-- section for "Colors" tab -->
<a href="Colors" />
... content of Colors "tab" here ...
<hr size="1" />

<!-- section for "Engines" tab -->
<a href="Engine" />
... content of Engine "tab" here ...
<hr size="1" />
... etc ...
```

Working Around the Lack of AutoPostBack

Without client-side script support, we can't depend on `AutoPostBack` to automatically submit the page to our server as the user interacts with the controls. Instead, we insert a normal `<input type="submit">` button within each section of the page, with the caption **Update** and a suitable pop-up tool-tip created by the `title` attribute:

```
<input id="btnUpdate1" type="submit" runat="server"
       value="Update" OnServerClick="NoScriptUpdate"
       title="Calculate and Update the price and other details" />
```

The `OnServerClick` attribute points to a server-side event handler named `NoScriptUpdate` that we've added to the page:

```
Sub NoScriptUpdate(oSender As Object, oArgs As EventArgs)
   CalculateCarPrice()
End Sub
```

All this does is force the price of the vehicle to be updated. The 'change' event handlers that we include in the list controls on the page are still defined, for example we still have the attribute `OnSelectedIndexChanged="SelectExtras"` on the `CheckBoxList` control that implements the list of optional extras for the vehicle.

Without `AutoPostBack`, of course, these 'change' events are not immediately raised on the server when an item is selected, but they are still raised when a postback does occur. So they will still execute and update the page just as they do in the script-enabled version.

Replacing the TreeView Control

We can't use a `TreeView` control without client-side script support, because the nodes are hyperlinks that execute a client-side JavaScript URL function to cause the selected nodes of the tree to be expanded and contracted. Instead, we chose to just display all the data from our source XML files as hierarchical lists:

Vehicle Details:	Equipment	Safety
	- Power Steering	- Airbags: 2
	- Tinted windows	- Side airbags: 2
	- Electric mirrors	- Rollbar
	- Heated screen/mirrors	- Side impact bars
	Mechanical	**Security**
	- Rear wheel drive	- Remote locking
	- Anti-lock brakes	- Dead locks
	- Traction control	- Factory alarm
	- Limited slip diff	- Immobiliser
	Interior	**Dimensions**
	- Number of seats:2	- Width: 79"
	- Front headrests	- Height: 56"
	- Cup holders: 2	- Length: 139"
	- Electric seat adjust	- Weight (lb): 1,322
	Costs	**Capacities**
	- Insurance rate: 19	- Fuel: 12 gallons
	- Cost per mile: $2.26	- Luggage: 4.3 cu.ft.
	- Service 12,000 miles	

As we no longer have a fixed-size 'tabbed dialog', the length of the lists is not really important. To display the XML content, we take advantage of another control that we briefly mentioned in Chapter 6 – the ASP.NET `Xml` server control.

The ASP.NET Xml Web Forms Control

The ASP.NET `Xml` control is designed to make it easy to display XML in a web page, or the result of transforming XML into another format (usually HTML) with an XSL or XSLT stylesheet. The control has only a few properties that are associated with generating output:

Property	Description
Document	A reference to an `XmlDocument` object that contains the XML document we want to display or transform.
DocumentContent	A string containing the text of the XML document we want to display or transform.
DocumentSource	A string that contains the physical or virtual path to the XML document we want to display or transform.
Transform	A reference to an `XslTransform` object that contains the XSL or XSLT stylesheet to use for transforming the XML document before displaying it.
TransformSource	A string that contains the physical or virtual path to the XSL or XSLT stylesheet we want to use for the transformation.
TransformArgumentList	A reference to an `XsltArgumentList` object that contains the arguments to be passed to the stylesheet.

When the control comes to render its content to the output, any required XSL or XSLT transformation takes place automatically. So all we have to do is specify the XML and XSLT documents that we want to use, and the control does the rest.

In the HTML section of our page, we removed the declaration of the two `TreeView` controls from the 'Details' 'tab', and replaced them with two `asp:Xml` controls:

```
<!-- section for "Details" tab -->
<table border="0" cellpadding="6">
  <tr>
    <td valign="top"><a name="Details" />
      <font face="Tahoma,Arial,Helvetica,sans-serif" size="2">
      <span style="body-text"><b>Vehicle Details:</b></span></font></td>
    <td>   </td>
    <td valign="top">
      <font face="Tahoma,Arial,Helvetica,sans-serif" size="1">
      <span style="small-text">
      <asp:Xml id="xmlDetailLeft" runat="server" />
      </span></font></td>
    <td>   </td>
    <td valign="top">
      <font face="Tahoma,Arial,Helvetica,sans-serif" size="1">
      <span style="small-text">
      <asp:Xml id="xmlDetailRight" runat="server" />
      </span></font></td>
  </tr>
</table>
```

Populating the Xml Controls

One point to watch out for, however, is that the control properties and its output is not maintained automatically in the viewstate of the page, so we have to specify the properties of the control each time the page loads. Therefore, we added this code to the `Page_Load` event so that it runs every time the page loads:

```
...
' specify XML source files and the matching XSLT
' stylesheets for the two asp:Xml controls
' have to do this on every page load as the result
' is not persisted in the viewstate
Try
  xmlDetailLeft.DocumentSource = "xmldata/tvdata-left-" & sCarID & ".xml"
  xmlDetailLeft.TransformSource = "xmldata/cardetail.xslt"
  xmlDetailRight.DocumentSource = "xmldata/tvdata-right-" & sCarID & ".xml"
  xmlDetailRight.TransformSource = "xmldata/cardetail.xslt"
Catch
  lblMessage.Text = "Error loading XML data for car details."
End Try
...
```

The XML Documents and the XSLT Stylesheet

We looked at the XML documents that contain the vehicle details in the previous chapter. The document format is like that shown in the next listing:

tvdata-left-1.xml

```
<?xml version="1.0"?>
<TREENODES>
  <TreeNode Text="Equipment">
    <TreeNode Text="Power Steering" />
    <TreeNode Text="Cruise control" />
    <TreeNode Text="Tinted windows" />
  </TreeNode>
  <TreeNode Text="Mechanical">
    <TreeNode Text="Front wheel drive" />
    <TreeNode Text="Anti-lock brakes" />
  </TreeNode>
  <TreeNode Text="Interior">
    <TreeNode Text="Number of seats: 4" />
    <TreeNode Text="Cup holders: 2" />
    <TreeNode Text="Electric seat adjust" />
  </TreeNode>
  <TreeNode Text="Costs">
    <TreeNode Text="Insurance rate: 9" />
    <TreeNode Text="Cost per mile: $ 0.89" />
    <TreeNode Text="Service 12,000 miles" />
  </TreeNode>
</TREENODES>
```

To transform this into a hierarchical list is easy using XSLT. We don't have room for an XSLT primer here, so you may have to go off and consult other suitable books if you are not familiar with it (we suggest *XSLT Programmer's Reference 2nd Edition* (ISBN 1-86100-506-7, also by Wrox Press) as a good starting point).

Our XSLT stylesheet, named `cardetail.xslt`, contains a template that matches the root of the XML document (`match="/"`). This template then selects all the `TreeNode` elements in the document that are child nodes of a `TREENODES` element (remember that XML is case-sensitive). These `TreeNode` elements represent the top-level headings, and the template that matches them outputs the value of the `Text` attribute wrapped in HTML `<b>` and `</b>` tags and followed by a `<br />` element.

Then it selects all the `TreeNode` child nodes of the current top-level node, and applies a template to these. The only template that matches in this case is the last one (`match="*"`). In this template the content of the `Text` attribute is output without the HTML `<b>` and `</b>` tags, indented by preceding it with a hyphen, and followed by a `<br />` element:

cardetail.xslt

```
<?xml version='1.0'?>
<xsl:stylesheet xmlns:xsl="http://www.w3.org/1999/XSL/Transform" version="1.0">

<xsl:template match="/">
  <xsl:apply-templates select="child::TREENODES/child::TreeNode"/>
</xsl:template>

<xsl:template match="TREENODES/child::TreeNode">
  <b><xsl:value-of select="attribute::Text"/></b><br />
  <xsl:apply-templates select="child::TreeNode"/>
</xsl:template>

<xsl:template match="*">
  - <xsl:value-of select="attribute::Text"/><br />
</xsl:template>

</xsl:stylesheet>
```

Because of the recursive nature of the process in XSLT, the result is that the child nodes of each top-level node are processed immediately after that top-level node, and before the next top-level node. So we get the output you see in the last screenshot.

Managing Without the setOptionButtons Function

The three remaining issues we have to face when there is no client-side script support are relatively minor, and have little effect on the way our page behaves. The omission of the `setOptionButtons` routine that automatically selects the appropriate option button in the 'Finance' section of the page simply means that users have to remember to select the required option when they select the number of months or enter their maximum payment amount, and before they click the Calculate button:

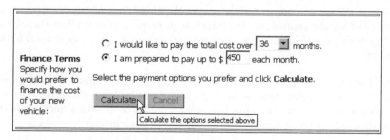

Managing Without the mainWindowPage Function

One area that does lose some useful functionality without client-side script support is being able to manage navigation from the 'Model Details' window to another window. There are a couple of times when this is really useful:

❑ If the user has 'lost' their current session (by not accessing a page within the timeout period), we have to redirect them to the `default.aspx` page to start a new session and collect (or generate) the user ID. But we need to open this page in the main window, not in the pop-up window that contains the 'Model Details' page.

❑ When users save a quotation (and in the instructions at the foot of the window) it's nice to be able to provide a link that opens the 'My Cars' page in the main window and closes the 'Model Details' window.

We can't do any of this without client-side scripting. In response to the 'lost' session, all we can do is display a message to the user telling them how to restart their session. You can see the differences between the code in the `Page_Load` event handler in this page, and the code in the script-enabled version highlighted in the next listing:

```
' get stylesheet size from Session
sStyleSize = CType(Session("WccStyleSize"), String)

' if no value, session has expired or user entered
' site at page other than 'Home' page
If sStyleSize = "" Then

    ' write client-side code that reloads 'Home' page and closes
    ' window to browser, plus message for non-script clients
    Dim sReload As String = "<html><body><center>" _
      & "<b>Your session has expired.</b><p />" _
      & "<b>Please close this window and reload the Home page</b>" _
      & "</center></body></html>"

    ' then prevent rest of page from being processed
    Response.Write(sReload)
    Response.Flush()
    Response.End()
    Exit Sub

End If
```

Even though we did not use client-side script to open the 'Model Details' window from the main window as a pop-up, the window does remember who its parent is (this is where the value for the `window.opener` property comes from). However, we can't access this value or use it without script support.

As to the issue of the navigation to the 'My Cars' page, all we can do here is again provide a helpful message, without the hyperlinks. And, as our page is likely to be longer than the user's screen depth, they won't be able to see the bottom of the page after a postback to save a quotation. Therefore we display the information (or error) message at the top of the page instead:

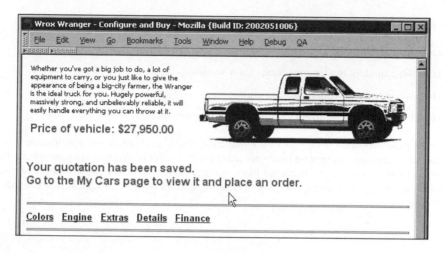

Managing Without a Close Button

Well, what can we say? How will we manage without a **Close** button? Just hope that the user is clever enough to use the normal Windows 'close' button at the top right of the window? If you think it's necessary, you can always put some text in the page to remind them of this.

Summary

At last we've covered all aspects of our 'Model Details' page. While devoting three chapters to a single web page might seem excessive, we've tried to provide the information in a way that makes it easy to understand what the page does, how it works, and why we designed and built it the way we did.

The previous two chapters covered this overview and looked at the basic page structure, including exploring the database we use to power the application, as well as a detailed look at how the bulk of the code that provides the interactive interface works.

This chapter has been devoted to a more narrow range of topics. We looked at how we calculate the price of a vehicle, including all the user selections such as the color range, engine type, and optional extras. We also showed you how we calculate the payment terms for the selected finance package.

Then we moved on to look at how we save the current vehicle configuration to the database as a quotation. In this part of the chapter we included an aside to discuss the use of transactions to protect the validity of a database during updates, and saw how we can implement connection-based transactions using ADO.NET.

Finally, we explored the differences between the two versions of the 'Model Details' page – one that is designed for script-enabled browsers, and one that is designed to work as well as possible in non-script-enabled browsers and other user-agents.

The topics we looked at were:

❑ How we calculate the price of a vehicle as the user configures it

❑ How we calculate the finance terms for a vehicle

❑ How we save the configuration as a quotation

❑ How the non script-enabled version of the page works

Having saved a quotation for a vehicle to the database, the next stage in our application is to see how the user can view that quotation and place an order for the vehicle. All this is accomplished in the 'My Cars' page, but before we can get there we have to think about the other requirements of most web applications – allowing users to register, and managing authentication and authorization through a 'login' feature.

WANTED
WEB DEVELOPER

11

The Login and Register Page

With the completion of the 'Model Details' page in the previous chapter, visitors to our example Wrox Car Company site can now see our range of vehicles, compare their performance, check out the features of each one, and configure them to suit their own requirements. They can also save this configuration as a quotation. However, there is one more feature of the site that we haven't yet considered.

We want to allow our visitors to come back at any time and view the quotations they have saved. We also want them to be able to place an order for a vehicle based on a quotation they received. And, having purchased one or more vehicles from us, we'd like them to be able to see their purchase history as well.

OK, so selling cars over the Web is not a common activity (though it is happening), although the features we've just been discussing are in common use on most e-commerce sites today. The quotation is just a glorified 'shopping cart', and the ability to view previous order history is available at most sites. So, while our example may appear a little esoteric, it is close to the actual real-world requirements for many sites. In this and the next chapter, we'll see how we implement these features in our Wrox Car Company site.

In this chapter, the aims are to look at:

- ❏ The ASP.NET and other techniques we use for authentication and authorization
- ❏ How we identify 'anonymous' users as they browse and then log into our site
- ❏ How we collect and store information about our visitors when they register
- ❏ How we force users that have already registered to provide 'logon' details
- ❏ How the 'login and register' page in our example Wrox Car Company site works

We start with a brief review of the way that web servers and our site normally deal with 'anonymous' visitors. This involves three technical terms, which we'll define and describe first – Authentication, Authorization and Impersonation.

Web Site Users and Identities

Most web sites are designed to allow users to visit without having to present any credentials. This is ideal, because usually we want to encourage as many visitors as possible to come to our sites (and buy something as well, if that's the purpose of the site). So, most of our visitors are 'anonymous', in that they do not have to provide any information about their identity before they can view the pages.

Of course, as with most web sites out there, not all of the pages are suitable for anonymous access. Where we allow the user to place an order, download information, access resources they are supposed to pay for, or even administer the site itself, we'll usually force them to identify themselves so that we can see if they should be permitted to carry out these actions.

The topic of identifying users and allowing only certain users to access specific resources involves three topics that are fundamentally separate, but which become intertwined when we implement restricted access to our pages:

- ❑ **Authentication** is the process of discovering the **identity** of a user, either automatically by using some persistent identification feature (such as a cookie or a client certificate) or by prompting them to provide some information or characteristic that we recognize. This information or characteristic could be a username and password, a smart card, a fingerprint scan or a scan of the retina of their eye, or whatever else you may have seen in recent sci-fi movies. As long as it is something that only they can provide, we can use it to authenticate them.

- ❑ **Authorization** follows on from authentication. Once we know exactly who a user or visitor is, we can decide if they should be allowed to access the resource they requested. Information about who can access what resources can be stored in a variety of ways. For a Windows disk file, or many other Windows resources, it is an Access Control List (ACL) that is defined within the operating system. For other resources, the list of users and their individual permissions (such as READ and/or WRITE) can be stored in a database or in some other storage system such as an XML document, Active Directory, and so forth.

- ❑ **Impersonation** is related to authentication, in that it allows a user to access resources as though they were someone else. An obvious example is the 'anonymous user' account that Internet Information Server uses to access resources on behalf of visitors to a web site who are not individually authenticated. We'll look at this topic in more detail soon.

This book is not about web server or web site security, and so we will not be exploring all the related topics in detail. However, we will look at how we use the three features for controlling access that we've listed above – both generally and in relation to our **Wrox Car Company** site.

Authentication

The first step in implementing any kind of restricted access to resources or a web site is to be able to identify each user when they send a request for that resource. Even when we allow anonymous access to resources, the browser or user agent automatically sends some information about the user to our server. This includes things like:

- ❑ The IP address of the user's browser, proxy server or ISP, so that we can send the response back to them.

❑   The user agent string that identifies what type of browser or user agent software they are using, so that we can send back appropriate content to suit their browser.

❑   The various content types that their browser will accept, such as HTML, images, and so on. Again, this allows the server to tailor the output to suit that type of client.

What the browser doesn't do by default is send details of the actual user, for example their name and address or their e-mail address. Neither does it automatically send a username and password that allows us to uniquely identify the *user* (rather than the browser). If we want this to happen, we have to specifically set up the server or configure the site to not accept 'anonymous' visitors (and hence prompt for the user's credentials).

In the **Wrox Car Company** site, you'll recall that we allocate each user an ID when they first come to the site. This is done in `default.aspx`, and the ID is stored in their ASP.NET session, and in a persistent cookie that we store on their machine. If the user has visited our site before, we look in the cookie for this ID (in the code in `default.aspx`), and reuse this for all subsequent visits. If this is their first visit to the site (or if they have destroyed the cookie since their last visit or are using a different machine), we create a new 'anonymous' ID for them.

So, each user can be identified by the user ID we allocate to them. However, as you can see from the above, this is not really any use in **authenticating** them. It may indicate that they have been here before (if there is a cookie with the ID in it), but that really only identifies the machine where we stored it. It could be a different person who is using the machine this time.

So, to actually identify the user, we have to get them to provide some form of unique characteristic that we can check against a list of existing users. In our case, we use the most common technique – we ask for a combination of user name and password. Once they provide these, we can look them up against our database of registered users, and identify them uniquely.

Authorization

While authentication allows us to identify the user, we also need to see if they are allowed to access the resource they requested. In our **Wrox Car Company** site there is only one level of authorization. If a user can be authenticated, they can access the 'My Cars' page. If they cannot be authenticated, they have to register and provide the details we need to authenticate them in the future. Once this is done, they become authorized to access the 'My Cars' page.

In most web sites, this level of authorization is sufficient for the 'public' parts of the site. However, you may also have areas of the site that are not available for even registered users. For example, if your site administration tasks (adding new items, setting prices, and suchlike) are performed via pages in the site, then you will definitely want to limit access to a more controlled subset of users.

In terms of 'registration' for these users, it is likely to be the site administrator who creates the list of users that will have access, and even what level of access each one should have. Some may be able to upload new content, while others will only be able to view reports on the site's performance. In many ways, this is similar to the concept of Windows' own file access security, where some users may have 'read/write' permission while others might only have 'read' permission.

For our site, the list of users that will have access to the 'My Cars' page is held in our database. We store the user name and the password (encrypted to prevent anyone being able to view the table contents and see the passwords). The table also contains the registered details of each user, such as their name, address, e-mail address, and so on. We collect all this information from them when they register:

Impersonation

We've talked about 'anonymous' access to our site, but you are no doubt aware that nobody can actually access resources on a server without being identified first. Then they must access the resources under the context of an existing account that is valid on the machine, or valid on the domain to which the machine belongs. When you specify the entry for **Everyone** in the security dialogs in Windows, what you are actually saying is 'every existing valid account'.

To allow users that are not authenticated to access content on a web site anonymously, Internet Information Server uses its own account (by default named IUSR_*machinename*) to access the resources on behalf of the anonymous (unauthenticated) user. In other words, the user is being impersonated as the IUSR account. There is also an account named IWAM_*machinename* that is used to execute components installed in Windows Component Services (or MTS under Windows NT4).

In ASP.NET, the IUSR and IWAM accounts continue to exist as before. However, unlike ASP 3.0 and earlier, all access to pages or resources that are processed by the ASP.NET Framework is (by default) under the context of an account named ASPNET. So our ASP.NET pages and other ASP.NET resources are accessed with the user being impersonated as the ASPNET account.

> Note that the ASPNET account is only used for ASP.NET resources. So, for example, `.doc`, `.zip`, image files and many other types of file are accessed under the context of the IUSR account and not the ASPNET account unless you specifically configure ASP.NET to handle these types of files (in **IIS Manager**, open the **App Mappings** page that from the **Configuration** button in the **Home Directory** page of the **Properties** dialog for the site). So any access limitations you want to specify for these types of file must be done against the IUSR account.

In some cases we will still use the IUSR and ASPNET accounts to access restricted resources, and use custom security methods or the built-in methods that are provided by ASP.NET to limit access. So the user is still being impersonated by that account. In other cases, we might abandon impersonation and force the user to provide details of a Windows account on the machine or domain that does have access permission for the resource they requested.

In the **Wrox Car Company** site we allow the default impersonation in IIS to be used, and access pages and resources under the context of the IUSR and ASPNET accounts. We identify our users through **ASP.NET Forms Authentication**, and then control access to resources with the associated built-in authorization features of ASP.NET. These two topics are the main focus of the later sections of this chapter.

Permissions for the Anonymous Accounts

The 'anonymous' accounts we've discussed earlier have only limited access to resources on the machine, providing a basic level of security so that visitors can only access the resources we specify (usually just the content of the web site) and any required components and temporary folders. By default, the IUSR and IWAM account can only read files and execute specified components. If we want to be able to write to the server's disk from within a web page, or access another service such as SMTP, we have to manually add this permission to the IUSR (and/or IWAM) accounts.

The ASPNET account has similar permissions to the IUSR and IWAM accounts, with a few extra added to allow it to access the .NET Framework class files and other folders it uses. So, to write to the server's disk from an ASP.NET page, for example, we have to give the ASPNET account the relevant 'write' or 'modify' permission.

ASP.NET Authentication Methods

ASP.NET provides three types of authentication and authorization. The following table shows these (together with the default of using only the features of IIS itself). We're only going to be discussing Forms authentication in depth in this book, but we will briefly indicate how the other types work so that you can see if they better suit your own requirements:

Type	Name	Description
Windows built-in authentication	Windows	The initial authentication is performed by IIS through Basic, Digest, or Integrated Windows authentication. The requested resources are then accessed under the context of the account that the user presents credentials for. The web.config file can specify the accounts that are valid for the whole or parts of the application.
Passport-based authentication	Passport	This option uses a centralized web-based authentication service provided by Microsoft, which offers single-sign-on (SSN) and core profile services for member sites.
Forms-based authentication	Forms	Unauthenticated requests are automatically redirected to an HTML form page using HTTP client-side redirection. This is similar to custom authentication methods used in previous versions of ASP, but it provides much of the functionality as part of the framework of ASP.NET. The user provides their login credentials and submits the form. If the application authenticates the request, the system issues a cookie that contains their credentials (in fact, a key for re-acquiring the identity). The client browser then sends the cookie with all subsequent requests, and the user can access the application while they retain this cookie. Access to requested resources takes place within the context of the ASPNET account.
Default (IIS) authentication	None	*The default.* Impersonation can still be used, but access control is limited to that specified within IIS. Resources are accessed under the context of the special ASP.NET process account, or the IUSR account if impersonation is enabled.

To specify the type of authentication we want to use in an ASP.NET virtual application or virtual directory we provide the **Name** shown above in the `<authentication>` section of the `web.config` file for that site or directory:

```
<configuration>
...
<system.web>

  <authentication mode="Windows|Passport|Forms|None">
    authentication options used for the application
  </authentication>

  <authorization>
    users and roles that have access to the application
  </authorization>

  <identity>
    if application should run under a different account
  </identity>

</system.web>
...
</configuration>
```

The other two elements shown here within the `<system.web>` section of `web.config` are used to specify how access control should be carried out. The `<authorization>` section is used to specify which users or groups can and cannot access the application. The `<identity>` section is used to specify if impersonation is enabled – in other words, whether to run under the user (or IUSR) account, the special ASPNET process account, or a different account that we specify.

Windows Authentication

If we want each user to be authenticated against an existing Windows account, the best choice is **Windows authentication**. We simply configure machine-level or domain-level accounts in Windows using the built-in account management tools. Users provide their user name and password when they access the restricted pages in the site. In fact, if they have logged onto their local machine with these credentials, they are used automatically without the logon dialog appearing.

Obviously, this approach is not usually suitable for a public web site, as you would then have to set up domain or local accounts within Windows for each user. Besides which, many browsers (other than Internet Explorer 5 and above) cannot use the Digest authentication method that is required. Windows authentication is more suited to an intranet situation, or perhaps an extranet where you have only a limited set of users and can specify which browser they use to access the site.

Setting Up Windows Authentication

To set up an application or a section of an application to use Windows authentication, we simply specify this authentication mode and then turn on impersonation within the `<identity>` element:

```
<configuration>
...
<system.web>
  <authentication mode="Windows" />
  <identity impersonate="true" />
```

```
    </system.web>
    ...
  </configuration>
```

Now, each user will access resources under the context of the account that they were authenticated with by IIS.

Passport Authentication

Microsoft provides a 'Passport Service' that can be used to authenticate users on any passport-enabled site, anywhere on the Internet. When they log onto a participating site, their browser or user agent sends their credentials to the passport service, which authenticates them and places a secure cookie on their machine. Then, when they access another participating site, the browser presents this cookie to the passport service to prove that the user has already been authenticated. The passport service then indicates who that user is to the new site so they can be properly authorized – that is, the new site can check if this user has permission to access the resource they've requested.

So, the power of the passport service is that a user can present the same credentials to any participating site, while only having to log in once during a session. When they close their browser, or indicate that they wish to log off, the cookie is destroyed. They must then log on again to re-access resources on any of the participating sites.

Setting Up Passport Authentication

To set up passport authentication you must subscribe to the 'Passport Service', and install special software on your web server to allow the process to work. Full details are available from http://www.microsoft.com/netservices/passport/. Once you've installed the software and subscribed to the service, you configure passport authentication in the web.config file:

```
<configuration>
...
<system.web>
  <authentication mode="Passport">
    <passport redirectUrl="internal|url" />
  </authentication>
</system.web>
...
</configuration>
```

The <passport> element supports a single attribute named redirectUrl. The default value (before you install and configure passport authentication) is internal, which means that unauthenticated requests will receive a generic error message created by your server. Any other string is assumed to be the URL of the passport service that unauthenticated requests will be redirected to for authentication.

Forms Authentication

Where the highest levels of security are not required, **Forms-based authentication** (sometimes referred to as cookie-based authentication) automates many of the tasks that we would normally perform ourselves in earlier versions of ASP to build custom authentication solutions. Forms-based authentication also removes the unintuitive Windows Logon dialog, allowing us to replace it with an attractive custom form, or integrate the login controls (basically two text boxes and a button) into existing pages.

The Forms authentication process generates a secure cookie when the user logs into the application, and sends it to the client. Then, if this cookie is present in subsequent requests, we know that the user has already been authenticated. The cookie contains their identity, and ASP.NET can check that this user is authorized to access the resource they requested. If they are, it returns this resource to them (for example, by executing an ASP.NET page). If not, they are denied access.

If the cookie is not present in the request headers, the user is automatically redirected to a custom login page that we create ourselves. The user enters their credentials into this login page and submits it to our application where these credentials are automatically checked to authenticate the user. If they are recognized, an authentication cookie is added to the headers and the request is sent to the next stage of the process. ASP.NET checks to see if this user is authorized to access the resource they requested, and if so sends it to them. If not, they are denied access.

Setting Up Forms-Based Authentication

Like all other ASP.NET security settings, Forms-based authentication is configured within the web.config file for an application or a virtual directory. The <authentication> section carries the value Forms for the mode attribute, and within the element itself we add more elements to specify how the authentication of users will be carried out:

```
<configuration>
...
<system.web>
  <authentication mode="Forms">
    <forms name="cookie-name"
           path="cookie-path"
           loginurl="url"
           protection="All|None|Encryption|Validation"
           timeout="number-of-minutes" >
      <credentials passwordFormat="Clear|SHA1|MD5">
        <user name="user-name" password="user-password" />
        <user name="user-name" password="user-password" />
        ... more users listed here ...
      </credentials>
    </forms>
  </authentication>
  <machineKey validationKey="AutoGenerate|key"
              decryptionKey="AutoGenerate|key"
              validation="SHA1|MD5"/>
</system.web>
...
</configuration>
```

The attributes of the <forms> element define:

❑ The name that will be assigned to the cookie.

❑ The path that the cookie is valid for. This is usually set to "/" to indicate the complete site. If not, and the site contains links that are not in the correct letter case (for example, an <a> element with href="mypage.aspx" where the actual page name is MyPage.aspx), the cookie will not be returned by some browsers. This will cause the login form to be displayed again.

❑ The `loginurl` that specifies the virtual path to the login form page.

❑ The `protection` level required for the cookie. The settings are: `All` (the default), which uses both data validation (based on the `<machineKey>` element) and encryption (Triple DES if available and if the key is at least 48 bytes long); `None` (should be used only for personalization purposes); `Encryption` (the cookie is encrypted but data validation is not performed); `Validation` (validation is performed but the cookie is not encrypted).

❑ The `timeout` in minutes before the cookie expires on the user's machine and the server.

Within the `<forms>` element is:

❑ An optional `<credentials>` element that specifies the encryption algorithm used to encrypt the user's password in the `web.config` file. Within this element there can be a series of optional `<user>` elements, which between them specify the users who will be able to access the protected resources.

We can also specify an optional `<machineKey>` element within the `<system.web>` section, which specifies the keys and method to be used to encrypt the cookie contents. In general we omit this element, and allow a key to be created automatically. However, it can be useful in a situation like a web farm, where we want all machines to use the same key. The key length must match the number of characters required for the encryption level and method that is used. This entry in the default `machine.config` file specifies that the keys are auto-generated:

```
<machineKey validationKey="AutoGenerate"
            decryptionKey="AutoGenerate"
            validation="SHA1" />
```

So, an example `web.config` file for Forms authentication might look like the following. Remember that the `<credentials>` and `<machineKey>` sections are optional. Our example also lists some users, and you can see that their passwords are encrypted:

```
<configuration>
...
<system.web>
  <authentication mode="Forms">
    <forms name="MyNewApp" path="/" loginUrl="/main/login.aspx"
           protection="All" timeout="30" >
      <credentials passwordFormat="SHA1">
        <user name="billjones"
              password="87F8ED9157125FFC4DA9E06A7B8011AD80A53FE1" />
        <user name="marthasmith"
              password="93FB8A49CC350BAEB2661FA5C5C97959BD328C50" />
        <user name="joesoap"
              password="5469541CA9236F939D889B2B465F9B15A09149E4" />
      </credentials>
    </forms>
  </authentication>
  <!-- keys usually only specified for a Web farm -->
  <machineKey validationKey="3875f9...645a78ff"
              decryptionKey="3875f9...645a78ff"
              validation="SHA1" />
</system.web>
...
</configuration>
```

Note that the `<identity>` element is not used in Forms-based authentication.

Hard-coding user details into the `web.config` file (within the `<credentials>` section) is fine if you only have a few users, or perhaps where you use generic accounts such as 'admin' or 'user' where all users in that 'group' log in with the same credentials. However, it soon becomes cumbersome when you have lots of users, or when you need to change the user list or their passwords regularly. In this case, it's better to use another technique for storing the list of users and their passwords. As you'll see later in this chapter, we prefer to use a database to store these details instead.

Specifying Users and Groups

The previous examples all show how we can use the built-in features of ASP.NET to **authenticate** users. However, we also want to be able to **authorize** them, by limiting access to resources to specific users. This is done within the `<authorization>` section of the `web.config` file, with a series of `<allow>` and `<deny>` elements. The general form of each of these elements is highlighted in the next listing:

```
<configuration>
...
<system.web>

  <authentication mode="Windows|Passport|Forms|None">
    authentication options used for the application
  </authentication>

  <authorization>
    <allow roles="comma-separated list of Windows account group names"
           users="comma-separated list of Windows user account names"
           verb="GET|POST|HEAD" />
    <deny roles="comma-separated list of Windows account group names"
          users="comma-separated list of Windows user account names"
          verb="GET|POST|HEAD" />
    users and roles that have access to the application
  </authorization>

  <identity>
    if application should run under a different account
  </identity>

</system.web>
...
</configuration>
```

The `<allow>` and `<deny>` element must contain either a `roles` or a `users` attribute. It does not have to contain both, and the `verb` attribute is always optional. To specify a domain user account, we include the domain name followed by a backslash and the username, for example MyDomainName\MyUserName. There are also special values that refer to Windows built-in account groups, such as Everyone, BUILTIN\Administrators, and so on.

To specify a local (machine) account we just use the machine name in place of the domain name. There is no way to specify a domain account without the actual domain (there is no short-cut that means 'use the local domain'), so we have to edit the list if we change the domain name or move the application to another domain.

There are also two special symbols that we can use:

❑ An asterisk (*) means all `users`, `roles`, or `verbs`, depending on which of these attributes it is used in.

❑ A question mark (?) means 'anonymous access'. In the case of Windows and Forms-based authentication, this is the account set up in IIS for anonymous access. This character can only be used within the `users` attribute.

You'll see the way that we use the last of these special symbols in our **Wrox Car Company** site later on in this chapter.

Specifying HTTP Access Types

We can also use the `<allow>` and `<deny>` elements to control the type of HTTP action that a user can take when accessing an application or directory by using the `verb` attribute:

```
<configuration>
...
<system.web>
  <authorization>
    <allow verb="GET" users="*" />
    <allow verb="POST" users="MyDomainName\MyAccount" />
    <deny verb="POST" users="*" />
  </authorization>
</system.web>
...
</configuration>
```

This example will allow the domain-level account named **MyAccount** to send `POST` requests to the application (submit an HTML form), but all other users will only be able to send `GET` requests. And, of course, we can combine this access control setting with the list of groups and users, by adding the `verb` attribute to the previous example that used the `roles` and `users` attributes.

Avoiding Nested ASP.NET Applications

ASP.NET does not allow us to share resources between different applications. Such resources include things like assemblies in the `bin` directory, user controls, session state, and so on. Neither can we carry session state into a separate application using the `Server.Transfer` method. This limitation even applies when we 'nest' applications – in other words when we make a sub-folder into a virtual application directory within an existing virtual application directory. Although the new application is nested within the existing one, the restrictions on accessing resources applies between these two applications.

However, (as we saw earlier) if we use a `web.config` file that includes the `<authentication>` element, we must place this in the root folder of an ASP.NET application. So, to limit access to a specific sub-folder using this approach would mean that this sub-folder would have to be a separate, nested ASP.NET application. But even if this folder is nested within the existing application, the two applications will not be able to share values, assemblies, or user controls.

Thankfully, we can easily get round this problem. The `<authentication>` and `<authorization>` sections *can* be in the same `web.config` file if we are limiting access to all the pages in all folders of the application. However, they can instead be placed in *separate* `web.config` files, in different folders, if we only want to limit access to certain folders and not all of them.

While the web.config file containing the <authentication> element **must always** be in a virtual application folder (the application root directory or the root folder of the web site), web.config files containing the <authorization> element can be placed in any sub-folder. They do not have to be placed in a virtual application folder. This means that we avoid the need for nested applications, and we can share all the resources across all the pages in all the sub-folders.

For more details of how authentication, authorization and impersonation work in ASP and IIS generally, you might like to look at these topics in Professional ASP 3.0 Web Techniques *(Wrox Press, ISBN 1-86100-321-8). It provides down-to-earth practical advice for setting up restricted access using IIS and Windows authentication methods. For full details of the ASP.NET authentication and authorization features, check out* Professional ASP.NET 1.0 *(Wrox Press, ISBN 1-86100-703-5).*

Wrox Cars Login and Register Process

We use Forms-based authentication in our example application, so that we force users to be authenticated before they can access the 'My Cars' page, where they can view previous quotations and place an order. To implement this, we have a sub-folder named secure that contains the 'My Cars' page. It also contains the 'logon' page (named login.aspx) that allows the user to log in and be authenticated.

The next schematic shows the layout of our site and the relevant web.config files. All the pages that can be accessed anonymously, without logging on, are in the root folder of the site (plus a few other sub-folders that contain the user controls, images, and XML data files):

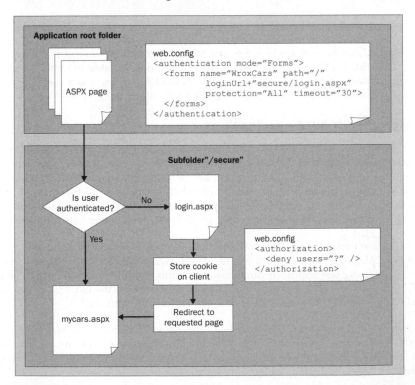

The Root Folder web.config File

The root folder named `wroxcars` of our application contains the following `web.config` file (we've omitted the `<session>` element that defines the way that sessions are supported from this listing for clarity):

```
<configuration>

  <system.web>

    <!-- specify that we will use Forms authentication -->
    <authentication mode="Forms">
      <forms name="WroxCars" path="/" loginUrl="secure/login.aspx"
             protection="All" timeout="30" >
      </forms>
    </authentication>

  </system.web>

</configuration>
```

We're using Forms-based authentication, and we specify that the name of the application is `WroxCars`. This name is used in the cookie we send to the client following successful authentication. We also specify that the cookie should apply to the complete site, so that it is sent back to our server with every request to a page from our site. In theory, we could specify only the `secure` sub-folder here, but (as we discussed earlier) it is generally more reliable to specify the whole site and thereby make sure that the cookie is always returned.

The `loginUrl` value is the path (relative to the location of the `web.config` file) of the page that visitors use to provide their login credentials. We also specify that we want all the normal encoding techniques to be used to protect the cookie contents, and that the cookie will expire in 30 minutes. So, if the user does not access a restricted page within 30 minutes, they will effectively be logged out automatically.

You'll notice that we don't specify a list of users in the `<authentication>` section of our `web.config` file. We could, and then ASP.NET will automatically check to see if the credentials provided are acceptable or not. However, we want to be able to add new users automatically and store more details about each one, without having to keep updating the `web.config` file (remember that each change to it will force a restart to our application). So, instead, we keep the user details in a database table, and perform the authentication checks ourselves.

The "secure" Sub-folder web.config File

The Forms authentication settings we specified in the root folder of the application (`wroxcars`) apply to all the folders and sub-folders within our application – our entire **Wrox Car Company** site. However, the default authorization settings (in `machine.config`) allow all users – anonymous or otherwise – to access all ASP.NET resources in these folders.

To protect a specific subfolder, all we need to do is specify the authentication options we require for that folder in a `web.config` file located there. In the `wroxcars/secure` sub-folder, we have the following `web.config` file:

```
<configuration>
<system.web>

  <authorization>
    <deny users="?" />
  </authorization>

</system.web>
</configuration>
```

This just prevents anonymous access to ASP.NET resources located in this folder. The special symbol "?" simply means 'anonymous users'. Now any visitor that wants to access the 'My Cars' page must be authenticated first, and then authorized by ASP.NET.

Looking at the lower section of the previous schematic, you can see that the Forms authentication process will automatically redirect unauthenticated users to the page named `login.aspx`. In that page, our job is to decide if the user is to be allowed access, and if so tell ASP.NET to generate the appropriate cookie and then redirect them to the page they originally requested (`mycars.aspx`).

> Remember that all the ASP.NET authentication and authorization processes only apply to resources that are accessed by ASP.NET. In other words, they only prevent anonymous access to file types that are mapped to the ASP.NET process in IIS Manager. By default, this **does not** include things like `.htm`, `.inc`, `.pdf`, `.doc` and `.zip` files, and so on.

Authentication for Cookie-Less Clients

Of course, while we've been getting excited about how easy all this is to achieve in ASP.NET, we have to consider one other scenario. Our site demands session support from users, and we implement this using cookie-less sessions (URL munging) for clients that don't support cookies. But what happens to Forms-based authentication when there is no client-side cookie support? The answer is simple – it doesn't work.

> For this reason, the `web.config` file in the root folder of the cookie-less version of the application (`cookieless-wroxcars`) does not contain an `<authentication>` or `<authorization>` section. And there is no `web.config` file in the `cookieless-wroxcars/secure` sub-folder.

In this case we have to provide some other mode of authentication and authorization. In the `cookieless-wroxcars` folder of the examples is the version of the **Wrox Car Company** application that works with clients that don't support cookies (or have them disabled). Here, we use one of the more traditional techniques for limiting user access and forcing them to log on before accessing restricted content.

Custom Authentication and Authorization Techniques

Before the advent of ASP.NET, most web sites had evolved techniques for forcing users to register and then log on before being allowed to access specific resources. The common techniques all use some 'token' value that indicates if a user has been authenticated, and this value is stored between page requests in a cookie, the query string, a hidden `<form>` control, or in the user's ASP.NET session.

The 'token' value is generated and persisted (using whichever technique is chosen from the list above) once the user has logged in. As each page is requested, a process (usually part of each page) checks that a suitable value exists to indicate that they were authenticated, and optionally checks to see if this user is authorized to view the page or resource. If they are, they receive the page or resource. If not, they are redirected to the login page.

Of course, when you think about it, this is just what ASP.NET Forms authentication does. Only it hides a lot of the difficult parts of the process and makes it much easer to implement. We don't need to worry about creating a suitable cookie or testing to see if it exists.

But when we have to manage without cookies, we will have to do all this work ourselves. We also have to find somewhere else to persist the 'token' value. We could add it to the query string as a name/value pair, but that makes it easy for a user to bookmark the page complete with the authentication 'token', and so they can avoid logging on at a later date. It's also easy for users to break in without being authenticated by simply typing the value themselves, so we would be forced to use some dynamic or random value that changes every time to prevent this.

Alternatively, and a little safer (but not much) is the use of a `hidden`-type HTML control to hold the 'token' value. However, while this is not immediately visible (and so it is not stored in web server, proxy server and router logs like the query string!) this can still leave us wide open to spoofing attacks by people who just build their own pages with the 'token' inserted into a `hidden`-type control using the `value` attribute.

Instead, where we are guaranteed session support (as in our **Wrox Car Company** site), the best option is to store the 'token' that indicates successful authentication in the user's session. That way it is never sent across the network, it will disappear when the user's session expires, and overall is generally a great deal more secure than the query string or `<form>` controls approach:

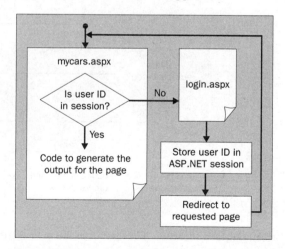

We still use the same login page to collect the values, and the same techniques to authenticate the user against the contents of our database table. The only differences are in the way that we store the 'token' that indicates successful authentication. You'll see how we implement this cookie-less approach when we look at the `login.aspx` page in detail soon.

The Process Step-By-Step

While we use two different techniques to perform the authentication and authorization process in our example site (depending on whether the client supports cookies, as we've just been discussing), the process as a whole is the same. In this section, we'll pull together all the aspects and requirements so that you can see exactly what our login and register page must achieve. We'll first summarize the steps, and then look at the whole thing in more detail. Here's the obligatory schematic:

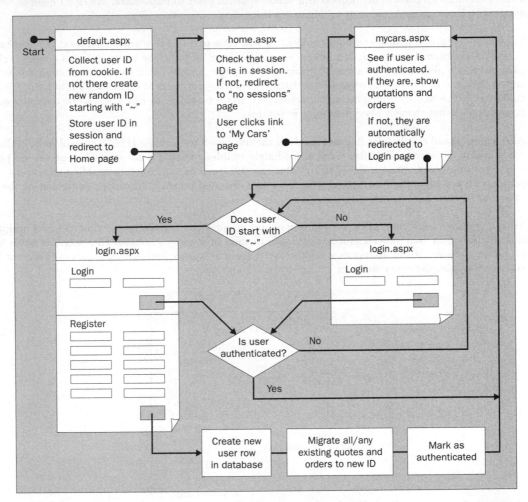

The process steps are also summarized in a little more detail in the next section, which should help to make it all clearer:

❑   In default.aspx we either collect the existing ID from a cookie sent with the request when the user first enters our site, or we generate a new random user ID if there is no cookie. The user ID is then stored in the user's ASP.NET session.

❑ In the 'Home' page we check that there is a user ID in the session. If not, we redirect the user to a page that indicates the problem, and asks them to either enable cookies or use the alternative cookie-less version of the application.

❑ When the user attempts to access a page in the secure folder (mycars.aspx), we check to see if they have been authenticated (in other words, have they logged on to the application yet?). In the 'standard' version of the application, ASP.NET Forms-based authentication does this for us. In the cookie-less version, we look for a session value to indicate this.

❑ If they have been authenticated, we can display their quotations and orders and allow them to place an order.

❑ If they have not yet been authenticated, we redirect them to the 'Login' page. Here we check to see if they are using an 'anonymous' User ID or not. Anonymous user IDs (ones we generate randomly the first time they visit the site or if they have no existing cookie containing a user ID) start with the "~" character.

❑ If this is an anonymous user ID, we display both the 'login' controls and the 'register' controls. If they already have registered, but 'lost' the cookie containing their user ID, they can enter the details of the account that they created when they registered, and log on using this. Or they can register if they have not done so before:

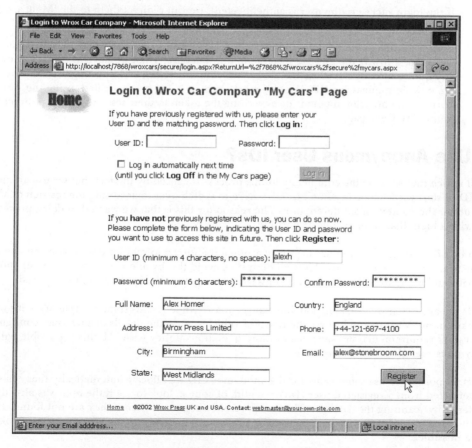

❑ If this is not an anonymous user ID, we know that they have already registered and so we just display the 'login' controls:

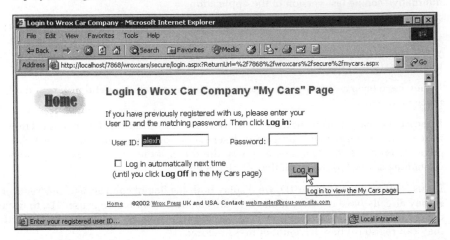

❑ If the login succeeds (the user is authenticated), we can redirect them to the 'My Cars' page. If the login fails, we just redisplay the same set of controls on the login page again.

❑ If the user fills in their details and registers (rather than logging in using an existing account), we create a row in the tblUsers table in our database. Then we have to check if they have any quotes already stored against their anonymous user ID, and if so migrate these across to the new permanent user ID. We also mark them as being authenticated (using the ASP.NET Forms authentication methods or by writing the token to their session) before redirecting them to the 'My Cars' page.

Why Use Anonymous User IDs?

You'll notice that some of the complexity in this process is caused by the fact that we use an anonymous user ID to start with. Then, in some cases, we have to switch over to accessing the restricted 'My Cars' page under the context of a different user. The reason for this is that we wanted to delay presenting the user with a login dialog for as long as possible.

It can be off-putting, when you are browsing a site, to be forced to register before you can examine the products and decide what to buy. Most modern sites avoid this by allowing you to fill your shopping cart without having to register or log in. Only when you get to the checkout is this required.

This is the approach we've taken, and you can see that – while it adds some complexity – it's not really that hard to do. Visitors can browse the range of vehicles, view the details of each one, configure them to suit their requirements, and save one or more quotations if they wish. All this is possible with an anonymous user ID or a registered user ID.

The main point is to use some value for the anonymous ID we allocate automatically that can easily be differentiated from a registered user ID. We could, of course, look to see if the user was already registered by scanning the database table, and present a register screen if they are not found. However, we felt that our approach was easier and more efficient in the long run, avoiding database lookups where possible.

Storing the user ID in a cookie on the user's machine (where cookies are supported) also allows us to automatically pick it up whenever they access our site, and display it in the login page so that they only have to type their password. OK, you may decide for security reasons *not* to pre-fill the user ID text box, but that depends on your requirements for the site and whether you think that the risk it adds outweighs the benefit to the user.

Why Use a Combined Login and Register Page?

You can also see that we use a combined 'login' and 'register' page. Many sites implement different pages for these two features, so that every user sees the login page first. This login page contains a link to a separate page where the user can register if they haven't done so before. If we implement custom input validation techniques client-side, using separate pages is often easier to manage. It also means that we can submit the user's value to different pages if required – one for logging in and a different one for registering.

However, in ASP.NET, we have the postback architecture. It does its utmost to persuade us to submit pages back to themselves for processing, rather than to a different 'handler' page. Meanwhile, we can benefit from the extra capabilities that the ASP.NET server controls provide to make the work of handling the user input, validating it, and storing it much easier.

There are a couple of downsides to this approach, however – although we work round them in our example site. As you'll see later on, we've had to abandon client-side validation because we can't decide which 'set' of controls the user will fill in when they first load the page. They might have 'lost' their user ID cookie, but remember their login details. In this case they would enter these details and click **Login**. However they might not have registered before, and so they will use the other 'set' of controls and click **Register**. With ASP.NET client-side validation enabled, one 'set' of controls will always be invalid, preventing the page from being submitted.

Secondly, having two "submit" buttons (**Login** and **Register**) on the same page can cause some confusion if the user presses the *Return* key instead of clicking the appropriate button. In traditional ASP pages, we can use separate `<form>` sections with only one submit button on each `<form>`. The browser submits the `<form>` that contains the input focus when the *Return* key is pressed; so (assuming that the user typed values into one of the text boxes on that form before pressing the *Return* key) the appropriate one is submitted.

However, ASP.NET only allows us to include one server-side `<form>` section in a page, so both controls are on the same form. Only the first one (in the order of the HTML declarations) can be 'pressed' using the *Return* key, so if our user fills in the 'register' section controls and presses *Return* they will get an error because they have effectively clicked the **Login** button.

In our `login.aspx` page we get round this (where possible) by disabling the buttons using interactive client-side script to achieve the same effect. When the user types in a text box, we disable the 'submit' button for the other 'set' of controls. You'll see how when we look at this page in detail next.

The Login and Register Page

In this section of the chapter, we'll explore the workings of our 'login and register' page in detail. We start with a quick look at the HTML declarations, and a discussion of the way we use the ASP.NET Validation controls to check our user's input. Then we'll move on and look at the code in the page that makes it all work.

The HTML Page Declarations

Basically, the structure of the 'login and register' page (login.aspx) is simple. We use exactly the same formatting, stylesheet declaration and 'skip to' links as we do in the pages you've seen in previous chapters. In the login.aspx page, the main difference is within the single server-side ASP.NET <form> section. Here we have a two-column single-row table that contains the link back to the 'Home' page in the left-hand column, and all remaining page content in the right-hand column. The login and register controls make up this content, consisting of:

❑ A section containing the username and password textboxes and Login button for visitors that have already registered

❑ A section containing an ASP.NET ValidationSummary control that displays any validation errors

❑ A section containing an ASP.NET Panel control, which encloses the textboxes and Register button for visitors who have not previously registered

An outline view of the page structure is shown next:

login.aspx

```
...
<form runat="server">

<table width="100%" border="0" cellspacing="0" cellpadding="10">
<tbody>
 <tr>
  <td valign="top" width="110px">
    <a Title="Back to List of Models" href="../home.aspx">
     <img src="../images/btn_home.gif" width="100" height="49" hspace="3"
          vspace="2" alt="Home Page" border="0" /></a>
  </td>
  <td align="left">
    <a name="content" />
    <font face="Arial,Helvetica,sans-serif" size="4" color="#b50055">
    <p class="large-red-text">
      <b>Login to Wrox Car Company "My Cars" Page</b></p></font>

    <!-- "Login" controls for existing user -->
    <!-- HTML and validation controls go here -->

    <!-- summary of validation errors -->
    <!-- ASP.NET ValidationSummary control here -->
```

```
        <asp:panel id="pnlRegister" Visible="False" runat="server">
          <!-- "Register" controls for new user -->
          <!-- HTML and validation control declarations here -->
          <!-- not visible by default, displayed as required -->
        </asp:panel>

      </td>
    </tr>
  </tbody>
</form>
...
```

The ASP.NET Validation Controls

We're using the ASP.NET Validation controls to check the user's input and make sure that it complies with the 'rules' we've established. For example, a user ID must be between 4 and 20 characters in length and cannot contain any spaces. These controls make it really easy to perform both server-side and client-side validation in an ASP.NET page.

However, as we noted towards the end of the previous section of this chapter, we are not using client-side validation at all. This is because we have two distinct 'sections' of input controls on our page, and the user can fill in either section. The validation controls can only be enabled and disabled when a postback occurs, but if client-side validation is enabled the user won't be able to submit the page without filling in values for both sets of controls.

It also means that we have to 'manually' enable and disable the validation controls server-side, as well as validating the controls individually, rather than relying on the automatic validation that occurs by default (like we did when validating an e-mail address in the 'Home' page). However, this approach demonstrates just how versatile the controls are, and how you can use them in a range of situations for specific and non-standard validation requirements.

The 'Login' Section of the Page

The top section of the page contains the two textboxes where users can log in if they have previously registered. There are two validation controls attached to each of these textboxes, one to force a value to be entered (a RequiredFieldValidator control) and one to check that the entry meets our criteria for that field (a RegularExpressionValidator control). We also specify a range of attributes for each of the textboxes to make it easier for the user to see what we expect them to enter into that textbox. The next listing shows the introductory text for this section of the page, and declarations for the first (User ID) textbox:

```
<!-- "Login" controls for existing user -->
<font face="Tahoma,Arial,Helvetica,sans-serif" size="2">
<span class="body-text">
If you have previously registered with us, please enter your<br />
User ID and the matching password. Then click <b>Log in</b>:</span>
<table cellpadding="5" cellspacing="5" border="0">
  <tr>
    <td colspan="2" align="center" nowrap="nowrap">
      <font face="Tahoma,Arial,Helvetica,sans-serif" size="2">
```

```
    <span class="body-text">User ID:</span>
    <asp:TextBox id="txtLogonUserID" CssClass="body-text"
        TabIndex="1" Columns="15" runat="server"
        ToolTip="Enter your registered user ID"
        onkeypress="disableSubmit('Register')"
        onfocus="javascript:window.status='Enter registered userID'" />
    <asp:RequiredFieldValidator id="valRequLogonUserID" runat="server"
        ControlToValidate="txtLogonUserID" Display="dynamic"
        ErrorMessage="You must provide your User ID">
      *
    </asp:RequiredFieldValidator>
    <asp:RegularExpressionValidator id="valRegexLogonUserID" runat="server"
        ControlToValidate="txtLogonUserID" Display="dynamic"
        ValidationExpression="\S{4,20}"
        ErrorMessage="User ID must be 4 - 20 characters with no spaces">
      *
    </asp:RegularExpressionValidator>    
    ...
```

The TextBox Control Attributes

Amongst the attributes for the textboxes you can see that we specify:

❑   The TabIndex, allowing us to control the order in which the input focus moves through the controls when the user presses the *Tab* key.

❑   The number of Columns (the physical size of each textbox).

❑   The ToolTip that provides the pop-up tool-tip when the mouse hovers over the control.

❑   A value for the onkeypress event handler attribute, which executes the client-side JavaScript function named disableSubmit when the user types in this textbox. We'll look at this function later on.

❑   A value for the onfocus event handler attribute, which executes a JavaScript URL statement that displays a useful tip in the status bar of the browser when this control receives the input focus.

The Validation Control Attributes

The attributes we include for the validation controls depend on the type of control. For the RequiredFieldValidator we must specify the ControlToValidate attribute to indicate which control we want to validate, and the ErrorMessage to display when the content is invalid. We also specify that the Display of the content of the control (an asterisk) should be "dynamic", so that it does not take up space on the page when the input control content is valid.

For the RegularExpressionValidator we also provide the ControlToValidate, Display, and ErrorMessage attribute values. We also have to provide a value for the ValidationExpression attribute to define what content is valid. As we saw in the 'Home' page, this value is a regular expression that evaluates to True or False, depending on the contents of the validated control. Our regular expression, "\S{4,20}", specifies that the value must be between 4 and 20 non-space characters.

A guide to the syntax and general techniques for using regular expressions can be found in the .NET SDK at:
ms-help://MS.NETFrameworkSDK/cpguidenf/html/cpconcomregularexpressions.htm

The Password Textbox and Validation Controls

The next listing shows the section that declares the **Password** textbox and associated validation controls. You can see that it is virtually the same as the previous declaration for the **User ID** controls, with the notable difference that this time the `TextMode` attribute is added and set to `"Password"` so that the control displays asterisks as the user enters their password (it is rendered on the client as an `<input type="password">` control):

```
...
    <span class="body-text">Password:</span>
    <asp:TextBox id="txtLogonPWord" CssClass="body-text"
        TabIndex="2" TextMode="Password" Columns="10" runat="server"
        ToolTip="Enter the password you provided when you registered"
        onkeypress="disableSubmit('Register')"
        onfocus="javascript:window.status='Enter password provided ...'" />
    <asp:RequiredFieldValidator id="valRequLogonPWord" runat="server"
        ControlToValidate="txtLogonPWord" Display="dynamic"
        ErrorMessage="You must provide your password">
      *
    </asp:RequiredFieldValidator>
    <asp:RegularExpressionValidator id="valRegexLogonPWord" runat="server"
        ControlToValidate="txtLogonPWord" Display="dynamic"
        ValidationExpression="\S{4,20}"
        ErrorMessage="Password must be 4 - 20 characters with no spaces">
      *
    </asp:RegularExpressionValidator></font>
  </td>
</tr>
...
```

Allowing Persistent Authentication

Next comes the declaration of the checkbox (captioned **Log in automatically next time**). This allows the user to persist the login even when they leave the site, close their browser, and then come back another time:

```
...
<tr>
 <td align="left" nowrap="nowrap">
  <font face="Tahoma,Arial,Helvetica,sans-serif" size="2">
  <span id="spnHideChecbox" runat="server">
  <asp:CheckBox id="chkPersist" CssClass="body-text" TabIndex="3"
       runat="server" />
  Log in automatically next time<br />
  (until you click <b>Log Off</b> in the My Cars page)</span></font>
 </td>
 ...
```

By default, a user's authenticated 'session' expires automatically when the login `timeout` value is reached, or when they close their browser. In both cases, the cookie containing the authentication token is destroyed. However, we can cause the cookie to be stored on their machine with a long timeout (5 years), so they can return to the site and be automatically authenticated without having to log in again.

Only when we specifically destroy the cookie (or if the user destroys it themselves) do they need to log in again. You'll see how we destroy the cookie and 'log off' the user when we look at the 'My Cars' page in the next chapter.

Persistent logins can present a security risk (a different user could access the site from their machine, or even hijack the cookie by copying it to another machine), but they are useful in applications where the security level requirement is low. We include the feature here mainly to demonstrate how it is achieved, should you wish to incorporate it into your pages.

The Login Button and Message Label

The final two controls in this section of our page are the Login button and a Label where we display status messages (for example, if there is a data access problem). Validation errors are not displayed here – that's the job of the ValidationSummary control you'll see shortly.

The Button control that implements the Login button is shown next, and you can see that we again include a ToolTip and TabIndex attribute. The OnClick attribute specifies that the server-side event handler named DoLogin will be executed when the button is clicked:

```
...
<td align="right" valign="bottom">
 <font face="Tahoma,Arial,Helvetica,sans-serif" size="2">
 <asp:Button id="btnLogon" Text="Log in" CssClass="body-text"
      runat="server" ToolTip="Log in to view the My Cars page"
      TabIndex="4" OnClick="DoLogin" /></font>
 </td>
</tr>
...
```

The message label completes this section of the page. We turn off viewstate support so that any error messages will not be persisted across postbacks and confuse the user:

```
...
<tr>
 <td colspan="2" align="center" nowrap="nowrap">
  <font face="Tahoma,Arial,Helvetica,sans-serif" size="2">
  <b><asp:Label id="lblLoginMsg" CssClass="body-text"
         EnableViewState="false" runat="server" /></b></font>
 </td>
</tr>
</table>
...
```

The next screenshot shows the Login section of the page, with the tool-tip for the button and the status message from the User ID textbox visible:

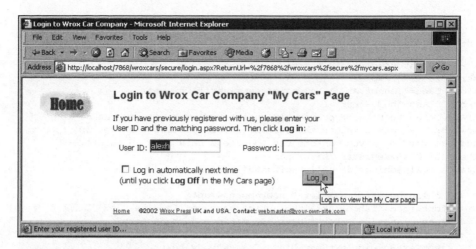

The ValidationSummary Control

Our page contains two separate sections of controls, but only one `ValidationSummary` control. This will display validation errors from whichever section of the page the user submitted (**Login** or **Register**). Therefore we placed it between the **Login** and **Register** sections so that the content is always displayed near to any controls that may contain an error.

The only attribute we provide for the `ValidationSummary` control is the `HeaderText` to display above the list of validation errors:

```
...
<!-- summary of validation errors -->
<font face="Tahoma,Arial,Helvetica,sans-serif" size="2">
<asp:ValidationSummary id="valSummary" runat="server"
    HeaderText="<hr /><b>Sorry, your values cannot be accepted.</b><br />
              The following errors were found. Please check<br />
              the values you entered (marked with '*')</b>" />
</font>
...
```

The 'Register' Section of the Page

The **Register** section of the page contains many more controls than the **Login** section, but the declarations are just about identical. For each textbox we specify the `Columns`, `TabIndex`, `ToolTip`, `onkeypress`, and `onfocus` attributes just as before. We also have (with one exception) the same two validation controls per textbox – a `RequiredFieldValidator` and a `RegularExpressionValidator`.

The next listing shows the declaration of the introductory text for this section, followed by the **User ID** textbox and associated validation controls. Notice that all this section of the page is enclosed in an ASP.NET `Panel` control (which creates a `<div>` or a `<table>` depending on the client type). We set the `Visible` attribute to `False` for this `Panel`, so that the content will not be included in the page by default. When we want to display the **Register** controls, we just have to set the `Visible` property to `True` at runtime:

```
...
<asp:panel id="pnlRegister" visible="False" runat="server">

<!-- "Register" controls for new user -->
<hr size="1" /><p />
<font face="Tahoma,Arial,Helvetica,sans-serif" size="2">
<span class="body-text">
If you <b>have not</b> previously registered with us, you can do so
now.<br />Please complete the form below, indicating the User ID
and password<br />you want to use to access this site in future.
Then click <b>Register</b>:</span>
<table cellpadding="5" cellspacing="5" border="0">
 <tr>
  <td colspan="4" align="left" nowrap="nowrap">
    <font face="Tahoma,Arial,Helvetica,sans-serif" size="2">
    <span class="body-text">User ID (minimum 4 characters,
    no spaces):</span>
    <asp:TextBox id="txtUserID" CssClass="body-text"
        TabIndex="5" Columns="15" runat="server"
        ToolTip="Enter a User ID (4 to 20 characters, no spaces)"
        onkeypress="disableSubmit('Logon')"
        onfocus="javascript:window.status='User ID to log on in future'" />
    <asp:RequiredFieldValidator id="valRequUserID" runat="server"
        ControlToValidate="txtUserID" Display="dynamic"
        ErrorMessage="You must provide a User ID">
      *
    </asp:RequiredFieldValidator>
    <asp:RegularExpressionValidator id="valRegexUserID" runat="server"
        ControlToValidate="txtUserID" Display="dynamic"
        ValidationExpression="\S{4,20}"
        ErrorMessage="User ID must be 4 - 20 characters with no spaces">
      *
    </asp:RegularExpressionValidator></font>
  </td>
 </tr>
 ...
```

Comparing Control Values

To save space and repetition, we haven't listed all the other control declarations here. However, there are a few points worth noting. We have a textbox for the user to enter the password they want to use, and another one to confirm this password by entering it again.

The second of these textboxes has a `RequiredFieldValidator` attached to force a value to be entered, but instead of a `RegularExpressionValidator` we attach a `CompareValidator` control that compares the values in the two textboxes. To achieve this, we just set the `ControlToCompare` attribute to the ID of the first textbox, and specify that the comparison `Type` is to compare the two values as strings:

```
<asp:CompareValidator id="valCompPWordCheck" runat="server"
     ControlToValidate="txtPWordCheck" Display="dynamic"
     ControlToCompare="txtPWord" Type="String"
     ErrorMessage="Password and confirmation do not match">*
</asp:CompareValidator></font></td>
```

Other Regular Expressions

The regular expression we used for the user ID and password is of the form `"\S{4,20}"`. This specifies that the value must contain non-space characters (and be between 4 and 20 characters long in this case). However, when validating other controls, such as the name, address, and so forth, we want to allow spaces to be included in the value. So, in these controls, we specify a regular expression of the form `".{4,20}"` instead. The full stop means 'any alphanumeric character' rather than 'any non-space alphanumeric character'.

When validating the e-mail address in the 'Home' page we used a fairly simple regular expression:

```
".*@.*\..*"
```

This basically limits entries to [*any alphanumeric characters*]@ [*any alphanumeric characters*] . [*any alphanumeric characters*]. So many non-valid values could be entered, though it does ensure that we get something that resembles an e-mail address. If you want to be more specific, and lock down the possible range of values that can be entered, you can use one of the many regular expressions that are listed on different web sites, or are in common use. This one more closely limits acceptable values to the standard formats for an e-mail address:

```
"([a-zA-Z0-9_\-\.]+)@(([a-zA-Z0-9\-]+\.)+)([a-zA-Z0-9]{2,4})"
```

The Register Button and Message Label

Finally, the Register section contains a `Button` control to submit the page and a `Label` control to display messages – much like we saw earlier in the Login section. The `Button` control calls a server-side event handler named `DoRegister` when clicked:

```
...
  <td colspan="2" align="right" nowrap="nowrap">
   <font face="Tahoma,Arial,Helvetica,sans-serif" size="2">
   <asp:Button id="btnRegister" Text="Register" CssClass="body-text"
        runat="server"
        ToolTip="Click to register details and access the My Cars page"
        TabIndex="15" OnClick="DoRegister" />
   </font>
  </td>
 </tr><tr>
  <td colspan="4" align="center" nowrap="nowrap">
   <font face="Tahoma,Arial,Helvetica,sans-serif" size="2">
   <b><asp:Label id="lblRegisterMsg" CssClass="body-text"
        EnableViewState="false" runat="server" /></b></font>
  </td>
 </tr>
</table>

</asp:panel>
...
```

The next screenshot shows the page when the current user has a temporary user ID. The controls to register are visible this time:

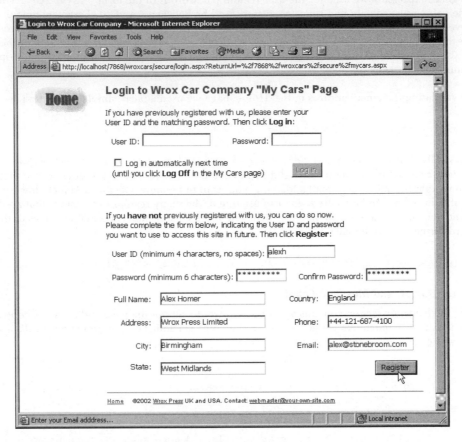

The Client-Side Script Functions

It's a nice touch in a page where the user has to enter values to set the input focus to the first control on the page, ready for them to start typing. And if there might be an existing value in that control, it's even nicer to select it so that they can just type a new value without having to delete the existing one, or press *Tab* to go to the next control.

The <body> element in our page defines a client-side event handler named setUserIDFocus that will be executed when the page has finished loading:

```
<body ... onload="setUserIDFocus()">
```

This function simply moves the input focus to the first User ID textbox on the page, using the focus method, and then selects the entire content of that control to give the effect we want:

```
<script language="JavaScript">
<!--
function setUserIDFocus() {
  var txtUserID = document.forms[0].elements['txtLogonUserID'];
  txtUserID.focus();
  txtUserID.select();
}
...
```

Disabling the Submit Buttons

We discussed earlier, when explaining why we include both the Login and Register sections in the same page, how having two 'submit' buttons on the same <form> can cause confusion if the user presses the *Return* key instead of clicking on the appropriate 'submit' button. To solve this, we include a client-side function in our page that disables the 'submit' button for the section that they are not interacting with.

All the textboxes in the Login section of our page contain the following onkeypress attribute, which executes the client-side function named disableSubmit when the user types in the textbox. They pass in a String that indicates which section the user is interacting with:

```
onkeypress="disableSubmit('Logon')"
```

Likewise, all the textboxes in the Register section contain this onkeypress attribute:

```
onkeypress="disableSubmit('Register')"
```

The disableSubmit function simply has to detect which section is being used, and then enable and disable the appropriate 'submit' buttons by setting their (client-side HTML) disabled property. Notice that we check if the controls actually exist on the page first to prevent a script error. While the Login button should always exist, the Register button may not be included if this user already has a permanent user ID:

```
...
  function disableSubmit(sAction) {
    var btnLogin = document.forms[0].elements['btnLogon'];
    var btnRegister = document.forms[0].elements['btnRegister'];
    if (btnRegister == null) return;
    if (sAction == 'Logon') {
      btnRegister.disabled = false;
      btnLogin.disabled = true;
    }
    else {
      btnLogin.disabled = false;
      btnRegister.disabled = true;
    }
  }
//-->
</script>
```

Not all browsers support the disabling of controls, and the function will have no effect in these browsers. However, it does work in Internet Explorer 4 and above. And, because the `disabled` property is part of the specification for controls in the HTML DOM version 2 and CSS2, it works in the 'version 6' browsers from Mozilla, Netscape, and Opera (Opera does not 'gray out' disabled buttons, but it does prevent them from being used).

The ASP.NET Server-Side Code

Having seen the HTML and client-side code in our 'login and register' page, the next step is to look at the server-side ASP.NET code that it contains. We declare three page-level variables to hold values that we'll use throughout the page. The sStyleSize and sConnect values are used in exactly the same way as in other pages we've already looked at. The user ID will be extracted from the user's session and stored in the sUserID variable:

```
' page-level variable to hold style size
Dim sStyleSize As String = "Standard"

' page-level variable to hold current user ID
Dim sUserID As String

' page-level variable to hold DB connection string
Dim sConnect As String
```

The Page_Load Event Handler

When the page loads, the first thing we must do is ensure that we still have an active ASP.NET session. We do this in the same way as we have in other pages you've seen in previous chapters, by testing for the presence of the current user ID in the session (recall that we stored it there in `default.aspx` when the user first entered our site). If it's not there, we know that the session has expired, and so we redirect them to `default.aspx` to reestablish it:

```
Sub Page_Load()

  ' get current UserID from Session
  sUserID = CType(Session("WccUserID"), String)
  If sUserID = "" Then

    ' not in Session so browser does not support
    ' sessions or did not load default.aspx first
    Response.Clear()
    Response.Redirect("../default.aspx")
    Response.End()

  End If
  ...
```

Next, we extract the stylesheet size from the user's session so that it can be inserted into the <link> element to select the correct stylesheet (as in all the earlier pages we've examined). Then we can extract the connection string for our database from the `web.config` file:

```
...
' get style sheet size from Session
sStyleSize = CType(Session("WccStyleSize"), String)

' get database connection string from web.config
sConnect = ConfigurationSettings.AppSettings("WroxCarsConnectString")
...
```

Displaying the 'Register' Section

Next, we decide if we need to display the section containing the Register controls. Anonymous user IDs (for visitors who have not yet registered) start with "~", so we just have to check for this. For an anonymous ID we make the Panel containing the Register controls visible. For a permanent user ID, we hide the Panel and pre-fill the User ID textbox with the value we extracted from this user's session earlier on:

```
...
' if this is a temporary login name, may need to register
If sUserID.Substring(0, 1) = "~" Then

  ' make register controls visible
  pnlRegister.Visible = True

Else

  ' hide register controls
  pnlRegister.Visible = False

  ' display this user's ID in login textbox
  txtLogonUserID.Text = sUserID

End If
...
```

Of course, if a user chooses as their permanent ID one that starts with this character, they will always see the Register controls, but that seems to be an unlikely situation so we don't check for it. If you want to prevent this, just change the regular expression in the validation control for the txtUserID textbox to prevent them choosing one that starts with "~".

Disabling the Validation Controls

We've already decided that we will have to 'manually operate' the validation controls to allow for our page to contain two distinct sets of controls, only one set of which may be filled with valid values each time. So, in the Page_Load event handler, we disable the controls completely by turning off client-side validation and server-side validation for every control in the page.

One nice feature when we use the ASP.NET validation controls is that the Page object exposes a collection of all the validation controls (Page.Validators), which allows us to easily iterate through them. This saves us from having to iterate through all the controls in the Page.Controls collection and check to see if each one is a validation control or not.

For each validation control we find, we set the `EnableClientScript` and `Enabled` properties to `False`:

```
. . .
' disable client-side validation and disable the default
' automatic validation to allow page to be submitted
' when only some of the controls are visible/filled
Dim oValidator As BaseValidator
For Each oValidator In Page.Validators
  oValidator.EnableClientScript = False
  oValidator.Enabled = False
Next
. . .
```

Of course, we could have disabled client-side validation for the controls by including the attribute `EnableClientScript="False"` in the control declarations. However, we have to iterate through them to set the `Disabled` property each time, as we change this value elsewhere in the page and it will be maintained in the viewstate otherwise.

Adapting the Page for Cookie-Less Clients

The last task in the `Page_Load` event handler is a minor diversion to ensure that we cope correctly with clients that do not support cookies. If we are using cookie-less sessions, we must set the 'authenticated' flag value in the session to indicate that the user is not currently authenticated. Also, because we can't use cookies, we cannot offer persistent authentication. So we hide the checkbox where the user would normally be able to select this option:

```
. . .
' see if we are using cookie-less sessions
If Session.IsCookieless Then

  ' set authentication flag in session to "no"
  ' set to "yes" after successful login/registration
  Session("WCCUserAuthenticated") = "no"

  ' hide the persistent cookie auto-logon option
  ' as this only applies to Forms-based authentication
  spnHideChecbox.Visible = False

End If

End Sub
```

The DoLogin Event Handler

When the user enters the user ID and password for an existing 'account' in the top section of the page, and clicks the Login button, the `DoLogin` routine is executed. In it, we first have to validate the values they entered, and we do this by manipulating the validation controls that we declared within this section of the page.

We used a specific set of ID values for these validation controls, as you can confirm from the listings we showed earlier. The two in the Login section have the string "Logon" in their control ID: for example, ValRequLogonPWord. The controls in the register section do not contain this string.

So we can iterate through the Page.Validators collection and examine the ID of each one to see if it contains this string. If it does, we first have to enable it, and then call its Validate method to perform the validation:

```
Sub DoLogin(oSender As Object, oArgs As EventArgs)
' check if User ID and password exist in database
' and redirect them to the 'My Cars' page if valid

   Dim oValidator As BaseValidator
   Dim sValidatorID As String
   For Each oValidator In Page.Validators
     sValidatorID = oValidator.ID
     If sValidatorID.IndexOf("Logon") > 0 Then

        ' this is a validator for the "Login" controls
        ' so enable it and perform validation
        oValidator.Enabled = True
        oValidator.Validate()

     End If
   Next
   ...
```

Now the IsValid property of the Page object will be set depending on the results of the validation, but only for any enabled validation controls. So, the next step is to see if there were any validation errors. If there were, the ValidationSummary control will display the values of the ErrorMessage property for each enabled validation control, and we don't have to do any more. The page will be redisplayed with the errors visible to the user ready for corrective action.

If there were no validation errors, we can continue and check if this user can be authenticated. However, our AuthenticateUser routine (which is located elsewhere in this page, and described in detail later) returns the permanent user ID of the current user by updating the sUserID variable to this value.

This means that – if the user has already registered, but they entered the site without the cookie that holds their permanent user ID – they will currently have a temporary 'anonymous' user ID in their session and in the variable sUserID. So if they have saved any quotations before reaching the login page, these quotations will have been saved using the anonymous ID. It means that we need to save this ID in another variable so that we can migrate these quotations across to their permanent user ID afterwards:

```
   ...
   ' see if validation controls indicate that all values
   ' in appropriate set of controls on page are valid
   ' if not, page will display validation errors
   If Page.IsValid Then
```

```
     ' if user has already registered but entered site this time
     ' with a temporary UserID we need to save this temporary ID
     ' so that we can migrate any quotes they received before
     ' switching over to their registered user name
     Dim sAnonID As String = ""
     If sUserID.Substring(0, 1) = "~" Then
        sAnonID = sUserID
     End If
     ...
```

Now we can call our `AuthenticateUser` routine, and if it returns `True` we know that the user was successfully authenticated. Then, if they were using a temporary 'anonymous' ID, we call another routine in our page named `MigrateExistingRows`. This simply swaps the user ID value of any rows that contain this user's 'anonymous' ID to their registered permanent user ID:

```
     ...
     If AuthenticateUser() Then

        ' after authentication sUserID contains registered User ID
        ' if they were using an anonymous ID then now need to migrate
        ' any existing quotes to registered user ID they provided
        If sAnonID > "" Then
          MigrateExistingRows(sAnonID, sUserID)
        End If
        ...
```

All that remains now is to redirect the user to the 'My Cars' page. If they are using cookie-less sessions, it means that ASP.NET Forms authentication is not actually being used. So we have to create our own routine to mark them as being authenticated and then redirect them to the 'My Cars' page. You'll see this routine, named `RedirectFromCookielessLoginPage`, described shortly:

```
     ...
     ' redirect to page originally requested (mycars.aspx)
     ' depends on what session support we are using
     If Session.IsCookieless Then

        ' using custom session-based authentication
        RedirectFromCookielessLoginPage(sUserID)

     Else
     ...
```

However, if they are using Forms authentication, we have a couple of things to do. We have to make sure that the cookie stored on their machine contains the current registered User ID (in case they 'lost' the original cookie and are using a temporary one). A routine named `UpdateUserIDCookie` that we've included in our page does this, and we provide the user ID we want to store in the cookie as a parameter.

Then we can simply call the `RedirectFromLoginPage` method of the `FormsAuthentication` object, providing as the first parameter the ID of the user we want to be marked as authenticated. This method creates the ASP.NET authentication cookie and places it on the client, then redirects the user to the page that they originally requested. In our case, this will be the 'My Cars' page. Notice that we specify the value of the 'persistent authentication' checkbox as the second parameter when we call this method. If this is `True` (checked), a long-term **persistent** cookie will be created instead of a short-term **session** cookie that expires when the browser is closed or the `timeout` period ends:

```
...
Else
  ' using Forms-based authentication
  ' update cookie to reflect current user name
  UpdateUserIDCookie()

  ' redirect to page they originally requested
  ' create persistent cookie if selected in page
  FormsAuthentication.RedirectFromLoginPage(sUserID, _
                                   chkPersist.Checked)

    End If

  End If

End If

End Sub
```

The `DoLogin` event handler that we've just been looking at uses four other routines to perform its magic. We described briefly what these routines do in the previous section, and we'll look at each one in more detail next. The four routines are:

❑ `AuthenticateUser`, which searches in our `tblUsers` table for an existing user ID and password combination, and returns the actual user ID from the database if a match is found.

❑ `MigrateExistingRows`, which changes the value of the user ID in the `tblQuoteOrders` table from a temporary 'anonymous' user ID to the correct permanent registered user ID for all rows that match a specified 'anonymous' user ID.

❑ `RedirectFromCookielessLoginPage`, which marks a user as being authenticated, and then redirects them to the 'My Cars' page. It is used when the browser does not support cookies.

❑ `UpdateUserIDCookie`, which simply writes a new cookie to the client's machine containing the specified user ID.

Authenticating an Existing User

The `AuthenticateUser` routine is shown next. In it we first collect the user ID from the textbox on the page and remove any leading or trailing spaces. In theory the validation controls will prevent the user entering any spaces, but it does no harm to be sure! Then we specify the name of a stored procedure in our database that will select the matching user, and create our connection and command objects as usual – setting the `CommandType` to indicate that we're using a stored procedure:

```
Function AuthenticateUser() As Boolean
' check if this UserID/password is valid

  ' get login User ID specified in form controls
  ' and remove any stray spaces from start and end
  Dim sLogonID As String = txtLogonUserID.Text
  sLogonID = sLogonID.Trim()

  ' specify the stored procedure name
  Dim sProcName As String = "AuthenticateUser"

  ' create connection and command objects
  Dim sqlConn As New SqlConnection(sConnect)
  Dim sqlComm As New SqlCommand(sProcName, sqlConn)
  sqlComm.CommandType = CommandType.StoredProcedure
  ...
```

The stored procedure we use, named `AuthenticateUser`, is relatively simple. It expects to be supplied with two parameters – the user ID and password – and it returns from the database the value of the user ID for the row that contains the specified user ID and password. This means that, if the user enters their user ID in a different letter case (they are not case sensitive), we will return it in the correct case:

```
CREATE PROCEDURE AuthenticateUser
@UserID varchar(20), @UserPW varchar(255) AS
SELECT UserID FROM tblUsers WHERE UserID = @UserID AND UserPW = @UserPW
```

By default SQL Server and most other databases are not case-sensitive when selecting or matching text values. However, if you have installed and/or configured your database to run in case-sensitive mode, the user ID will be case sensitive unless you add code to convert it to a specific case (probably all lower-case) when storing and retrieving it each time.

Encrypting the Password

So now we can think about where the other parameter for our stored procedure, the user's password, comes from. We are storing the passwords in our database in encrypted form, and so we have to encrypt the password that the user entered into the textbox before we can use it as a parameter for our stored procedure, and in the `WHERE` clause of that stored procedure.

The delightfully named `HashPasswordForStoringInConfigFile` method of the `FormsAuthentication` object can convert a text string into the equivalent SHA1 or MD5 **hash** equivalent value, and this is how we convert our user's password. The great thing about using encrypted hash values is that they are automatically case-sensitive, so (for example) the hash for `"Alex"` is completely different from the hash for `"alex"`. Therefore our password check is case-sensitive, because we are actually comparing two hash values in our stored procedure's `WHERE` clause.

The next line of our `AuthenticateUser` routine creates the password hash, and then we can add the parameters we need to the `Command` object's `Parameters` collection:

```
  ...

  ' create SHA1 hash of password provided (could use "MD5" instead)
  Dim sPWHash As String
```

```
sPWHash = FormsAuthentication.HashPasswordForStoringInConfigFile _
                                    (txtLogonPWord.Text, "SHA1")

' add the parameters to the Command object
sqlComm.Parameters.Add("@UserID", sLogonID)
sqlComm.Parameters.Add("@UserPW", sPWHash)
...
```

As a brief diversion here, it's worth mentioning one problem that does arise when storing passwords only in 'hashed' form. A hash is a mathematical function that is easy to perform one way (creating the hash) but extremely difficult to perform the other way (extracting the original value from the hashed value). This is intentional, as it is the whole reason for using a hash to encrypt the value.

However, many sites offer a "Forgotten your password?" feature that e-mails the account password to the e-mail address that the account is registered for. We could e-mail our users the encrypted hash but that would be no help, as they could not tell from that what the original password was. And neither can we, so we can't offer this kind of feature. All we could do is implement some system for allowing them to provide a new password and then updating the database table with the hash of this password.

Executing the Stored Procedure

Now we can execute the stored procedure. We know that it returns a rowset that should contain only one row, and that row has a single column (the user ID). So, for speed and efficiency, we can use the `ExecuteScalar` method rather than creating and returning a `DataReader` object. The `ExecuteScalar` method returns just the value of the first column in the first row of the resulting rowset.

Therefore, if the result returned by `ExecuteScalar` is the same as the value of the user ID stored in the `sUserID` variable, we know that the user exists and that they provided the correct password. All we then have to do is update the page-level `sUserID` variable to the actual (letter-case correct) user ID, and store it in the user's ASP.NET session as well. Then we can return `True` to indicate successful authentication. However, if we don't get a match on the user ID and password, we display a message in the `Label` control in this section of the page and return `False`:

```
...
Try

  ' execute the stored procedure
  sqlConn.Open()
  If sqlComm.ExecuteScalar() = sLogonID Then

    ' found matching row so use new logon as UserID and update session
    sUserID = sLogonID
    Session("WCCUserID") = sUserID
    Return True

  Else

    ' no matching row found
    lblLoginMsg.Text = "* Invalid User ID or password, try again..."
    Return False

  End If
```

```
    Catch objError As Exception

      'display error details
      lblLoginMsg.Text = "* Error while accessing database.<br />" _
                          & objError.Message & "<br />" & objError.Source

      Return False

    Finally

      sqlConn.Close()

    End Try

  End Function
```

The remainder of the code is the Catch section of our Try...Catch construct (where we display the error details), and the Finally section that closes the database connection irrespective of whether there was an error or not.

Migrating Existing Quotations to the New User ID

The next routine we use in the DoLogin event handler is responsible for migrating any existing quotes that have been saved with an 'anonymous' user ID to the user's permanent registered user ID. For this we use a simple stored procedure named MigrateQuotes, which accepts two parameters: the old (anonymous) and the new (registered) user ID:

```
CREATE PROCEDURE MigrateQuotes
@AnonUserID varchar(20), @NewUserID varchar(20) AS
UPDATE tblQuoteOrder SET UserID = @NewUserID WHERE UserID = @AnonUserID
```

The related child table named tblQuoteOrderExtras is linked to the tblQuoteOrder table by a primary key/foreign key constraint. The primary key of the tblQuoteOrder table is an IDENTITY value that is created automatically, and not the user ID (which could occur many times in the tblQuoteOrderExtras table). Therefore the user ID is not included in the tblQuoteOrderExtras table, and so we don't need to update any rows in this table.

The MigrateExistingRows routine receives the two values we need when it is called, and returns a Boolean result to indicate success or failure. All the code uses well-tried techniques that are identical to many other routines we've seen in other pages of our site.

As there could be zero or more existing quotations for this user, we can't use the number of rows that were updated to check for success or failure of the stored procedure. However, it will raise an error if the update process itself fails (for example, if you do not grant the correct permissions or the connection fails). So we return True if the ExecuteNonQuery method does *not* cause an error, or False if it does:

```
Function MigrateExistingRows(sAnonID As String, sNewID As String) _
                                              As Boolean
  ' migrate existing quotes in database for anonymous user
  ' to the new user ID they specified when registering
```

```
        ' specify the stored procedure name
        Dim sProcName As String = "MigrateQuotes"

        ' create connection and command objects
        Dim sqlConn As New SqlConnection(sConnect)
        Dim sqlComm As New SqlCommand(sProcName, sqlConn)
        sqlComm.CommandType = CommandType.StoredProcedure

        ' add parameters to Command
        sqlComm.Parameters.Add("@AnonUserID", sAnonID)
        sqlComm.Parameters.Add("@NewUserID", sNewID)

        Try

            ' execute the stored procedure
            sqlConn.Open()
            sqlComm.ExecuteNonQuery()
            Return True

        Catch objError As Exception

            Return False

        Finally

            sqlConn.Close()

        End Try

    End Function
```

Redirecting Cookie-Less Clients

When we are dealing with clients that do not support cookies, we can't use ASP.NET Forms authentication. So we have to build our own version of the RedirectFromLoginPage method that the FormsAuthentication object exposes (and which we use in the DoLogin event handler for clients that do support cookies).

Our custom RedirectFromCookielessLoginPage routine is called after we have authenticated a user, and its task is to mark the user as being authenticated and then redirect them to the appropriate page. All that's involved is to store the token value "yes" in the WCCUserAuthenticated session variable, then perform our redirection:

```
Sub RedirectFromCookielessLoginPage(sUserID As String)
' custom routine to redirect client to mycars.aspx page after
' successful authentication when using cookieless sessions

    ' set session flag to indicate registration succeeded
    Session("WCCUserAuthenticated") = "yes"
    Response.Clear()
    Response.Redirect("mycars.aspx")
    Response.End()

End Sub
```

Notice that we hard-coded the page URL for redirection into the code, as we know that we will only ever redirect to the 'My Cars' page. This is the only page (other than the 'login and register' page) in our `secure` folder, and the only one for which access is restricted and authentication is required.

This is in contrast to the `FormsAuthentication.RedirectFromLoginPage` method, which automatically redirects the user to the page that they originally requested (the one that they were trying to view when they were redirected to the 'login' page). When this redirection to the login page takes place, the URL of the original page is appended to the query string, and so the `RedirectFromLoginPage` method can tell which page it needs to redirect the user to after successful authentication. You can see this in the **Address** bar in the following screenshot:

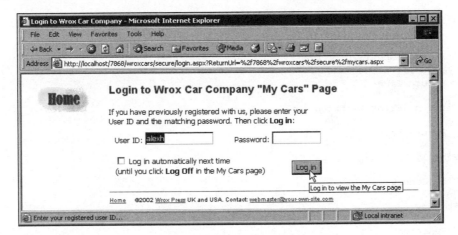

We could, of course, replicate this behavior in our custom `RedirectFromCookielessLoginPage` routine if required. We would have to add the URL of the current page to the query string in the page that causes the login page to be loaded (in our case the 'My Cars' page), but this can easily be extracted from the `Request.Path` property. Then, in the `RedirectFromCookielessLoginPage` routine, we could extract this URL from the query string and perform the appropriate redirection.

Updating the User ID Cookie

The final routine that we call from the `DoLogin` event handler is responsible for writing the cookie containing the user ID to the client's machine. If we have changed the user ID from an 'anonymous' one to a registered one as they logged into the site, we have to do this so that their next visit will take place under the context of the correct user ID.

The code is just the same as we used to create the cookie in the `default.aspx` page. We create a new `HttpCookie` object, setting the name and value within the constructor, and then specify that it should apply to our entire site and that it should not expire for 5 years. Then we add it to the `Cookies` collection for this page:

```
Sub UpdateUserIDCookie()
' write new cookie with UserID to client's browser

   Dim oCookie As New HttpCookie("WccUserID", sUserID)
   oCookie.Path = "/"
   Dim dNow As DateTime = Now()
```

```
     oCookie.Expires = dNow.AddYears(5)
     Response.Cookies.Add(oCookie)

End Sub
```

*Remember that this cookie is **not** the same as the authentication cookie that is created automatically by the Forms authentication process. The cookie we create in the routine listed above only contains the user ID, and is used to persist it between visits to our site.*

The DoRegister Event Handler

The other event handler in our page, `DoRegister`, is executed when the user clicks the **Register** button rather than the **Login** button. The task here is more complex, because we have to:

❑   Validate the registration values that the user entered

❑   Insert the new user into the database

❑   Migrate any existing quotes to the new user ID

❑   Mark the user as being authenticated

❑   Redirect them to the 'My Cars' page

Luckily (or perhaps due to good design), we already have routines that we can use to perform several of these tasks. We used these in the `DoLogin` event handler we've just been looking at.

Validating the User's Values

The first step in our `DoRegister` event handler is much the same as we saw in the `DoLogin` event handler. We validate the values that the user entered, but this time for the controls in the lower (**Register**) section of the page. The technique is just the same, but we test for validation control IDs that do *not* contain the string "`Logon`":

```
Sub DoRegister(oSender As Object, oArgs As EventArgs)
' runs when the "Register" button is clicked
' add user to database, migrate any existing quotes
' and redirect them to the "My Cars" page

  ' cause appropriate set of validation controls to
  ' check the values of the controls on the page
  Dim oValidator As BaseValidator
  Dim sValidatorID As String
  For Each oValidator In Page.Validators
    sValidatorID = oValidator.ID
    If sValidatorID.IndexOf("Logon") < 0 Then

      ' this is a validator for the "Register" controls
      ' so enable it and perform validation
      oValidator.Enabled = True
      oValidator.Validate()
```

```
    End If
Next
...
```

Now we can see if validation succeeded, and if so we save the temporary 'anonymous' user ID just as we did in the DoLogin event handler:

```
...
' see if validation controls indicate that all values
' in appropriate set of controls on page are valid
' if not, page will display validation errors
If Page.IsValid Then

  ' save existing "anonymous" user ID
  Dim sAnonID As String = sUserID
  ...
```

Inserting the New User Details

Next we attempt to insert our new user's details into the tblUsers table in our database. We use a separate routine named InsertNewUser (elsewhere within this page), which returns True or False depending on whether the new values can be inserted. We'll look at this routine later on:

```
    ...
    If InsertNewUser() Then
      ...
```

Providing that we did successfully add our new user to the database, we can now migrate any existing quotations they may have saved to their new registered user ID. We use the same MigrateExistingRows routine as we did in the DoLogin event handler, and specify the old and new user ID values as parameters:

```
      ...
      ' inserted new user into tblUsers in DB so now
      ' update any existing quotes for old temporary
      ' anonymous user ID to new registered user ID
      MigrateExistingRows(sAnonID, sUserID)
      ...
```

The remainder of the DoRegister routine is again remarkably similar to the DoLogin routine we saw earlier. If the client does not support cookies we use the custom RedirectFromCookielessLoginPage routine to update the 'authenticated flag' value in this user's session and then redirect them to the 'My Cars' page.

If the client does support cookies (and therefore supports Forms-based authentication), we update their cookie and call the RedirectFromLoginPage method of the FormsAuthentication object to mark them as being authenticated and redirect them to the 'My Cars' page. Notice that this time we specify the value False for the persistent login parameter to the RedirectFromLoginPage method, as this is safer. They can decide to switch on persistent login when they next log into our site if they wish:

```
...
' redirect to page originally requested (mycars.aspx)
' depends on what session support we are using
If Session.IsCookieless Then

    ' using custom session-based authentication
    RedirectFromCookielessLoginPage(sUserID)

Else

    ' using Forms-based authentication
    ' update cookie to reflect new user name
    UpdateUserIDCookie()

    ' do not create persistent authentication cookie this time
    FormsAuthentication.RedirectFromLoginPage(sUserID, False)

End If

Else

    'display error details
    lblRegisterMsg.Text = "* The User ID you specified is already in use"

End If

End If

End Sub
```

Inserting a New User into the Database

The only remaining section of code in the 'login and register' page that we haven't discussed yet is how we insert a new user into the `tblUsers` table of our database. As you'll be expecting by now, we use a stored procedure to perform the row insert. This stored procedure, named `InsertNewUser`, accepts nine parameters that are equivalent to the nine columns in the table for which we must provide values:

```
CREATE PROCEDURE InsertNewUser
@UserID varchar(20), @UserPW varchar(255), @UserName varchar(50),
@Address varchar(60), @City varchar(30), @State varchar(20),
@Country varchar(30), @Phone varchar(20), @Email varchar(50) AS
INSERT INTO tblUsers(UserID, UserPW, UserName, Address,
                     City, State, Country, Phone, Email)
VALUES (@UserID, @UserPW, @UserName, @Address,
        @City, @State, @Country, @Phone, @Email)
```

We execute this stored procedure using the `ExecuteNonQuery` method of the `Command` object, just as we've done so many times before in other pages. The only twist here is that we need to create the appropriate 'hash' of the password before we add it to the `Parameters` collection:

```
Function InsertNewUser() As Boolean
' add a new user to the database
```

```
    ' specify the stored procedure name
    Dim sProcName As String = "InsertNewUser"

    ' create connection and command objects
    Dim sqlConn As New SqlConnection(sConnect)
    Dim sqlComm As New SqlCommand(sProcName, sqlConn)
    sqlComm.CommandType = CommandType.StoredProcedure

    ' create SHA1 hash of password provided (could use "MD5" instead)
    Dim sPWHash As String
    sPWHash = FormsAuthentication.HashPasswordForStoringInConfigFile _
                                            (txtPWord.Text, "SHA1")

    ' get proposed new UserID from text box
    Dim sNewUserID As String = txtUserID.Text

    ' add parameters to Command
    sqlComm.Parameters.Add("@UserID", sNewUserID)
    sqlComm.Parameters.Add("@UserPW", sPWHash)
    sqlComm.Parameters.Add("@UserName", txtName.Text)
    sqlComm.Parameters.Add("@Address", txtAddr.Text)
    sqlComm.Parameters.Add("@City", txtCity.Text)
    sqlComm.Parameters.Add("@State", txtState.Text)
    sqlComm.Parameters.Add("@Country", txtCountry.Text)
    sqlComm.Parameters.Add("@Phone", txtPhone.Text)
    sqlComm.Parameters.Add("@Email", txtEmail.Text)
    ...
```

We then execute the stored procedure, and if the result is one (one row was updated) we know that the process was successful and we can return True. Otherwise, or if there is an error, we return False. Then, in the Finally block, we just have to close our database connection:

```
    ...
    Try

        ' execute the stored procedure
        sqlConn.Open()
        If sqlComm.ExecuteNonQuery() = 1 Then

            ' new user insert succeeded so update session and variables
            sUserID = sNewUserID
            Session("WCCUserID") = sNewUserID
            Return True

        Else
            Return False
        End If

    Catch objError As Exception
        Return False
    Finally
        sqlConn.Close()
    End Try

End Function
```

Summary

Another long chapter, and more complicated concepts and code – or so it may seem. In fact, the techniques we've used in this chapter are not really that complicated, but they can seem confusing at first. ASP.NET Forms authentication is extremely powerful (we've really only shown you the simplest ways of using it here), and saves a lot of work on our behalf when writing code. Once you become familiar with the process it forces you to follow, it all makes a great deal of sense.

In this chapter, we started by reviewing the basic concepts of access control, in particular how they relate to a web site. We followed this with a brief summary of the ASP.NET authentication and authorization configuration options, before concentrating in more detail on how Forms-based authentication works and how we use it in our example Wrox Car Company site.

Forms-based authentication is a great time-saver, but falls down if there is no support for cookies in the client. However, we discussed other 'traditional' ASP techniques for controlling access, and for checking if a user has been authenticated, and used one of these techniques (storing a 'flag value' in the user's session) in our example site. We saw how we can interweave it with Forms-based authentication to get the best of both worlds.

We also discussed how we can work with the ASP.NET validation controls in a more controlled and specific way to achieve 'managed' validation where our page contains more than one set of input controls that must be validated. And, related to this discussion, we saw how we can get round a couple of problems caused by only having one `<form>` section on a page, instead of separate ones as was the traditional approach in ASP 3.0 and earlier.

Finally, we worked through the code for the 'login and register' page in our example site, seeing how it all fits together – and picking up a few other tips on the use of encrypted passwords, and providing persistent login rather than having the authentication expire when the browser is closed or the session times out.

The topics we discussed in this chapter were:

- ❑ The ASP.NET and other techniques we use for authentication and authorization
- ❑ How we identify 'anonymous' users as they browse and then log into our site
- ❑ How we collect and store information about our visitors when they register
- ❑ How we force users that have already registered to provide 'logon' details
- ❑ How the 'login and register' page in our example Wrox Car Company site works

In the next and final chapter, we look at the remaining page in our site where the user can view their quotations and place orders for our vehicles. It's the pinnacle we've been working towards (and the one feature that would pay for our site if it wasn't just a fictional example!).

Quotations and Orders

In this final chapter, we'll look at the one remaining page of our **Wrox Car Company** that we haven't yet discussed. The 'My Cars' page allows visitors to see quotations they have saved, and place an order for a vehicle based on one of these quotations. Of course, placing an order in a real-world site usually involves a great deal of backend processing such as verifying payment details, registering the order, and updating the customer's account details.

This book aims to show how we can use ASP.NET Web Forms and server controls to build interfaces, so we will not be looking at this backend processing. We'll take a shortcut to placing an order, with a simple update to our database. However, you will see how we can use ASP.NET to build a useful and informative interface easily, including how we can bind the list controls that are provided with ASP.NET to sets of nested data, as well as to simple data tables.

So, the aims of this chapter are to show:

❑   How we can bind related sets of data to a range of list controls

❑   How we can easily display hierarchical data in nested form

❑   How we built the 'My Cars' page

❑   How we handle the placing of an order for a vehicle

We start with a look at the concepts of binding to related and hierarchical sets of data.

Binding List Controls to Related Data

ASP.NET provides a useful range of server controls that can display lists, using a data source that contains repeated 'rows' or 'items' of data. Examples that we've already seen in this book include the CheckBoxList, RadioButtonList, DropDownList, Repeater, DataList, and DataGrid.

Binding to a Single Data Source

In all of the previous examples that use these list controls, we bound the control to a single data source such as a `DataTable` or `DataView`. Then, in some of the examples, we interacted with the control by hooking into the `ItemDataBound` event and used code in this event handler to read, modify, and even insert new content into the output for the control for one or more of the 'rows' it creates.

For example, in the 'Home' page, we interact with the `DataGrid` control to change the URL of the hyperlinks in the output generated by this control. This allows us to detect if the current user's browser supports client-side scripting – and, if so, change the URLs so that they use a JavaScript function to open the new window rather than a traditional hyperlink:

home.aspx

```
Sub SetNavigateUrl(oSender As Object, oArgs As DataGridItemEventArgs)
    If bCanScript And (oArgs.Item.ItemType = ListItemType.Item _
                Or oArgs.Item.ItemType = ListItemType.AlternatingItem) Then

        ' it's a data row that is being bound so create appropriate
        ' URLs for hyperlinks and remove Target attributes
        Dim sCarID As String = oArgs.Item.DataItem("CarID")
        Dim sHref As String = "javascript:openWindow('" _
                        & InsertSessionId(Request.Path) _
                        & "/cardetail.aspx?id=" & sCarID _
                        & "', '" & sCarID & "')"

        ' update HRef in controls to new value
        CType(args.Item.FindControl("lnkCarImage"), Hyperlink).NavigateUrl = sHref
        CType(args.Item.FindControl("lnkCarImage"), Hyperlink).Target = ""
        CType(args.Item.FindControl("lnkCarName"), Hyperlink).NavigateUrl = sHref
        CType(args.Item.FindControl("lnkCarName"), Hyperlink).Target = ""

    End If
End Sub
```

However, while this might just seem like a useful technique for modifying the content of a control, it is actually a lot more useful and powerful than that. It allows us to interact with the content of the 'template' section that generates the output in its entirety. We can insert new controls, show and hide existing controls, update almost any of the properties of existing controls, and thereby change the output that the list control generates in almost any way we like.

Binding Nested List Controls

From the above, you can probably see how we can use this technique to display related or nested data within an ASP.NET list control. During the `ItemDataBound` event, we can interact with other list controls that are declared within the templates of the main list control (or generated dynamically), binding them to the appropriate data source and even selecting the appropriate value(s) within these nested list controls.

To see what we mean, we'll look shortly at an example that is not actually part of the Wrox Car Company site. However, to give you a flavor for where we're going, take a look at the next screenshot of the 'My Cars' page in our Wrox Car Company site. Within the list we display a list of the optional extras that were specified for each vehicle when the quotation was saved. However, these optional extras are in a related child table, and not in the table containing the quotations. To create this nested (hierarchical) display, we have to interact with the list control that creates the page content during the ItemDataBound event:

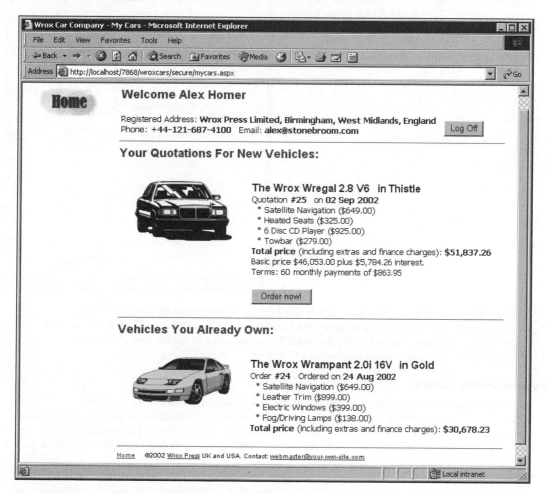

An Example of Nested Bound Controls

To help you understand how we can databind nested list controls that are located within another list control, we've provided a simple example page named nested-binding.aspx. You'll find this in the nested-binding sub-folder of the sample files for this book. It demonstrates how three different types of ASP.NET list control can be used within a DataGrid control, though the principles are applicable to any other combination of list controls.

The screenshot here shows the final page. We've placed a DataGrid control on the page, and you can see that it contains three columns: Select Engine, Select Extras, and Select Color. Each of the three rows in the DataGrid contains three list controls: a RadioButtonList, a CheckBoxList, and a DropDownList. The third column in each row also contains an ASP.NET Image control. The Image control reflects the selection in the DropDownList control above it:

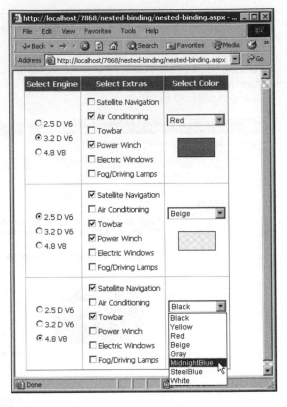

*Note that we are **not** handling postbacks in this page, so selecting in the list controls has no effect. The aim of this example is to demonstrate how we construct these nested lists. There is a server-side <form> in the page, but this is only because it is required when we use the CheckBoxList, RadioButtonList, and DropDownList controls.*

The DataGrid Declaration

The declaration of the DataGrid control contains the styling information, and sets the AutoGenerateColumns attribute to False because we want to generate our own custom column content. The <Columns> element contains the definition of the columns we want to display, and in this case you can see that we've used three TemplateColumn elements to define the three columns we want:

nested-binding.aspx

```
<asp:DataGrid id="dgrNesting" runat="server"
    AutoGenerateColumns="False"
    CellPadding="4" Font-Size="10"
    Font-Name="Tahoma,Arial,Helvetica,sans-serif"
    HeaderStyle-HorizontalAlign="center" HeaderStyle-BackColor="#b50055"
    HeaderStyle-ForeColor="#ffffff" SelectedItemStyle-BackColor="#ffffcc"
    ItemStyle-HorizontalAlign="center" HeaderStyle-Font-Bold="True">

  <Columns>
```

```
        <asp:TemplateColumn HeaderText="Select Engine">
          <ItemTemplate>
            <asp:RadioButtonList style="font-size:12px"
                 id="radEngine" runat="server" />
          </ItemTemplate>
        </asp:TemplateColumn>

        <asp:TemplateColumn HeaderText="Select Extras">
          <ItemTemplate>
            <asp:CheckBoxList style="font-size:12px"
                 id="chkExtras" runat="server" />
          </ItemTemplate>
        </asp:TemplateColumn>

        <asp:TemplateColumn HeaderText="Select Color">
          <ItemTemplate>
            <asp:DropDownList style="font-size:12px"
                 id="selColor" runat="server" /><p />
            <asp:Image id="imgColor" border="1" runat="server" />
          </ItemTemplate>
        </asp:TemplateColumn>

      </Columns>

    </asp:DataGrid>
```

The content of each column is just an empty list control of the appropriate type, a `RadioButtonList`, a `CheckBoxList` or a `DropDownList`. The third column also contains an `Image` control with no value set for the `ImageUrl` (the source of the image to display). We'll fill the lists, select some values at random, and set the `ImageUrl` property of the `Image` control within the event handler that we attach to the `DataGrid` control.

The Data Sources for the Lists

We've reused part of the code that builds the `DataSet` from our 'Model Details' page in this example. The `DataSet` we generate contains three tables: `CarDetails` contains a list of car/engine combinations, `CarExtras` contains a list of extras that are available for the selected vehicle, and `CarColors` contains a list of the colors that are available for the selected vehicle.

When we generate the `DataSet` within the `Page_Load` event, we specify the value `"5"` for the `CarID` so that we get back a `DataSet` containing the three rows that define the three possible car/engine combinations for the **Wrox Wranger** truck, and the extras and colors available for this vehicle:

```
Sub Page_Load()

  ' get DataSet from function elsewhere in this page
  oCarsDS = GetCarDetailsDS("5")
  ...
```

Then we can bind the default view of the `CarDetails` table (a `DataView` object) to the main `DataGrid` control named `dgrNesting`:

```
...
' display details of this vehicle
dgrNesting.DataSource = oCarsDS.Tables("CarDetails").DefaultView
dgrNesting.DataBind()

End Sub
```

However, this only gives us an empty `DataGrid`, as you can see in the next screenshot. The `RadioButtonList` and `CheckBoxList` controls have no content (no `ListItems`, because we have not specified a `DataSource`), and so they generate no visible output. The `DropDownList` does appear, but again it has no content so the list is empty. And, as we didn't specify the `ImageUrl` for the `Image` control, this shows no image:

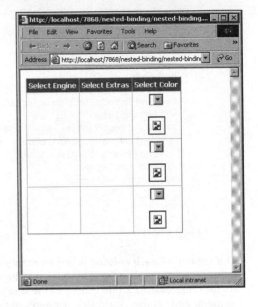

Handling the OnItemDataBound Event

What we need to do now is handle the `ItemDataBound` event, just as we did in several examples of using list controls in earlier chapters. We add an event handler named `FillLists` to the page, and specify that this should be executed when each row in the `DataGrid` is databound to the source data, by adding it to the declaration of the `DataGrid` (highlighted in the next listing):

```
<asp:DataGrid id="dgrNesting" runat="server"
    AutoGenerateColumns="False"
    CellPadding="4" Font-Size="10"
    Font-Name="Tahoma,Arial,Helvetica,sans-serif"
    HeaderStyle-HorizontalAlign="center" HeaderStyle-BackColor="#b50055"
    HeaderStyle-ForeColor="#ffffff" SelectedItemStyle-BackColor="#ffffcc"
    ItemStyle-HorizontalAlign="center" HeaderStyle-Font-Bold="True"
    OnItemDataBound="FillLists">
```

Now, in our `FillLists` event handler, we can interact with the controls in each row of our `DataGrid` as the `DataBind` method we execute in the `Page_Load` event handler binds these rows to the source data from the `CarEngines` table. The next listing shows the first part of the declaration of our `FillLists` event handler. As in earlier examples, we must make sure that we only execute code in response to the event when the source of the event is an `Item` or an `AlternatingItem` row. (Even if we don't specify an `AlternatingItem` template in the definition of a list control, the event is still raised as an `AlternatingItem` row event for alternate rows.):

```
Sub FillLists(oSender As Object, oArgs As DataGridItemEventArgs)
' runs when the OnItemDataBound event occurs
' used to bind nested list controls and select values
' in this example, values selected at random but could come from rows

  ' make sure its an Item or AlternatingItem row
  If oArgs.Item.ItemType = ListItemType.Item _
  Or oArgs.Item.ItemType = ListItemType.AlternatingItem Then
    ...
```

Referencing the Nested List Controls

Our next step involves getting references to the controls in the current row of the DataGrid – in other words the row that is currently being bound to the main CarDetails data source. We use the FindControl method of the current Item (the row being bound, as exposed by the Item property of the DataGridItemEventArgs object that is passed to our event handler), and specify the ID of the control we want to find:

```
    ...
    ' get references to the three list controls and Image in this row
    Dim oRadioList As RadioButtonList _
         = CType(oArgs.Item.FindControl("radEngine"), RadioButtonList)
    Dim oCheckList As CheckBoxList _
         = CType(oArgs.Item.FindControl("chkExtras"), CheckBoxList)
    Dim oDropList As DropDownList _
         = CType(oArgs.Item.FindControl("selColor"), DropDownList)
    Dim oImage As Image = CType(oArgs.Item.FindControl("imgColor"), Image)
    ...
```

Binding the Nested List Controls

Now we can bind the list controls in this row to the relevant data sources. The RadioButtonList control shows the list of engines that can be bound to the same CarDetails table as the parent dgrNesting list control, as this will provide the three engine types for this vehicle.

We use the DataTextField and DataValueField properties to set the captions of the radio buttons and their values, just as we have in earlier examples, and then call the DataBind method to display the data. The fact that we're now inside the event handler for the ItemDataBound event, rather than in the Page_Load event handler for a single control located directly on the page (as we've used in earlier examples) makes no difference. It works in just the same way:

```
    ...
    ' set DataSource and DataBind the RadioButtonList control
    oRadioList.DataSource = oCarsDS.Tables("CarDetails").DefaultView
    oRadioList.DataTextField = "EngineName"
    oRadioList.DataValueField = "EngineID"
    oRadioList.DataBind()
    ...
```

Likewise, we can bind the other list controls to the appropriate data sources. We bind the list of optional extras to the CarExtras table, and the list of available colors to the CarColors table. Again we specify the DataTextField so that the controls know which column contains the text to display, and for the DropDownList control we also specify the DataValueField property (remember that the CheckBoxList control does not actually use the DataValueField property, as we discovered in earlier examples):

```
...
' set DataSource and DataBind the CheckBoxList control
oCheckList.DataSource = oCarsDS.Tables("CarExtras").DefaultView
oCheckList.DataTextField = "ExtraText"
oCheckList.DataBind()

' set DataSource and DataBind the DropDownList control
oDropList.DataSource = oCarsDS.Tables("CarColors").DefaultView
oDropList.DataTextField = "Color"
oDropList.DataValueField = "ColorID"
oDropList.DataBind()
...
```

This is all we need to do to populate the three list controls in our page. The next screenshot shows the results. Of course, we haven't specified the ImageUrl of our Image control in each row, so this still doesn't display anything. And the lists are all 'unselected' or set to the first value in the data source, as so far we haven't specified what value these controls should have:

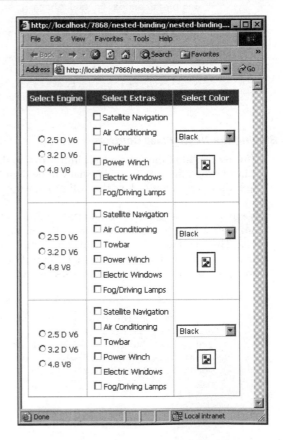

Setting the Values of Nested List Controls

So, the next step is to look at how we set the values of the controls in each row. You have probably figured this out already, but we'll work through the code we used just to confirm this. We first have to decide what the values of each control should be. In applications that allow users to edit data, the values of the controls in each row will be the current values in the source data row.

For example, if the `DataGrid` was displaying a list of customers, a drop-down list of country names should be set to the name of the country in the database table for that customer. The user can change this, but if they don't the page reflects the underlying data – which is what you would expect.

The value of the underlying data in the row that is currently being bound can be obtained within the `ItemDataBound` event from the `DataItem` property that is exposed by the arguments to the event handler. In our 'Home' page, for instance, we extracted the value of the `CarID` from the current row (which we use to build the `href` for each link) as our `DataGrid` was being data bound using:

home.aspx

```
Dim sCarID As String = oArgs.Item.DataItem("CarID")
```

You'll find plenty of examples of using these techniques to display and allow the user to update data in our sister book ASP.NET Distributed Data Applications *(Wrox Press ISBN 1-86100-492-3, see* http://www.daveandal.com/books/4923/ *for more details).*

In our example, however, we just generate random values for the list controls to demonstrate the techniques for setting the control values. We generate five integers, with their ranges of value depending on the maximum number of items in each list control (note that the `Random.Next` method returns an `Integer` that is **less than** the value of the second parameter):

nested-binding.aspx

```
    ...
    ' create random values for the controls
    Dim iEngine As Integer = oRandom.Next(0, 3)
    Dim iExtra1 As Integer = oRandom.Next(0, 6)
    Dim iExtra2 As Integer = oRandom.Next(0, 6)
    Dim iExtra3 As Integer = oRandom.Next(0, 6)
    Dim iColor As Integer = oRandom.Next(0, 8)
    ...
```

Selection Based on a SelectedIndex Value

If the value we have can be treated as the `SelectedIndex` of the nested control, it's easy to set the control value. We just assign it to the `SelectedIndex` property of the control:

```
    ...
    ' select RadioButton in "Engines" RadioButtonList control
    oRadioList.SelectedIndex = iEngine
    ...
```

This will often be the case if the control uses a set of consecutive zero-based values from a table designed to contain control values, as in our list of engines in the 'Model Details' page. And, in a RadioButtonList, we can only select one item. However, in a CheckBoxList we might be required to select more than one item. This could be the case if the values come from a linked child table, as with the optional extras for our vehicles. In this case, we can set the Selected property of the matching ListItem controls within the Items collection of the control, based again on their index within the control:

```
...
' select three CheckBoxes in "Extras" CheckBoxList control
oCheckList.Items(iExtra1).Selected = True
oCheckList.Items(iExtra2).Selected = True
oCheckList.Items(iExtra3).Selected = True
...
```

For a drop-down list, we use the same technique as the RadioButtonList. Like the RadioButtonList, the DropDownList control only allows one item to be selected – so we can set the SelectedIndex property of the control directly:

```
...
' if we know the SelectedIndex value
oDropList.SelectedIndex = iColor
...
```

However, if we were using a ListBox control rather than a DropDownList control, and the declaration included the attribute SelectionMode="Multiple", users would be able to select more than one item, as with a CheckBoxList. In this case, to set multiple values in our event handler, we'd use the same technique as shown earlier for the CheckBoxList control – setting the Selected property of the appropriate ListItem objects within the control's Items collection.

Selection Based on a Value that Appears in the Control

Often, the value we want to select in a nested list control is not equivalent to the SelectedIndex of the control. This is regularly the case when we get the value from the underlying DataRow that the current template row is based on. The value we want to select may, for example, be the Text of the ListItem object within a DropDownList control that we want to select, or (more likely) the Value of that ListItem object.

To do this, we have to iterate through the control's Items collection and examine each ListItem to see if the Value (or Text) matches the value we want to select. When we find a match, we set the Selected property of that ListItem object:

```
...
' select item(s) in a list control by iterating through values to find
' a match for a specific value if it is one of those shown in the list
Dim oItem As ListItem
For Each oItem In oDropList.Items
  If oItem.Value = iColor Then oItem.Selected = True
Next
...
```

Setting the ImageUrl of the Image Control

The final step in our event handler in this example sets the `ImageUrl` property of the `Image` control in the third column of our `DataGrid` control to the same color as is selected in the `DropDownList` of colors above it.

Code that ran earlier within this event handler (as shown above) set the `SelectedIndex` of the `DropDownList` to the (random) color value we require. To show how we can access the nested controls in exactly the same way as we do when they are not within another list control, we now extract the color name from the `DropDownList` control – simply by using the `SelectedItem` property to return a reference to the currently selected item in the list, and then accessing the `Text` property of this item. This returns the name of the color, and we can use it to build the URL of the image we want to display:

```
...
' get text from drop-down list and use to set Image source
Dim sColorName As String = oDropList.SelectedItem.Text
oImage.ImageUrl = "../wroxcars/images/colors/" & sColorName & ".gif"

  End If

End Sub
```

Here's the final result again, and you can see that it does provide some great ways to display data in list form:

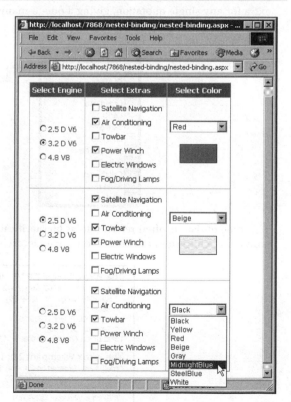

Binding to Hierarchical Data

So far, we've demonstrated how we can use list controls (and other controls) nested within a parent list control, and access these nested controls to fill them with data, select values, and set their properties. However, there is another specialist situation we often have to handle that is related to the techniques we've just seen.

In fact 'related' is a good term to use, because the example we've just seen uses only 'un-related' data as a source for the list controls. Each control is bound to a set of data that is un-related to the data used for the parent list control. OK, so we used the same data for the parent control and one of the nested list controls in the previous example, but only because that table contained the data we required for both list controls.

Another common scenario when databinding list controls to data is when the data consists of **related rows**. For example, it could be a list of orders and a list of the lines for each order. Or, in our Wrox Car Company example (as you've seen in the previous chapter and in the screenshot near the start of this chapter), we have a table containing a list of quotations and a related child table containing the list of optional extras for all the quotations.

Each optional extra row in the table named `tblQuoteOrderExtras` is related to only one quotation row in the table `tblQuoteOrder`. Of course, there could be (and is likely to be) more than one optional extra for any single quotation, giving a one-to-many relationship between the `tblQuoteOrder` table and the `tblQuoteOrderExtras` table:

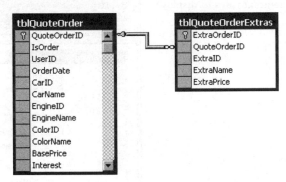

This type of data is often referred to as **hierarchical**, probably because – when listed in the page – the parent and child rows are nested to form a hierarchy of information:

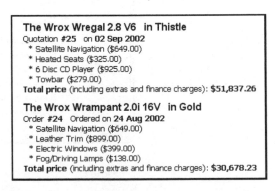

Hierarchical Binding in the 'My Cars' Page

As you've seen, the 'My Cars' page in our **Wrox Car Company** site displays the details of each user's quotations and previous orders in the hierarchical form shown earlier. We'll use this page to demonstrate how we perform this kind of databinding, though you can easily adapt the technique to suit your own requirements.

As with the nested binding examples we showed earlier, the declaration of the controls to perform hierarchical binding is simple enough. We have a parent list control, which must support templates, and one or more nested child list controls. In the 'My Cars' page, we use `Repeater` controls for both the parent and the nested child rows.

The big differences between nested and hierarchical databinding are in the content of the `DataSet` we use as the data source for the controls, and the way we extract the rows that form the data source for the nested child control.

Specifying a DataRelation Within a DataSet

In the `ItemDataBound` event handler, at the point where we come to bind the nested list control, we need to extract a set of child data rows from our `DataSet` that are related to the current parent row (the row being bound to the parent list control). To achieve this, we must specify a relationship between the two data tables that we place in the `DataSet`.

ADO.NET allows us to place more than one `DataTable` into a `DataSet`, and then optionally create relationships between these tables (`DataRelation` objects). When we create the relationship, the existing rows are automatically examined to ensure that they can be related without causing an error. For example, there must be only one parent row for every child row, the parent rows must be uniquely identifiable on their primary key, and there cannot be any 'orphan' child rows that have no related parent row.

The constructor for a `DataRelation` object specifies the name of the relationship, and references to the columns in the parent and child tables that implement this relationship:

```
Dim MyRelation As New DataRelation("name", parent-column, child-column)
```

Then we add the new relationship to the `Relations` collection of the `DataSet` object:

```
DataSet.Relations.Add(MyRelation)
```

Extracting the Related Child Rows

Once there is a relationship in place within the `DataSet`, we can use it to extract related child rows given a parent row. This requires the parent row to be available as a `DataRowView` object. The `ItemEventArgs` object that is passed to our event handler as a parameter contains a reference to the data row that is currently being bound to the parent list control, as the `Item.DataItem` property, and we can convert this into a `DataRowView`. In VB.NET, as you've seen in previous examples, we use a `CType` statement:

```
MyDataRowView = CType(oArgs.Item.DataItem, DataRowView)
```

In C#, we can do it like this:

```
DataRowView MyDataRowView = (DataRowView)oArgs.Item.DataItem;
```

Once we've got a `DataRowView`, we can use its `CreateChildView` method to get a `DataView` object based on the related child table, which contains only the related child rows. We specify as a parameter to the `CreateChildView` method the name of the relationship we want to use:

```
MyChildDataView = MyDataRowView.CreateChildView("relation-name")
```

Then we can bind this `DataView` to the nested list control in the current row. This list control will display only the rows in the child table that are related to the row currently being displayed by the parent list control. Exactly what we are after! You'll see this code in use in the following description of the 'My Cars' page.

Building the 'My Cars' Page

The remainder of this chapter is devoted to looking at the structure, content, and code that makes up the 'My Cars' page. Here we display the user's quotations and existing orders in two lists, with their name and address details at the top of the page. For any quotation they have received, they can place an order simply by clicking the 'Order now!' button:

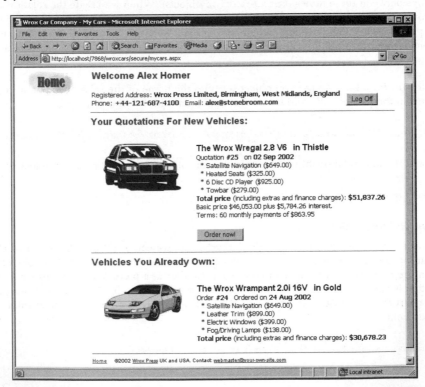

The HTML for the 'My Cars' Page

Much of the outline structure of this page is the same as the pages we've seen in earlier chapters, so we won't be listing and describing all the ways that we specify the style information, the 'skip to' links, or the link back to the 'Home' page. Instead, we'll concentrate on what is actually different from the other pages we've seen.

The entire content of the page is wrapped in a server-side `<form>` so that we can perform postbacks when the user places an order. Inside this `<form>` is a two-column, single-row HTML table that controls the layout of the content. The left-hand cell contains just the link back to the 'Home' page. The right-hand cell contains the user's address details and the Log Off button, plus the two lists of their quotations and previous orders.

Here's an outline of the HTML for the `<form>` section, with the section for the user's name and address, the Log Off button, and the templates for the list controls removed for clarity:

mycars.aspx

```
...
<form runat="server">

<table width="100%" border="0" cellspacing="0" cellpadding="10">
<tbody>
 <tr>
  <td valign="top" width="110px">
    <!-- link to Home page here -->
  </td>
  <td align="left">

    <!-- user's name/address details and Log Off button here -->

    <!-- message for feedback when placing an order here -->

    <!-- caption for list of quotes here -->

    <!-- list of quotes -->
    <asp:Repeater id="repQuotes" runat="server"
        OnItemDataBound="QuotesListDatabound" OnItemCommand="PlaceOrder">
      ...
      ... templates here...
      ...
    </asp:Repeater>

    <!-- caption for list of orders here -->

    <!-- list of orders -->
    <asp:Repeater id="repOrders" runat="server"
        OnItemDataBound="OrdersListDatabound">
      ...
      ... templates here...
      ...
    </asp:Repeater>
```

```
     <!-- page footer here -->
   </td>
  </tr>
 </tbody>
 </table>

 </form>
 ...
```

The Name and Address Details, and Log Off Button

The top part of this section of the page contains an HTML table where we display a 'welcome' message that includes the user's name, their registered address details, and the button to log off and destroy the cookie (including a persistent cookie) that performs authentication when using ASP.NET Forms authentication. If the current session is supported by the ASP.NET cookie-less sessions mechanism, the Log Off button will destroy the existing authentication flag that is stored in the user's session instead:

Welcome Alex Homer

Registered Address: **Wrox Press Limited, Birmingham, West Midlands, England**   Log Off
Phone: **+44-121-687-4100**   Email: **alex@stonebroom.com**

The section of HTML that generates this part of the page is listed next. You can see the two ASP.NET Label controls we use. The Label control with the ID of lblHeading displays the 'welcome' text, and the Label with ID value lblDetail displays the two lines containing the user's address details, phone number and e-mail address.

Then comes the <input type="submit"> button that we use to implement the Log Off button. We chose to use an HtmlInputButton control here, but we could equally well have used an ASP.NET Button control instead. Notice that the OnServerClick attribute is specified so that the event handler named DoSignOut will execute when the button is clicked (causing a postback to the server):

```
    ...
    <!-- user's name/address details and Log Off button -->
    <table border="0" width="95%">
     <tr>
      <td align="left"><a name="content" />
        <font face="Arial,Helvetica,sans-serif" size="4" color="#b50055"><b>
        <asp:Label id="lblHeading" CssClass="large-red-text"
              runat="server" /></b></font><p />
        <font face="Tahoma,Arial,Helvetica,sans-serif" size="2">
        <asp:Label id="lblDetail" CssClass="body-text" runat="server" />
        </font>
      </td>
      <td align="right" valign="bottom">
        <font face="Tahoma,Arial,Helvetica,sans-serif" size="2">
        <input type="submit" Value="Log Off" runat="server"
              OnServerClick="DoSignOut"
              title="Log off and cancel automatic logon for this site" />
        </font>
      </td>
```

```
        </tr>
      </table>
  ...
```

The Messages Label

Next we have a `Label` that we use to display status and error details. For example, after the user places an order, we display this message:

> **Thank you for placing your order. An email confirmation has been sent to you with delivery and payment details.**

The `Label` control declaration includes the CSS style definition for large red text, and we've enclosed it in a `<font>` element for older browsers (as we've done throughout the application):

```
   ...
<!-- message for feedback when placing an order -->
<font face="Arial,Helvetica,sans-serif" size="4" color="#b50055"><b>
<asp:Label id="lblMessage" CssClass="large-red-text"
     EnableViewState="False" runat="server" /></b></font>
   ...
```

The Caption for the Quotations Section

The remaining two sections of the HTML implement the two lists – one for quotations and one for orders. They are fundamentally similar, so we'll examine the quotations list and then point out the differences when we come to the list of orders.

The quotations list is preceded by a `Label` control that contains the horizontal rule to separate the page content, and the caption for the list. Initially it has the `Visible` attribute set to `False` so that the horizontal rule and caption are not displayed in the page. We can change this later, in our code, when we see if there are any quotations to show:

```
   ...
<!-- caption for list of quotes -->
<asp:Label id="lblQuotesHeading" CssClass="large-red-text"
     Visible="False" EnableViewState="False"
     runat="server"><hr size="1" />
  <font face="Arial,Helvetica,sans-serif" size="4" color="#b50055">
  <b>Your Quotations For New Vehicles:</b>
</asp:Label></font><p />
   ...
```

The following screenshot shows the caption, followed by the output from the first of the `Repeater` controls:

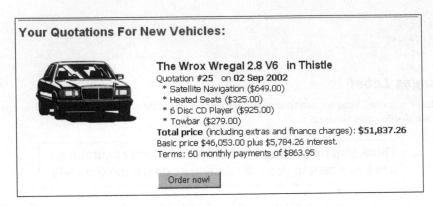

The List Control for the Quotations Section

The list shown in the previous screenshot (OK, so there's only one quotation in the list, but there could be several) is implemented by the following HTML declaration of the `Repeater` control. We start by declaring the attributes that will cause two event handlers to be executed: one when each item in the list is bound to the source data (`OnItemDataBound`), and one that is executed when any control within the rows of the list causes a postback to our server (`OnItemCommand`):

```
...
<!-- list of quotes -->
<asp:Repeater id="repQuotes" runat="server"
    OnItemDataBound="QuotesListDatabound"
    OnItemCommand="PlaceOrder">
...
```

The HeaderTemplate Section

Next, we declare the templates that will create the visible output from the source data. We want to generate an HTML table that will contain all the items in our list, with each item in a separate row of this table. So we start with a `HeaderTemplate` that generates the opening `<table>` element:

```
...
<HeaderTemplate>
  <table border="0" cellpadding="7" cellspacing="7">
</HeaderTemplate>
...
```

The ItemTemplate Section

Each row of the output is generated by successive iterations of the `ItemTemplate`, and in this we create the table row. We place an image of the current vehicle in an ASP.NET `Image` control within the first cell of this row, using the `Eval` method to create the appropriate `ImageUrl` and `ToolTip` attributes:

```
...
<ItemTemplate>
  <tr>
    <td valign="top">
      <asp:Image runat="server" hspace="10"
```

```
            ImageUrl='<%# DataBinder.Eval(Container.DataItem, _
                        "CarName", "../images/{0}150.gif") %>'
            ToolTip='<%# DataBinder.Eval(Container.DataItem, _
                        "CarName", "The Wrox {0}") %>' />
    </td>
    ...
```

Next comes the second cell of the table row for this item in our list. In it we have a series of elements that generate the output containing the model name, engine name, and color name. The quotation number, date, and order ID follow. All these values are taken from the rows of the parent table named `tblQuoteOrder` (via a stored procedure that you'll see later):

```
    ...
    <td valign="top">
      <font face="Arial,Helvetica,sans-serif" size="3">
      <b>The Wrox <%# Container.DataItem("CarName") %>
      <%# Container.DataItem("EngineName") %>   in
      <%# Container.DataItem("ColorName") %></b></font><br />
      <font face="Tahoma,Arial,Helvetica,sans-serif" size="2">
      Quotation #<b>
      <asp:Label id="lblOrderID">
        <%# Container.DataItem("QuoteOrderID") %>
      </asp:Label></b>  
      on <b><%# DataBinder.Eval(Container.DataItem, "OrderDate", _
                        "{0:dd MMM yyyy}") %></b><br />
      ...
```

The Nested Repeater Control for the Optional Extras

Now we come to the interesting part. To display the list of optional extras in this quotation, we use a nested `Repeater` control. This is declared next, and you can see that we use an `ItemTemplate` that outputs the details of the optional extras in the data source that it will be bound to. These details are in the related child table named `tblQuoteOrderExtras`, and again are extracted from the database by a stored procedure that you'll see later:

```
    ...
    <!-- list of extras for each vehicle -->
    <asp:Repeater id="repQuoteLines" runat="server">
      <ItemTemplate>
          * <%# Container.DataItem("ExtraName") %>
        ($<%# DataBinder.Eval(Container.DataItem, "ExtraPrice", _
                        "{0:#,##0.00}") %>)<br />
      </ItemTemplate>
    </asp:Repeater>
    ...
```

The Price and Finance Details

After we've listed all the optional extras for this quotation, we add some more values from the main `tblQuoteOrder` table columns. We display the total price, followed by a `Label` control that wraps the basic price, interest, number of months, and monthly payment details. This `Label` control has the attribute `Visible="False"`, so these values will not be visible unless we change the `Visible` property to `True` in our code. We'll do this only if there are finance terms saved for the quotation:

```
...
<b>Total price</b> (including extras and finance charges):
<b>$<%# DataBinder.Eval(Container.DataItem, "TotalPrice", _
                    "{0:#,##0.00}") %></b><br />
<asp:Label id="lblFinance" Visible="False" runat="server">
  Basic price $
  <%# DataBinder.Eval(Container.DataItem, "BasePrice", _
                    "{0:#,##0.00}") %> plus
  $<%# DataBinder.Eval(Container.DataItem, "Interest", _
                    "{0:#,##0.00}") %> interest.<br />
  Terms: <%# Container.DataItem("PaymentMonths") %>
  monthly payments of
  $<%# DataBinder.Eval(Container.DataItem, "PaymentAmount", _
                    "{0:#,##0.00}") %>
</asp:Label><p>
...
```

The 'Order now!' Button

The final control in our `ItemTemplate` is the 'Order now!' button. We specify a `ToolTip` for this button, and then set the `CommandName` attribute to the ID of the current quotation. When we handle events raised by controls within a list control (such as our `Repeater` control), we can use the `CommandName` and `CommandArgument` properties to pass text values to the event handler.

In general, we use this feature to pass the row 'key' for the current row, so that we can identify in our event handler which row caused the event to occur. You'll see how we retrieve this value when we look at the event handler for the `ItemCommand` event later in this chapter:

```
      ...
      <asp:Button id="cmdOrder" Text="Order now!" runat="server"
          ToolTip="Place an order for this vehicle now"
          CommandName='<%# Container.DataItem("QuoteOrderID") %>' />
      </p></font>
    </td>
  </tr>
</ItemTemplate>
  ...
```

The FooterTemplate Section

The final template in our `Repeater` control declaration is the `FooterTemplate` section. This just has to output the closing `</table>` tag for the table we've been creating within our main (parent) `Repeater` control:

```
  ...
  <FooterTemplate>
    </table>
  </FooterTemplate>
</asp:Repeater>
  ...
```

The 'Orders' Section

The next section of our page is the list of existing orders for our user. Most of the declaration of the caption and the `Repeater` controls are the same as in the quotations section, with a few minor differences. For example, we don't want to remind our customers how much interest they paid when they bought their last car, so we don't show the breakdown of the finance terms. Neither, for obvious reasons, do we want to show the 'Order now!' button:

In the code declarations for the 'Orders' section we have a different event handler attached to the `ItemDataBound` event, and we do not define an event handler attribute for the `ItemCommand` event (there are no controls in this list that can cause a postback):

```
...
<!-- list of orders -->
<asp:Repeater id="repOrders" runat="server"
    OnItemDataBound="OrdersListDatabound">
    ...
    ... as shown for quotations list control
    ...
```

We still have a nested 'child' `Repeater` for the list of optional extras, but there are no bound controls for the finance terms in the `ItemTemplate` section of the main 'parent' `Repeater`:

```
      ...
      <!-- list of extras for each vehicle -->
      <asp:Repeater id="repOrderLines" runat="server">
        <ItemTemplate>
            * <%# Container.DataItem("ExtraName") %>
          ($<%# DataBinder.Eval(Container.DataItem, "ExtraPrice", _
                          "{0:#,##0.00}") %>)<br />
        </ItemTemplate>
      </asp:Repeater>
      <b>Total price</b> (including extras and finance charges):
      <b>$<%# DataBinder.Eval(Container.DataItem, "TotalPrice", _
                      "{0:#,##0.00}") %></b><br />
      </font>
    </td>
  </tr>
</ItemTemplate>
...
```

The Code for the 'My Cars' Page

In the `<script>` section of the page, we declare the customary variables to hold the stylesheet size, the current user ID, and the database connection string. We also have a variable to hold the `DataSet` containing all of this user's quotation and order details that we extract from our database:

```
...
' page-level variable to hold style size
Dim sStyleSize As String = "Standard"

' page-level variable to hold current user ID
Dim sUserID As String

' page-level variable to hold DB connection string
Dim sConnect As String

' page-level variable to user and order details DataSet
Dim dsDetails As DataSet
...
```

Before we look at the `Page_Load` event handler, however, we'll see how we extract the details of the user and their quotations and orders from the database and fill the `DataSet` that we use throughout the remainder of the page.

Generating the DataSet of User Details

We need to create three tables of data within our `DataSet`. These are:

❑   Details of the user from the `tblUsers` table – their registered name and address, phone, and e-mail address. This table within our `DataSet` is named `UserDetail`.

❑   A list of quotations and orders from the `tblQuoteOrder` table for this user. This table within our `DataSet` is named `Orders`.

❑   A list of all the optional extras for all this user's quotations and orders, taken from the `tblQuoteOrderExtras` table. This table within our `DataSet` is named `OrderLines`.

The Stored Procedures to Extract the Data

We use three stored procedures to extract the data we need from the database. To get the user details for the `UserDetail` table, we select all the columns from the `tblUsers` table in our database for the row with the matching `UserID`:

```
CREATE PROCEDURE GetUserDetails @UserID varchar(20) AS
SELECT * FROM tblUsers WHERE UserID = @UserID
```

To extract the list of quotations and orders for the `Orders` table, we select all the columns from the `tblQuoteOrder` table in our database for all rows with the matching `UserID`:

```
CREATE PROCEDURE GetUserOrders @UserID varchar(20) AS
SELECT * FROM tblQuoteOrder WHERE UserID = @UserID ORDER BY OrderDate DESC
```

To extract the list of optional extras for all of the user's quotations and orders, for the OrderLines table in our DataSet, we need to join the tblQuoteOrder and tblQuoteOrderExtras tables on the QuoteOrderID value. This allows us to select the columns we want from the tblQuoteOrderExtras table in our database for all rows where the parent row in the tblQuoteOrder table contains a matching UserID:

```
CREATE PROCEDURE GetUserOrderLines @UserID varchar(20) AS
SELECT tblQuoteOrder.QuoteOrderID, ExtraName, ExtraPrice
FROM tblQuoteOrder JOIN tblQuoteOrderExtras
   ON tblQuoteOrder.QuoteOrderID = tblQuoteOrderExtras.QuoteOrderID
WHERE UserID = @UserID
```

The GetUserDetailsDS Function

The function named GetUserDetailsDS, which uses these three stored procedures and returns a DataSet, is very similar to previous examples. We define the stored procedure names, create the Connection and Command objects, set the single @UserID parameter for our stored procedures, and then fill the DataSet with the three tables returned by these stored procedures:

```
Function GetUserDetailsDS() As DataSet
   ' function to get current user's details as a DataSet

   ' to hold DataSet for the results
   Dim dsUserDetail As DataSet = Nothing

   ' to hold stored procedure names
   Dim sDetailsProc As String = "GetUserDetails"
   Dim sOrdersProc As String = "GetUserOrders"
   Dim sOrderLinesProc As String = "GetUserOrderLines"

   Dim sqlConn As New SqlConnection(sConnect)
   Dim sqlComm As New SqlCommand(sDetailsProc, sqlConn)
   sqlComm.CommandType = CommandType.StoredProcedure
   sqlComm.Parameters.Add("@UserID", sUserID)

   Try

      ' create a new empty DataSet for the results
      dsUserDetail = New DataSet()

      ' and fill it from the database
      Dim daUserDetail As New SqlDataAdapter(sqlComm)
      sqlConn.Open()
      If daUserDetail.Fill(dsUserDetail, "UserDetail") = 1 Then

         ' found details for a single user as expected so fill other
         ' tables in DataSet with all quotation and order details
         sqlComm.CommandText = sOrdersProc
         daUserDetail.Fill(dsUserDetail, "Orders")
         sqlComm.CommandText = sOrderLinesProc
         daUserDetail.Fill(dsUserDetail, "OrderLines")
         ...
```

Creating the Relationship Between the Tables

However, before we finish, we must add the DataRelation to our DataSet that will allow us to extract the related child rows for each parent row when we come to bind the nested Repeater controls in our lists of quotations and orders. We need a relationship between the parent Orders table and the child OrderLines table in our DataSet.

We showed you how this is done earlier in the chapter. In this example, the new relationship is named relOrders, and we specify references to the QuoteOrderID column of the parent and child tables as the second and third parameters to the DataRelation constructor. Then we add the new relationship to the DataSet object's Relations collection:

```
      ...
      ' create relationship between Orders and OrderLines tables
      ' and add it to the DataSet object's Relations collection
      Dim oRelation As New DataRelation("relOrders", _
            dsUserDetail.Tables("Orders").Columns("QuoteOrderID"), _
            dsUserDetail.Tables("OrderLines").Columns("QuoteOrderID"))
      dsUserDetail.Relations.Add(oRelation)

   Else

      dsUserDetail = Nothing

   End If

   Catch
      dsUserDetail = Nothing

   Finally
      sqlConn.Close()

   End Try

   ' return DataSet - will be Nothing if there was an error
   Return dsUserDetail

End Function
```

Now (as you can see in the code above) we can return our DataSet, or return Nothing if there was an error. We also have to remember to close our database connection. We opened it ourselves, so it remains open when the three calls to the Fill method have completed.

There is no point in storing the DataSet in the user's ASP.NET session, as we did in the 'Model Details' page, because it is only used once – to fill the lists of quotations and orders. If there is a postback to the server, it's because the user placed an order. In this case the data in the database will change, and so we will have to refill the DataSet anyway.

The Page_Load Event Handler

Now that we know where our data comes from, we'll look at the remaining code routines in the 'My Cars' page. The `Page_Load` event handler has several tasks to carry out, including some we've seen in many of the other pages. This includes setting the CSS style size, checking if an ASP.NET session exists for this user, and collecting the database connection string from `web.config`:

```
Sub Page_Load()

  ' get stylesheet size from Session
  sStyleSize = CType(Session("WccStyleSize"), String)

  ' if no value, session has expired or user entered
  ' site at page other than 'Home' page
  If sStyleSize = "" Then
    Response.Clear()
    Response.Redirect("../default.aspx")
    Response.End()
  End If

  ' get connection string from web.config
  sConnect = ConfigurationSettings.AppSettings("WroxCarsConnectString")
  ...
```

Checking If the User Has Been Authenticated

Now we can make sure that the user was authenticated. We set a `Boolean` flag variable to `False` as the default, then check which kind of session support we are using. If this user's browser or user-agent does not support cookies, and is using the cookie-less version of the application, we check if they were authenticated by looking in their ASP.NET session for the authentication value `WCCUserAuthenticated="yes"`.

If we find this, we can set our 'authenticated' flag to `True`, and collect the ID of this user from the session variable named `WCCUserID`. This value was stored there in the Login page. If we don't find the authentication value in the session, we redirect the user to the Login page instead:

```
  ...
  ' flag for checking if user is authenticated
  Dim bAuthenticated As Boolean = False

  ' check what type of session support we are using
  If Session.IsCookieless Then

    ' cookie-less sessions, so look in session
    If CType(Session("WCCUserAuthenticated"), String) = "yes" Then
      bAuthenticated = True
      sUserID = CType(Session("WCCUserID"), String)
    Else    'not authenticated
      Response.Clear()
      Response.Redirect("login.aspx")
      Response.End()
    End If
    ...
```

Alternatively, if the user's browser or user-agent does support cookies, we know that the ASP.NET Forms authentication system was used to authenticate them, and that they have a valid ASP.NET authentication cookie on their machine. If not, they would have been automatically redirected to the Login page, and would not have got this far.

Once the user has been authenticated in this way, we can take advantage of another feature of the ASP.NET security model. We can access the default User object for this page instance, and from its Identity.Name property get the ID that was used for authentication. This is the user ID value we'll be using later in our page code:

```
   ...
   Else

     ' get name of authenticated current user from Forms
     ' authentication system - User ID can be extracted from
     ' the User object implemented by Forms authentication
     bAuthenticated = User.Identity.IsAuthenticated
     sUserID = User.Identity.Name

   End If
   ...
```

Setting the Webmaster E-mail Address

In our other site pages, we take advantage of the custom user control we built to create the page footer containing the links to other pages and the link to send e-mail to the webmaster of our site. However, in the 'My Cars' page we only have a single link – to the 'Home' page – and so we have implemented the page footer directly within the HTML declaration of this page. This means that we need to extract the e-mail address of the webmaster from the web.config file, and set the NavigateUrl and Text of the hyperlink in the page footer when our page loads:

```
   ...
   ' set the e-mail address of the webmaster in the page footer
   Try
     Dim sWebmasterEmail As String = _
                 ConfigurationSettings.AppSettings("WroxCarsWebmasterEmail")
     lnkWebmaster.NavigateUrl = "mailto:" & sWebmasterEmail _
                           & "?subject=Wrox Cars Web Site"
     lnkWebmaster.Text = sWebmasterEmail
   Catch
   End Try
   ...
```

Displaying the Page Content

Now we can display the main content of the 'My Cars' page. We check that our user was authenticated (in theory we know that they will be, but it is worth checking to be sure in case someone changed the web.config file).

If this page load is not occurring through a postback (in other words, it's the first time that the page has been loaded), we can collect the DataSet of values using the GetUserDetailsDS function we've just been looking at. Providing that it returns a DataSet, we can then call two other routines in our page to display the content:

```
    ...
    If bAuthenticated Then

      If Not Page.IsPostback Then

        ' this is the first time the page has been loaded
        ' get user's details and quotes from database
        dsDetails = GetUserDetailsDS()
        If dsDetails Is Nothing Then

          lblDetail.Text = "<b>* Could not access database.</b>"

        Else

          ' display registered user's details, quotes, and orders
          DisplayUserDetails(dsDetails)
          DisplayUserVehicles(dsDetails)

        End If

      End If

    Else

      lblDetail.Text = "<b>* Not authenticated</b>"

    End If

  End Sub
```

If we don't get a `DataSet` back, or if the user was not authenticated, we just display suitable messages in the `lblDetail` control on the page instead.

Displaying Details of the User

The first of the routines we call from the `Page_Load` event, `DisplayUserDetails`, simply extracts the user's registration details from the single row (at index zero) in the `UserDetail` table of the `DataSet`, and builds up a couple of `String` values containing these details. These `String` values are then inserted into the two `Label` controls in the top section of the page:

```
Sub DisplayUserDetails(dsDetails As DataSet)
  ' extract user's name/address/etc from DataSet
  ' and display them at the top of the page

  Dim drDetails As DataRow = dsDetails.Tables("UserDetail").Rows(0)
  lblHeading.Text = "Welcome " & drDetails("UserName")
  lblDetail.Text = "Registered Address: <b>" _
    & drDetails("Address") & ", " & drDetails("City") _
    & ", " & drDetails("State") & ", " _
    & drDetails("Country") & "</b><br />Phone: <b>" _
    & drDetails("Phone") & "</b>   Email: <b>" _
    & drDetails("Email") & "</b>"

End Sub
```

Displaying Details of the User's Vehicles

The second of the routines we call from the Page_Load event handler is DisplayUserVehicles. To display the details of the user's quotations and orders, we have to bind the data in the Orders table of our DataSet to the two Repeater controls on the page. To decide if a row in the Orders table is a quotation or an order, all we have to do is filter the table on the IsOrder column, which is set to 'one' for an order or 'zero' for a quotation.

So, after getting a DataView from the DefaultView property of the table, we apply a filter to it that selects only the rows that have zero for the IsOrder column. Then we can check to see if there are any quotations by examining the Count property of the DataView. If there are one or more quotations, we make the horizontal rule and the large red text caption for this table visible (you'll recall that these are declared within the Label control with ID value lblQuotesHeading):

```
Sub DisplayUserVehicles(dsDetails As DataSet)
   ' extract lists of quotes and orders for this user from
   ' DataSet and display in Repeaters in this page

   ' get a filtered DataView of just the quotations
   Dim dvQuotes As DataView = dsDetails.Tables("Orders").DefaultView
   dvQuotes.RowFilter = "IsOrder = 0"
   If dvQuotes.Count > 0 Then

      ' at least one quote so make Quotes heading visible
      lblQuotesHeading.Visible = True

   End If
   ...
```

Then we can bind the filtered DataView to the Repeater control to display the quotations. Remember that we only bind the parent Repeater to the data extracted from the Orders table here. We will fill in the nested list of child 'optional extra' rows in the ItemDataBound event handler, as you'll see shortly:

```
   ...
   ' bind quotations Repeater control to display them
   repQuotes.DataSource = dvQuotes
   repQuotes.DataBind()
   ...
```

Then we can repeat the process to display any orders for this user. This time the row filter selects only rows that have the value 'one' in the IsOrder column:

```
   ...
   ' get a filtered DataView of just the orders
   dvQuotes.RowFilter = "IsOrder = 1"
   If dvQuotes.Count > 0 Then

      ' at least one order so make Orders heading visible
      lblOrdersHeading.Visible = True

   End If
```

```
   ' bind orders Repeater control to display them
   repOrders.DataSource = dvQuotes
   repOrders.DataBind()

End Sub
```

The ItemDataBound Event Handlers

The routine we've just looked at is responsible for binding the two 'parent' Repeater controls on our page to the list of quotations and orders in the Orders table of our DataSet. However, when we declared these two Repeater controls, we specified event handlers for their OnItemDataBound attributes.

So, when the ItemDataBound event occurs as each row is bound to the source data, the event handlers will be invoked. We have defined two different event handlers, named QuotesListDatabound and OrdersListDatabound. While they are fundamentally similar, they have to access different sets of controls. We could have used some If...Then constructs within a single event handler to work with both lists, but this would have made it harder to see what's happening.

Handling the ItemDataBound Event for the Quotations List

In the QuotesListDatabound event handler, we first check that we are reacting to the event only for an Item or an AlternatingItem row. We have two distinct tasks to accomplish in this event handler. We want to show the contents of the Label control that contains the finance details if the user specified these when saving the quotation. We also have to get the appropriate set of 'optional extra' rows from our DataSet and bind these to the nested 'child' Repeater control.

To see if the user saved any finance details with their quotation, we can check the value of the PaymentMonths column in the Orders table. If it is greater than zero, we have details to show so we set the Visible property of the Label control that contains the finance details for this row of the Repeater output:

```
Sub QuotesListDatabound(oSender As Object, oArgs As RepeaterItemEventArgs)
  ' runs for each row in Quotes Repeater as it is databound

  ' see if it is an item or alternating item row
  If oArgs.Item.ItemType = ListItemType.Item _
  Or oArgs.Item.ItemType = ListItemType.AlternatingItem Then

    ' show Finance terms section only if not zero
    If oArgs.Item.DataItem("PaymentMonths") > 0 Then
      CType(oArgs.Item.FindControl("lblFinance"), Label).Visible = True
    End If
    ...
```

Now we can get the list of optional extras for this quotation. As you saw in the earlier sections of this chapter, we need to convert the DataRow that is exposed by the Item.DataItem property of the arguments to the event handler into a DataRowView, and then execute its CreateChildView method to get a DataView containing the related child rows from the OrderLines table in the DataSet.

So, we start by getting a reference to the nested 'child' Repeater control using the FindControl method (the ID of the Repeater control is repQuoteLines). Then we pass the name of the DataRelation in the DataSet to the CreateChildView method. The resulting DataView is assigned to the DataSource property of our Repeater control. A call to the DataBind method of this control is enough to cause it to display these rows:

```
...
    ' get DataView of related child rows from OrderLines table
    ' (tblQuoteOrderExtras in database) and bind to nested Repeater
    ' control that appears in each row of the parent Repeater
    Dim oLinesRep As Repeater _
        = CType(oArgs.Item.FindControl("repQuoteLines"), Repeater)
    oLinesRep.DataSource = CType(oArgs.Item.DataItem, _
                                DataRowView).CreateChildView("relOrders")

    oLinesRep.DataBind()

  End If

End Sub
```

Handling the ItemDataBound Event for the Orders List

The event handler named OrdersListDatabound for the Repeater control that displays the list of orders is shown in the next listing. We don't display the finance terms when we list a user's existing vehicle orders, so we don't need to worry about showing these. We just have to bind the nested 'child' Repeater control in each row of this list, in exactly the same way as we did in the previous code listing:

```
Sub OrdersListDatabound(oSender As Object, oArgs As RepeaterItemEventArgs)
    ' runs for each row in Orders Repeater as it is databound

    ' see if it is an item or alternating item row
    If oArgs.Item.ItemType = ListItemType.Item _
                Or oArgs.Item.ItemType = ListItemType.AlternatingItem Then

        ' get DataView of related child rows from OrderLines table
        ' (tblQuoteOrderExtras in database) and bind to nested Repeater
        ' control that appears in each row of the parent Repeater
        Dim oLinesRep As Repeater _
                    = CType(oArgs.Item.FindControl("repOrderLines"), Repeater)
        oLinesRep.DataSource = CType(oArgs.Item.DataItem, _
                                    DataRowView).CreateChildView("relOrders")

        oLinesRep.DataBind()

    End If

End Sub
```

Logging Out of the Application

We include a feature in our 'My Cars' page that allows a user to 'log out' of the application if they wish. You'll recall that the ASP.NET Forms authentication mechanism places a **session cookie** on the user's machine. This cookie contains encoded authentication information, which allows the user to access pages that are not available to 'anonymous' visitors. When they close their browser (or when the authentication session times out) this cookie disappears, and they have to log in again when they next visit the site.

Users can also specify that we should place a **persistent cookie** on their machine, by ticking the 'Log in automatically next time' checkbox on the Login page. This cookie survives the user closing their browser, and allows them to access the protected pages without having to log in again next time.

However, it's good practice to allow users to 'log off' if they wish – especially if they are going to be leaving their machine running or allow other people to use it. And, if they have previously specified the 'persistent cookie' option, they can destroy this cookie by logging off.

If the user's browser does not support cookies, however, we are performing all of the authentication tasks ourselves, and storing an authentication flag value in the user's ASP.NET session. In this case, clicking the Log Off button simply has to clear this flag value within the session, requiring the user to log on again when they come back to the 'My Cars' page.

The Log Off Button Code

As you've seen in the earlier screenshots, we provide a Log Off button near the top of the 'My Cars' page. When clicked, this button causes a postback to the server and executes a routine named DoSignOut. While we could test what kind of session support is in use, we chose to simply execute all of the tasks required to log out a user for both kinds of sessions – it only involves a few lines of code in all.

To destroy the Forms authentication cookie, we just call the SignOut method of the FormsAuthentication object. To clear the cookie-less sessions authentication flag, we just set the session variable WCCUserAuthenticated to "no". Then, irrespective of the type of session support in use, we have to redirect the user to the appropriate page outside the secure folder of our application. We chose to redirect them to the 'Home' page:

```
Sub DoSignOut(objSender As Object, objArgs As EventArgs)
  ' runs when the "Log Off" button is clicked

  ' destroy the users authentication cookie
  FormsAuthentication.SignOut()

  ' clear authenticated flag in session
  Session("WCCUserAuthenticated") = "no"

  ' redirect them to the Home page
  Response.Clear()
  Response.Redirect("../home.aspx")
  Response.End

End Sub
```

Placing an Order

When the user clicks the 'Order now!' button in any of the quotation rows (if there are any displayed), a postback is initiated and our event handler named PlaceOrder is executed. We defined this event handler in the OnItemCommand attribute of the Repeater control that displays the list of quotations. When this event occurs, we want to convert the current quotation (the one containing the 'Order now!' button that was clicked) into an order.

We use a simple stored procedure to convert a quotation into an order. It just has to set the `IsOrder` column value of the specified row in the `tblQuoteOrder` table in our database to 'one'. We pass the order ID into the stored procedure as a parameter:

```
CREATE PROCEDURE ConvertToOrder @QuoteOrderID int AS
UPDATE tblQuoteOrder SET IsOrder = 1 WHERE QuoteOrderID = @QuoteOrderID
```

We call this stored procedure from our `PlaceOrder` event handler. The first step here is to figure out which quotation we want to convert into an order. You'll recall that we set the `CommandName` property of the 'Order now!' buttons in our `Repeater` declaration using the following code:

```
<asp:Button id="cmdOrder" Text="Order now!" runat="server"
    ToolTip="Place an order for this vehicle now"
    CommandName='<%# Container.DataItem("QuoteOrderID") %>' />
```

The highlighted line shows that each 'Order now!' button will have as its `CommandName` the ID of the order for the row it is located within. To get this value within our event handler, we query the `CommandSource` property of the arguments passed into the routine. This returns a reference to the control that caused the postback, and we convert this to a `Button` object then access the `CommandName` property. This returns a `String` value, but we want an `Integer` to pass to our stored procedure, so we have then to parse it to an `Int32` type:

```
Sub PlaceOrder(oSender As Object, oArgs As RepeaterCommandEventArgs)
    ' simple routine to convert a Quote into an Order
    ' in reality would probably collect payment information first

    ' get order ID from routine arguments
    Dim sOrderID As String = CType(oArgs.CommandSource, Button).CommandName
    Dim iOrderID As Integer = Int32.Parse(sOrderID)
    ...
```

Executing the Stored Procedure

Now we can define the name of our stored procedure, create the `Connection` and `Command` objects, specify the parameter we require, and execute the stored procedure just as we've done in many other previous examples:

```
    ...

    ' to hold stored procedure name
    Dim sProcName As String = "ConvertToOrder"

    Dim sMessage As String
    Dim sqlConn As New SqlConnection(sConnect)
    Dim sqlComm As New SqlCommand(sProcName, sqlConn)
    sqlComm.CommandType = CommandType.StoredProcedure
    sqlComm.Parameters.Add("@QuoteOrderID", iOrderID)

    Try
```

```
sqlConn.Open()
If sqlComm.ExecuteNonQuery() = 1 Then
    ...
```

Displaying the Results

If the stored procedure succeeds in updating one row in the table, we know that the quotation has been converted into an order. The next thing is to redisplay the page content to show that this is the case. However, because the stored procedure has changed the content of the database we have to reload our `DataSet` by calling the same `GetUserDetailsDS` function as we did in the `Page_Load` event handler when we first loaded the page. Then we can execute the `DisplayUserVehicles` routine again with the new `DataSet` to display the updated information:

```
    ...
    ' update to an order from a quote succeeded
    ' get DataSet with updated values and display them
    dsDetails = GetUserDetailsDS()
    DisplayUserVehicles(dsDetails)
    ...
```

Next we inform the user that their order has been placed, by sending them an e-mail message using a separate routine named `SendEmailConfirmation` within this page. We just provide the `OrderID` and it does the rest – we'll see how shortly. Then we create a suitable message to display in our page, depending on the outcome of the database update:

```
    ...
    ' send e-mail confirmation of order
    SendEmailConfirmation(sOrderID)
    sMessage = "<p>Thank you for placing your order. " _
            & "An email confirmation<br />" _
            & "has been sent to you with delivery and " _
            & "payment details.</p>"

  Else

    sMessage = "* Sorry, this quotation could not be located."

  End If

Catch

  sMessage = "* Sorry, the database could not be accessed."

Finally

  sqlConn.Close()

End Try

  ' display message in Label on page
  lblMessage.Text = sMessage

End Sub
```

At the end of this code, after making sure that the database connection is closed, we display the message we created in the `Label` control between the two `Repeater` controls on our page (you can see it in the next screenshot – in this case the list of quotations is now empty).

Sending Order Confirmation E-mail Messages

After an order has been successfully placed, the 'My Cars' page displays a message and sends the user an e-mail to confirm this. You can see this message in the next screenshot. We have just placed an order for the Wrox Wregal 2.8 V6 in 'Thistle', with a few optional extras:

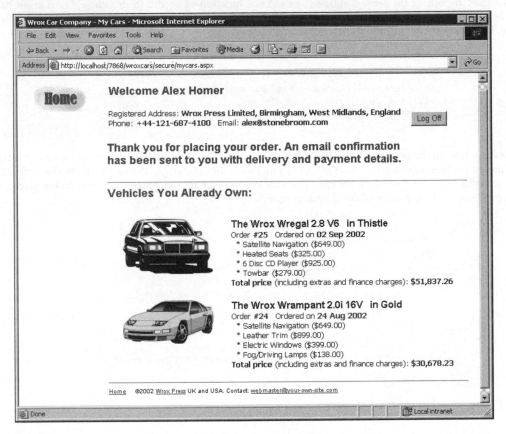

To send the confirmation e-mail, we take advantage of the same `sendmail.ascx` user control that we use in our 'Home' page to send confirmation messages to visitors when they join our mailing list.

> *As discussed in previous chapters, we discovered that the ASP.NET classes, which interact with the CDO objects in Windows 2000, often fail when placed in a folder that is not an application root directory, and so we placed the `sendmail.ascx` user control in the root folder of our application.*

We register the `sendmail.ascx` control at the top of our 'My Cars' page:

```
<%@Register TagPrefix="wcc" TagName="sendmail" Src="../sendmail.ascx"%>
```

Then we insert it just before the closing `</body>` tag:

```
<!-- control containing the routine to send email messages -->
<wcc:sendmail id="ctlMail" runat="server" />
```

Now we can use it just like we did in our 'Home' page, by setting the `FromAddress`, `ToAddress`, `MessageSubject`, and `MessageBody` properties, and then calling the `SendEmail` method.

Creating the Confirmation E-mail Message

The message we create is reasonably complex because we want to include all of the order details, including a list of the optional extras and the finance terms. We build up the message body as a series of `String` values, and then concatenate them with the remaining text to form the complete message.

So, first we collect the user's registered details from the `UserDetail` table in our `DataSet`:

```
Sub SendEmailConfirmation(sOrderID As String)
    ' routine to send e-mail confirmation of placing an order

    Try

        ' build parts of message as strings
        ' get user details from single row of UserDetail table in DataSet
        Dim drDetails As DataRow = dsDetails.Tables("UserDetail").Rows(0)
        Dim sUser As String = "Name: " & drDetails("UserName") & vbCrlf _
            & "Address: " & drDetails("Address") & vbCrlf _
            & "City: " & drDetails("City") & vbCrlf _
            & "State: " & drDetails("State") & vbCrlf _
            & "Country: " & drDetails("Country") & vbCrlf _
            & "Phone: " & drDetails("Phone") & vbCrlf _
            & "Email: " & drDetails("Email") & vbCrlf
        ...
```

Next, we filter the `Orders` table to select just the order specified in the parameter passed to the `SendEmailConfirmation` routine. In this case we're using the `Select` method of the table to return an array containing the single row we want at index zero:

```
        ...
        ' create a criteria and select the matching row in the Orders table
        ' in the DataSet, then extract order details
        Dim sFind As String = "QuoteOrderID = " & sOrderID
        Dim arrOrders As DataRow() = dsDetails.Tables("Orders").Select(sFind)
        Dim drOrder As DataRow = arrOrders(0)
        ...
```

Using the values in this row, we build the next `String` containing the date, the order number, the model name, the engine name, and the color for the vehicle:

```
...
Dim dDate As DateTime = drOrder("OrderDate")
Dim sOrder As String = "Order #" & drOrder("QuoteOrderID") _
    & " placed on " & dDate.ToString("dd MMM yyyy") & vbCrlf
Dim sModel As String = "Model: The Wrox " & drOrder("CarName") _
    & vbCrlf & "Engine: " & drOrder("EngineName") & vbCrlf _
    & "Color: " & drOrder("ColorName") & vbCrlf
...
```

Listing the Optional Extras

Now we want a list of optional extras. We create a suitable filter to select the rows from the `OrderLines` table that have the current `OrderID` value, and then (providing that we found some rows) iterate through them adding each one to the `String` that describes the vehicle:

```
...
' select the matching rows in the OrderLines table
' in the DataSet, then extract 'extras' details
Dim fPrice, fInterest, fPayment As Decimal
Dim drOrderLine As DataRow
arrOrders = dsDetails.Tables("OrderLines").Select(sFind)
If arrOrders.Length > 0 Then
    sModel &= "Optional extras included in your order:" & vbCrlf
    For Each drOrderLine In arrOrders
        fPrice = drOrderLine("ExtraPrice")
        sModel &= "* " & drOrderLine("ExtraName") & " ($" _
            & fPrice.ToString("F2") & ")" & vbCrlf
    Next
End If
...
```

Showing the Price and Finance Details

The next part of our e-mail message is the price and any saved finance terms. We can collect all this information from the row referenced by the `drOrder` variable, which we set when we were extracting the model details earlier in our code. To see if there were any finance terms saved with the quotation we just have to check the value of the `PaymentMonths` column, as we did when displaying the quotation details in our page earlier on:

```
...
fPrice = drOrder("TotalPrice")
Dim sPrice As String = "Total Price including extras " _
                & "and finance charges: $" _
                & fPrice.ToString("#,##0.00") & vbCrlf
If drOrder("PaymentMonths") > 0 Then
    fPrice = drOrder("BasePrice")
    fInterest = drOrder("Interest")
    fPayment = drOrder("PaymentAmount")
```

```
        sPrice &= "Basic price: $" & fPrice.ToString("#,##0.00") _
            & " plus $" & fInterest.ToString("#,##0.00") _
            & " interest." & vbCrlf & "Terms: " _
            & drOrder("PaymentMonths").ToString() & " monthly payments of $" _
            & fPayment.ToString("#,##0.00") & vbCrlf
        End If
        ...
```

Building the Message Body and Sending the Message

With all the parts of our message body complete, we can build up the final message as a `String` named `sMessage`. Then we set the `FromAddress` property of our user control to the e-mail address of the webmaster (again extracted from `web.config`), set the `ToAddress` property to the user's e-mail address (extracted from the 'user details' table row), set the `MessageSubject` property to a suitable value, and assign the `sMessage` string to the `MessageBody` property. To send the message we just have to call the `SendEmail` method of the user control:

```
    ...
    Dim sMessage As String = "Thank you for placing your order with the " _
        & "Wrox Car Company." & vbCrlf & vbCrlf _
        & "Your order details are:" & vbCrlf & vbCrlf _
        & sOrder & vbCrlf & sUser & vbCrlf _
        & sModel & vbCrlf & sPrice & vbCrlf _
        & "We will contact you as soon as your vehicle " _
        & "is ready for delivery and arrange payment " _
        & "and shipping details." & vbCrlf & vbCrlf _
        & "NOTE: Wrox Cars are a fictitious organization " _
        & "designed only to promote the Wrox Press book " _
        & "Professional Web Form Techniques (ISBN 1-861" _
        & "007-86-8) from Wrox Press (http://www.wrox.com/). " _
        & "For more details see http://www.daveandal.com/books/7868/"

    ' use ASCX control in root folder of application to send the message
    ctlMail.FromAddress _
            = ConfigurationSettings.AppSettings("WroxCarsWebmasterEmail")
    ctlMail.ToAddress = drDetails("Email")
    ctlMail.MessageSubject = "Wrox Car Company Order Confirmation"
    ctlMail.MessageBody = sMessage
    ctlMail.SendEmail()

    Catch
    End Try

End Sub
```

As a result of ordering the vehicle you saw in the previous screenshot, we get an e-mail confirmation that looks like this:

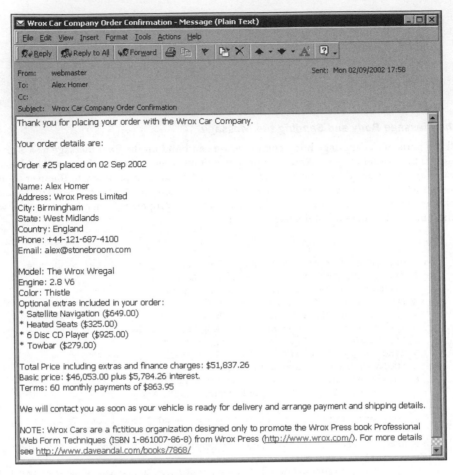

All we have to do now is write even more books so that we can pay the monthly premium!

Summary

In this final chapter, we've completed our study of both the Wrox Car Company example site, and the techniques we use within it to build interactive and attractive user interfaces with ASP.NET. Hopefully you can now see why we believe that ASP.NET, with its postback architecture, automatic page state maintenance, huge range of useful server controls, and the backing of the whole .NET Framework class library, makes it the obvious choice for developing modern web applications.

In this chapter, we concentrated on the remaining page of our site, the 'My Cars' page where a visitor can view quotations they have saved, and place orders for our exciting range of vehicles. We demonstrated a few new techniques – including binding un-related and related sets of data to nested list controls. We also showed you how we can interact with the Forms authentication system we introduced in the previous chapter to protect pages from unauthorized access.

The topics for this chapter were:

- ❏ How we can bind related sets of data to a range of list controls
- ❏ How we can easily display hierarchical data in nested form
- ❏ How we built the 'My Cars' page
- ❏ How we handle the placing of an order for a vehicle

So, now it's your turn to take up your ASP.NET editor, and go build great web sites and web applications.

WANTED

WEB DEVELOPER

Index

A Guide to the Index

The index is arranged hierarchically, in alphabetical order, with symbols preceding the letter A. Most second-level entries and many third-level entries also occur as first-level entries. This is to ensure that users will find the information they require however they choose to search for it.

C

O

X

Notes

Notes

C# Today

The daily knowledge site for professional C# programmers

C#Today provides you with a weekly in-depth case study, giving you solutions to real-world problems that are relevant to your career. Each one is written by a leading professional, meaning that you benefit from their expertise and get the skills that you need to thrive in the C# world. As well as a weekly case study, we also offer you access to our huge archive of quality articles, which cover every aspect of the C# language. www.csharptoday.com

C#Today has built up an archive of over 170 articles, in which top authors like Kaushal Sanghavi, Matthew Reynolds and Richard Conway have tackled topics ranging from thread pooling and .Net serialization to multi-threaded search engines, UDDI, and advanced techniques for inter-thread communication.

By joining the growing number of C#Today subscribers, you get access to:

- a weekly in-depth case study
- code heavy demonstration of real world applications
- access to an archive of over 170 articles
- C# reference material
- a fully searchable index

Visit C#Today at: www.csharptoday.com

p2p.wrox.com

The programmer's resource centre

A unique free service from Wrox Pres

With the aim of helping programmers to help each oth

Wrox Press aims to provide timely and practical information to today's programmer. P2F is a list server offering a host of targeted mailing lists where you can share knowledge with four fellow programmers and find solutions to your problems. Whatever the level of your programming knowledge, and whatever technology you use P2P can provide you wi the information you need.

ASP
Support for beginners and professionals, including a resource page with hundreds of links, and a popular ASP.NET mailing list.

DATABASES
For database programmers, offering support on SQL Server, mySQL, and Oracle.

MOBILE
Software development for the mobile market is growing rapidly. We provide lists for the several current standards, including WAP, Windows CE, and Symbian.

JAVA
A complete set of Java lists, covering beginners, professionals, and server-side programmers (including JSP, servlets and EJBs)

.NET
Microsoft's new OS platform, covering topics such as ASP.NET, C#, and general .NET discussion.

VISUAL BASIC
Covers all aspects of VB programming, from programming Office macros to creating components for the .NET platform.

WEB DESIGN
As web page requirements become more complex, programmer's are taking a more important role in creating web sites. For these programmers, we offer lists covering technologies such as Flash, Coldfusion, and JavaScript.

XML
Covering all aspects of XML, including XSLT and schemas.

OPEN SOURCE
Many Open Source topics covered including PHP, Apache, Perl, Linux, Python and more.

FOREIGN LANGUAGE
Several lists dedicated to Spanish and German speaking programmers, categories include. NET, Java, XML, PHP and XML

How to subscribe:

Simply visit the P2P site, at http://p2p.wrox.com/

Got more Wrox books than you can carry around?

Wroxbase is the new online service from Wrox Press. Dedicated to providing online access to books published by Wrox Press, helping you and your team find solutions and guidance for all your programming needs.

The key features of this service will be:

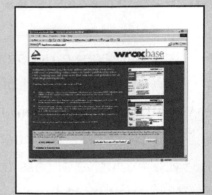

- Different libraries based on technologies that you use everyday (ASP 3.0, XML, SQL 2000, etc.). The initial set of libraries will be focused on Microsoft-related technologies.
- You can subscribe to as few or as many libraries as you require, and access all books within those libraries as and when you need to.
- You can add notes (either just for yourself or for anyone to view) and your own bookmarks that will all be stored within your account online, and so will be accessible from any computer.
- You can download the code of any book in your library directly from Wroxbase

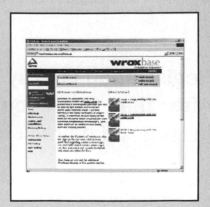

Visit the site at: www.wroxbase.com

Programmer to Programmer™

Registration Code: | 7868X99TNGAK3P01

Wrox writes books for you. Any suggestions, or ideas about how you want
information given in your ideal book will be studied by our team.
Your comments are always valued at Wrox.

Free phone in USA 800-USE-WROX
Fax (312) 893 8001

UK Tel.: (0121) 687 4100   Fax: (0121) 687 4101

Professional ASP.NET Web Forms Techniques– Registration Card

Name _____

Address _____

_____

_____

City _____ State/Region_____

Country _____ Postcode/Zip_____

E-Mail _____

Occupation _____

How did you hear about this book?

☐ Book review (name) _____

☐ Advertisement (name) _____

☐ Recommendation _____

☐ Catalog _____

☐ Other _____

Where did you buy this book?

☐ Bookstore (name) _____ City_____

☐ Computer store (name) _____

☐ Mail order_____

☐ Other _____

What influenced you in the purchase of this book?

☐ Cover Design   ☐ Contents   ☐ Other (please specify):

_____

How did you rate the overall content of this book?

☐ Excellent   ☐ Good   ☐ Average   ☐ Poor

What did you find most useful about this book? _____

_____

_____

What did you find least useful about this book? _____

_____

Please add any additional comments. _____

_____

What other subjects will you buy a computer book on soon?

_____

What is the best computer book you have used this year?

_____

Note: This information will only be used to keep you updated
about new Wrox Press titles and will not be used for
any other purpose or passed to any other third party.

7868

Check here if you DO NOT want to receive support for this book ▌ 7868

wrox

Programmer to Programmer™

Note: If you post the bounce back card below in the UK, please send it to:

Wrox Press Limited, Arden House, 1102 Warwick Road,
Acocks Green, Birmingham B27 6HB. UK.

Computer Book Publishers

BUSINESS REPLY MAIL

FIRST CLASS MAIL   PERMIT#64   CHICAGO, IL

POSTAGE WILL BE PAID BY ADDRESSEE

WROX PRESS INC.,
29 S. LA SALLE ST.,
SUITE 520
CHICAGO IL 60603-USA